Routledge History of Philosophy
Volume III

Volume III is devoted to the Middle Ages. It considers the rich traditions of Arab, Jewish and Latin philosophy, which began to flourish in the ninth century and continued, in the Latin West, until the early seventeenth century. Among the philosophers treated in detail are Avicenna and Averroes, Maimonides, Eriugena, Anselm, Abelard, Grosseteste, Aquinas, Henry of Ghent, Duns Scotus, Peter Aureoli, William of Ockham, Wyclif and Suárez. An introductory chapter discusses Boethius, the late antique thinker who was enormously influential in the medieval Latin West. Special attention has been given to many lesser-known, but important figures in each period, as well as to medieval logic and to the cultural context of medieval philosophy, both in Islam and the Christian West.

This volume provides a comprehensive analysis of the main areas of medieval philosophy by the experts in each field. It offers fresh perspectives on a complex and rapidly changing area of research, in which Arab and Jewish philosophy are considered in their own right, rather than as sources for Latin thinkers, and the thirteenth century (the time of Aquinas) is not viewed as dominating the earlier and later parts of the period.

John Marenbon is a fellow at Trinity College, Cambridge, where he works on medieval philosophy. His recent books include *The Philosophy of Peter Abelard* (1997), *Aristotelian Logic, Platonism and the Context of Early Medieval Philosophy in the West* (2000), and *Boethius* (2003). He is preparing a new edition of the *Introduction to Medieval Philosophy* for Routledge (forthcoming).

Routledge History of Philosophy
General Editors – G. H. R. Parkinson and S. G. Shanker

The *Routledge History of Philosophy* provides a chronological survey of the history of Western philosophy, from its beginnings in the sixth century BC to the present time. It discusses all the major philosophical developments in depth. Most space is allocated to those individuals who, by common consent, are regarded as great philosophers. But lesser figures have not been neglected, and together the ten volumes of the *History* include basic and critical information about every significant philosopher of the past and present. These philosophers are clearly situated within the cultural and, in particular, the scientific context of their time.

The *History* is intended not only for the specialist, but also for the student and general reader. Each chapter is by an acknowledged authority in the field. The chapters are written in an accessible style and a glossary of technical terms is provided in each volume.

Each volume contains 10–15 chapters by different contributors.

Routledge History of Philosophy
Volume III

Medieval Philosophy

EDITED BY

John Marenbon

Routledge
Taylor & Francis Group

LONDON AND NEW YORK

First published 1998
by Routledge
2 Park Square, Milton Park, Abingdon, Oxon OX14 4RN

Simultaneously published in the USA and Canada
by Routledge
270 Madison Ave, New York NY 10016

Reprinted 2000

First published in paperback 2003

Reprinted 2004

Transferred to Digital Printing 2009

Routledge is an imprint of the Taylor & Francis Group, an informa business

Typeset in Garamond by RefineCatch Ltd, Bungay, Suffolk
Printed and bound in Great Britain by
TJI Digital, Padstow, Cornwall

British Library Cataloguing in Publication Data
A catalogue record for this book is available from the British Library

Library of Congress Cataloging in Publication Data

ISBN 10: 0-415-05377-3 hbk
ISBN 10: 0-415-30875-5 pbk

ISBN 13: 978-0-415-05377-8 hbk
ISBN 13: 978-0-415-30875-5 pbk

Contents

CONTENTS

Preface to the
paperback edition

The success of the first edition of the **Routledge History of Philosophy,** which has led to the publication of this new paperback edition, fully justifies the thinking behind this project. Our view at the time that we planned this collection was that the history of philosophy has a special importance for contemporary philosophers and philosophy students. For the discipline demands that one develop the rigorous techniques required to grasp the significance of a philosopher's ideas within their historical framework, while constantly assessing the relevance of the problems or theories discussed to contemporary issues. The very persistence of these 'perennial problems in philosophy' is an indication, not just of their enduring relevance, but equally, of how important it is to be thoroughly grounded in their history in order to grasp their full complexity. We would like to take this opportunity to thank once again all of the authors involved, each of whom has produced such a lasting contribution to the history of philosophy, and also, our editors Richard Stoneman and Muna Khogali, for their role in making the **History** such an indispensable resource.

G. H. R. P. Reading, 2002
S. G. S. Toronto, 2002

General editors' preface

The history of philosophy, as its name implies, represents a union of two very different disciplines, each of which imposes severe constraints upon the other. As an exercise in the history of ideas, it demands that one acquire a 'period eye': a thorough understanding of how the thinkers whom it studies viewed the problems which they sought to resolve, the conceptual frameworks in which they addressed these issues, their assumptions and objectives, their blind spots and miscues. But as an exercise in philosophy, we are engaged in much more than simply a descriptive task. There is a crucial critical aspect to our efforts: we are looking for the cogency as much as the development of an argument, for its bearing on questions which continue to preoccupy us as much as the impact which it may have had on the evolution of philosophical thought.

The history of philosophy thus requires a delicate balancing act from its practitioners. We read these writings with the full benefit of historical hindsight. We can see why the minor contributions remained minor and where the grand systems broke down: sometimes as a result of internal pressures, sometimes because of a failure to overcome an insuperable obstacle, sometimes because of a dramatic technological or sociological change and, quite often, because of nothing more than a shift in intellectual fashion or interests. Yet, because of our continuing philosophical concern with many of the same problems, we cannot afford to look dispassionately at these works. We want to know what lessons are to be learnt from the inconsequential or the glorious failures; many times we want to plead for a contemporary relevance in the overlooked theory or to reconsider whether the 'glorious failure' was indeed such or simply ahead of its time: perhaps even ahead of its author.

We find ourselves, therefore, much like the mythical 'radical translator' who has so fascinated modern philosophers, trying to understand an author's ideas in his and his culture's eyes, and at the same time, in our own. It can be a formidable task. Many times we fail in the historical undertaking because our philosophical interests are so strong, or lose sight of the latter because we are so enthralled by the former. But the nature of philosophy is such that we are compelled to master both techniques. For learning about the history of philosophy is not just a challenging and engaging pastime: it is an essential element in learning about the nature of philosophy – in grasping how philosophy is intimately connected with and yet distinct from both history and science.

The *Routledge History of Philosophy* provides a chronological survey of the history of Western philosophy, from its beginnings up to the present time. Its aim is to discuss all major philosophical developments in depth, and with this in mind, most space has been allocated to those individuals who, by common consent, are regarded as great philosophers. But lesser figures have not been neglected, and it is hoped that the reader will be able to find, in the ten volumes of the *History*, at least basic information about any significant philosopher of the past or present.

Philosophical thinking does not occur in isolation from other human activities, and this *History* tries to situate philosophers within the cultural, and in particular the scientific, context of their time. Some philosophers, indeed, would regard philosophy as merely ancillary to the natural sciences; but even if this view is rejected, it can hardly be denied that the sciences have had a great influence on what is now regarded as philosophy, and it is important that this influence should be set forth clearly. Not that these volumes are intended to provide a mere record of the factors that influenced philosophical thinking; philosophy is a discipline with its own standards of argument, and the presentation of the ways in which these arguments have developed is the main concern of this *History*.

In speaking of 'what is now regarded as philosophy', we may have given the impression that there now exists a single view of what philosophy is. This is certainly not the case; on the contrary, there exist serious differences of opinion, among those who call themselves philosophers, about the nature of their subject. These differences are reflected in the existence at the present time of two main schools of thought, usually described as 'analytic' and 'continental' philosophy. It is not our intention, as general editors of this *History*, to take sides in this dispute. Our attitude is one of tolerance, and our hope is that these volumes will contribute to an understanding of how philosophers have reached the positions which they now occupy.

One final comment. Philosophy has long been a highly technical subject, with its own specialized vocabulary. This *History* is intended not only for the specialist but also for the general reader. To this end, we have tried to ensure that each chapter is written in an accessible

Notes on contributors

Stephen Brown (Boston College, Mass.) works mainly on the history of philosophy and theology in the thirteenth and early fourteenth centuries. His many publications include studies and editions of William of Ockham and Walter Burley.

Brian Davies OP (Fordham University, New York) works mainly on the philosophy of religion and medieval philosophy. His books include *The Thought of Thomas Aquinas* (1992), *An Introduction to the Philosophy of Religion* (2nd edn, 1993) and *Philosophy of Religion: A Guide and Anthology* (2000).

Stephen Dumont (University of Notre Dame) works especially on Duns Scotus and has published many articles on him.

Sten Ebbesen (Institute for Greek and Latin, Copenhagen University) works on a wide area of medieval Latin and Greek philosophy, with a special interest in logic and the Parisian arts masters. His publications include *Commentators and Commentaries on Aristotle's 'Sophistici Elenchi'* (1981) and many editions of logical texts.

Stephen Gersh (Medieval Institute, University of Notre Dame) works especially on the Platonic tradition in late ancient and early medieval philosophy. His books include *From Iamblichus to Eriugena* (1978) and *Concord in Discourse: Harmony and Semiotics in Late Classical and Early Mediaeval Platonism* (1996).

Arthur Gibson (Roehampton Institute) has interests stretching over a wide area of modern philosophy and the history of philosophy and logic. His publications include *Biblical Semantic Logic: A Preliminary Analysis* (1981).

Jorge Gracia (State University at Buffalo) has worked especially on the theory of individuation and its history in the early and late

Middle Ages, Suárez and also on modern Latin American philosophy. His publications include *Introduction to the Problem of Individuation in the Early Middle Ages* (2nd edn, 1988) and, as editor, *Individuation in Scholasticism: The Later Middle Ages and the Counter-Reformation (1150–1650)* (1994).

Alfred Ivry (New York University) specializes in medieval Jewish and Islamic philosophy. His publications include an edition of Moses Narboni's *Treatise on the Perfection of the Soul* and of Averroes' Middle Commentary on Aristotle's *On the Soul*.

Jean Jolivet (Ecole pratique des hautes études, Paris) writes both on Latin philosophy from the ninth to twelfth centuries, and on Islamic philosophy. Among his many books are *Arts du langage et théologie chez Abélard* (1969), *L'Intellect selon Kindi* (1975) and, as editor, *Multiple Averroes* (1978).

Zénon Kaluza (Ecole pratique des hautes études, Paris) specializes in late medieval philosophy in the Latin West. His publications include *Les querelles doctrinales à Paris: Nominalistes et réalistes aux confins du XIVe et XVe siècles* (1988), 'Nicolas d'Autrécourt' and numerous articles.

John Marenbon (Trinity College, Cambridge) works on medieval philosophy. His most recent publication is *The Philosophy of Peter Abelard* (1997).

Steven Marrone (Tufts University) works especially on thirteenth-century philosophers and theologians and their attitudes to scientific method. His books include *William of Auvergne and Robert Grosseteste: New Ideas of Truth in the Early Thirteenth Century* (1983) and *Truth and Scientific Knowledge in the Thought of Henry of Ghent* (1985).

Rosamond McKitterick (University of Cambridge) specializes in the history of culture, manuscripts and literacy in early medieval Europe. Her many publications include *The Carolingians and the Written Word* (1989) and, as editor, *Carolingian Culture: Emulation and Innovation* (1993).

Chris Schabel (University of Cyprus) specializes in philosophical theology of the later Middle Ages. His publications include a study, with texts, of the quarrel over future contingents involving Peter de Rivo in fifteenth-century Louvain (1995–6).

Colette Sirat (Paris, Ecole pratique des hautes études) is a specialist in medieval Jewish philosophy as well as a leading palaeographer. Her publications include *A History of Jewish Philosophy in the Middle Ages* (1985).

Paul Vincent Spade (Indiana University) has worked extensively on later medieval logic. Besides many articles and editions of logical texts, he has published translations of William Heytesbury on insolubles (1979), of texts on the problem of universals (1994) and a catalogue of *Insolubilia* literature (1975).

Acknowledgements

I am most grateful for the patience of the contributors, many of whom had to wait for far longer than they would have expected for the whole volume to be ready. Chris Schabel and Arthur Gibson rescued the whole enterprise when they agreed to step in at very short notice to provide a replacement for two chapters promised by a scholar who eventually was unable to supply them. Richard Stoneman has been a tolerant and encouraging editor throughout the whole project, and Harry Parkinson, one of the general editors of the *Routledge History of Philosophy*, provided a draft on which I based the Chronological chart. Laura Pieters Cordy has helped throughout with scanning and setting out complex material, and I have been most fortunate to have in Mary Dortch a scrupulously intelligent copy editor, undaunted by the challenge of so many different authors, styles and even languages.

Abbreviations

AL	*Aristoteles Latinus* (various publishers), 1939–
BGPTMA	Beiträge zur Geschichte der Philosophie und Theologie des Mittelalters
CC c.m.	Corpus Christianorum continuatio medievalis
CHLMP	*The Cambridge History of Later Medieval Philosophy*, ed. A. Kenny, N. Kretzmann and J. Pinborg, Cambridge, 1982
CHRP	*The Cambridge History of Renaissance Philosophy*, ed. C. B. Schmitt *et al.*, Cambridge, 1988
CIMAGL	*Cahiers de l'Institut du Moyen Âge grec et latin* (a journal printing a large number of relevant texts)
MPL	J.-P. Migne, *Patrologia Latina*
PIMSST	Pontifical Institute of Mediaeval Studies, Studies and Texts
SIEPM	Société Internationale pour l'étude de la philosophie médiévale

Chronology

This chronology runs from the birth of Boethius, the first author treated in the volume, to shortly after the death of Suárez, in the early seventeenth century. No attempt, however, has been made to treat the fifteenth, sixteenth or early seventeenth centuries in any detail (a more detailed chronology for this period will be found in Volume IV), but merely to indicate the chronological position of the latest writers in the medieval tradition and their relation to some of the most important writers in other, contemporaneous traditions. A (?) indicates that a date is approximate.

Politics and society		Religion	
		496	Baptism of Clovis
		519	Acacian schism resolved
526	Theoderic d.		
		570	Muhammad b.
		590–604	Gregory the Great Pope
		596	Gregory sends Augustine to England
		610	Muhammad's first visions
711–12	Muslim conquest of Spain	735	Venerable Bede d.
750	Overthrow of Ummayad caliphate; first 'Abassīd caliph		
762	Baghdad capital of 'Abassīd caliphate		
778	Charlemagne defeated at Roncevaux		
		786	Iconoclasm condemned at Council of Nicaea
		793	Vikings raid Lindisfarne
800	Charlemagne crowned Emperor in Rome		
814	Charlemagne d.		
		817	Systematization of Benedictine rule by St Benedict of Aniane officially approved
840	Charles the Bald becomes king		

Education and the arts		Philosophy and theology	
		480	Boethius b.
		500 (?)	fl. pseudo-Dionysius
		523 (?)	Boethius, *Consolation of Philosophy*
		525 (?)	Boethius d.
529	Justinian closes Platonic School at Athens	529	John Philoponus, *On the Eternity of the World*
532 (?)	Athenian Neoplatonists set up school at Harrān;		
532–7	Hagia Sophia built, Constantinople		
		538 (?)	Simplicius writing commentaries at Harrān
546–8	San Vitale built, Ravenna		
		562	Cassiodorus, *Institutiones*
		575 (?)	John Philoponus d.
		633	Isidore of Seville d.
		662	Maximus the Confessor d.
		709/10	Aldhelm d.
		754 (?)	John Damascene d.
781	Alcuin meets Charlemagne		
		791 (?)	*Libri Carolini*
800 (?)	The Book of Kells		
		804 (?)	Alcuin d.
		808	Ḥunayn ibn Isḥāq b.
830–3	Einhard, *Life of Charlemagne*		

Politics and society		Religion	
		863	Cyril and Methodius begin their mission to the Slavs
		867	Photian schism
875	Charles the Bald d.		
908–10	Fātimid dynasty founded	909	Monastery of Cluny founded
		962	Great Lavra (monastic community) on Mt Athos founded
987	Louis V, last Carolingian King of France, d. Accession of Hugh Capet	988	Vladimir, ruler of Russia, establishes Christianity as the official religion
		999	Gerbert of Aurillac becomes Pope Sylvester II

Education and the arts	Philosophy and theology	
	849	Gottschalk's views on pre-destination condemned at Synod of Quiercy
	850–1	Eriugena, *On predestination*
	855	Council of Valence condemns Eriugena's *On predestination*
	859	Council of Langres condemns Eriugena's *On predestination*
	860 (?)	Ratramnus of Corbie, *De anima ad Odonem*
	861–6	Eriugena, *Periphyseon*
	865	al-Rāzī b.
	866(?)	Gottschalk d.
	868	Ratramnus of Corbie d.
	870 (?)	al-Kindī d.
871–99 Alfred the Great, King of Wessex, promotes ecclesiastical reform and the revival of learning	871 (?)	Eriugena d.
	873	Ḥunayn ibn Isḥāq d.
	882	Saadiah b.
884 (?) Notker, *Liber hymnorum*		
	893–908 (?)	Remigius of Auxerre expounds Martianus Capella and Boethius
908 (?) Remigius of Auxerre d.		
	925	al-Rāzī d.
	942	Saadiah d.
	950	al-Fārābī d.
	972–83	Gerbert at the School of Rheims; expounds the *logica vetus*
	980 (?)	Avicenna (Ibn Sīnā) b.
1001–3 (?) Hrotsvitha d.		
	1003	Gerbert d.
	1018	Michael Psellos b.

Politics and society		Religion	
		1054	Patriarch of Constantinople anathematizes Roman Church
1066	Battle of Hastings; William of Normandy becomes King of England		
1071	Turks defeat Byzantines at battle of Manzikert		
		1076	Pope Gregory VII deposes and excommunicates Emperor Henry IV
		1077	Henry IV submits to Pope at Canossa
		1084	Carthusian order founded
		1085	Pope Gregory VII, driven from Rome by Henry IV, dies at Salerno
1086	England: Domesday survey		
1087	William the Conqueror d.		
		1088	Work begins on great church at Cluny
		1093	Anselm, Archbishop of Canterbury; Durham Cathedral begun
		1095	Pope Urban II proclaims First Crusade
		1098	Foundation of Abbey of Cîteaux
		1099	Crusaders capture Jerusalem

Education and the arts	Philosophy and theology	
1025–33 (?) Guido d'Arezzo reforms musical notation		
	1033	Anselm b.
	1037	Avicenna d.
	1050	Synod of Vercelli condemns Ratramnus' views on the Eucharist
	1054–8	Solomon ibn Gabirol d.
1071 William IX of Aquitaine, Provençal poet, b.		
	1072	Peter Damian d.
	1076	Anselm, *Monologion*
	1077–8	Anselm, *Proslogion*
	1079	Peter Abelard b.
	1080 (?) (?)	Gilbert of Poitiers b. William of Conches b.
	1088	Berengar of Tours d.
	1090	Bernard of Clairvaux b.
	1092	Roscelin accused of tritheism
	1093 (?)	al-Ghazālī, *Incoherence of the Philosophers*
	1094–8	Anselm, *Cur Deus Homo*
	1109	Anselm d.
	1116 (?) (?)	Abelard of Bath, *De eodem et diverso*; Abelard, *Dialectica*
	1120	Abelard, *Theologia summi boni*, discusses Trinity
	1121	Council of Soissons condemns Abelard's views on the Trinity

Politics and society	Religion	
	1122	Suger elected Abbot of Saint-Denis
	1140 (?)	Gratian, *Decretum* (collection of Canon law)
	1143	Translation of Qur'ān into Latin
	1144	Suger's choir, St Denis, consecrated
	1146	Bernard of Clairvaux preaches Second Crusade
	1147–8	Second Crusade
1152 Frederick Barbarossa becomes Emperor		
	1163	Cathedral of Notre Dame, Paris, begun
	1170	Murder of Archbishop Becket, Canterbury St Dominic b.
	1181	St Francis of Assisi b.
1187 Saladin captures Jerusalem		
	1189–92	Third Crusade

Education and the arts		Philosophy and theology	
		1122	William of Champeaux d.
		1125 (?)	Roscelin d.
		1126 (?) (?)	Averroes (Ibn Rushd) b.; Abelard, *Theologia Christiana*; William of Conches comments on *Timaeus*
1127	William IX d.		
		1133 (?)	Abelard, *Theologia scholarium*
		1138	Maimonides (Moses ben Maimon) b.; Abelard, *Ethics*
		1140	Council of Sens condemns Abelard's views on the Trinity
		1142 (?)	Hugh of St Victor d. Abelard d.
		1144 (?)	William of Conches, *Dragmaticon*
1145–55	Winchester Psalter		
		1148	Council of Rheims examines Gilbert of Poitiers' views on the Trinity in his commentary on Boethius' *Theological Treatises*
		1153	Bernard of Clairvaux d.
		1154 (?)	Gilbert of Poitiers d. William of Conches d.
		1155–7	Peter Lombard, *Sentences*
		1159 (?)	John of Salisbury, *Policraticus*
		1160 (?)	Peter Lombard d. John of Salisbury, *Metalogicon*
1170 (?)	musical school of Notre Dame		
		1173	Richard of St Victor d.
1177–81	Chrétien de Troyes, *Lancelot*		
1178–82	Walter of Châtillon, *Alexandreis*		
		1180	John of Salisbury d.; Maimonides, *Mishneh Torah*
1182–3	Alan of Lille, *Anticlaudianus*		

Politics and society		Religion	
		1190	Barbarossa d. when on Crusade
		1194	Cathedral of Chartres destroyed by fire; new cathedral begun
		1198	Innocent III becomes Pope
		1202	Fourth Crusade diverted from Egypt, its original objective, to Constantinople
		1204	Crusaders sack Constantinople and establish Latin Empire
		1209	Establishment of Franciscan Friars
		1209–18	Southern France: Crusade against the Albigenses
1215	England: Magna Carta granted by King John	1215	Innocent III convokes Fourth Lateran Council
		1216	Innocent III dies; Establishment of Dominican Friars
		1217–21	Fifth Crusade at Damietta (Egypt)
1220	First Mongol attacks on Europe	1221	St Dominic d.
		1226	St Francis d.
		1228–9	Crusade of Frederick II; Jerusalem recovered by negotiation
		1232	Papal Inquisition established by Gregory IX
		1233	Gregory IX instructs the Inquisition to complete the eradication of the Albigensian heresy
		1235	Robert Grosseteste becomes bishop of Lincoln
1236	Ferdinand III of Castile captures Cordoba from Muslims		

CHRONOLOGY

Education and the arts		Philosophy and theology	
		1190	Maimonides, *Guide of the Perplexed*
		1198	Averroes d.
1200	First charter concerning University of Paris		
?1200–10	Wolfram von Eschenbach, *Parzival*		
		1204	Maimonides d.
1207	*Cantar de mío Cid*		
1210 (?)	Aristotle's *Metaphysics* and natural science proscribed in Paris arts faculty; Gottfried von Strassburg, *Tristan*		
1214	Earliest known Charter of Oxford University	1214	David of Dinant d.
1215	First statutes of University of Paris	1215	Fourth Lateran Council proclaims orthodoxy of Lombard's *Sentences*
1222	Foundation of University of Padua		
		1225 (?)	Thomas Aquinas b.
1231	First Charter of Cambridge University		

Politics and society		Religion	
1238	James I of Aragon captures Valencia		
1241	Mongols reach Hungary and the Adriatic		
1244	Muslims capture Jerusalem		
1248	Ferdinand III of Castile captures Seville	1248	Louis IX of France leads a crusade
1250	Egypt: 'Abassīd dynasty replaced by Mamluk	1250	Louis IX captured in Egypt; Grosseteste at Rome; speech 'De corruptelis ecclesiae'
1258	Mongols capture Baghdad		
1260	Mongols defeated by Mamluks at Ain Jalut		
1261	Byzantine forces regain Constantinople; end of Latin, and restoration of Greek empire		
		1270	Louis IX dies on Crusade
		1274	Second Council of Lyons achieves a union of the Churches, which lasts until 1289

Education and the arts		Philosophy and theology	
1237	Guillaume de Lorris, (beginning of) *Roman de la rose*		
1240 (?)	Cimabue b.		
1243	Foundation of University of Salamanca		
		1244	Aquinas becomes a Dominican
1245	Foundation of University of Rome	1245	Alexander of Hales d.; Albert the Great, master of theology at Paris
1248	Albert the Great founds *studium generale* at Cologne		
		1249	William of Auvergne d.
		1253	Grosseteste d.
		1254/5	Bonaventure, master of theology at Paris
		1256–9	Aquinas's first period as master at Paris
		?1260–70	William of Moerbeke, translations of Aristotle
		1264	Aquinas, *Summa contra Gentiles* completed
1265	Dante b.	1265 (?)	Siger of Brabant lectures on *On the Soul*
		1266	Aquinas, *Summa theologiae* begun
1267 (?)	Giotto b.	1267	Bacon, *Opus maius*
		1268	Bacon, *Opus minus* and *Opus tertium*
1270–80	Jean de Meun, (continuation of) *Roman de la rose*	1270	Tempier's condemnation of errors, including unity of intellect;
		(?)	Boethius of Dacia, arts master at Paris
		1274	Aquinas d. Bonaventure d.
		1276–92	Henry of Ghent teaches at Paris

Politics and society	Religion

1291 Fall of Acre, last Crusader outpost	
	1302 Bull of Boniface VIII, *Unam sanctam*, affirms universal jurisdiction of Pope
	1309–77 Papacy at Avignon
1315–17 Famine in Europe	
	1324 Marsilius of Padua, *Defensor pacis*, criticizes Papacy
	1326 Eckhart accused of heresy; appeals to Pope
	1327 Marsilius excommunicated
1328 Charles IV, last Capetian King of France, d. Succeeded by Philip VI, first Valois king	
	1329 After the death of Eckhart, Pope John XXII condemns 28 of his theses

Education and the arts		Philosophy and theology	
		1277	Stephen Tempier, Bishop of Paris, condemns 219 articles in theology and natural philosophy; Peter of Spain d.
		1280	Albert the Great d.
		1284	Siger of Brabant d.
		1292	Roger Bacon d.
		1293	Henry of Ghent d.
		1296–7	Dietrich of Freiberg, master of theology at Paris
		1300 (?)	Duns Scotus working on *Ordinatio of Sentences* commentary
1302 (?)	Cimabue d.	1302	Duns Scotus leaves Oxford for Paris
		1302–3	Eckhart's first period as master in Paris
1304	Petrarch b.	1306–9	Dante, *Convivio*
		1308	Duns Scotus d.
1310 (?)	Dante begins *Divina Commedia*		
1313	Boccaccio b.		
		1317–19	William of Ockham lectures on *Sentences* at Oxford
		1317–29	Gersonides, *Wars of the Lord*
		1320–2	Walter Burley master of theology at Paris
1321	Dante d.	1322	Peter Aureoli d.
		1322–3	Walter Chatton comments on *Sentences* at Oxford
		1324	Ockham summoned to Avignon to answer charges of heresy
		1326–34	Robert Holcot at Oxford
		1328	Ockham excommunicated; Eckhart d.; John Buridan, rector of Paris University
		1331	Ockham expelled from his order

Politics and society	Religion
1337 Beginning of Hundred Years War between England and France	
	1342 Marsilius of Padua d.
1345 English defeat the French at Crécy	
1347–50 First wave of the Black Death (bubonic plague) in Europe	
1354 Turks occupy Gallipoli, obtaining a footing in Europe	
1358 Jacquerie (peasant uprising in France)	
1361 Beginning of second wave of the Black Death	
	1377 Pope Gregory XI condemns Wyclif's view (*De civili dominio*) that the civil power may deprive clergy of their endowments; Pope Gregory XI returns to · Rome from Avignon
	1378–1417 Great Schism: Western Christendom divided by the creation of anti-Popes

Education and the arts		Philosophy and theology	
		1334	Durand of St-Pourçain d.
1337	Giotto d.		
1339	Ban on Ockhamism in Paris		
		1340	Gregory of Rimini, commentary on *Sentences*;
		1340–55	Richard Swineshead active
1341	Petrarch crowned with laurels at Rome		
		1344	Chatton d.;
			Gersonides d.;
		(?)	Burley d.;
		(?)	Thomas Bradwardine, *De causa dei*
		1345–60	Nicholas Oresme active
1347	University of Prague founded	1347	Ockham d.
		1349	Bradwardine d.
			Holcot d.
		1350 (?)	Richard of Campsall d.
		1351 (?)	Nicholas of Autrecourt d.
		1355 (?)	John of Ripa active in Paris
		1358	Adam Wodeham d.;
			Gregory of Rimini d.;
		(?)	Buridan d.;
			Nicholas Aston master of theology at Oxford
		1360	Berthold of Moosburg, commentary on *Proclus*
		1361	Richard Kilvington d.
1364	University of Cracow founded		
1365	University of Vienna founded		
		1372 (?)	Heytesbury d.;
			John Wyclif, master of theology
1374	Petrarch d.		
1375	Boccaccio d.	1375–1406	Coluccio Salutati, Chancellor of Florence
1377	Guillaume de Machaut d.		

Politics and society		Religion	
1381	Peasants' Revolt, England		
		1415	Jan Hus burned at Council of Constance
1453	Fall of Constantinople to Turks		
1492	Final defeat of Moors at Granada		
		1517	Luther's 95 theses
		1540	Loyola founds Jesuits
		1545–63	Council of Trent

Education and the arts		Philosophy and theology	
		1381	Wyclif's theory of the Eucharist condemned by the University of Oxford
		1382	Nicole Oresme d. Wyclif's doctrines condemned at the Council of Blackfriars, London
		1384	Wyclif d.
1385 (?)	Chaucer, *Troilus and Criseyde*	1390	Albert of Saxony d.
1400	Chaucer d.		
		1410	Hasdai Crescas d.
		1420	Peter of Ailly d.
		1429	John Gerson d.; Paul of Venice d.
1434	Jan van Eyck, Arnolfini Wedding picture		
		1440	Nicholas of Cusa, *De docta ignorantia*
		1469–74	Ficino, *Theologia Platonica*
1481	Nominalist ban at Paris lifted		
		1548	Francisco Suárez b.
		1549	Gabriel Vázquez b.
		1596	Descartes b.
		1597	Suárez, *Disputationes metaphysicae*
		1599	Pedro Fonseca d.
		1600	Luis de Molina d.
		1604	Vázquez d.
		1605	Francis Bacon, *The advancement of learning*
		1612	Suárez, *De legibus*
		1617	Suárez d.
		1637	Descartes, *Discours de la méthode*

Introduction

John Marenbon

❧❧❧

Medieval philosophy, the subject of this volume, is a distinct tradition within the history of Western philosophy. Its four sub-traditions are 'Arab' philosophy – which took place in Islamic lands and was written usually in Arabic, though sometimes in Persian; 'Jewish' philosophy – the work of Jews in Islamic and Christian countries, written in Arabic or Hebrew; 'Latin' philosophy – produced in the countries of Christian Europe where Latin was the main language of higher learning and usually, though not always, written in Latin; and (of rather less importance) 'Byzantine' philosophy – written in Greek in the Christian empire of Byzantium. Medieval Arab philosophy begins with the first philosophical writings in Arabic in the ninth century; it ends, as a tradition of importance, with the death of Ibn Rushd (Averroes) in 1198, after which growing religious intolerance scarcely permitted the practice of philosophy as it had been known. Medieval Jewish philosophy begins in Islam not long after the Arab tradition, with which it is closely connected. It went on to flourish also in the Jewish colonies of Christian Europe and declined in the fifteenth century. Philosophy in the medieval Latin West begins in the late eighth century, at the court of Charlemagne. The tradition has no clear chronological end point and its final centuries coincide in time with the different, though related, tradition usually described as 'Renaissance philosophy'. Fifteenth- and sixteenth-century universities continued to produce philosophical work firmly in the medieval tradition (often, indeed, consciously restating the ideas of one or another great master of the thirteenth or fourteenth century), and in late sixteenth- and early seventeenth-century Spain there was a flowering of philosophy which, though with differences of emphasis, is distinctively medieval in its sources, techniques and concerns. In Byzantium, it is hard to place any but an arbitrary boundary between late ancient Neoplatonism

1

and medieval Greek philosophy. The tradition was brought to a clear end, however, when Constantinople fell to the Turks in 1453.

Why, though, speak of a single, distinct tradition of 'medieval philosophy' when four different traditions, developed in different languages and cultures, appear to be involved? And why include works written in Persia and the Middle East, in non-European languages, in the history of *Western* philosophy? These seem difficult questions, but the answer is simple (although it is wrong to use the description 'Western philosophy' in a cavalier way: the importance of works in Arabic for medieval philosophy should make historians ask how Western 'Western philosophy' is[1]). The four traditions are interlinked so closely that, whilst their differences are important, they are best understood as a whole. First, all use a common heritage of ancient Greek philosophy, especially that practised in the Neoplatonic schools of late antiquity, although with a greater emphasis on the complete works, rather than just the logic, of Aristotle. Second, in their development, the traditions are interconnected. Medieval Jewish philosophers were deeply influenced by the Arab thinkers they read, and translations of Arabic writing transformed the study of philosophy in the Latin West from the late twelfth century onwards. The Byzantine tradition was less open, although there were some translations from Latin into Greek late in the Middle Ages. Third, all four traditions belong to cultures dominated by a monotheistic, revealed religion: Islam, Judaism or Christianity. Although the relations between religious doctrine and philosophical speculation varied both from one tradition to another, and at different periods within each tradition, the questions posed and constraints exercised by revelation were similar in all three religions and exercised a profound influence on the philosophical work produced within their ambit.

It is this third feature – its close connection with revealed religion – which, more than anything else, explains a final, extrinsic characteristic which applies to the medieval tradition of philosophy as a whole: its comparative neglect. The *Routledge History of Philosophy* itself provides an illustration. This volume, devoted to the Middle Ages, must consider roughly twice the length of time covered by the following seven volumes, dealing with Renaissance and modern philosophy. But the allocation of space to medieval philosophy by the general editors is, none the less, unusually generous by the standards usually accepted today. The more common estimation of the Middle Ages among professional philosophers is indicated by a recent, and in most other respects excellent, textbook designed to introduce students both to philosophy as it is practised today, and to the history of philosophy. The editor explains to his readers that:

2

For a very long period – roughly from the fourth to the seventeenth centuries AD – thought in the West was dominated by Christianity. This does not mean that there was no philosophy; far from it; but much of it served theology or at least (except in such cases as logic) it was constrained by theological considerations.[2]

Medieval (and Renaissance) philosophy is, apparently in consequence, eliminated from the book entirely, except for a fleeting reference to Aquinas. The historical section jumps from the Greeks to Descartes without further comment.

The historiography of medieval philosophy (especially medieval Latin philosophy, which has dominated historians' attention) can be seen as a series of reactions and counter-reactions to the dismissive approach to the area illustrated here in a modern and extreme form, but widespread in many variations, at least since the eighteenth century.[3] The earliest serious historians of medieval philosophy, in the nineteenth century (such as Victor Cousin and Barthélemy Hauréau) were willing to concede the principle on which the dismissive approach, adopted by those who would ignore medieval philosophy altogether, was founded. The dominance of Christianity and its influence on the thought of philosophers was, they granted, a grave defect in medieval philosophy; but not so grave that the period was without interest. Cousin, for instance, argued that in the Middle Ages ecclesiastical authority was absolute and medieval philosophy – 'scholasticism' as he called it – was used 'in the service of faith, under the aegis of religious authority: it moved within a circle that was not of its own devising, but had been imposed on it by an authority other than its own' ([Intr. 1] 28). Yet philosophy still retained something of its own nature, and Cousin believed that even medieval scholasticism took the four forms he found in each epoch of philosophy: idealism, sensualism, scepticism and mysticism. The approach produced richer results than its apologetic tone would seem to promise, aided perhaps by Cousin's belief in a clear, though non-linear, development of philosophy from antiquity to his own day.

From the late nineteenth century until nearly the present, however, most work on medieval philosophy has been carried out from a very different point of view.[4] Historians strongly committed to orthodox Catholicism, many of them in holy orders, were quick to build on a long tradition of medieval scholarship within the Church (especially among religious) and take up the new interest in medieval philosophy. Understandably, however, they were opposed to the approach followed by Cousin and other 'rationalist' historians (as they described them). Yet they did not, as might have been expected, counter it by arguing that the influence of revealed religion on medieval philosophy was not cramping, but beneficial. Rather, they insisted that the great medieval thinkers (pre-eminently, Thomas Aquinas) recognized a distinction between philosophy and theology. They were, indeed, great theologians; but they were also great philosophers, who elaborated rational systems of philosophy independent of revelation. It is, they argued, the job of the historian of medieval philosophy to isolate and explain these philosophical systems. Part of the stimulus behind this approach may well have been provided by the problem which many Catholic thinkers and churchmen in the late nineteenth and earlier twentieth century believed modern philosophical movements posed for them. They saw most contemporary philosophy as hostile to the claims of religion and hoped to find in medieval thinkers a system which could be set against the current schools of thought. For this purpose, it was essential that, although scholastic philosophy should be fully compatible with Christian doctrine and lead naturally towards it, it should also be recognized as a fully independent philosophy, separable from revealed doctrine and able to compete on equal terms with other schools of thought. The advantage of this approach is that it brought an interest to medieval thinkers which was neither condescending nor merely antiquarian. Its disadvantage is that the distinction between philosophy and theology in the Middle Ages (even just in the Latin tradition) was neither clear-cut nor undisputed nor unchanging, and that the modern scholastic philosophy elaborated on the basis of medieval models is intellectually feeble.[5]

In recent decades, three trends have been particularly important in shaping approaches to medieval philosophy. All areas of medieval study have become more and more professional, and there has been an increasing emphasis on the need for research on the raw material of medieval scholarship: the large, still in many parts unexplored collections of manuscripts in libraries throughout Europe. So much remained, and remains, to be done in the way of editing works of medieval philosophy, studying their diffusion, establishing chronologies and tracing influences that many scholars have devoted their careers to this type of work. What they achieve, so long as they are technically competent, is of enormous value; indeed, a good edition is likely to go on being used and appreciated long after the best of interpretative studies have been left to gather dust. There is, however, a tendency among some scholars to see these sort of tasks as constituting the main business of historians of medieval philosophy. Once the manuscripts have been studied and edited most of the historian's work, they feel, has been done: it remains only to present the medieval philosopher's thoughts in terms as close as possible to his own; any attempt at deeper analysis or, God forbid, criticism is disparaged as 'unhistorical'. In this way, the pursuit of scholarly goals, so valuable in itself, is made to obstruct the *understanding* of medieval philosophy.

This emphasis on technical historical and editorial scholarship occurs mostly among scholars who regard themselves primarily as medievalists (and often belong to history or to literary faculties in universities). A very different trend is to be found among the scholars of medieval philosophy in the philosophy faculties of universities in Britain, North America and Australasia. Whereas medieval philosophy has usually had a place in philosophy courses in continental Europe, up until the 1950s it was almost entirely ignored by English-speaking analytical philosophers, working in the tradition of Frege and Russell. Then a number of pioneers – medievalists who had taught themselves logic, such as Ernest Moody; logicians with medieval interests, such as Peter Geach and Arthur Prior – began to point out the remarkable parallels between modern and medieval logic.[6] Many of the medieval logicians' ideas could be clarified by using modern symbolic logic to describe them, and it became apparent that in some fields they had anticipated the discoveries of the twentieth century. More broadly, the highly technical, unrhetorical, logically-based manner of addressing philosophical issues in the medieval universities – which had often been another cause of neglect – was seen to be uncannily close to the methods of the twentieth-century analytical school. Since the 1960s or 1970s a group of philosophers, mainly in North America, led by Norman Kretzmann, have brought the interests, technical training and clarity of the analytical method to bear on a range of mostly thirteenth- and fourteenth-century philosophy and, especially, logic. *The Cambridge History of Later Medieval Philosophy*, edited by Kretzmann, Jan Pinborg and Anthony Kenny (whose career has combined original work in modern philosophy with studies of ancient and medieval philosophers), is both a manifesto of this approach, and a monument to its achievements in the years up until 1982.[7] It remains the single most important modern book on medieval philosophy.

The 'analytic' approach to medieval philosophy championed by these scholars searches for passages of philosophical interest in medieval works, extracting them where necessary from their wider theological or other context. The aim is to set out as clearly as possible the arguments used by medieval philosophers, especially where they relate to concerns shared by modern philosophers, and to examine them critically, in much the same way as a philosopher now would examine the arguments of one of his contemporaries. The great success of this method is that it enables the medieval philosophers to be understood. Understanding a philosophical argument or position involves being able to explain the claims it makes and the distinctions it involves, and being able to see what would count as an argument against it.

Most non-analytical discussions of medieval philosophy fail to do this, both from lack of close attention to the stages of each argument and from the decision not to attempt translation of medieval terms into modern ones, which we now can meaningfully manipulate in our reasoning. In this sense, the analytical method sets a standard which any conscientious student of medieval philosophy should emulate: to retreat from its demands is to seek refuge in antiquarian obscurantism.

None the less, there is reason to doubt that the analytical method, without further development and change, provides the path which will lead medieval philosophy, as the editors of the *Cambridge History* hoped ([Intr. 8] 3), from the 'philosophical ghetto' and make its study 'intellectually continuous' with the activity of contemporary philosophy. Despite the impression to the contrary that the last two paragraphs might have engendered, the study of medieval philosophy is *not* flourishing in English-speaking philosophy departments. Its exponents there are few and thinly spread. For most students of philosophy, and professional philosophers, medieval philosophy is a non-subject, while medieval historians continue to approach philosophical texts in ignorance of the analytical method or hostility to it. The failure of the analytical approach to medieval philosophy to win many converts may be blamed partly on academic narrow-mindedness, but partly it must be traced to the nature of its results. Although the analytical approach has made a number of medieval arguments and positions comprehensible, it has done little to show why it is worth studying and understanding them. At best, the medieval authors are demonstrated to have anticipated modern discoveries. More often, their arguments, although ingenious, are exposed as flawed. The analysts are, indeed, eager to emphasize, despite these results, the greatness of the best medieval philosophers as philosophers, but philosophy students, even if convinced by these protestations, might be excused for preferring to study other great philosophers of the past, whose overall positions link up more obviously with modern concerns, whilst historians will be left puzzled about what exactly all this detailed scrutinizing of argument and counter-argument is supposed to have revealed. At the root of the problem is the way in which the analytical approach strips away the context of medieval discussions and pays scant regard to the overall aims and presuppositions of the writers, in order to isolate a core of philosophical argument. Yet, it might be thought, its exponents have no alternative. Whereas the wider contexts of early modern and, strangely, ancient philosophical arguments have strong connections with modern concerns, the contexts of the medieval arguments – very often theological – seem irremediably strange and foreign to present-day concerns. This judgement, however, is too swift. The wider contexts of medieval philosophical arguments need to be grasped

6

thoroughly and in their relation to general problems and tensions in medieval culture, rather than seen superficially and in isolation. Then their interest, and their connections with modern concerns, will emerge.

A third trend, evident in the work of some of the leading scholars of medieval philosophy in Europe (such as Kurt Flasch, Alain de Libera, Ruedi Imbach and Burkhard Mojsisch),[8] shows just such a willingness to explore and explain the wider contexts of medieval philosophy. Each of these scholars has concentrated especially on areas which have traditionally been thought marginal to medieval philosophy: the Platonic tradition which flourished in late thirteenth- and fourteenth-century Germany, philosophical works written for or by laymen, philosophical writing in the vernacular by figures such as Dante and Eckhart. Their claim is not merely that this material deserves attention, but also that it helps to provide a new picture of the underlying concerns and aims, and of the range, of medieval philosophy.

This volume does not seek to represent any one method of treating medieval philosophy. Its contributors were chosen because of their specialist knowledge of the individual areas they discuss, and also with the aim of producing a book which would *not* follow a single approach to the area, but show something of the diversity of approaches now current. The various approaches have, however, been carefully matched to the subject-matter, so as to provide different points of entry to the subject for readers from different academic backgrounds. To take just the most striking examples. Later medieval logic and the work of Ockham are the two areas of medieval philosophy with the most obvious links with modern analytical philosophy. The chapters devoted to them (17 and 14) have been written by scholars able to bring out and explain these links; readers from an analytical background might wish to begin here. In his chapter on Eriugena and Anselm (6), Stephen Gersh has drawn on a different strand of modern philosophy, the semiotic theories originating in France. These theories are not to everyone's taste (Gersh himself makes clear how distant his own approach is from the editor's!), but Eriugena's work, especially, raises questions about reading, interpretation and polysemy, which are now of wide interest and have rarely been recognized in medieval philosophy. Latin philosophy of the early Middle Ages is often anonymous and needs to be studied not just by looking at individual texts and authors, but also by a careful examination of the manuscript evidence of teaching and learning. Rosamund McKitterick brings a manuscript specialist's attention to this area. Readers with a historical background may find her chapter (5) a good starting place or, if they are interested in broader questions about the relation between religion and the transmission of culture, they might look to the chapter on Boethius (1), or that by Jean Jolivet on earlier Arab philosophy (2) or by Zénon Kaluza on late medieval philosophy (18). The general reader, unsure perhaps whether or not medieval philosophy has anything at all to offer, could not do better than begin with the chapter (11) on the most celebrated medieval thinker of all, Aquinas, where Brian Davies brings out, in simple, non-technical terms, some of the themes in his work which are still important today.

The chapters of this volume may, then, be taken individually, as essays in different styles on various, related (and chronologically ordered) subjects. But there is also a way in which this volume should be seen and used as a whole. Both those coming new to medieval philosophy, and those already familiar with the area, need a chronological and geographical/linguistic map of the subject. This volume offers a map of the subject as it is seen now by specialists – and it is a map strikingly different in two ways from that offered by existing general histories of medieval philosophy in English.[9] First, most histories treat Arab and Jewish philosophy almost exclusively with regard to their influence on Latin philosophy, almost as if Avicenna, Averroes and Maimonides had written so that one day they could be studied by Aquinas and Duns Scotus. By contrast, the chapters on Arab and Jewish philosophy here are the work of experts in Arab and Jewish thought and culture and emphasize both the cultural context of these philosophers and their achievement in absolute terms.[10] Second, in most histories of medieval philosophy, the thirteenth century is seen as the period of greatest achievement in Latin philosophy, epitomized by the work of Thomas Aquinas, with the centuries before leading up to it by way of preparation and the centuries after representing a decline, slow at first, then steep. In this *History*, by contrast, the early medieval period and twelfth century is seen as an important area of philosophy in its own right, and the later medieval centuries are not overshadowed by the thirteenth. Although Aquinas is recognized as an outstandingly great thinker, his work is seen as belonging to the first generation of Latin philosophers who had thoroughly absorbed the new translations of Aristotle and the Arab and Jewish writers: the tradition of medieval philosophy became more sophisticated in the century following his death and it remained lively (despite the vicissitudes of the fifteenth and sixteenth centuries) until the early 1600s.

 NOTES

1   This point is brought out very clearly in de Libera [Intr. 9].
2   A. C. Grayling (ed.) *Philosophy: a Guide through the Subject*, Oxford, 1995, p. 3.

3   Hostility to medieval philosophy (and especially to medieval logic) goes, of course, far further back: to the fourteenth century, when early humanists began to attack what they perceived as the obscurity and barbarous Latin of the university logicians. But these critics did not complain about the connections between philosophical concerns and revealed doctrine. On the historiography of medieval philosophy, see also Marenbon [Intr. 10, 83–90] and Van Steenberghen [Intr. 13] and, especially, Imbach and Maierù [Intr. 6].

4   The most distinguished recent exponent of the approach described in this paragraph is Fernand Van Steenberghen (see, for example, [Intr. 12]). His approach has influenced English-language readers both through translations of his work (for instance [Intr. 13]) and through David Knowles's widely read textbook [Intr. 8] which is heavily indebted to Van Steenberghen.

5   There is not space here properly to consider Etienne Gilson, whose work still provides many with their first and only glimpse of medieval philosophy. Gilson was both a remarkable scholar and a brilliant, independent (and often idiosyncratic) thinker, influenced by modern philosophers, especially Heidegger. In the course of his life, he moved further and further away from the model of medieval philosophy as a discipline separable from Christian doctrine, as he developed his notion of 'Christian philosophy', impossible without revelation, yet distinct from theology. See A. de Libera, 'Les Etudes de philosophie médiévale en France d'Etienne Gilson à nos jours', in Imbach and Maierù [Intr. 6] at 22–33.

6   Especially important pioneering books are Geach [Intr. 3] and Moody [Intr. 11].

7   There have, of course, been many important studies of medieval philosophy using the analytical method in the fifteen years since then. Two of the most impressive are Marilyn McCord Adams's two-volume study of Ockham [14.12] (discussed in Chapter 14) and Simo Knuuttila's work on modality [1.21]. (For complicated historical reasons, philosophy in Finland has tended to belong to the English-language analytical school, though without the indifference towards the history of philosophy, found in many English and American philosophy departments.)

8   See Flasch [Intr. 2] and Imbach [Intr. 5]. For the work of de Libera and Mojsisch, see especially Chapter 10. This chapter is intended merely as a digest of some of the important ideas proposed by these scholars, and to provide basic information on Bonaventure and the translations which would not otherwise have been included in the volume. Its author is not a specialist in the area!

9   It is close, however, to that provided by Alain de Libera in [Intr. 9], which is strongly recommended to all who can read French.

10 The space allocated to Arab and Jewish philosophy here is, however, less than it deserves. And Byzantine philosophy, although less important, ought not, practical considerations aside, to have been excluded (for a good survey, see de Libera [Intr. 9] 9–51). My excuse as editor is that, given severe pressures on the space available, it seemed sensible to angle the volume towards the material which would be most readily accessible, in translation and in the original, to readers.

 BIBLIOGRAPHY

Intr. 1 Cousin, V. *Cours de Philosophie par M. V. Cousin: introduction à l'histoire de la philosophie*, Paris, 1828.

Intr. 2 Flasch, K. *Das philosophische Denken im Mittelalter: Von Augustin zu Macchiavelli*, Stuttgart, 1986.

Intr. 3 Geach, P. T. *Reference and Generality: an Examination of Some Medieval and Modern Theories*, Ithaca, NY and London, 1962; amended edn, 1980.

Intr. 4 Gilson, E. *A History of Christian Philosophy in the Middle Ages*, London, 1955.

Intr. 5 Imbach, R. *Laien in der Philosophie des Mittelalters: Hinweise und Anregungen zu einem vernachlässigten Thema* (Bochumer Studien zur Philosophie 14), Amsterdam, 1989.

Intr. 6 Imbach, R. and Maierù, A. *Gli studi di filosofia medievale fra otto e novecento* (Storia e letteratura, studi e testi 179), Rome, 1989.

Intr. 7 Kenny, A., Kretzmann, N. and Pinborg, J. *The Cambridge History of Later Medieval Philosophy, from the Rediscovery of Aristotle to the Disintegration of Scholasticism, 1100–1600*, Cambridge, 1982 (hereafter abbreviated to *CHLMP*).

Intr. 8 Knowles, D. *The Evolution of Medieval Thought*, 2nd edn, ed. D. E. Luscombe and C. N. L. Brooke, London and New York, 1988.

Intr. 9 Libera, A. de *La Philosophie Médiévale*, 2nd edn, Paris, 1995.

Intr. 10 Marenbon, J. *Later Medieval Philosophy (1150–1350): an Introduction*, rev. edn, London and New York, 1991.

Intr. 11 Moody, E. A. *Truth and Consequence in Mediaeval Logic*, Amsterdam, 1953; repr. Westwood, Conn., 1976).

Intr. 12 Van Steenberghen, F. *La Philosophie au XIIIe Siècle*, Louvain, 1966.

Intr. 13 —— *Aristotle in the West*, 2nd edn, trans. L. Johnston, Louvain, 1970.

Intr. 14 —— *Introduction à l'Étude de la Philosophie Médiévale*, Louvain, 1974.

CHAPTER 1

Boethius: from antiquity to the Middle Ages

John Marenbon

Boethius is a difficult figure to place in the history of philosophy. Considered just in himself, he clearly belongs to the world of late antiquity. Born in 480, at a time when Italy was ruled by the Ostrogoths under their king, Theoderic, Boethius was adopted into one of the most distinguished patrician families of Rome and bene-fited from an education which made him at home not only in classical Latin culture but also in Greek literature and philosophy. Although most historians doubt that Boethius actually went to Alexandria or Athens to study, he certainly knew the work of Greek Neoplatonists of the immediate past: Proclus, Porphyry and probably Ammonius. Although a Christian, writing in Latin, he therefore falls into a tradi-tion stretching back directly to Plotinus and, ultimately, to Aristotle and Plato. Yet considered as a late antique philosopher, his impor-tance is limited. Most of Boethius' ideas and arguments derive from his Greek sources; his own contribution lay more in choosing, arranging and presenting views than in original thinking. By contrast, from the perspective of medieval philosophy, Boethius looms large. Only Aristotle himself, and perhaps Augustine, were more important and wide-ranging in their influence. Besides providing scholars in the Middle Ages with two of their most widely-read textbooks on arithmetic and music,[1] through his translations, commentaries and monographs Boethius provided the basis for medieval logic. His short theological treatises helped to shape the way in which logical and philosophical techniques were used in discussing Christian doctrine. His *Consolation of Philosophy*, read and studied from the eighth century through to the Renaissance, and translated into almost every medieval vernacular, was a major source for ancient philosophy in the early

11

Middle Ages and its treatment of goodness, free will and eternity continued to influence thirteenth- and fourteenth-century thinkers. In short, it would be hard to understand the development of philosophy in the medieval Latin West without looking carefully at Boethius' work – and it is for this reason that, although he falls outside its chronological limits, a chapter on his work (with glances forward at its medieval influence) begins the present volume.

❧ THE LOGICAL WORKS ❧

In one of his logical commentaries ([1.4] II: 78–9), Boethius announces that he is planning to translate into Latin all the works of Aristotle's he can find, and all of Plato's dialogues, and to provide commentaries for each of his translations. Only for Aristotle's logic was the project, at least in large part, realized. Boethius translated the whole of Aristotle's logical *organon*, along with the *Isagoge* ('Introduction') by Porphyry. The translations, executed in meticulous word for word fashion, remained the standard versions of the *organon* until the end of the Middle Ages, except in the case of the *Posterior Analytics*, where his version was lost. In addition, Boethius wrote two commentaries each on the *Isagoge* and on *On Interpretation*, a commentary on the *Categories* and scholia on the *Prior Analytics*; there are grounds for thinking he also wrote a commentary on the *Topics*, although it does not survive.[2]

In formulating his project, Boethius was strongly influenced by the common attitude among late Neoplatonists to Plato and Aristotle. Although they looked to Plato as the originator of the philosophy which gave understanding of the intelligible world and which they pursued in their most ambitious works, Neoplatonists from Porphyry onwards recognized a distinct place for the study of Aristotelian logic; and in the Alexandrian school, Neoplatonists such as Ammonius devoted most of their public teaching to Aristotle's logic. This logic was seen to be concerned with language as used to describe the world we perceive with our senses. So long as students of logic were aware that they were not dealing with a complete description of reality as the Neoplatonists envisaged it, they could pursue the subject with profit. Plato and Aristotle could be reconciled, once their different spheres of interest were recognized (it is no surprise that Boethius himself planned to write a monograph showing the agreement of Plato and Aristotle). In the logical commentaries he kept scrupulously to the Aristotelian approach, even where he produced two commentaries to the same text.[3] Although he speaks of writing a second, 'Pythagorean' commentary on the *Categories*, he seems never to have done so.[4]

Some scholars have argued that Boethius' logical commentaries are merely direct translations of marginalia he found in his manuscripts of the Greek texts, but this view is implausible. Boethius gives every indication of having worked from a small number of sources, among which Porphyry was his favourite, selecting, arranging, paraphrasing and from time to time adding his own reflections.[5] It remains true that these commentaries are thoroughly unoriginal works, but they were all the more valuable for that reason to medieval thinkers. Rather than giving them the views of just one logician, the commentaries opened to them a whole tradition of late antique thinking over a wide range of subjects, since the commentaries go far beyond the discussion of strictly logical questions, to consider matters of metaphysics, meaning and the philosophy of mind. Unlike the Neoplatonic students or Boethius himself, however, the medieval readers did not suppose that the approach to philosophical problems taken in the commentaries was a deliberately limited one, to be complemented and superseded by an investigation of intelligible reality. As a result, medieval Western philosophy was given a strong bias towards Aristotelian ways and aims, even before Aristotle's metaphysical, scientific and ethical works became available.

There are many illustrations of this phenomenon. An obvious example is the influence of Boethius' discussion of universals in his second commentary on the *Isagoge* ([1.3] 159: 10–167: 20). Porphyry himself had skirted over the problem of universals as one too difficult for the beginners to whom the *Isagoge* was addressed. He left just a set of unanswered questions, which suggest that, understandably for a Neoplatonist, were he teaching more advanced students he would have wished to raise and defend the existence of Platonic universals, existing independently of particulars and incorporeally. Boethius, however, presents the view of Alexander of Aphrodisias, which he considers to be the solution in accord with Aristotle. His argument, identifying the universal with the form which makes any particular of a given species the sort of thing it is, and which can be grasped mentally by abstracting from accidental differences, has been criticized by modern commentators as muddled – and was perceived as such by many medieval readers. But it presented a realism quite distinct from Platonic realism, and in the medieval debate, dominated by refinements of Boethius' position and nominalist attacks on it, Platonic realism played almost no part.[6] Or, to take another example, Boethius' discussion of perception, the mind and language at the beginning of his second commentary on *On Interpretation* introduced many of the themes which Aristotle explored in his *On the Soul*.

Boethius' work as a logician went beyond his plan of translating and commenting on Plato and Aristotle. He wrote a series of logical monographs, on categorical syllogisms, hypothetical syllogisms, division and topical reasoning, as well as a commentary on Cicero's *Topics*. The short treatise *On Division* deals with some of the material of the *Isagoge* and *Categories*. In writing about categorical syllogisms (syllogisms the premises of which are non-complex statements) – in his earlier *On Categorical Syllogisms* and his later, unfinished *Introduction to Categorical Syllogisms* – Boethius follows Aristotle closely, though adding some post-Aristotelian developments concerning negative terms. The other two treatises introduce new, non-Aristotelian areas of logic. A hypothetical syllogism is a syllogism where one or both of the premises are molecular statements: statements consisting of more than one simple statement joined together by a connective. These are not just conditionals (as the word 'hypothetical' may suggest) but also conjunctions and disjunctions. Whereas the variables in categorical syllogisms are terms, the variables in hypothetical syllogisms are statements. *On Hypothetical Syllogisms* goes beyond Aristotle, who had restricted himself to the logic of terms, by exploring the logic of statements (propositional logic), although it seems not to draw on the most sophisticated ancient exponents of this branch of logic, the Stoics. To a modern reader, some of the inference schemata Boethius proposes will seem strange, since – unlike most modern logicians – he assumes that it cannot be the case that, if p then q is true, it is also true that if p then not-q.[7] For medieval logicians, however, *On Hypothetical Syllogisms* was one of the two important bases from which they went on to elaborate a logic of statements.

The other basis was Boethius' *On Topical 'differentiae'*. The theory of topics was seen originally as a way of discovering arguments: in the case of Aristotle's *Topics*, arguments for use in dialectical argument-contests, in the case of many later writers (including Cicero in his *Topics*) for use in legal oratory. By Boethius' time, topics were considered to be both what were called 'maximal propositions' – obviously true, universal generalizations – and the *differentiae* by which the whole genus of maximal propositions is divided into subordinate genera and species. For instance, one of Boethius' maximal propositions is that 'things whose definitions are different are themselves also different' and its *differentia* is 'from definition'. Themistius and Cicero had each divided up the maximal propositions differently, producing two alternative sets of *differentiae*. *On Topical 'differentiae'* explains the theory of topics, sets out the two schemes of *differentiae* and compares them. The use of the treatise as an aid to constructing (and, by extension, to confirming) informal arguments is obvious. The link with formal logic arose because, in addition to maximal propositions expressing what might, at best, be thought of as common-sense generalizations ('what seems true to everyone or to many or to the wise should not

14

be denied'), there are others which put forward some of the fundamental principles which are needed for logical deduction, such as *modus ponens* (if *p* then *q*, and *p*, then *q*) and *modus tollens* (if *p* then *q*, and not-*q*, then not-*p*). Some medieval logicians would see the theory of topics, as set out by Boethius, as providing the laws both for syllogistic inference and for the logic of statements.

❧ THE THEOLOGICAL TREATISES ❧

Boethius' reputation as a theologian depends on five short treatises, called in the Middle Ages the *Opuscula sacra*. Only three of them are of importance: no. 2 is a briefer, probably preliminary version of part of no. 1, whilst no. 4 ('On faith') – sometimes, but probably wrongly, supposed inauthentic – is a straightforward confession of faith, containing nothing of Boethius' own thoughts. No. 5, a refutation of the opposing extreme Christological views of Nestorius and Eutyches, was probably the first to be written (after 512). Christology was a controversial issue in Boethius' day. The statement of the Council of Chalcedon (451), which affirmed that Christ was made known in two natures, but without division or separation, was accepted in the West, but challenged in the East by the followers of Nestorius, who emphasized the distinctness of Christ's two natures, and by monophysites, who held that in the person of Christ there is only a single, divine nature. Acacius, the patriarch of Constantinople (471–89) issued a document, the *Henotikon*, which condemned Nestorius and also condemned the extreme monophysite, Eutyches, but failed to reaffirm the Council of Chalcedon's statement about the number of natures in Christ. This failure provoked a schism (the 'Acacian schism') with the Latin Church. Boethius' treatise was stimulated by the attempt in 512 of a group of Greek bishops to draw up a compromise position which would be acceptable to the papacy (see [1.31]). Boethius – who was more willing than the Pope to go along with the Greek bishops' position – clearly wished to contribute to the debate, though less perhaps by the view he stated, than by the manner in which he put it forward. He adopted the precise, scholastic style of theological writing which had become popular in the Greek East, but went against usual practice in the Latin West. He carefully defined his terms – 'essence', 'subsistence', 'substance', 'person' and 'nature' – and proceeded to argue that his heterodox opponents were guilty of logical, as well as doctrinal, error (see [1.14]). Boethius' treatises on the Trinity (1 and 2) also seem to owe their origin to events connected with the Acacian schism. In 519, a group of Scythian monks, loyal to Chalcedon, came to Rome to try to gain acceptance of the formula

15

'one of the Trinity suffered in the flesh', which had been rejected by the authorities in Constantinople. Boethius approaches the question of divine triunity more generally, trying to show that a careful application of logical tools, especially Aristotle's theory of the ten categories, shows how God can be both three persons and yet one God.

Boethius' theological treatises were studied intensely, glossed and commented on, from the ninth century onwards. Their importance for medieval scholars was unrelated to the doctrinal controversies from which they arose: although there were many theological controversies in the medieval Western Church, they were rarely on the questions of Christology and trinitarian doctrine which were so important in late antiquity. Medieval thinkers, rather, found in the *opuscula* a valuable source of information about ancient philosophical doctrines. To take two examples. Boethius' definition of 'nature' in treatise no. 5 introduced them to ideas from Aristotle's *Physics*. A discussion early on in treatise no. 1 ([1.7] 10: 21–12: 58) discusses in detail the relations between God, form, matter and being. God, says Boethius, is not just form without matter, he is also (the only) non-composite pure form. Physical objects are concrete wholes of form and matter but, Boethius insists, the embodied forms are merely images of other, disembodied forms. Much twelfth-century metaphysics is an effort to clarify and develop this three-layered hierarchy of pure, non-composite form, disembodied forms and the images of these forms in material things. Medieval thinkers were also greatly influenced by the method of these treatises. They suggested that logical tools and precisely defined philosophical terms could both clarify difficult points of Christian doctrine and provide the means to demonstrate that, given certain fundamental points of doctrine (accepted by all parties), heterodox positions involved logical error. These two patterns of logically-competent, philosophically-informed theological speculation were two of the main models for Christian thinking from the ninth century to the fifteenth.

The third of the theological treatises is different in character from the others. In the Middle Ages it was known as *De hebdomadibus* ('On the groups of seven') from the reference in its first sentence to a work, since lost, by Boethius called the 'Hebdomads'. The treatise is intended to clarify a problem considered there: how is it that all things are 'good in that they are', although they are not 'substantial goods'? There is nothing explicitly Christian in its content. Boethius begins with a list of philosophical axioms which modern scholars have been able to interpret in the light of late antique Neoplatonism, but which perhaps proved all the more stimulating to medieval commentators by their obscurity.[8] The discussion which follows is, in effect, an unravelling of the ambiguity of the phrase 'good in that it exists'. One way in which something can be good in that it exists is to be 'a substantial good'. God is a substantial good because he cannot be conceived except as good. Everything else is good in that it exists, but in a different way. All things derive their existence from God (and could not exist unless they did so), and because God is good, they are good by virtue of the existence they derive from him. It is true, therefore, that they cannot exist without being good. They, however, unlike God, could be conceived as not being good. They are not, therefore, substantial goods. Some of the considerations Boethius raises here would be explored in a wider context as part of medieval discussion of the transcendentals – those attributes, including goodness, which everything was considered to have by virtue of existing.[9]

❧ 'ON THE CONSOLATION OF ❧ PHILOSOPHY': THE HIGHEST GOOD

Although they lived under the rule of a barbarian king committed to a heretical Arian Christianity, Boethius and his aristocratic Roman contemporaries were allowed to retain many of the trappings of importance and authority and, if they chose, to exercise real power as officials of Theoderic. Boethius combined – as a man of his rank would have been expected to do – public service with his private devotion to scholarship. Until near the end of his life, however, writing and translating was his primary concern, and his political activities were confined to Rome and the Senate, away from the court of Theoderic at Ravenna.[10] In 522 Boethius was given the almost unprecedented honour of both his sons being appointed as consuls together. In the same year, Boethius himself was appointed to be 'Master of the Offices', an important and influential position at the Ravenna court. He had not held the post for long when he was arrested, imprisoned and eventually (probably in 525, but possibly in 524 or 526) executed, on charges of treason against the Gothic regime and sorcery. Boethius himself dismisses all these accusations and attributes his downfall to the intrigues of enemies created by his uprightness and his defence of the weak as a court official. The underlying reasons for Boethius' execution – followed soon by that of his respected father-in-law, Symmachus – seem, however, to lie in Theoderic's growing doubts over the loyalty to him of the Roman aristocracy, after the strongly pro-Catholic Emperor Justin acceded to the Byzantine throne in 518 and the Acacian schism had finally been resolved in 519.

While in prison, Boethius wrote the work by which he is most remembered, *On the Consolation of Philosophy* (*De consolatione Philosophiae*). Here he deserts his usual simple presentation and dry style for the elaborate literary form of a *prosimetrum* (a work in prose

interspersed with verse passages), which allows his personal circumstances to give urgency to the philosophical questions he tackles. The
Consolation is an imaginary dialogue between Boethius and Philosophy,
a female personification of the tradition of philosophical wisdom
which, despite the attempts of different schools to sunder it (her clothes
are torn, because each philosophical sect has tried to take some of
them for itself), is a unified one, stretching back to Socrates and Plato.
Boethius represents himself at the beginning of the dialogue as overcome by grief and self-pity: he bewails the injustice of the accusations
against him and the turn of fortune which has brought him from a
position of importance to prison; he longs for death to put an end to
his suffering. Philosophy treats him as someone suffering from an
illness. The shock of his fall from power has made him forget the
wisdom which, from his youth, he had learned from her. He still
retains the knowledge (I, prose 6) that there is a God who rules the
universe, but he no longer knows to what end all things move. He
believes that, whereas the workings of nature follow a rational order,
in human affairs the evil are left free to triumph and oppress the good.
Philosophy begins with what she calls 'lighter remedies', a series of
arguments to show him that his personal downfall is not the disaster
he takes it to be. In particular, she insists that he cannot blame fortune
for instability, since it is the very nature of fortune to be unstable,
and of the goods of fortune, such as riches, power, honour and fame,
to be transitory.

Boethius is now prepared for Philosophy's 'weightier remedy', her
argument about the highest good (bk III). When people seek to obtain
the various goods of fortune, she argues, they are motivated by a
genuine desire for the good – we desire only what we consider to be
good – but are misled by ignorance about the nature of the good.
Each of the goods of fortune, taken on its own, is worth little and
does not last. People's mistake is to seek these goods individually,
rather than trying to gain the single good from which all these other
goods derive. This highest good is happiness (*beatitudo*); but, since
God (III, pr. 10) is that than which nothing better can be thought,
he is perfectly good. Therefore the highest good, which everyone seeks
but most, ignorant of its undivided nature, fail to gain, is God himself.
Philosophy goes on (bk IV) to explain why, despite appearances, it
is not the case that the wicked enjoy power while the good are left
impotent. She distinguishes the will to obtain something and the power
to be able to do so. Everyone, she says, wants happiness. The good
have the power, by being good, to gain happiness, whereas the evil
are unable to gain it. By contrast with Boethius-the-character's earlier
view of a universe in which God has abandoned humankind to its
own devices, Philosophy explains that divine providence arranges all

things; fate is simply the working out as actual events of this providential plan which is conceived 'in the purity of God's intellect' (IV,
pr. 6).

The thumbnail sketch in the last paragraph of Philosophy's arguments does little justice to the reasoned manner in which she is made
to develop her points. Yet the impression of looseness and question-
begging which may emerge is not misleading. At almost every stage,
Philosophy makes assumptions which an interlocutor less docile than
Boethius-the-character would have questioned, and the views she
reaches, although sweeping, are far from clear. To take just two examples. Central to Philosophy's argument is the idea that there is a perfect
good, from which the imperfect goods of fortune are derived. She
argues that the existence of a perfect good follows from the existence
of imperfect goods, because (III, pr. 10) 'if in any genus there seems
to be something which is imperfect, it is necessary that there is also
something perfect in it'. She supports this view by asking from where
the imperfect thing would derive its existence, did a perfect one not
exist. This principle may, indeed, have been one which Neoplatonists
of Boethius' time would accept, but is not the obvious truth which
Philosophy claims it to be. Another central idea is that the good man
is happy because he is able to gain the highest good, God. But in
what does this grasp of the highest good consist? What seems to be
called for is some idea of a beatific vision, either in this life or beyond
it. Philosophy, however, provides no such explanation. Yet it may not
be right to criticize Boethius-the-author for merely indicating the shape
of a philosophical position, rather than describing and justifying it in
detail. The full arguments for Philosophy's views, he might argue, are
to be found in the tradition of writing she personifies. The *Consolation*
merely sets out the main conclusions of the way of thought which the
character Boethius had supposedly forgotten in his grief; five short
books cannot be expected to provide a substitute for his years of
Neoplatonic study.

'ON THE CONSOLATION OF PHILOSOPHY:' DIVINE PRESCIENCE AND HUMAN FREE WILL

In Book V, the manner of the *Consolation* changes. The ornate language
of the earlier books all but disappears in favour of a more technical
style, close to that of the logical commentaries; and it is the Aristotelian
logical tradition which now gives Boethius his starting point. After
a short discussion of chance, the dialogue takes up the question of
God's omniscience and human freedom. Here the issue is strictly God's

fore*knowledge*: his providential pre*destination*, executed in time through fate, as discussed in Book IV, does not enter into consideration.

Intuitively, divine omniscience seems to pose a threat to human free will. If God knows everything, then he knows what I will do tomorrow. Whether I drink red wine or white wine with my dinner tomorrow might appear to be something I can choose by my free will. But if God knows *now* which I shall drink, is not my free will over the choice illusory? If God knows now that I shall drink white wine – and it is knowledge, not just a good guess – then it seems that the possibility that I shall drink red has already been closed. I have no choice but to drink white. One way of trying to formalize this train of thought is what might be called the 'knowledge-brings-determinism' argument. Part of the definition of 'knowledge' is that it is true belief. So, if I know *p*, then *p* is true. Since this follows from a definition, it is a matter of necessity. Just as it is a matter of necessity that, if I am a bachelor, I am unmarried, so it is a matter of necessity that if I know *p*, *p* is true. God knows everything, and so for *p* we can substitute any true statement about the past, present or future, including statements about future events such as my drinking the white wine. If God knows that I will drink white wine tomorrow, then necessarily I will drink white wine tomorrow, and similarly for any statement about the future – there are therefore no future contingents; all that will happen will happen by necessity.

The knowledge-brings-determinism argument, however, is invalid. It commits what would now be called a scope fallacy, by failing to distinguish whether the whole complex statement, or rather just an element of it, should be qualified by 'necessarily'. Consider the analogy of the bachelor. It is not the case that, if someone is a bachelor, then necessarily he is unmarried. He might well have married before now, although he has not. Rather, we ought to say: necessarily, if he is a bachelor, he is unmarried. Similarly, the definition of 'knowledge' shows merely that necessarily, if God foresees *p*, then *p*. Allowing that the whole conditional (if God foresees *p*, then *p*) is necessarily true in no way implies that *p* itself is necessarily true, and so it presents no threat to contingency or to human free will.

Boethius is often credited with showing the fallaciousness of the knowledge-brings-determinism argument and contrasted with earlier thinkers, such as Augustine who, though upholding free will, thought the logic of this argument irrefragable.[11] The basis of the claim is a distinction Boethius makes near the end of his discussion of divine prescience (V, pr. 6) between 'simple necessity' and 'conditional necessity'. As an example of strict necessity Boethius gives the necessity that all men are mortal; as an example of conditional necessity, that 'if you know someone is walking, it is necessary that he is walking'. He goes on to explain that, in such a case of conditional necessity, it is not the nature of the matter, but the 'adding of the condition' which brings about the necessity; and conditional necessity, he says, does not imply simple necessity. At first sight, especially in light of his terminology, Boethius *does* seem to be distinguishing between simple (non-composite) necessary statements, and the necessity of a whole conditional; and it is this distinction which is needed to expose the fallacy of the necessity-brings-determinism argument, by contrasting the whole conditional 'If God knows *p*, then *p*', which is necessary, with the simple statement *p*, the consequent of this conditional, which is not necessary. But closer scrutiny of the text does not support this reading.[12] Boethius is not talking about different types of statement but about different types of necessity. He is saying that the fact that men are mortal is necessary according to simple necessity, whereas, if you know someone is walking, the fact that he is walking is necessary, but only according to conditional necessity. Simple necessity, he believes, constrains – men cannot but die some time; but not conditional necessity – the man might have chosen to remain still.

Boethius' idea of conditional necessity is bound up with his view, inherited from the Aristotelian tradition, of the necessity of the present. Immediately after he has used the example of knowing (you know he is walking) to illustrate conditional necessity, he moves on to another example, which he apparently considers parallel: 'No necessity compels a walking man that he should will to walk although at that time when he is walking, it is necessary that he walks.' Here, too, Boethius believes, is an example of conditional necessity: the fact that he is walking at time *t* becomes necessary, conditionally though not simply, by the addition of the condition that it is now time *t*. Modern philosophers would say that, although it is not possible that he walk and not walk at *t*, it is possible that, although he is walking at *t*, he might not have been walking at that time: there is another possible world in which he stayed still at that moment. Boethius had no such conception of synchronous alternative possibilities.[13]

The link Boethius makes between conditional necessity and the necessity of the present renders the way in which he goes about tackling the question of divine prescience and human free will explicable. At the beginning of the discussion (V, pr. 3) the character-Boethius puts to Philosophy a version of the knowledge-brings-determinism argument, as applied to divine prescience. He considers the counter-argument made by some, that there is no causal relation between divine prescience and future events, but he replies to it by saying that, though there is no causal relation, none the less, divine prescience renders future events necessary. In her reply (which presumably gives Boethius-the-author's considered view), Philosophy begins by arguing that

21

Boethius was wrong to dismiss the counter-argument. If divine prescience does not cause future events to take place, it does *not* determine them. She recognizes, however, that there is something troubling about the idea that God knows now what I shall do tomorrow. Since, if the action in question is one I shall freely decide on it is not certain now what it will be, it seems as if there can be no foreknowledge about it, merely opinion. Philosophy's way of dealing with this problem (V, pr. 4–5) is to explain that beings of different levels cognize in different ways. God's 'intelligence' is unlike our reason, just as our reason differs from the senses. To see how God's intelligence works, we must realize (V, pr. 6) that for God to be eternal means that he enjoys 'the entire and perfect possession at once of unending life' (*interminabilis vitae tota simul et perfecta possessio*). God therefore knows all things, past, present and future, as if they were present. Only after having established this point at length, does Philosophy introduce briefly the distinction between simple and conditional necessity. The idea of God's timelessness – which would have been entirely superfluous were this distinction Boethius' way of noticing the scope fallacy which underlies the knowledge-brings-determinism argument – is, then, central to his treatment of prescience and free will for two reasons. First, it enables him to answer the epistemological problem about how an uncertain future could be *known*: for God, the object of knowledge is not future (or past), but present. Second, it allows him to resolve the logical problem which troubled the Boethius-the-character-in-the-dialogue, by assimilating God's present-tense knowledge of *p* to the more general case of *p* being true at the present time. Both cases are seen to involve an added condition ('GOD KNOWS *p*'/ '*p* WHEN *P*'). Boethius accepted the necessity of the present, but also knew that no one thought it a constraining necessity, and so it was now easy for him to characterize both it and the necessity implied by God's omniscience as a special sort of non-constraining 'conditional necessity', to be distinguished from constraining simple necessity.

From the thirteenth century onwards, detection of the scope fallacy involved in the knowledge-brings-determinism argument was routine. Statements of the form 'if *p*, then necessarily *q*' were said to exhibit 'necessity of the consequent' (*necessitas consequentis*), as opposed to statements of the form 'necessarily, if *p* then *q*', which exhibited 'necessity of the consequence' (*necessitas consequentiae*) ('*consequentia*' was the word for an 'if . . . then . . .' statement). This awareness was, however, often put in terms of Boethius' simple and conditional necessity, as if Boethius had shared it. Moreover, Boethius' treatment of God's timeless eternity was widely discussed. Some, such as Aquinas, adopted it (in the *Summa Theologiae* Aquinas states verbatim Boethius' definition of eternity as 'the entire and perfect possession at once of unending life' and defends it); other, later thinkers argued vigorously against it. Aquinas also found an important use for this view of timeless eternity in tackling an argument from divine prescience to determinism which Boethius had not anticipated. If God foreknows everything, then it is not just that God knows that tomorrow I shall drink white wine, not red: it is also true that it *has* come to God's knowledge that I shall drink white wine, not red, tomorrow. 'It has come to God's knowledge that *p*' implies *p* and, since it is a statement about the past and the past cannot be changed, if it is true, it seems it must be necessarily true; what a necessary truth implies is itself necessarily true; and so, the argument goes, my drinking the white wine is necessary.[14] There are various ways of attacking this argument, but Boethius provides Aquinas with a very straightforward one: if God knows in a timeless eternity, then it is not the case that God *has come to know* anything. As with many aspects of Boethius' work, medieval thinkers found more in his argument about divine prescience and human free will than he had explicitly put there. This may be a tribute to a certain undeveloped philosophical insight in Boethius – an inexplicit feel for important problems and the moves needed to deal with them – as well as to the cleverness of his medieval readers.

❧ 'ON THE CONSOLATION OF ❧ PHILOSOPHY': NEOPLATONISM AND CHRISTIANITY

The most remarkable feature of the *Consolation* is something it omits: any explicit reference to Christianity. Boethius' discussion of the highest good, which is God, and his treatment of providence, fate and prescience, would have been as acceptable to a pagan Neoplatonist as to a Christian, and of uniquely Christian doctrines such as the Trinity and incarnation there is not a mention. But few scholars nowadays believe that Boethius omitted Christian dogma from the *Consolation* because, when he wrote it, he had abandoned Christianity. Such a conversion to paganism is implausible, and there are several biblical echoes in the *Consolation*, at least one of which appears deliberate, since Philosophy echoes closely the phrasing of the Book of Wisdom and Boethius-the-character comments that, not merely what she has said, but the 'very words' she has used, delight him (III, pr. 12). Why, then, is the *Consolation* not more openly Christian? Perhaps because Boethius envisaged his task as presenting a *philosophical* justification of the providential ordering of the universe by a supremely good deity: a justification in which none of the premises is based on revelation. His training and writing had been as a logician and philosopher, and even his theological works had been exercises in philosophical analysis. It is not surprising that he should seek to come to terms with his downfall by writing as a philosopher, though he remained in his faith a Christian.

None the less, there are moments in the *Consolation* when Boethius' Neoplatonism does sit uncomfortably with Christian doctrine. At a central point in the work, before she concludes her argument identifying God with the highest good, Philosophy makes a solemn prayer. The poem (III, metrum 9) is an epitome of the *Timaeus*, the favourite Platonic dialogue of the Neoplatonists. It speaks without reservation of Platonic doctrines, such as reincarnation and the World Soul, which are clearly incompatible with Christianity. Possibly Boethius thought that, in the context of a poem, they need not be taken literally. Later, however, in his discussion of divine prescience (V, pr. 6), he champions the view that the world has endured for ever: it is what many would call 'eternal', although Boethius prefers to describe it as 'perpetual', reserving 'eternal' to describe the timeless eternity of God. Boethius' view was that of the pagan Neoplatonists of his time. Christians insisted that the world had a beginning and, writing shortly after Boethius' death, the Greek Christian philosopher John Philoponus would devise a set of intricate arguments, drawing on Aristotle's ideas about infinity, to support this position. Yet Boethius cannot have seen his own view as unacceptable for Christians, since he had already referred to it in his painstakingly orthodox *On the Trinity* (section IV).[15]

Although medieval writers drew on almost every aspect of the *Consolation*, none was more important than the work's uncertain status as a text by a Christian writer without explicitly Christian doctrines, and with some ideas which seemed distinctly pagan. The most popular strategy for commentators was to discover an explicitly Christian meaning implicit within the text, especially in sections like III, m. 9 which, at first sight, were hardest for Christian readers to accept. But there were dissenters, such as Bovo of Corvey in the tenth century, who insisted on a literal reading.[16] For some writers, such as the Middle English poet, Chaucer, the *Consolation* seems to have provided a model for writing about serious issues in a way which presupposes no commitment to Christianity, a philosophical precedent for the use of a pagan setting in literary fiction.

❧ EPILOGUE ❧

In the Latin West, Boethius' death marks the end of the ancient tradition of philosophy. There were writers – for instance, Cassiodorus (*c.* 485–580), Boethius' more politically-compromising successor as Master of the Offices, and Isidore (before 534–636), Bishop of Seville – who helped to pass elements of ancient teaching to medieval readers. But they were educators and encyclopaedists, rather than thinkers. The seventh- and eighth-century scholars in England and Ireland included some enthusiastic grammarians, but no logicians; the philosophical elements in patristic texts aroused little interest from them. The medieval Latin philosophical tradition would begin at the court of Charlemagne, in the 790s.

In the Greek tradition of philosophy, however, Boethius' death by no means marks a boundary. The Christian, John Philoponus, would produce important and influential philosophical work a little later in the sixth century.[17] Nor had pagan Neoplatonism come to an end. When in 529, shortly after Boethius' death, the Emperor Justinian closed the Platonic school at Athens, its philosophers sought refuge at the court of the Persian king, Chosroes. When, a little later, Chosroes concluded a peace treaty with Byzantium, it included a provision that the pagan philosophers be allowed to return to Byzantine lands and practice their form of philosophy unhindered. They took up residence at Harran, near to the Persian border, in about 532 and there Simplicius wrote most of his work.[18] The pagan Neoplatonic school at Harran survived at least until the tenth century, although very little is known of its later work. By then, the Middle East had been transformed by the preaching of Muhammad in the seventh century and the rapid rise of Islam. It is the tradition of philosophy which grew up in Islam from the ninth century onwards that this *History* will first consider.

 NOTES

1 For these works (and possible works on geometry and astronomy), which fall outside the scope of this discussion, see Chadwick [1.12] 69–107 and the articles in Gibson [1.16] by Caldwell, Pingree and White.

2 See J. Barnes, 'Boethius and the study of logic', in Gibson [1.16] 73–89. Barnes points out (p. 87) that Boethius himself ([1.1] 1191A, 1209C, 1216D) claims to have written such a commentary. Barnes also points to a thirteenth-century commentary which mentions a commentary by Boethius on the *Posterior Analytics*; but this medieval remark, not otherwise supported, carries little weight.

3 The first commentary on the *Isagoge* is an early work, which uses Marius Victorinus' translation rather than Boethius' own; the second commentary gives his maturer thoughts on the text. Boethius composed the two commentaries on *On Interpretation* together, putting simpler material in the first and more complex (but no less Aristotelian) discussion in the second.

4 See [1.1] 160AB and S. Ebbesen, 'Boethius as an Aristotelian commentator' in Sorabji [1.32], esp. 387–91.

5 See J. Shiel, 'Boethius' commentaries on Aristotle' in Sorabji [1.32] 349–72 for the view that Boethius translated marginalia, and Ebbesen's article, cited in the previous note, pp. 375–7, for strong arguments against it.

6 See the wide-ranging discussion in de Libera [1.22] (pp. 128–32 for Boethius).

7 See Barnes, 'Boethius and the study of logic' in Gibson [1.16] 83–4, Dürr [1.15] and Martin [1.23] 379–86.

8 On the medieval influence of *De hebdomadibus*, see Schrimpf [1.30].

9 There is a collection of articles on the transcendentals in medieval philosophy in *Topoi* 11 (1992) (guest editor, J. Gracia).

10 See J. Matthews, 'Anicius Manlius Severinus Boethius' in Gibson [1.16] 26–9.

11 See, for instance, C. Kirwan, *Augustine*, London, 1989, p. 98.

12 Knuuttila ([1.21] 60–1) briefly mentions exactly this point; I shall try to develop and justify it in the following paragraphs. Pike [1.28] 72–6) attributes to Boethius a different and more powerful argument either than the traditional interpretation criticized above, or than the one proposed here. But it is hard to believe, from the way Boethius develops his ideas in the text, that the argument really is his.

13 The lack of a conception of synchronous alternative possibilities in Boethius and other ancient writers, and the gradual introduction of this notion from the twelfth century onwards, is one of the main themes of Knuuttila [1.21].

14 This argument is stated in, for instance, Aquinas' *De veritate* q.12, a.12. For discussion of it, see Kenny [1.19] and Prior [1.29].

15 See Courcelle [1.13] 221–31 for a comparison between Boethius' views on the eternity of the world and those of his Christian and pagan near contemporaries.

16 See Chapter 5, pp. 110–11.

17 A good introduction to Philoponus' work is given in R. Sorabji (ed.) *Philoponus and the Rejection of Aristotelian Science*, London, 1987.

18 See I. Hadot, 'La vie et oeuvre de Simplicius', in I. Hadot (ed.) *Simplicius: Sa vie, son oeuvre, sa survie* (Peripatoi 15), Berlin and New York, 1987, pp. 3–39; but not all scholars accept this reconstruction of events.

❖ BIBLIOGRAPHY ❖

Original Language Editions of Boethius

1.1 *Works* in *MPL*, 63–4, Paris, 1847.

1.2 Translations of Aristotle in *AL* 1, 2, 3, 5, ed. L. Minio-Paluello et al., Bruges and Paris, 1966–9; 6, ed. B. Dod, Leiden and Brussels, 1975 (hereafter *AL*).

1.3 Commentaries on Porphyry's *Isagoge*, ed. S. Brandt (Corpus scriptorum ecclesiasticorum latinorum 64), Vienna and Leipzig, 1906.

1.4 Commentaries on Aristotle's *On Interpretation*, ed. C. Meiser, Leipzig, 1877–80.

1.5 Scholia on *Prior Analytics*, in *AL* 3.

26

1.6 Commentary on Cicero's *Topics*, ed. J. C. Orelli and J. G. Baiter in *M. Tulli Ciceronis opera omnia* V, 1, Zurich, 1833 and *On Hypothetical Syllogisms*, ed. L. Obertello, Brescia, 1969.

1.7 *Theological Treatises (Opuscula sacra)*, ed. H. F. Stewart, E. K. Rand, S. J. Tester (with *On the Consolation of Philosophy*), London and Cambridge, Mass., 1973.

1.8 *On the Consolation of Philosophy*, ed. L. Bieler (Corpus christianorum 94), Turnhout, 1957.

English Translations of Boethius

1.9 *On Topical Differentiae*, trans. E. Stump, Ithaca, NY and London, 1978.

1.10 *Boethius' 'In Ciceronis topica'*, Ithaca, NY and London, 1988.

1.11 *On Division*, in N. Kretzmann and E. Stump (eds) *Cambridge Translations of Medieval Philosophical Texts: Logic and the Philosophy of Language*, Cambridge, 1988, pp. 11–38.

1.7 contains a parallel English translation of the *Theological treatises* and also a translation of *On the Consolation of Philosophy*. Many other translations of the *Consolation* exist.

Boethius Studies

1.12 Chadwick, H. *Boethius: the Consolations of Music, Logic, Theology and Philosophy*, Oxford, 1981.

1.13 Courcelle, P. *La consolation de philosophie dans la tradition littéraire: antécédents et posterité de Boèce*, Paris, 1967.

1.14 Daley, B. 'Boethius' theological tracts and early Byzantine scholasticism', *Mediaeval Studies* 46 (1984): 158–91.

1.15 Dürr, K. *The Propositional Logic of Boethius*, Amsterdam, 1951.

1.16 Gibson, M. (ed.) *Boethius: His Life, Thought and Influence*, Oxford, 1981.

1.17 Gruber, J. *Kommentar zu Boethius De Consolatione Philosophiae*, Berlin, 1978.

1.18 Huber, P. *Die Vereinbarkeit von göttlicher Vorsehung und menschlicher Freiheit in der Consolatio Philosophiae des Boethius*, Zurich, 1976.

1.19 Kenny, A. 'Divine foreknowledge and human freedom', in A. Kenny (ed.) *Aquinas: a Collection of Critical Essays*, Notre Dame, Ind., 1969, pp. 273–96.

1.20 Klingner, F. *De Boethii Consolatione Philosophiae*, (Philologische Untersuchungen 27), Berlin, 1921.

1.21 Knuuttila, S. *Modalities in Medieval Philosophy*, London and New York, 1993.

1.22 Libera, A. de *La querelle des universaux: De Platon à la fin du Moyen Âge*, Paris, 1996.

1.23 Martin, C. J. 'Embarrassing arguments and surprising conclusions in the development of theories of the conditional in the twelfth century', in J. Jolivet and A. de Libera (eds) *Gilbert de Poitiers et ses contemporains* (History of Logic 5), Naples, 1987, pp. 377–400.

1.24 Minio-Paluello, L. 'A Latin commentary (trans. ?Boethius) on the *Prior Analytics* and its Greek sources', *The Journal of Hellenic Studies* 77 (1957): 93–102 (repr. in *Opuscula* 347–56).

1.25 —— 'Les traductions et les commentaires aristotéliciens de Boèce', *Studia Patristica II*, Texte und Untersuchungen zur Geschichte der altchristlichen Literatur 64 (1957): 358–65 (repr. in *Opuscula* 328–35).

1.26 —— *Opuscula: the Latin Aristotle*, Amsterdam, 1972.

1.27 Obertello, L. *Severino Boezio*, 2 vols, Genoa, 1974.

1.28 Pike, N. *God and Timelessness*, London, 1970.

1.29 Prior, A. 'The formalities of omniscience', in *Papers on Tense and Time*, Oxford, 1968, pp. 26–44.

1.30 Schrimpf, G. *Die Axiomenschrift des Boethius, De Hebdomadibus als philosophisches Lehrbuch des Mittelalters* (Studien über die Problemgeschichte d. antike u. mittelalterlichen Philosophie 2), Leiden, 1966.

1.31 Schurr, V. *Die Trinitätslehre des Boethius im Lichte der 'Skythischen Kontroversen'* (Forschungen zur christlichen Literatur und Dogmengeschichte 18.1), Paderborn, 1935.

1.32 Sorabji, R. (ed.) *Aristotle Transformed: the Ancient Commentaries and their Influence*, London, 1990.

CHAPTER 2

From the beginnings to Avicenna

Jean Jolivet

❧

Arabic philosophy began at the turn of the second and third centuries
of the Hegira, roughly the ninth and tenth centuries AD. The place
and the time are important. It was in 133/750 that the 'Abbāssid
dynasty came to power. The 'Abbāssids, like the Ummayads whom
they had driven out, were Arabs; but they had been aided by eastern
powers: Persians and Shi'ite Muslims. The symbolic capital of the
empire changed from Damascus to Baghdad, founded in 145/762 by
the second 'Abbāssid caliph, al-Manṣūr. Now Islamic power stretched
from the Atlantic to central Asia. Damascus and Baghdad were areas
which had been Hellenized for a millennium and where Byzantium
and Persia had faced each other. Now the Arabs had been victorious
over them both, overturning the Sassanids, who had already been
forced back towards the East by Byzantium, and taking from
Byzantium not only Egypt but also its Asian provinces, where the
monophysite Christians were in schism with the Orthodox Church
and persecuted by the imperial authorities. These conquests took place
between 634 and 650 (the second and third decades of the Hegira).
These historical circumstances foreshadow several essential features of
Arabic philosophy to which we shall return. First, there was a gap in
time between the revelation of the Holy Book, which was 'handed
down' in an un-Hellenized area of Arabia, and the beginning of Arabic
philosophy (contrast the development of Christian thought, where
Hellenistic elements are to be found even in the earliest documents).
Second, the emergence of Arabic philosophy coincided with a change
of dynasty brought about with the help of non-Arabs: the political,
religious and, in particular, literary aspects of this change would develop

29

in the third/ninth century into the movement which was called the *shuʿūbiyya* (after the *Koran*, 49, 13: 'Men . . . we have set you up as peoples, *shuʿūban*). Third, Arabic philosophy developed in a milieu linked, in language, culture and belief, by age-old ties both to Greece and to Asia – and, as we shall see, it was thanks to Christian scholars that it found its particular direction.

✦✦ THE TRANSLATIONS ✦✦

For two centuries, Christians had been employed to translate Greek works into Syriac, a type of Aramaic that had been developed into a literary language. In this way there began, even before the birth of Islam, the great enterprise of translation which would provide the opportunity for the first works of Arabic philosophy and the results of which would provide its subject-matter and foundation. The history of this movement, especially its earliest stage, has not yet been written in full. We can say, however, that between the fifth and seventh centuries AD translations were made from Greek into Syriac, particularly translations of medical works and, even more, of logical works. The first books of Aristotle's *Organon* were, then, not merely translated but received a number of commentaries. The majority of the translators were Nestorians, but they also included Jacobites. At the end of the first/seventh century, the Muslims took over the Fertile Crescent and the Umayyad caliph ʿAbd al-Malik decided that Arabic would be the official language of the empire. The work of the translators was enlarged. Translation from Greek to Syriac continued to be their main task, but there were also translations made from Greek into Arabic and from Syriac into Arabic. This third route was used only in the fourth/tenth century when even the educated no longer knew Greek, and when in any case the translation movement came to a halt.

Not only was there a change in the languages from which, and to which, translations were made; there was variation over time in the method and type of translation. Translators into Syriac changed from giving paraphrases to making literal versions. The greatest of them were the two Christian Nestorians Ḥunayn ibn Isḥāq and his son Isḥāq ibn Ḥunayn, whose work in Syriac and Arabic dates from the third/ninth century. Acute in establishing their texts and rigorously accurate in translating from one language to another, Ḥunayn and his son ended by creating 'a technical Arabic capable of closely reflecting the structure of the Greek' ([2.27]). There were many other translators too in their century and the one before, some of them very fine. Rather than list them, it is more useful to step back in time and mention the names of ʿAbd Allāh ibn al-Muqaffaʿ (d. 140/757) and of the Syrian

Ibn Bahrīz, who lived at the time of the caliph al-Ma'mūn (d. 218/833). Both wrote epitomes of logical works (al-Muqaffa' on Porphyry's *Isagoge* and the first books of the *Organon*; Ibn Bahrīz on the whole *Organon*). We can see in these works the first attempts to develop an Arabic philosophical vocabulary ([2.27], [2.43]).

In this way an enormous library of philosophical and scientific works was built up and revealed to the curiosity and interests of new readers. The last Umayyad caliphs and the first of the 'Abbāssids were especially strong in their support for this work of translation. In the case of the 'Abbāssids, this enthusiasm was motivated in part by a political motive, since Greek philosophy and science provided a cultural counterbalance to the theology of the Islamic Arabs and to the ancient heritage of the Persians. The intellectual (and, particularly, philosophical) market-place was thus stocked with a complex mixture of goods: an Arabic Plato (the details of which still remain unclear), an Arabic Plotinus attributed to other authors, collections of philosophical comments and aphorisms in which authentic pronouncements mingle with apocrypha, and above all the complete works of Aristotle, without the *Politics* but with various, especially Neoplatonic, pseudepigrapha. This Aristotle is omnipresent in Arabic philosophy, yet its presence was the result in the main of a choice made several centuries earlier by the Syriac translators: 'it was not the Arabs who chose Aristotle, but the Syriacs who imposed [him on them]' ([2.43]; cf. [2.20], [2.38], [2.41], [2.44]).

❧ AL-KINDĪ ❧

Arabic philosophers drew extensively, then, on Aristotle's work and thought. Yet they were not Aristotelians in the strict sense of the word. This is already clear in the work of the first of them, Abū Yūsuf Ya'qūb ibn Ishāq al-Kindī (born end of second century/beginning of eight century; died after 256/870) ([2.19], [2.11]). Al-Kindī was a philosopher, no doubt; but he was primarily a wide-ranging scholar and scientist (and it was just as such that, half a thousand years later, Ibn Khaldūn would remember him). The biographer and bibliographer Ibn al-Nadīm (fourth/tenth century) provides a *catalogue raisonné* of his works: almost 250 of them in all, of which only about a tenth survive. Ibn al-Nadīm divides them into seventeen categories. Classifying them, rather, by subject areas, we find that al-Kindī devoted about 50 treatises to philosophy and logic, but nearly a hundred to the various branches of mathematics (including astrology), and 35 to medicine and the natural sciences. The others do not concern us here. His scholarly and scientific work was thus extensive and varied; we might mention, for instance, in passing his contributions to optics and pharmacology. As a philosopher, he quotes by name hardly any authors besides Plato and Aristotle. We do not know precisely how great his knowledge was of Plato, but he wrote a treatise listing the works of Aristotle ([2.23]). Of the major works only the *Politics* is, as we should expect, absent. The list includes two apocrypha (*On Plants, On Minerals*), but not the *Theology of Aristotle*, a work by an unknown author, probably Porphyry, consisting of considerably adapted extracts from Plotinus' later *Enneads*. Its absence is all the more striking because al-Kindī had corrected an Arabic translation of it made by Ibn Nā'ima for the son of the caliph al-Mu'taṣim (218/833 to 228/842). And indeed al-Kindī's philosophy is a branch of Neoplatonism, but not one which is disguised by being based on Aristotelian apocrypha of Neoplatonic origin.

Among the handful of philosophical works of al-Kindī's which have survived, the most important is the *Book of First Philosophy* (*Kitāb al-falsafah al-ūlā* ([2.2]); note how the Greek *philosophia* is transcribed as *falsafah*; similarly *philosophos* becomes *faylasūf*, plural *falāsifah*). Of this book with its Aristotelian title we have only the first part (divided into four chapters). It is a Neoplatonic work in the sense that the main concepts of Aristotelianism (the categories, the predicables, causes) are made part of a theory of the one, into which al-Kindī's ontology is absorbed. In this rich discussion, new ideas and new methods are found in every chapter. We shall consider merely a few significant themes of various sorts. Chapter 1 forms a veritable manifesto, decked out with quotations from Aristotle (who is not named: the passages are mostly from the *Metaphysics* A 1). Al-Kindī provides an apologia for philosophy which, he says, has been formed over the course of centuries. We must gather what remains and bring it to fruition. It matters little, he says, that it comes from elsewhere. We must adapt it into our own language and to our own traditions, since it does not differ in content from the messages of the prophets: it is knowledge of God's unity and sovereignty, of virtue and of what in general we should seek and avoid. The ending of chapter 2 provides a characteristic example of al-Kindī's method and his liberty with regard to Aristotle. Using the method of geometry, he shows that the body of the world, movement and time can exist only if they are simultaneous with each other. They are, therefore, finite, because the world is finite. Aristotle's view that the world is eternal is thus rejected. Chapter 3 ends with a dialectical treatment of the one and the many based in detail, yet also very freely, on Proclus (*Platonic Theology* II, 1), who none the less is not named ([2.29]). Finally, chapter 4 demonstrates that the True One is transcendent: above every genus, category and ontological structure. It is he who gives to everything which is 'accidentally one' the unity which makes it exist, and this being-made-one, 'the flowing of unity from the True One' is a being-made-to-exist (*tahawwī*). (The noun *tahawwī* is derived from the pronoun *huwa*, 'him', which by its very meaning implies reference to an existing being and from which is also derived the word *huwiyya*, 'substance' or 'existence' depending on the context. Al-Kindī's vocabulary includes a number of neologisms, some of which were not used by his successors; it bears witness to the state of Arabic philosophical vocabulary which was still being constructed, especially by the translators.) At this point the known part of the *First Philosophy* concludes. It is an important work, which shows how al-Kindī fits together the major systems of Greek philosophy, especially Neoplatonism. The concepts of the one and of transcendence are, in particular, common to this philosophical school and to Muslim theology. The Muʿtazilites especially would make it one of their main themes, and there is independent evidence that al-Kindī was close to them.

The doctrinal themes of the *First Philosophy* can be compared to those contained in other works by al-Kindī: explicitly or implicitly, the main aspects of his thought are to be found in this central work. First, the idea of the underlying harmony between revelation and prophecy is also found in the main discussion of the *Letter on the Number of Aristotle's Bodies* ([2.23]): the 'divine knowledge' which God gives, from his free choice, to the prophets opens to them the knowledge of visible and invisible substances, whereas men usually have to labour long and hard, using logic and mathematics, to gain it. Thus the final verses of sourate 36 (*Yā ʿSīn*) provide illuminating teaching on creation, the sequence of life and death and on contraries in general. Al-Kindī expounds at length the philosophical content of what divine revelation condenses into a few words. Second, as has already been explained, knowledge is gained through science and mathematics. This is an important theme of the *Letter*, which is proposed and argued at the beginning and taken up again near to the end. In both places, mathematics is put first, and it is this method which is used in chapter 2 of the *First Philosophy*. The discussions there are taken up in three other letters about the finitude of the world. Elsewhere too al-Kindī's arguments often have a rigorous, detailed structure based on the mathematical method. Third, the cosmological theme is developed by the same method in the *Letter on the Prostration of the Farthest Body*, which takes a text from the Koran (55: *al-Raḥmān*, 6) – 'The star and the tree prostrate themselves' – as its point of departure. Al-Kindī begins with a semantic analysis of the words 'prostration' and 'obedience', which he says mean the same in this context. Then he explains in detail how God's will works in the world, which he envisages according to Greek cosmology and Aristotle's physics (except that he does not consider it eternal); once they have been created, the heavens are put into motion, and from this there comes about time and then coming-to-be. The heavens live, think and are the agent cause of all coming-to-be. The *Letter on the True, First and Perfect Agent Cause, and the Imperfect Agent Cause [which is called agent] by Extension* explains that true agency is reserved for God alone, who creates the first sphere of the heavens and puts it into motion and, through it, puts all the other spheres into motion: but what comes to be from it is not action, but being-acted-upon (*infi'al*) ([2.31]).

We should also mention two topics which are implied in the *First Philosophy* but not discussed there. One of these is the soul, the subject of a metaphysical, exhortatory treatise, which gathers together ideas from various sources, in particular ones taken from Platonism, Neoplatonism and Hermeticism ([2.22]). Another is intellectual knowledge, treated in the *Letter on the Intellect*, one of the few works by al-Kindī translated into Latin (twelfth century). Here al-Kindī differentiates four types or levels of the intellect, according to the reinterpretation of Aristotle's theory of intellectual knowledge by the early Neoplatonic school (Porphyry) and John Philoponus ([2.28]). Finally, the *Letter on How to Dispel Sadness* ([2.40]) is a lengthy moral exhortation which includes spiritual advice, written in the common philosophical style of the first centuries AD. In this work al-Kindī shows much less of his characteristic turn of mind than elsewhere, where he subjects what he has gathered from the Greek philosophers to his own treatment.

❧ AL-RĀZĪ AND AL-FĀRĀBĪ ❧

The most idiosyncratic figure in the history of Arabic philosophy is, without question, that of Abū Bakr Muḥammad ibn Zakariyyā al-Rāzī (251/865–313/925), who was also an outstanding writer on medicine. The most important of his many medical works, *al-Hāwī* (known in Latin as *Continens*) has a significant place in the history of medicine, in Christian Europe as well as in Islam, and it was translated into Latin twice (end of thirteenth century and in the sixteenth century). He took his inspiration as a philosopher more closely and constantly from the Greeks than from other sources. He looked to Socrates as the master of all philosophers in his way of life; he knew and quoted Plato, Aristotle, Porphyry, John Philoponus and others. He did not think that philosophy always remains one and the same. It progresses through the very differences between those who follow it, and to be a philosopher does not, he believed, mean to have the truth but to try to reach it – a view of intellectual history entirely other than al-Kindī's. The basis of al-Rāzī's ethics is reason and its aim is the ordering of conduct and the subjugation of the passions. His theology is explicitly philosophical. The world is an emanation from God; and not only God, but also the world soul, prime matter, space and time are eternal. Al-Rāzī believed in the transmigration of souls, which could rise to higher moral and metaphysical levels in successive reincarnations. And he denied that there was such a thing as prophecy. God inspires all men equally, but they are not all equal in taking advantage of it. Clearly, these views were not acceptable to the Islamic faithful. Only a few rather short treatises of al-Rāzī survive, and the work where he denies the existence of prophecy is known only through the quotes made in order to attack it by his contemporary and compatriot, the Ismāʿīlite missionary, Abū Ḥātim al-Rāzī. Despite the controversial nature of his philosophical ideas, al-Rāzī was allowed to be the doctor in charge of the hospital at Baghdad.

Abū Bakr al-Rāzī's place in the history of *falsafah* is therefore a strange one, the very opposite of that held by al-Kindī, another Neoplatonist. Different again is that held by Abū Naṣr Muḥammad ibn Muḥammad al-Fārābī, who was born at about the same time as al-Kindī died and who lived until 339/950 ([2.11]). He maintained the same high level of philosophical thinking as his great predecessor, but he moved it definitely into a new direction, opening up a fresh path for its development. One feature of his work was his great interest and ability in logic. Here he was the beneficiary of the work done by the translators and commentators (most of them Christians), such as Abū Bishr Mattā and Yuḥannā ibn Ḥaylān, his masters at the Aristotelian school at Baghdad, whom he considered to belong to the tradition of the Greek commentators. But he went further, especially in the attention he gave to the structure of reasoning and the types of argument. Among his works of logic are books based on, or commenting on (often very freely), all the books of the *Organon*, as well as Porphyry's *Isagoge* and in accord with the practice of the School of Alexandria, the *Rhetoric* (though not, like them, the *Poetics*, which remained on the edges of the Arab philosophical tradition). He also wrote introductory logical works and, more interestingly, a *Little Book of Reasoning according to the methods of the mutakallimūn and the fuqahā*, which examines critically, according to logical criteria alone, the methods of argument used by the theologians and the lawyers. Al-Fārābī begins with a systematic exposition of Aristotle's logic. In his prologue, al-Fārābī explains that he will use 'terms known to those who speak Arabic and examples familiar to our contemporaries'. This method might be taken as one especially designed for teaching, but it might also be seen in terms of a more far-reaching principle of logico-grammatical analysis. Before giving a complete survey of logic and placing it within the whole domain of knowledge, the *Book of Terms*

Used in Logic lists the words which are joined to nouns, to verbs and to noun-verb combinations: that is to say, tool-words. In this list are found purely logical terms (such as quantifiers) but especially invariable words, some of which correspond to terms in Greek, others of which have a place only in Arabic. There is, then, here a tension between the universality implied by the return to Greek philosophy, and the particularity of the language of *faylasūf*. In this light, al-Fārābī's work can be seen as an attempt to introduce certain particular features of the Arabic language into the historical development of logic ([2.9], [2.25]).

Here we see the deep structure of al-Fārābī's thought: more emphatically than al-Kindī's, it is based on the attempt to combine ideas of different sorts – Greek and Arabic, philosophical and religious – into a whole which is both systematic and historical. Another witness to this way of thinking and writing is the strange *Book of Letters* (*Kitāb al-ḥurūf*). 'Letters' has two different (but compatible) meanings here. It provides the work's title first because the book is a set of loose variations, in al-Fārābī's usual manner, on Aristotle's *Metaphysics*, which was sometimes called in Arabic *Kitāb al-ḥurūf* (from the fact that its books are each designated by a Greek letter). But, second, the title refers to the fact that, just like the *Book of Terms Used in Logic*, this treatise contains a study of various tool-words; and these are what grammarians call *ḥurūf*, 'letters'. Here, however, the list is occupied mainly by terms which are used in philosophy, whether words like 'when' and 'how' or the names of the categories, predicables and so on. In this context, al-Fārābī examines the copula in attributive propositions which, in Arabic, poses problems unknown to Greek logicians. (It is wrong, however, to draw – as has been done – the conclusion that this difference in the way being is expressed caused a radical separation between 'Arab thought' and 'Greek thought'. The Greek attributive proposition can easily do without the copula, and Arabic philosophers were perfectly comfortable in ontology.) This treatise also dwells on, among other things, the relation between philosophy, religion, language and the whole course of civilization, considered in the most general way. Altogether, it examines in depth concepts and themes from the whole field of philosophy: the status of concepts, the categories, the vocabulary of being, epistemology and scientific method. In one way or another it includes the subject-matter of various Aristotelian works along with subjects such as the history of culture and the theory of religion which Aristotle did not consider systematically. Here perhaps is a third reason for its title. To al-Fārābī, this book occupied a place among his works similar to that of the *Metaphysics* (devoted to being *qua* being, and to theology) among Aristotle's writings.

In logic, then, al-Fārābī's project was to found the Greek on the Arab and the Arab on the Greek. In political philosophy, his second main interest, his procedure is the same, although it involves more material that is rooted in cultural particularities. Political philosophy includes consideration of the relations between philosophy and religion, which for al-Fārābī meant the defence of philosophy. A number of his works fit into this class. *The Enumeration of the Sciences* surveys the encyclopaedia of scientific knowledge which the Arabs have built up through their philology, their translations from the Greek and their own creative work: grammar and linguistics, logic, mathematics (in the broad sense of the quadrivium along with mechanics), physics, metaphysics, politics and two exclusively Islamic branches of knowledge: *fiqh* or jurisprudence and *kalām*, defensive or polemical theology (about which al-Fārābī manifests considerable reserve, whereas he recognizes the usefulness of *fiqh*). Although the chapters on these two Islamic subjects seem not to fit in with the rest of the work, al-Fārābī had promised, in his prologue, to deal with the branches of knowledge 'which are being followed at the present time', a qualification which now is seen to have its rationale. *The Agreement of the Two Sages* is intended to show that, despite appearances to the contrary, Plato and Aristotle do not contradict each other. This subtle, at times even enigmatic work, is at least clear in its aim. Starting from a definition and analysis of the content of philosophy, it attempts to reveal a deep unity among the main doctrines which make it up and so to assert its value against those who attack it, and guarantee its place in the field of knowledge and thought. Side by side with this treatise is the collection consisting of *The Attainment of Happiness*, *The Philosophy of Plato* and *The Philosophy of Aristotle* ([2.3], [2.4]).

During the course of his life, al-Fārābī was able to observe the crumbling of the 'Abbāssid caliphate's power. In every part of the empire minor, practically independent princely dynasties sprang up. During al-Muqtadir's caliphate (298/908 to 320/930) there were thirteen vizirs, amd two rival caliphates were formed: the Fatimid in Egypt and the Umayyad in Spain. Between al-Muqtadir's death and al-Fārābī's own, four caliphs were overthrown or assassinated. Not unexpectedly, then, al-Fārābī was aware of the importance of politics and the philosophical problems posed by it. They formed the subject of many of his works, and were emphasized even in books of his which also dealt with other areas. His most extensive political work is called *Principles of the Opinions of the Citizens of the Best City*. Here al-Fārābī considers the city and its government by placing it within a wider scheme of macrocosm and microcosm, in which the structure of the greater and lesser worlds is seen to be similar at every level. This structure is hierarchical: its elements (the celestial spheres, the faculties of the soul, the bodily organs, the inhabitants of cities) are each seen to depend on something superior, which is the basis for their initial and continuing existence. Al-Fārābī gives a clear description of the emanation of the celestial intelligences and their spheres, one which Avicenna will copy and fill out in detail. The city should be organized and run by a legislator who combines being 'wise, prudent and a philosopher'. From the agent Intellect there come into the legislator's potential intellect the intelligible forms which make up his knowledge, whilst also putting his imagination to work so that he becomes an 'annunciatory prophet', who can inculcate the best laws in the people through persuasion and thus achieve the aim of political science: to establish the happiness of the city. The legislator will, then, be both philosopher and prophet: he will combine philosophy and religion. Especially in the *Book of Letters* and the *Book of Religion*, al-Fārābī asserts the priority of philosophy to religion, which 'follows' it: 'good religious laws are subordinate to the universal principles of practical philosophy'. Religion is subordinate to philosophy in the way that imagination is to the intellect, and persuasive discourse to demonstration. These ideas are linked to various ancient philosophical themes: Platonic (the role of the legislator) and Aristotelian (the position of rhetoric). Al-Fārābī is certainly nearer than al-Rāzī to the Islamic view of religion and the state, in that he accepts the existence of prophets and gives a rational explanation for it. But, by sharp contrast with al-Kindī, his doctrine is laicized: it keeps the form of Islam but subverts its content. The philosophical religion about which he theorizes ends by placing the philosophical theology of the Greek philosophers above the teaching of God's messengers ([2.8]).

This is not the place for a history of Islamic theology (the *kalām*), nor even a sketch of it. This kind of speculative theology began even before the end of the first century, the product of the need to express and defend in formal language the truths first formulated in the Qu'rān. Its main themes included the structure of created being, the relation of human actions to God's absolute power and how God should be conceived. Only the Mu'tazilite school, which began in the second century, need be mentioned here, since it was the first to deal with the central points of theology and arrange them into a doctrinal whole; and since, moreover, its exponents were accused of being close to the *falāsifah*. The Mu'tazilites – who differed between themselves on many matters – were agreed that the good can be known by reason, apart from revelation; that man creates his own acts. They emphasized the absolute unity of God: his names are many, but not his attributes. And some of them engaged in profound speculations about the status of non-existing things (for instance, things before God created them, or those things which God knows will never exist). These are genuinely philosophical themes, and it is legitimate to speak of a metaphysics or physics of the *kalām* – but one which has a characteristic vocabulary, set of concepts and structure different from those of *falsafah*. Their paths are different but, quite often, they intersect. Without some knowledge of the *kalām*, there are important features of Arabic philosophy which will not be properly understood ([2.21], [2.39]).

At the same period there were other writers connected in one way or another with the central tradition of *falsafah*. First, the collective work of the Ikhwān al-Ṣafā' (Brothers of Purity) should be mentioned. It was produced throughout the tenth century AD. It consists of fifty-two letters, written in a style which is more accessible and persuasive than that of the philosophers and theologians. Taken together, the letters make up an encyclopaedia which is Neoplatonic in its arrangement and concepts, spiritual in content and religious in its basis. The Ikhwān should be placed within Shi'ism or, rather, on its edges, since they were Isma'īlites. Theirs was an hierarchical organization of initiates. Although they therefore have a rather special place within Islam as a whole, their method of speculation illustrates how the Shi'ites accepted far more readily than the Sunnis the connection between philosophy and religion. Like the Mu'tazilites, the Ikhwān held that truth was originally given in a divine revelation witnessed by the philosophical sages as well as the prophets. Whilst it is just to compare this idea to late Neoplatonism, it also has a precise place in the intellectual and spiritual history of Islam in this particular period. On the one hand, it provided a way to recognize the value of ancient traditions, especially those in what was now the eastern part of the empire, which seemed to pre-date Islam. On the other hand, it was a means of legitimating the philosophy derived from the Greeks, following the path opened by al-Kindī but with greater historical precision. As a result the sages of antiquity (Empedocles and Pythagoras were thought the most venerable) were considered to have lived at the same period as David and Solomon and to have profited from their wisdom; this wisdom, which emanated from 'the tabernacle of prophecy' was successively passed to Socrates, then to Plato and even went as far as Aristotle. The heyday of this historico-ideological doctrine was the second half of the tenth century AD, a time when several emirs of the Shi'ite Buyid dynasty, with its capital at Shīrāz, acted as patrons of learning and science. There is a certain uniformity to the philosophy of this period. Ancient philosophy was well and accurately known, but it did not stimulate any really creative thought. Rather, it was linked to a taste for learning and for expounding the stock of ancient wisdom. Writers of this sort include Abū Sulaymān al-Sijistānī (died *c.* 990), Abū Ḥayyān al-Tawḥīdī (died in 399/1099) and Ibn Fātik al-Mubashshir, all of them men of great learning. Among the works typical of this tendency is the *Eternal Wisdom* of Abū 'Alī Aḥmad ibn Miskawayh (died in 421/1030), chancellor of the Buyid emir, 'Aḍud al-Dawla. This work claims to be a translation of an old Persian book and collects pronouncements attributed to ancient Persian, Indian, Arab and Greek sages. For the exponents of this current of thought, the truth has been available ever since its original revelation. Such a conception comes down to applying to philosophers the principle by which the prophets all transmit the same revelation; but, for this reason, philosophy, having been made sacred, becomes merely a matter of retrospection. Al-Kindī's explicit view was very different, but his idea of a deep agreement between philosophers and prophets left the way open for the notion of eternal wisdom and so may have perhaps contradicted his own theory of progress ([2.18], [2.33], [2.34]).

❧ AVICENNA ❧

The traditional (perhaps not completely exact) date for the birth, near Bukhara (in present day Uzbekistan) of Abū 'Alī al-Ḥusayn ibn 'Abdallah ibn Sīnā is 370/980. Ibn Sīnā, known as 'Avicenna' in the West through the twelfth-century Latin translations, is a giant in the history of thought. A polymath, he was in particular an outstanding physician, and it was in this capacity or as a vizier that he served various princes in the eastern parts of Islam. His life was thus far from calm and, at times, it was dramatic. He died at Hamadān in 429/1037 as a result of taking a wrongly made-up medicine. Some of his works have been lost, but what remains is still substantial. It includes treatises on various subjects, especially medicine; writings in which he wraps philosophical views in fiction, in a way reminiscent of Plato's myths; and a set of encyclopaedias, some of which are more or less schematic, whilst others are fairly or extremely detailed. The detailed, lengthier encyclopaedias are *The Direction* (*al-Hidāya*), *The Cure* (*al-Shifā*) – by far the longest of them, *The Salvation* (*al-Najāt*) and *Instructions and Remarks* (*al-Ishārāt wa-l-tanbīhāt*). These are all in Arabic, whilst a fifth large encyclopaedia, the *Book of Knowledge* (*Dānesh-nāme*) is in Persian. Two rules of method guide the composition of these works. First, they follow in general the scheme of the branches of knowledge traditionally recognized in Aristotelianism: logic, physics, mathematics, and theology or metaphysics. This does not mean that all Ibn Sīnā's encyclopaedias follow exactly this order. For instance, the *Book of Knowledge*, as well as another work in Persian, the *Philosophy for 'Alā' al-Dawla*, places metaphysics before physics, in accord with the idea of metaphysics as the study of the general properties of being. Avicenna's other encyclopaedias place metaphysics after physics, which prepares the ground for understanding it. The second rule is what follows from the progress of knowledge and Ibn Sīnā's own decisions on theoretical questions. The result of these two principles is that Ibn Sīnā expounds his own views, following Aristotle but not repeating him; thus in the *Shifā* the material of the *Meteorologica* is differently arranged among different books, and the *Metaphysics* follows Aristotle's plan only distantly. The only works on which he actually wrote commentaries are Aristotle's *Metaphysics* Λ and *On the Soul,* and also the apocryphal *Theology of Aristotle.* These commentaries belonged to the *Book of Right Judgement* (*Kitāb al-Inṣāf*), which survives only in fragments (the complete text was lost when the prince whom Ibn Sīnā served as physician and vizier was defeated in battle). In this way there disappeared almost the whole of what has been taken as Ibn Sīnā's last philosophy, what he called an 'Eastern philosophy', distinct from that of 'Westerners'. There has been much speculation about the nature of this 'Eastern philosophy'. Some have seen it as a definite turning towards what would later be called 'philosophy of illumination'. Others point out that a treatise which Ibn Sīnā actually calls *Logic of the Easterners* is not particularly different from his other writings. They consider that the term 'Easterners' refers to an Aristotelian school at Khurāsān. Moreover, in the *Instructions,* which are later than the lost *Book of Right Judgement,* there is no mention of 'Eastern philosophy' ([2.10], [2.24], [2.25]).

As a young man, Ibn Sīnā read and learnt everything there was to read and learn. But for the formation of his thought the most important of all the books he read were the *Letters* of the Ikhwān al-Ṣafā', and the works of al-Fārābī, which were particularly important in allowing him to grasp the point of Aristotle's *Metaphysics* by showing him the deep connection between the theology and the ontology of forms which this text brings together. His interest in the Ikhwān is understandable in the light of his spiritual sympathy (perhaps even adherence) to Ismaʿīlism; his father was himself an Ismaʿīli. With regard to al-Fārābī, there is no difficulty in drawing up a list of parallels with Ibn Sīnā's views. The two thinkers shared a universal vision of a hierarchy of being with God at the head of it, and (following the accumulated teaching of the Aristotelian commentators and of al-Kindī) an analysis of the intellect which, using the notions of act and potency, divides it into several ontologically distinct levels. To this, they both linked a doctrine of prophecy; and they also shared an interest in logic. But Ibn Sīnā treated these traditions as he did Aristotle: he handled their various features in his own personal way. A fuller study would need to take these differences into account, listing and analysing them. For instance, in logic Ibn Sīnā combined the rules for attributive propositions and those for hypothetical ones into a more complete synthesis than had been previously achieved ([2.35], [2.37],

[2.42]). Similarly, Ibn Sīnā's thinking about the origin of things goes further than al-Fārābī's. According to Ibn Sīnā 'the Being which is necessary by its essence' is an Intelligence which thinks itself and so is at once thinking and thought. The thought which it has of itself is productive of being. The first being produced in this way therefore exists necessarily and yet, in its own essence, it is contingent. It too is an Intelligence (the First Intelligence) which (1) thinks the Necessary in itself and also thinks itself in its two aspects: (2) in its own necessary existence and (3) in its contingent essence. From Thought (1) there emanates a second Intelligence placed directly below this first Intelligence; whilst from Thought (2) there emanates a form, and from Thought (3) matter, which are respectively the soul and body of the first Intelligence's sphere. The second Intelligence produces the soul and body of its own sphere, and the third Intelligence; and this process continues down to the last Intelligence, that of the sphere of the moon. From it there emanate into the sublunary world the forms which human intellects receive in different ways and the matter which is 'prepared' to receive these forms. The ideas implied by this scheme of cosmic emanation are at the very heart of Avicenna's metaphysics – none more so than the correlated notions of necessity and contingency.

Aristotle had established the existence of a pure Act, the First Mover 'on which depend the heavens and all nature'; al-Kindī that of a True One, the 'cause of unity' and so of the existence of 'all beings which are unitary'. Ibn Sīnā bases his own argument on a division of being according to logical modality. All beings of whose existence we are aware are contingent by their very essence, since it includes no necessity: they can without contradiction be conceived as not-existing. Moreover, their existence is ultimately linked by causal relations to the celestial spheres which are themselves also contingent in essence. But it is impossible that a chain of causes should go on for ever from one contingent thing to another, since what is contingent is, by definition, something which can equally be or not be: contingent existence tends in itself towards non-existence in so far as it is not founded on something which exists necessarily. There is, therefore, a first term in the causal chain which is necessary in its very essence – that is to say, whose essence includes that mark of necessity which is lacking in all other things and which can also be expressed as the identity in it of essence and existence. In this way, the cosmogony sketched above is given a philosophical basis. Just as the whole system of the world comes about from the thought which the Necessary Being has of itself, so this being, in thinking itself at the same time thinks everything in the universe: it thinks 'the higher (that is, heavenly) beings, each in its individuality, and the being of the sublunary world in the universals under which they are classified' ([2.6]).

The distinction between essence and existence is another feature of Ibn Sīnā's thought which is his own; he did not take it from al-Fārābī, as was long thought because of the misattribution of a short treatise (*Fuṣūṣ al-ḥikam*, which might be translated as *Precious Aphorisms*) which continues Ibn Sīnā's own formulation of the distinction. In all contingent things, Ibn Sīnā differentiates, on the one hand, the fact of having a certain quiddity (*māhiyyah*: *mā* is translated into Latin as *quid*, thus producing the word *quidditas*) or, as he is also willing to say, a *ḥaqīqah*, meaning 'truth' – what this thing which exists really is; and, on the other hand, the very fact that it exists, its *wujūd* or *huwiyya*. (The word *huwiyya* is made up from the pronoun *huwa* which means 'him' but also acts as the copula in attributive propositions; al-Kindī, who also uses *wujūd*, had already used *huwa* as the basis for another word, *tahwid*, as noted above.) The standard contrast essence and existence in Western philosophy is, then, a good rendering of Ibn Sīnā's distinction between *māhiyya* and *wujūd*. In existing things essence does not imply existence, otherwise they would exist necessarily. The one exception, as we have seen, is God, and this structural distinction has its place at the level of the ultimate origin of things. But it also gives rise to an idea relevant to the ontology of forms. What sort of being does essence have? It has no effect on existence as such, but essence determines its status in each existing thing. In itself, essence is neither universal nor particular, neither singular nor plural, neither present in existence nor just a concept in the mind: but it can be any of these. To use Ibn Sīnā's own example: the universal 'horse' signifies something which is distinct from its universality: 'horseliness' (*equinitas* in the Latin translations) or 'just horseliness' (*equinitas tantum*). This horseliness can be attached to the 'conditions' of existence in actual horses, or not: in itself, it is removed from any condition and only a 'divine being' can be attributed to it, as Ibn Sīnā says in an enigmatic comment which should certainly be linked to what he says about the origin of the world in God's thought. Methodologically, this doctrine of being supports one of Ibn Sīnā's favourite procedures. He engages in an imaginary experimentation with combinations of forms, an inspection of the 'thingness' (his word too) of a given object, from which one can see what is or is not compatible with its nature and so what should be thought about it. In this theory of essence, Ibn Sīnā can be seen to be following on from the theological speculations about non-existing things mentioned above in connection with the Mu'tazilites ([2.32]).

There remains one area where Ibn Sīnā is close to al-Fārābī: the theory of prophecy, its nature and function. Prophetic revelation is an outstanding example of the joining of the human soul with the separated Intelligences. Intellectual understanding is the most common

43

instance of this joining, but whereas ordinary men proceed through discursive thought, the prophet is, he said, 'informed of what is invisible; an angel speaks to him'. The function of prophecy is to ensure the social ties which are necessary for men by giving them laws and laying down religious obligations. But it can only inculcate the truth which it contains through symbols which are accessible to simple minds. It is not a matter of the prophets' hiding the truth but of expressing it in another language. Thus the descriptions of the happiness of heaven are allegories of the spiritual pleasures of the separated soul. Besides its use in interpreting prophecies, Ibn Sīnā uses his idea of symbolic expression in two ways. Sometimes he employs it to give philosophical readings of verses from the Qur'ān: for instance, in *Instructions and Remarks* he interprets the famous verse about light (Sourate 24, *Light*, v, 35) as an imagistic description of the intellectual faculties of the soul and their hierarchy, from the material intelligence up to the intelligence in act which is in contact with the Agent Intellect. In the same work, Ibn Sīnā refers to the *Story of Salāmān and Absāl* (about which he also wrote a letter): they are two figures, he says, who represent the soul of man ('yourself') and its level of mystical knowledge, a subject treated in detail in the *Instructions*. Or again – this is the second way in which he treats symbols – he himself composes stories which put into the form of images the adventures of the soul desiring 'light' (*Ḥayy ibn Yaqzān*) and in search of truth (*The Story of the Bird*) ([2.1], [2.7], [2.36]).

ᕫᕫ CONCLUSION ᕫᕫ

Without doubt Ibn Sīnā is the most widely known of the great Eastern *falāsifah*, because of the extent of his work and the variety of fields, including medicine and literary composition, in which he excelled. Knowledge of al-Kindī and al-Fārābī is more restricted to specialist historians of philosophy, but it would be unjust not to recognize al-Kindī's pioneer role and his genius as a scholar and philosopher, or al-Fārābī's penetration and power of synthesis. Not, of course, that there is any question of drawing up an order of merit. The task of these concluding remarks is, rather, to give a general picture of this period of *falsafah*. It was a lively, creative period, and many lesser but highly able authors, unmentioned in this account, were active. Its central problems resulted from the interplay between two different oppositions. On the one hand, there was the opposition between the Prophet of Islam's revelation and a body of teaching originating in another language and a different spiritual atmosphere. On the other hand, there was the opposition between tradition and progress, which in some ways repeats the first opposition, but in others suppresses it by looking to a wisdom which has always been the same. Leaving aside this illusory solution, there are two different ways in which the main opposition – between religion and philosophy – was resolved. One way was to reconcile their differences in some way or other. This was al-Kindī's procedure (although his historical view of philosophy did not fully resolve the tension between the terms of the second opposition, tradition and progress). Ibn Sīnā, too, proceeded in this way. He combined a theology which was philosophical in a highly technical way with exegetical and mystical meditations. The other way involved subordinating religion and making the philosophical tradition the solid basis for progress. Al-Rāzī went the furthest in this direction; al-Fārābī tried to have the best of both worlds, but his philosophy of religion has philosophy of mind and political science, rather than the Koran, as its main constituents.

These, then, were the main themes and tensions in the first period of *falsafah*: the first period because, after Ibn Sīnā, Arab and Islamic philosophical and religious thought took on a new configuration. During the fifth/eleventh century, the Seljuk Turks conquered Iran bit by bit, moving from East to West, and they entered Baghdad in 447/1055. They did not suppress the caliphate which had long been in decline, but they put it beneath their authority and presented themselves as its defenders against the various Shiʿite regimes of the Near East and Egypt. As a necessary accompaniment to this military/religious programme, there was ideological reform. Its outstanding exponent was Abū Ḥāmid al-Ghazzālī (458/1058 to 505/1111). His work took many forms (theoretical, mystical, political), but here we need note merely his hostility to *falsafah*. His main work in this area is the *Incoherence of the Philosophers* (*Tahāfut al-falāsifah*), in which he refutes twenty theses held by al-Fārābī and Ibn Sīnā. These theses, he says, express in one way or another three points of view which are directly opposed to the faith: that the world has existed for eternity; that God knows only universals; and that bodies will not be resurrected. Physics and metaphysics are thus to be rejected; the only valuable parts of philosophy left are mathematics and logic. Al-Ghazālī's attack, which took place in a political climate hostile to whatever fell outside strict theological and juridical tradition, put an end to three centuries of vigour in the *falsafah* of the Near East. *Falsafah* would go on as such for a while in the extreme West of Islam, the Maghreb and Spain, where there was already a well-established scientific and philosophical tradition. And, in the East, the legacy of Ibn Sīnā would continue, but in a way where (starting especially with Shihāb al-Dīn Yaḥyā al-Suhrawardī, of Alep, put to death in 587/1191) its mystical tendencies were emphasized. There followed a brilliant line of philosophers whose

Bibliographies

2.10 Janssens, J. L. *An Annotated Bibliography of Ibn Sīnā (1970–1989)*, Leuven, 1991.
2.11 Rescher, N. *Al-Fārābī: an Annotated Bibliography*, Pittsburgh, Pa., 1962.
2.12 —— *Al-Kindī: an Annotated Bibliography*, Pittsburgh, Pa., 1964.

General Surveys

2.13 Badawi, A. *Histoire de la philosophie en Islam, II*, Paris, 1972.
2.14 Butterworth, C. E. 'The study of Arabic philosophy today', in T. A. Druart (ed.) *Arabic Philosophy and the West*, Washington, DC, 1988, pp. 55–140.
2.15 Corbin, H. *Histoire de la philosophie islamique*, Paris, 1964.
2.16 Fakhry, M. *A History of Islamic Philosophy*, 2nd edn, London and New York, 1983.
2.17 Hitti, P. K. *History of the Arabs*, 8th edn, London, 1964.
Since this chapter was written there has also been published:
Nasr, S. H. and Leaman, O. *History of Islamic Philosophy*, 2 vols (Routledge History of World Philosophies I), London and New York, 1996.

Studies

2.18 Arkoun, M. *Contribution à l'étude de l'humanisme arabe au IV/Xe siècle: Miskawayh, philosophe et historien*, Paris, 1970.
2.19 Atiyeh, G. N. *Al-Kindi: the Philosopher of the Arabs*, Rawalpindi, 1966.
2.20 Fakhry, M. 'The Arabs and the encounter with philosophy', in T. A. Druart (ed.) *Arab Philosophy and the West*, Washington, DC, 1988, pp. 1–17.
2.21 Frank, R. M. *The Metaphysics of Created Being according to Abū l'Hudhayl al-'allāf*, Istanbul, 1966.
2.22 Genequand, C. 'Platonism and hermetism in al-Kindī's *Fī al-nafs*', *Zeitschrift für Geschichte der arabisch-islamischen Wissenschaften* 4 (1987–8): 1–19.
2.23 Guidi, M. and Walzer, R. *Studi su al-Kindi, I: uno scritto introduttivo allo studio di Aristotele*, Rome, 1940.
2.24 Gutas, D. *Avicenna and the Aristotelian Tradition: Introduction to Reading Avicenna's Philosophical Works*, Leiden, 1988.
2.25 Hasnaoui, A. 'Fārābī et la pratique de l'exégèse philosophique (Remarques sur son *Commentaire au De Interpretatione d'Aristote*)', *Revue de Synthèse* 106 (1985): 27–59.
2.26 —— 'Aspects de la synthèse avicennienne', in M. A. Sinaceur (ed.) *Penser avec Aristote*, Toulouse, 1991, pp. 227–44.
2.27 Hugonnard-Roche, H. 'L'intermédiaire syriaque dans la transmission de la philosophie grecque à l'arabe: le cas de l'*Organon* d'Aristote', *Arabic Sciences and Philosophy* 1(2) (1991): 187–209.
2.28 Jolivet, J. *L'Intellect selon Kindī*, Leiden, 1971.
2.29 —— 'L'intellect selon al-Fārābī, quelques remarques', *Bulletin d'etudes orientales* 29 (1977): 211–19.

2.30 —— 'Pour le dossier du Proclus arabe: al-Kindī et la *Théologie platonicienne'*, *Studia Islamica* 49 (1979): 55–75.

2.31 —— 'L'action divine selon al-Kindī', *Mélanges de l'Université Saint-Joseph* 50, Beirut (1984): 313–29.

2.32 —— 'Aux Origines de l'ontologie d'Ibn Sīnā', in J. Jolivet and R. Rashed (eds) *Etudes sur Avicenne* Paris, 1984, pp. 11–28.

2.33 —— 'L'Idée de la sagesse et sa fonction dans la philosophie des 4e et 5e siècles', *Arabic Sciences and Philosophy* 1, 1 (1991): 31–65.

2.34 Kraemer, J. L. *Philosophy in the Renaissance of Islam: Abū Sulaymān al-Sijistānī and his Circle*, Leiden, 1986.

2.35 Maróth, M. *Ibn Sīnā und die peripatetische 'Aussagenlehre'*, Leiden, 1989.

2.36 Michot, J. *La Destinée de l'homme selon Avicenne: le retour à Dieu (Ma'ad) et l'imagination*, Louvain, 1986.

2.37 Moussaoui, A. 'Le Problème des fondements de la logique chez les penseurs musulmans médiévaux: la logique d'Ibn Sīnā', unpublished Ph.D. thesis, University of Paris I, 1987–8.

2.38 Peters, F. E. *Aristotle and the Arabs*, New York, 1968.

2.39 Pines, S. *Beiträge zur islamischen Atomenlehre*, Berlin, 1936; repr. New York and London, 1987.

2.40 Ritter, H. and Walzer, R. *Studi su Al-Kindī II: uno scritto morale inedito di Al-Kindī (Temistio peri alypias?)*, Rome, 1938.

2.41 Rosenthal, F. *Greek Philosophy in the Arab World*, London, 1990.

2.42 Shehaby, N. *The Propositional Logic of Avicenna*, Dordrecht and Boston, 1973.

2.43 Troupeau, G. 'Le Rôle des syriaques dans la transmission et l'exploitation du patrimoine philosophique et scientifique grec', *Arabica* 38 (1991): 1–10.

2.44 Walzer, R. *Greek into Arabic*, Oxford, 1962.

CHAPTER 3

Averroes

Alfred Ivry

Abū'l Walīd Muḥammad ibn Aḥmad ibn Rushd (1126–98) needs to be known only as Averroes to be familiar to students of philosophy in the West. Greatly respected as a commentator on Aristotle's writings, Averroes was also strongly attacked for what were perceived to be his theologico-political and metaphysical views. He was accused of holding a double-truth theory, in which religion had its own truths which could contradict, though not invalidate, the truths of reason; and accused as well of believing that our minds belong essentially, and return at death, to a single eternal intelligence, a doctrine known as monopsychism.

'Averroism' came to be synonymous with these views, though the 'double truth' accusation is a distortion of his position. Averroes, however, cannot be faulted for the particular view of him that the Latin West had, which it chose to have, on the basis of the translations of his work that it privileged. For Christian Europe may be seen to have been so taken with Averroes as the disciple and interpreter of Aristotle, that it disregarded his indigenous Islamic identity. The Muslim Ibn Rushd, however, is very concerned to show that the teachings of philosophy are not antithetical to those of Islam, that religion not only has nothing to fear from philosophy, but that philosophy endorses its teachings as a popular expression of its own. At the same time, Averroes' argument with his co-religionists may be seen as a plea for toleration of dissent within Islamic society.

Averroes was able to take this stand because he was deeply rooted in the religious establishment of his day. Born into a Cordoban family of learned jurists, Averroes studied and wrote on Islamic law and eventually became chief judge of Cordoba, following in the family tradition. As a young intellectual he also studied theology, and his familiarity with the writings of al-Ghazzālī (d. 1111) in particular were critical to his later defence of philosophy against the latter's criticisms.

In addition to mastering the traditional 'religious sciences' of Islam, Averroes avidly studied the full range of the 'secular sciences' of his day. Besides Arabic poetry, these subjects were basically the heritage of Greek learning (in Arabic translation), and featured mathematics, astronomy, medicine and philosophy. He achieved prominence as a physician, and wrote a medical treatise, known in the Latin West as *Colliget* (from *al-Kulliyāt*, the Arabic for 'generalities' or principles).

Averroes' major scholarly effort, however, went into the study of philosophy, which for him meant the writings of Aristotle. For him, as for others from Andalusian Spain (Maimonides, for example), Aristotle was 'the master of those who know', and Averroes dedicated himself to expounding peripatetic views. In so doing, he set himself against both the competing influence of Neoplatonic ideas, which had made considerable inroads in the Muslim East, and the domestic opposition of anti-philosophical theologians, the *mutakallimūn*.

Averroes' philosophical position attracted the Almohad caliph, Abū Ya'qūb Yūsuf (reigned 1163–84).[1] The caliph, while apparently interested in understanding and cultivating science and philosophy, was no doubt also interested in having philosophers at court for reasons of state, perhaps as a check on the influence of the more traditionally-oriented theologians and lawyers. Averroes' repeated criticism of these people, and of al-Ghazzālī in particular, bespeak the author's confidence in royal support, which he in fact enjoyed for many years.

It was the Prince of the Believers, Abū Ya'qūb himself, who (in 1168–9) comissioned Averroes to summarize Aristotle's corpus, and who then appointed him to various high offices, first as a qadi and then, from 1182, as court physician. Averroes remained at court during the reign of Abū Yūsuf, the son of Abū Ya'qūb, and was able to complete, under apparently favourable conditions, what had become a monumental task of philosophical exegesis.

In 1195, however, the caliph turned against Averroes and other philosophers, apparently deferring to the conservative majority in his regime. For a brief time the study of philosophy was prohibited, Averroes was banished from court and placed under house arrest, his books banned and ordered burnt. Having made his point, the caliph then relented, and Averroes was a free and respected person when death took him in 1198.

Islamic philosophy of the sort Averroes advocated died with him, however, in a Muslim climate which had become increasingly conservative. Averroes had no significant Muslim disciples, and his books were largely ignored by Arab readers, some writings disappearing in their original language. Fortunately, interest in Averroes and in Aristotelian thought remained high among Jews and Christians; the

Jews reading him in Judaeo-Arabic (Arabic in Hebrew characters) and then Hebrew translation, the Christians in Latin. Averroes' commentaries on Aristotle were read alongside the original works from the thirteenth century on, and themselves engendered supercommentaries; while a Latin (and, to a lesser extent, Hebrew) Averroism emerged which claimed him as its progenitor.

Today, Muslim scholars, particularly in North Africa, are reclaiming Averroes for their culture, appreciating his contribution to Western philosophy while viewing him within the social and political context of Almohad Andalusia and the Maghreb. An international consortium of learned societies is engaged in publishing critical editions, with concordances, of his Aristotelian commentaries in Arabic, Hebrew and Latin, the languages in which they circulated in the Middle Ages; they bring to fruition the project first proposed by Harry Wolfson in 1931.

Averroes wrote thirty-eight commentaries in all, mostly two and sometimes three per Aristotelian work.[2] The commentaries differ in length, and are called 'short', 'middle' and 'long' accordingly. The short or 'epitomes' are free-standing summaries, apparently Averroes' initial effort to digest the arguments of Aristotle and his successors, both Greek and Muslim, on a given text. There are only five long commentaries, for the *Posterior Analytics*, *Physics*, *On the Heavens*, *On the Soul* and *Metaphysics*, and they are exhaustively detailed and uncompromising studies, quoting Aristotle in full and commenting on his every sentence. Comparison of Averroes' middle and long commentaries on *On the Soul* and *Metaphysics* has raised the possibility that the middle are abridgements and somewhat revised versions of the long. It seems likely that Averroes wrote the long commentaries for himself and the few who would have the training and patience to follow him, while composing the middle commentaries in a relatively shorter and somewhat more accessible and hence popular form, presumably for the edification of the caliph and his educated retinue.

Besides these commentaries, Averroes composed a number of smaller independent treatises, particularly on issues relating to epistemology and physics, both terrestrial and celestial. He also wrote two defences of philosophy, against the critical onslaught of al-Ghazzālī and the theologians of Islam.

In these *apologia*, Averroes insists upon respecting the dogmas of Islam, while presenting himself as a dedicated philosopher, and offering a spirited defence of the religious obligation to pursue philosophy. Refraining on principle from deliberating upon the truth value of articles of faith in general, Averroes yet asserts the political and ethical necessity of affirming traditional religious beliefs.

Though this non-judgemental attitude to religious claims may be seen as disingenuous, it could as well be argued that Averroes was simply applying the same criterion to religion that he applied to other fields of enquiry, namely, that it had its own premisses, which, as premisses, were non-demonstrable. Moreover, he knew that the particular nature of the claims made in Islam, as in all revealed religions, based as they were on a belief in miracles, did not comply with the natural and empirical foundations which he saw as necessary for logical, rational discourse.

Accordingly, the theology which Averroes allowed himself is of the philosophical kind, in which the particular affirmations of Islam are relevant only at the most universal and impersonal level, concerned with the existence and nature of God, creation and providence. Averroes' God is thus the philosophers' God, with no historical or ethnic identification. As a medieval philosopher, however, Averroes works within a modified Aristotelian view of the deity, such that God relates to the world more directly and affectedly than Aristotle thought.

Averroes' logical commentaries attest to the advanced state of the art in the Islamic world by the twelfth century, with full understanding of the technical aspects of syllogistic proof as well as of the political purposes to which logical argument could be put. Viewing, with his predecessors, the *Poetics* and *Rhetoric* as part of the *Organon*, Averroes has less sympathy with poetry as a vehicle for expressing the truth than he has for rhetoric, recognizing the common and even necessary use of rhetoric in traditional religious discourse ([3.4] 73, 84). Dialectical reasoning is both criticized, when used by the *mutakallimūn* as a self-sufficient methodology; and praised, when treated by the *falāsifah* as an effective stepping-stone to demonstrative proof. It is the demonstrative proof, with its necessary premisses, which remains the ideal form of argument for Averroes, though he may well have suspected it was an ideal not often realized. As al-Ghazzālī insisted, foreshadowing Hume, many of the philosophers' physical and metaphysical premisses, and hence proofs, were not necessarily true.

Nevertheless, Averroes' physics and metaphysics follow Aristotle mainly in integrating the principles of being in the sublunar and supralunar spheres. As much as is possible, Averroes presents a uniform picture of the universe. The same principles obtain in the celestial and terrestrial realms, despite the matter of the heavens being considered as eternal. Even where Averroes acknowledges the special properties of the heavens, and even more so of God, and qualifies his descriptions as 'equivocal', and 'analogous' language, it appears he believes in the universal applicability and intelligibility of his ontological principles.

Developing Aristotle's hylomorphic perspective, Averroes posits a prime matter which, through its connection with an initial amorphous 'corporeal form', is conceived of as an existing substantive potentiality ([3.12] 51–4). This, because the corporeal form for Averroes is an indeterminate tridimensional extension, an actual substance of sorts. Prime matter thereby represents being in a perpetual state of becoming.

At the other end of the spectrum of being – and part of that spectrum for Averroes – the first mover or God is conceived as an immaterial substance, both fully actual and the very principle of actuality, the actual state of every being deriving ultimately from him. In this way, while representing the very principle of being, God functions to facilitate continuous change and becoming in the world.

Every substance in the universe in this view is regarded as the product of these eternal formal and material principles of being, and each substance exists in actual and potential states. At the extremes there is no absolutely separate existence either, prime matter not being found without a corresponding 'corporeal form', and God's very existence 'proven' only in relation to the motion of the heavens, for which he is a first and necessary cause.

Averroes gets this view of God partly from Aristotle, together with Aristotle's conceptualization of the first mover as an immaterial and intelligent being: a mind the essential being and sole activity of which is thought, treated in the post-Aristotelian tradition as equivalent to knowledge. For Averroes, as for his Muslim predecessors, this divine knowledge is not purely self-referential; in thinking himself, God was believed to think and hence to know the essential forms (i.e. the species) of all beings ([3.9] 155). While not subscribing to a Neoplatonic emanationist view, and instead believing that all forms are intrinsic to the substance in which they appear, Averroes yet believes that the actualization of each form depends ultimately on the first cause.

For Averroes, the physical dependency of the world upon God is couched not only in terms of intelligence and knowledge, but also desire and even love ([3.9] 154). The heavenly bodies were each thought to have intellects which functioned as their immaterial, formal principles. For Averroes this meant that each intellect 'knew' the place and role of its sphere in the cosmos, both in relation to the other spheres, and to the unmoving first cause itself. This knowledge could also be expressed as a desire in the intellect to realize itself as perfectly as it could, which for the spheres took the form of perfectly circular and hence eternal motion.

Averroes does not seriously posit the existence of a soul in addition to an intellect for each sphere, believing he had no need for a second immaterial principle to explain the motion of the planets ([3.9] 149). For him, the intellect alone could both think or know its object, and desire or love it, desire being the external manifestation of its knowledge, intellect in action. Moreover, the intellects of the spheres could be said to 'know' events on earth, inasmuch as their movements, and particularly the heat of the sun, affected the generation of substances here. This knowledge Averroes judged 'accidental' or incidental to the 'essential' knowledge or function of the spheres, which was to maintain their own, more immediate perfection, expressed by perfect circular motion ([3.9] 38).

Averroes clung to the Aristotelian model of circular planetary motion, though aware that astronomical theory had long since modified it. He thereby shows his fundamental if anachronistic loyalty to Aristotle as the arbiter of scientific truth. At the same time, Averroes modified his Aristotelian stance, or appears to have done so, as circumstances required. A striking example of this occurs in his treatment of the process of intellection, at the juncture where mortal and immortal intellects, transient and eternal thoughts, supposedly meet.

This is a subject about which Aristotle was notoriously vague in *On the Soul* 3.5, and for which the post-Aristotelian tradition had proposed a number of theories. The fundamental question was whether the potential human intellect, being formed and informed by the imaginative and sensory faculties of the soul, could transcend these physical origins and become an independent and hence immortal substance. Averroes formulated different responses to this question throughout his life ([3.31] 220–356), and it appears his final position is that the individual intellect is only 'accidentally' related to the other corporeal faculties of the soul, belonging 'essentially' to a universal immaterial 'Agent Intellect'. Put another way, the Agent Intellect is 'essentially' a single immaterial actual substance, 'accidentally' related, as a potential or material intellect, to many corporeal beings.

The Agent Intellect for the peripatetic post-Aristotelian tradition is that intellect which is the last of the heavenly intelligences, its sphere of operation our earth. For Averroes, it acts in much the same way that God does in the universe as a whole, as the actualizing principle for all innate forms, including and especially the form of human beings, their intellects. The Agent Intellect thus actualizes the potential and natural intelligibility of all objects here, and the potential knowledge of all persons who exercise their minds. The philosopher's knowledge, his 'acquired intellect', may be considerable indeed, when directed towards and conjoined with the Agent Intellect, his ultimate goal; yet this conjunction does not, for Averroes, render the individual intellect itself immortal. Its truths are not personal, though its knowledge is its own, as long as the person lives. The immortality that the individual may anticipate is as part of the sum of universal truths, identified with the Agent Intellect. For Averroes this knowledge, however inadequate it may seem to the person seeking a personal immortality or mystical union with the deity, yet provides the philosopher with a sense of great felicity and fulfilment.

The uncompromising teachings of Averroes' commentaries are modulated in the works he composed in his own name in defence of philosophy. The *Faṣl al-Maqāl*, paraphrased in English as 'Averroes on the harmony of religion and philosophy',[3] was probably written about ten years after Averroes received his mandate from the caliph to explain and summarize Aristotle's works, i.e. in a period when Averroes enjoyed the caliph's support and felt confident in presenting philosophy's claim to religious legitimacy before its detractors.

The *Harmony* has a logical and legal focus, Averroes arguing before his fellow jurists that while rooted in the Qur'ān, Islamic law is as much of an innovation or post-Qur'ānic development within Islam as is philosophy, and that therefore both are equally permissible expressions of the faith. For Averroes, the Qur'ān demands that one reflect upon, hence study the world, which he takes as an obligation to pursue philosophy, for those capable of it. This means, in effect, those who appreciate the difference between demonstrative and non-demonstrative arguments, people (i.e. philosophers) who can argue apodictically ([3.11] 45).

Persons such as these are relatively few in any society, Averroes recognizes, and he readily accepts the use of the less conclusive and more popular forms of religious discourse, expressed dialectically and rhetorically. Averroes believes the Qur'ān appeals to people on all three levels, though its demonstrative arguments may only be alluded to, and that only by understanding the text allegorically. Averroes has no hesitation in doing so, his philosophical – here meta-physical – convictions dictating his interpretation of God's word ([3.11] 58).

The *Harmony* is in this respect a dogmatic assertion of the superiority of scientific, i.e. demonstrable, philosophical discourse, to all other forms of reasoning. Averroes could scarcely expect to persuade his critics of the virtues of philosophy in this manner, and his writing simply attests to his complete conviction and self-confidence.

Averroes' claims for philosophy are buttressed in this book by a brave *de facto* attack upon one of the institutions of Islamic faith, the concept of *ijmā'* or consensus, which when invoked has the status of law. To his critics, there is a consensus in Islam that philosophy is an irreligious and hence unacceptable pursuit. Averroes, in response, claims that a unanimous consensus does not exist on this issue, simply because there may always be private reservations to positions publicly declared, undermining theoretically the seeming unanimity; while this is true in many areas, it is particularly so for philosophy, which has always had an esoteric tradition of its own ([3.11] 52).

Averroes in fact insists upon the private nature of philosophical instruction, claiming it wrong to teach the masses philosophy or the allegorical meaning of Scripture, since they would misunderstand the philosophers and be led to unbelief. It is better to have them believe in ideas which approximate and imitate the truth, thereby preserving society and their own (and the philosophers') well-being ([3.11] 66).

While it would be too much to claim that Averroes is fully preaching toleration, within the limits of his society he may be seen as advocating a fair measure of freedom of speech. He is not beyond branding as heretics disbelievers in creation, prophecy and the after-world, but insists, without going into much detail, that the traditional understanding of these concepts should not be the only permissible ones.

Averroes addresses these particular issues more fully in the *Tahāfut al-Tahāfut* (*The Incoherence of the Incoherence*), his major defence of philosophy against the theological attack of al-Ghazzālī. Here the polemical side of Averroes takes a back seat to his gift for philosophical argument, his sights set on Avicenna (d. 1037) as much as on al-Ghazzālī. For it is Avicenna's philosophy which al-Ghazzālī had first summarized, in his *Maqāsid al-Falāsifah* (*The Intentions of the Philosophers*), and then attacked, in his *Tahāfut al-Falāsifah* (*The Incoherence of the Philosophers*).

The incisiveness of al-Ghazzālī's attack may well have contributed to the declining fortunes of philosophy in the Muslim East, and eventually in the Muslim world as a whole. In Andalusia, however, the rational philosophical tradition lived on through the twelfth century, and Averroes' *Incoherence* may be seen as a last hurrah for a rigorous Aristotelianism within Islamic culture. Averroes may have hoped that in discrediting Avicenna's Neoplatonically inclined approach to philosophy he could defuse al-Ghazzālī's critique of philosophy in general, not appreciating the fact that if Avicenna's more religiously compatible philosophy was refuted, his own more uncompromising approach would be even more at risk in Islamic society.

As does his *Harmony*, Averroes' *Incoherence* daringly insists on the legitimacy, if not necessity, of his interpretation of creation, providence and the afterworld, though realizing the philosopher's political and moral obligation to uphold conventional beliefs in these issues. Accordingly, he gives sufficient lip-service to traditional religious locutions to permit wildly divergent assessments of his views on these matters in contemporary scholarship.

Averroes' *Incoherence of the Incoherence* is a detailed response to al-Ghazzālī's *Incoherence of the Philosophers*, containing a verbatim transcript of the former work. As such, it offers, among other things,

Averroes' proofs for the eternity of the world, so presented as to be compatible with the notion of God as creator; Averroes' utilization of positive predication of divine attributes in the one God; and Averroes' rejection of the Avicennian distinction between essence and existence, as well as of the Neoplatonically inspired emanationist ontogony which Avicenna adopted. In place of Avicenna's scheme, Averroes advocates a more immanentist role for God in the cosmos, modifying thereby Aristotle's self-centred deity.

Averroes' physics, both celestial and terrestrial, is basically Aristotelian, as is his closing defence of the logical necessity for believing in causation, directed against al-Ghazzālī's Occasionalism. Averroes' final remarks defending his views on immortality of the soul and resurrection are very abbreviated, and perhaps indicative that he knew how difficult it was to make them acceptable to his critics, though ostensibly he claims these are not topics amenable to philosophical investigation.

For al-Ghazzālī, the notion of the eternity of the world poses two main difficulties: it challenges God's role as sole creator of the universe, and pre-empts the exercise of his free will. Al-Ghazzālī thus attempts both to discredit the notion of eternal motion and the philosophers' use of the concept of divine will. He claims, using arguments which may be traced to John Philoponus, that the different rates of motion of the supposedly eternal heavenly bodies would create disparate and hence impossible infinite numbers; while a divine will in an eternal universe would have to act for that which already is and always has been existent, chaining its will to necessity and thereby rendering it otiose.

Averroes' response to the problem of different infinities distinguishes between actual and potential states of being; as all actual movements are finite, infinity is predicable only of non-actual or potential movements, which as such are non-quantifiable ([3.18] 10). As for the divine will, Averroes acknowledges that its action is indeed eternal and necessary, but that it is nevertheless a real will, not the same as ours, though equivocally predicable ([3.18] 90).

'Creation' for Averroes is the term for an eternal process in which God is the agent directly responsible, as the first and final cause, for the motion of the heavenly bodies; and indirectly responsible, through those motions, for the formal and efficient causality which determines the nature of all objects. Even matter may be said to come within God's purview, through the forms with which all matter is connected ([3.18] 108).

This eternally created world is viewed as the willed effect of God's knowledge, which 'knowledge' is tantamount to the creative act itself. God thus 'knows' the world, in so far as he is its creator. This knowledge is of the world as it is, the actual world, with its corresponding real potentialities, integral to the nature of every actual being. God's knowledge accordingly is of that which is necessary, being actual, though full knowledge of that entails, for Averroes, knowledge as well of non-necessary or possible alternative states of being.

Averroes' assurance in the divine awareness of logically possible alternative orders in the universe encourages him to speak of the divine will as 'choosing' to act in the manner which he does, though the choice is eternally foreknown and necessary. The divine will is thus, for Averroes, the external realization of a theoretically more comprehensive divine knowledge. These and other attributes may be predicated of God, since as immaterial properties they pose for Averroes no quantifiable challenge to the divine oneness ([3.18] 188, 212).

Nor do such distinct notions as knowledge and will, or power and life, for example, introduce differentiation into the divine essence for Averroes, since in that essence they are undifferentiated ([3.18] 257). It is we who, assessing the multiple effects of God's presence in the world, attribute diverse faculties to him. God's nature remains unique, though it is not necessary therefore to strip it of all meaningful predication, and to distance God from the world physically and logically. God's involvement in the world is thus a necessary part of his very being, even as the full nature of every object includes the effect it has upon others.

Averroes is, accordingly, more willing than other medieval philosophers to detail God's manifold presence in the world, a presence which allows him to speak even of God's knowledge of individuals, though such statements must not be taken without qualification ([3.18] 207). A frequent form of qualification for Averroes, used in many contexts as we have seen, is the distinction he employs between 'essential' and 'accidental' states of being, though both are necessary for the full description of the object discussed. Thus, it may be said that God's knowledge is essentially one (or single) though accidentally many (or diverse).

Averroes' political philosophy is known to us from a variety of sources, not least his commentary on Plato's *Republic*.[4] This work is particularly intriguing, being included, presumably intentionally, within the corpus of his Aristotelian commentaries. Admittedly, Averroes' choice of the *Republic* was determined in part by his unfamiliarity with Aristotle's *Politics*, a text which was unavailable to him in Spain, and largely unknown throughout the Islamic world. However, that fact may itself indicate the status which the *Republic* enjoyed among the Muslim *falāsifah*, particularly Averroes' predecessor, al-Fārābī (d. 950). As the pre-eminent textual representative of Greek political philosophy, the *Republic* thus had to be included in the canon of philosophical texts which Averroes was charged to present, with his commentaries, to the caliph.

The paraphrase of the *Republic* which Averroes offers his readers is, however, imbued with Aristotelian perspectives, and shows the influence of the Stagirite's *Organon* as well as his *Nicomachean Ethics* ([3.30] 17–45). The metaphysical and dialectical underpinnings of the *Republic* all but disappear, and the examination of personal and civic virtue which Plato describes is pursued by Averroes for essentially instrumental purposes. Political philosophy is treated primarily as a practical science, though surely Averroes knew the kind of state Plato advocated was impractical and totally unrealistic for a Muslim society.

Though it is not necessary to believe Averroes endorsed everything he reports Plato as recommending in the *Republic*, it is quite clear that he is sympathetic to many of Plato's teachings there. Averroes' own affinities can be discerned from the style of his composition, both in his omissions and elaborations, as well as in his comparisons of Plato's teachings with references to the situation obtaining in the cities or states of his own time.

Averroes omits the opening and closing Books of the *Republic*, with their dialectical, poetic and mythic emphases, and omits also the discussion of the Ideas and of the divided line in Book 6 of Plato's work; substituting for it an attack upon the world view and methods of the *mutakallimūn*, a critique which may be seen as an indirect way of affirming Aristotelian nominalism and logic. There as elsewhere in this commentary, Averroes emphasizes Aristotelian distinctions between demonstrative and non-demonstrative forms of reasoning. While preferring demonstrative arguments, Averroes acknowledges the necessity of presenting philosophical truths to the masses in less rigorous ways. Suspicious of the dialectical arguments of the *mutakallimūn* and of the themes and excesses of much of poetic discourse, and recognizing the limited scope of demonstrably necessary argument in this field, Averroes would apparently consider the *métier* of political discourse, if not of political philosophy in general, to be rhetoric.

This non-literal interpretation of Averroes' approach to the *Republic* may help the reader understand his stunning indifference to the conventions of Muslim society. Daringly, Averroes follows Plato in considering religion from a political perspective only. It is seen as a structural component of all societies, part of the legal and moral composition of each city, with Islam and its Prophet accorded no special priority ([3.13] 48). Prophecy as an institution is not placed above the leadership and laws bestowed by the philosopher-king or *imām* (the one Muslim term which Averroes uses, though treating it as a mere synonym for Plato's ideal leader) ([3.13] 72). Nor is Averroes particularly sensitive to the strictures of Islamic law, in apparently advocating equal rights and responsibilities for both sexes, and in seeming agreement with Plato's views on the engendering and upbringing of the guardian class.

Again, Averroes does not hesitate to convey and apparently concur with Plato's remarks about the necessity for political leaders to lie to their subjects on occasion, presenting abstract or impersonal truths in fictive dress. While Averroes is sympathetic to the particular teachings of popular Islam, with its personal and providential God, and after-world beliefs, he considers them only from a neutral political perspective, risking thereby the wrath of his community ([3.13] 24). Here it would appear that his philosophical zeal has overwhelmed his political prudence.

On the other hand, a conventional Islamic influence on Averroes may be discerned in his treatment of Plato's views on warfare ([3.13] 12). Unlike the Greek philosopher's defensive (if pre-emptive) military strategy, which Averroes sees as a racially biased attempt to keep the barbarians at bay, the war which the Cordoban *faylasūf* advocates is a *jihād* or 'holy war'; this is intended, however coercively, to bring the virtues of good government and civilization to all those capable of being educated, particularly the young.[5] Averroes, we could thus assume, did not ponder the destabilizing effects upon society of a permanent state of warfare, and this despite the ample evidence from the cities of his own time.

We know, however, from his legal compendium *Bidāyat al-Mujtahid wa-Nihāyat al-Iqtiṣād* (which may be loosely translated as *The Proper Rational Initiative of a Legist*), written for the most part well before his *Republic* commentary, that Averroes had considered *jihād* in all its ramifications, including the advisability, under duress, of declaring a truce, in effect making peace. His remarks in the *Republic* commentary should therefore not be taken as a realistic assessment of or prescription for Islamic society, but as a commentary on an ideally imagined state, as loosely Muslim as Plato's was Greek.

This commentary, like many other commentaries of his, leaves the reader wondering which of Averroes' remarks are meant to be taken as truly his, and to what degree we must see him adopting a rhetorical stance, and for what ultimate purpose. Fundamentally, Averroes has an appreciation for the philosopher-king model of leadership, with all its stratification and manipulation for the common good; and he has an elitist but apparently egalitarian view of society. It would be surprising if he did not know that this Platonic political philosophy was anything but a practical or implementable document, and that therefore this commentary, as all his philosophical writings, were primarily intended for theoretical reflection, the path to happiness for him best reached through intellectual pursuits.

 NOTES

1 Cf. the description of Averroes' momentous encounter with the caliph, as given by Hourani [3.11] 12.
2 Cf. the inventory of these commentaries assembled by Harry Wolfson [3.29].
3 The full title more literally would be 'The Book of the Distinction of Discourse and Determination of the Connection between Religious Law and Philosophy', cf. Hourani [3.11] 1.
4 Averroes' commentary on the *Nicomachean Ethics* is only partially extant; for his paraphrase of Plato's work see Ralph Lerner [3.13].
5 Cf. Rudolph Peters [3.14] 21 (the chapter on *Jihād* from Averroes' legal handbook *Bidāyat al-Mujtahid*).

 BIBLIOGRAPHY

This is an abbreviated bibliography, owing to the large number of editions, translations and studies of Averroes' philosophical writings. A complete listing to date may be found in the Rosemann and Druart-Marmura entries given in the bibliographical section below.

Complete Editions of Arabic Original, and of Hebrew and Latin Translations

3.1 *Aristotelis opera cum Averrois Commentariis*, 9 vols and 3 supplements, Frankfurt-on-Main, Minerva, 1962. Reprint of *Aristotelis omnia quae extant Opera . . . Averrois Cordubensis in ea opera omnes, qui ad haec usque tempora pervenere, commentarii*, Venice, 1562.
3.2 *Corpus Commentariorum Averrois in Aristotelem*. Ongoing series, published by the Mediaeval Academy of America, Cambridge, Mass. until 1974, Arabic editions since then published in Madrid and Cairo, Hebrew editions in Jerusalem, and Latin editions in Cologne, under the auspices of learned academies in each country. Nine editions published to date, three each in Arabic, Hebrew and Latin.
The American Research Center in Egypt has sponsored the publication of various Arabic commentaries on the *Organon*, edited by C. Butterworth *et al.*

Editions and Translations of Single Works

3.3 Bland, K. (ed. and trans.) *The Epistle on the Possibility of Conjunction with the Active Intellect by Ibn Rushd with the Commentary of Moses Narboni*, New York, Jewish Theological Seminary of America, 1982.
3.4 Butterworth, C. (ed. and trans.) *Averroes' Three Short Commentaries on Aristotle's*

Topics, Rhetoric, *and* Poetics, Albany, NY, State University of New York Press, 1977.

3.5 —— (trans.) *Averroes' Middle Commentaries on Aristotle's* Categories *and* De Interpretatione, Princeton, NJ, Princeton University Press, 1983.

3.6 —— (trans.) *Averroes' Middle Commentary on Aristotle's* Poetics, Princeton, NJ, Princeton University Press, 1986.

3.7 Davidson, H. 'Averrois Tractatus de Animae Beatitudine', in R. Link-Salinger (ed.) *A Straight Path*, Washington, DC, Catholic University of America Press, 1988, pp. 57–73.

3.8 Freudenthal, J. and S. Fränkel, 'Die durch Averroes erhaltenen Fragmente Alexanders zur Metaphysik des Aristoteles untersucht und übersetzt von J. F. Mit Beiträgen zur Erläuterung des arabischen Textes von S. F.', *Abhandlungen der Königlichen Akademie der Wissenschaften zu Berlin* aus dem Jahre 1884; repr., New York, Garland, 1987.

3.9 Genequand, C. (trans.) *Ibn Rushd's Metaphysics*, Book Lam, Leiden, E. J. Brill, 1984.

3.10 Goldstein, H. (trans.) *Averroes' Questions in Physics*, Dordrecht, Boston and London, Kluwer, 1991.

3.11 Hourani, G. (trans.) *Averroes on the Harmony of Religion and Philosophy*, London, Luzac, 1961; repr. 1976.

3.12 Hyman, A. (ed. and trans.) *Averroes'* De substantia orbis, Cambridge, Mass. and Jerusalem, Medieval Academy of America and Israel Academy of Sciences and Humanities, 1986.

3.13 Lerner, R. (trans.) *Averroes on Plato's* Republic, Ithaca, NY and London, Cornell University Press, 1974.

3.14 Peters, R. (trans.) Chapter on *Jihād* from Averroes' legal handbook *Bidāyat al-mujtahid*, in *Jihad in Mediaeval and Modern Islam*, Leiden, E. J. Brill, 1977, pp. 9–25.

3.15 Puig, J. (trans.) *Averroes, 'Epitome in Physicorum Libros'*, Madrid, Instituto Hispano-Arabe de Cultura, 1987. (Pages 14–24 contain a bibliography.)

3.16 Rosenthal, E. (ed. and trans.) *Averroes' Commentary on Plato's Republic*, Cambridge, Cambridge University Press, 1956; repr. with corrections 1966 and 1969.

3.17 Van den Bergh, S. (trans.) *Die Epitome der Metaphysik des Averroes*, Leiden, E. J. Brill, 1924 (repr. 1970).

3.18 —— (trans.) *Averroes' Tahafut al-Tahafut* (*The Incoherence of the Incoherence*), London, Luzac, 1954 (repr. 1969, 2 vols).

Bibliographies

3.19 Cranz, F. E. 'Editions of the Latin Aristotle accompanied by the commentaries of Averroes', in E. Mahoney (ed.) *Philosophy and Humanism. Renaissance Essays in Honor of Paul Oskar Kristeller*, Leiden, E. J. Brill, 1976, pp. 116–28.

3.20 Druart, T.-A. and Marmura, M. 'Medieval Islamic philosophy and theology: bibliographical guide (1986–1989)', *Bulletin de Philosophie Médiévale* 32, ed. SIEPM (1990): 106–11.

3.21 Rosemann, P. 'Averroes: a catalogue of editions and scholarly writings from 1821 onwards', *Bulletin de Philosophie Médiévale* 30, ed. SIEPM (1988): 153–215.

3.22 Vennebusch, J. 'Zur Bibliographie des psychologischen Schriftums des Averroes', *Bulletin de Philosophie Médiévale* 6 (1964): 92–100.

Surveys

3.23 Badawi, A. *Histoire de la philosophie en Islam, II: les philosophes purs*, Paris, Vrin, 1972, pp. 737–870.

3.24 Cruz Hernández, M. *Abu-l-Walîd Ibn Rušd (Averroes): Vida, obra, pensamiento, influencia*, Cordoba, Caja de Ahorros, 1986.

3.25 Fakhry, M. *A History of Islamic Philosophy*, London and New York, Longman and Columbia University Press, 1970, 2nd edn 1983, pp. 270–92.

3.26 Gätje, H. 'Averroes als Aristoteleskommentator', *Zeitschrift der Deutschen Morgenländischen Gesellschaft* 114 (1964): 59–65.

3.27 Jolivet, J. (ed.) *Multiple Averroès*, Paris, Les Belles Lettres, 1978.

3.28 Schmitt, C., 'Renaissance Averroism studied through the Venetian editions of Aristotle-Averroes (with particular reference to the Giunta edition of 1550–2)', in *L'Averroismo in Italia*, Rome, Accademia Nazionale dei Lincei, 1979, pp. 121–42.

3.29 Wolfson, H. 'Revised plan for the publication of a *Corpus Commentariorum Averrois in Aristotelem*', *Speculum* 38 (1963): 88–104; 39 (1964): 378, corrections.

Studies

3.30 Butterworth, C. 'Ethics and classical Islamic philosophy: A study of Averroes' *Commentary on Plato's Republic*', in R. Hovannisian (ed.) *Ethics in Islam*, Malibu, Calif., Undena, 1985, pp. 17–45.

3.31 Davidson, H. *Alfarabi, Avicenna, and Averroes, on Intellect*, New York and Oxford, Oxford University Press, 1992, pp. 220–356.

3.32 Hourani, G. 'Averroes on good and evil', *Studia Islamica* 16, (1962): 13–40.

3.33 Hyman, A. 'Aristotle's theory of the intellect and its interpretation by Averroes', in D. O'Meara (ed.) *Studies in Aristotle*, Washington, DC, Catholic University of America Press, 1981, pp. 161–91.

3.34 Jolivet, J. 'Divergences entre les métaphysiques d'Ibn Rušd et d'Aristote', *Arabica* 29 (1982): 225–45.

3.35 Kogan, B. *Averroes and the Metaphysics of Causation*, Albany, NY, State University of New York Press, 1985.

3.36 Mahdi, M. 'Averroes on divine law and human wisdom', in J. Cropsey (ed.) *Ancients and Moderns*, New York and London, Basic Books, 1964, pp. 114–31.

3.37 Merlan, P. *Monopsychism – Mysticism – Metaconsciousness*, The Hague, Nijhoff, 1963, 2nd edn, 1969, pp. 85–113.

3.38 Sabra, A. I. 'The Andalusian revolt against Ptolemaic astronomy: Averroes and Al-Bitrûjî', in E. Mendelsohn (ed.) *Transformation and Tradition in the Sciences*, Cambridge, Cambridge University Press, 1984, pp. 133–53.

3.39 Wolfson, H. 'Averroes' lost treatise on the Prime Mover', *Hebrew Union College Annual* 23, 1 (1950/1): 683–710.

3.40 —— 'Avicenna, Algazali, and Averroes on divine attributes', *Homenaje a Millás-Vallicrosa*, Barcelona, Consejo Superior de Investigaciones Científicas, vol. 2 (1956): 545–71.

CHAPTER 4

Jewish philosophy

Colette Sirat

❦

❦ INTRODUCTION ❦

The history of medieval Jewish philosophy can be divided into two consecutive periods. The first, beginning in the ninth century and ending roughly with the death of Maimonides in 1204, occurred in Islamic lands. The second, which lasted from the twelfth century until the end of the Middle Ages, took place in Christian Europe.

Whether they lived among Muslims or Christians, Jews centred their lives on the Torah, a word which was used beyond its strict meaning to designate, not just the Pentateuch, but the whole scriptural tradition: the twenty-four books of the Hebrew Bible, their commentaries and also (except for the Karaites) the oral law: the *Mishnah* and *Guemarah* which make up the Talmud.

In Jewish schools the Torah was studied in Hebrew and, for the believer, the world was built around the revealed text. From the creation, God has guided the course of universal history. The sun and the planets are subject to his will. The God of the Bible is a moral agent who wills and decrees. To man, whom he has created 'in our image and likeness', he gives commandments and issues prohibitions. Humans can grumble to God, plead with him, make him change his mind. Moses speaks to God man to man: there is a dialogue between them. God is free to reply or not, but he is visibly and audibly in the presence of the prophets, appearing as a majestic king or sending his angels.

God has made a pact with the Jewish race. They are the chosen people, especially close to God. Other peoples are God's instruments, whom he uses to punish the people of Israel and bring them back to the right course. God has given his people, through Moses, his Law, the Torah. Even for the later prophets, who considered that God was king over all humanity, it was the Bible which enshrined divine will.

This text, revealed just once in human history contained all God's commands and all his prohibitions. For Jews the Torah, regarded as eternal and complete truth, given once and for all, was the criterion for all other truths. To turn against it would be to turn against God himself.

Philosophy came from outside. It was enshrined in Greek texts, translated into Arabic and, from the twelfth century onwards, into Hebrew. It appears that, at the very start, the Jews made use of doxographies; but the texts of Plato and Aristotle, along with Arabic commentaries, very soon became available to them. Arabic was the language which the Jews in Islamic lands spoke and wrote (sometimes, using Hebrew characters). For the whole of the first period of Jewish philosophy, philosophical texts were written in Arabic. Philosophy also included science and was a requisite for many physicians, astronomers and astrologers. It was not taught in the Jewish schools but by private tutors, and so it was available only to the better off

Yet the majority of philosophers who had a significant influence on Jewish thought in general were also rabbis, talmudic scholars and leaders of their communities. Although they were sometimes attacked for their opinions, the philosophers remained none the less within the Jewish community. This was possible, perhaps, because there are no articles of faith in Judaism. Orthodoxy is based, rather, on the Bible, which is far from monolithic and contains various passages that can be interpreted in more than one way. It is well known that, with regard to the Law, from early times oral teaching gave room for variety, nuance and innovation on the basis of the written text. The teaching was then recorded in writing and itself expounded and glossed until it formed an enormous (and even today still-expanding) body of material. Its importance shows how new problems were resolved without going against the old texts. And this use of allegory and symbolism as tools for interpretation allowed different systems of thought – philosophical, kabbalistic or ascetic – to remain within Judaism.

JEWISH PHILOSOPHY IN ISLAMIC LANDS

Jews in Islamic lands divided into the same philosophical schools as the Muslims: the *kalām*, Neoplatonism and Aristotelianism. Similarly, the questions which Jewish philosophers set themselves were, to a large extent, the same as those discussed by their Muslim counterparts.

The kalām

The *kalām* or, to be precise, the Mu'tazilite school, provided the context for rabbinic thought for a number of generations, and it lasted even longer among the Karaite Jews. Dāwūd ibn Marwān al-Muqammiṣ (ninth century) is the first rationalist Jewish thinker whose work survives. His *'Ishrūn Maqāla* (*Twenty Chapters*) expounds ideas inspired by the *kalām* but strongly influenced by Christianity, to which – for part of his life – he was a convert. His treatise is modelled on treatises of the *kalām*, except for his vigorous defence of Judaism and his arguments against other religions.

By contrast, other Jewish thinkers adopted only some ideas from the *kalām*, in particular, the definition of reason as a universal moral law transcending race and religion, which man finds within himself, and which applies to God, assuring us that there exists a good God in whom we can trust. Among the Karaites, Abū Yūsuf Ya'qūb al-Kirkisānī (Jacob al-Kirkisani) gave the fullest theoretical discussion of this doctrine, whilst Japheth ben Ali made a translation of the Bible into Arabic, accompanied by a commentary where these ideas emerge in the reading of the text. Both thinkers lived in the tenth century. Their great contemporary among rabbinic Jews was Saadiah ben Joseph Gaon (882–942), who was born in Egypt and moved to Babylon; there, in 928, he became *Gaon*, the head of the Talmudic academies. He was extremely prolific in every field: as a grammarian and lexicographer, a translator of the Bible into Arabic and commentator on it, as a liturgical poet and compiler of a prayer book, as a Talmudist and a jurist, as a writer on the calendar and chronology. Saadiah philosophized and engaged in polemic to prove the absolute truth of rabbinical Judaism against the claims of the Karaites and dangers posed by other religions, and by the various schools of philosophy and by scepticism in its different forms.

Arguments based on reason are found in most of Saadiah's works, but it is in two of them that they receive a systematic exposition. They are the *Commentary on the Book of Creation* (*Tafsīr Kitāb al-Mabādī, Peroush Sefer Yetzira*), which was translated into Hebrew several times and used especially in the eleventh and twelfth centuries; and the *Book of Doctrines and Beliefs* (*Al-Amānāt Wa-l'I'tiqādāt, Sefer Emunot Wede'ot*), which still remains today one of the fundamental works of Jewish theology.

Saadiah makes especial use of arguments taken from the *kalām*, as the plan of the *Amānāt* shows. Its first two chapters discuss the unity of God, the topic with which exponents of *kalām* usually begin their treatises, whilst the seven following chapters consider God's justice, the second main theme of the *kalām*. None the less, Saadiah does not adopt one of the central ideas of the *kalām*, that of atomism and the renewal of creation by God at every instant (the corollary of which is the denial that there are laws of nature). He chooses instead a somewhat vague Aristotelian understanding of the physical world.

In the introduction to his *Amānāt*, Saadiah proposes a theory of knowledge. Conviction (*i'tiqād*) arises from three sources: external reality, reason (that is to say, knowledge of good and evil) and what reason deduces necessarily from the reality of things and from the knowledge of good and evil. To these three Saadiah adds 'the truthful tradition', that of the Torah (including the oral Torah, the Talmud). The truthfulness of this tradition has been proved, Saadiah says, by signs, prodigies and, in particular, by the miraculous feeding of the Children of Israel with manna during their flight from Egypt. Whereas miracles and prodigies might be illusory or simulated, the miracle of the manna could not have been simulated, since it lasted for forty years and was so public an event that any idea of a carefully contrived lie is implausible. Nor could it have been a natural phenomenon which Moses was able to produce, since the philosophers would also have known about it and made use of the technique themselves. The 'truthful tradition', the fourth source of knowledge, is therefore based on the historical experience of the Jewish people. And Saadiah's argument gains added strength since none of the other religions questions the historical reality of the exodus from Egypt and the Jews' wanderings in the desert.

The Torah itself asks us to seek to understand the teachings it transmits. It does so for two reasons: first, so that the knowledge transmitted by tradition becomes firmly fixed in the intellect; and, second, so that we can reply to those who call the Law into question. Now, the knowledge which rational, scientific investigation uncovers turns out in fact to conform to traditional knowledge. Saadiah was thus able to represent the Torah and scientific knowledge as two twigs from the same branch. They can in no way contradict one another. Any apparent contradictions are the result either of mistakes in our reasoning, or of our failure to interpret Scripture correctly.

The structure of the *Amānāt* reflects this identity between tradition and reason. Each chapter begins with an introduction to the problem. Then follows an examination of biblical texts which confirm the thesis and, finally, there is a rational analysis of the problem and a refutation of opposing theses.

In his chapter on the creation, Saadiah begins by setting out the way in which this enquiry should be pursued. Here the senses cannot be of any help. Only rational arguments can be used. Whatever the hypothesis – the eternity of the world, the eternity of matter, and so on – an attempt must be made to establish it by reason.

Saadiah's deep intuition is that the world is limited and changing. Only the infinite action of God can sustain and explain this constant change, the perceptual generation of a world both spatially and temporally finite. The world and man, limited and imperfect, bear witness to a perfect and infinite being and lead us to a rational knowledge of the one God, creator of the world. In the introduction to the chapter on the unity of God, Saadiah lists all the objections which were made in his time to this rational way of thought and refutes them all ([4.3] 78, 80):

> Our Lord (be He exalted and glorified) has informed us
> through the words of His prophets that He is One, Living,
> Powerful and Wise, and that nothing can be compared unto
> Him or unto His works. They established this by signs and
> miracles, and we accepted it immediately. Later, speculation
> led us to the same result. In regard to His Unity, it is said,
> 'Hear O Israel, the Lord our God, the Lord is One'.
>
> (Deut. 6: 4)

God, the creator of the world, is therefore one; but who is he? And, when we say of him that he is one, about what unity are we speaking? What is the knowledge he possesses, on account of which we say he is knowing, and what are the actions which are attributed to him, on account of which we say that he acts? The rabbinical Jews replied to these questions with verses from the Bible which often use in connection with God not only such adjectives as 'powerful', 'good and merciful', 'jealous', but also attribute to him bodily movements – 'God rises', 'God comes down' and even parts of the body – 'God's arm', 'God's hand'. But Saadiah strongly opposes any notion of divine corporeality. One of the central aims in his thought is to purify the idea of God and demonstrate that God is incorporeal and transcendent. Everything in our world can be defined according to the Aristotelian categories. Even the soul and 'divine Glory' are definable substances and so more or less corporeal, because for Saadiah body and substance are one and the same thing. God, however, cannot be defined by any of the Aristotelian categories. He transcends them all; and there is nothing in common between finite, composite bodies, which are subject to change, and God, who is immaterial and always remains exactly what he is. Whilst his attributes, power and knowledge, signify that God is not lacking in power or knowledge, power and knowledge such as they are found in man cannot be applied to God because, in God, attributes are identical to essence. Men gain knowledge by learning over a period of time: it comes to be where it was not previously, and in old age it decreases, at death it disappears. But God has knowledge for all eternity. When we talk about God using positive attributes, in reality we are talking about 'something other', about which we can only form a vague notion and of which we know only that it does not resemble what exists here below. God's attributes are identical to his essence (or quiddity), and none is outside his essence. God is absolute unity.

Since we can arrive by reasoning at a refined and exact knowledge of God, why was it necessary to send the prophets? According to Saadiah, God, in his supreme knowledge, has acted 'for the good'. He does nothing in vain. The 'justice of God' (*'adl*), as conceived in the second of the Mu'tazilites' theses, shows why the very nature of God makes prophecy legitimate. Saadiah then goes on to explain why revelation was necessary for mankind. First, it sets out the actions which allow the very general moral laws, dictated by reason, best to be put into practice. Second, it includes other commandments, which are of value and which reason does not teach. Third, it allows people to act immediately, whereas reason, although based on the same principles, takes time to arrive at its conclusions. Moreover, some men never reach the level of rational knowledge, because of their imperfection or their disinclination to study, or because of the doubts which trouble them.

The Bible, however, is often written in anthropomorphic terms, which contradict what reason teaches us: that God is one and incorporeal. Yet tradition is drawn from the same source as rational knowledge and so it cannot be contrary to reason. A rational explanation must therefore be given for the whole of scriptural revelation, and especially for the visions of the prophets. Three principles guide this explanation:

1   All the manifestations of the supernatural are the work of God and God alone. Prophecy is a grace, a gift which God has put into a human receptacle, who is then called a prophet. The prophet is mortal like other men. He cannot do without food or drink. He leads a normal married life. He cannot predict the future. Nor can he perform miracles, except under exceptional conditions – otherwise it would be necessary to suppose that he had superhuman capacities. The prophet is merely an instrument of God's will, the receiver of supernatural visions.

2   God, who is unknowable and incorporeal, makes manifest his created Glory, the first of his creations, an air which is finer and more subtle than the visible air: the 'Second Air'. This Second Air is audible and visible, filled with light and colour, striking in its splendour. It is through the Second Air that the created word was produced which Moses heard, and the Ten Commandments heard in the visible air by the whole people of Israel on Mount Sinai.

It is the Second Air which the prophets saw and called the Throne of Glory and Cherubim, Angels, Seraphim . . .

3   God makes his glory visible in the manner of a teacher going from the easier to the more difficult. He created man in such a way that he was free to obey or disobey his commandments. His wish was that man should merit the highest reward, the world to come, and it is to this end that he made his orders and prohibitions. Among them are some which reason would have shown us were necessary, and others which revelation alone teaches us (though none of them is contrary to reason). These purely religious laws allow the faithful to prove their obedience and merit the reward which God wishes to give them: immortality and resurrection at the time of the Messiah.

Saadiah Gaon's thought remains very close to tradition, both in his conception of God and his exegesis of texts. His charm and optimism cannot fail to allure the modern reader. His simplicity ensures that he will remain for ever young.

Jewish Neoplatonists

Isaac Israeli (born 850, died by 932, or perhaps *c.* 955) was a slightly older contemporary of Saadiah's. He was a famous doctor, and he has the credit of having introduced into medieval Jewish thought texts and ideas taken directly from the Greeks. Like al-Kindī, he also used Greek texts which have not survived to modern times. His type of Neoplatonism is based on emanation. Between the perfection of God and the imperfection of the world below there are interposed more or less perfect essences which link the incorporeal deity to the world of matter. According to Isaac Israeli first matter and first form come from God. Intellect is engendered from these. From Intellect emanates the world of souls (that is, of the rational soul, the animal soul and the vegetative soul). There follows the world of the spheres, then the sublunary world with its four elements and what is made from them. Our earth is a mixture of the four elements: earth, water, air and fire. It is at the centre of the universe and without motion. The spheres, which are made of a more perfect matter, the quintessence, revolve around the earth and create by their movements the composite beings which are bodies.

Other Neoplatonists held that first form and matter emanated from God in a manner which was involuntary and outside time. But Isaac Israeli lays great stress on the creation. God creates first matter and first form. He makes them come to be from nothing, something which God alone can do. Isaac is, however, in agreement with other Neoplatonists in believing that first matter is intelligible, that is to say, absolutely incorporeal. First form contains all other forms which come into existence, but in a perfect way. Intellect, which is light and splendour, comes from the conjunction of first form and first matter. From Intellect emanates the rational soul, which is the human soul. The Intellect holds a high rank in the scale of being, since its source is a pure light, more elevated and brilliant than any body, even one as perfect as the sphere of the heavens. The so-called 'metaphysics of light' play an important role in this description of the higher world, and it is because the soul is part of this world that it is able to climb back up again towards its former habitation. The start of this return is knowledge of the higher world and certainty of the truth.

God, by his will and his power, has created and made manifest first matter and first form from nothingness. But it is by emanation – a necessary action – that Intellect, which is the source of souls and the universe, comes from these two created beings. Intellect and souls act in a different way from that found in the celestial sphere and the sublunary world. It can be said to create, in that nothing is lost of the essential light and lower beings are created from the shadow of this light. But in the world of the spheres and below, natural action is by generation and corruption, since the source of action is changed and diminished by the action itself which it carries out on bodies with qualities opposed to it. Below the celestial sphere all beings come into being from the four simple elements: fire, air, water and earth. Whereas in other bodies one or another of these elements predominates, in man they are in harmonious equilibrium. Every creature made of the elements is given a soul according to its capacity and each finds pleasure in bringing itself closer to the principal element in it.

The three degrees of the soul – intellectual, animal and vegetative – are not absolutely separate. For instance, certain animals have almost as much intelligence and prudence as man. All this is due to the inclination of one soul towards another. Sometimes, the rational soul tends towards the animal soul and its actions tend towards those of the animal soul which desires eating, drinking and pleasure. In the same way, the animal soul has a tendency to assimilate its actions to those of the rational soul when it is instructed and influenced by it. The rational soul tends to draw itself near to the Intellect and reach perfection, in which case it will be clear and pure, and it will seek good and true things such as knowledge and understanding, purity and saintliness, service of God and nearness to him. This all comes about from the influence of the higher substance.

Since man of his own accord raises himself towards the Intellect, and so towards God, what part does revelation play? Isaac Israeli divides mankind into types according to which of each of the three souls is dominant: the rational soul, the animal soul or the vegetative soul. Only a small proportion of the human race is, therefore, truly close to the light of the Intellect. These are the privileged individuals whom God will use as intermediaries in order to bring the divine word to humankind.

One of Isaac Israeli's pupils, Dunash ben Tamin, brings out his train of thought when he discusses Moses. Moses differs from the other prophets because he heard the word of God in the way described in Exodus 32: 11: 'the eternal one spoke to Moses face to face.' Moses' soul was superior to that of other men: it was subtle, light and, even before it was separated from Moses' body, it was united with the world of the rational soul. For when souls are separated from their bodies, they remain alive and are united with the world above: the soul becomes intellect and, in an incorporeal, spiritual union, the intellect is united with light.

Prophetic visions are no longer conceived as real, external phenomena which are seen and heard, but as internal visions which reflect spiritual rather than sensory reality. So far from being inferior to sensory reality, spiritual reality is as much superior to it, as the soul is superior to the body:

> One whose rational soul has withdrawn itself [i.e. from the lower souls] and upon whom intellect causes its light and splendour to emanate becomes spiritual, god-like, and longing exceedingly for the ways of the angels, as far as lies within human power. The Creator, exalted and blessed be He, therefore chose from among His creatures one qualified in this manner to be His messenger, caused him to prophesy, and showed through him His truthful signs and miracles. He made him the messenger and intermediary between Himself and His creatures, and caused His true Book to descend through him.
>
> ([4.20] 139)

The Bible is not, however, a work of philosophy. It includes narratives which have a sense which is far from intellectual (and some which can hardly be understood at all!). The reason for this, Israeli explains, is that God speaks the language of men so that all will understand him. He bases his language on the capacities of his audience. Those among them able to discern the pure sense will find it; because they are distant from material things and their minds are detached and luminous, they will see God's words and his light. Those who are still incapable of seeing the light will ask the sages to expound the Bible to them and, little by little, thanks to their expositions, they will understand and will come nearer to the source of purity until they are so close to the Intellect that it will print its form in their soul. God himself provides the example which the Intellect follows. God puts himself within reach of human understanding: the Intellect imitates this divine way of teaching when it wishes men to know future events, and the philosophers in their turn take the same course when they explain *viva voce* what their pupils cannot understand in their written work. The superior beings are like a ray of light which penetrates through the entire breadth of a solid body. The Intellect, the prophets and the philosophers all follow God's own footsteps as they incline themselves towards lower beings and help each of them, so far as he is able, to climb the ladder of light.

It was not only philosophers who developed such themes: the quest for purity, freedom from bodily desires, and the desire for union with the Intellect. They were also taken up by scholars, rabbis, poets and courtiers during the tenth to twelfth centuries: for instance, Haï Gaon (938–1038, Babylon), president of the Talmudic academy; Baḥyā ibn Paqudah (*c.* 1050–80, Andalusia), a judge on the rabbinical tribunal and author of the famous devotional work, *Guide to the Duties of the Heart*; the famous poet, Moses ibn Ezra (1055–*c.* 1135, Spain); Abraham ibn Ezra (*c.* 1092–1167, Spain then Italy and France), also a famous poet and biblical commentator; Joseph ben Jacob ibn Ẓaddik (died 1149 at Cordoba), a judge on the rabbinical tribunal and a philosopher; Abraham bar Ḥiyyah (died after 1136 at Barcelona), an astronomer and mathematician who held an important post at the court of Alphonsus I of Aragon and of the counts of Barcelona; and Solomon ibn Gabirol and Judah Halevi.

Solomon ben Judah ibn Gabirol (*c.* 1022 to 1054/8, Spain) is well-known for his Hebrew poetry, both sacred and secular. His philosophy is expounded in a treatise which has not survived in its Arabic original but in the Latin translation, *Fons Vitae* (*Source of Life*) made by John of Spain and Dominicus Gundissalinus in the mid-twelfth century. The *Fons Vitae* was widely read by thirteenth-century Christian theologians, who knew its author as 'Avicebron' or 'Avencebrol' and took him to be an Arab – or even a Christian – thinker. In addition, there survive some extracts from the work, translated into Hebrew, made in the thirteenth century by Shem Tov ibn Falaqera. These do not preserve the dialogue form found in the *Fons Vitae*. Gabirol's treatise was known to Neoplatonic Jewish philsophers and was fiercely criticized by the first Jewish Aristotelian, Abraham ibn Daud. Then it was almost entirely forgotten until 1846, when Solomon Munk showed that the extracts made by Falaqera were from the work translated into Latin as the *Fons Vitae*, and so that 'Avicebron' was none other than the famous Hebrew poet, Solomon ibn Gabirol.

Gabirol's system is Neoplatonic. Through knowing his own soul, man can know nature, free himself from it and return to the spiritual world, his place of origin. Knowledge is knowledge of being. There are only three sorts of being: (1) primary substance, (2) primary matter and form, (3) God and the Will, which is an intermediary between God and matter-with-form. Man is able to grasp these types of being because he finds within himself equivalents of them: his understanding corresponds to primary substance, his soul to the Will and his matter and form to primary matter and form. Man can know God's actions but not his essence apart from his acts, since it is infinite and above all things. In the order of emanation, primary matter and form are the nearest to the divine Will. From them together is engendered Intellect, then Soul, and from Soul Nature, which is the last of the simple substances. It is from Nature that bodily substance derives.

The path which will take the soul back to Intellect goes by the knowledge of composite beings: spiritual beings which are called 'simple' although they are in fact composite. Indeed, 'simple' and 'composite' are relative terms: a being is simple with regard to that which is lower than it, and composite with regard to that which is above it. The entirety of things can thus be regarded as if it were arranged in a line, beginning with universal matter and form. The further it is from its source, the more composite a being is with regard to that which goes before it, although it remains simple in relation to that which follows it.

Matter, form and the Will are the true subject-matter of the *Fons Vitae*. Gabirol describes at length the various types of matter and form, universal and particular, which make up the universe. Beings are individuated in the first place by forms, material or spiritual, whereas matter is one and universal. But to the unity of form there corresponds a unity of matter and, in another passage, Gabirol makes it clear that the diversity of beings is not brought about because of form, since form is one and entirely spiritual, but by matter which can be perfect and subtle or thick and heavy.

The Will is the ultimate goal of man's quest. This Will is identical to the Wisdom of God and his *logos*. Conceived apart from its acts, the Will is indeed identical to the divine essence, but it is distinguished from it when its acts are considered. In the former case, it is infinite, but finite in the second. It is an intermediary between the divine essence and form and matter. It penetrates all things and is their efficient cause; itself without motion, it is the cause of spiritual and bodily movement.

In Gabirol's philosophy, as in other Jewish Neoplatonic (and later Aristotelian) philosophies, God can be approached only through rational knowledge. Prophets and philosophers imitate God by their intellect, in thought, and prophetic visions are no longer considered to be dialogues with God or his angels but rather internal illuminations. Bodily acts have no value in themselves: they prepare the soul to separate from the body, since only then will it be able to fulfil its destiny.

It is this very approach to philosophy which Judah Halevi (born before 1075, died 1140) wishes to supersede in his *Kuzari*. Written in Arabic, the *Book of Refutation and Proof, in Defence of the Despised Faith* is a dialogue between the king of the Khazars and the defenders of philosophy, of Islam, Christianity and Judaism. From the beginning, Judah Halevi insists that good intentions are not sufficient to please God, who also cares about which rites and observances are used.

Above the natural manner of action, there is the supernatural way of acting of the *Amr Ilahi* (God's word and action): God has revealed himself in history, in his choice of a people, a land and a language. This choice is the only real proof of God's existence, and it is part of the order of the world. On to the mineral, vegetable, animal and rational kingdoms, there is added, in the hierarchical order, the prophetic order, that of Adam and his sons, of Noah and then of the whole people of Israel.

Man is able, by his own strength, to rise as far as the level of the Intellect. To do so, he must follow the discursive path, that of philosophy. But, in order to be marked out by the *Amr Ilahi*, he needs to follow the supernatural path, that of the Torah. God has reserved this path for his elect. In every generation since Adam there was one pure man, worthy of the *Amr Ilahi*; but then the whole people of Israel and it alone was chosen by God.

Along with the choice of the people of Israel goes the choice of the land of Israel and of its holy language, Hebrew. The land of Israel has a special place in Judah Halevi's work, and his Hebrew poems about Jerusalem are among the most beautiful of all Jewish literature. They are still recited today, and Judah Halevi's thought, with its particularist view of Judaism, remains as popular among modern Jewry as the thought of Maimonides.

The most original writing of the twelfth century, however, steps aside from debates between religion and philosophy. It is that of Abu'l-Barakāt al-Baghdādī, who lived in Iraq and died, at a very old age, after 1164. Towards the end of his life he converted to Islam. His *Kitāb al-Mu'tabar*, a sort of reply to Avicenna's philosophy, is based on his own personal reflections. He upholds the unity of the soul, denying that there is a distinction between it and the intellect. In his view, there is just one time, which measures *esse* and is similar for all beings, including God. Space is three-dimensional and infinite. Abu'l-Barakāt had a deep influence on Arab philosophy but none on Jewish thought, and his works were not translated into Hebrew.

Maimonides

Moses ben Maimon was born in 1138 at Cordoba, where his father was a rabbinical judge. In 1148 Maimon and his family fled from the religious persecution which took place after the town fell to the Almohades. After wandering from town to town in Spain, and perhaps also in Provence, in 1160 they arrived at Fez in Morocco. In about 1165 the whole family fled from Fez and set off to Acre. For five months, Maimon and his children lived in the land of Israel, then they went to Cairo and settled at Fostat. Maimon's son Moses rose rapidly in Egyptian Jewish society, helped perhaps by family ties with some of the important people there. For about five years from 1171 he was 'Leader of the Jews'. He was subsequently deprived of this post, but twenty years later he regained it and kept it until his death.

Maimonides earned his living by practising and teaching medicine, which he had studied in north Africa. His fame reached its peak in 1185 when he was chosen as one of the official doctors of Al Fadil, Saladin's vizier. At the same time as he followed his profession and composed his medical treatises, Maimonides completed two great works, the *Mishneh Torah* in 1180 and the *Guide of the Perplexed* in 1190, as well as conducting a lengthy correspondence with the many Jewish communities of Egypt and in other countries. His death in 1204 was the occasion for public mourning among Jews everywhere.

With the exception of the *Mishneh Torah*, all Maimonides' works were written in Arabic. They were almost immediately translated into Hebrew. The *Guide of the Perplexed* was translated by Samuel ibn Tibbon in 1204, and a second, less precise, more literary translation was made a few years later by Judah al-Harizi. It formed the basis for the Latin translation used by Christian scholastics such as Thomas Aquinas.

Maimonides' reputation rests, in the first place, on his contribution to law. It was as a legal authority that he was first known to the Jews of the diaspora and still today many eastern Jewish communities follow his juridical and religious rulings.

The comparison between Maimonides and Averroes is inescapable, and one difference between the two thinkers is striking. By contrast with Averroes, who held that philosophy should be carefully hidden from the ignorant, Maimonides is a philosopher in all his works, legal as well as philosophical, in the texts intended for the general public as much as in those written for students of philosophy. After Aristotle, al-Fārābī was Maimonides' real master. His influence is visible in a youthful work, the *Milot-ha-Higayon*, 'A Logical Vocabulary', written at the age of 16, and it remains in Maimonides' last work, the *Guide*. In a letter written to Samuel ibn Tibbon a year or two before he died, Maimonides told him:

> Aristotle's intellect [represents] the extreme of human intellect, if we except those who have received divine inspiration. The works of Aristotle are the roots and foundations of all works on the sciences. But they cannot be understood except with the help of commentaries, those of Alexander of Aphrodisias, those of Themistius, and those of Averroes, I tell you: as for works on logic, one should only study the writings of Abū Naṣr al-Fārābī. All his writings are faultlessly excellent.
> One ought to study and understand them. For he is a great man.

On Avicenna, his view is more qualified:

> Though the work of Avicenna may give rise to objections and are not as [good] as those of Abu Nasr [al-Fārābī], Abu Bakr al-Sāigh [Ibn Bājjah] was also a great philosopher, and all his writings are of a high standard.
>
> ([4.13] lix–lx)

And to read the other Jewish and Arab philosophers was, he thought, a waste of time.

The philosophical school to which Maimonides says he belongs, and which he recommends to Samuel ibn Tibbon, is that of the Andalusian philosophers, who strictly separated scientific knowledge from religion. Maimonides, however, did introduce philosophical principles into all his works, including those intended for the simple believer, such as Book I, part one of his *Mishneh Torah*, the *Book of Precepts* and the commentary on the *Mishnah*. These principles, thirteen in all, which are discussed afresh in the *Guide*, are presented by Maimonides as truths which everyone should accept by authority because they are the beliefs of the Jewish people, the necessary condition for belonging to it:

> When a man has accepted these principles and truly believes in them, he forms part of the community of Israel; and it is incumbent upon us to love him, to care for him and behave towards him as God has ordered us to do: to love and comfort him; if he sins because of his corporeal desires or his bad instincts, he will receive the punishment proportioned to his crime, and he may [afterwards] have the part [that belongs to him in the world to come], he is a sinner within the community of Israel. But if someone casts doubt on one of these principles, he has foresworn his faith, he is a renegade, a heretic, an unbeliever, he has rebelled against God and it is a duty to hate him and to cause him to perish.
>
> ([4.7] 148–9)

The 'Thirteen Principles' are divided into three groups. The first five are concerned with God, who is one and incorporeal; the following four with prophecy and the Law; the last four with reward and punishment, the coming of the Messiah and the resurrection of the dead.

The principles include certain articles of faith which were far from being unanimously accepted by the Jewish community, especially in these two respects:

(1) Divine incorporeality implies the rejection or allegorization of many biblical passages and of a certain number of texts which are an integral part of the oral Law. Maimonides was not the first to declare that God is not corporeal, but he was the first to exclude from the people of Israel those Jews who took the anthropomorphic comments in the Bible in their literal sense.

(2) By 'the world to come' Maimonides understands the immortality of the soul, and he does not make clear whether this is a matter of individual immortality. Traditional texts use two other expressions to talk about man after death: 'the days of the Messiah' and 'the resurrection of the dead'. For Maimonides, 'the days of the Messiah' means political independence of the Jews and their return to the land of Israel. The Messiah will easily be recognized, since his coming will coincide with a new period of history, totally different from the time of the diaspora. As for the corporeal resurrection of the dead, Maimonides holds that it is neither necessary from a scientific point of view, nor theoretically impossible. If one believes in divine omnipotence, it is a possibility. Clearly, this bodily resurrection is not of great importance to Maimonides, especially since it would be followed by a bodily death. Samuel ben Eli, Gaon of Baghdad, attacked Maimonides sharply for failing to insist on the resurrection of the dead and the survival of the individual human soul. In his final work, *The Letter on the Resurrection of the Dead*, Maimonides repeats his earlier view, unchanged, often with fierce irony.

A fourteenth-century versification of the Thirteen Principles became part of the daily prayers of almost every Jewish community, except for the Ashkenazim, thus impressing themselves on the great majority of Jews and definitively shaping the Jewish notion of God.

The Guide of the Perplexed is the Jewish philosophical work most known outside Judaism. By contrast with Maimonides' other works, which are models of clarity and order, the *Guide* is avowedly difficult to understand. Like the Torah, the prophetic books and the *Aggadot* of the Talmud, it is constructed in such a way as simultaneously to hide and reveal its inner sense. The difficulties of its plan and the ambiguities in its expressions can be traced back to the obscurities of the texts it discusses.

Maimonides suggests, moreover, that his book should not be studied chapter by chapter, but rather problem by problem. He asks that it should not be read in the light of preconceptions, but that the reader should first have studied all that ought to be studied, and that he should not explain it to others.

The book is intended neither for the ignorant, nor for philosophers – neither of these are in difficulties – but for those who, like Maimonides' follower, Joseph ben Judah, have studied science, mathematics, astronomy and then logic, and who pose themselves questions about the Bible and its interpretation. Take the example of God's incorporeality. From the conceptual point of view, belief in the existence of God is inseparable from his absolute unity and his absolute unity is inseparable from his incorporeality. But it is quite otherwise when seen from the pedagogical or historical angle. The Law of Moses, a political law like every other religious law, was given to the Jewish people at a certain point in its history. For it to be accepted, it had to take into consideration the beliefs to which the people were accustomed. If it had not done this, the political and intellectual good it brought would have been lost. Before insisting on the existence of an incorporeal God it was necessary to bring about acceptance of the existence of God himself. When they fled from Egypt, the only type of existence which the Jews could conceive was that of a corporeal being: 'The minds of the multitude were accordingly guided to the belief that He exists by imagining that he is corporeal and to the belief that he is living by imagining that He is capable of motion' (I, 46; [4.13] 98). 'God, may He be exalted above every deficiency, has had bodily organs figuratively ascribed to Him in order that His acts should be indicated by this means' ([4.13] 99). What was a gain in understanding at the time of Moses had become an inexcusable fault by the time of Maimonides: those who believe that God is corporeal were, as we have seen, to be excluded from the Jewish community. The Sages themselves had never committed this fault: 'the doctrine of the corporeality of God did not occur even for a single day to the Sages, may their memory be blessed and ... this was not according to them a matter lending itself to imagination or confusion' ([4.13] 102).

The problem which the *Guide* is intended to resolve is, therefore, that of the Law's double character. Sometimes its external sense, which results from the historical situation at the time when it was granted, serves to introduce and helps to discover the internal sense, which alone is true. Sometimes the external sense prevents the reader from reaching 'the knowledge of the Law in its reality' and is contrary to reason. The object of the *Guide* is to bring to light the two senses of the Bible: through this duality alone can knowledge from science and revelation be reconciled.

In the *Guide* there can be found the elements of the method which allows the cloak of divine, scriptural allegory to be removed:

> Know that the key to the understanding of all that the prophets, peace be on them, have said, and to the knowledge of its truth, is an understanding of the parables, of their import, and of the meaning of the words occurring in them. You know what God, may He be exalted, has said: *And by the ministry of the prophets have I used similitudes* (Hos. 12: 11). And you know that He has said: *Put forth a riddle and speak a parable* (Ezek. 18: 2).
>
> ([4.13] 10–11)

The first half of Book I treats in general the expressions in the Bible and the Talmud which cannot be taken in their literal sense. In the second half, God's attributes are described and the *Mu'takalimun*, among them Saadiah, are attacked. Book II discusses philosophical doctrines, then prophecy. Book III begins with an allegorical explanation of the 'Account of the Chariot' and then considers providence and the fact that the world will end and not continue eternally. Maimonides gives a psychological explanation of the book of Job, a history of religions and types of worship, and he goes on to talk about religious commands.

Clearly, it is beyond the scope of this survey to examine the great variety of interpretations of the *Guide*. Our discussion must be limited to mentioning a few of the especially important points in its doctrine.

(1) *God and his attributes* According to Maimonides, only negative attributes can be applied to God. Any relation between two terms implies something they have in common. But there can be nothing in common between a being which is totally separate and another being which depends on every other being. Even existence is not common to them both, because 'existence' does not describe the same thing when one speaks of God and when one speaks of a created being, because God is a necessary existence and a created being a possible existence.

For Moses, the prince among the prophets, as for man in general, to know God means, not to know anything of his essence but to know his actions. Through the speculative method which God showed to Moses, it is possible to make progress in knowing the unknowability of God's essence. As we deny attributes of God, we understand better his supereminence and the lack of relation between his perfection and ours. To deny that God has emotions is already to be closer to the truth about him than just to deny that he has a body. To deny not only that he has emotions but that there is any relation between him and other beings is to take another step on the path of negative theology, a step which brings us closer to the idea that God is above all our categories of thought. We should, therefore, say nothing about God, and true prayer – the only prayer which is befitting to God – is silence, since every positive praise in fact consists of attributing to him what, to us, is perfection and, for him, a defect. Maimonides quotes with great praise a Talmudic story (*Babylonian Talmud Berakhot* 33b) where a worshipper adds eulogistic adjective to eulogistic adjective in his prayers. Rabbi Haninah tells him that these praises are as unfitting as if one were to praise a king for all the silver coins he possessed, when his treasury was full of gold. Indeed, Maimonides says, were we left to follow reason alone, we would use none of these adjectives. We do so because men have need for images in order to understand and also just because the Torah used them. Since they were written in the Torah, we are allowed to read them as part of the biblical text. But we use them in our prayers only on the authority of the men of the Grand Synod, since they have taken the responsibility for this decision. Verbal prayer is, in fact, a concession to human weakness.

'Knowing God's actions' is the second aspect of knowledge of God. By knowing his creation, we learn what we should deny of God. Every branch of knowledge can teach us something about this. Arithmetic and geometry teach us that God's unity is not like the unity to which we add or which can be multiplied. Physics and astronomy teach us how God puts the world into motion through the intermediary of separated intellects, in a perfect and absolute manner. It is only because we have a tendency to describe God in anthropomorphic terms that certain of God's, or nature's, actions seem beneficent and certain others seem destructive. In reality, God's action is intended to maintain the immutable order of nature, which includes the preservation of the human race as of other species of living things.

(2) *God's understanding* In Part I, Chapter 68 of the *Guide*, Maimonides proposes a theory of understanding which seems to contradict his negative theology.

> Now when it is demonstrated that God, may He be held precious and magnified, is an intellect *in actu* . . . It is accordingly also clear that the numerical unity of the intellect, the intellectually cognizing subject, and the

intellectually cognized object, does not hold good with reference to the Creator only, but also with reference to every intellect. Thus in us too, the intellectually cognizing subject, the intellect and the intellectually cognized object, are one and the same thing wherever we have an intellect *in actu*.

(I, 68, [4.13] 165–6)

Contrary, then, to the views of Aristotle and al-Fārābī, Maimonides holds that God does not merely know his own essence but also every intelligible thing and the laws of nature: 'for through knowing the true reality of His own immutable essence, He also knows the totality of what necessarily derives from all His acts' (*Guide*, III, 21, [4.13], 485) The commentators have not found a convincing explanation for this contradiction.

(3) *The origin of the world*   In the *Mishneh Torah*, the proof of God's incorporeal existence is based on the perpetual movement of the sphere and so on the eternity of the world. In the *Guide*, Maimonides shows the extent to which the philosophical point of view contradicts the religious one:

> [T]he belief in eternity the way Aristotle sees it – that is, the belief according to which the world exists in virtue of necessity, that no nature changes at all, and that the customary course of events cannot be modified with regard to anything – destroys the Law in its principle, necessarily gives the lie to every miracle, and reduces to inanity all the hopes and threats that the Law has held out . . .
>
> If, however, one believed in eternity according to the second opinion we have explained – which is the opinion of Plato – . . . this opinion would not destroy the foundations of the Law and would be followed not by the lie being given to miracles, but by their becoming admissible. It would also be possible to interpret figuratively the texts in accordance with this opinion. And many obscure passages can be found in the texts of the *Torah* and others with which this opinion could be connected or rather by means of which it could be proved. However, no necessity could impel us to do this unless this opinion were demonstrated. In view of the fact that it has not been demonstrated, we shall not favor this opinion, nor shall we at all heed that other opinion.

(II, 25, [4.13] 328–9)

Commentators have interpreted these passages in opposing fashions. Some take them to be a clear statement in favour of creation, whereas for others they seem rather to disguise Maimonides' view, which he proposes clearly elsewhere, in favour of the eternity of the world. Shlomo Pines, in the most recent discussion of the problem, suggests that problems of method came to occupy Maimonides increasingly as his thought matured, which can be summarized as follows:

1 Aristotle's physics are true so far as the sublunary world is concerned, but dubious with regard to the heavens and the order of intelligences.
2 Man cannot reach the level of intellectual understanding except through the imagination, through the *phantasmata* of bodily things which, according to a quotation he makes from al-Fārābī's Commentary on the *Nicomachean Ethics*, implies the denial of the immortality of the soul. (The only happiness would be a political one.)

Maimonides' extreme intellectualism was not an easy doctrine to live with: his son, Abraham, who followed as head of the Jewish community in Egypt adopted a *sufi*-like mysticism and gathered around him a group of spiritually intense pietists. The descendants of Maimonides continued to practise this mystical approach to religion for two hundred years.

Ibn Kammūnah (thirteenth century) may be considered the last Jewish philosopher living in Islamic lands. In the fifteenth century, however, there was a sort of renaissance of Jewish philosophy, accompanied by mysticism, in the Yemen.

❧ JEWISH PHILOSOPHY IN ❧ CHRISTIAN LANDS

From the twelfth century onwards, Christians and Jews discovered a whole body of Greek texts and their Arabic commentaries. They were translated into Hebrew for the use of Jews, just as they were put into Latin for Christian readers.

Jewish philosophy in Christian lands was based on Greek and Arabic sources, but also on the works of Jews who had written in Arabic. Maimonides had seen no need to use texts written by other Jews, since Greek and Islamic works provided what was essential in disciplined knowledge. But his successors, who lived among Christians, wanted to know this Jewish philosophy, and there were translators – often dynasties of translators – who worked to make these texts available to them. The first of them was Judah ben Saul ibn Tibbon. He translated works by Baḥyā ibn Paqudah, Judah Halevi and Saadiah. In 1204 Samuel ibn Tibbon put Maimonides' *Guide* into Hebrew. The work came as a revelation to educated Jews. All of a sudden, the passages of the Bible which offended reason became clear and rational. Maimonides, as the spiritual leader of Judaism, was already celebrated for his religious learning. Now, with the *Guide*, he showed that he was also a consummate philosopher, who accepted the true path of scientific knowledge – that of Aristotle – and showed that true Judaism was the religion which fostered this knowledge. The *Guide* became a manual of philosophy.

Aristotle could not be studied without a commentary, and Maimonides himself had recommended those of Averroes. From the beginning of the thirteenth century, Averroes' commentaries were translated into Hebrew but also, in the middle of the century, popularized through encyclopaedias: the *Midrash ha-Hokhma* of Judah ben Solomon ha-Cohen, the *Sha'ar ha Shamayim* of Gerson ben Solomon of Arles and the *De'ot ha-philosophim* of Shem Tov ibn Falaqera. Besides Averroes, there are frequent references to Aristotle, Plato, Alexander of Aphrodisias, Themistius, al-Fārābī, Avicenna, Ibn Bājjah, and Greek and Arabic mathematical, astronomical and medical texts. The Jewish philosophers were deeply affected by their reading of Averroes and this coloured their interpretation of Maimonides. Very often, Averroist ideas were preferred to those of Maimonides, thereby sharpening the opposition between philosophy and religion. Except in Italy, no Christian author is named and the influence of Christian scholasticism is not explicitly acknowledged. Indeed, the universities were Christian institutions to which the Jews had no access. Jews spoke the vernacular (French, Provençal, Italian or Catalan), but these spoken languages did not give them knowledge of Latin. Whereas Jewish philosophers in Islamic countries benefited from all the sources of inspiration open to their Muslim colleagues, those in Christian lands were limited to Hebrew texts. This gave a certain homogeneity to Jewish philosophy, but also limited it. In contrast with what had happened in Islamic lands, Jewish philosophy developed in parallel, but separately, from Christian thought, and the connections between the two are not easy to discern. Often they share common problems; their answers are usually different.

During the thirteenth century, many philosophical works were written. Along with pursuing the sciences, authors engaged in the philosophical explanation of traditional texts, as Maimonides had shown, and of their anthropomorphic expressions. Philosophy was no longer the preserve of a learned or rich minority, but became available to a large section of society. An enlightened middle class had grown up in the south of France and Provence, in Catalonia, Spain and Italy. The existence of towns, material prosperity and the extensive links between the various Jewish communities encouraged the growth of a milieu where science and philosophy were keenly studied, and where scholars were numerous and influential within the community. Philosophy became the subject of public sermons. True, Jacob Anatolio was forced, by the opposition of some of his community, to abandon the set of philosophical sermons he had been giving on Saturdays in the synagogue. But the very fact that he had begun to give them, with the agreement of a certain number of the community, shows well how public philosophical teaching had become.

Both the upholders of traditional Judaism and the exponents of the kabbalah, which was developing in this period in Catalonia and Provence, were violently opposed to this surge of interest in philosophy. There was fierce anti-philosophical polemic in the Jewish communities during the whole of the thirteenth century, which reached its climax at several points: in 1202, about the resurrection of the dead (even before the *Guide of the Perplexed* had been translated), in 1240–2 and then at the very end of the century. This controversy about studying philosophy itself came to an end when the Jews were expelled from France in 1305, but the underlying differences of view continued until the end of the Middle Ages.

In the fourteenth century, Maimonides remained the fixed point of reference and provided the framework for Jewish thought. The central problems, however, and the way of tackling them began to be affected by the scholastic philosophy of the Christian universities: for instance, the question of individual forms in Yedaya ha-Penini, at the very beginning of the century; that of future contingents in the 1320s and 1330s; that of non-Aristotelian (Parisian) physics at the end of the century. In the second half of the fourteenth century, translations from Latin into Hebrew were more often of medical than philosophical texts, but they began to include works of logic. There was also a resurgence of interest in astrology, with a Neoplatonic emphasis.

Gersonides and Crescas

The dominant Jewish philosopher of the fourteenth century was Gersonides. Gersonides (Levi ben Gerson, Leo of Bagnols) (1288–1344) seems never to have left the south of France, where he lived at Bagnol-sur-Cèze, in Languedoc, in Avignon and in Orange. He is often considered the greatest Jewish philosopher after Maimonides. Like Maimonides, he was a philosopher and a Talmudist, as well as being learned in the sciences.

Besides works on astronomy (where he attacks some of the fundamental principles used by Ptolemy and proposes his own solutions) and biblical commentaries, Gersonides wrote (still mostly unpublished) commentaries on the epitomes and *Middle Commentaries* of Averroes. They were composed between 1319 and 1324 and cover the greater part of Aristotle's oeuvre. These are purely philosophical works and do not deal with questions linked to religion. In the excursus, where Gersonides expresses his own ideas, he refers readers to his *Wars of the Lord*. This work, divided into six books, took ten years to write and was finished in January 1329. Its introduction shows how much it differs from Maimonides' writings both in method and in its thoughts:

> I would like to examine in this book several important yet difficult questions on which many crucial doctrines relevant to man's intellectual happiness are based. First, is the rational soul immortal when it has achieved [only] some perfection? Second, when a man is informed by dreams or divination or prophecy of future events, is he informed of them essentially or accidentally? ... Third, does God know existent things? ... Fourth, is there divine providence over existent things? ... Fifth, how do the movers of the heavenly bodies move these bodies, and how many movers are there, as far as we can know? ... Sixth, is the universe eternal or created? ...
>
> Now it is without doubt essential that the reader of this book be familiar with the mathematical science, the natural sciences, and metaphysics. Of the questions mentioned so far, some belong to the sciences, others to metaphysics, and others require a knowledge of mathematics [including astronomy].
>
> ([4.14] 91–4)

Gersonides has therefore written a work about science, and he deals with mathematical, physical and metaphysical – that is to say, philosophical – questions. His intended audience are those who are plunged into perplexity by scientific questions to which previous philosophers have found no solution. It is not the letter of the biblical text which causes problems:

> The reader should not think it is the Torah that has stimulated us to verify what shall be verified in this book, [whereas in reality] the truth itself is something different. It is evident, as Maimonides (may his name be blessed) has said, that we must believe what reasoning has proved to be true. If the literal sense of the Torah differs from it, it is necessary to interpret those passages and accord them with reasoning. Accordingly, Maimonides (may his name be blessed) explains the words of the Torah that suggest that God (may He be

blessed) is corporeal in such a way that reason is not violated. He, therefore, maintains that if the eternity of the universe is demonstrated, it would be necessary to believe in it and to interpret the passages of the Torah that seem to be incompatible with it in such a way that they agree with reason. It is, therefore, evident that if the course of speculation causes us to affirm doctrines that are different from what appears to be the literal sense of Scripture, we are not prohibited by the Torah to pronounce the truth on these matters, for this is not incompatible with the true understanding of the Torah. The Torah is not a political law that forces us to believe false ideas; rather it leads us to the truth to the extent that is possible . . .

([4.14] 98)

In Gersonides' view, most of the prophets did not have revelations about things to do with the intelligible world. So Abraham did not know how many stars there are, because this number was not known in his day. Ezekiel thought that he had heard the voice of the celestial spheres, because this is how people thought of it in his times. Nor did the prophets have a political role (and here Gersonides rejected the whole Arab and Jewish political tradition); the purpose of dreams, divination and prophecy is to reveal the future, especially future contingents which will happen to individual human beings. These future events seem accidental. In fact, they can be known in advance, by dream, divination or prophecy, because they have been determined and arranged. The fact that accidental events are part of an order is proved by the existence of men who are said to have been born under a good star. They are granted every success whilst for other men misfortune is heaped on misfortune. But, if good or bad fortune were accidental, they would be distributed in fairly equal measure. Another argument is that, as the most eminent of creatures, man is taken care of by the celestial substances to such an extent that his actions and thoughts come from them. So astrologers know what people think and their predictions are often correct. When they predict wrongly, this is because of the distance of the stars from us and the limitations of the astrologers' knowledge. Since that which, for man, is an accident, is ordered and determined for the stars, these human events are in fact ordered and determined.

There are, however, acts which cannot be foreseen in the ordering of the stars: those which are freely chosen by men. But such acts are few. Indeed, almost all the thoughts of men and their movements are determined by the stars. Men are the most noble creatures and the order of the stars is intended for the good, and so men benefit more than other animals from the beneficent influence of the stars. It is rare that men set themselves against this order and, in fact, the great majority of events which we call accidental are determined and knowable. They are therefore the objects of scientific knowledge: of God's knowledge, eminently perfect; of the more partial knowledge of the Agent Intellect; and of the very limited and incomplete knowledge of man – a degree of knowledge which, none the less, gives him immortality.

God's thought is directed not merely toward himself but also to the law, order and organization of beings, which he considers in a single, unified concept. All the attributes which he has disseminated to the pure forms are perfect within him. To him then can be attributed those attributes which are the reflection of the perfection of the divine being in us: essence, existence, unity, substantiality, understanding, the joy which accompanies doing good and so on.

Gersonides discusses the creation of the world from an astronomer's point of view. God created the world by beginning with a first body lacking in form and therefore not being. This first body, entirely in potency, neutral and lifeless, has an existence which is known to the senses. It is the fluid body between the spheres and sometimes it is opposed to form. It can be seen in the spheres, where God has given it a geometrical form along with the ability to keep this form; whilst, in the sublunary world, it has the form of the elements and the ability to receive every form.

God created the world in time. Gersonides rejects the definition of the present instant as that which separates the past from the future. An instant can be the beginning or the end of an interval of time. In order to support the idea that the world was created in time, Gersonides also brings in the argument that history is still going on and is far from having reached its conclusion; consider the history of the branches of knowledge, or of the dissemination of God's law, or the history of languages.

Although he was deeply convinced of the truth of astrology, Gersonides upholds the existence of human free will, as all the other Jewish philosophers had done. The problems of determinism and future contingents which, in Christian scholastic philosophy, had taken a clear form in the work of Peter Aureoli, were raised in Jewish circles by Abner of Burgos. Abner's unqualified determinism was the justification for his conversion to Catholicism in the 1320s.

It is all the more astonishing to find an equally complete determinism in the thought of Hasdaï Crescas. Hasdaï Crescas was the leader of the Jewish community in Barcelona, already well known in 1367. His only son was killed in the anti-Jewish uprisings of 1391, though he himself survived. The wave of conversions to Catholicism which would go on through the whole of the fifteenth century had already begun, and Crescas dedicated himself to combating it and to reconstructing the Jewish communities which had been destroyed. His two polemical works were written in Catalan and his philosophical book in Hebrew.

Aristotelian philosophy was accused of having disturbed people's minds and of having driven the heads of communities – rich men who were often interested in philosophy – to convert and take with them other Jews. *The Light of God (Or Adonaï)* was planned by Crescas as just the first part of a more extensive project, intended to replace the whole of Maimonides' work, both in philosophy and rabbinical jurisprudence. But the second part of it was never written. According to Crescas, the very root of Maimonides' philosophy, like that of any thinker basing himself on Aristotle, was false. The route to God is not intellectual understanding, but fear and love.

The final purpose of human existence is the fulfilment of the divine commands given by God himself to the children of Israel, in order that they should love and fear him. Scientific knowledge, a preliminary to the knowledge and understanding of the commandments, must be based on a physics different from Aristotle's, because his physics is false. Book I of the *Light of God* is devoted to a critique of Aristotelian physics as it is expounded by Maimonides in the twenty-five propositions which precede Book II of his *Guide*.

Crescas argues that Aristotle gives to the infinite the characteristics of finite bodies, and conceives the infinite only in relation to the finite. If it exists, the infinite is not contained within bounds. It has neither weight nor lightness, neither form nor shape. If it has a circular movement, it is not around a centre and, although it moves itself voluntarily, it has no need of any external object to bring about its movement. It can just as well be a simple being as a composite one. Similarly, place in the Aristotelian definition is the place of the elements, not the place of the world as a whole. Crescas holds that it is necessary to dissociate body and space. Space can be empty of bodies. In this case, the definition of the place of the world as being its external boundary no longer applies, and we can conceive an infinite space. Space is no longer the relation between bodies, but, as pure extension, it exists before bodies. The finite corporeal world is situated within an infinite void. Crescas does not deny the possibility of an infinite number of worlds and this hypothesis, although not explicitly adopted, is perhaps implied by his citation of a passage from the Talmud. In the same way, Crescas refuses to define time as the measure of movement: time is also a measure of rest.

If we can conceive an infinity of time and an infinite numerical series, we can no longer accept the proof of God's existence based on showing that he is the Prime Mover because this proof is based on the assertion that a series of causes cannot be infinite and so must end in a first cause.

Crescas' central intuition, then, is that, because God is infinite, space and time are infinite, and a numerical series can be extended infinitely. The human mind cannot reach the essence of an infinite God either through philosophy or through revelation. God is unknowable in his essence. But, like Gersonides, Crescas asserts the existence of positive divine attributes. Yet, for him, there is no possible relation or comparison between God and his creatures. We gain our idea of God's attributes in the way in which we gain our idea of the infinite from the finite. Equally, the number of divine attributes is itself infinite. Just as the final aim of human existence is not understanding, so our joy in God cannot be the contemplation or understanding of his essence: it is the joy of a gift, of the Good which gives of itself. God is the true agent of all creatures. He makes them act through will and intention, and maintains them always in being through the emanation of his goodness. God likes to spread goodness and perfection and his joy is that of always giving the being which he spreads over the whole of creation, in the most perfect way that can be.

The joy which God experiences in an infinite and essential way is a giving; it is also love and desire. God has loved and desired the patriarchs, and he loves and desires the love of Israel. God's power is infinite. If it has given rise to a finite world, that is a result of will and choice. It is not merely infinite in potentiality but also in act. God's omnipotence, which reason shows to be infinitely strong in act, is revealed in the biblical miracles, when substances are created or destroyed, as when Moses' rod was changed into a snake.

As a result of God's omnipotence, there is no place for free will. Only the feeling of freedom differentiates freedom from compulsion. All human acts are made necessary by their causes. The will of the agent who causes an act is itself determined by causes which might be external or internal or both. Divine commands and the rewards or punishments which follow obedience to them or their disregard are themselves links in the causal chain which leads to a human act. A man is said to act 'voluntarily' when a cause is internal and not perceived by him, and 'involuntarily' only when an external cause is perceived as forcing him, despite his internal dissent, to such and such an action. Joy accompanies the fulfilment of God's commandments as an effect accompanies a cause, but only when the soul has acted voluntarily, without any external obligation which it regards as contrary to it.

Beliefs, especially true beliefs, are obligations on the soul, not results of its will, since their reality constrains the soul to accept them. Beliefs, then, give rise neither to reward nor punishment, and they are unrelated to the knowledge of intelligible things. Nor are the intelligibles what one calls 'the survival of the soul'. Reward – joy – is brought by the effort towards knowledge, the desire to know, the wish to understand.

The goal of the Torah is to enable men to acquire perfection in behaviour and belief, material happiness and happiness of the soul. Most important is the happiness of the soul. This is the ultimate aim of God's law. The soul's eternal happiness is the love and fear of God. Love and fear of God are the final stage, not only of the Torah, but also of true philosophy.

❧ EPILOGUE ❧

In Crescas' thought, we can see the influence not only of Christian scholasticism, but also of the kabbalah, which became more and more important in Jewish thought, the worse became the political situation of Jews in Spain and the more eagerly they returned to the sources of their religion. It became necessary to define precisely what were the principles of Judaism. It is not correct to speak of 'dogma' in Judaism. Jewish tradition, the Bible and the Talmud, was considered as a whole, over a long period. It had to be accepted in its entirety, since belief was involved in each of the commandments. It was in confrontation with other religions that Judaism found itself obliged to clarify and systematize the principles of the faith. This problem was marginal up until the end of the fourteenth century, but it became a burning issue in the fifteenth century, culminating with Albo (c. 1366–1444?). Albo places his assertion of the superiority of the Torah within the context of a consideration of the different types of law: natural, conventional and divine. The Torah alone, he believes, is divine law, because it guides men towards the true good: the immortality of the soul.

Traditionally, the fifteenth century is taken to mark the end of medieval Jewish philosophy. Yet as many philosophical works were written as they had been during the previous two hundred years. Here – as in the history of medieval Jewish philosophy in general – history has been distorted in favour of the 'great philosophers', whose works were printed in the sixteenth century and so widely diffused. Here in this chapter an anachronistically disproportionate weight has been given to the better known philosophers, in order to avoid too thin a treatment of too many figures. More obscure philosophers, whose works are still unprinted, deserve to have a more important place. We would then see that the fifteenth century, far from being a barren period, witnessed a real renewal of all the types of philosophy which had previously flourished: the Aristotelian current with Joseph ben Shem Tov ibn Shemtob and his son Shem Tov, Abraham ben Yomtob Bibago,

Isaac Abraham and, in the area of Padua, Elias del Medigo and his circle. In Italy, the Neoplatonic current was represented especially by Judah Abraham. In Provence, Africa and Turkey, as well as the Yemen, medieval philosophical texts were still read and taught to a wide audience. True, kabbalistic ideas came little by little to figure in the work of most philosophers. No longer did intellectual understanding play the only important part in the philosophers' systems – too many political and religious events had shaken the philosophers' ivory tower. But philosophical ideas (the most important of which is that of God's incorporeality) had taken root in the Jewish community, and to this day they remain an integral part of Judaism.

(translated by John Marenbon)

 BIBLIOGRAPHY

English translations of the most important texts are given here, followed by some English studies.

Translations

Karaite thinkers

4.1   *Karaite Anthology*, ed. L. Nemoy, New Haven, Conn., 1952; repr. 1980.

Saadiah Gaon

4.2   *The Book of Beliefs and Opinions*, a translation of the *Amanat* by S. Rosenblatt, New Haven, Conn., 1948.
4.3   *The Book of Doctrines and Beliefs*, an abridged translation of the *Amanat* by A. Altmann, in I. Heinemann (ed.) *Three Jewish Philosophers*, New York, 1969.

Solomon ben Judah ibn Gabirol

4.4   *The Fountain of Life*, Book III, trans. H. E. Wedeck, London, 1963.

Judah Halevi

4.5   *Book of Kuzari*, trans. by H. Hirschfeld, New York, 1946; also in I. Heinemann (ed.) *Three Jewish Philosophers*, New York, 1969.

Maimonides

4.6   *Mishneh Torah: The Book of Knowledge*, trans. M. Hyamson, Jerusalem, 1962.

4.7   Intoductions to *Commentary on the Mishnah*, in *Ethical Writing of Maimonides*, trans. R. L. Weiss and C. E. Butterworth, New York, 1975.

4.8   *Crisis and Leadership: Epistles of Maimonides*, trans. and notes by A. Halkin, discussions by D. Hartman, Philadelphia, Pa., New York and Jerusalem, 1985.

4.9   'Maimonides' Arabic treatise on logic', trans. M. ha-Higgayon, ed. E. Efros, *Proceedings of the American Academy for Jewish Research* 34 (1966), supplementing a previous publication ibid., vol. 8 (1938).

4.10   *Letters of Maimonides*, trans. and ed. with introduction and notes by L. D. Stitskin, New York, 1977.

4.11   'The first letter on astrology', in 'The Correspondence between the Rabbis of Southern France and Maimonides about Astrology', ed. and trans. by A. Marx, *Hebrew Union College Annual* 3 (1926): 311–58.

4.12   'The second letter on astrology', trans. R. Lerner, in 'Maimonides' Letter on Astrology', *History of Religions* 8 (1968): 143–68.

4.13   *The Guide of the Perplexed*, trans. S. Pines, Chicago, 1963.

Gersonides

4.14   *The Wars of the Lord*, Book One: *Immortality of the Soul*, trans. and with introduction and notes by S. Feldman, Philadelphia, Pa., 1984.

4.15   *The Wars of the Lord*, Book Two: *Dreams, Divination and Prophecy*; Book Three: *Divine Knowledge*; Book Four: *Divine Providence*, trans. with appendix and notes by S. Feldman, Philadelphia, Pa., New York and Jerusalem, 1987.

4.16   *The Creation of the World according to Gersonides*, J. J. Staub, Book VI, part 2, ch. 1, of *The Wars of the Lord*, Chico, Calif., 1982.

Joseph Albo

4.17   *Sefer ha-Ikkarim (Book of Principles)*, critical edn with trans. by I. Husik, Philadelphia, Pa., 1929.

Isaac Abrabanel

4.18   *Isaac Abravanel: Six Lectures*, ed. J. B. Trends and H. Loewe, Cambridge, 1937.

Studies

Saadiah Gaon

4.19   Malter, H. *Saadia Gaon: his Life and Works*, New York, 1929.

Isaac Israeli

4.20 Altmann, A. and Stern, S. M. *Isaac Israeli, a Neoplatonic Philosopher of the Early Tenth Century*, Oxford, 1958.

Abu'l-Barakāt al-Baghdādī

4.21 Pines, S. *Studies in Abu-l-Barakat al-Baghdadi: Physics and Metaphysics. Collected Works*, vol. I, Jerusalem, 1979.

Solomon ben Judah ibn Gabirol

4.22 Loewe, R. *Ibn Gabirol*, London, 1989.

Maimonides

4.23 Yellin, D. and Abrahams, I. *Maimonides, his Life and Works*, repr. with notes by J. I. Dienstag, New York, 1972.

4.24 Goiten, S. D. 'Moises Maimonides, man of action: a revision of the master's biography in light of the Geniza documents', in G. Nahon and C. Touati (eds) *Hommage à Georges Vajda*, Louvain, 1980.

4.25 Efros, I. *Philosophical Terms in the Moreh Nebukhim*, New York, 1924, repr. 1966.

4.26 Fox, M. *Interpreting Maimonides: Studies in Methodology, Metaphysics and Moral Philosophy*, Chicago, Ill., 1990.

4.27 Hartman, D. *Maimonides, Torah and Philosophical Quest*, Philadelphia, Pa., 1976.

4.28 Kellner, M. *Maimonides on Human Perfection*, Atlanta, Ga., 1990.

4.29 —— *Maimonides on Judaism and the Jewish People*, Albany, NY, 1991.

4.30 Leaman, O. *Moses Maimonides*, London, 1990.

4.31 Hyman, A. (ed.) *Maimonidean Studies*, with bibliography (1950–86) by D. R. Lachterman, New York, 1990.

4.32 Strauss, L. 'The literary character of the Guide for the Perplexed', in *Persecution and the Art of Writing*, Glencoe, Ill., 1976.

4.33 Reines, A. J. *Maimonides and Abrabanel on Prophecy*, Cincinnati, Oh., 1970.

Isaac Abrabanel

4.34 Natanyahu, B. *Don Isaac Abravanel, Statesman and Philosopher*, Philadelphia, Pa., 1953.

4.35 Sarachek, J. *Don Isaac Abravanel*, New York, 1938.

Crescas

4.36 Wolfson, H. *Crescas' Critique of Aristotle*, Cambridge, Mass., 1929.

CHAPTER 5

Philosophy and its background in the early medieval West

*Rosamond McKitterick and
John Marenbon*

◆◆❖◆◆

'Libraries, schools and the dissemination of texts' is by Rosamond McKitterick; the 'Introduction' and 'Philosophical themes' are by John Marenbon.

➤➤ INTRODUCTION ➤➤

The period from 800 to 1100 is even more neglected by historians of medieval Western philosophy than the rest of the Middle Ages. The neglect has not, however, been total. Two figures – John Scottus Eriugena, who wrote between *c.* 850 and *c.* 870, and Anselm of Canterbury, whose writings date from 1060 to 1100 – have long been picked out for special treatment. But Eriugena has most usually been regarded as a solitary genius closer to Greek late antiquity or even to nineteenth-century currents of thought than to his own time, whilst Anselm has been conveniently seen as the precursor of a twelfth-century intellectual awakening. In consequence, the attention received by these two thinkers has done little to stimulate interest in their contemporaries. Eriugena and Anselm *are*, indeed, the two outstanding philosophers of the time, and their thought is discussed in detail in the following chapter. But many of the problems they tackled and methods they used were common to their contemporaries. This chapter is designed to fill in some of this often forgotten background.

The names of some of those besides Eriugena and Anselm who considered philosophical questions in the early Middle Ages are known: for instance, Alcuin (the Englishman who became one of Charlemagne's main advisers in the 790s, and Alcuin's pupils Candidus Wizo and Fredegisus of Tours); Ratramnus of Corbie and Gottschalk of Orbais (mid-ninth century); Remigius of Auxerre and Bovo of Corvey (late ninth and early tenth century); Abbo of Fleury, Notker of St Gall and Gerbert of Aurillac (end of tenth century); Berengar, Lanfranc and Peter Damian (eleventh century). Yet much of the material from which a history of philosophy during this time must be constructed is anonymous, and an important part of it consists, not of independent works or even free-standing commentaries, but of glosses written in the margins and between the lines of the manuscripts of ancient or late antique textbooks. Indeed, since a good deal of the philosophical activity of these centuries consisted, not in original speculation, but in absorbing the ideas of ancient texts, the best evidence for it is often not a particular piece of writing, but information as to which centres of learning possessed manuscripts of what philosophical and theological works at which times. For these reasons, the study of manuscripts and their transmission is fundamental to the history of early medieval philosophy. The next section, therefore, presents an expert's summary of the state of knowledge in this area; it is followed by a brief survey of some of the outstanding philosophical themes of the period.

➷ LIBRARIES, SCHOOLS AND THE ➷ DISSEMINATION OF TEXTS

Sometime before 814, Archbishop Leidrad of Lyons presented a comprehensive collection of philosophical treatises to his cathedral library. The manuscript, now in Rome, Casa dei padri maristi A. II. 1, is datable on palaeographical grounds to the late eighth or early ninth century. It contains Porphyry's *Isagoge*, the *Ten Categories* (a paraphrase-cum-commentary of Aristotle's *Categories* wrongly attributed to Augustine), pseudo-Apuleius *Perihermenias* and Boethius' first commentary on Aristotle's *On Interpretation* ([5.17] 83, [5.20] 417, [5.75] 52–3). It was written for Leidrad and is the oldest surviving collection of works on dialectic. Not only does it contain the ancient texts; it also includes Alcuin's verses dedicating the *Ten Categories* to Charlemagne. In consequence, Bischoff linked this collection to the court library ([5.31] 157). Similarly, the Frankish royal court in the late eighth century and the cathedral library of Lyons are implicated in the transmission of Plato's *Timaeus* (in the translation by Calcidius). Paris, Bibliothèque Nationale lat. 2164, for example, written in north-east France *c.* 800, can be connected with the group of classical manuscripts in the court library of Charlemagne ([5.32] 158 and [5.55] 89). Its textual twin Lyons 324 also contains the commentary on the *Timaeus* by Calcidius and may have reached Lyons by the same route as Bishop Leidrad's philosophical and dialectical collection.

That Lyons, famous for its participation in the antique book trade, a notable centre of learning in the seventh century and possessor of many fifth-, sixth- and seventh-century codices in its libraries, should play a role in the transmission of ancient philosophical texts is certainly credible.[1] Charlemagne's remarkable collection of rare classical texts, moreover, is usually identified as listed on spare leaves in a late eighth-century grammatical collection, Berlin, Deutsche Staatsbibliothek Diez B. Sant. 66, emanating from the court circle. Such texts are now generally regarded as the fruit of an appeal for copies of remarkable or rare books sent out in about 780 ([5.32] 162–6, 154–6). In the case of the books associated with Leidrad, and with other classical texts linked with the court, the extant manuscripts are copies made from books sent to the Carolingian court, or, at a further remove, copies of the court transcriptions.

Although not all surviving manuscripts of philosophical and dialectical works have court connections, it is certainly the case that it is from the Carolingian period that our earliest copies of most of the principal works survive. We have in fact very little with which to fill the gap between late antiquity and the Carolingian period as far as any classical texts are concerned. Certainly, knowledge of ancient philosophy was also transmitted through the medium of patristic and Christian writers such as Augustine, Maximus the Confessor and Marius Victorinus, of whose work copies survive from the fifth to eighth centuries in relative abundance. It is from Carolingian copies, however, that most witnesses to classical literature and learning descend ([5.22], [5.31]). Nevertheless, it would be unwise to assume that no study was made of, or interest shown in, such texts in Italy or Gaul between the sixth and the late eighth centuries. In the eighth and ninth centuries we see classical texts, including those concerned with logic and philosophy, that have gained a sufficient readership and attracted enough interest for a copy or copies to be made of them. A wider intellectual context must therefore be envisaged. We may surmise indeed that Carolingian manuscripts containing philosophical texts reflect not random survival but deliberate preservation. They are the outcome of choices made in the eighth and ninth centuries in relation to distinct intellectual preferences, even if the initial survival of an ancient text beyond the fifth century had an element of chance in it. Thus, as Marenbon has established, the difference in popularity between the *Ten Categories* and Aristotle's *Categories* can be accounted for in that the former accords better with the intellectual preoccupations of thinkers in the ninth and tenth centuries ([5.75] and see also below, pp. 108–9).

Even so, intellectual preferences and an apparent encouragement of this type of intellectual activity and branch of learning cannot be assumed to be the natural outcome of the Germanic groups establishing successor states within the old Roman empire. Why should philosophy and logic have become a focus of scholarly interest within early medieval Western Europe, especially in light of the prevailing scholarly preoccupations with Christian theology and exposition of the Bible? Before attempting to answer this question, let us survey the evidence, in terms of extant manuscript distribution, firstly, that philosophy texts were more widely available throughout the eighth, ninth and tenth centuries, and secondly, that philosophy was studied in the early medieval schools.

In establishing the intellectual context for the study of philosophy in the early Middle Ages principal considerations are what texts were known and available, whether we can document the introduction of particular texts to a wider audience or region, and how ideas could be disseminated. Were particular centres noted for the study of philosophy and how did they come to be in such a position? The principal texts in question are: Plato's *Timaeus*; Boethius' *On the Consolation of Philosophy*, logical writings and the Latin translation of Aristotle's *Categories*; the composite translation of the *Categories* with Boethius' *lemmata*; the early medieval paraphrase of the *Categories* known as the *Ten Categories*; pseudo-Apuleius's *Perihermenias*; Macrobius' commentary on Cicero's *Dream of Scipio*; the *Topics* of Cicero.

If the Lyons philosophical collection and the Lyons *Timaeus* highlight the recognizable role played by the Carolingian royal court in the dissemination of philosophical texts, other centres also played a role, apparently independently of the court. Analysis of the textual tradition of Latin versions of the *Timaeus*, for example, indicates a special role for Ferrières and Corbie for the translation by Cicero, and for Rheims and St Amand for Calcidius's version (see [5.56]). Such specialization of book production in terms of types of text copied is an observable phenomenon of the Carolingian period, with classical literary texts concentrated in the Loire, Picardy and Lake Constance regions, mass books particularly associated with St Amand, Bibles and Gospel books of a distinctive format with Tours and a remarkable preoccupation with Augustinian theology at Carolingian Lyons (see [5.54]).

The earliest manuscripts of Boethius' translation of the *Categories* of Aristotle, whether complete or in fragmentary form, date from the late tenth and eleventh centuries.[2] They were produced at such centres as Corbie, Fleury, St Gall, Echternach and St Vaast, and were presumably based on earlier exemplars, or, conceivably, one common ancestor. The date of these, whether sixth or ninth century, is a matter for speculation. Three ninth-century manuscripts of the composite translation are extant, apparently from regions as diverse as the Lake Constance area, Picardy and northern Italy. Such distribution suggests either originally widely-dispersed texts or else the consequence of specific contacts between individuals in these areas in the ninth century. The *Ten Categories* survives in no fewer than nineteen ninth- and tenth-century manuscripts, many of them with extensive glosses ([5.75] 116–38, 173–206). Auxerre is an important centre of production, as is Fleury, but there are examples also from St Gall and Corbie, from as far east as Freising and as far west as Wales, with some French and Italian representatives in the eleventh and twelfth centuries. Examination of the manuscript transmission of other key texts reveals a similar pattern.

Porphyry's *Isagoge* in the translation by Marius Victorinus, for example, survives in fragments, now Munich, Bayerische Staatsbibliothek Clm 6403, written at Freising. In Boethius' translation, on the other hand, it is to be found in many copies of ninth and tenth century date (including Clm 6403), often coinciding with the *Ten Categories*. It is found, moreover, in such dialectical collections as the Lyons corpus belonging to Leidrad ([5.75] 173). Marenbon, furthermore, has ascertained that Ratramnus of Corbie, John Scottus Eriugena, Heiric of Auxerre and Remigius of Auxerre knew the *Ten Categories*. Thus Auxerre again figures very prominently, as indeed it does in all branches of intellectual life in the Carolingian world, but representatives of the *Isagoge* and *Ten Categories* are to be found in other cultural centres within the Frankish kingdoms, north and east, some of which had connections with Auxerre (see [5.24]). Again a similar pattern emerges when the manuscript tradition of the *Isagoge* and logical collections and Boethius' two commentaries on the *Isagoge* are considered. One ninth-century copy of the first commentary (in dialogue form) is extant in BN lat. 12958 of the late ninth or early tenth centuries used at Corbie, though not written there, in order to compile BN lat. 13955. The commentary survives in five tenth-century manuscripts whose origins indicate a wide dissemination of the text thereafter, though not necessarily emanating from Corbie itself (*Aristoteles Latinus* 1, 6–7, p. xxi). Pseudo-Apuleius' *Perihermenias*, too, has a largely Frankish circulation in the early Middle Ages ([5.66]) while Auxerre plays a particularly important role in the transmission of Macrobius' commentary on Cicero's *Dream of Scipio* ([5.22] 22–32). BN lat. 6370, moreover, although from Tours, has corrections written in the hands of Heiric of Auxerre and Lupus of Ferrières. Other ninth-century manuscripts of Macrobius survive also from Tours, Fleury and Corbie with dissemination thereafter into southern Germany and southern Italy. Similarly, work on the 'Leiden corpus' of Cicero's philosophical works has established that Corbie, Ferrières and possibly Rheims in the ninth century as well as Monte Cassino in the eleventh are implicated in the transmission of Cicero's *Topics* (see [5.25], [5.27] and [5.22] 124–30).

The textual links among the Carolingian copies of the various philosophical works studied in the early Middle Ages and between these and descendants of later date from elsewhere are sometimes strong, suggesting that individual contacts played a crucial role at some stage in the late tenth and early eleventh centuries, if not earlier. Equally, it is remarkable, within the traditions of the texts, how many independent lines of transmission there are. Although the evidence indicates a group of centres in the early Middle Ages which concentrated much attention on those philosophical texts, there is enough surviving from elsewhere to suggest that study of philosophy was not confined to centres such as Auxerre, Fleury or Corbie but that there were pockets of interest scattered elsewhere, notably in southern Germany. Further, although some of the later centres evincing interest in these texts in the tenth and eleventh centuries are clearly connected with the older Carolingian centres, others are not, and may therefore be the earliest extant witnesses to a far more widespread interest in and study of philosophical texts in Western Europe in the early Middle Ages than the available evidence now permits us to reconstruct.

We may have to envisage, moreover, a considerable survival of late antique exemplars. Traces of their existence can sometimes be deduced, as in the copy of Macrobius owned by Symmachus, whose subscription in his book is transmitted in no less than ten of the later copies. Other examples are the sixth-century geographical miscellany which travelled from Ravenna to Gaul and provided the exemplar for the copy (Vatican lat. 4929, fos 79v–159r) made in the circle of Lupus of Ferrières and Heiric of Auxerre; the ancient papyrus codex of Boethius' commentary on the *Topics* of Cicero borrowed by Lupus of Ferrières from Tours, the late antique texts of Terence and the Aratea copied at Rheims and in Lotharingia in the ninth century such as BN lat. 7899 and Leiden Voss. lat. Q79, and the famous Virgil texts thought to have been possessed by St Denis and Lorsch in the Carolingian period.[3] Certainly if one augments the core texts defined in this chapter with texts of related interest and content, as well as the evidence provided by library catalogues of the ninth, tenth and eleventh centuries, the number of centres possessing them is very considerably enhanced. The royal court of the Carolingians, moreover, figures with some prominence (see [5.15] 1005, [5.18], [5.53]).

The *scriptoria* of the monasteries and cathedrals were, therefore, obviously active in the provision of texts. From glosses and commentaries on philosophical texts dating from the ninth century onwards, moreover, it is clear that such provision was clearly related to, and supplied the needs of, libraries and schools (see [5.30], [5.38], [5.78]). Such specialized book production facilitated study and the intellectual activity of individuals, as is evident from the occasional indications we get of personal libraries, such as that of Gerward of Lorsch or the books added to the library of Murbach by Abbot Iskar (see [5.16], [5.21], [5.29]). Similarly the requirements of individuals or even institutions stimulated copying activity, in that the network of communications between the various centres established the canon of texts necessary for a particular library to possess as well as furnishing information about where exemplars of desired texts might be obtained (see [5.53]). The personal interests of Hadoardus of Corbie, Lupus of Ferrières and Murethach, Haymo, Heiric and Remigius of Auxerre determined to a very considerable degree the direction of study at the schools and within the groups of scholars with which they were associated.[4]

Other Carolingian masters elsewhere were as active. At Laon, Martin of Laon, as is evident from the number of school texts he annotated, taught script, Greek, law, history, grammar and *computus*. One of his most famous teaching compilations, Laon Bibliothèque Municipale 468, also used by his successors as masters of the school at Laon, Bernard and Adelelm, includes texts on the life of Virgil and commentaries on Virgil, on the liberal arts and 'On philosophers, poets, the sibylls and magicians'. The overriding emphasis of two of Martin's other teaching manuals, Laon Bibliothèque Municipale 444 and 464, is on grammar (see [5.36], [5.38] and more generally [5.44]). At Reichenau, among the many teachers there, one, Walafrid Strabo, reveals his interests to us in his personal compilation of texts (St Gall Stiftsbibliothek 878) (see [5.28]). It contains a rich miscellany of grammatical texts, short treatises on metrics and computus, Bede's *On the Nature of Things* and works on time extracts from ecclesiastical histories and an excerpt from a letter by Seneca. If we compare this selection with the school texts listed at the end of the Reichenau library catalogue for 821, there is a similar emphasis on grammar and computus (see [5.18]). In very few Carolingian centres, notably Auxerre in the ninth and tenth centuries and Rheims in the tenth century, was philosophy in any sense formally part of the curriculum. Gerbert of Rheims, for example, is said to have taught Porphyry's *Isagoge* in the translations of Marius Victorinus and Boethius, Aristotle's *Categories* and *On Interpretation* and Cicero's *Topics* as well as to have provided instruction in the arts of metrics, rhetoric, arithmetic, geometry and astronomy.[5]

In the tenth century at St Gall it was Notker III Labeo (950–1022) who was the first to translate philosophical texts from the

Latin into German vernacular for the sake of his German-speaking pupils at the school of St Gall. According to a letter written to Hugh, bishop of Sitten, Notker translated Boethius, *On the Consolation of Philosophy*, the *Categories* and *On Interpretation* of Aristotle (translated from Boethius' Latin version) and the first two books of Martianus Capella's *On the Marriage of Mercury and Philology* as well as the *Quicumque vult*, the Psalter and the Book of Job. Notker III composed one treatise, *On Music*, in German and wrote a number of others in Latin, such as *On the Art of Rhetoric, On the Parts of Logic, On Disputation* and *Computus*, which were subsequently translated into German. Not all these have survived but among those that are extant are, in the literal translation they provide, invaluable indications of pedagogical methods in an early medieval school, with every assistance being offered to aid understanding of the text, guides to rhetorical figures and dialectical techniques and a wealth of miscellaneous general information about etymology, history, zoology and astronomy.[6] There are, moreover, some fascinating witnesses to the dissemination of texts from Auxerre mentioned above: to these translations, notably of the *On the Consolation of Philosophy* of Boethius and Martianus Capella, were appended commentaries, some of which were based on, if not actually translations of, the expositions of Remigius of Auxerre.

The combination of Notker's texts, as with the range of topics addressed by Walafrid Strabo, Martin of Laon, Gerbert of Rheims and other Carolingian masters, is in fact typical of the different emphases within the school curriculum in the early Middle Ages. It is not feasible to think in terms of philosophy playing a separate role within the school curriciulum in the Carolingian period. Rather, elements of philosophy and the discipline of logic would develop out of the emphasis on the structure of language and grammar and be incorporated into the general teaching of the *artes* as the foundation for a deeper understanding of scripture and the teaching of the fathers (see [5.41], [5.46]). Thus Notker translated texts relating to all aspects of the *trivium* (grammar, dialectic and rhetoric), the *quadrivium* (arithmetic, geometry, astronomy and music) and to the Bible and liturgy.

At other schools in France, Germany and Italy a similarly rich mixture within the school curriculum is to be observed. In the episcopal schools of Germany, such as those of Trier, Augsburg, Eichstätt and Utrecht, Würzburg, Regensburg, Cologne and Liège, and many more, the Carolingian school curriculum was taught, with only occasionally the instruction in philosophy being noted (see [5.39], [5.60]). Ohtrich of Magdeburg, for example, was noted as one of the famous philosophers of his day.[7] Bruno of Cologne, instructed at Utrecht under Bishop Balderich, kept abreast with the newest developments in 'history, rhetoric, poetry and philosophy'.[8] Even at Auxerre, where philosophy is such a major part of the intellectual activity of its leading scholars, it is important to remember that this was also the centre which produced the *Deeds of the Bishops of Auxerre*, *Miracula*, homiliaries, biblical exegesis of lasting importance, and lives of saints.

Nevertheless it would appear, in fact, that philosophy became a more dominant part of the school curriculum in the course of the tenth century, and became still more important in the schools of the eleventh and twelfth centuries, at least in France. In the later ninth and tenth centuries, moreover, there is a discernible increase in the importance of cathedral schools in both the West and the East Frankish kingdoms, notably, by way of example, at Rheims and Liège and the German episcopal schools mentioned above. The lines of institutional continuity between the cathedral and monastic schools of the East and West Frankish kingdoms in the ninth and tenth centuries to the schools of Paris in the twelfth century are clear [5.60]. It is no surprise that we find in the teaching of the schools of Laon, Chartres and Paris in the eleventh and twelfth century the same mixed curriculum, designed according to a similar structure, and methods of teaching which have their roots in the early Carolingian period. At Chartres, for example, it was possible to study medicine, geometry, computus, music and logic; a manuscript from Fulbert of Chartres' time, Chartres Bibliothèque Municipale 100, was a compilation of familiar texts, namely, the *Isagoge*, the *Categories*, the *Topics* of Cicero and other related texts, including a poem by Fulbert on the difference between rhetoric and dialectic [5.60]. In the glossing methods employed by Anselm of Laon, of Peter Lombard, or Hugh of St Victor, the development of distinctive layout of text and gloss to accommodate these new developments, and in the philosophical discussion of such authors as Thierry of Chartres, we witness a similar blend of older curriculum and scholarly methods with a response to the new influences in learning and currents of thought, wonderfully elucidated long since by Southern ([5.63], [5.64]). No doubt this was due in part to the availability of a greater variety of classical texts, especially by Plato and Aristotle but to these should be added the work of the contemporary authors, discussed in the various chapters in this volume. The extant library catalogues of the twelfth century and the reconstruction of twelfth-century libraries such as those of Zwiefalten, demonstrate more clearly than any other sources the extent both of the Carolingian foundations of the school curriculum and their intellectual emphases and the innovations of the eleventh and twelfth centuries (see [5.17], [5.23]). Corbie's library, for example, although including a large corpus of philosophical works, with many of Boethius' works, a commentary on Martianus Capella by John Scottus Eriugena, the *Timaeus*, and the philosophical works of William of Conches, and the library of Cluny with its copies of the *Isagoge*, Martianus Capella, the *Categories* of Aristotle, Boethius' commentary on Cicero's *Topics*, Calcidius and many more, still contain an overwhelming preponderance of patristic texts and biblical exegesis. The primary focus of intellectual endeavour remained the Bible, but philosophy had a secure place in the intellectual activities of many of the leading scholars of Europe.

That learning, including the study of philosophy, enjoyed such a prominent position within the life of the monasteries and cathedrals of Western Europe in the early Middle Ages is a phenomenon to which we have become accustomed, even though the preoccupation with scholarship within a monastic context might appear anomalous (see [5.44], [5.52] 19). The acceptance of intellectual endeavour as an essential part of a society's activity and the primary focus of its culture is nevertheless a remarkable characteristic of early medieval culture and merits some discussion.

Let us consider, therefore, the role of the royal court signalled at the beginning of this chapter in order to explore, first, the political dimensions of the promotion of education and learning and, second, the implications of patronage – royal, aristocratic, episcopal and monastic – not only in promoting education and the study of philosophy but also in helping to shape particular cultural imperatives that became an accepted part of a society.

Within the Germanic kingdoms Lupus of Ferrières offers a clue, in that he laments, in a letter to Einhard, the passing of Charlemagne:

> within your memory there has been a revival of learning,
> thanks to the efforts of the illustrious emperor Charles to
> whom letters owe an everlasting debt of gratitude. Learning
> has indeed lifted up its head to some extent ... In these days
> [*c.* 836] those who pursue an education are considered a
> burden to society ... men have consequently shrunk from this
> endeavour, some because they do not receive a suitable reward
> for their knowledge, others because they fear an unworthy
> reputation.[9]

Lupus lauded the activities of Charlemagne's grandson Charles the Bald and his support of scholarship in many of his other letters. Further, such authors as Notker Balbulus of St Gall testify to the extent to which the Carolingian rulers actively promoted scholarship.[10] We may add to this the emphasis on correct texts of the Christian liturgy, canon law and the Bible, education and learning in Carolingian legislation and directives from the king to his abbots and bishops, such as the *Admonitio Generalis* of 789 and the *De litteris colendis* of *c.* 800.[11] Although the main aim of such learning was a fuller understanding of the Christian faith, and the provision of an educated administrative class of clerics and lay magnates, sufficient latitude is provided to those responsible for carrying out the wishes of the ruler with respect to teaching and the provision of correct texts for all Christian learning to benefit. Certainly, the subsequent production and dissemination of all kinds of text, apparently in response to the ruler's initiative, is well documented (see [5.54]).

What should also be reckoned with is the personal interest of the rulers themselves in matters of higher learning and the degree to which they actively promoted scholarship, the liberal arts and philosophy by means of patronage. From the books associated with the Carolingian rulers it is apparent how they gathered together scribes and artists, not only to produce books which reflect the personal piety and private interests of the king but also as a strategy of royal piety and largesse (see [5.31], [5.32], [5.43], [5.53], [5.55]). As Lupus implies in the extract from his letter to Einhard quoted above, the king's patronage held the promise of material reward. It is clear from the surviving evidence of scholarly activity associated with the court, and the dedications of many works to the king, that many sought such patronage. The essential material support for learning, in other words, was provided by secular rulers as well as by the Church to satisfy particular as well as general goals.

The role of the king in creating the social imperatives that made an exercise of secular patronage in this particular sphere of activity so acceptable is all important. We are not observing merely the consequences of personal intellectual and aesthetic predilections. Certainly the presence of early Carolingian manuscripts with court connections, such as the Lyons dialectical collection or Plato's *Timaeus*, seems to testify to the gathering of rare classical works, and suggests that there are deeper motives in royal patronage to be discerned. What is apparent above all is the sheer organization and determination behind the dissemination of particular texts to do with the Christian faith and learning, and the explicit association of this activity with the exercise of Christian kingship made by the rulers. Thus it is not simply that King Charles the Bald enjoyed his lessons with Walafrid Strabo and derived intellectual pleasure and stimulus from the presence of such scholars as Manno of St Ouen, Lupus of Ferrières or John Scottus Eriugena in his kingdom, or even at his court. Nor is it that scholars who enjoyed royal patronage were thereby able to pursue their intellectual activities; and many had considerable influence on succeeding generations of pupils and scholars. Among them were Alcuin of Tours, Hrabanus Maurus of Fulda and Mainz, John Scottus Eriugena, or Lupus, who was part of the dynamic intellectual milieu focused on Auxerre and Fleury in the mid-ninth century. What is essential is that intellectual activity was recognized to be a fundamental part of the spiritual and cultural goals of all Christians; the king as Christian ruler therefore had a duty to foster this as much as he enlarged the kingdom, promoted the administration of justice and the use of agreed weights and measures or guaranteed the stability and value of the coinage.

The example of the high priority given to intellectual activity and culture set by rulers to future generations, moreover, is not to be underestimated. Of course, the Carolingians were not the first to exercise patronage in this way. Nevertheless, they were arguably the first to take such an effective interest in the correctness of the Christian texts in use in the churches, chapels and monasteries of their kingdoms, and the first whose patronage was more than an occasional interest in benefactions. The Carolingian rulers actually sustained groups of artists, scribes and craftsmen over a long period of time in order to create artefacts or carry out their particular cultural objectives (see [5.55]). It was an example, if not actually followed, then certainly emulated by other rulers, and by lay and ecclesiastical magnates. In Anglo-Saxon England, for example, Asser's *Life of King Alfred* recounts the great interest the king took in learning and how he himself translated, as well as commissioning translations from others, many crucial texts, not least Boethius' *On the Consolation of Philosophy* (see [5.34], [5.48]). Cnut is also attested as a patron of some stature (see [5.43], [5.51]). If in the tenth and eleventh centuries on the Continent the Carolingian, Capetian and Saxon kings of the West and East Franks were rather less active in the promotion of scholarship and patronage of learning, the baton fell above all to the bishops. The bishops of Liège, Trier and Hildesheim are cases in ponit. Liège was celebrated for its learning under Bishops Ebrachar and Notker but they were following a tradition established in the time of Bishop Hartgar, who acted as patron and offered a refuge to the Irish scholar Sedulius Scotus (see [5.42], [5.50]). Many manuscripts, ivories and some remarkable pieces of metalwork have been associated with Egbert, bishop of Trier from 977 to 993, and Bernward of Hildesheim, which were produced in ateliers both in their own dioceses and elsewhere (see [5.43]). Mayr-Harting has highlighted these bishops' acknowledgement of their reflection of kingly rule, and the way in which they visibly manipulated, or commanded, spiritual power by commissioning book covers and reliquaries wrought in gold and studded with bright jewels, and manuscripts resplendent with fine painting, decorated initials and beautiful script (see [5.59] 57–97).

The display of wealth that was one obvious outcome of the patronage of culture and learning was also a demonstration of power and might. It is of crucial importance for our understanding of the intellectual culture of the early Middle Ages to see that patronage operated so effectively and constructively in the cultural as well as in the political and military spheres. Indeed, these various activities were seen to interlock and to be many facets of one society. Thus social and political imperatives from the pinnacle of authority, displays of wealth and power, the enhancing of authority, and the incorporation of a further, cultural, dimension within the ideals of political and social leadership had repercussions for the particular cultural preoccupations and intellectual aspirations of early medieval society. Patronage played a crucial role in establishing such preoccupations within the intellectual horizons and educational traditions of Western Europe. We thus observe an essential interplay between political authority, economic resources and intellectual endeavour.

❦ PHILOSOPHICAL THEMES ❦

There were three main fields of philosophical activity in the early medieval period: the study of logic, the reading and reaction to ancient and late antique philosophical texts and the analytical discussion of problems about Christian doctrine. The manuscript background to the first two has been explored in the previous section; the following paragraphs offer a quick sketch of some of the main themes in each area.

Logic

The earliest evidence for medieval interest in and use of logical techniques is found in the *Libri Carolini*, the statement of the Western position on the worship of icons prepared at Charlemagne's court *c.* 790, probably by Theodulf of Orleans. The longest logical passages here borrow material from Boethius and Apuleius on semantics and on the relations between the truth-values of differently quantified sentences (see [5.10] IV 28, pp. 216–21). It was Alcuin, who apparently established himself as Charlemagne's leading intellectual in the 790s, who gave early medieval logic its twist towards metaphysical and theological concerns. In his *De dialectica* ('On logic'), the first medieval logical textbook, Alcuin gives pride of place to the doctrine of the ten categories, as expounded in the *Ten Categories*, attributed at this time to Augustine. Aristotle's discussion of the categories is less a piece of logic than an exercise in fundamental metaphysics, an analysis of the different types of entity (universal and particular substances, universal and particular accidents). Augustine had already put the doctrine to theological use in his *On the Trinity*, and Alcuin borrowed and emphasized this theme in his *On the Faith of the Holy Trinity*.[12] The *Ten*

Categories became the most eagerly studied logical textbook in the ninth and tenth centuries, and the question of whether God could be fitted into them, already raised by Alcuin, was taken up by his pupils and explored in depth by Eriugena (see [5.6]; cf. [5.75] 50–3, 72–86). The glosses to the *Ten Categories*, which vary from manuscript to manuscript, show a definite pattern of development. The late ninth-century glossators tended to use the text as a springboard for Eriugena-inspired metaphysical and theological comments, only loosely related to the logical subject-matter. Tenth- and eleventh-century glossators became less and less interested in such speculation and more concerned to reach an understanding of basic Aristotelian ideas such as the distinctions between substance and accident, and between univocal and equivocal words, or the nature of space and time.[13] Gradually, a translation of Aristotle's own text came to replace the pseudo-Augustinian paraphrase, giving scholars the chance to use Boethius' commentary and, through it, to master the argument of the text and consider the difficult problems about the status of Aristotle's discussion (is it about words, or things, or what?) which would concern twelfth-century logicians.[14]

The *Isagoge* ('Introduction') by Porphyry, a short guide to the notions of genus, species, differentiating property (*differentia*), distinguishing characteristic (*proprium*) and accident, long regarded as an introduction to Aristotle's *Categories*, was also known from the time of Alcuin. Glosses to the *Isagoge* – at least those so far investigated – draw heavily on Boethius' commentaries.[15] Porphyry's famous allusion to the disputed status of universals, which became the focus for medieval debates from the twelfth century onwards, seemed to excite no controversy. One of the few early medieval writers to discuss universals, Ratramnus of Corbie, exponent of a somewhat inchoate conceptualism, turned, not to the *Isagoge*, but the first of Boethius' commentaries on it and also to Boethius' *Theological Treatises*.[16] Aristotle's *On Interpretation*, although known, was found forbiddingly difficult by most logicians until the eleventh century: glosses are rare and derivative (see [5.78] 101). But, by about 1000, Abbo of Fleury, Notker of St Gall and Gerbert of Aurillac included it within their teaching, and Abbo compiled his own introduction to syllogistic reasoning, drawing on Boethius' textbooks.[17]

Aside from Anselm's *De grammatico*, there is disappointingly little *direct* evidence for logical studies for most of the eleventh century itself.[18] Material dating from 1100 or just before shows a sophistication in dealing with the *Isagoge*, *Categories* and *On Interpretation*, and a facility in handling syllogisms and topical inferences which cannot have been suddenly acquired; this is a surmise strongly supported by the confident use in doctrinal controversy and discussion of notions from both the *Categories* (as in the dispute between Lanfranc and Berengar) and *On Interpretation* (as in Anselm's *Cur Deus Homo* and Peter Damian's *Letter on God's Omnipotence*).[19]

Reading Ancient Philosophy

Although some early medieval writers criticized logic as a distraction from religious devotion, no one could claim that the ancient logical textbooks were themselves a challenge to the faith; and, indeed, in his *Theological Treatises* (much read and glossed in these centuries) Boethius had shown how logical techniques could be used against heresy in support of orthodox doctrine. By contrast, Latin texts of ancient philosophy posed what might seem as a direct challenge to Christian belief, by proposing a view at least in some respects incompatible with them. Yet it was not, in fact, any of the three main pagan philosophical books available from the ninth to the eleventh centuries that became the focus of controversy. Plato's *Timaeus* (in Calcidius' partial translation) was found too difficult for sustained discussion; the two introductory books of Martianus Capella, preceding the handbooks to the individual disciplines, were too obviously an allegory to cause problems; and Macrobius' commentary on Cicero's *Dream of Scipio* tended to be looked on as a source of information about natural science, especially astronomy, to which further information of like nature should be appended by glossators. And so, strangely, it was in connection with the work of a Christian author that scholars from the ninth to the eleventh centuries considered most carefully how to react to ancient philosophy. After writing his logical translations, commentaries and translations, and his *Theological Treatises*, Boethius, in prison and awaiting execution, wrote his final work, *On the Consolation of Philosophy*. The *Consolation* not only avoids any explicit reference to Christian revelation. It also contains passages which present ancient Platonic ideas which, taken literally, are incompatible with Christianity. In particular, the ninth metrum (or verse passage) of Book III, a prayer incanted at the very climax of the argument, is an epitome of the *Timaeus*, and it refers both to the idea of reincarnation and to that of the World Soul.

What should the Christian reader make of such passages?[20] The most forthright reaction was that of Bovo (d. 916), a monk of Corvey, who recognized clearly that, although Boethius had written elsewhere on Christian doctrine, he was setting out here to present Platonic and not Christian teaching ([5.5]). Using Macrobius – he seems not to have known the *Timaeus* itself – he gives a clear explanation of the ideas behind the compressed phrases of Boethius' poem. Although this

110

approach had its followers, it was not the most common one. At much the same time as Bovo, Remigius of Auxerre had composed his commentary ([5.14]), not just to this metrum, but to the whole *Consolation*, drawing on earlier glosses (just as he would do in his extensive commentary on Martianus Capella) but developing them in his own way. His effort was to find an explicitly Christian meaning hidden in the apparently Platonic phrases of Boethius.[21] About a hundred years later, Adalbold of Utrecht pursued a similar Christian-izing line in his commentary on Book III, metrum 9 ([5.1]), although he allegorized less thoroughly than Remigius and ended with an un-intendedly strange amalgam of orthodox Christianity and Platonic teaching.[22] Twelfth-century scholars, especially William of Conches, would follow and sophisticate the approach pioneered by Remigius and Adalbold, applying it to genuinely pagan texts as well as to the *Consolation*.[23]

Problems Raised by Christian Doctrine

From the twelfth century onwards, much of the best philosophical thinking took place in the context of theology, the systematic investi-gation of Christian doctrine which would be typified in the universities by the commentaries on the *Sentences* of Peter the Lombard. In the ninth to eleventh centuries, it is difficult to talk of 'theology' in this sense. But philosophical discussion still arose in connection with various types of writing concerned primarily with Christian doctrine: sermons and biblical exegesis were inclined to be unargumentative (though Eriugena's are an exception), but other works about doctrine, stimulated by controversy or responding to particular questions, often contain interesting material for the historian of philosophy.

One of the fiercest controversies in the ninth century was insti-gated by Gottschalk, a monk first of Fulda, then Reichenau, then Orbais.[24] In a series of writings from the 830s onwards, Gottschalk championed the idea, which he claimed (with some justice) to be Augustine's, that God's predestination is dual: of the good to bliss and of the wicked to damnation. He found many well-educated supporters, but others in the Church feared that his teaching would discourage people from trying to act well by making them think that, regardless of anything they did, they were from eternity predestined to hell or to heaven. Two important churchmen – Hrabanus Maurus, archbishop of Mainz and prolific scriptural exegete and encyclopaedist, and Hincmar, archbishop of Rheims – wrote against Gottschalk; and they also commissioned an attack from a scholar attached to the court of the emperor, Charles the Bald; this would be John Scottus

Eriugena's first treatise, his *On Predestination*.[25] Although Hrabanus' and Hincmar's pieces (not, however, John's) amass patristic quotations, all three involve argument and analysis, and together they provide the earliest medieval attempt to explore notions such as free will, evil and punishment.

All three writers challenged Gottschalk's formula of dual predestination by saying that God *predestines* in one way alone – the good to salvation – but he *foresees* both the salvation of the good and the damnation of the wicked. Only those predestined to salvation can be saved, because for salvation God's grace is needed. Yet God cannot be said to 'predestine' the wicked; rather, he fails to predestine them. Eriugena also adds the argument ([6.4] 62: 27–65: 123), based on the Platonic view that evil is not a thing but a deficiency, that God *could* not possibly predestine anyone to a wicked life or to eternal punishment because, as evils and therefore deficiencies, they have no cause. (This last is a particularly silly argument: the emptiness of my glass is just as clearly caused by my having drunk the wine as its fullness was caused by my having poured wine into it from the bottle!) So far all three writers have hardly distanced themselves more than verbally from Gottschalk, since on their view people will still be damned, whatever they do, if God fails to predestine them. Hrabanus and Hincmar are aware of this problem but try to dodge it, stressing God's inscrutability or, in the case of Hincmar, suggesting that God withholds grace from those whose future misuse of their wills he has foreseen. Eriugena does not resolve the central issue: how can an individual human being be held responsible for the evil actions which, without the help of grace, he cannot but perform? Rather, he concentrates on relieving God of any responsibility for unjustly punishing those who are not responsible for their wickedness by an astonishingly bold move. He claims that God does not punish anybody [[6.4] 63: 42–66: 155). Sinners are punished (through ignorance, or through the knowledge that they lack beatitude, or through the frustration of their desire to become nothing at all), but not by God, who is merely the framer of just laws.

There were various doctrinal controversies in the two following centuries which stimulated philosophical discussion, most notably the dispute in the mid-eleventh century between Lanfranc and Berengar over the eucharist.[26] But even more interesting for the history of philosophy is a work written at much the same time (*c.* 1067), as part not of a public controversy but of a private debate. Peter Damian was unwilling to accept Jerome's statement, put to him by a friend, that 'whilst God can do all things, he cannot restore a virgin after she has lost her virginity' and he wrote his *Letter on Divine Omnipotence* ([5.11]) to explain why not. Damian is known as an ascetic, contemptuous of pagan philosophy, and historians have often interpreted his rejection of Jerome's position in this light: as an extreme manifestation of his anti-philosophical stance, according to which he claims that God can undo the past, making what has happened not have happened and thus violating the fundamental logical law of non-contradiction. On a careful reading, however, the argument of the letter is seen to be quite different.[27] Damian contends that, by nature, it is impossible to restore her virginity to a virgin who has lost it. By this he means that there is no way of repairing the ruptured membrane. The only way, then, that by nature a non-virgin could become a virgin would be if the past were changed, so that her virginity never had been lost. But, Damian goes on, this – changing the past – is *impossible* absolutely, even for God and certainly by nature. Making a non-virgin into a virgin by repairing her virginity (not by changing the past) *is* possible, however, for God, though it is impossible by nature. Here, then, Damian seems to be distinguishing between the physically impossible, which is possible for God, and the logically impossible, which even for God is impossible. But, at one point ([5.11] 619A–620C), he asks whether God could make it that Rome had never existed and answers that God could. He goes on to explain that, since God lives in an eternity which is timeless, to say that God could now make it that Rome never existed is equivalent to saying that God could have from the beginning shaped a providence which did not include the existence of Rome. Damian's position is defensible, though when clarified it becomes less bold than it at first seems. He makes two arguable claims: (1) that God might have chosen a providence other than the one he has in fact chosen – a providence in which, for instance, Rome never existed; (2) that God's choice of providences does not take place at any moment in time, but in timeless eternity. (1) would be accepted by most Christian thinkers; the meaningfulness of (2) can be queried, but the position has had many adherents, from Boethius' time until now. Taken together, (1) and (2) lead to the conclusion that God could make it (tenseless) that Rome never existed. Since God exists timelessly, any verb which is applied to him is timeless: the apparently paradoxical 'God is able to make it that Rome never existed' is no different in meaning from the straightforward 'God was able to make it that Rome never existed'.

 NOTES

1 See Cavallo [5.35], Kleberg [5.49] 44, Lowe [5.19] and cf. Eddius Stephanus, *Life of Bishop Wilfrid*, Cambridge, 1985, ch. 6.
2 See Minio-Paluello's introduction to his edition of the *Categories* in *Aristoteles Latinus* (I, 1–5), Bruges and Paris, 1961, pp. xiv, xxiii, xxxii, xxxv.

3 See Reynolds [5.22] 225 and Bischoff [5.33]; for Lupus's borrowing, see the edition of his letters by L. Levillain, Paris, 1964, pp. 214–15.

4 See Bischoff [5.27] (Hadoardus), Beeson [5.25] and Gariépy [5.40] (Lupus), and on Heiric see [5.24] as well as the editions of his *Collectanea* by R. Quadri, Fribourg, 1966, and of his excerpts from Valerius Maximus by D. Schullian, *Memoirs of the American Academy in Rome* 12 (1935): 155–84.

5 See Marenbon [5.75] and Richer's *History of France*, ed. R. Latouche, Paris, 1967, II, p. 46.

6 See P. Piper, *Die Schriften Notkers und seiner Schule*, Freiburg and Tübingen, 1882–3, I, pp. 859–61 for Notker's letter, and cf. J. Knight Bostock, *A Handbook on Old High German*, 2nd rev. edn, Oxford, 1976; see also below, Chapter 6, p. 132, for Notker.

7 *Life of St Bernward*, ch. 1 in H. Kallfelz (ed.) *Lebensbeschreibungen einiger Bischöfe des 10.–12. Jahrhunderts*, Darmstadt, 1973.

8 Ruotger, *Life of Bruno*, ch. 5, in H. Kallfelz (ed.) *Lebensbeschreibungen einiger Bischöfe des 10.–12. Jahrhunderts*, Darmstadt, 1973.

9 Translated in G. W. Regenos, *The Letters of Lupus of Ferrières*, The Hague, 1966.

10 Notker, *Gesta Karoli*, ed. H. Haefele, Berlin, 1959, 1.1.

11 Monumenta Germaniae Historica, Capitularia, ed. A. Boretius, Hanover, 1830, I, nos 22, 29, 30, 53, 79–81.

12 *De dialectica* is printed in [5.2] 101, cols 951–76 and *On the Faith of the Holy Trinity* at cols 13–54; see esp. col. 22; cf. Marenbon [5.75] 31 and the additions and corrections to this view in J. Marenbon, 'Alcuin, the Council of Frankfort and the beginnings of medieval philosophy', in *Das Frankfurter Konzil von 794*, ed. R. Berndt, Mainz, 1997, II, 603–15.

13 [5.75] 116–38; for some additions and corrections, see Marenbon [5.78] 100.

14 See L. Minio-Paluello, 'Note sull'Aristotele latino medioevale: xv – Dalle *Categoriae Decem* pseudo-Agostiniane (Temistiane) al testo vulgato aristotelico Boeziano', *Rivista di Filosofia Neoscolastica* 54 (1962) 137–47, reprinted in Minio-Paluello [5.83] 448–58; and, for glosses and commentaries to *Categories* see Marenbon [5.78] 82–3, 100–1, 109–10 and 26–7. A paraphrase/commentary of the *Isagoge* and *Categories* from the early eleventh century has been edited by G. d'Onofrio: *Excerpta Isagogarum et Categoriarum*, Turnhout, 1995 (CC c.m. 120). See also Marenbon [7.67].

15 The *Isagoge* glosses from one manuscript have been edited by C. Baeumker and B. von Walterhausen: *Frühmittelalterlichen Glossen des angeblichen Jepa zur Isagoge des Porphyrius* (BGPMA 24,1), Münster, 1924; for a list of glossed manuscripts and their relations, see Marenbon [5.78] 99.

16 See Ratramnus [5.12] for the text and cf. Marenbon [5.75] 67–70.

17 For bibliography and further discussion of Abbo, Notker and Gerbert, see below, Chapter 6.

18 For Anselm's *De grammatico*, see below, Chapter 6.

19 Peter Damian's *Letter* is discussed below, pp. 112–13; for the use of Aristotle here and by Anselm, see also Marenbon [5.79].

20 For a survey of the influence of the *Consolation*, see Courcelle [5.68]; see also Troncarelli [5.82], [5.83].

21 Useful extracts are printed in Remigius [5.14]; cf. Courcelle [5.68] 278–90, and Marenbon [5.76] 78–9.

22 See T. Gregory, *Platonismo medievale: studi e ricerche* (Istituto storico Italiano per 51 medioevo, studi storici 26–7), Rome, 1958, pp. 1–15.

23 See below, Chapter 7, pp. 172–3.

24 On Gottschalk, see esp. Jolivet [5.74]; on the predestination controversy, see Ganz [5.70] and Schrimpf [5.81]. For Gottschalk's theological works, see [5.8].

25 See also below, Chapter 6, p. 120 on the background and reaction to *On Predestination*. Hrabanus puts his views in letters to Bishop Noting of Verona (*MPL* 112, cols 1530–53) and to Count Eberhard of Friuli (Monumenta Germaniae Historica, Epistolae Karolini Aevi III, pp. 481–7). Hincmar's contribution before Eriugena entered the controversy was a letter to his parishioners, ed. W. Gundlach, 'Zwei Schriften des Erzbischofs Hinkmar von Reims', *Zeitschrift für Kirchengeschichte* 10 (1889): 258–309. For a full account of Hincmar's part in the controversy and his various writings connected with it, see J. Devisse, *Hincmar, Archevêque de Reims, 845–882*, Geneva, 1975–6, pp. 115–79.

26 This is well discussed in Holopainen [5.73] 44–118; cf. also Gibson [5.72].

27 This is the reading proposed by Holopainen [5.73] 6–43. See also the discussion of the modal notions involved in this discussion in Knuuttila [1.21] 63–7.

❧❧❧ BIBLIOGRAPHY ❧❧❧

Original Language Editions

5.1 Adalbold of Utrecht, Commentary on Book III, metrum 9 of Boethius, *On the Consolation of Philosophy*, in Huygens [5.9].

5.2 Alcuin, Works in MPL 100–1.

5.3 Anonymous glosses to *Ten Categories*, in Marenbon [5.75] 185–206.

5.4 Anonymous glosses to Boethius, *Theological Treatises*, in E. K. Rand, *Johannes Scottus*, Munich, 1906.

5.5 Bovo of Corvey, Commentary on Book III, metrum 9 of Boethius, *On the Consolation of Philosophy*, in Huygens [5.9].

5.6 Candidus Wizo, Theological and philosophical passages, in Marenbon [5.75] 152–70.

5.7 Fredegisus of Tours, *On the Substance of Nothing and on Shadows*, in *Monumenta Germaniae Historica*, Epistolae, IV, pp. 552–5.

5.8 Gottschalk of Orbais, *Oeuvres théologiques et grammaticales de Godescalc d'Orbais*, ed. D. C. Lambot, Louvain, 1945.

5.9 Huygens, R. B. C. (ed.) 'Mittelalterliche Kommentare zum *O qui perpetua* ...', *Sacris Erudiri* 6 (1954): 373–427.

5.10 *Libri Carolini*, ed. H. Bastgen, *Monumenta Germaniae Historica*, Concilia II, Supplementum, Hanover and Leipzig, 1924.

5.11 Peter Damian, *Letter on God's Omnipotence*, ed., with French translation, by A. Cantin (Sources chrétiennes 191), Paris, 1972.

5.12 Ratramnus of Corbie, *Liber de anima*, ed. D. C. Lambot, Namur and Lille, 1952.

5.13 Remigius of Auxerre, *Commentary on Martianus Capella*, ed. C. Lutz, Leiden, 1962–5.

5.14 Remigius of Auxerre, Commentary on Boethius, *On the Consolation of Philosophy* (extracts) in Appendix to E. T. Silk (ed.) *Saeculi noni auctoris in Boetii consolationem philosophiae commentarius*, Rome, 1935.

Bibliographies, Catalogues and Handbooks

A bibliography of the philosophical material is given in Marenbon [5.76] 164–91. Bibliographies for the various areas of cultural history from *c.* 780 to *c.* 900 are found in McKitterick [5.57].

5.15 Becker, G. *Catalogi bibliothecarum antiqui*, Bonn, 1885.

5.16 Berschin, W. and Geith, K. E. 'Die Bibliothekskataloge des Klosters Murbach aus dem IX. Jahrhundert', *Zeitschrift für Kirchengeschichte* 83 (1972): 61–87.

5.17 Delisle, L. *Le Cabinet des manuscrits de la Bibliothèque Impériale/Nationale*, Paris, 1868–81.

5.18 Lehmann, P. *Mittelalterliche Bibliothekskataloge Deutschlands und der Schweiz*, I, *Die Diözesen Konstanz und Chur*, Munich, 1918.

5.19 Lowe, E. A. *Codices Lugdunenses antiquiores*, Lyons, 1924.

5.20 —— *Codices Latini antiquiores*, IV, Oxford, 1957.

5.21 Milde, W. *Der Bibliothekskataloge des Klosters Murbach aus dem 9. Jahrhundert. Ausgabe und Beziehungen zu Cassiodors 'Institutiones'*, Beiheft to *Euphorion, Zeitschrift für Literaturgeschichte* 4, Heidelberg, 1968.

5.22 Reynolds, L. D. (ed.) *Texts and Transmissions: a Survey of the Latin Classics*, Oxford, 1983.

5.23 von Borries-Schulten, S. *Katalog der Illuminierten Handschriften der Württemburgischen Landesbibliothek Stuttgart*, 2, *Die Romanischen Handschriften*, Part I, *Provenienz Zwiefalten*, Stuttgart, 1987.

Studies

Manuscript transmission, schools and cultural background

5.24 [Auxerre] *Intellectuels et artistes dans l'Europe Carolingienne ix–xi siècles*, Auxerre, 1990.

5.25 Beeson, C. H. *Lupus of Ferrières as Scribe and Text Critic*, Cambridge, Mass., 1930.

5.26 —— 'The Collectaneum of Hadoard', *Classical Philology* 40 (1945): 201–22.

5.27 Bischoff, B. 'Hadoardus and the manuscripts of classical authors from Corbie', in S. Prete (ed.) *Didascaliae: Studies in Honor of Anselm A. Albareda*, New York, 1961; repr. in German in Bischoff, *Mittelalterliche Studien* 1, Stuttgart, 1965, pp. 49–63.

5.28 —— 'Eine Sammelhandschrift Walahfrid Strabos (Cod. Sangall. 878)', *Mittelalterliche Studien* 2, Stuttgart, 1967, pp. 34–51.

5.29 —— *Lorsch im Spiegel seiner Handschriften*, Munich, 1974.

5.30 —— 'Die Bibliothek im Dienst der Schule', in *Mittelalterliche Studien* 3, Stuttgart, 1981, pp. 213–33.

5.31 —— 'Panorama der Handschriftenüberlieferung aus der Zeit Karls des Grossen', *Mittelalterliche Studien* 3, Stuttgart, 1981, pp. 5–38.

5.32 —— 'Die Hofbibliothek Karls des Grossen', *Mittelalterliche Studien* 3, Stuttgart, 1981, pp. 49–70.

5.33 —— 'Paläographie und frühmittelalterliche Klassikerüberlieferung', in *Mittelalterliche Studien* 3, Stuttgart, 1981, pp. 55–72.

5.34 Bullough, D. 'The educational tradition in England from Alfred to Aelfric: teaching *utriusque linguae*', in his *Carolingian Renewal: Sources and Heritage*, Manchester, 1991.

5.35 Cavallo, G. *Libri, editori e pubblico nel mondo antico: Guida storica e critica*, Rome, 1977.

5.36 Contreni, J. J. *The Cathedral School of Laon from 850–930: its Manuscripts and Masters*, Münchener Beiträge zur Mediävistik und Renaissance-Forschung, Munich, 1976.

5.37 —— *Codex Laudunensis 468: a Ninth-century Guide to Virgil, Sedulius and Liberal Arts*, Armarium Codicum Insignium III, Turnhout, 1984.

5.38 —— *Carolingian Learning, Masters and Manuscripts*, Aldershot, 1992.

5.39 Fleckenstein, F. 'Königshof und Bischofsschule unter Otto dem Grossen', *Archiv für Kulturgeschichte* 38 (1956): 38–62; repr. in J. Fleckenstein, *Ordnungen und Formende Kraft des Mittelalters. Ausgewählte Beiträge*, Göttingen, 1986, pp. 168–92.

5.40 Gariépy, R. J. 'Lupus of Ferrières: Carolingian scribe and text critic', *Medieval Studies* 30 (1976): 90–105.

5.41 Glauche, G. *Schullektüre im Mittelalter: Entstehung und Wandlungen des Lektürekanons bis 1200 nach den Quellen dargestellt*, Münchener Beiträge zur Mediävistik und Renaissance-Forschung, Munich, 1970.

5.42 Hellmann, S. *Sedulius Scottus*, Munich, 1906.

5.43 Heslop, T. A. 'The production of *de luxe* manuscripts and the patronage of King Cnut and Queen Emma', *Anglo-Saxon England* 19 (1990): 151–95.

5.44 Hildebrandt, M. M. *The External School in Carolingian Society*, Leiden, New York and Cologne, 1992.

5.45 Hoffmann, H. *Buchkunst und Königtum im ottonischen und frühsalischen Reich* (Monumenta Germaniae Historica Schriften 30), Stuttgart, 1986.

5.46 Illmer, D. *Formen der Erziehungs und Wissensvermittlung im frühen Mittelalter. Quellenstudien zur Frage der Kontinuität des abendländischen Erziehungswesens*, Münchener Beiträge zur Mediävistik und Renaissance-Forschung, Munich, 1971.

5.47 Iogna-Prat, D., Jeudy, C. and Lobrichon, G. *L'Ecole Carolingienne d'Auxerre de Murethach à Remi 830–908*, Paris, 1991.

5.48 Keynes, S. and Lapidge, M. *Alfred the Great*, Harmondsworth, 1983.

5.49 Kleberg, T. *Buchhandel und Verlagswesen in der Antike*, Darmstadt, 1969.

5.50 Kurth, G. *Notger de Liège et la civilisation au Xe siècle*, Paris, 1905.

5.51 Lapidge, M. 'Artistic and literary patronage in Anglo-Saxon England', *Committenti e produzione artistico-letteraria nell'alto medioevo occidentale*

(Settimane di Studio del Centro Italiano di studi sull 'alto medioevo 39), Spoleto, 1992, pp. 137–91.

5.52 Leclercq, J. *The Love of Learning and the Desire for God*, London, 1978.

5.53 McKitterick, R. *The Carolingians and the Written Word*, Cambridge, 1989.

5.54 —— 'Carolingian book production: some problems', *The Library*, 6th series 12 (1990): 1–33.

5.55 —— 'Royal patronage of culture in the Frankish kingdoms under the Carolingians: motives and consequences', *Committenti e produzione artistico-letteraria nell'alto medioevo occidentale* (Settimane di Studio del Centro Italiano di Studi sull'alto medioevo 39), Spoleto, 1992, pp. 131–91.

5.56 —— 'Knowledge of Plato's *Timaeus* in the ninth century: the implications of Valenciennes Bibliothèque Municipale MS 293', in H. J. Westra (ed.) *From Athens to Chartres, Neoplatonism and Medieval Thought: Studies in Honour of Edouard Jeauneau*, Leiden, New York and Cologne, 1992.

5.57 —— (ed.) *Carolingian Culture: Emulation and Innovation*, Cambridge, 1993.

5.58 —— (ed.) *The New Cambridge Medieval History*, vol. II, Cambridge, 1995.

5.59 Mayr-Harting, H. *Ottonian Book Illumination: an Historical Study*, 2 vols, London, 1992.

5.60 Riché, P. *Les Ecoles et l'enseignement dans l'occident chrétien de la fin du v siècle au milieu du xi siècle*, Paris, 1979.

5.61 *La Scuola nell'Occidente Latino nell'alto medioevo*, Settimane di Studio del Centro Italiano di studi sull'alto medioevo, Spoleto, 1972.

5.62 Sot, M. *Haut Moyen-Âge: Culture, éducation et société*, Paris, 1990.

5.63 Southern, R. *The Making of the Middle Ages*, London, 1953.

5.64 —— *Medieval Humanism and Other Studies*, Oxford, 1970.

5.65 Sullivan, R. E. (ed.) *'The Gentle Voices of Teachers': Aspects of Learning in the Carolingian Age*, Columbia, Oh., 1955.

5.66 Thomas, P. (1908) *Apulei Opera quae supersunt* III, Leipzig, 1908.

Philosophical studies and monographs on particular texts and authors

5.67 Bouhot, J. P. *Ratramne de Corbie*, Paris, 1976.

5.68 Courcelle, P. *La Consolation de philosophie dans la tradition littéraire*, Paris, 1967.

5.69 Delehaye, P. *Une controverse sur l'âme universelle au IXe siècle*, Louvain, 1950.

5.70 Ganz, D. 'The debate on predestination', in M. Gibson and J. Nelson (eds) *Charles the Bald. Court and Kingdom*, 2nd edn, London, 1990, pp. 283–302.

5.71 Gibson, M. (ed.) *Boethius: His Life, Thought and Influence*, Oxford, 1981.

5.72 —— *Lanfranc of Bec*, Oxford, 1978.

5.73 Holopainen, T. *Dialectic and Theology in the Eleventh Century* (Studien und Texte zur Geistesgeschichte des Mittelalters 54), Leiden, New York and Cologne, 1996.

5.74 Jolivet, J. *Godescalc d'Orbais et la trinité*, Paris, 1958.

5.75 Marenbon, J. *From the Circle of Alcuin to the School of Auxerre* (Cambridge Studies in Medieval Life and Thought, 3rd series 15), Cambridge, 1981.

5.76 —— *Early Medieval Philosophy (480–1150): an Introduction*, 2nd edn, London, 1988.

5.77 —— 'John Scottus and Carolingian theology: from the *De praedestinatione*, its background and its critics, to the *Periphyseon*, in M. Gibson and J. Nelson (eds) *Charles the Bald: Court and Kingdom*, 2nd edn, London, 1990, pp. 303–25.

5.78 —— 'Medieval Latin commentaries and glosses on Aristotelian logical texts, before ca. 1150 AD', in C. Burnett (ed.) *Commentaries and Glosses on Aristotelian Logical Texts: the Syriac, Arabic and Medieval Latin Traditions* (Warburg Institute Surveys and Texts 23), London, 1993, pp. 77–127.

5.79 —— 'Anselm and the early medieval Aristotle', in J. Marenbon (ed.) *Aristotle in Britain during the Middle Ages*, Turnhout, 1996, pp. 1–19.

5.80 Minio-Paluello, L. *Opuscula: the Latin Aristotle*, Amsterdam, 1972.

5.81 Schrimpf, G. 'Der Beitrag des Johannes Scottus Eriugena zum Prädestinationsstreit' in H. Löwe (ed.) *Die Iren und Europa im früheren Mittelalter*, Stuttgart, 1982.

5.82 Troncarelli, F. *Boethiana aetas*, Alessandria, 1987.

5.83 Troncarelli, F. *Tradizioni perduti*, Padua, 1981.

CHAPTER 6

John Scottus Eriugena and Anselm of Canterbury

Stephen Gersh

❧

❧ INTRODUCTION ❧

by John Marenbon

John Scottus Eriugena came from Ireland, as his name indicates ('Scottus' meant 'Irishman' in the Latin of this period, and 'Eriugena', a neologism invented by John himself, is a flowery way of saying the same thing). He worked on the Continent, however, under the patronage of Charles the Bald. The first mention of him, in a letter of 851 or 852 about the predestination controversy, is as 'an Irishman at the royal court'. After the disastrous reception of his own contribution to this dispute, *On Predestination* (discussed in Chapter 5), it seems to have been Charles's protection which saved Eriugena from punishment and ensured he could continue his work. Glosses survive by Eriugena on Martianus Capella's *On the Marriage of Mercury and Philology*, a late antique handbook of the seven liberal arts widely studied in the ninth century, and it is likely that these represent some of his teaching at the palace school in the late 840s.[1] Already his comments show some of the characteristic themes of his thought. For instance, a reference by Martianus to the myth of Orpheus, who tries to rescue his wife, Eurydice, from the underworld, is glossed in terms of the relation between the beauty of sound (represented by Orpheus) and the art of music 'in its profoundest reasons' (represented by Eurydice), which the musician must seek by descending into the depths of his discipline.

Eriugena's intellectual horizon was greatly enlarged in the 850s when Charles commissioned him to translate from Greek the writings which had been issued as (and were taken to be) by Dionysius, the learned pagan converted by St Paul, though they were in fact the work of a fifth-century Christian deeply influenced by the Neoplatonism of Proclus. The manuscript of pseudo-Dionysius had been sent as a present by the Byzantine emperor to Charles's father, Louis the Pious. An obscure translation had been made at the time by Hilduin, Abbot of St Denis. Eriugena had taught himself Greek much better and succeeded, not merely in producing a comprehensible translation which would be used for the next three centuries, but also in absorbing the ideas he found in the text. He went on to translate various other Greek Christian texts, by Gregory of Nyssa and the seventh-century Maximus the Confessor. All these influences, along with his wide reading of the Latin fathers (especially Ambrose and Augustine) and his enthusiasm for logic (especially as found in the pseudo-Augustinian *Ten Categories*), are combined in his masterpiece *Periphyseon* ('About Nature'; it is also sometimes known as *De divisione naturae*, 'On the division of nature'), written in the 860s. The *Periphyseon* has been seen by some as continuing a tradition of Greek Neoplatonic thought, and by some as anticipating nineteenth-century German Idealist philosophy; whilst other scholars have concentrated on placing the work within the context of Carolingian thought.[2] Yet other approaches, too, are possible (as Stephen Gersh's discussion below will illustrate) – a diversity of interpretation encouraged by a text of remarkable breadth and audacity, where bold strokes of the imagination sometimes stand in for rigour of argument and suggestiveness of imagery for clarity of thought.

The *Periphyseon* begins by setting out a fourfold division of universal nature – discussed below in greater depth by Stephen Gersh – into: (1) that which is not created and creates, (2) that which is created and creates, (3) that which is created and does not create, and (4) that which is not created and does not create. God, as creator, constitutes (1); the primordial causes – which are both like Platonic Ideas and the Stoic seminal reasons Eriugena learnt about in Augustine's *Literal Commentary on Genesis* – make up (2); (3) is the created world of men, animals and things and (4), like (1), is identified with God, but God as the Final Cause to which all things return. The underlying course of universal history, seen as the progress from (1) to (4), is described in the five books of the work, which takes the form of a dialogue between master and pupil. Book I is mainly devoted to showing that God does not belong to any of Aristotle's ten categories. Drawing on pseudo-Dionysius' negative theology, Eriugena argues that God does not even belong to the first category, that of *ousia* (substance or essence) as Augustine had held. The remaining four books are structured round an exegesis of the story of creation and fall in Genesis, in which Eriugena discovers not only an account of divisions (2) and (3) but also that of the return of all things at the end of time to the uncreated and uncreating God of (4). Unusual positions abound: that (following Maximus) sexual differentiation arose only as a consequence of the fall; that the nothing from which God created all things is God himself who, being beyond all description, is nothing rather than something; that (continuing the line of thought from *On Predestination*, but hedging it around with qualifications and even contradictions) there will be no Hell, at least in the ordinary sense.

Eriugena also composed a commentary on pseudo-Dionysius' *Celestial Hierarchy*, a homily on the prologue to John's Gospel and the beginning of a commentary on that Gospel. The homily provides a short and beautifully written summary of some of the main themes of his later work.

Anselm was born at Aosta in Italy in 1033. He became a monk of Bec in Normandy in 1059, where he was taught by Lanfranc, whom he went on to succeed as Abbot (in 1078) and as Archbishop of Canterbury (in 1093). He died in 1109, after a stormy tenure of the archbishopric in which he tried to assert the power and independence of the Church. Anselm did not begin to write his theological and philosophical works until he was over 40. From then up almost until his death he produced a series of writings distinguished by an extraordinary elegance of thought and clarity of purpose. Unlike almost every other medieval thinker, Anselm makes no parade of philosophical or theological authorities, although he clearly knew as well as anyone of his time the logical texts of Aristotle, Porphyry and Boethius then available, and he had studied deeply Augustine's more philosophical writings.[3]

Anselm's two earliest monographs, the *Monologion* (1076) and the *Proslogion* (1077–8), are both concerned to provide rational arguments for the existence and attributes of God, although he assumes that his readers will be Christians who already accept by faith the truth of the assertions which he is setting out to prove. The *Monologion* uses a variety of arguments designed to show that there exists a triune God. The *Proslogion* uses a single line of argument and does not attempt to argue for triunity, but restricts itself to the not specifically Christian divine attributes such as omniscience, omnipotence, perfect goodness and eternity. The piece is built around the notion of that-than-which-nothing-greater-can-be-thought: what, for simplicity's sake, may be called the notion of a 'maximal being'. Most of the work is devoted to showing that, in the case of each presumed divine attribute, it must belong to a maximal being because, without it, the being would not be maximal. But this would merely show that, *if* it existed, a maximal being would be omnipotent, omniscient and so on. By far the greatest attention, in Anselm's time and ever since, has been given to the argument placed at the beginning (often called Anselm's 'onto-logical proof') to demonstrate that a maximal being does actually exist. Anselm advances two premisses: (1) that a maximal being does at least exist in thought, and (2) that to exist in reality and thought is greater than to exist in thought alone. He considers (1) to be proven by the fact that even someone who denies the existence of a maximal being (such as the fool of Psalm 14, who denies that God exists) has the mental concept of such a being; and he takes (2) for granted. He then argues that it must be false to claim that a maximal being *A* exists in thought and *not* in reality, because such a being would be less great than a being *B* exactly like it except that it existed in thought and also in reality, and so *A* would not be a maximal being. Therefore, given that a maximal being exists in thought, it must exist in reality too. The classic objection to this argument, that existence is not a predicate, is not very powerful, since Anselm's argument is based on the contrast between *ways* of existing, in thought and in reality. His premiss (2) may not be convincing, but it is not obviously false or meaningless. Modern re-workings of the ontological proof usually adapt premiss (1) to read: '"God exists" is possibly true', and, in order to make a plausible argument, they need to add another claim (3), that if a maximal being exists, it must exist in such a way that it cannot not exist: it must exist necessarily. (3) is found in the next chapter of the *Proslogion*, but as a further argument rather than as an additional premiss to the proof that a maximal being exists. It remains a matter for dispute among philosophers whether any version of the ontological argument, strengthened in this way, is sound.[4]

Besides writing a detailed reply to the criticisms raised by Gaunilo, a monk of Marmoutier, to his ontological proof, Anselm went on to write, among others, works *On Truth, On Free Will* and on the compat-ibility of grace and divine prescience with human freedom. His *Cur Deus homo (Why God became man,* 1094–8) is especially ambitious: basing himself on Scripture, but only on that part of it accepted by Jews and Muslims as well as Christians, Anselm tries to show that God needed to become incarnate if he was to remain just but also maintain the benevolent purpose of his creation. Two works of Anselm also survive which are more purely philosophical in content: *De gram-matico*, an intricate logical discussion, following on from Aristotle's *Categories* and Boethius' commentary, of the semantics of denomina-tive words such as *grammaticus* ('literate'), and the 'Philosophical fragments', which examine modal notions and sketch out a philosophy of action.[5]

❧ QUESTIONS OF METHOD ❧

Like any other object of critical analysis, the literary production of those writers of the ninth to eleventh centuries who are usually styled 'philosophers' is approachable from various perspectives. One such viewpoint, dominant in medieval philosophical scholarship until quite recently, has been that of orthodox Thomism. However, the notion that pre-thirteenth-century intellectual figures should primarily be valued for their tentative movements towards certain doctrines of high scholasticism is nowadays losing its appeal. There is obviously neither the sociopolitical pressure nor the metaphysical conviction to sustain it.

John Marenbon's survey, published in 1983 ([6.33]), makes the pre-scholastics speak, at least to a degree, in an idiom intelligible to a late twentieth-century audience. That he should emphasize their preoccupation with problems of language is therefore perfectly understandable. This is documented by their elaboration of the doctrine in Aristotle's *On Interpretation* about words, thoughts, and things ([6.33] 21–2, 32–3, 101–2) and by their rediscovery of the distinction between sense and reference of terms ([6.33] 102–3, 106 ff.).[6] One only needs to adopt a more comprehensive notion of the linguistic – including the structural element and the overlap with the semiotic – in order to see such preoccupation in greater relief. However, that he should limit their claim to be called 'philosophers' is perhaps too drastic.

A careful reading of *Early Medieval Philosophy* reveals its author's personal conviction about the nature of philosophy. For him, it is primarily methodological in a sense opposed to ontological realism and system building ([6.33] 6, 10, 15–16, 81). The methodology consists of arguments from premises to conclusions (pp. 4, 58), the premises being generally open to doubt but ideally self-evident either to observation or reason rather than textually given, the conclusions being unknown in advance (pp. 4, 12). Philosophy also employs terms which are literal rather than metaphorical and univocal rather than equivocal in its discussions (pp. 5–6, 9–10). Since these criteria define a discipline recognizable to Bertrand Russell but not to early medieval writers, Marenbon is left with relatively few illustrations of genuine philosophy before the twelfth century. Although the traditions of logic and of logic's application to theology represented by certain passages in Augustine and Boethius are to be excepted (pp. 10, 47–8), a substantial portion of the late antique and early medieval literature fails to meet one or more criteria. The Latin translation of Plato's *Timaeus* is too metaphorical (pp. 5–6), the Latin Platonic material of late antiquity too much concerned with system building and metaphorical expression (pp. 9–10, 15–16). Likewise, Eriugena's thought involves too much system building (p. 81), too many premises derived from texts (p. 58), and too much equivocal language (pp. 65–9), Anselm of Canterbury's too many conclusions known in advance (pp. 95–7).

Despite the persuasiveness of this discussion, a different approach to the philosophical writing of the ninth to eleventh centuries is possible. This would involve equal attention to the linguistic component but – since history shows this term to imply not universality but family resemblance – fewer prior assumptions about the meaning of 'philosophy'. What follows is an attempt to investigate samples of Carolingian and post-Carolingian philosophical literature from such a viewpoint. I shall suggest that these materials, in their concern for systematic construction, pre-existing textual data, and the polysemy of etymology and metaphor, exhibit not intellectual weaknesses but intellectual strengths.

❧ ERIUGENA ❧

In some respects, Western medieval philosophy can be viewed as beginning with the brilliant and controversial ninth-century thinker John Scottus Eriugena.[7] Marenbon values him for his ability to reason abstractly yet criticizes his tendency to system building. However, it is Eriugena's notion of structure which perhaps makes him closer to modern writers than to other medieval ones.

Few would deny that a particular concept of 'structure' is one of the intellectual paradigms of our era.[8] This involves a priority of relation to related terms, such relations being either of opposite to opposite where one opposite exists through or is understood through the other, or else of whole to part where the whole exists through or is understood through the part, or vice versa.[9] Originating in linguistics, where it determined both the phonological and semantic spheres – for example as the Saussurian concept of 'value',[10] the theory regarding presence (+) or absence (–) of distinctive features elaborated by Trubetzkoy and Jakobson,[11] and the Hjelmslevian notion of 'form'[12] – it has passed into the currency of historical, anthropological, literary, psychoanalytic, and other studies. Although avoiding the term 'structure' itself, Eriugena builds his metaphysical system with identical components. Priority of relation is underlined by his discussion of the Aristotelian categorical doctrine in *Periphyseon* I where the category of 'relation' (*relatio, ad aliquid*) or of 'condition' (*habitus*) is found to be present in all the other categories.[13] Contrast of opposite with opposite is a recurrent theme of Eriugena's writing, as instanced by the negative and affirmative predicates applied to God (I. 458A–462D, II. 599B–600A, III. 684D–685A, etc.) and the five dichotomies constituting nature (II. 529C–545B); contrast of whole with parts is only slightly less frequent, an instance being God's status with regard to created things of which man's is the microcosmic reflection (IV. 759A–B. Cf. II. 523D–524D). Strict relatedness is clearly the writer's underlying assumption in such cases, since each binary term is said to be dependent ontologically and epistemologically on its counterpart (V. 953C–954A, V. 965A–B).

Eriugena exploits the notion of structure in developing his own variant of the classical Platonic Theory of Forms. The expression of this doctrine, acquired through intermediary Greek and Latin patristic sources, combines ontological and semiotic criteria.

From the ontological viewpoint,[14] there exists a set of transcendent i.e. atemporal and non-spatial principles. These are termed 'reasons' (*rationes*) in Latin, and 'Ideas' (*ideai*), 'prototypes' (*prōtotypa*), 'predestinations' (*proorismata*), or 'divine volitions' (*theia thelēmata*) in Greek.[15] They possess a metaphysically intermediate status since they depend upon a prior cause: God (the technical term for such dependence being 'participation' (*participatio*)), while subsequent terms, created objects, depend on them.[16] According to Eriugenian textual exegesis, when the Bible describes God as making heaven and earth 'in the beginning', it means that the first principle establishes the reasons or Ideas of intellectual or sensible creatures within its Word.[17] Examples of the transcendent principles are Goodness, Being, Life, Wisdom, Truth, Intellect, Reason, Power, Justice, Salvation, Magnitude, Omnipotence, Eternity, and Peace (II. 616C–617A).

From the semiotic viewpoint,[18] Eriugena proposes an analysis of the term 'nature' (*natura*) using a combination of traditional logical principles like the square of opposition[19] and the division of genus into species versus the partition of whole into parts.[20] Within nature, four 'differences' (*differentiae*) are posited: creating (A), not created (D), created (B), and not creating (C), these combining to form four 'species' (*species*): creating and not created (1), both created and creating (2), created and not creating (3), and neither creating nor created (4).[21] The relations between 1 and 3 and between 2 and 4 are described as 'opposition' (*oppositio*), those between A2 and A1, between B3 and B2, between C3 and C4, and between D4 and D1 as 'similarity' (*similitudo*), and those between B2 and D1, between C3 and A2, between B3 and D4, and between C4 and A1 as 'dissimilarity' (*dissimilitudo*) (I. 441A–442A, II. 523D–528B). This semiotic analysis is applied to metaphysics when species 1 is identified with God as the beginning of the cosmic process, species 2 with the reasons or Ideas, species 3 with the effects of the reasons or Ideas, and species 4 with God as end of the cosmic process.[22]

By endorsing the thesis that there is an analogy between the cosmos and a book, Eriugena can pass easily from assumptions about the structure of reality to assumptions about the structure of texts.[23] That he has a systematic approach to texts is suggested by the possibility of dissolving *Periphyseon* into a mosaic of citations.[24] Of course, he presents no formalized theory concerning the relations between a literary text, its reader, and antecedent texts comparable with those developed in connection with modern fiction by Bakhtin, Kristeva and others.[25] Nevertheless, the combination of quotations in his writing indicates several interpretative strategies.

Among Eriugena's citations,[26] a considerable number come from the Greek Fathers. Taking them in chronological order of authorship, there are lengthy passages from Origen on the end of the world (V. 929A–930D), from Gregory of Nyssa on man as the image of God (IV. 788A–801C), from pseudo-Dionysius the Areopagite on the divine names and on the celestial hierarchies,[27] and from Maximus the Confessor on the fivefold division of nature (II. 529C–542B). Two Latin Fathers contribute textual materials of importance: Augustine on miscellaneous questions[28] and Ambrose on the interpretation of Paradise (IV. 815B–816C). Among Eriugena's further quotations, a large group comes from Latin secular authors. Considering these also in chronological order of authorship, there are substantial extracts from pseudo-Augustine on the ten categories,[29] from Martianus Capella on the measurement of the cosmos,[30] and from Boethius on the nature of number.[31] The incorporation of all these antecedent texts into *Periphyseon* reflects one paramount exegetical purpose. This is to make them agree in meaning so that, when two texts are perceived to disagree on the denotative level, agreement must be sought in some connotative meaning;[32] and when they are seen to disagree on the connotative level, the denotative meaning of one text should be accepted, its selection being founded on a hierarchy of socio-political value.[33] The application of this exegetical principle can be documented by many examples. Latin Christian and Greek Christian writings are held to agree when Augustine and pseudo-Dionysius discuss the divine ignorance beyond knowledge (II. 597C–598A), Latin secular and Greek Christian when 'Plato', Virgil and Gregory of Nyssa describe the four elements,[34] Latin secular and Latin Christian when 'Plato' and Augustine interpret the world soul as principle of life (III. 727C–728D), and Latin secular, Greek Christian and Latin Christian when 'Aristotle', pseudo-Dionysius and Augustine discuss the ten categories.[35] Disagreement on the denotative level overcome by shifting to the connotative level of one or both texts is instanced among Latin Christian and Greek Christian authors when Ambrose, Augustine, pseudo-Dionysius and Maximus describe the indirect perception of God through theophany;[36] disagreement on the connotative level overcome by concentrating on the denotative level of one text only is illustrated among Latin Christian and Greek Christian authors when pseudo-Dionysius and Maximus but not Augustine discuss the threefold division of the soul into substance, power and activity,[37] and among Latin Christian and Latin secular authors when Pliny and Martianus Capella but not Augustine calculate the measurements of the cosmos (III. 719A, 721C. Cf. III. 724A–C).

Eriugena obviously exploits the notion of multiple meanings in texts. That this is in the late twentieth century part of the definition of literariness would hardly be questioned,[38] and that it is nowadays also a fundamental problem in philosophy is the legacy of Gadamer, Derrida and others.[39] But it is important to find the exact coordinates of Eriugena's position. Of the theoretically possible views of meaning which are relevant here, one would connect the polysemy of individual texts with an ultimate monosemy – metaphysical truth – and establish a limit for hermeneutical activity and a distinction between denotation and connotation.[40] This was the attitude of medieval theologians.[41] Another view would connect the polysemy of individual texts with an ultimate polysemy – a linguistic 'reality' – and establish no limits for hermeneutical activity and no distinction between denotation and connotation. Such is the position of modern deconstruction.[42] A careful study of Eriugena's philosophical methodology reveals him supporting neither the first nor the second viewpoint exclusively but oscillating between the two: a most unusual approach for a Western medieval thinker.

The evidence for Eriugena's concept of polysemy consists primarily of various statements about thought and language.[43] Clearly the notion that polysemy is a property to be exploited rather than a defect to be overcome in the pursuit of philosophy requires a fusion rather than a separation of the cognitive and the verbal. Eriugena explicitly advocates such a fusion in several instances while commenting on Martianus Capella and Maximus the Confessor.

Among Eriugena's comments on the text of Martianus Capella, those dealing with the meaning of its initial allegory are particularly relevant. This narrative depicts the god Mercury's search for a bride, culminating in his choice of the mortal Philology, and then the preparations for the marriage of Mercury and Philology, including a ritual of Philology's deification. Since Eriugena quite plausibly interprets Mercury and Philology as figures of language and reason respectively, the marriage of the two protagonists for him indirectly signifies the fusion of discourse and thinking.[44] Naturally, this represents a primary rather than exclusive meaning of such an inherently polysemous text.[45]

Among Eriugena's developments of Maximus the Confessor's teaching, those concerned with a threefold psychological process are particularly important. Here, Eriugena sometimes contrasts two inner cognitive functions: intelligence and thinking with an outer expressive function: sensation = sign-manipulation,[46] but sometimes describes three inner cognitive and expressive functions: intelligence = non-interpretation, reason = expression, and interior sensation = quasi sign-manipulation.[47] The shift between the first and second formulations – tantamount to replacing the traditional contrast of thought and language with a more unusual combination of the two – results from the contextual pressure of a Trinitarian analogy in the latter case.[48] Just as God expresses himself to himself and to creation through his Word, so does man reflect the same processes on a lower level of being.

In order to appreciate these developments, one should pause momentarily to recall Aristotle's theory in *On Interpretation* that spoken words are signs – *symbola* or *sēmeia* – of mental affections and that, although mental affections are identical for all mankind, spoken words are different.[49] Thanks to Boethius' translation and commentary on this text, the radical cleavage between thinking and language which it advocated became a medieval commonplace.[50] However, modern linguistic theory in the tradition of Saussure's *Cours de linguistique générale* would insist that the acoustic image – the signifier, and the concept – the signified, are inseparable components of one wholly arbitrary linguistic sign.[51]

Further evidence for his concept of polysemy is provided by the writer's practice in connection with etymology. Here, Eriugena follows the doctrine, established by the Stoics and transmitted to the Latin West by Isidore of Seville, that study of the forms and derivations of words leads to knowledge of the things which they represent.[52] The *Periphyseon* contains numerous examples of simple etymologies exploited in this way. Because *metochē* ('participation') is composed of *meta* ('after') plus *echein* ('to have'), it indicates the derivation of an essence from a superior one (III. 632B) and because *stereōma* ('firmament') is composed of *stere* ('solid') plus *hama* ('together'), it indicates the common boundary of all corporeal things (III. 694B). Similarly the noun *ousia* ('substance') comes from the verb *eimi* ('I am') and therefore signifies subsistence of each thing in its transcendent causes whereas the noun *phusis* ('nature') comes from the verb *phuomai* ('I am born') and therefore signifies the generation of each thing in some material substratum.[53] When Eriugena alternates etymologies of a single term, the fusion of real and verbal begins to predominate over the separation of the two.[54] For example, the word *theos* ('God') is derived both from the verb *theōrō* ('I see'), so that God is the one who sees all things in himself, and from the verb *theō* ('I run'), so that he is that which itself runs through all things. (I. 452B–C). The word *angelos* ('angel') is connected both with the preposition *engus* ('near'), meaning that angels are the creatures immediately after God, and with the verb *engigno* ('I engender'), meaning that they are the creatures who transmit divine illuminations.[55] When Eriugena connects etymologies of different terms, the fusion of real and verbal completes its ascendancy over the separation of the two. Because *bonitas* ('goodness') comes from the verb *boō* ('I call'), while *boō* is synonymous with *kalō*, from which comes the adjective *kalos* ('beautiful'), the God who is both goodness and beauty can be understood as calling all created things from non-existence into existence.[56]

The writer's practice in connection with metaphor provides yet more evidence for his concept of polysemy.[57] For Eriugena, 'metaphor' (*metaphora/translatio*) represents the application to something of a name normally applied to something else (see I. 458C, 461C, 463B, 464D, 512B–D, 522A, etc.). This is a notion derived from such textbooks as the pseudo-Ciceronian *To Herennius*, although Eriugena does not specify the ground of this transference of names in the perceived similarity between the objects concerned.[58] 'Metonymy' (*metōnumia*) is defined as a more specific version of the above, involving the application to the contained of a name normally applied to the container (I. 480B. Cf. *To Herennius* IV. 32. 43). 'Synecdoche' (*sunekdochē*) is a more specific version of the above, involving the application to the part of a name normally applied to the whole, or else the application to the whole of a name normally applied to the part (II. 560A–B, III. 706B, IV. 744C. Cf. *To Herennius* IV. 33. 44). When Eriugena advocates such transferences of terms either between a created thing and God[59] or between one created thing and another, he remains within the traditional theory. When he treats these transferences as simultaneously metaphors, metonymies and synecdoches (I. 480B, III. 706B) he is perhaps metaphysically rationalizing certain imprecisions in that established teaching. But when he understands such transferences of terms not as unilateral between a literal and a figurative sense but as bilateral between two literal-figurative senses,[60] he passes beyond the traditional doctrine. In fact, the writer seems to have developed this notion of 'reciprocal metaphor' (*reciproca metaphora*) (III. 706A) against a twofold background. Within his theory of divine names, a given term e.g. 'goodness' can be applied to the creator but is normally applied to the creature while that same term can be applied to the creature but is ultimately grounded in the creator.[61] In connection with his theory of the Incarnation, a certain term e.g. 'air' can be applied to a higher element but is normally applied to a lower one, while another term e.g. 'light' can be applied to a lower element but is normally applied to a higher one. This example is particularly interesting since air and light are already metaphors of human and divine respectively.[62] Also in connection with his theory of the Incarnation, a certain term relating to salvation e.g. 'flesh' may be applied to the redeemed but is normally applied to the fallen, while another term e.g. 'spirit' may be applied to the fallen but is normally applied to the redeemed.[63]

The understanding of metaphor emerging from such texts moves away from that implying comparison of two spheres of meaning, and associated with the classical tradition from Aristotle to Quintilian and beyond, towards that based on fusion of two spheres of meaning and advocated by Richards and other modern critics.[64] Such a viewpoint has one important consequence which Eriugena intuitively grasps: that the traditional distinction between the verbal and the real is becoming questionable. This is because the metaphorized and metaphorizing terms are no longer contrasted as verbal and real but as equally verbal-real. The same viewpoint has another consequence which he explicitly states: that the habitual distinction between 'figurative' and 'literal' language is almost unworkable (see III. 705Aff.).

It is because of this deliberate rather than accidental role of polysemy in his thought that we should be less ready than some have been to accuse Eriugena of philosophical confusion. For example, Marenbon finds serious fault in the handling of substance ([6.33] 65–70). He rightly notes that Eriugena's substance is primarily universal but, since he has confused two distinct types of universal: (a) classes of things where whatever distinguishes their members is present wholly in each one, and (b) universal qualities where whatever is characteristic of individuals is present to different degrees in each, concludes that this substance is a notion vitiated by ambivalence. However, it is also reasonable to see deliberate polysemy rather than unconscious confusion here.[65] Eriugena's 'substance' is simply a lexeme whose semantic properties enter into numerous configurations, forming a simple structure where it is opposed to non-substance (I. 461A–464A) – the affirmative and negative theologies. It forms a more complex structure where the opposition of universal and particular is discovered within it and it is opposed to accident (I. 467D–468B, 470Dff.) – the Aristotelian categories. It forms the most complex structure where it is combined with form, opposed to quality in combination with form, metaphorically fused with 'dry land', and opposed to quality metaphorically fused with 'water' (III. 698Cff.), the exegesis of Genesis 1: 9–10. Any structure may actualize semantic properties logically inconsistent with those of other structures. That inconsistencies are an ineradicable feature of natural languages and of all literature and philosophy derived from them is a fact which Eriugena perhaps saw more clearly than did most of his contemporaries and successors.

It had always been assumed by nineteenth-century historians of philosophy that Eriugena exercised little influence over later thinkers. Although various attempts have been made to counter this negative assessment in recent times,[66] the only hitherto undiscovered influences

131

to be brought to light have been those on the immediately subsequent generation. Thus, Eriugena's studies of the Latin Fathers are known to have influenced one set of Carolingian glosses on Augustine's *De Musica* (edited by Boeuff [6.45]) and his studies of Latin secular authors of various glosses of the same period on the pseudo-Augustinian *Ten Categories*.[67] These latter glosses have been extensively discussed in recent scholarship. From passages now published it is possible to see that various commentators had grasped the semiotic ramifications of Eriugena's work. Indeed, certain glosses recall the structural preoccupations of his thought in elaborating the notion of 'nature',[68] and others its polysemic tendency by applying ideas concerning homonymy, synonymy, and paronymy or etymological arguments to metaphysics.[69]

If Eriugena *had* exercised influence over later thinkers, it would undoubtedly have run counter to the norm of medieval intellectual development. In general, writers of this period went back directly to antique sources for their material, and during the tenth and eleventh centuries this meant primarily Boethius, whom Eriugena had only partially exploited.[70] For example, Notker Labeo makes extensive use of Boethius' translation of Aristotle's *Categories* (see [6.63]), Abbo of Fleury of the Boethian monographs on logical division and on various kinds of syllogism (see [6.64]), Gerbert of Aurillac of Boethius' first commentary on Porphyry's *Isagoge*, etc. Gerbert is arguably the most important member of this group.[71] His treatise *De rationali et ratione uti* (*On 'rational' and 'to use reason'*) is a discussion of logical problems surrounding the extension of the two predicates 'rational' and 'using reason' ([6.16] 1. 299) more interesting for the ideas arising *en route* to the solution than for the solution itself. Here, Gerbert reveals the structural preoccupation of a typical Platonist in establishing three 'semiotic' categories:[72] act without potency, act with potency, and potency without act, which are applied to hierarchies of physical and metaphysical principles,[73] yet a desire to reduce polysemy more characteristic of the re-emergent Aristotelianism ([6.16] 9. 304).

❧ ANSELM OF CANTERBURY ❧

The next major figure in the Western intellectual tradition and the dominant thinker of the late eleventh century is Anselm of Canterbury.[74] Marenbon arrives at an ambivalent judgement in his case, on one hand denying him the title of 'philosopher' because his argumentation does not arrive finally at its conclusions but assumes them from the outset, and on the other conceding it in recognition of his contributions to the study of the language–thought relation and of the logic of possibility and necessity. Yet it is possible to reevaluate Anselm's philosophical contribution under the three headings proposed earlier: structure, text and polysemy (see p. 125).

Anselm exploits the notion of structure in developing a variant of the classical Platonic Theory of Forms during the early chapters of *Monologion* which combines ontological and 'semiotic' criteria. The ontological viewpoint is clearly indicated when he describes a set of transcendent i.e. atemporal and non-spatial principles, each of which is termed an 'exemplar' (*exemplum*), 'form' (*forma*), or 'rule' (*regula*) (*Monologion* 9, 24. 7–20). It is either present in the divine mind or an aspect of the divine essence,[75] and is somehow the cause of lower i.e. spatio-temporal things.[76] The semiotic viewpoint is adopted implicitly when Anselm introduces the set of transcendent principles with a discourse based on semantic permutation.[77]

In the first place, there is an argument in the abstract. This is founded on the following inventory of semantic elements: two terms – the plurality of things having property x ($a_1, a_2 \ldots$) and the single property x (b); two relations constitutive of terms – effect of another (R→) and effect of itself (R←); two terms constituted by relations – the plurality of things having property x through another (aa$_1$, aa$_2$ ...) and the single property x through itself (bb); and three relations – greater than (R>), less than (R<), and equal to (R=). The inventory is activated gradually as the argument proceeds through six stages:

1   There are things having property x [$a_1, a_2 \ldots$];
2   A thing having property x to greater, lesser, or equal degree than another thing having property x has this through the property x [(a_1 R $\gtreqless$ a_2) R→ b];
3   The property x is itself x [b R←];
4   Things having property x are things having property x through another [$a_1, a_2 \ldots$ R = aa$_1$, aa$_2$ ...];
5   The property x is the property x through itself [b R = bb];
6   The property x through itself is greater than things having property x through another [bb R> aa$_1$, aa$_2$ ...].

In the second place, the argument is applied to three concrete instances: where property x is identified with 'good' sensed or understood, 'great' sensed or understood, and 'existent' sensed or understood respectively.[78]

Important features of Anselm's philosophical method are revealed here. For example, it seems that there is less an alternation of premisses and conclusions – as in formal logic – than a permutation of semantic properties. In fact, the whole discourse can be understood in semantic terms with the exception of the idea (point 3 above) that the property x is itself x. This is purely ontological in character, since it makes no sense to say that the semantic property x has the semantic property

133

x.[79] Furthermore, it appears that the permutation of semantic properties follows a largely symmetrical pattern, the clearest indication of a writer's thinking in structural terms.

It would be inappropriate to seek the relation to textual authorities here which was apparent in Eriugena. The difference between the two philosophers seems extreme, given that Anselm's works – especially *Monologion* and *Proslogion* – are attempts to construct a discourse 'by reason alone' (*sola ratione*) without explicit dependence on sources.[80] Nevertheless, Anselm's relation to textual authorities is different from that of his predecessor rather than non-existent.

Although numerous Latin patristic sources are mentioned in the extant letters, the only authority cited in the treatises themselves is Augustine. But this citation is of overwhelming interpretative significance. In the preface to *Monologion*, the writer diverts potential criticism that he is advocating novel or false teachings by stressing the complete agreement between the doctrines of his book and those of Augustine's *On the Trinity* ([6.11] I: 8. 8–14). Some modern scholars would interpret this as the typical statement of a medieval writer endeavouring to conceal the novelty of his thought behind a declaration of traditionalism. However, Anselm's remarks are more than a rhetorical commonplace. This becomes clear on analysing the *Monologion* into an assemblage of Augustinian materials reorganized according to the structural principles described above.

Anselm's relation to textual authorities is even indicated by the *Proslogion*, which cites no source at all. This treatise contains a famous passage where a premiss that God is 'something than which nothing greater can be thought' (*aliquid quo nihil maius cogitari possit*) is postulated as self-evident, the premiss then being used as the starting point for an argument allegedly proceeding by the application of reason alone to the conclusion that God exists ([6.11] I: 101. 1–4, 104. 7). But even if one were to concede the premiss to be self-evident – a dubious point in itself – one could not consider it independent of textual background. In fact, the premiss corresponds to a definition of God found in Christian texts like Augustine's *On the Customs of the Catholic Church and those of the Manicheans* ([6.11] I: 11. 24) and Boethius' *On the Consolation of Philosophy* ([6.11] I: 10, 57–8), and in secular works like Cicero's *On the Nature of the Gods* ([6.11] I: 77) and Seneca's *Natural Questions*[81] to name only the most obvious parallels. So Anselm's purpose was perhaps to recommend the faith to non-Christians by deducing it from a premiss stated by Christian and non-Christian authors alike.

Anselm obviously does not exploit the notion of multiple meanings in texts; indeed, the ideal of univocity would seem more consistent with his method. Nevertheless, some of his ideas about signification, had they been extended in a different direction, would have supported the exploitation of polysemy.

One suggestive idea is the distinction between appellation and signification elaborated in the treatise *De grammatico*. Here, he argues that in statements like 'the horse is white', the adjective is 'appellative' (*appellativum*) of the white thing but 'significative' (*significativum*) of its possession of the property ([6.11] I: 159. 12–15, 161. 21). Since he stresses that what is appellated is an existent object but what is signified is not, the distinction seems to approximate that between reference and sense in modern linguistic theory.[82] However, any Platonist would maintain that in the statement 'the horse is x', the x signifies a transcendentally existent x-ness in which Socrates participates. This is the viewpoint which also seems to underlie the argument about divine attributes in *Monologion* 1–4.[83]

Another aspect of Anselm's theory of signification conducive to the systematic exploitation of polysemy is his notion of a 'speaking' (*locutio*) within the divine nature. By explaining that the exemplar in the divine mind according to which all things are created is a speaking (see p. 133), he follows traditional patristic teachings regarding the Word as second person of the Trinity.[84] However, the use of the term 'speaking' also requires a rational justification. Anselm therefore proposes to distinguish three ways of speaking about an object:[85]

1   Speaking of things by employing sensible signs in a sensible manner e.g. signifying a man by using the word 'man' – such signs being unmotivated and non-universal;[86]
2   Thinking by employing sensible and external signs in an insensible and internal manner e.g. silently thinking the word 'man' – these signs also being unmotivated and non-universal;
3   Speaking things themselves by employing sensible signs in neither a sensible nor an insensible manner e.g. perceiving a man either by imagining his sensible shape or by thinking his universal essence 'animal, rational, mortal' – such signs being motivated and universal.[87]

It is the third type of speaking which can be attributed to the divine mind.[88] The exemplar in the latter, according to which all things are created, can therefore be described as a thinking process coextensive with rather than anterior to the manipulation of signs.[89] With this argument, Anselm points towards that elimination of the distinction between cognitive and verbal characteristic of post-Saussurian linguistic theory albeit from a restricted theological perspective (cf. pp. 128–9).

Another suggestive idea is the application of metaphor to philosophical method underlying the entire *Monologion*. Towards the end of that text Anselm raises an important question: given that the divine nature surpasses human understanding and is accessible only through words whose meaning is transformed, how true are all the inferences constructed from such words in respect of the divinity?[90] He answers that there is a certain truth in things signified 'not properly but through some likeness' (*non proprie ... sed per aliquam similitudinem*). The passage should be noted by those modern scholars who agonize over the cogency of Anselm's arguments about God, since he shows clearly that the 'logic' which they contain is intended to be not the embodiment but only the reflection of truth.[91] Apparently, logical metaphor is to logic in the *Monologion* what arithmetical metaphor was to arithmetic in Eriugena's exposition of the divine names.

 NOTES

1   See Leonardi, 'Glosse eriugeniane a Marziano Capella in un codice leidense', in Roques [6.57].
2   For Eriugena and Greek Neoplatonism, see esp. Beierwaltes [6.44] and Gersh [6.49]. Dermot Moran [6.54] explores the connections with German Idealism; cf. also W. Beierwaltes, 'Zur Wirkungsgeschichte Eriugenas im deutschen Idealismus. Ein kurze, unsystematische Nachlese', in [6.44] 313–20. Accounts more directed to the historical context will be found in Jeauneau [6.51], Marenbon [5.75] and Schrimpf [6.59].
3   On Anselm's knowledge of logic, see Henry [6.69] and his editions of *De grammatico* [6.14 and 6.15].
4   See Bibliography [6.75–6.82] for some modern treatments of the ontological proof.
5   On *De grammatico*, see the works by Henry listed in n. 3 above; on Anselm's theory of modality and philosophy of action, see Serene [6.73].
6   In addition, Marenbon stresses the relation between logic and language in general explored by Fredegisus (p. 51), Gottschalk (pp. 55, 105), ninth-century writers at St Gall (p. 105), the anonymous eleventh-century glossator of Priscian (p. 106ff.), etc.
7   The most useful books providing a general introduction to Eriugena's life and works are Cappuyns [6.24] and Moran [6.54]. See O'Meara and Bieler [6.55], Allard [6.38], Beierwaltes [6.42] and [6.43], Jeauneau [6.51], for essays on specific aspects of his thought.
8   This is true not only of the original 'structuralists' but also of the semioticians and even the deconstructionists who have followed them.
9   On these criteria see Lévi-Strauss, C., *Structural Anthropology*, English trans., New York, 1964, pp. 279–80 and Greimas, A. J., *Structural Semantics*, English trans., Lincoln, Neb. 1983, pp. 18ff.
10 See Saussure, F. de *Course in General Linguistics*, English trans., New York, 1959, pp. 114–15.
11 This theory is conveniently summarized by Barthes, R., *Elements of Semiology*, English trans., London, 1984, pp. 135ff.

12 See Hjelmslev, L., *Prolegomena to a Theory of Language*, English trans., Madison, Wis., 1961, p. 23.

13 Eriugena, *Periphyseon* I. 466A–467C. References to Eriugena's work give the column numbers of Floss's edition [6.1] which are reproduced in the modern editions and translations and so provide a standard form of reference. Because of his interpretation of pseudo-Augustine: *The Ten Categories*, Eriugena allows the separate Aristotelian categories of relation and condition to coalesce. On Eriugena's theory see Flasch [6.48].

14 In discussing both Eriugena's and Anselm's notions of structure, I shall distinguish 'ontological' and 'semiotic' components. By the former is meant any aspects of the metaphysical system stated in the texts, by the latter those aspects corresponding to elements in the notion of structure described earlier. Of course, neither Eriugena nor Anselm could have made such a distinction.

15 II. 529A–C. Elsewhere, Eriugena calls these 'primordial causes' (*causae primordiales*). See III. 622Bff.

16 II. 616B. 'And they are said to be the principles of all things since all things whatsoever that are sensed or understood either in the visible or invisible creation subsist by participation in them, while they themselves are participations in the one cause of all things: that is, the most high and holy Trinity'. Cf. III. 630A–C, III. 644A–B, III. 646B–C, III. 682B–C.

17 II. 546A–B. 'But on considering the interpretations of many exegetes, nothing strikes me as more probable or likely than that in the aforesaid words of Holy Scripture – that is, within the meaning of "heaven" and "earth" – we should understand the primordial causes of the entire creature which the Father had created before the foundation of all other things in his only begotten Son who is designated by the term "beginning", and that by the word "heaven" we should hold the primal causes of intelligible things and celestial essences to have been signified, but by the word "earth" those of the sensible things in which the entire corporeal world is completed'.

18 See note 14. That Eriugena was aware of the linguistic even if not semiotic starting point of his analysis is suggested by his reference to nature as a 'generic term' (*general nomen*) rather than as a generic entity. See Cristiani, M., 'Natureessence et nature-langage. Notes sur l'emploi du terme "natura" dans le "Periphyseon" de Jean Erigène', *Miscellanea Mediaevalia* 13/2: *Sprache und Erkenntnis im Mittelalter*, Berlin and New York, 1981, pp. 707–17.

19 The square of opposition was a classificatory schema applied by Greek writers of late antiquity to (a) substance and accident and (b) the numbers 1–10. Thus, in (a) four terms: of a subject (A), not in a subject (D), in a subject (B), not of a subject (C) are grouped into four combined terms: of a subject but not in a subject (1), both in a subject and of a subject (2), in a subject but not of a subject (3), neither of a subject nor in a subject (4) where 1 = universal substance, 2 = universal accident, 3 = particular accident, 4 = particular substance. See Porphyry, *On the Categories* 78, 25ff. In (b) four terms: generating (A), not generated (D), generated (B), not generating (C) are grouped into four combined terms: generating but not generated (1), both generated and generating (2), generated but not generating (3), neither generating nor generated (4) where 1 = the numbers one, two, three, and five, 2 = the number four, 3 = the numbers six, eight, and nine, 4 = the number seven. See Theo of Smyrna, *Exposition of*

Mathematical Matters 103. 1–16. Such schemata were repeated in Latin texts and thereby transmitted to Eriugena and others: see Marius Victorinus, *To Candidus* 8. 1–21, Macrobius' commentary on Cicero's *Dream of Scipio* I. 5. 16, Martianus Capella, *On the Marriage of Mercury and Philology* VII. 738, Boethius, *Commentary on Aristotle's Categories* I. 169Bff. The square of opposition in antiquity has been discussed by Hadot [6.31] 148ff., Libera, A. de, 'La sémiotique d'Aristote', in *Structures élémentaires de la signification*, ed. F. Nef, Brussels, 1976, pp. 28–55. The square of opposition in Eriugena has been examined most recently by Onofrio [6.56] and Beierwaltes [6.43] 17–38. An analogous schema applied to propositions was also traditional and certainly known to Eriugena; see Martianus Capella, *On the Marriage of Mercury and Philology* IV. 400–1.

20 See Martianus Capella, *On the Marriage of Mercury and Philology* IV. 352–4.

21 I. 441A–442B. Eriugena himself seems to envisage a diagram in the form:

The notation A, B . . . 1, 2 . . . is not provided by Eriugena.

22 I. 442A–B, II. 525A, II. 526C–527A, II. 527C. The fourfold schema is repeated later in *Periphyseon* but with no additions to the basic doctrine. Cf. III. 688C–689A, IV. 743B–C, V. 1019A–B.

23 See Eriugena, *Homily on the Prologue to John* [6.9] 14, 291B–C. The analogy between the cosmos and a book was derived from Maximus the Confessor, *Ambigua* 1245A–1248A. See Duclow [6.47] 131–40.

24 Eriugena is here elevating a standard Carolingian literary practice – illustrated by Alcuin, Hrabanus Maurus, Ratramnus of Corbie, etc. – to a more philosophical level.

25 For example, see Kristeva, J., *Sēmeiōtikē. Recherches pour une sémanalyse*, Paris, 1969, pp. 143ff., 181–2, etc.

26 A complete inventory can be found in Madec [6.53].

27 I. 509B–510B, II. 617A–620A. Cf. Eriugena, *Commentary on pseudo-Dionysius' Celestial Hierarchy*, passim.

28 For the Augustinian citations see Madec [6.53]. These are peculiar in being (a) extremely frequent, (b) generally brief, and (c) somewhat oblique.

29 I. 463Aff. This text is paraphrased rather than quoted. Eriugena associates the material with 'Aristotle', and tends not to quote secular authors verbatim.

30 III. 716B–719A. Paraphrase only.

31 III. 654A–655C. Paraphrase only. For Eriugena, naturally, Boethius ranks among the Christian authors. However, his *On Arithmetic* – the only text cited in *Periphyseon* – is thoroughly secular in character.

32 On connotation and denotation in Eriugena see below.

33 The hierarchy is as follows: Greek Christian writers are preferred to Latin Christian writers, and Christian writers to pagan writers.

34 I. 476C–477B. 'Plato' may be considered a Latin author, since Eriugena knew only Calcidius' Latin translation of the *Timaeus*.

35 I. 458Aff. 'Aristotle' may be treated as a Latin author, since Eriugena relied entirely on Aristotelian testimonia in pseudo-Augustine and others.

36 I. 446A–451C. A 'theophany' is an appearance of God. Eriugena held that God is *never* cognized directly, but only in theophanies.

37 I. 486B–D, II. 567Aff. Cf. II. 602D–603C, 610B–611A. It is highly significant that the references to the Greek Fathers are made by the 'Teacher' and those to the Latin Fathers by the 'Student' in the *Periphyseon*'s dialogue.

38 For example, see Barthes, R., *SZ*, English trans., New York, 1974, pp. 1–16.

39 For example, see Derrida, J. *Margins of Philosophy*, English trans., Brighton, 1982, pp. 209ff.

40 I shall follow the predominant usage of modern semantic theory where the 'denotation' of a term is a primary meaning, the 'connotation' a secondary one. In realist semantics, where denotation can be associated with a term's 'reference' to an object and connotation with its 'sense' – using Frege's nomenclature – the distinction between denotation and connotation is easy to maintain; but in strict nominalism where denotation cannot be associated with a term's 'reference' to an object, the distinction between denotation and connotation becomes problematic.

41 Given that early medieval theologians assume (a) that a spiritual meaning resides behind the literal meaning of biblical texts and (b) that the spiritual meaning is the ultimate truth underlying the derivative truth of the literal meaning, they share one important assumption with the realist semantic theory discussed above: that there is an ontologically grounded primary meaning. On the relation between medieval exegesis and polysemy see Eco, U., *Semiotics and the Philosophy of Language*, London, 1984, pp. 147–53.

42 See Eco, *Semiotics*, pp. 153ff.

43 Eriugena's contribution to the understanding of this question – and therefore to medieval semantic theory in general – has not been studied to date. However, there are some useful comments in Beierwaltes [6.41].

44 Eriugena, *Commentary on Martianus Capella* [6.2] pr. 3, 16–22. 'Wishing to write about the seven liberal arts, he invented a certain story about the marriage of Philology and Mercury. And this was not without the display of a most subtle intelligence, for Philology represents the love of reason and Mercury the eloquence of speech. If these have come together as though by a certain marriage in the souls of those pursuing the study of wisdom, it is possible to arrive without any difficulty at knowledge and possession of the liberal arts.'

45 The impact of the polysemous tendency initiated by Martianus Capella on medieval writers has gone largely unnoticed. Thus Kristeva, *Sēmeiōtikē*, pp. 168–9, contrasts a 'Menippean' polysemy with the theocentric monosemy of the medievals. Yet *On the Marriage of Mercury and Philology* is one example of ancient Menippean satire which became standard reading in medieval schools.

46 I. 454B 'For our intellect, too, before it enters into thought and memory is not unreasonably said not to be. It is invisible in itself and known to nobody besides God and ourselves. But when it has entered into thoughts and acquires form in certain phantasies, it is not undeservedly said to come into being. For it comes to be in the memory when it acquires certain forms of things, sounds, colours, and other sensibles, having had no form before it entered into memory. Then it receives a kind of second formation when it is formed in certain signs

of forms or sounds – I mean letters which are signs of sounds and figures which are signs of mathematical forms – or in other sensible indicators by which it can be introduced into the senses of those who are sentient.'

47 II. 572C–573B 'There are three universal motions of soul of which the first is according to mind, the second according to reason, and the third according to sense. The first is simple, above the nature of the soul itself, and devoid of interpretation: that is, knowledge of that around which it moves. "Through it, the soul moves around the unknown God but, because of his excellence, in no way has knowledge of him derived from anything which exists" as to what he is – that is, it cannot find him in any essence or substance or in anything which can be said or understood, for he surpasses everything which is or is not and cannot be defined in any manner as to what he is. The second motion is that by which the soul "defines the unknown God as being the cause" of all things. For it defines God to be cause of all things, this motion being within the nature of soul. It is that "through which the soul moved naturally imposes on itself through the activity of knowledge all the natural reasons formative of all things which subsist as having been eternally made in him who is known only causally" – for he is known because he is cause: that is, it expresses them in itself through its knowledge of them, this knowledge itself being born in the second motion from the first. The third motion is "the composite one through which the soul comes into contact with eternal things and reforms the reasons of the visible in itself as though through certain signs." It is described as composite not because it is not simple in itself as the first and second motions are simple but because it begins to know the reasons of sensible things not through themselves.' In this passage, a good example of Eriugena's intertextual method, the words of Maximus appear between quotation marks.

48 The Trinitarian analogy will be more explicit in Anselm of Canterbury's development of the same theme. See p. 135.

49 Aristotle, *On Interpretation* 1, 16a1ff. See Kretzmann, N. 'Aristotle on spoken sound significant by convention', in J. Corcoran (ed.) *Ancient Logic and its Modern Interpretations*, Dordrecht, 1974, pp. 3–21; Lieb, H. 'Das "semiotische Dreieck" bei Ogden und Richards. Eine Neuformulierung des Zeichenmodells von Aristoteles', in H. Geckeler (ed.) *Logos Semantikos*, Berlin, 1981, pp. 137–56; and Weidemann, H. 'Ansätze zu einer semantischen Theorie bei Aristoteles', *Zeitschrift für Semiotik* 4 (1982): 241–57.

50 This influence is documented in standard works on the history of medieval semantics. See especially, Kretzmann, N., 'Semantics, History of', in P. Edwards (ed.) *The Encyclopedia of Philosophy*, vol. 7, New York, 1967, pp. 362–3, 365ff.; Pinborg [6.36] 29ff. and Eco [6.29].

51 See Saussure, *Course in General Linguistics*, pp. 65–70, 111ff. The same fusion occurs in the semiotic theory of Peirce. See Peirce, C. S., *Collected Papers*, vol. 5, ed. C. Hartshorne and P. Weiss, Cambridge, Mass., 1931–58, p. 314, etc.

52 See Klinck [6.32] for the medieval tradition in general.

53 V. 867A–B. These etymologies are all based on the Greek. However, Eriugena also explores Graeco-Latin etymologies at III. 697A (*ouranos/caelum*), V. 954D–955A (*aidēs/infernus*). An etymology based on the Latin occurs at I. 494D–495A.

54 This situation is naturally conducive to polysemy. Fusion of real and verbal

parallels and complements the fusion of cognitive and verbal described on p. 128.

55 III. 668C–D. Cf. *Commentary on 'Celestial Hierarchy'* 4. 314–25.

56 II. 580C–581A. The passage is particularly interesting when combined with III. 624A–625A. Since this states that the order of the divine names is – according to Eriugena's philosophical idealism – partially dependent on the human mind's perception, the etymological activity of II. 580Cff. must be not only the discovery but also the positing of 'reality' itself. There is another complex etymology at V. 1003B–D.

57 The precise nature of metaphor is a matter of controversy. However, it clearly represents a specific application of the concept of polysemy where the primary meaning of a metaphorized term is the secondary meaning of the metaphorizing term and vice versa.

58 See *To Herennius* IV. 34. 45, Quintilian, *Institutes of Oratory* VIII. 6. 4ff., Martianus Capella, *On the Marriage* IV. 359–60, Isidore of Seville, *Etymologies* I. 37. 5, etc.

59 See I. 458C, I. 461C, I. 463B, etc. This application of metaphor is discussed by Beierwaltes, W., 'Negati affirmatio. Welt als Metapher. Zur Grundlegung einer mittelalterlichen Ästhetik durch Johannes Scotus Eriugena', *Philosophisches Jahrbuch* 83 (1976): 237–65.

60 Traditionally, synecdoche occurs in two forms – transference from whole to part and transference from part to whole – and is therefore already bilateral. See *To Herennius* IV. 33. 44.

61 I. 459C. 'But since the divine significations which are predicated of God by transference from the creature to the creator in Holy Scripture – if indeed it is rightly said that anything can be predicated of him (which we should consider elsewhere) – are innumerable and cannot be discovered or collected together in the smallness of our reasoning, only a few such divine names should be set down by way of illustration'; I. 461C. 'For the statement "It is Truth" does not affirm that the divine nature is Truth in a proper sense but that it can be called by such a name in a metaphor from the creature to the creator. It clothes the divine essence which is naked and devoid of all proper signification with such words'; I. 463B–C. 'But as we have said above, just as almost all things which are properly predicated of the nature of created things can be said metaphorically of the creator of things in order to signify, so also the significations of the categories which are discerned properly in created things can be uttered not absurdly concerning the cause of all – not to signify properly what it is but to suggest in a transferred mode what we should reasonably think about it when investigating it in some fashion'; I. 480B. 'So if all things which are are rightly predicated of God not properly but by a kind of transference since they derive from him, why is it surprising that all things which are in place – since they seem to be enclosed everywhere by greater things – can be called places although none of them is properly a place but is contained within what is place in its proper nature?' Cf. III. 624A–625A.

62 I. 480B–C. 'We see that those things which are contained are named after the things which contain them through metonymy – that is, transferred naming – although they are not so contained by them that they are unable to subsist in their natural limits without them. It is the common practice of mortals to call

the wife or the family a "house" although these things are naturally distinct. For it is not the house which confers substantial existence on the wife or the family but the place of their own nature. Yet because they possess that existence in the house they are accustomed to be named after it. Likewise the things which contain are named after the things which are contained. For example: air contains light, and so air which is illuminated is called "light"; the eye is called "sight" or "vision" although according to its proper nature it is neither sight nor vision'. Cf. I. 450A–B, I. 515B–C, V. 876A–B, V. 1021B.

63 III. 706A–B. 'Not unreasonably, given that it is the most common practice of Holy Scripture to signify the natural subsistences and reasons of invisible things with words signifying visible things, in order to train pious philosophers. And this is not surprising, since the same practice has the very frequent custom of suggesting corporeal and sensible things with the names of spiritual and invisible things. Since there are many and innumerable examples of this reciprocal metaphoricity and they are very well known to all those trained in Holy Scripture, it would appear to be a lengthy and superfluous task to amass them in the present discussion. However, let us use a few illustrations: "That which is born of flesh is flesh" – here the entire man born in original sin is called by the name "flesh" – "And that which is born of the spirit is spirit" – the entire man reborn through regeneration in Christ is expressed by the term "spirit". And if somebody says that it is not the entire man but only the flesh of a man that is born of flesh, I shall reply that it is therefore not the entire man but only the soul that is born of spirit and if so it follows that there is no grace to benefit the baptized bodies. But if the entire man, namely soul and body, is reborn in Christ and becomes spirit, then necessarily the entire man is born of flesh in Adam and is flesh, from which it is concluded that the flesh is called spirit and the spirit flesh. The Word of God is called flesh and flesh the Word, and there are similar cases where both synecdoche and metaphor are understood simultaneously.'

64 See Richards, I. A., *The Philosophy of Rhetoric*, New York, 1936, pp. 89ff. The distinction between 'comparison' and 'fusion' theories of metaphor owes something to Black, M., *Models and Metaphors*, Ithaca, NY, 1962, pp. 25ff., who sets out a complete typology consisting of substitutive, comparative, and interactive approaches.

65 The problems associated with polysemy were formally discussed in pseudo-Augustine, *Ten Categories* 9. 135, 13ff., a text with which Eriugena was particularly familiar. Cf. Martianus Capella, *On the Marriage* IV. 355–7.

66 The volume of essays, Beierwaltes [6.42], setting out to prove that Eriugena exercised significant influence over later medieval thinkers, has not achieved the desired result. In fact, the following conclusions now seem to have been established: (1) Eriugena's influence was considerable for one or two generations after his time (the evidence: Heiric of Auxerre, Remigius of Auxerre, and other glossators); (2) In the eleventh century there are only a few traces of his influence, e.g. in Hrotsvitha of Gandersheim; (3) Eriugena's influence becomes more noticeable from the beginning of the twelfth century but only in certain respects: (a) His ideas influence many in a negative sense (the evidence: copies of Eriugenian MSS, polemic against him), (b) He is influential as translator of pseudo-Dionysius, (c) His ideas influence a few in a positive sense (the evidence:

Honorius Augustodunensis, 'Marius', *On the Elements*). See also Lucentini [6.52].

67 Edited by Marenbon [5.84] 173ff. Eriugena also influenced the gloss tradition on Martianus Capella in a manner now difficult to describe precisely; see Schrimpf [6.58].

68 Gloss I in Marenbon's edition.

69 Gloss IIIb in Marenbon's edition.

70 On the Boethian logical tradition in the Middle Ages see van de Vyver [6.37] and Minio-Paluello [6.34].

71 On Gerbert's work in general see the collection *Gerberto, Scienza, Storia e Mito* [6.61]. This includes papers by Riché [6.62] – stressing the important of Boethius – and Frova [6.60].

72 On the term 'semiotic' see note 14.

73 Gerbert, [6.16] 6, pp. 301ff. Gerbert here systematizes material in Aristotle, *On Interpretation* 13. 23a 21–5.

74 The most useful book providing a general introduction to Anselm's life and works is Hopkins [6.22]. Among other modern studies, Kohlenberger [6.70] and Evans, G. R., *Anselm and Talking about God*, Oxford, 1978 should be mentioned.

75 The first interpretation predominates at 9, 24. 7 to 10, 25. 27, the second at 1, 13. 1 to 4, 18. 3. Both are perfectly standard in the Augustinian tradition which Anselm represents.

76 The type of causality (efficient) is discussed at 6, 18. 18 to 7. 22, 10.

77 The semiotic always implies the semantic even though the reverse is not the case.

78 [6.11] I: 14. 5ff. 'It is therefore easy for someone to say to himself silently: Since the goods are so numerous whose great diversity we both perceive through the bodily senses and discern by the reason of the mind, should we believe that there is one thing through which alone whatever things are good are good or are things which are good good through one another? But it is absolutely certain and clear to all those willing to pay attention that whatever things are called something in such a way as to be called this in greater or lesser or equal degree in respect of one another, are called this through something which is understood not differently in different things but the same in each case, whether it be considered as equally or unequally present in them ... Therefore, since it is certain that all good things, if compared to one another, are either equally or unequally good, it is necessary that all good things are good through something which is understood as the same in different things, although sometimes good things seem to be called good through one another ... But who would doubt that that through which all good things are good is a great good? So it is good through itself, since every good is good through it. Therefore it follows that all other goods are good through something other than that which they are themselves, and that only this other is good through itself. But no good which is good through another is equal to or greater than that good which is good through itself. So that alone is supremely good which is only good through itself, for that is supreme which so excels others that it has neither an equal nor a superior.'

79 This is one feature reinforcing the picture of Anselm as a Platonic realist. That he was moving away from this position was argued by Schmitt [6.72]. However, the only evidence for such an interpretation is an apparently non-realist handling

of abstract terms to be discussed on p. 135. Anselm's position as a Platonic realist is examined by Flasch [6.67] and Adams [6.65].

80　In Anselm's writing, the term *ratio* itself has a multiplicity of connotations given by the earlier textual tradition: ontological, theological, epistemological, psychological and logical. See Gersh [6.68].

81　[6.11] I, pr. 13 On the textual background to Anselm's argument see Audet [6.66] and Nothdurft [6.35].

82　The modern discussion seems to have begun with Frege about 1892. See Frege, G., 'On sense and reference', pp. 118–40 and Russell, B., 'On denoting', pp. 143–58, both in F. Zabeeh (ed.) *Readings in Semantics*, Urbana, Ill., 1974.

83　Cf. note 79. To the question whether Anselm saw any inconsistency between these two positions the answer is uncertain. However, since he probably viewed the signifieds of *De grammatico* but apparently not the transcendent properties of *Monologion* as universals in the logical sense, the philosophical problems raised by the two treatises were more easily separated for him than they are for his modern reader. The issue of universality is first raised at *Monologion* 27, [6.11] I. 45. 1–22.

84　See Augustine, *On the Trinity* X. 1ff., XV. 10–16. On the history of this theory see Colish [6.28] 50–1, 99.

85　The threefold division in this text: sensible signs + sensible manner, sensible signs + insensible manner, sensible signs + neither sensible nor insensible manner, juxtaposes semiotic categories in a manner recalling Eriugena. See n. 19.

86　Anselm does not himself employ the terms 'unmotivated' and 'non-universal' here. However, he clearly views the first type of sign as defined negatively with respect to the third type. The latter will be specified as motivated and universal.

87　Anselm says that the third type of sign is 'natural' (*naturalis*) apparently meaning that it is motivated. In modern linguistic theory, a motivated sign is one whose signifier and signified are related analogically. See Barthes, *SZ* pp. 114ff.

88　*Monologion* 10 [6.11] I:24. 29ff. 'It is noted in common usage that we can speak of a single thing in three ways. We speak of things either by using sensible signs – that is, signs which can be perceived by bodily senses – in a sensible manner; or by thinking the same signs which are sensible externally in an insensible manner within ourselves; or by neither using these signs in a sensible nor an insensible manner but by speaking of the things themselves inwardly in our mind through imagination of the bodily or through a rational understanding in place of the diversity of things themselves. For I speak of the man in one way when I signify him with the name "man", in another when I think the same name silently, and in another when my mind contemplates that same man either through an image of the bodily or through reason. It is through an image of the bodily when the mind imagines his sensible shape, but it is through reason when it thinks his universal essence which is "animal, rational, mortal". Of these three ways of speaking each consists of its own kind of words. However, the words of that speech which I have posited as third and last – when they are of things which are not unknown – are natural and the same among all races.' In this passage, Anselm develops the theory which he found in Aristotle's *On Interpretation*; see p. 129.

89　Anselm states unambiguously that even the third type of speaking constitutes sign-manipulation of a sort.

90 *Monologion* 65 [6.11] I: 75. 17–65, 77. 3. The reference to transformation of meaning indicates metaphoricity.

91 It is possible to treat the statement at *Proslogion* 15 [6.11] I: 112. 12–17 that God is 'something greater than can be thought' (*quiddam maius quam cogitari possit*) as a correction of the famous premiss of *Proslogion* 2 [6.11] I: 101. 4–5. If so, Anselm is pointing out that the ontological argument is in the final analysis only an image of the truth.

BIBLIOGRAPHY

Original Language Editions

Eriugena

6.1 Floss, H. J. (ed.) *Joannis Scoti opera quae supersunt omnia* (MPL 122), Paris, 1853.

6.2 Lutz, C. E. (ed.) *Annotationes in Marcianum*, Cambridge, Mass., 1939.

6.3 Jeauneau, E. (ed.) Commentary on Martianus, Book I, in Oxford, Bodleian Auct. T. II. 18, in *Quatre thèmes érigéniens*, Montreal and Paris, 1978.

6.4 Madec, G. (ed.) *De praedestinatione*, (CC c.m. 50), Turnhout, 1978.

6.5 Sheldon-Williams, I. P. (ed.) *Periphyseon* I–III with facing English translation, Dublin, 1968–81 (Scriptores latini hiberniae 7, 9, 11). (On this problematic edition, see P. Lucentini, 'La nuova edizione del "Periphyseon" dell'Eriugena', *Studi medievali*, 3a serie, 17(1), 1976.)

6.6 Jeauneau, E. (ed.) *Periphyseon* IV with facing English translation by J. J. O'Meara and I. P. Sheldon-Williams (Scriptores latini hiberniae 13), Dublin, 1995.

6.7 —— (ed.) *Periphyseon* I (CC c.m. 161), Turnhout, 1996.

6.8 Barbet, J. (ed.) *Expositiones in Ierarchiam Coelestem* (CC c.m. 31), Turnhout, 1975.

6.9 Jeauneau, E. (ed.) *Homélie sur le Prologue de Jean* with parallel French translation (Sources chrétiennes 151), Paris, 1969.

6.10 —— (ed.) *Commentaire sur Jean* with parallel French translation (Sources chrétiennes 180), Paris, 1972.

Anselm

6.11 Schmitt, F. S. (ed.) *Opera omnia* I, II, Edinburgh, 1946. (These volumes contain all the philosophical works except for those in [6.12].)

6.12 Philosophical fragments, edited in F. S. Schmitt and R. W. Southern, *Memorials of St Anselm*, Oxford, 1969.

6.13 Charlesworth, M. J. *Proslogion* with parallel English translation and commentary, Oxford, 1965.

6.14 Henry, D. P. *The De Grammatico of St Anselm: The Theory of Paronymy*, Notre Dame, Ind., 1964.

6.15 —— *Commentary on De grammatico: the Historico-logical Dimensions of a Dialogue of St Anselm's*, Dordrecht and Boston, 1974. (Both [6.14] and [6.15] contain the text, translation and detailed commentary on this dialogue.)

Gerbert

6.16 Olleris, A. (ed.) *Oeuvres de Gerbert*, Clermont-Ferrand and Paris, 1867.

English Translations

Eriugena

6.17 Sheldon-Williams, I. P. (but issued under the name of J. J. O'Meara), *Periphyseon (The Division of Nature)*, Montreal and Washington, 1987.
6.18 Homily on Prologue to John, translated in J. J. O'Meara, *Eriugena*, Oxford, 1978.

Anselm

6.19 Hopkins, J. and Richardson, H. *Anselm of Canterbury* I–IV (complete philosophical and theological works), London, Toronto and New York, 1974–6.

Bibliographies, Concordances and Handbooks

6.20 Brennan, M. *A Guide to Eriugenian Studies*, Fribourg and Paris, 1989.
6.21 G. H. Allard (ed.) *Periphyseon – indices générales*, Montreal and Paris, 1983.
6.22 Hopkins, J. *A Companion to the Study of St Anselm*, Minneapolis, Minn., 1972.
6.23 Evans, G. R. (ed.) *A Concordance for the Works of St Anselm*, 4 vols, Millwood, NY, 1984.

Biographies

6.24 Cappuyns, M. *Jean Scot Erigène. Sa vie, son oeuvre, sa pensée*, Louvain and Paris, 1933.
6.25 Southern, R. W. (ed. and trans.) *The Life of St Anselm, Archbishop of Canterbury, by Eadmer*, London, 1962.
6.26 —— *St Anselm and his Biographer: a Study of Monastic Life and Thought 1059–c.1130*, Cambridge, 1963.
6.27 —— *Anselm, a Portrait in a Landscape*, Cambridge, 1990.

General and Background Studies

6.28 Colish, M. *The Mirror of Language: a Study in the Medieval Theory of Knowledge*, 2nd edn, Lincoln, Neb., 1983.
6.29 Eco, U. 'Denotation', in [6.30] 43–77.
6.30 Eco, U. and Marmo, C. (eds) *On the Medieval Theory of Signs*, Amsterdam and Philadelphia, Pa., 1989.

6.31 Hadot, P. *Porphyre et Victorinus*, Paris, 1968.

6.32 Klinck, R. *Die lateinische Etymologie des Mittelalters*, Munich, 1970.

6.33 Marenbon, J. *Early Medieval Philosophy (480–1150): an Introduction*, 2nd edn, London, 1988.

6.34 Minio-Paluello, L. *Opuscula: the Latin Aristotle*, Amsterdam, 1972.

6.35 Nothdurft, K. D. *Studien zum Einfluss Senecas auf die Philosophie und Theologie des zwölften Jahrhunderts*, Leiden and Cologne, 1963, pp. 192–7.

6.36 Pinborg, J. *Logik und Semantik im Mittelalter. Ein Überblick*, Stuttgart and Bad Cannstatt, 1972.

6.37 Vyver, A. van de 'Les étapes du développement philosophique du haut moyen âge', *Revue belge de philologie et d'histoire* 8 (1929): 425–52.

Studies on Eriugena

6.38 Allard, G.-H. (ed.) *Jean Scot écrivain*, Montreal and Paris, 1986.

6.39 Beierwaltes, W. 'Negati affirmatio. Welt als Metapher. Zur Grundlegung einer mittelalterlichen Ästhetik durch Johannes Scotus Eriugena', *Philosophisches Jahrbuch* 83 (1976): 237–65; repr. in Beierwaltes [6.44], 115–58.

6.40 —— (ed.) *Eriugena. Studien zu seinen Quellen*, Heidelberg, 1980.

6.41 —— 'Language and object: Reflections on Eriugena's valuation of the function and capacities of language', in [6.38] 209–28.

6.42 —— (ed.) *Eriugena Redivivus: Zur Wirkungsgeschichte seines Denkens im Mittelalter und im Übergang zur Neuzeit*, Heidelberg, 1987.

6.43 —— (ed.) *Eriugena: Begriff und Metapher*, Heidelberg, 1990.

6.44 —— *Eriugena. Grundzüge seines Denkens*, Frankfurt, 1994.

6.45 Boeuff, P. le 'Un commentaire érigénien du "De musica"', *Recherches Augustiniennes* 22 (1987): 271–309.

6.46 Cristiani, M. 'Nature-essence et nature-langage: notes sur l'emploi du terme "natura" dans le "Periphyseon" de Jean Erigène', *Sprache und Erkenntnis im Mittelalter* (Miscellanea Mediavalia 13, 2), Berlin and New York, 1981, pp. 707–17.

6.47 Duclow, D. F. 'Nature as speech and book in John Scotus Eriugena', *Mediaevalia* 3 (1977): 131–40.

6.48 Flasch, K. 'Zur Rehabilitierung der Relation: Die Theorie der Beziehung bei Johannes Eriugena', *Philosophie als Beziehungs – Wissenschaft (Festschrift Schaaf)*, Frankfurt-on-Main, 1971, pp. 1–25.

6.49 Gersh, S. *From Iamblichus to Eriugena*, Leiden, 1978.

6.50 —— 'Omnipresence in Eriugena: Some reflections on Augustino-Maximian elements in Periphyseon', in Beierwaltes [6.40] 55–74.

6.51 Jeauneau, E. *Etudes érigéniennes*, Paris, 1987.

6.52 Lucentini, P. *Platonismo medievale: Contributi per la storia dell'Eriugenismo*, Florence, 1979.

6.53 Madec, G. 'Jean Scot et ses auteurs', in Allard [6.38] 143–86.

6.54 Moran, D. *The Philosophy of John Scottus Eriugena*, Cambridge, 1989.

6.55 O'Meara, J. J. and Bieler, L. (eds) *The Mind of Eriugena*, Dublin, 1973.

6.56 Onofrio, G. d' 'Über die Natur der Einteilung: Die dialektische Entfaltung von Eriugenas Denken', in Beierwaltes [6.43] 17–38.

6.57 Roques, R. (ed.) *Jean Scot Erigène et l'histoire de la philosophie*, Paris, 1977.
6.58 Schrimpf, G. 'Zur Frage der Authentizität unserer Texte von Johannes Scottus' "Annotationes in Martianum"' in [6.55] 125–38.
6.59 —— *Das Werk des Johannes Scottus Eriugena im Rahmen des Wissenschaftsverständnisses seiner Zeit. Eine Hinführung zu Periphyseon* (BGPTMA 23), Münster, 1982.

Studies on Gerbert and his contemporaries

6.60 Frova, C. 'Gerberto *philosophus*: Il *De rationali et ratione uti*', in [6.61] 351–77.
6.61 *Gerberto, Scienza, Storia e Mito, Atti del Gerberti, Symposium*, Bobbio, 1985.
6.62 Riché, P. 'L'enseignement de Gerbert à Reims dans le contexte européen', *Gerberto. Scienza, Storia e Mito* [6.61] 51–69.
6.63 Rijk, L. M. de 'On the curriculum of the arts of the Trivium at St Gall from *c.* 850–*c.* 1000', *Vivarium* 1 (1963): 35–86.
6.64 —— 'Les oeuvres inédites d'Abbon de Fleury', *Revue bénédictine* 47 (1935): 125–69.

Studies on Anselm

6.65 Adams, M. M. 'Was Anselm a realist? The *Monologium*', *Franciscan Studies* 32 (1972): 5–14.
6.66 Audet, T. A. 'Une source augustinienne de l'argument de saint Anselme', in J. Maritain *et al. Etienne Gilson, philosophe de la Chrétienté*, Paris, 1949, pp. 105–42.
6.67 Flasch, K. 'Der philosophische Ansatz des Anselm von Canterbury im *Monologion* und sein Verhältnis zum augustinischen Neuplatonismus', *Analecta Anselmiana* 2 (1970): 1–43.
6.68 Gersh, S. 'Anselm of Canterbury', in P. Dronke (ed.) *A History of Twelfth-century Western Philosophy*, Cambridge, 1988, pp. 255–78.
6.69 Henry, D. P. *The Logic of St Anselm*, Oxford, 1967.
6.70 Kohlenberger, H., *Similitudo und ratio. Überlegungen zur Methode bei Anselm von Canterbury*, Bonn, 1972.
6.71 Koyré, A. *L'idée de Dieu dans la philosophie de saint Anselme*, Paris, 1923.
6.72 Schmitt, F. S. 'Anselm und der (Neu-)Platonismus', *Analecta Anselmiana* 1 (1969): 39–71.
6.73 Serene, E. 'Anselm's modal conceptions', in S. Knuuttila (ed.) *Reforging the Great Chain of Being* (Synthese Historical Library 20), Dordrecht and Boston, 1981.
6.74 Vuillemin, J. *Le Dieu d'Anselme et les apparences de la raison*, Paris, 1971.

Studies of the Ontological Argument

6.75 Gale, R. M. *On the Nature and Existence of God*, Cambridge, 1991, pp. 201–37.
6.76 Gombocz, W. 'Zur neueren Beiträgen zur Interpretation von Anselms Proslogion', *Salzburger Jahrbuch für Philosophie* 20 (1975): 131–5.
6.77 Henry, D. 'The *Proslogion* proofs', *Philosophical Quarterly* 5 (1955): 147–51.

6.78 Hick, J. and McGill, A. C. *The Many-Faced Argument*, New York, 1967.

6.79 La Croix, R. R. *Proslogion II and III: a Third Interpretation of Anselm's Argument*, Leiden, 1972.

6.80 Lewis, D. K. 'Anselm and actuality', in *Philosophical Papers* I, New York, 1983.

6.81 Malcolm, N. 'Anselm's ontological arguments', *Philosophical Review* 69 (1960): 41–62.

6.82 Plantinga, A. 'God and necessity', in *The Nature of Necessity*, Oxford, 1974.

CHAPTER 7

The twelfth century

John Marenbon

∾ INTRODUCTION ∾

The twelfth century began and ended with events which mark it off, at least symbolically, as a discrete period in the history of Western philosophy. It was in about 1100 that Abelard – the most wide-ranging and profound philosopher of the period – arrived in Paris to study, and very soon to teach, logic. The competing, quarrelling, disorganized schools of Paris, whose growth Abelard did so much to stimulate, would be the setting for much of what was liveliest and most sophisticated in twelfth-century philosophy. It was in the year 1200 that Philip Augustus issued the privilege to the schools of Paris which, symbolically at least, marks the beginning of Paris University. The schools would henceforth become a more homogeneous and tightly-regulated organization, imposing a rigid framework on thirteenth- and fourteenth-century scholastic thought. Works newly translated from the Greek and Arabic gradually entered the curriculum and the work of almost all the twelfth-century philosophers was rapidly forgotten.

Modern historians of philosophy have set out to repair this neglect. But (at least until very recently) they have characterized the period in two main ways, each of which leaves in question whether twelfth-century philosophy itself contains much worth studying. The first way has been to see the time as one of beginnings. Between 1100 and 1200, it is said, the ground was prepared for the great flourishing of scholasticism in the mid- and late thirteenth century. Such a description might well suggest that the twelfth century, fascinating as it may be for the intellectual historian who wishes to see how, and against what background, ideas develop, produced little of independent philosophical interest.

The second way of characterizing the twelfth century has been in terms of its 'humanism' (and, closely linked to this, as a time of

150

'renaissance'). The period is presented as one of revived activity in all branches of learning, closely connected with a respect for the classical past and a wish to rediscover its literature in all its various branches, poetic, scientific, legal and philosophical. The achievements of the thirteenth century are presented as being narrower: its sophistication in logic, philosophy and theology must be balanced against the aridity of the scholastics' style, their rejection of the variety and complexity in form found in twelfth-century writing, their apparent contempt for poetry and fine latinity. Such a contrast can easily be turned against the thinkers of the twelfth century by the modern reader of philosophy. They are suspected of being dilettantes; their writings, full of interest to the literary historian, are thought to lack the precision and single-mindedness necessary for good philosophy.[1]

There is some truth in the rationale behind each approach. Twelfth-century scholars did, indeed, elaborate the logical and theological techniques which served the philosophers of the thirteenth- and fourteenth-century universities. Many were attentive to the literary form of their writings and enthusiasts of ancient literature as well as ancient philosophy. And even the sharpest-minded of them, such as Abelard, can be clumsy or imprecise in their technical vocabulary and sometimes inattentive to the complexity of the issues they are treating; whilst some well-known thinkers of the time, especially those most influenced by Platonism, are more inclined to system building than to detailed argument and analysis. Yet there is a substantial body of twelfth-century thought sufficiently rigorous to require careful philosophical analysis and certainly interesting and unusual enough to deserve attention in its own right, rather than just as the forerunner of something else. Much of it is linked to the most striking feature of intellectual life in the period: the importance of the 'trivium': the three language-based disciplines of grammar, rhetoric and, most prominently, logic. (Indeed, the humanistic interest in ancient literature and in rhetoric was part of a general enthusiasm for the verbal arts, among which logic was dominant.)

This chapter must be selective. More than half of it is devoted to the outstanding philosophers of the time: Peter Abelard and his near-contemporary, Gilbert of Poitiers. The section following this one looks more briefly at four important masters working at the turn of the century. A later section sketches the Platonic current in twelfth-century thought, looking especially at the work of William of Conches and Thierry of Chartres. The concluding sections provide a quick introduction to the logical schools and theological methods of the period from 1150 to 1200, a time still far less well investigated than the previous half century.

ᕥ FOUR MASTERS AT THE BEGINNING ᕥ
OF THE CENTURY

Four masters, already established by 1100 or shortly afterwards, indicate the most important directions philosophy would take in the century which followed. Three of them, Garlandus of Besançon, Roscelin of Compiègne and William of Champeaux, were logicians, although Roscelin also put forward controversial views on the Trinity and William would write on moral and theological topics, such as natural law, sin and free will. Bernard of Chartres, however, was a grammarian, interested both in grammatical theory and in careful reading of ancient pagan philosophical texts, in particular Plato's *Timaeus*.

The tradition of medieval logic was well established by the late eleventh century. Like other branches of study in the Middle Ages, it was based on ancient texts. Six were in common use by 1100: Aristotle's *Categories* and *On Interpretation*, Porphyry's *Isagoge* (all in Boethius' translations, and approached using Boethius' commentaries) and Boethius' own *On Division*, treatises on categorical and hypothetical syllogisms and *On Topical 'differentiae'*. Taken together, these works provided an introduction to constructing and analysing arguments. The *Isagoge* and the *Categories* could be read as guides to the various sorts of term which can appear as subject or predicate in a statement. *On Interpretation* explained how terms are combined to make statements, and how statements are related to each other as, for instance, contraries ('All men are bald' – 'No man is bald') or contradictories ('All men are bald' – 'Some man is not bald'). Students could then learn from Boethius' own textbooks how to construct syllogistic arguments, either using atomic statements as premisses so as to form categorical syllogisms or molecular statements as premisses to form hypothetical syllogisms, and they could study arguments based on 'topics', commonly accepted maxims of reasoning.[2] These texts, especially the two by Aristotle, also contain far more than such an introduction. The *Categories* can be read as the concise statement of an ontology, whilst the *On Interpretation* raises problems about the nature of truth and meaning, about perception and knowledge, and about modality and free will. Sporadic evidence – occasional glosses, and passages in Peter Damian and Anselm of Canterbury – suggests that eleventh-century scholars were already aware of some wider implications of the logical texts. But the main emphasis at this stage seems to have been on mastering the basic skills of logic through careful study of the texts. If more digressive discussion was wanted, the earliest commentators were happy to turn to Boethius and copy passages of his commentaries verbatim.[3]

Garlandus of Besançon is known for his *Dialectica*, a comprehensive textbook on logic which was probably written at the turn of the twelfth century. Some scholars have described Garlandus as an early nominalist: an exponent of the view that nothing exists which is not a particular. But it is more accurate to see him as following a particular interpretative method in his approach to the *Isagoge* and the *Categories*. In common with a number of other scholars of the time (including the young Abelard), Garlandus read these texts *in voce* rather than *in re*: as talking not about things but about words.[4] For instance, when Porphyry writes about genera or about accidents, Garlandus takes his remarks as concerning words such as 'animal' and 'whiteness'. Roscelin's views can be surmised only from allusions (usually hostile) by other writers. The most famous of these is Anselm of Canterbury's comment that, according to Roscelin, universals are merely the puffs of air made when we speak. This might be just a jibe which draws out the consequences of *in voce* exegesis. But some scholars – especially Jean Jolivet – have given a more ambitious reconstruction of Roscelin's thinking, using other evidence too. Roscelin, they say, focused on the reference a word has to an individual, whole object in the world. In the case of the words 'genus' and 'species', he would have argued that there is no individual object in the world to which they refer, so their reference is just to other words (such as 'animal', 'man') – and, considered as things, words are just puffs of air. Whether Roscelin ever propounded this view coherently, and if so when (he was still alive in the early 1120s), is uncertain.[5]

The earliest *definite* signs of a serious interest in the semantic and metaphysical problems about universals comes from those logicians who adopted a realist view. William of Champeaux, who taught at the school of Notre Dame in Paris, was one of their leaders. For modern philosophers, the problem of universals concerns properties and relations. But William and his contemporaries approached the question mainly in the context of a remark in Porphyry's *Isagoge* about species and genera, that is to say, universal substances. They had then to consider primarily the semantics not of sentences such as 'Socrates is white', but of those such as 'Socrates is a man'. A simple view, derived from Boethius, held that there is a universal essence shared by all men, who are then individuated by their accidental attributes (being six foot tall, sitting just here at six o'clock). William was forced to abandon this theory ('material/essential essence realism') by the attacks of his former pupil, Abelard, and then espoused an 'indifference theory', according to which the many particulars of the same species are at the same time one in that they are 'not different' from each other in respect of their nature. William's interests as a logician were not, however, confined to speculations about universals. He was probably the author of a general *Introduction* to logical method, and it is clear from Abelard's *Dialectica* that he discussed the problems raised by the different meanings of the verb 'to be' – as the copula and as implying present existence.

William was a theologian as well as a logician. He studied under Anselm of Laon, a leading scriptural exegete. Like Anselm's, William's theological teaching survives in the form of 'Sentences' (*sententiae*), ranging in length from a couple of lines to several hundred words, which may originally have been stimulated by dispute over the interpretation of a passage from the Bible, but take the form of free-standing discussions of a problem. William is more speculative and more analytical than Anselm, ranging over topics such as intentions and acts, the ontological status of evil, and implicit faith. He approaches the question of divine prescience ([7.28] 195–6) and human free will in the manner of a logician, trying (though not very successfully) to show that the statement, 'It is possible for things to happen other than as they will happen' does not imply 'It is possible for God [who foresees all things] to be mistaken.'

Bernard, master at the cathedral school of Chartres in the first two decades of the century, represents a different tradition of early medieval teaching. He concentrated, not on logic, but on grammar. Part of his work as a grammarian was connected with the theory of grammar, as expounded by Priscian in his elaborate *Institutiones grammaticae*. Eleventh-century scholars had already composed a running commentary (the *Glosule*) to the *Institutiones*, which dealt with philosophical questions about semantics far more thoroughly than Priscian himself had done. Unfortunately, Bernard's work in this area is known only through a few remarks made, long after his death, by John of Salisbury.[6] John also records how Bernard commented on the Latin classics, drawing out their moral teaching and he commemorates him as the leading Platonist of his time. Bernard's Platonism seems to have owed a good deal to Boethius' *Theological Treatises*, especially in its introduction of secondary forms, enmattered images of the immaterial primary forms. But there was one work by Plato himself that was available to him and other twelfth-century scholars: the *Timaeus* in Calcidius' partial Latin translation. Recently, a strong argument has been made for attributing to Bernard a commentary on the *Timaeus*. Although these *Glosae in Platonem* are for the most part straightforwardly literal and heavily reliant on the commentary Calcidius had written, they contain Bernard's characteristic views about secondary forms and they exercised an influence on later twelfth-century exegesis of the work.[7]

❧ PETER ABELARD ❧

Peter Abelard is probably better known than any medieval philosopher, not as a thinker but as the husband of Heloise and participant in a remarkable exchange of love-letters which have held their appeal from the time of Petrarch to the present. It was in fact the castration plotted by Heloise's relatives and its consequences which gave Abelard's career its distinctive shape, splitting it roughly into two halves. From about 1102 until his castration in 1117, Abelard was a brilliant teacher of logic in Paris and in Melun and Corbeil, small towns both connected with the royal court. He had studied under both Roscelin and William of Champeaux – and quarrelled with both. Although he did teach Christian doctrine, it was a relatively unimportant part of his work. The *Dialectica*, a textbook of logic, independent in form but closely linked to exegesis of the six standard ancient texts, probably dates from the end of this period. The *Logica* ('*Ingredientibus*') – logical commentaries, of which those on the *Isagoge*, *Categories*, *De interpretatione* survive in full – was probably written up a little later, but it too reflects his teaching at this time.[8]

After the castration, Abelard became a monk of St Denis. Although he continued to teach logic, theological questions came more and more to occupy him. The first fruit of this new interest was the *Theologia summi boni*, a treatise on the Trinity, rich in philosophical discussion, which was promptly condemned at the Council of Soissons in 1121. Undeterred, Abelard greatly extended the work, developing his logical analysis of Trinitarian relations and adding a long eulogistic account of the ancient philosophers and their virtues, to form the *Theologia Christiana*. One logical work dates from the same time (the *Glossulae* on Porphyry, often called the *Logica Nostrorum petitioni sociorum*), but Abelard's main energies were given to theology and, increasingly, to ethical questions within theology. His *Collationes (Dialogue between a Christian, a Philosopher and Jew)*, probably written *c.* 1130, discuss the virtues, evil and the highest good. By this time, Abelard – who had left St Denis and, for a time, taught students at his own monastic/eremitic foundation, the Paraclete – was abbot of St Gildas, a monastery on a remote peninsula in Brittany. His attempts to reform the Breton monks proved disastrous and, from about 1133 to (probably) 1140, Abelard was teaching again in Paris. Although he gave some lectures on logic, he devoted most of his energy to developing his ethically-based theological system. The final version of his *Theologia*, the *Theologia scholarium*, a commentary on St Paul's letter to the Romans, *Sententie* recording his theology lectures, and (from *c.* 1138 to 1139) *Scito teipsum* (or, as he also called it, his *Ethics*) are the most important works from this highly productive period. At the same time, Abelard wrote extensively at the request of Heloise, who had taken over the Paraclete as abbess of a group of nuns, providing her with sermons, letters, scriptural exegesis, answers to theological queries and poetry.

Even as a young logician in Paris, Abelard had been a controversial figure, competing with William of Champeaux for students and reputation and patronized by William's enemies in the Church and at court. From the time of the Council of Soissons onwards he became a target for the hostility of the reforming party in the Church and, by the late 1130s if not earlier, for that of its leader, Bernard of Clairvaux. His campaign culminated in the Council of Sens of 1140, where Abelard was accused of nineteen heresies listed by Bernard. Abelard denied all charges of heresy, but the charges were upheld by the Pope. Abelard, now sick, spent the last two years of his life at the great abbey of Cluny and one of its dependencies. There the abbot, Peter the Venerable, ensured that the sentence of excommunication was lifted and engineered a reconciliation with Bernard.

Perhaps because of the controversies which accompanied and ended his career, Abelard has gone down in the history of philosophy as a brilliant, daring but unconstructive thinker: powerful as a logician but, otherwise, to be blamed or praised for merely applying the tools of logic to theology. This judgement is unjust, but it does reflect an important difference between Abelard, the most wide-ranging and inventive Western philosopher of the twelfth century, and the great thinkers of the thirteenth and fourteenth centuries. Unlike Aquinas, Duns Scotus and Ockham, Abelard did not combine his developments in different areas of philosophy into a single, coherent and distinctive pattern. Rather, his work falls into two separate parts, corresponding roughly to the division in his career. In his logical works he not only makes startling discoveries of a technical nature; he also reconsiders the metaphysical questions raised by Porphyry and Aristotle in the light of his nominalism, trying to arrive at an account of the basic structure of things and tackling the various aspects, semantic and metaphysical, of the problem of universals with great sophistication. In his theological writing he concentrates on developing a philosophical ethics which, where necessary, shapes the understanding of Christian doctrine to suit its requirements.

The following pages can give only an impression of some of the most philosophically interesting aspects of a thinker whose originality and breadth of vision would entitle him to much more space in a *History of Philosophy* had it not been his misfortune to live in the Middle Ages. First, his ideas on two areas connected with the more formal side of logic will be sketched: his treatment of conditionals, and his analysis of modal statements. (Many other of his more formal developments are also of great interest: for instance, his treatment of 'impersonal statements', such as 'It is good that you are here', and his discussion of the copula.)[9] Second, after a glance at his basic metaphysics, Abelard's approach to the problem of universals will be examined. Third, his account of a central area in ethics, the ethical act, will be discussed and set in context.

Abelard developed his ideas about conditionals ('if . . . then . . .' statements) mainly in considering the theory of 'topical arguments' put forward by Boethius in *On Topical 'differentiae'*.[10] He did not, however, believe that what Boethius said there about inferences could be applied directly to conditionals, partly because many of Boethius' maxims were concerned to provide probable, rhetorically convincing arguments rather than irrefragable ones, partly because – unusually for a medieval thinker – Abelard clearly distinguished between the validity of an argument and the truth of a conditional. For the truth of a conditional, his requirement was more stringent even than the modern notion of strict implication (it is impossible for the antecedent to be true and the consequent false): he also insisted on a strict criterion of relevance. For Abelard, 'if p then q' is true if and only if p 'of itself requires' q, by which Abelard means that the sense of q must be contained in that of p (Abelard [7.19] 284: 1–4). One of Abelard's reasons for imposing this criterion was that, from conditionals which fail this criterion (for instance, 'If it's a man, it's not a stone', based on the topic 'from opposites'), Abelard was able to infer a conclusion of the form 'if p, then not-p', and he looked on this as a *reductio* (although most modern logicians would certainly not).[11] Unfortunately for Abelard, his great rival and critic in the 1130s, Alberic, was able to show that, even observing Abelard's criterion, arguments could be constructed which led to 'if p, then not-p'. Abelard appears to have had no answer to this problem, which would exercise the next generation of logicians (see below, pp. 175–6).

Abelard also thought deeply about the semantics of conditionals.[12] On what does the truth of 'if p, then q' depend? He rules out two apparently promising answers: that the truth of a conditional is based on a relation between thoughts, or that it is based on the things to which the conditional refers. Thoughts cannot provide the basis, Abelard considers, since one can think of a true statement without thinking of all the numberless statements it entails. Nor can things provide the basis, because (for instance) the conditional 'If it is a rose, it is a flower' would remain true even if there were no roses or flowers of any kind. Abelard concludes that the truth of conditionals is based on *dicta*: on 'what is said' by statements. 'It is a rose' says of something that it is a rose. 'It is a flower' says of something that it is a flower. 'If it's a rose, it's a flower' is true because *that* something is a rose not only cannot be true unless it is also true *that* it is a flower, but also it requires *that* it is a flower. What, then, are *dicta*? Often, Abelard treats them rather as some modern philosophers treat propositions. They are non-linguistic bearers of truth and falsity. At other times Abelard seems to regard them more as states of affairs, truth-makers rather than truth-bearers. At all times, however, he insists that *dicta* are not things. This position, too, is far from clear, since it suggests that statements about *dicta* must be analysed into statements using some other terms, but it is hard to see what these terms could be.

Abelard discussed modal logic in the *Dialectica* and, in greater detail, in his *Logica* commentary on the *On Interpretation*.[13] He was the first medieval logician clearly to distinguish between the *de dicto* (or '*de sensu*') and *de re* readings of modal statements such as 'It is possible that the sitting man stands'. *De dicto* this is read as a false statement: 'Possibly the man is sitting and standing.' *De re* it is read as a statement which (provided the man actually *is* sitting) is true: 'The man is sitting and possibly he is standing.' But the exact interpretation of the *de re* reading gave Abelard difficulties.

To a considerable extent, he shared an ancient view of modality which did not allow for synchronous alternative possible states of affairs. According to this view,

1   The man is sitting at t and possibly he is standing at t'

(where t' is any time other than t) is, under the right circumstances, true, but

2   The man is sitting at t and possibly he is standing at t

must be false. The *de re* modal statement 'The man is sitting and possibly he is standing' must therefore be interpreted as (1). Yet Abelard also believes that anything, according to its nature (the sort of thing it is), always has various potencies: a man, for instance, can sit or stand at any time. This view, it might seem, should have led him to acknowledge synchronous possible states of affairs. Instead, Abelard prefers to think about possibility just in terms of what is possible *for* some thing, according to its nature, without thinking about the possibility or impossibility of states of affairs involving the thing. For instance, being able to walk is part of human nature. Therefore, Abelard believes, it is possible for a man who has had his legs amputated to walk; but he does not think that this commits him to holding that the man might actually walk at some time in the future, nor does he explicitly recognize any possible state of affairs in which the man has not lost his legs, synchronous with the actual state of affairs in which the man is without them ([7.20] 229: 34–6, 273: 39–274: 18). Such an approach may be rather unsatisfactory, but it had its advantages when Abelard came to the theological problem of predestination. Is it possible for God to save a man who is predestined to damnation? Abelard thought not. God would predestine to damnation only those fitting to be damned, and it is not possible for God not to damn someone fit for damnation. Yet, Abelard insisted, it is possible for the man to be saved, since this is a possibility open to any man ([7.18] 521: 669–79).

Abelard approached the question of what things there are with the presumption of nominalism already firmly in mind. Everything, he believed, is a particular. He thought he had strong arguments for rejecting any of the positions according to which his contemporaries held that there are some things which are not particulars but universals.[14] As a consequence, Abelard had to make a radical adaptation of what might be called the 'traditional' metaphysics of his time, taken over from Aristotle's *Categories* and Porphyry's *Isagoge*. Here is a sketch of this traditional metaphysics. It is not intended to give an accurate account of Aristotle's or Porphyry's intentions, but rather an impression of how their textbooks tended to be read by early twelfth-century scholars. According to the traditional ontology, things are of four basic sorts (see Figure 1). There are particular substances: the particular members of natural kinds (such as this man, or Socrates, to take the standard twelfth-century example of a particular substance). Natural kinds like water which do not obviously divide into particular members tend to be ignored. There are universal substances, the natural kinds themselves such as Man and Animal. Then there are what were called 'accidents': non-essential properties, and relations, of substances. Like substances, accidents were considered to be universal or particular; so, for instance, Socrates would be white by his own particular whiteness. In practice, however, particular accidents were rarely mentioned. These, then, are the four basic sorts of things: particular substances, universal substances, particular accidents and universal accidents. Man-made objects (houses, ships and so on) were considered to be composites of natural substances.

This picture derives mainly from the *Categories*. The *Isagoge* added to it Porphyry's famous 'tree' (see Figure 2). Universal substances are arranged into a hierarchy of genera and species. 'Genus' and 'species'

	SUBSTANCE	ACCIDENT
UNIVERSAL	Animal, Man	colour, whiteness
PARTICULAR	Socrates, this man	this whiteness

Figure 1

differentia		*genus/species* substance	*differentia*
corporeal	body	incorporeal substance	*incorporeal*
being alive	living thing	non-living body	*not having a soul*
having *sense-perception*	animal	plant	*not having sense-* *perception*
rational	rational animal	irrational animal	*irrational*
mortal	man	(pagan) god	*immortal*

Figure 2

are relative terms: Man is a species of Animal, and so Animal is the genus of Man, but Animal is itself a species of Living Thing. Each species is distinguished from its genus by a specifying characteristic or, as it was called, *differentia*: having-sense-perception is, for instance, what differentiates Animal from Living Thing.

As a nominalist, Abelard had to make some drastic changes to this traditional scheme.[15] Holding that every thing is a particular, he simply cancels out the first line in Figure 1. For him, things are of just two sorts: particular substances and particular accidents (and *differentiae*). And Abelard stresses that although particular accidents cannot exist except in dependence on a particular substance, they are each separate things, which might have been attached to different substances from those to which in fact they are attached.[16] Since there are no universal substances, there cannot be a hierarchy of genera and species. But Abelard translates Porphyry's tree into the structure of particular things. He regards *differentiae* as particular, non-substance things, exactly like accidents (he had a convenient word which meant either an accident or a *differentia*: a 'form'), except that each substance of a given kind must have attaching to it certain given sorts of *differentiae*, as indicated by Porphyry's tree: for instance, a man cannot be without rationality, mortality, having-sense-perceptions and so on.

This scheme is not without problems. It might seem to imply that a particular substance of a given kind is not really one thing at all, but rather a bundle of *differentiae*. Some of Abelard's discussions do appear to favour a bundle theory, in which these bundles would be attached to body, which would be regarded as fundamental rather than as just one type of substance. But elsewhere Abelard explicitly recognizes that particular substances exist in a way which, in theory, is independent from the *differentiae* which must attach to them (see esp. [7.19] 420: 30–421: 8, and cf. [7.68] 128–30). Another difficulty concerns accidents. Aristotle had given nine classes of accidents, which

160

included, for instance, relations, time and posture. Abelard initially accepted that even accidents in these categories are particular things. In the mid-1120s – after he had done his most important work as a logician – he came to think it implausible that a relation such as father-hood is a thing of any sort. He therefore revised his treatment of accidents and accepted the existence of particular accidental forms only in some categories; but he was left (at least to judge by surviving texts) without an account of accidents in the remaining categories.[17]

Abelard's basic metaphysics set the problem which his treatment of universals had to answer.[18] As a nominalist, his explicit answer to the question which his contemporaries usually posed – 'Are there universal things or just universal words?' – was unequivocal: only words could be universals. How then, he had to explain, could universal words be used meaningfully? His theory of the semantics of universals is designed to answer this question, and does so with remarkable success. But there still remained a metaphysical question for Abelard to tackle: if species and genera are not things, what is the real basis for the system of natural kinds, which Abelard recognized as a feature of reality, not a mind or language-imposed construct? Abelard's answer to this question, less satisfactory than his treatment of the semantic one, ends by taking an unexpected turn.

To begin, however, with the semantic problem. It is not, as a modern philosopher might expect, a problem about deciding the *reference* of predicates. For Abelard (along with most of his contemporaries), in a statement 'S is P', the reference of 'S' and 'P' is the same. Latin grammar makes this position plausible: there are no articles, and an adjective 'φ' always includes the meaning of φ-man/woman/thing, according to its gender. So in '*Socrates est homo*', '*Socrates*' and '*homo*' ('a/the man') are thought to refer to the same thing: Socrates; and similarly in '*Socrates est albus*', '*albus*' ('a/the white man') is taken to refer to Socrates. There is no difficulty about any of this for a nomi-nalist, since Socrates is a particular thing, a perfectly acceptable referent for words. The nominalist's problem concerns, rather, the *signification* of universal words. To signify *x* to someone is to cause there to be a thought of *x* in his mind. Twelfth-century logicians were primarily concerned with signification in their semantic analyses. It is through the signification of the predicate, they held, that the speaker conveys his meaning: that Socrates is a man (not a donkey), that he is white (not turquoise or indigo). And, whilst Socrates is a man on account of particular *differentiae* of rationality and mortality, and white by a particular accident of whiteness, in the statement 'Socrates is white' the signification of 'white' is universal: it produces a thought of white-ness in general, not of the particular whiteness by which Socrates happens to be white. But, according to Abelard, there is nothing which is whiteness in general (or man-ness in general): there are just particular accidents of whiteness, just particular men. So there seems to be no *x* of which universals can produce a thought when they signify.

Abelard's earlier way of tackling this problem, in the *Logica* ([7.20] 20: 15–22: 24), is to posit an *x* which is not a thing. When universal words are heard, they produce a thought (which is a thing – a particular accident – Abelard holds). They also cause a mental image which, Abelard says, is not a thing at all, but a figment. (Abelard's explanation of why it is not a thing shows that he thinks of the image solely in terms of its content: my mental image of a castle cannot be a thing because it is not really made of stone, and so on.) In the case of universal words, the mental image is a common, undifferentiated one, of man rather than of Socrates. It is these common mental images or conceptions which, he says, are the objects of the thoughts produced by universal words. Abelard can therefore claim both that universal words signify – there is an *x* of which they produce a thought – and that there is no *thing* which they signify. In the *Glossulae* ([7.20] 530: 24–531: 29) Abelard simplifies this picture. There he argues that a word signifies so long as it produces in its hearers thoughts with content. The content of the thoughts produced by universal words is (or, at least, can be) universal, derived from particulars by a process of abstraction. And so universal words signify, but it does not follow from this that there are any universal things which they signify.

Although any account of signification must involve the mind, in both Abelard's earlier and his later theories universal words have their signification as a result of how things really are. We form a common conception of man – or, in the later theory, abstract a universal thought content for man – because men are really alike. But, although the signification of universal words is based on how things really are, it is not always based on a complete understanding of how they really are. Abelard takes it for granted that we unproblematically group things correctly according to their natural kinds, but he considers that only in some cases do we know the structure of *differentiae* characteristic of a given natural kind. There is another semantic relationship, however, which does link universal words to this very structure in all cases: Abelard calls it 'imposition'. He envisages the first user of a word 'imposing' a certain group of sounds on a particular substance and every substance of the same kind. The impositor may well not know what is the structure of *differentiae* that characterizes the substance in question, but when he imposes the word he does so according to the structure the substance really has, whatever that may be. He thus creates a link – though an open, unspecified one – between the universal word and the real structure of the objects to which it can be used to refer and on which its signification is based.[19]

The metaphysical side of the problem of universals for Abelard is to explain in what the real resemblance between members of a kind consists, given that there are no real universals. He tackles it with his notion of *status* ([7.20] 19: 21–20: 14). Men, for instance, are alike in sharing the *status* of man; and this, he explains, means just that they are alike in being men or in that they are men. And the *status* of man (being a man), he insists, is not a thing of any sort.

There is nothing wrong with this explanation, but it raises another question in its turn. On what in reality is the *status* of man founded? What is involved in being a man? Abelard has all along made it clear that what characterizes men is a certain structure of particular *differentiae*. No one is a man who does not have (his own particular) *differentiae* of mortality, rationality and so on. Abelard might, at this stage, have proposed a variety of resemblance nominalism, which would hold that particular *differentiae* of a given sort are exactly similar and this similarity is unanalysable. Each *status* would be defined as having a certain structure of such particular *differentiae*; x would share the *status* of y if and only if his particular *differentiae* were exactly similar to y's. Surprisingly, in the only discussion ([7.20] 569: 32–573: 5] where he directly answers the question of what makes different particular *differentiae* of the same sort similar, Abelard opts for a different solution. He suggests that, whilst a man may have been rational by any one of infinitely many actual or hypothetical particular rationalities, there is a *universal differentia* of rationality, which no man can lack. He goes on to say that, in a sense, this universal *differentia* is the same as a particular *differentia*, since it differs from it not as one thing from another, but merely by 'definition' – a type of difference Abelard had introduced in discussing the Trinity and never entirely clarified.[20] Although this discussion therefore remains obscure, it suggests that, pressed to give the metaphysical basis of his theory of universals, Abelard has sacrificed much of the nominalist ground he so strenuously defends at every other stage.

Abelard developed his ethical theory on three different levels. He attempted (especially in the *Collationes*) to answer the most general questions about the nature of good and evil and their relation to God (see [7.65] and [7.68] 233–50). Whereas Abelard's contemporaries and medieval and patristic predecessors tended to argue, in Neoplatonic fashion, that evil is a privation not a thing, Abelard was ready to admit that there are evil things – particular accidents of, for instance, pain or sorrow – although not evil substances. He reconciled this position with God's goodness and omnipotence by explaining that, when we assert the goodness of God's providence, we are predicating 'good' not of things but of *dicta*: 'it is good that there are evil things' ('good' is predicated of the *dictum* that-there-are-evil-things) and does not entail 'evil things are good'. In some of his sermons and poetry, the Rule he wrote for Heloise and her nuns and a long poem of advice to his son (the technocratically-named Astralabius), Abelard developed the practical implications of his ethics and examined the tensions between moral standards and the thoughts and feelings of individuals in difficult, ethically problematic circumstances.[21]

At the centre of Abelard's moral theory, however, is his discussion of the ethical act; and, although his treatment of virtues and merit is also interesting and innovative, it is Abelard's treatment of sin which, rightly, has attracted the interest of historians of philosophy.[22] Yet it has often been misconstrued. Historians have frequently described it as 'intentionalist' and contrasted it with a crude, externalist approach to ethical judgement, where a person's guilt is judged solely according to the sort of acts he performs, as assessed by an outside observer. A moralist can be an 'intentionalist' in one or both of two ways. The intentionalism may concern *what* is judged ethically (object intentionalism). The object non-intentionalist considers that external acts alone are to be judged, whereas the object intentionalist considers that agents' intentions must be judged as well as, or instead of, their acts. Or the intentionalism may concern the basis for ethical judgement (subject intentionalism). The subject intentionalist will hold that an agent's own beliefs about what is right and wrong are an important element to be taken into account in reaching a judgement; the anti-intentionalist will minimize their role or exclude them. Abelard is certainly both an object and a subject intentionalist. But his object intentionalism needs to be set alongside the different object intentionalism of his contemporaries, not contrasted with an imaginary externalism, and his subject intentionalism does not have the extreme consequences which it might at first seem to threaten.

In their treatments of sin, Abelard's contemporaries put great weight on the intentions accompanying a sinful act. The most popular theory envisaged them as mental acts preceding the external sinful act itself. Its exponents analysed the psychological stages of committing a sin, from contemplating the action, being tempted, indulging the temptation to performing the act. Although these theorists held that the performance of the external act added to the gravity of the sin, they considered that, already at an early stage of contemplating the sinful action with pleasure, the agent would be sinning to some degree, even if he went on successfully to resist the temptation. They held, then, that it is worse actually to sleep with a married woman than to be ready and about to do so but prevented by the unexpected arrival of the husband. But they would also consider that a man would have sinned to some degree if he merely thought with pleasure about sleeping with her, even if he would never have considered making any practical move to do so.

164

By contrast, Abelard held that neither the performance of the external act itself, nor any of the thoughts or feelings preceding it but not directly linked to its real or planned performance need be considered in judging sin. Before we perform an action, he believed, we perform a mental act of willing it or (in the terminology he finally used, in *Scito teipsum*) 'consenting' to it. Consenting to an act means being entirely ready to perform it, and so I can consent to an act which I do not perform because it is thwarted. For Abelard, it is acts of consent – not any other type of mental events, and not external actions – which alone can be sins. The thwarted adulterer sins no less, having consented to adultery, than the successful one; whilst, if he is inflamed with passion for a married woman and incessantly imagines with pleasure the idea of sleeping with her, but he resists the temptation to do so, then not only does he not sin, he wins merit in the sight of God for his successful struggle.[23]

The contrast made above between external acts and mental events preceding them omits what many philosophers now would consider the most important element in any theory of action: the idea that we act under a description, which is linked to various of our mental and external acts, both before and after the act in question. To some extent Abelard seems to have grasped this idea. He is very concerned to distinguish between consent and what he calls 'willing'. When a man consents to adultery, he does not will to commit adultery if he would prefer it were the woman in question unmarried. When a man murders his feudal overlord in self-defence, knowing that his supporters will certainly try to take their revenge on him, he certainly does not will to commit murder, although he consents to it and, for Abelard, he would therefore be guilty of murder, just as, in the first example, he would be guilty of adultery ([7.21] 6: 24–8:20, 16: 16–32). What does Abelard mean by this notion of reluctant action, in which I do not will to perform what I do in fact perform? Although he does not develop the idea explicitly, he seems to have in mind that most acts fit a number of descriptions. The adulterer does not will to commit adultery since he would not choose to perform the act just under the description of 'sleeping with a married woman' (or 'committing adultery'), nor the murderer his act just under the description of 'killing one's overlord'. In each case the agent consents to the act on account of other relevant descriptions of it such as sleeping with the woman one desires, or saving one's life.

What determines for Abelard which acts of consent are sinful and which not? We sin, Abelard believes, by showing contempt for God (e.g. [7.21] 4: 31–2). He explains what it is to show contempt for God in two different ways: either as (a) doing what is not fitting (e.g. [7.21] 4: 27–8) or as (b) not doing what we believe we should do for God (e.g. [7.21] 6: 3–6). The juxtaposition of two so different accounts may seem puzzling. In any case, it seems that only (b) fits the equation of sin with contempt of God. If I do what is unfitting but believe that it *is* what I should do for God, I cannot be showing contempt for him (unless my contempt consists in not having found out what really is fitting and unfitting). The puzzle is solved, however, by Abelard's beliefs about natural law.[24] Abelard considered that all mentally competent adults (who alone he held capable of sinning) at all periods of history naturally know the general moral precepts laid down by God, such as the prohibitions of murder, adultery and theft. He also believed that they all have the power of conscience, which he saw as an ability to see how particular actions fall under the general commands and prohibitions of moral law. There is then, for Abelard, no gap between what is fitting for moral agents to do and what they believe they should do for God. Although he is a subject intentionalist, he thus avoids the danger of having to allow that someone might not sin whatever action he performed simply by virtue of not believing that the action is sinful.

There are, of course, difficulties about his view. Although, in his discussions of ethics in practice, Abelard is acutely aware of the possibility of moral conflict – where one and the same action is both enjoined and forbidden by divine law – for theoretical purposes he ignores such dilemmas. Moreover, Abelard has to account not just for natural law, but for the revealed laws of the Old and the New Testament. The Old Law raises a special difficulty for him. He considers, as in consistency he must, that a Jew who accepts the Old Law and breaks one of its special precepts, not contained in natural law, such as the dietary laws, commits a sin because he is showing contempt for God by his action ([7.16] 306: 311–25). This, he grants, applies to a twelfth-century Jew as much as to a biblical one. But Abelard also considers that the twelfth-century Jew is mistaken to believe that God now enjoins the dietary laws on him or on anyone. In practice, the point is of little importance. But in principle the gap which Abelard has allowed between moral belief and the truth about divine precepts upsets his whole theory, for it is hard to see what limit he could place on the beliefs which people or groups of people might sincerely hold about what are God's special laws for them.

❦ GILBERT OF POITIERS ❦

Next to Abelard, the most profound and adventurous thinker of the twelfth century was Gilbert of Poitiers (1085/90–1154). Gilbert enjoyed the successful and comparatively undramatic career for which

Abelard might have hoped. A native of Poitiers, he was taught at Chartres by Bernard and at Laon by Anselm. He became a canon and then chancellor of Chartres, and taught both there and in Paris. In 1142 he was made bishop of Poitiers. Like Abelard, Gilbert was the object of Bernard of Clairvaux's suspicion and hostility. Gilbert was forced to defend his views on the Trinity and the Incarnation, first in front of Pope Eugene III (April 1147) and then at a consistory after the Council of Rheims (March 1148). As he had done with Abelard, Bernard used underhand tactics to try to ensure Gilbert would be condemned. But this time he was unsuccessful and Gilbert was allowed to return to his diocese without harm to his reputation.[25]

Gilbert did not write prolifically. He produced biblical commentaries (on the Psalms and the Pauline Letters), where he kept close to the specifically Christian doctrinal themes, eschewing the opportunities for ethical speculation so eagerly followed by Abelard. A set of theological *Sententie* survives (in two versions). But they do not seem to offer a close account of his lectures, and certainly incorporate the views of other masters. Gilbert was an accomplished logician as well as a theologian, and he gave rise to a distinctively Porretan school of logic; but no logical work of his own is known. Gilbert's contribution to philosophy emerges only from his long and intricate commentary on Boethius' *Theological Treatises* (*Opuscula sacra*), probably written early in the 1140s. Since Gilbert's technique as a commentator is to gloss every word of the original text, the character of Boethius' treatises has a deep influence on his work, but in ways that are unexpected.

Gilbert does *not* take over many of Boethius' views or arguments directly, even though he is supposedly explaining them. Rather, he strains to fit Boethius' words into his own often very different arguments, at the cost of an unwieldily profuse terminology and frequent obliqueness or obscurity in exposition. In his *Opuscula*, Boethius had been concerned in the main to use logical and metaphysical ideas rather straightforwardly as ways of elucidating and confirming orthodox Christian doctrine about the Trinity and Christology. Gilbert, however, insists that different principles of argument and ways of arguing must be used in different disciplines. He claims that arguments devised in connection with natural things (natural science), or in the course of analysing them into their in reality inseparable constituents (what Gilbert calls 'mathematics'), cannot be used directly in talking about God (theology). But these arguments can be used indirectly, by 'proportionate transumption', a process in which some of what a natural or mathematical argument establishes is accepted as applicable to God, but not all.[26] This framework gives Gilbert the chance to develop his philosophical account of the natural world more fully than

Boethius had done. But, in developing his natural and mathematical arguments, Gilbert is always at least in part concerned with how to 'transume' them proportionately so as to serve his, and Boethius', ultimate theological aims. Gilbert's main philosophical discussions – of topics such as predication, parts and wholes, individuation and the relation between body and soul – are all coloured in this way, and sometimes their rationale becomes clear only in the light of his doctrinal objectives. Yet it would be wrong to see Gilbert merely as a theologian propounding quasi-philosophical arguments to illustrate Christian doctrine. Parts of his thinking take up the type of philosophical questions which had been stimulated by the ancient logical texts and which had fascinated Abelard; and nowhere more clearly than in his complex and original treatment of the metaphysical structure of things.[27]

Gilbert makes a fundamental distinction between what he calls *quo est* ('from which it is') and *quod est* ('what it is') (7.10] 91: 51–8, 116: 47–9).[28] (Driven by the requirements of exegesis, he also uses a bewildering variety of other terms to describe this distinction.) Examples of what Gilbert considers *quod ests* are Socrates, this man, that dog, this white thing. What he has in mind, it seems, are concrete wholes made of substances along with their accidents. Although a denominative word such as 'white thing' (*album*) is the word for a *quod est*, Gilbert assumes that in any given case when it is used its reference will be the same as that of a substance word and, often, of a proper name. So, for instance, the *quod est* in question might be this white thing, this labrador, Fido. (Gilbert does not envisage instances where a denominative might sort things differently for purposes of reference, for instance, 'this white thing' referring to Fido and the white ball in his mouth taken together; nor does he indicate how he thinks about man-made objects.) *Quo ests* are, for instance, whiteness, bodiliness, rationality, humanity, Socrateity. They are not, however, universal forms. Every *quo est* is singular (or one in number: Gilbert uses the two notions interchangeably), and every *quod est* is what it is from its own singular *quo ests* ([7.10] 144: 58–60, 145: 95–100). So, for instance, I am rational (supposing I am) and six-foot tall from a singular rationality and a singular being-six-foot-tall which are each *quo ests* numerically distinct from Socrates' rationality and being-six-foot-tall.

As this account suggests, by '*quo ests*' Gilbert means something very close to what Abelard and others had in mind when they spoke of particular forms (accidents or *differentiae*). So, for example, Abelard would talk of the particular being-six-foot-tall and the particular rationality attaching to Socrates by which he is six-foot tall and rational. Yet there are important differences between the two philosophers' schemes. Abelard thinks of particular forms attaching to substances and, although one element of his discussion (the 'bundle theory') points in a different direction, he accepts that, were a substance *per impossibile* stripped of all forms, it would still retain an identity. For Gilbert, however, the relationship between *quo ests* and *quod ests* is causal and correlative. A *quod est* is made what it is by its *quo ests* and there can be no *quo ests* apart from a *quod est* ([7.10] 278: 8–279: 12). The notion of bare substance may be problematic, but that of a bare *quod est* would be simply ungrammatical, because a *quod est* must be a 'what' (a white thing, a rational thing, Socrates), made what it is by a *quo est* (whiteness, rationality, Socrateity). Gilbert's scheme thus avoids some of Abelard's problems (but at a price, since the notion of making or causing involved is thoroughly obscure: what the *quo est* makes into the *quod est* cannot be the *quod est* itself – so what is it?).

Another important development in Gilbert's scheme has already been indicated by mentioning the *quo ests* humanity and Socrateity. As well as all his simple *quo ests*, such as rationality, mortality and being-six-foot-tall, which make Socrates something which is mortal, rational and six-foot tall, there are also his complex *quo ests*, composed of two or more of the simple *quo ests*; so, for instance, his humanity – that by which he is a man – would be composed of the *differentiae* of the species man and of the *differentiae* of all the genera of that species (rationality, mortality, having senses, being alive, being bodily). The most complex of all these composite *quo ests* is called by Gilbert the 'collected property' or 'whole form' of Socrates ('Socrateity', for short). It is composed of all the *quo ests* 'which both in actuality and by nature have been, are and will be' those of Socrates ([7.10] 144: 73–8, 274: 75–95).

Gilbert uses this idea of whole forms to make one of his most characteristic distinctions. As already mentioned, Gilbert holds that every *quo est* is singular; even composite *quo ests*, such as this humanity or Socrateity, are singular ([7.10] 167: 7–19, 301: 86–95). So too is every *quod est* singular. It is singular, Gilbert says, because the *quo est* which makes it into a *quod est* is itself singular ([7.10] 144: 58–62). To be singular is not, however, for Gilbert to be individual. In his view everything which is individual is singular. But only those singulars which are not 'dividuals' are individual. Whatever is exactly similar (*conformis*) to something else, or could possibly be exactly similar to something else, is a dividual. Although the *quo ests* by which Socrates is rational and six-foot-tall are singular and distinct from the singular *quo ests* by which Plato is rational and six-foot-tall, each *quo est* of rationality and each *quo est* of being-six-foot-tall is exactly similar to every other such *quo est*. The same is true of almost every *quo est*, whether simple (mortality, whiteness) or complex (animality, humanity). Even if it should happen that as a matter of fact there is not, never has been nor ever will be a *quo est* exactly similar to a simple or complex *quo est*, then in almost every case it is possible that there might be one exactly similar ([7.10] 143: 52–144: 78, 270: 73–271: 82). No one, suppose, has ever had or will ever have a nose quite the same shape as mine; but 'by nature' – hypothetically – there might be such a person. Or consider the complex *quo est* sun-ness which makes something into a sun. Gilbert thought (wrongly, of course) that there was and would be only one thing like this: sun is a species which contains only one member, the Sun. But by nature, he believed, there is nothing to prevent there being infinitely many suns, all made into what they are by *quo ests* of sun-ness, each singular but exactly similar to each other. The (as a matter of fact unique) *quo est* of sun-ness is therefore dividual just as the very many *quo ests* of humanity are dividual ([7.10] 273: 53–71).

There is just one type of *quo est* which, Gilbert claims, is not dividual because it is not actually or possibly exactly similar to any other *quo est*: the whole form of a *quod est* (for instance, Socrateity). Whole forms, then, are individuals, and so are their *quod ests*, that is to say, every *quod est*, since every *quod est* has a whole form. Where, then, for Abelard (who makes no distinction between particularity, singularity and individuality) a form such as this whiteness or that rationality is no less a particular thing than Socrates himself, Gilbert is able to discriminate more finely: this whiteness, that rationality and Socrates are each singular, but only Socrates (and his whole form, Socrateity) is individual.

Gilbert's idea of individuality also provides him with his approach to the problem of universals. Complex dividual *quo ests* fall into groups, the members of each of which, although themselves all singular, are completely similar to every other member of the group. In virtue of this complete similarity all the members can be regarded as one universal, a species: for example, humanity. Again, many complex dividual *quo ests* are completely similar not just to some other *quo ests* in every respect, but also to some in some respects; for instance, every *quo est* of humanity and every *quo est* of horse-ness are completely similar in respect of being bodily, being alive and having senses. They can therefore be further grouped into what is also regarded as one universal, the genus animality ([7.10] 269: 34–50, 312: 95–113). True to the emphasis of the discussion at the time, Gilbert considers just universals in the category of substance; presumably, though, he would also consider that groups of exactly similar simple *quo ests* (such as whitenesses or rationalities) are universals in other categories. Gilbert, therefore, is a realist over universals, but his real universals are all *quo ests* which cannot exist except in conjunction with *quod ests* which, because they are individual, cannot be universal. To the objection that his real universals must, like any real universal, be contradictorily both one and many, Gilbert could reply that, whereas it would be a contradiction to assert of many individuals that they are one, it is permissible to say of many singulars that they are one because of their complete similarity to each other.[29]

All this rests on the presumption that whole forms are indeed individual: there is nothing else to which any of them is, or could possibly be, exactly similar. What entitles Gilbert to make this presumption? Gilbert gives no explicit answer, but it is worth looking carefully to see what, if anything, he had in mind. It seems obvious to relate the individuality of whole forms to the principle that no two bodily objects can be in the same place at the same time: they cannot therefore have exactly similar accidents in these respects. Gilbert's comments in a different context ([7.10] 77: 5–78: 13, 148: 88–92) show that he was highly aware of this point. Yet, at first sight, such an explanation seems not to fit Gilbert's view (see above, p. 169) that the whole form of Socrates is composed, not only of all the *quo ests* that have, do and will make him what he is, but also of all those that he has 'by nature'. The spatio-temporal dissimilarity principle does not rule out Plato having by nature the very same space-time accidents as Socrates actually has. Indeed, if Socrates' complex *quo est* is composed of all the *quo ests* he has 'by nature', it seems that it must include every sort of *quo est* that can attach to a man, and that therefore the whole form of each member of a species is exactly similar to that of every other member of that species – and therefore, contrary to what Gilbert maintains, is dividual.

What must be implicit, it seems, in Gilbert's view is a distinction between *quo ests* which apply to alternative, different ways things might be (or, at least, a distinction between those *quo ests* which something has in actuality, and those which it has only by nature). This would accord with Simo Knuuttila's view that Gilbert was one of the earliest thinkers who, influenced by the doctrine of divine omnipotence, was willing to admit synchronous alternative possible state of affairs, each belonging to different providential programmes, any of which God could put into effect although only one is the actual programme he chooses.[30] Gilbert would, then, be able to insist that, in any given providential scheme – and so in whatever scheme is the actual one – Socrates does not share his spatio-temporal *quo ests* with anyone else, and that therefore his whole form is not the same as anyone else's. None the less, Gilbert did not in fact think out his views on modality this far; had he done so, he might not have wished to accept the many difficulties this view brings with it.[31]

➤ THE PLATONIC CURRENT ➤

Most of the main twelfth-century thinkers owed something to Plato. Abelard, for instance, argued that the description of the World Soul in the *Timaeus* was an allegory of the Holy Spirit, and he used this surmise as evidence that the pagan philosophers knew of the Trinity before the coming of Christ. He also took the few comments about the *Republic* at the beginning of the *Timaeus* and used them as the basis for his own political ideal of cities where everything is done for the common good ([7.68] 304–7). Abelard's Platonism, however, is opportunistic. He takes themes from Plato and transforms them for his own purposes, using them within a structure of thought which itself owes remarkably little to Plato. Some scholars have argued that there is an important Platonic element in Abelard's treatment of universals and *dicta* (see [7.61] 149 and [7.56]). The interpretation offered here does not support that view. Similarly, historians have often held, contrary to the reading advanced here, that Gilbert rests his metaphysics on a notion of Platonic Ideas. There is, at any rate, room for dispute about the Platonism of Abelard and Gilbert, but neither continues the tradition of Bernard of Chartres in the direct way that was done, as John of Salisbury recognized, by William of Conches.

William of Conches was already teaching and writing in the early 1120s and appears to have remained active until the 1150s; he taught perhaps at Paris or, so some have argued, at Chartres, and later taught at the court of the Duke of Normandy. Like Bernard, he was a grammar teacher. He wrote a commentary on Priscian's *Institutiones grammaticae* (*Principles of grammar*), drawing extensively on the anonymous eleventh-century *Glosule* to Priscian; and he made detailed commentaries on a series of classical texts. These include poetry (he is known to have glossed Iuvenal) but he concentrated on Platonic writers: Boethius' *Consolation of Philosophy*, Macrobius' commentary on Cicero's *Dream of Scipio* and, most important, the *Timaeus* itself. In interpreting these texts, William drew on the already well-established medieval tradition of reading pagan texts as allegories of Christian truth. He went beyond his predecessors in the thoroughness with which he applied this method. He would admit, if necessary, that, being pagans, the ancient authors could not be trusted in everything they said. Usually, however, he discovered a satisfactory reading. He shared with Abelard (and may have taken from him – but the chronology is not clear) the identification of Plato's World Soul with the Holy Spirit. But unlike Abelard, for whom it carried important implications about the knowability of God, he was willing to drop the identification. For William, it was merely a convenient reading of an ancient text, which could if necessary be sacrificed.

The ideas in his texts which William took most were scientific, rather than philosophical or theological ones.[32] The *Timaeus* and Macrobius were regarded as important sources for natural science, and William developed this interest independently, in his *Philosophia* (*c.* 1125) and his later dialogue (part extension, part more cautious revision of the *Philosophia*), the *Dragmaticon* (between 1144 and 1149). In these works he also made use of, and sometimes combined or developed in an original way, medical and scientific sources translated from the Arabic and Greek. In the *Philosophia* and the *Dragmaticon*, and in the commentary to the *Timaeus*, William tried to show how all things came into being through the natural interaction of the four elements (fire, air, water and earth). Only the creation of the human soul required a separate intervention by God. William was firmly committed to this search for naturalistic explanations: he accused of pride and ignorance those who wished to explain everything by divine intervention, and claimed that he illustrated God's power by his explanations of how God worked through nature ([7.31] 39–40).

The other leading Platonist of the mid-twelfth century (he was described by a pupil, Hermann of Carinthia, as 'the soul of Plato restored to mankind from heaven') was Thierry 'the Breton', known also as Thierry of Chartres, where he was chancellor in the 1140s; previously he had taught both there and almost certainly at Paris. As well as an interest in rhetoric, logic and the various branches of mathematics, Thierry shared William of Conches's penchant for naturalistic explanation of what many of their contemporaries would have described in terms of direct divine intervention. But Thierry gave his most distinctive philosophical teaching – and that which shows his Platonism most clearly – in the course of commenting on Boethius' *Theological Treatises*.[33] A commentary known as *Librum hunc* (written late 1140s; incipit 'Inchoantibus librum hunc') can be shown to be fairly closely based on this teaching. Together with two other commentaries on the work from the same period (Incipit 'Intentio auctoris' and 'Aggreditur propositum'), which contain close parallels to it and each other but also differ sharply in some of their doctrines, *Librum hunc* shows how Plato's Theory of Ideas was adopted and transformed.

The first stage in the transformation was Boethius' doubling of the forms: 'From those forms which are beyond matter', writes Boethius, 'come those forms which are in matter and make the body' – forms which therefore, more properly, should be called 'images'. All three commentaries go on to argue that only the images which come into contact with matter are many, and that the forms from which they derive are really one form, God, the form of forms. The argument is developed in two main ways. *Librum hunc* asserts that the forms of all things 'emanate' (*emanare*) from the one, simple divine form. These forms have it in common with the one true form that they are an 'equality of being'. By this he apparently means that a particular substance *s* is what it is (an *s*) from its form *f*, so that *f* can be called 'the equality of being an *s*'. God's form, 'the wholeness and perfection of all things', stands in the same relation to God as *f* to *s*. None the less, the commentator insists that all forms besides that of God are not really forms, but simply the images of form. Plurality, he goes on to explain, arises solely through the coming together of form, which is one, and matter, which is also in itself one.[34] In the two other commentaries, the talk is not of emanation but rather of God's thinking.[35] When an artificer wishes to produce a mental exemplar of what he will make, he must think of the material of which it will be made: the exemplar is not itself enmattered, but it must be conceived in relation to matter. Similarly, God, who is himself the form of forms, conceives the forms of all things in relation to their matter. He then unites them with matter, at which point they cease to be forms and become images.

In the second half of the century, the Platonic current (no longer closely connected with exegesis of the *Timaeus* or with natural science) intermingles often curiously with other influences. For example, there survives a fragment (itself book-length) of a very lengthy commentary on a work by the fifth-century Greek Neoplatonist known as 'pseudo-Dionysius' (because he issued his works under attribution to Dionysius, the Areopagite converted by St Paul). The commentary was written between 1169 and 1177 by William of Lucca. William was probably the author of a logical textbook based on Abelard's teaching (see below, p. 175); he was certainly deeply influenced in his theology by Gilbert of Poitiers; and, like Thierry of Chartres, he formulated his thoughts about Platonic Ideas (which, in what remains of his commentary, are far from clear) with Boethius' *Theological Treatises* in mind.[36] Alan of Lille (see below, pp. 177–8) provides another example of late twelfth-century syncretic Platonism.

❧ THE LOGICAL SCHOOLS OF THE LATER ❧ TWELFTH CENTURY

In the second half of the twelfth century, logicians divided themselves into a number of self-consciously distinct schools, all probably based in Paris.[37] Each of these schools derived from one of the leading logical masters of the preceding period. The Porretani (or Gilebertini) were the followers of Gilbert of Poitiers (who was called Gilbert Porretanus). Abelard's followers were called the Nominales.[38] The Parvipontani (or Adamitae) were the followers of another influential logical, Adam of

Balsham (d. 1159), called Parvipontanus because his school was at the Petit-Pont, whose *Ars disserendi* (*c.* 1132) offers a highly innovative approach to logic, both in its terminology and arrangement of material. The Meludinenses or Robertini were almost certainly the followers of Robert of Melun, although at present only Robert's work as a theologian, not as a logician is known. Another important logician of the 1130s and 1140s was Alberic, a determined opponent of Abelard's. Although no surviving text can be definitely assigned to him, his views are frequently and respectfully cited in the logical commentaries of the 1140s, some of which can be closely linked to him.[39] The logicians who called themselves the Albricani were certainly his followers; whether they can be identified with the Montani (from the Mont Ste Geneviève, where Alberic, but also Abelard and others taught) is unclear.

The later twelfth-century masters who ran these schools remain anonymous, but a number of texts survive which show their sophistication and ingenuity. From the Porretans there is a substantial textbook of logic (called by its editors the *Compendium logicae Porretanum*), probably written between 1155 and 1170. William of Lucca's *Summa dialetice artis* (where Abelard is throughout the supreme authority, called the Philosophus) illustrates the thinking of the nominalists; the *Introductiones montane maiores* that of the Montani; the *Ars meliduna* – the longest and most sophisticated of all – the work of the Melidunenses.[40]

The division of these logicians into schools is not a mere convenience of the historian: it reflects how the scholars thought of themselves. For each school there was a set of basic theses to which all those who belonged had to subscribe. The Porretan *Compendium* takes the form of a commentary of each of the Porretani's theses, and there survive similar lists of theses with discussion for the Melidunenses and the Nominales.[41] Most of the theses concern controversies which arose in connection with the *Isagoge*, *Categories* and *On Interpretation* over topics such as universals, predication, parts and wholes and entailment. Often they are stated in a deliberately paradoxical fashion; for instance, according to the Melidunenses, 'Socrates and Plato are not Socrates and Plato'; according to the Nominales, 'Nothing grows'. The divisions between the schools emerge very clearly in the differing solutions each proposed to the objection Alberic had raised to Abelard's theory of conditionals (see above, pp. 157–8). Alberic's argument begins from the principle that, if p implies q, then p and r implies q, and it chooses as an exemplification of this argument-pattern one in which the conjunction of p and r is an impossibility. The Porretani rejected this argument-pattern, because it leaves one of the conjuncts without a role in the implication, whilst the Montani refused to accept conditionals where the antecedent is impossible. The Nominales, Abelard's own followers, seem (not surprisingly) to have been left in some confusion; the Melidunenses argued that nothing follows from a false statement; whilst the Parvipontani alone did not treat Alberic's argument as a *reductio*, but accepted it along with its conclusion and therefore the paradoxes of strict implication: from an impossibility anything follows, and a necessity follows from anything.[42]

It would be very wrong, however, to imagine that the logicians of the later twelfth century did no more than react to and systematize the ideas of their founders. First, even on the most closely discussed questions of the previous decades, the new masters had their own thoughts. So, for example, the *Ars meliduna* proposes a sophisticated Platonic theory. Universals are all 'intelligible things'. What the mind grasps when it considers a universal is not, though, a relation of similarity, but the 'coming together' (*communio*) of things which – in the case of genera and species (Animal, Man), but not that of other universals (white, rational) – brings it about that what participates in it is something.[43]

Second, the later twelfth century was a time when previously unknown Aristotelian logical texts (the *logica nova*) first became known: the *Prior Analytics*, the *Topics* and *On Sophistical Refutations*. All three, for instance, are used in the *Ars meliduna*. This development is less important, however, than it might seem. It was only the third of these texts, Aristotle's treatise on sophisms (arguments which are incorrect but superficially plausible) that was studied enthusiastically. *On Sophistical Refutations* was known before the others, by the 1120s; Alberic and his followers were greatly impressed by it; and it continued to fascinate logicians for the rest of the century. Although its value in detecting logical fallacies in theological arguments may have initially recommended the treatise, it came to fuel a growing interest in the principles of deductive argument.[44]

The third and most important development of the years 1150–1200 may help to explain the generally slight impression made by the *logica nova*. It was in this period that medieval logicians broke away from the framework of study set by the ancient authorities. For instance, whereas Abelard's *Dialectica* had mainly followed the pattern of the textbooks by Aristotle, Porphyry and Boethius, both the Porretan *Compendium* and the *Ars meliduna* reorganize the whole subject-matter of logic into four parts: terms, statements (*propositiones*), what terms signify, what statements signify (see [7.77] II, 1, 539). The new approach went beyond matters of organization. Almost all the branches of what would be called the *logica modernorum* – those parts of logic not covered in the ancient texts – began to be developed at this time: besides the theory of conditionals (which Abelard had already begun to develop), the theory of the (semantic) properties of terms; the study of sophisms and of words such as 'only', 'except', 'begins', 'ceases'; the treatment of semantic paradoxes and the special sort of logical disputation called 'obligations'.[45]

❧ PHILOSOPHICAL THEMES IN LATER ❧ TWELFTH-CENTURY THEOLOGY

The divisions between schools were less clear-cut among the theologians than the logicians. There were, certainly, those who followed Gilbert of Poitiers either very closely or with more freedom. Abelard, too, was highly influential; but his more controversial theological doctrines were usually rejected and his distinctive ethics adopted piecemeal, if at all. Although there are a number of references to Nominales in theological contexts, they seem not to be to any distinctively nominalist *theology*, but rather to nominalist logical positions which were used in a theological discussion.

There was, by contrast, far more variety in the manner of pursuing theology than was the case for logic, even leaving aside the monastic theologians such as William of St Thierry, Ailred of Rievaulx and Bernard of Clairvaux himself, who distanced themselves from the schools. At the Abbey of St Victor in Paris, where William of Champeaux had founded a theological tradition, which was carried on in the 1130s and 1140s especially by Hugh (of St Victor), Richard (of St Victor) wrote, sometime after about 1150, a long and carefully-worked *De trinitate*. Its aim is to show (rather as Anselm had tried in the *Monologion*) that there are strong rational grounds for holding, not merely that God exists, but that he is triune. Richard, however, writes to illuminate the faithful, not to convince non-believers. If he figures less in the history of philosophy than some of his contemporaries, it is not because his arguments lack sophistication but rather because his views are not easily detached from their theological context.

In the theology of the schools – mainly the schools of Paris – there were two main approaches to method. Gilbert of Poitiers' idea that each branch of knowledge, including theology, has its own fundamental rules, combined with the axiomatic method used in the third of Boethius' *Theological Treatises* (and Gilbert's own use of it in his commentary on that treatise), led to the attempt to produce an axiomatic theology. Peter of Vienna (or of Poitiers) places near to the beginning of his *Summa* (*c.* 1150) a set of rules which apply to created things (many of them read like the theses of the logical schools) but according to some of which we may also gain knowledge about God. In his *Regulae caelestis iuris* (*c.* 1170–80) Alan of Lille sets out no fewer than 134 special theological rules, which he expounds and attempts to justify in the work, sometimes deriving one from another.[46] Axiomatic theology turned out, however, to be a passing fashion. The most influential of all twelfth-century theological works turned out to be the *Sentences* written by Peter the Lombard in about 1155–7. Glosses began to be written on the Lombard's *Sentences* in the later twelfth century and, from the thirteenth to the fifteenth centuries, commentary on what were simply called 'the *Sentences*' was the vehicle for much of the most important theological and philosophical work (see pp. 194–5). The Lombard probably based his *Sentences* on the discussion of doctrinal difficulties which took place in his lectures on the Bible, but he drew together his material in a systematic way, to provide an orderly consideration, problem by problem, of the whole area of theological debate.

The Lombard's *Sentences* were valued, above all, for their orthodoxy – although many passages show a powerful logical mind, fully abreast of the subtleties of an Abelard or a Gilbert of Poitiers. Some of those who followed his methods were far more openly enthusiastic for logical analysis; few more so than his pupil, Peter of Poitiers (not to be confused with the Porretan Peter, also from Poitiers). Peter's discussion of divine omnipotence ([7.23] 48–68) in his *Sentences* (*c.* 1176) provides a good example of this logically intricate approach to doctrinal problems, since Peter borrows some of the best ideas of theologians from the past two decades and also adds his own.[47]

Like Abelard, he argues that 'God is omnipotent' does not mean that he can do all things, since he cannot walk or eat or sin, but rather (following Augustine) that God can do whatever he wills. Peter adds to this the requirement, mentioned by Peter the Lombard, that 'nothing whatsoever can be done to God' (which would seem to entail that he can not do whatever he does not will to do). Peter does not explain why, but this extra requirement would overcome the objection that Augustine's definition is too weak since it makes omnipotent whoever limits his wishes to his capabilities. He goes on to consider the position (Abelard's, but he is not named) that God can do only what he does, which is supposedly entailed by a variety of considerations of the form: God does only and all what is good (what is fitting, what his justice requires). Peter's solution is to distinguish between 'good' predicated of men and of God. Men are good because what they do is good, but what God does is good because it is done by God. He can then – making a similar distinction to that used by Abelard between *de dicto* and *de re* modalities – distinguish two senses of 'God can do only what it is good to be done by him'. They are a composite (*de dicto*) sense: 'God can do only that-which-if-done-by-him-is-good'; and a divided (*de re*) sense: 'God can do only that which is good: i.e. he cannot do that which is now bad.' Only the composite sense yields a true statement, and the composite sense does not limit what God can do, but merely affirms that whatever he in fact does is good (because he does it). Peter then works through a number of more purely logical fallacies which seem to limit God's power. Peter finishes the section with a long discussion of God's power to alter natural necessities. God, he argues, can bring about what is impossible according to natural causality, for instance, that a man is an ass. But 'the man is an ass' is true only if it is interpreted as saying that, according to natural causes, he is man, but according to a higher cause, he is an ass.

❧ CONCLUSION: OLD SOURCES, NEW ❧ SOURCES AND THE ACHIEVEMENTS OF TWELFTH-CENTURY PHILOSOPHY

The preceding sections will have given the impression that, in most important respects, twelfth-century thinkers used only a narrow range of ancient and late antique texts, most which had been available since the ninth century: the *logica vetus*, Plato's *Timaeus*, Boethius' *On the Consolation of Philosophy* and *Theological Treatises*, complemented by Latin philosophical and scientific texts by Cicero, Macrobius and Martianus Capella; the only exception seems to be Aristotle's *On Sophistical Refutations*, the one work of the *logica nova* which was taken up with enthusiasm in this period. The twelfth century thus appears to present a stark contrast to the thirteenth, when philosophy in the Latin West was transformed by contact with the whole range of Aristotle's writings, and with work by the great medieval Arab and Jewish thinkers, such as Avicenna, Averroes and Maimonides.

In one way, this impression is misleading. A number of the translations which would be influential during the thirteenth century were made in the years from 1150, especially in Toledo (see pp. 226–7). One of the most important of these translators, Dominicus Gundissalinus (d. after 1181), wrote a number of independent works which combine the influence of Avicenna and Latin authors such as Boethius.[48] There were writers such as Adelard of Bath (writing between *c.* 1110 and 1145) and Hermann of Carinthia (fl. 1138–43) who learned Arabic and exploited Arabic sources – though their interests were more scientific than philosophical.[49] The *Liber de causis* (*Book about Causes*), a translation of an Arabic adaptation of the late Neoplatonist Proclus' *Elements of Theology*, was known to Alan of Lille. Some of Aristotle's non-logical works were being used in Salerno late in the century; around 1200 or shortly afterwards, David of Dinant, who had travelled in Greece, translated and used passages from Aristotle's scientific writings, and John Blund wrote a *De anima* (*On the Soul*) using Aristotle and, especially, Avicenna.[50]

Despite these reservations, it would still be right to conclude that the main achievement of twelfth-century philosophy was not related to newly available ancient or Arabic material. Nor, indeed, despite many of these scholars' great reverence for the ancients, should it be seen in terms of a deeper assimilation of the ancient texts previously known, or even of a new approach to them. The great writers of the first half of the century – Abelard, Gilbert of Poitiers (and some would wish to add William of Conches and Thierry of Chartres) – posed and tackled philosophical questions with an originality which makes the model of assimilation inappropriate. The second half of the century did not produce any philosophers of the same stature, but it saw two important developments, largely unrelated to ancient sources: the development of a systematic, argumentative method of theology, and the elaboration of sophisticated logical techniques for semantic analysis and the study of argument. It would be these, along with the effects of the new Aristotelian and Arabic material, that would provide the framework for the impressive philosophical developments in thirteenth- and fourteenth-century Paris and Oxford.

 NOTES

1   For a fuller sketch of the historiography of twelfth-century philosophy, see Marenbon [7.66] 101–6.
2   See Chapter 1, pp. 14–15 for fuller discussion.
3   See Marenbon [7.42] 80–4; for a wider study of the themes in early medieval commentaries and glosses on Aristotle and Porphyry, see Marenbon [7.67].
4   For the identification of Garlandus and material on *in voce* exegesis, see Iwakuma [7.52] 47–54; for this interpretation, see Marenbon [7.68] 108–16.
5   See Jolivet [7.57] where the material is collected and this interpretation advanced; cf. de Libera ([7.61] 142–5) and M. Tweedale, 'Logic: to the time of Abelard' in Dronke [7.49] 204–5.
6   John of Salisbury [7.13] III, 2, pp. 124–5; trans. in [7.34] 151–2.
7   The arguments for attributing the *Glosae* to Bernard, along with a full account of Bernard's life and the testimony (mainly from John of Salisbury) to his teaching, are given by Dutton, in his edition of the *Glosae* [7.7] 21–45, 239–49.
8   The dating of the *Dialectica* is controversial: see Mews [7.70] 74–104 and Marenbon [7.68] 41–3.
9   On impersonal statements, see Jacobi [7.53]; on the copula, see de Rijk [7.76] (acute discussion and full bibliography on the question).
10 Christopher Martin (see especially [7.69]) has been the first modern scholar to explain Abelard's theory of entailment. He also brings out the parallels between

Abelard's approach and that in modern 'relevant' logics. The following paragraph depends entirely on his work. On the theory of topics, see above, Chapter 1, pp. 14–15.

11 On the close connection between the principle observed by Boethius (see above, Chapter 1, p. 14) that it is not possible that p implies q and p implies not-q, and the principle that it is not possible that p implies not-p (arguably the two principles are equivalent), see Martin [7.69] 381.

12 See esp. Abelard [7.19] 153: 33–160: 36 and [7.20] 365: 13–370: 3 and cf. de Libera, 'Abélard et le dictisme' in [7.44] 59–92; Martin, 'The logic of the *Nominales*', in Courtenay [7.48] 110–26; de Rijk, 'La signification de la proposition (dictum propositionis) chez Abélard', in [7.74] 547–55; Marenbon [7.68] 222–9.

13 See Abelard [7.19] 199–210 and Abelard [7.14] (entirely on modality). On this subject, see Knuuttila [7.59] 82–96 and Marenbon [7.68] 221–5.

14 He presents these at Abelard [7.20] 10: 17–16: 18, 513: 15–522: 9; cf. Tweedale [7.81] 89–132.

15 Abelard develops this ontology in the *Dialectica* and the *Logica*: for a full discussion and references, see Marenbon [7.68] 117–37.

16 See Abelard [7.20] 129: 33–6 and (on *differentiae*: see below) 84: 14–21, 92: 22–9; cf. Marenbon [7.68] 119–22.

17 See esp. Abelard [7.17] 342: 2434–344: 2532; the whole question is discussed and other texts are given in Marenbon [7.68] 138–61.

18 There is a large literature on Abelard's theory of universals. Among the important modern discussions are Tweedale [7.81], de Rijk, 'The semantical impact of Abailard's solution of the problem of universals', in Thomas [7.80] 139–50 and Jolivet [7.57]. The following paragraphs summarize the rather different view proposed in Marenbon [7.68] 174–201.

19 On imposition, see Abelard [7.19] 595: 11–31.

20 The fullest treatment of various types of difference is in the *Theologia Christiana*, Abelard [7.17], 247: 1677–255: 1936; cf. Marenbon [7.68] 150–5.

21 In Marenbon [7.68] 213–331, the three levels of Abelard's ethical theory are examined. The following section draws especially on chapters 11 and 12 (pp. 251–81).

22 Valuable discussions are given by Blomme [7.46] and M. de Gandillac, 'Intention et loi dans l'éthique d'Abélard' in [7.74] 585–608.

23 Abelard [7.21] 10: 28–14: 25. Abelard puts forward his analysis of the ethical act in a number of works, including the commentary on Romans and the *Sententie*. References here are made, wherever possible, to *Scito teipsum*, both because it contains Abelard's latest formulation of his ideas and it is easily accessible in good translation.

24 See esp. Marenbon [7.64]; Abelard develops his ideas about natural law especially in Book II of the *Theologia Christiana* and in the *Collationes*.

25 On Gilbert's life, see Nielsen [7.73] 25–39.

26 For Gilbert's distinction between the different disciplines, see esp. [7.10] 79: 43–88: 69; on proportional transumption, see e.g. 143: 42–7, 170: 87–93. On the whole question of Gilbert's method, see Marenbon, 'Gilbert of Poitiers', in Dronke [7.49] 330–6.

27 In my piece on Gilbert (cited in the previous note – esp. 329–30, 351–2) I lay

strong (in retrospect too strong) emphasis on the extent to which Gilbert's doctrinal aims shaped his arguments, without bringing out how Gilbert was also contributing to the philosophical debate of his times. De Rijk's criticism [7.75] 34–5, though mistaken in attributing to me a hostile intention towards Gilbert, is in this way very just.

28 Valuable analyses of Gilbert's theory of *quo est* and *quod est* are provided in de Rijk [7.75] and Gracia [7.50] 155–77.

29 Many scholars consider (on the basis, especially, of [7.10] 195: 100–7) that, for Gilbert, *quo ests* are images of disembodied Platonic Ideas. In 'Gilbert of Poitiers', in Dronke [7.49] 349–51, I argue that this is a misinterpretation: Gilbert introduces disembodied forms merely in his account of the creation of the elements, not as the archetypes of *quo ests*. For a different view again, see de Libera [7.58] 170–5.

30 See Knuuttila [7.59], esp. 211–17; Knuuttila discusses the passage in question at pp. 216–17.

31 On this view, 'Socrates' would have to be a rigid designator, picking out the individual Socrates in every possible world where he exists, however different he is from one world to another. But Gilbert's statement about the whole form comprising every *quo est* that belongs to the thing by nature seems to leave the room for variation disturbingly wide. There seems, for instance, no guarantee that Socrates must have the same parents from one possible world to another, and it becomes unclear how at all we should identify Socrates.

32 See esp. Elford, 'William of Conches', in Dronke [7.49] 308–27; more generally on William, see Gregory [7.51].

33 For reconstructions of Thierry's underlying ideas, see Dronke, 'Thierry of Chartres', in Dronke [7.49] 358–85 and Gersh, 'Platonism–Neoplatonism–Aristotelianism: a twelfth-century metaphysical system and its sources', in Benson and Constable [7.45] 512–34.

34 [7.27] 81: 1–7, 82: 25–33; this passage is analysed and its sources discussed by Gersh in the article cited in the previous note, pp. 517–24.

35 'Aggreditur propositum . . .' (printed as Thierry's *Glosa*), [7.27] 275: 11–276: 39 and 'Intentio auctoris . . .' (printed as Thierry's *Lectiones*), [7.27] 168: 76–170: 33, 176: 45–50, which in this discussion puts forward, somewhat less clearly, almost exactly the same view as 'Aggreditur propositum . . .'.

36 See William of Lucca, commentary on ps–Dionysius, ed. F. Gastaldelli, Florence, 1984, xcii–xciii for dating, and xxi–xxvii for the authorship of the *Summa dialetice artis*. For Platonic Ideas, see especially pp. 100–2. For further discussion of this and a related, unpublished text, see Marenbon [7.66] 114–17.

37 The various articles in Courtenay [7.48] provide the best guide to what is known about these schools. See especially Iwakuma and Ebbesen, 'Logico-theological schools from the second half of the twelfth century: a list of sources' (pp. 173–210), which I follow closely here. A very intelligent discussion of the material is given by de Libera [7.61] 132–7. A wealth of material is collected in de Rijk [7.77] II, 2. For a survey, see Jacobi, 'Logic: the later twelfth century', in Dronke [7.49] 227–51.

38 This has been disputed, but two contributions to Courtenay [7.48]: Normore ('Abelard and the school of the Nominales', pp. 80–96) and Iwakuma ('Twelfth-century Nominales: the posthumous school of Peter Abelard', pp. 97–109), put the identification beyond reasonable doubt.

39 See de Rijk [7.78] and Marenbon, 'Vocalism, nominalism and commentaries on the *Categories* from the earlier twelfth century', in Courtenay [7.48] 51–61, at 54–5.

40 Both the *Introductiones montane maiores* and the *Ars meliduna* remain unpublished; de Rijk discusses and prints extracts from them in [7.78] 12–22 and [7.77] II, 1, 264–390. For the *Summa dialetice artis*, see [7.32].

41 For the *Melidunenses*, the so-called *Secta Meliduna* (see de Rijk [7.77] II, 1, 282–6, where the list of these is printed); for the *Nominales*, the so-called *Positio 'nominalium'*, ed. Ebbesen [7.4] 430–2.

42 These observations are taken from Martin [7.69] 394–400, where much fuller details are given.

43 The most important parts of the discussion are printed by de Rijk [7.77] II, 1, 306–9; I am grateful to Dr Yukio Iwakuma for supplying me with a transcript of further material from the *Ars*. De Libera ([7.61] 158–67) discusses the treatment of universals in the *Ars* at length. He suggests that the theory had a further refinement, in that universals are *complex* intelligible structures, which are expressed not by common names but by complex expressions.

44 The reception of *On Sophistical Refutations* is examined in detail in de Rijk [7.77] I.

45 See below, Chapter 17, where most of these areas are discussed.

46 For a brief guide to the extensive bibliography on Porretan theologians, see my 'A note on the Porretani', in Dronke [7.49] 353–7. There is no space here to do justice to the varied work of Alan of Lille (*c.* 1120–1203), which includes philosophical allegories, sermons and two more straightforward theological textbooks; the best guide is in the introduction to Alan of Lille [7.3].

47 There is a fine analysis of discussions of this subject (and of Peter of Poitiers) in Boh [7.47]; I follow Boh in some of my discussion in the next paragraph.

48 See Jolivet, 'The Arabic inheritance', in Dronke [7.49] 134–45 for a detailed discussion and full bibliography.

49 See Burnett, 'Hermann of Carinthia', in Dronke [7.49] 386–404.

50 On David of Dinant, see Maccagnolo, 'David of Dinant and the beginnings of Aristotelianism in Paris', in Dronke [7.49] 429–42; on John Blund, see Jolivet, 'The Arabic inheritance', in Dronke [7.49] 146–7.

BIBLIOGRAPHY

Original Language Editions

7.1 Adam of Balsham *Ars disserendi*, in L. Minio-Paluello (ed.) *Twelfth-century Logic, Texts and Studies I*, Rome, 1956.

7.2 Alan of Lille *Regulae caelestis iuris*, ed. N. Häring, *Archives d'histoire doctrinale et littéraire du moyen âge* 48 (1981): 97–226.

7.3 Alan of Lille *Textes inédits*, ed. M.-T. d'Alverny (Etudes de philosophie médiévale 52), Paris, 1965.

7.4 Anonymous 'Two nominalist texts', ed. S. Ebbesen, *CIMAGL* 61 (1991): 429–40.

7.5   Anonymous *Compendium Logicae Porretanum*, ed. S. Ebbesen, K. Fredborg, L. Nielsen, *CIMAGL* (1983): 46.

7.6   Anonymous, twelfth-century logical works on sophisms and on properties of terms, in de Rijk [7.77], vol. I and vol. II, 2 respectively.

7.7   Bernard of Chartres (?) *Glose super Platonem*, ed. P. E. Dutton (PIMSST 107), Toronto, 1991.

7.8   David of Dinant *Quaternuli* (fragments), ed. M. Kurzialek (Studi mediewisty-czne 3), Warsaw, 1963.

7.9   Garlandus (of Besançon) *Dialectica*, ed. L. M. de Rijk, Assen, 1959.

7.10   Gilbert of Poitiers *Commentaries on Boethius*, ed. N. Häring (PIMSST 13), Toronto, 1966.

7.11   Hermann of Carinthia *De essentiis*, ed. C. Burnett, Leiden and Cologne, 1982.

7.12   John Blund *Tractatus de anima*, ed. D. A. Callus and R. W. Hunt (Auctores Britanni Medii Aevi 2), London, 1970.

7.13   John of Salisbury *Metalogicon*, ed. J. B. Hall (CC c.m. 98), Turnhout, 1991.

7.14   Peter Abelard, authentic ending of *De interpretatione* commentary, in L. Minio-Paluello (ed.) *Twelfth-century Logic II: Abaelardiana inedita*, Rome, 1958.

7.15   —— *Collationes*, ed. R. Thomas, Stuttgart and Bad Cannstatt, 1970.

7.16, 7.17, 7.18   published in *Petri Abaelardi opera theologica* (CC c.m. 11–13), Turnhout, 1969–1987:

7.16   Peter Abelard *Commentary on Romans*, ed. E. Buytaert (11).

7.17   —— *Theologia Christiana*, ed. E. Buytaert (12).

7.18   —— *Theologia summi boni, Theologia scholarium*, ed. E. Buytaert and C. Mews (13).

7.19   —— *Dialectica*, ed. L. M. de Rijk, 2nd edn, Assen, 1970.

7.20   —— *Logica* and *Glossulae* in B. Geyer (ed.) *Peter Abaelards philosophische Schriften* (BGPTMA 21), Münster, 1919–31.

7.21   —— *Scito teipsum (Ethics)*, ed. D. Luscombe, Oxford, 1971.

7.22   —— *Sententie*, ed. S. Buzzetti, Florence, 1983.

7.23   Peter of Poitiers *Sentences*, I and II (only these two vols published), ed. P. S. Moore and M. Dulong, Notre Dame, Ind., 1943, 1950.

7.24   Peter of Vienna (Poitiers) *Summa*, ed. N. Häring, as *Die Zwettler Summe* (BGPTMA n.f. 15), Münster, 1971.

7.25   Peter the Lombard *Sentences*, 2 vols (Spicilegium Bonaventurianum), Grottaferrata, 1971, 1981.

7.26   Richard of St Victor *De trinitate*, ed. G. Salet (Sources Chrétiennes 63), Paris, 1959.

7.27   Thierry of Chartres and others, Commentaries on Boethius, in N. M. Häring (ed.) *Commentaries on Boethius by Thierry of Chartres and his School* (PIMSST 20), Toronto, 1971.

7.28   William of Champeaux *Sententiae*, in O. Lottin, *Psychologie et morale aux XIIe et XIIIe siècles*, V, Gembloux, 1959, pp. 189–227.

7.29   William of Conches, Commentary on *Timaeus* (*Glosae super Platonem*), ed. E. Jeauneau, Paris, 1965.

7.30   —— *Dragmaticon*, ed. W. Gratarolus (as *Dialogus de substantiis physicis*), Strasbourg, 1567; repr. Frankfurt, 1967.

7.31   —— *Philosophia mundi*, ed. G. Maurach, Pretoria, 1980.

7.32 William of Lucca *Summa dialetice artis*, ed. L. Pozzi (Testi e saggi 7), Padua, 1975.

Translations

7.33 Anonymous *Abbreviatio montana*, in N. Kretzmann and E. Stump (eds) *Cambridge Translations of Medieval Philosophical Texts: Logic and the Philosophy of Language*, Cambridge, 1988, pp. 39–78.
7.34 John of Salisbury *Metalogicon*, trans. D. D. McGarry, Gloucester, Mass., 1971.
7.35 Peter Abelard, discussion of universals from *Logica* in P. Spade, *Five Texts on the Mediaeval Problem of Universals*, Indianapolis, Ind. and Cambridge, 1994, pp. 26–56.
7.36 —— *Theologia Christiana* (extracts), trans. J. R. McCallum, Oxford, 1948.
7.37 —— *Collationes*, trans. J. Payer (as *Dialogue between a Jew, a Christian and a Philosopher*) (Mediaeval Sources in Translation 20), Toronto, 1979.
7.38 —— *Scito teipsum*, in the edition by Luscombe [7.21].
7.39 —— selections (in French) in J. Jolivet, *Abélard ou la philosophie dans le langage* (Vestigia 14), Freiburg, Switzerland, 1994.
7.40 —— Letters and *Historia calamitatum*, trans. B. Radice, Harmondsworth, 1974.

Bibliographies, Catalogues and Biographies

7.41 Barrow, J., Burnett, C. and Luscombe, D. 'A checklist of the manuscripts containing the writings of Peter Abelard and Héloïse and other works closely associated with Abelard and his school', *Revue d'histoire des textes* 14–15 (1984–5): 183–302.
7.42 Marenbon, J. 'Medieval Latin commentaries and glosses on Aristotelian logical texts before *c.* 1150 AD', in C. Burnett (ed.) *Glosses and Commentaries on Aristotelian Logical Texts* (Warburg Institute Surveys and Texts 23), London, 1993, pp. 77–127.
7.43 Mews, C. and Jolivet, J. 'Peter Abelard and his influence', in *Contemporary Philosophy: a New Survey*, 6/1, Dordrecht, 1991, pp. 105–40.
Rich bibliographical information will be found in Dronke [7.49], especially in the bio-bibliographies, pp. 443–57.
For biographies, see the bio-bibliographies in Dronke [7.49] 443–557; for Abelard, see Marenbon [7.68] 7–35 and Mews [7.71].

Studies

7.44 *Abélard: Le 'Dialogus', la philosophie de la logique* (Cahiers de la revue de théologie et de philosophie 6), Geneva, Lausanne and Neuchâtel, 1981.
7.45 Benson, R. L. and G. Constable (eds) *Renaissance and Renewal in the Twelfth Century*, Oxford, 1980.
7.46 Blomme, R. *La Doctrine du péché dans les écoles théologiques de la première moitié du XIIᵉ siècle* (Universitas catholica Lovaniensis. Dissertationes ad

gradum magistri . . . consequendum conscriptae, series III, 6), Louvain and Gembloux, 1958.

7.47 Boh, I. 'Divine omnipotence in the early Sentences', in T. Rudavsky (ed.) *Divine Omniscience and Omnipotence in Medieval Philosophy* (Synthese historical library 25), Dordrecht, 1985, pp. 185–211.

7.48 Courtenay, W. (ed.) a collection of articles on twelfth-century nominalism, *Vivarium* 30 (1992).

7.49 Dronke, P. (ed.) *A History of Twelfth-Century Western Philosophy*, Cambridge, 1988.

7.50 Gracia, J. *Introduction to the Problem of Individuation in Early Medieval Philosophy*, Munich and Vienna, 1984.

7.51 Gregory, T. *Anima mundi: La filosofia di Guglielmo di Conches e la Scuola di Chartres*, Florence, 1955.

7.52 Iwakuma, Y. '"Vocales", or early nominalists', *Traditio* 47 (1992): 37–111.

7.53 Jacobi, K. 'Diskussionen über unpersönlichen Aussagen in Peter Abaelards Kommentar zu *Peri Hermeneias*', in E. P. Bos (ed.) *Mediaeval Semantics and Metaphysics* (Artistarium supplementa 2), Nijmegen, 1985, pp. 1–63.

7.54 Jeauneau, E. *Lectio philosophorum*, Amsterdam, 1973.

7.55 Jolivet, J. *Arts du langage et théologie chez Abélard*, 2nd edn (Etudes de philosophie médiévale 57), Paris, 1982.

7.56 —— 'Non-réalisme et platonisme chez Abélard: Essai d'interprétation', in J. Jolivet (ed.) *Abélard en son temps*, Paris 1981; repr. in Jolivet, *Aspects de la pensée médiévale: Abélard: doctrine du langage*, Paris, 1987.

7.57 —— 'Trois variations médiévales sur l'universel et l'individu: Roscelin, Abélard, Gilbert de la Porrée', *Revue de Métaphysique et de Morale* 1 (1992): 111–55.

7.58 Jolivet, J. and Libera, A. de *Gilbert de Poitiers et ses contemporains: aux origines de la 'logica modernorum'* (History of Logic 5), Naples, 1987.

7.59 Knuuttila, S. *Modalities in Medieval Philosophy*, London and New York, 1993.

7.60 Landgraf, A. *Introduction à l'histoire de la littérature théologique de la scolastique naissante*, French edn prepared by A.-M. Landry (Publications de l'institut d'études médiévales, Montreal 22), Montreal and Paris, 1973.

7.61 Libera, A. de *La Querelle des universaux: De Platon à la fin du Moyen Âge*, Paris, 1996.

7.62 Lottin, O. *Psychologie et morale au XIIe et XIIIe siècles*, V, Gembloux, 1959.

7.63 Luscombe, D. 'From Paris to the Paraclete: the correspondence of Abelard and Heloise', *Proceedings of the British Academy* 74 (1988): 247–83.

7.64 Marenbon, J. 'Abelard and natural law', in A. Zimmermann (ed.) *Miscellanea Mediaevalia* 21(2): *Mensch und Natur im Mittelalter*, Berlin and New York, 1992, pp. 609–21.

7.65 —— 'Abelard's ethical theory: two definitions from the *Collationes*', in H. J. Westra (ed.) *From Athens to Chartres*, Leiden, New York and Cologne, 1992, pp. 301–14.

7.66 —— 'Platonismus im 12. Jahrhundert: alte und neue Zugangsweisen', in T. Kobusch and B. Mojsisch (eds) *Platon in der abendländischen Geistesgeschichte: neue Forschungen zum Platonsimus*, Darmstadt, 1997, pp. 101–19.

7.67 —— 'Glosses and commentaries on the *Categories* and *De interpretatione* before Abelard', in J. Fried (ed.) *Dialektik und Rhetorik im früheren und hohen Mittelalter*, Munich, 1997, pp. 21–49.

7.68 —— *The Philosophy of Peter Abelard*, Cambridge, 1997.

7.69 Martin, C. J. 'Embarrassing arguments and surprising conclusions in the development of theories of the conditional in the twelfth century', in J. Jolivet and A. de Libera (eds) *Gilbert de Poitiers et ses contemporains* (History of Logic 5), Naples, 1987, pp. 377–400.

7.70 Mews, C. 'On dating the works of Peter Abelard', *Archives de l'histoire doctrinale et littéraire du moyen âge* 52 (1985): 73–134.

7.71 —— *Peter Abelard* (Authors of the Middle Ages II, 5: Historical and religious writers of the Latin West), Aldershot, 1995.

7.72 —— 'Nominalism and theology before Abelard: new light on Roscelin of Compiègne', *Vivarium* 30 (1992): 4–33.

7.73 Nielsen, L. O. *Theology and Philosophy in the Twelfth Century: A Study of Gilbert Porreta's Thinking and the Theological Expositions of the Doctrine of the Incarnation during the Period 1130–1180* (Acta theologica danica 15), Leiden, 1982.

7.74 *Pierre Abélard, Pierre le Vénérable* (Colloques internationaux du Centre National de la Recherche Scientifique 546), Paris, 1975.

7.75 Rijk, L. M. de 'Semantics and metaphysics in Gilbert of Poitiers: A study in twelfth-century metaphysics', *Vivarium* 26 (1988): 73–112; 27 (1989): 1–35.

7.76 —— 'Peter Abelard's semantics and his doctrine of being', *Vivarium* 24 (1986): 85–128.

7.77 —— *Logica modernorum* I and II, Assen, 1962, 1967.

7.78 —— 'Some new evidence on twelfth-century logic: Alberic and the school of Mont Ste Geneviève', *Vivarium* 4 (1966): 1–57.

7.79 Southern, R. W. 'Humanism and the school of Chartres', in *Medieval Humanism and Other Studies*, Oxford, 1970, pp. 61–85.

7.80 Thomas, R. (ed.) *Petrus Abaelardus (1079–1142): Person, Werk und Wirkung* (Trier theologische Studien 38), Trier, 1980.

7.81 Tweedale, M. *Abailard on Universals*, Amsterdam, New York and Oxford, 1976.

CHAPTER 8

The intellectual context of later medieval philosophy: universities, Aristotle, arts, theology

Stephen Brown

ORIGIN OF THE UNIVERSITIES

A number of medieval towns in the twelfth century owed a large portion of their renown to their schools. Chartres was both respected and criticized for its efforts to reconcile Plato and Aristotle. Reims was a centre for the study of Scripture and the Fathers. Anselm of Laon brought fame to his home as a centre of developing theology. Paris was a magnet attracting famous teachers: Abelard, the dialectician and theologian; Hugh, Richard, and Andrew of St Victor, who brought to their Parisian abbey a justly respected name in the study of Scripture and a reverential awe for its level of mysticism; and Peter Lombard, whose *Sentences* became, from the thirteenth to the sixteenth century, the ordinary textbook of theology. Toledo's cathedral school became a place of contact between the Christian and Muslim intellectual worlds and offered a home for translators and commentators. In that school Dominic Gundissalinus, Gerard of Cremona, the Scotsman Michael Scotus, and the Englishman Alfred of Sareschal provided translations of Aristotle and his Islamic commentators that would later serve as key curriculum texts in the nascent universities.[1] Bologna grew famous for the study of law, owing mainly to the stature of the legal advisers of Frederick Barbarossa and to the masters who explained Gratian's great canonical collection, the *Decretum*. Salerno drew students for medicine owing to the fame of Constantine the African, translator of the *Articelli* or *Art of Medicine*, a collection of texts that became the

188

heart of the medical curriculum. Under the leadership of Bartholomew of Salerno, Maurus and Urso of Calabria, Salerno stood as the centre for the study of medicine from 1050 to 1200 before yielding its place of primacy to Montpellier and Paris ([8.22] 65–88).

At the end of the twelfth and the beginning of the thirteenth centuries great consolidations occurred. If we limit ourselves to the consideration of theology, Paris led the way on the Continent. With the support of Popes Innocent III and Gregory IX, the University of Paris became the theological stronghold of the Christian world. The cathedral school of Notre Dame, the abbey of St Victor, the houses of the newly arrived Dominicans and Franciscans, formed an intellectual guild or corporation of masters and students, a *universitas magistorum et scholarium*. In the pursuit of their common interests they became a unified and autonomous community. This guild took the title 'University of Paris'. Across the Channel, Oxford outstripped the other English schools, owing mainly to the influence of Robert Grosseteste, student of scriptural wisdom, translator of Aristotle's *Nicomachean Ethics*, commentator on the Greek philosopher's *Posterior Analytics*, bishop of Lincoln, and chancellor of the young university ([8.21] 3–48).

❧ THE AUGUSTINIAN MODEL OF STUDY ❧

The programme of study for the cathedral, monastery and palace schools of the twelfth century, and for the early universities of the late twelfth and early thirteenth centuries, was inspired by St Augustine's *On Christian Doctrine*. Book II of Augustine's work viewed traditional pagan studies, if approached prudently, as helpful to those seeking understanding of the divine wisdom found in the sacred Scriptures. The seven liberal arts (the *trivium* of grammar, rhetoric and dialectic and the *quadrivium* of arithmetic, astronomy, geometry and music), along with geography, botany, geology and the mechanical arts all could assist those who read the Scriptures to attain a fuller grasp of the divine message. The twelfth-century schools of liberal arts became the faculties of arts in the universities of the thirteenth century. The arts faculty was a preparatory faculty, training students for further studies in law, medicine, and especially theology.

Richard Fishacre, in a sermon that he preached on the first day of class at Oxford in 1246, tells us that there is a threefold wisdom. The first kind of wisdom is that which is written in the book of life. This form of wisdom is the wisdom of God himself. To see God's meaning and plan for everything, to the degree that is possible for man, is the goal that all studies should strive to achieve. The way of attaining this goal is by carefully studying the two other books that manifest the divine wisdom found in the book of life: the book of the Scriptures and the book of nature. The Scriptures provide God's revelation to humankind of the riches of his own wisdom. The Bible is, thus, the principal help in coming to some understanding of divine wisdom. The Scriptures also give us a view of the book of nature that differs from the portraits of nature given by philosophers who are unaided by divine revelation. The Scriptures tell us that the natural world is a world created by and cared for by God. They likewise tell us that the created world provides vestiges and images of its Creator. The Bible uses natural things and the events of history to lead us to deeper understandings of God's wisdom. We must therefore study the Scriptures to learn what they themselves say of God; but we must also, guided by the Bible, study the natural world to see how richly it tells us about the God who creates and cares for it, and whose imprint it bears. Both the Bible and creation thus help us to discover 'the depths of the riches both of the wisdom and knowledge of God' (Rom. 11: 33) ([8.11] 23–36 and [8.20]).

This sermon of Richard Fishacre at Oxford, following the Augustinian model of study, shows the way of investigation in the early medieval universities. The final goal of all study is to come to a greater understanding of God's view of reality, by taking as primary source the sacred Scriptures, which reveal the divine wisdom. The secondary instrument for discovering divine wisdom is found in the created world, which provides all the analogies for coming to a fuller understanding of God. They are the analogies used in the Scriptures: 'The kingdom of heaven is like a mustard seed'; 'You are the salt of the earth'; 'Behold the lamb of God, who takes away the sins of the world'; 'My kingdom is not of this world.' All other studies serve as helps in pursuing the divine wisdom that lies hidden in such scriptural declarations and that is manifested in some way in the created images of mustard seeds, salt, lamb, and earthly kingdoms that the Scriptures employ to speak of the hidden things of God. All the human disciplines, principally those of grammar, rhetoric, dialectic, arithmetic, geometry, astronomy, music – and philosophy, in the more technical sense of the term – are handmaids to be put at the service of the mistress, the wisdom of the Scriptures ([8.11] 26–32).

❧ THE STUDY OF ARISTOTLE ❧

At the beginning of the universities, only in the area of dialectic (logic) did Aristotle fit into the traditional curriculum of studies that prepared students for the study of the sacred Scriptures. What became known as the *logica vetus*, or old logic, included Aristotle's *Categories* and *On Interpretation*. This old logic, available in Latin to the schools since the time of Boethius (480–525), also included the introduction to the *Categories* made by Porphyry and the commentaries on these two works of Aristotle done by Boethius himself. Before the middle of the twelfth century the *logica nova*, or new logic (the *Prior Analytics*, *Posterior Analytics*, *Topics* and *On Sophistical Refutations*) was also in use. Some of these works derived from the translation efforts of Boethius, but had been lost or neglected; others, by 1150, had been newly trans-lated by James of Venice.[2] Thus the whole of Aristotle's *Organon* or logic was available and had an ever deepening influence, transforming medieval Christian thinking from a sacramental or symbolic form of knowledge to a more scientific discipline through the study of various causal connections.

As the more properly philosophical works of Aristotle (e.g. *On the Soul*, *Physics*, *Metaphysics*, *Nicomachean Ethics* and *Politics*) were translated and began to be studied, more than the style or character of Christian knowledge was changed. The contents of Aristotle's works, his natural philosophy, slowly but surely also began to have their influ-ence: his view of man, his teaching on the eternity of the world, his portrait of the unmoved Mover or supreme Being, his doctrine of virtues, his focus on the natural fulfilment or end of man. For the first time since the patristic era, Christian thinkers encountered a pagan philosopher directly. Many were struck by the brilliance of his intel-ligence and the strength of his argumentation; others were troubled by those of his teachings that seemed incompatible with those of the Christian faith.[3]

➤➤ DIFFICULTIES WITH ARISTOTLE'S ➤➤ NATURAL PHILOSOPHY

Attempts at moderating the disturbing influence that Aristotle's philosophy might have were made a number of times. The first inter-vention came in 1210 from the Provincial Council of Sens, presided over by Peter of Corbeil; it forbade the reading of Aristotle's 'natural philosophy' at Paris. Five years later, the papal legate Robert de Courçon also prohibited the reading of Aristotle's 'natural philosophy'. In 1231, Pope Gregory IX appointed a commission of William of Auxerre, Simon of Authie and Stephen of Provins to correct the prohib-ited books. Since William of Auxerre died shortly thereafter, the commission never met. Furthermore, this effort made by Gregory to correct Aristotle gradually became viewed as an admission that Aristotle was not necessarily wrong, but only wrong on certain issues. Little by little the prohibition against his natural philosophy was ignored. By 1255, all the known works of Aristotle, at least at an introductory level of understanding, were required in the arts faculty of the University of Paris ([8.26] 132–81).

Aristotle's works were read at many different levels. There was the introductory or beginner's level, where a first approach was made to one of his texts. In this beginning *lectio*, or reading, the Aristotelian text was read aloud and the basic direction and outline of the work was indicated. In a more advanced *lectio*, the text was explained in detail. In commentaries on the philosopher's works, the text was sometimes evaluated and on certain points questions were posed and answered. At the more advanced level of study, 'questions' concerning a text usually involved a deeper examination of the philosophical issues raised. In such a questioning approach, both sides of a debate were presented, and then a solution to the conflict was offered by the master. As teachers and students became more and more familiar with Aristotle's texts and philosophical positions, more specific conflicts between what he seemed to teach and what were matters of Christian belief became more evident.

Some points of Aristotelian teaching that caused problems for Christians had been passed down from the patristic era. St Augustine, for instance, had attributed to Aristotle the position that the world was eternal and therefore was not created in time. This was one of the grounds for the prohibitions at Paris against the public reading, before correction, of the natural philosophy of Aristotle in the early thirteenth century. Teachers who saw benefits for Christian theology that might come from the study of Aristotle, argued, however, that Aristotle never dealt with the question of creation. Aristotle, according to their reading of his texts, was simply giving a physical explanation, claiming that time did not exist before the world itself came to exist. Philip the Chancellor and Alexander of Hales, for instance, claimed that metaphysics dealt with the issue of creation and that Aristotle did not pass metaphysical judgements on the nature of the world. According to their interpretation, Aristotle was only speaking as a physicist or natural philosopher: describing the world as it actually exists, not taking a position on whether it was created or not (see [8.16] 57–70).

Other problems concerning Aristotle's teachings none the less gradually came to the fore as Christian thinkers became more familiar with his positions and with the commentaries made on them by earlier authors, especially the often conflicting commentaries of the Arabic philosophers, Avicenna and Averroes. St Bonaventure, in his Lenten sermons at Paris in the late 1260s and early 1270s, pointed out a number of problems in Aristotelian teaching at the university. The disturbing views at times might not clearly be positions of Aristotle himself, but rather positions of those in the arts faculty who show the strong influence of Averroes' interpretations of the Greek philosopher. The principal difficulties were: (1) the unicity of man's intellect, implying no personal immortality, and thus undermining individual moral responsibility; (2) the eternity of the world, entailing its independence from divine creation and a denial of divine concern or providence; (3) the independent study of philosophy – pretending to be a supreme and definitive wisdom separated from Christian wisdom.[4]

The most detailed catalogue of the difficulties raised by the teaching of certain heterodox or radical Aristotelians in the arts faculty, however, is found in the list of 216 propositions condemned at Paris in 1277. They might be divided into two basic groups: (1) propositions concerned with the nature of philosophy and its relation to divinely revealed truths; (2) propositions of a specific kind that challenge particular truths of the faith. Among the first type of propositions we can find these condemned statements: (a) there is no more excellent state than to dedicate oneself to philosophy; (b) the only wise men of the world are the philosophers; (c) for a man to have any certitude about a conclusion, it is necessary for him to base his argument on self-evident principles; (d) nothing should be admitted as true unless it can be proved by a self-evident principle or by something based on self-evident principles; (e) man should not be content merely with authority if he is to achieve absolute certitude in regard to any question; (f) the Christian faith impedes learning; (g) there are fables and false things in the Christian religion just as in other faiths. Among the specific positions condemned we find the propositions: (a) God does not know anything but himself; (b) the world, including all the species that are contained in it, is eternal; (c) it is impossible to refute the reasons of the philosopher concerning the eternity of the world without admitting that the will of God contains incompatibles; (d) the intellect is numerically one for all men; (e) happiness is had in this life, not in another.

There were, then, in the late 1260s and throughout the 1270s– 1280s signs of a real challenge to the Augustinian model of study, which stressed the unity of Christian wisdom. This challenge, of necessity, also affected studies in the faculty of theology as teachers and students moved there after learning or teaching in the arts faculty.[5]

❧ THEOLOGY AS A DEDUCTIVE SCIENCE ❧

The 1253 university statutes at Oxford, confirming actually existing practice, indicate that a student could attain his degree in theology (which was considered a higher degree, as opposed to the degree taken earlier in the arts) by one of three routes: (1) he could study the Bible, a practice that usually entailed writing commentaries, using earlier exegetical efforts, on at least one book of the Old Testament and one book of the New Testament; (2) he could present a commentary on Peter Comestor's *Scholastic History* which presented a broader overview of all history, based primarily on the biblical account; (3) he could comment on the *Sentences* of Peter Lombard, a collection of doctrinal questions organized in four books according to logical principles. The same options in practice were available even earlier in Paris, as is clear not only from the statutes of the Dominican Order listing these three options, but also from the practices that were in vogue after Alexander of Hales made the *Sentences* of Lombard a course textbook. Generally, we can say that the third option, the commentary on Peter Lombard's *Sentences*, was the one most frequently followed in the universities by the 1250s, if not earlier. Theology, through this instrument, thus became more and more a logically organized or scientific discipline (see [8.1] 112, [8.2] 49).

The logical organization of doctrinal questions is evident in the many earlier authors, who followed Peter Lombard's *Sentences* by commenting in the margins of his text. His text was their text. It is also evident in the *Summae* of the late twelfth and early thirteenth centuries, which for the most part patterned themselves on his schema of questions. Explicit efforts to justify this procedure only come later. They can be found, for example, in the *Summa quaestionum* written by William of Auxerre in the 1220s, with its close structural correspondence to Lombard's *Sentences*. Lombard (d. 1160) provides no discussion or justification of his method; nor do the people who gloss his *Sentences* or write *summae quaestionum* that slightly alter Lombard's organization. William of Auxerre, living in a university world more strongly touched by Aristotle's logical works, tries to give a methodological justification for writing such a work. For William, theology starts with certain principles or premises and makes explicit, or deduces, the further knowledge implied in these premises. The primary premises in theology are the articles of the Christian faith. They are the starting points for theological reflection. They also set the boundaries for theological studies, in the sense that theology should not deviate from the articles of the faith nor pursue questions unrelated to basic Christian beliefs ([8.6] 17).

Other theologians immediately following William of Auxerre more deliberately attempted to set up parallel structures between Aristotle's model of science and their intellectual efforts in theology. Odo Rigaud, speaking of a 'science of the faith' maps out the correspondences and differences between the method he follows and the method sketched by Aristotle in the *Posterior Analytics* (see [8.23] II, 12–13). Thomas Aquinas set up a parallel between Aristotle's description of a subalternated science, like optics, which used principles borrowed from a higher or subalternating science such as geometry, and the subalternated science of theology that uses principles borrowed from the higher science possessed by God and the blessed – principles that God has revealed in the Scriptures. Just as geometry, which studies lines, helps the student of optics, which studies lines of vision, come to an understanding of the lines of vision, so God's knowledge of all that he has revealed provides the ultimate first principles which allow the student of theology to come to a knowledge or understanding of God and all things as they are related to him. Theology, then, is a science in the same way that optics is a science ([8.15] 67–92).

CRITIQUES OF THEOLOGY AS A DEDUCTIVE SCIENCE

As we have indicated, the intellectual atmosphere in the late 1260s and throughout the 1270s–1280s had altered. Argument had become more precise and hard-nosed. Godfrey of Fontaines, who was a student at Paris during most of Thomas Aquinas' second teaching period there (1269–72) attacked, in question 10 of his *Quodlibet IV* (1287), Aquinas' claim that theology was like a subaltern science. Godfrey distinguishes two kinds of certitude: the certitude based on evidence and the certitude based on faith. Technically, he calls them certitude of evidence and certitude of adherence. He then argues that if we start with principles or premises that we hold because of faith, then no matter how sure we are that the conclusions are true, still they will never be science, since science is based on evidence. Of course, a correctly argued conclusion can be a certain conclusion. Yet, since it still is based on faith, it is not an evident conclusion, and thus is not science. We might want to speak of the necessary way in which a faith conclusion flows from faith premises and argue that there is a science of the consequence. Yet this in no way supplies evidence for the consequent or conclusion.

Godfrey also contested the example given by Aquinas. He argues that where a subaltern science must rely on principles received from an expert in a higher science which, within the subaltern science, are believed but cannot be *known*, then the subaltern science is not truly a science at all. Yet this is the case in theology as Aquinas presents it: the principles of theology, in so far as they are revealed by God, are believed. Just as human authority begets opinion which is a state of mind lacking both kinds of certitude, so divine authority produces faith which is a state of mind that only has the certitude of adherence. Of what advantage is it, asks Godfrey, for a theologian who is relying on such principles, which he cannot know but must accept as a matter of faith, that they are known evidently and with certitude to the blessed and that, in themselves, they are evident and certain? This does not bring the believing theologian evidence. He remains essentially a believer, without evidence. Theology is not a science, at least in the sense that it brings evidence for theological truths (see [8.3] 260–4; cf. [8.25] 120–31).

Henry of Ghent (d. 1293) was also a critic of Thomas Aquinas. Whereas Godfrey of Fontaines criticized Aquinas from an Aristotelian viewpoint, Henry criticized him from an Augustinian one. One of Henry's main efforts in his approach to philosophy and theology was to show that Aristotle had a limited vision of reality, that he was deprived of the riches of Christian revelation, and that his philosophy was too pretentious in presenting itself as a complete human wisdom.

In his discussion of the nature of theology, Henry gave the strictest literal analysis of Aristotle's theory of subalternation, as found in the *Posterior Analytics*. Then he declared that none of the philosopher's types exactly fit what Thomas tried to make them fit. In effect, the philosopher never knew a case of subalternation of the kind that Thomas was speaking about (see [8.8] 52r–4r; cf. [8.12] 337–45, [8.14] 194–206).

❧ GODFREY'S AND HENRY'S ALTERNATIVES ❧ TO DEDUCTIVE THEOLOGY

Godfrey's critique of Aquinas argued that any conclusion deduced from premises held on faith could only be a conclusion of faith. In proceeding to such a conclusion or consequent we gain no evidence. The only way in which one might speak of any scientific progress is in the logical realm: we can by correct logical procedure guarantee science of the consequence. This critical side of Godfrey moved at least one later author to place Godfrey in the camp of those who held that theology is a science of consequences (see [8.25] 108). For Godfrey, however, theology is, beyond a science of consequences, a science of Sacred Scripture. In a way that a layman does not, a theologian develops a habit whereby he can show in the texts of Sacred Scripture the justifications or warrants for the truths of the Christian faith. He knows, for instance, that the Trinity and the Incarnation are taught or anticipated in such and such texts of the Old and New Testament. He thus knows not only the truths of the faith as presented in the Creed; he knows the scriptural bases on which the Church supports herself in teaching them. And this knowledge is not just a habit based on memorization. A theologian comes to understand the Scriptures and sees that sense cannot be made of certain passages unless one admits a plurality of persons in God and a plurality of natures in Christ.

Godfrey's full position might even claim more of a role for a theologian than what we have stated so far, but most later portraits of his stance limit him to holding that theology is a science of Sacred Scripture (see [8.4] 69–82; 4. [8.25] 155–67). Theology as a science of Sacred Scripture was far too restrictive for Henry of Ghent, since it seemed to leave aside any knowledge of the realities of which Sacred Scripture speaks. It seemed to him that Godfrey's position abandoned the study of reality to philosophers and awarded simply the study of the sacred texts to the theologians. In question 2 of *Quodlibet XII* (1288), Henry waged his attack on Godfrey:

> It is very striking that teachers in every other faculty do their best to praise their science. It is only certain theologians, in an effort to promote philosophy, who put down theology, saying that it is not properly a science and that it cannot make the realities we believe in truly intelligible in the present life. Such theologians block any way of knowing or understanding the things we believe in. They lead others to the point of having no hope of understanding these realities. Surely, this is pernicious, dangerous to those who hear it, and harmful to the Church.
>
> ([8.7] 485v, trans. SFB)

It is in reaction to Godfrey's main thesis, that theology is a science of Sacred Scripture, that Henry of Ghent was forced to pursue another route, which would admit a science of the realities spoken of in the Scriptures and presented by the Church for Christian belief. He claimed that theologians receive extra assistance from God to understand the realities of which the Scriptures speak.

It is important to realize that, for Henry, any certain knowledge that man might attain requires at least God's general assistance or illumination. A helpful analogy might be found by imagining a person inside a cathedral, looking at the colours and shapes of the stained glass windows. What that person immediately focuses on, of course, are the colours and shapes of the figures in the windows. When we reflect on the situation, however, we realize that this person could not see the colours or determine the shapes unless the sun, hidden from immediate perception, were present and active. Similarly, we would grasp nothing for certain, because of the darkness of the objects or the weakness of our sight, unless God, like the sun, were illuminating the objects and assisting our sight. For Henry, this is the general illumination required for any certain knowledge. In the case, however, when a theologian is dealing with the objects of faith, objects beyond man's natural perception even when aided with the general assistance of God's illumination, he needs a special assistance or illumination to grasp these supernatural objects of faith.

Henry presents this special light as a middle light between the light of faith, which elevates men with faith to know, by hearing the authority of Scripture, things that are above anything Aristotle ever grasped. It is also a light below that possessed by the blessed who behold the realities that at one time they may have only believed. This middle light is a special illumination given to theologians, as distinct from laymen and the blessed, to grasp the realities they believe in.

> In regard to the divine world, by knowing the natures of the terms of faith, such as 'Father', 'Son', and 'Holy Spirit', he can, by the intellect's search, with the aid of supernatural light [faith] and with special divine illumination [the middle light], come to know that the Holy Spirit proceeds from the Father and the Son, and not from the Father alone. And the same holds for other realities that are proper to the science of theology and that pertain to faith.
>
> ([8.8] 94v–95r, trans. SFB)

The science of theology as developed by Henry thus appeals to a middle light between the light of faith and the light of glory. Theology thereby is very definitely aimed beyond the study of the Scriptures as such to a study of the higher realities of which the Scriptures speak ([8.7] 485r–486v).

THE DECLARATIVE THEOLOGY OF PETER AUREOLI

Criticisms of Henry of Ghent's position were strong. Godfrey thought that Henry was placing theologians beyond academic accountability. They could merely claim a superior light that others lacked ([8.4] 71). John Duns Scotus points to a predecessor who wondered why students and teachers spent so much time in the classroom sweating over theological arguments rather than in chapel praying for this theological light ([8.9] 43). In brief, to many theologians Henry seemed to be claiming more than he could warrant.

Peter Aureoli (d. 1328) thought that the direction of theology had gone awry since the time of William of Auxerre, often acclaimed as the thirteenth-century apostle of deductive theology. Aureoli gives one of the most extensive discussions on the nature of theology that can be found among medieval authors. He presents in great detail the positions of Thomas, Godfrey, Henry and Duns Scotus, refutes each in terms of his own view of the character of theology, and then tells us what theology is really about.

When we say that he presents and criticizes the opinions of these theologians, he does not simply repeat the critiques others have given of these opinions. It is from his own perspective concerning the nature of theology that he produces his critique. What is that perspective? It is this: theologians develop many cognitive habits when they study theology. Since they make many deductions, they develop strong logical skills. Since they use among their premises, besides the premises of faith, materials from physics and metaphysics, they become very able in Averroes' philosophy of nature and Avicenna's metaphysics. Since they trace revealed truths back to their biblical sources, they become very knowledgable in the texts of the Scriptures. Theologians thus develop cognitive abilities in many fields of learning. Yet none of the intellectual habits that we have mentioned are the proper habit of a theologian. Most recent theology, according to Aureoli, has been led astray from what it is really about. It has been led astray by the limping analogy that the articles of the faith are principles or quasi-principles in theology. Theology in the proper sense is surely about the articles of the faith, but not as principles from which we deduce new truths. It is rather about the articles themselves. Properly speaking, theology is declarative: it brings light to these very articles of the faith.

When Aureoli says that theology is declarative, he means first of all that the theologian, using analogies and probable reasons taken from other sciences, is able to gain and offer some understanding of the things he believes in, and is able to overcome doubts raised against them. He can, furthermore, make clear the meanings of terms that are used to express the truths of the Christian faith, and can appeal to and explain the scriptural bases that sustain these truths. In brief, he is 'ready to render an account of those things that are in him by faith' (I Peter 3: 15). Now, none of these abilities makes him believe. His faith is the ground for accepting these truths. Theology is declarative: it is a habit that makes the theologian more clearly grasp with his mind the things that the Church believes in. In the words of St Augustine in Book XIV of *On the Trinity*, theology is the kind of 'knowledge by which the most wholesome faith is begotten, nourished, defended, and strengthened'.

According to Peter Aureoli, Augustine, Thomas Aquinas and all doctors of theology in their practice formed questions concerning the very articles of the faith. They asked: Is there only one God? Is there in God a trinity of persons? Is the incarnation possible? They tried to answer such questions in their *summae* or commentaries on Lombard's *Sentences*. It is not that they doubted their truth. The *question* as a learning instrument was not developed to undermine the faith, nor to produce faith. It was a method designed to bring greater clarity to what they already believed. Instead of speaking of the articles of the faith as principles or premises, as theologians have done since at least the time of William of Auxerre, Aureoli would have them speak of the articles of faith almost as conclusions. By responding to the *quaestio*, by clarifying the terms employed, by answering objections, by finding suitable analogies, and developing strong arguments, theologians not only make it clearer *that* there is one God, or *that* there are three persons in God, or *that* the incarnation is possible, but they make it clearer how these things are so ([8.10] 132–75; cf. [8.24] 20–78).

❧ GREGORY OF RIMINI'S CASE FOR ❧ DEDUCTIVE THEOLOGY

In the opening question of the prologue to his *Commentary on Book I of Lombard's Sentences* in 1342, Gregory of Rimini certainly had Peter Aureoli in mind when he tried to determine what is proper theological discourse. Proper theological discourse must focus, he contends, on the articles of the faith, not on the probable arguments that might be employed to bring some clarity to the articles of the faith. Probable arguments in themselves only beget opinion, and surely theology is not primarily a discipline aimed at producing opinion.

Gregory's own view of properly theological discourse is the type of argument made up of propositions contained in Sacred Scripture or propositions deduced from scriptural propositions. Everyone realizes, he argues, that something is proved theologically when it is proved from the words of Scripture. If a theologian proves that God is eternal and does so on the basis of the eternity of motion, as Aristotle does in Book XII of the *Metaphysics*, he is not involved in theological discourse. If he bases himself on John's Gospel ('In the beginning was the Word . . .' [John 1: 1]), then this is proper theological discourse. This is the kind of discourse that marks Augustine's arguments in *On the Trinity*: he does not prove the Trinity by probable propositions, but rather by the authority of Scripture. Likewise, when the Church determined as a matter of Christian belief that the Holy Spirit proceeds from the Father and the Son, it did not declare this to be an article of faith because of analogies or probable arguments. It was because the Church saw that this truth followed necessarily from the statements of Sacred Scripture. The ultimate resolution of all theological discourse, according to Gregory, is the truth of the sacred canon of the Scriptures.

It is from the truths of Scripture that all other theological truths are ultimately deduced. Theology, then, according to Gregory, properly is deductive, not declarative ([8.5] 13–23; [8.18] 610–44).

❦ THEOLOGY AS DECLARATIVE AND ❦ DEDUCTIVE

Some theologians, such as Peter of Candia, who commented on Lombard's *Sentences* at Paris in 1378–80, evaluated the declarative theology of Peter Aureoli and the deductive theology of Gregory of Rimini, and judged that both approaches were necessary. He argued that the articles of the faith can, in fact, be appreciated in themselves and also as premises for extending the domain of faith by deducing further legitimate conclusions. The method followed when the articles of the faith are considered in themselves is a direct or immediate approach to revealed truth: all the truths are seen as parts of a cohesive whole and are affirmed in an equal manner. When the articles of the faith are viewed as premises, then the theological conclusions drawn from them are not affirmed directly. The believer adheres to them as derived, and as due to his adherence to the premises from which they are derived and to which he directly assents. In admitting that both declarative and deductive theology are proper theological habits, Peter of Candia claims that he was following in the footsteps of John Duns Scotus and William of Ockham. He also was imitating the actual practice of almost all medieval university theologians up to the time of Gregory of Rimini (see [8.13] 156–90).

 NOTES

1   For the beginnings of the translation movement, see above, Chapter 7, pp. 179–80.
2   On the *logica vetus* and *logica nova*, see also above, Chapter 7, pp. 176–7.
3   See Dod [8.17] 45–79 and Lohr [8.19] 80–98. For a fuller account of the translations (and Arab commentaries), see below, Chapter 10, pp. 226–7.
4   See Van Steenberghen [8.27] 3–114. On Bonaventure, see also below, Chapter 10, pp. 227–30.
5   See Denifle-Chatelain [8.1] 543–60 for the relevant charters.

BIBLIOGRAPHY

Original Language Editions

8.1 Denifle, H. S. and Chatelain, A. *Chartularium Universitatis Parisiensis*, 4 vols, Paris, Delain, 1889–97.

8.2 Gibson, S. *Statuta antiqua universitatis Oxoniensis*, Oxford, Clarendon Press, 1931.

8.3 Godfrey of Fontaines *Les quatres premiers Quodlibets de Godefroid de Fontaines*, M. De Wulf and A. Pelzer (eds) *Les Philosophes belges*, vol. 3, Louvain, Institut Supérieur de Philosophie de l'Université, 1904.

8.4 —— *Le huitième Quodlibet, Le neuvième Quodlibet, Le dixième Quodlibet*, J. Hoffmans (ed.) *Les Philosophes belges*, vol. 4, Louvain, Institut Supérieur de Philosophie de l'Université, 1924.

8.5 Gregory of Rimini *Lectura super primum et secundum Sententiarum*, ed. A. D. Trapp and V. Marcolino (Spätmittelalter und Reformation. Texte und Untersuchung 6), Berlin and New York, De Gruyter, 1981.

8.6 William of Auxerre *Summa aurea*, J. Ribaillier (ed.) *Spicilegium Bonaventurianum*, vol. 16, Paris and Grottaferrata, Editions du Centre National de la Recherche Scientifique et Editiones Collegii S. Bonaventurae ad Claras Aquas, 1980.

8.7 Henry of Ghent *Quodlibeta*, Paris, I. Badius Ascensius, 1518.

8.8 —— *Summa quaestionum ordinariarum*, Paris, I. Badius Ascensius, 1520.

8.9 John Duns Scotus *Opera omnia*, vol. XV, Paris, Vivès, 1893.

8.10 Peter Aureoli *Scriptum super Primum Sententiarum*, ed. E. M. Buytaert, St Bonaventure, NY, Louvain and Paderborn, Franciscan Institute, E. Nauwelaerts and F. Schöningh, 1952.

Studies

8.11 Brown, S. F. 'Richard Fishacre on the need for "philosophy"', R. Link-Salinger, J. Hackett, M. S. Hyman, R. J. Long and C. H. Marekin (eds) *A Straight Path: Studies in Medieval Philosophy and Culture*, Washington, DC, Catholic University of America Press, 1988.

8.12 —— 'Henry of Ghent's critique of Aquinas' subalternation theory and the early Thomistic response', R. Työrinoja, A. I. Lehtinen and D. Føllesdal (eds) *Knowledge and the Sciences in Medieval Philosophy*, Helsinki, Annals of the Finnish Society for Missiology and Ecumenics, vol. 55, 1990.

8.13 —— 'Peter of Candia's hundred year "History" of the theologian's role', *Medieval Philosophy and Theology* 1 (1991): 156–90.

8.14 —— 'Henry of Ghent's *Reductio artium ad theologiam*', D. Gallagher (ed.) *Thomas Aquinas and his Influence in the Middle Ages*, Washington, DC, Catholic University of America Press, 1994.

8.15 Chenu, M.-D. *La Théologie comme science au XIIIe siècle*, Paris, Vrin, 1957.

8.16 Dales, R. C. *Medieval Discussions of the Eternity of the World*, Leiden, New York, Copenhagen and Cologne, E. J. Brill, 1990.

8.17 Dod, B. G. 'Aristoteles Latinus', in *CHLMP*.

8.18 Grassi, O. 'La questione della teologia come scienza in Gregorio da Rimini', *Rivista di filosofia neo-scolastica* 68 (1976): 610–44.

8.19 Lohr, C. 'The medieval interpretation of Aristotle', in *CHLMP*.

8.20 Long, R. J. 'The science of theology according to Richard Fishacre: edition of the Prologue to his *Commentary on the Sentences*', *Mediaeval Studies* 34 (1972): 71–98.

8.21 McEvoy, J. *The Philosophy of Robert Grosseteste*, Oxford, Clarendon Press, 1982.

8.22 Montero-Cartelle, E. 'Encuentro de culturas en Salerno: Constantino el Africano, Traductor', J. Hamesse *et al.* (eds) *Rencontres de cultures dans la philosophie médiévale*, Louvain and Cassino, Publications de l'Institut d'Etudes médiévales, 1990.

8.23 Sileo, L. *Teoria della scienza teologica*, Rome, Pontificium Athenaeum Antonianum, 1984.

8.24 Streuer, S. R. *Die theologische Einleitungslehre des Petrus Aureoli*, Werl in Westphalia, Franziskanische Forschungen, 1968.

8.25 Tihon, P. *Foi et théologie selon Godefroid de Fontaines*, Paris and Bruges, Desclée de Brouwer, 1966.

8.26 Van Steenberghen, F. *La Philosophie au XIIIe siècle*, Louvain and Paris, Publications Universitaires and Béatrice-Nauwelaerts, 1966.

8.27 —— *Thomas Aquinas and Radical Aristotelianism*, Washington, DC, Catholic University of America Press, 1980.

CHAPTER 9

Metaphysics and science in the thirteenth century: William of Auvergne, Robert Grosseteste and Roger Bacon

Steven Marrone

By the third decade of the thirteenth century there emerge the first signs of a new metaphysics. Alongside Neoplatonizing idealism we now see attempts to lay greater emphasis on the ontological density of the created world and to structure reality without resorting to the terms of a relation to the divine ideal. The ensuing philosophical reassessment was more systematic, more technically precise and more self-conscious than anything the medieval West had seen before. Given the catalysing role played by logic, it was only natural that much of this programme was carried out within the confines of an attempt to explain knowledge. For the early thirteenth century, metaphysics and epistemology went hand in hand.

The two figures who did the most to promote the new meta-physics, as well as a profoundly Aristotelianizing campaign to establish the criteria for knowledge, were masters whose important work was done between 1220 and 1235 in the schools of theology at the new universities. Robert Grosseteste (d. 1253) was born in England prob-ably before 1170, studied and taught the arts curriculum in provincial schools and perhaps at Paris and Oxford, and began to lecture on theology at Oxford after 1214 but no later than 1225. His activity as a philosopher effectively ended with his appointment as bishop of Lincoln in 1235. William of Auvergne (d. 1249) was born in France around 1180, went to Paris to study, and began teaching there first in arts and then by the 1220s in theology. He was named bishop of

Paris in 1228, although he continued to write about philosophical matters for some years thereafter.

In Grosseteste's earlier works there is, to be sure, no hint of the new attitude. His treatise *On Truth* (*De veritate*) offers an ontology still firmly grounded in the Neoplatonic world-view. Quoting Anselm, he defines truth as a kind of ontological obligation: the correctness (*rectitudo*) of objective things ([9.3] 135: 3–6). Such obligation is met inasmuch as things conform to God's eternal word, or, more specifically, to an idea or reason (*ratio, ratio aeterna*) in God's mind, eternally representing the object as it ought to be ([9.3] 137: 1–2, 139: 29–30).

This idealized notion of truth is directly manifest in Grosseteste's noetics. Drawing on an image commonplace in Latin Christian discourse since the time of Augustine, he explains that the intellect can attain the truth, its proper object, only in an intelligible light shining from God himself ([9.3] 137: 2–4). The image surely serves in part as shorthand for a more complicated epistemic argument. If objective truth is a quality arising out of the conformity between an object and its divine ideal, then the mind can seize the truth only when it perceives, and can compare, both thing (*res*) and idea (*ratio*) ([9.3] 138: 4–11). It is clear, however, that Grosseteste also takes quite literally the existence of a higher light in which truth must be known. He goes on to say that just as the eye can see a coloured body only when it is bathed in visible light, so the mind can know a thing in its truth only if the divine light is shining on it ([9.3] 137: 19–25).

Yet when Grosseteste came to analysing Aristotle's ideas about true knowledge, a dramatically different vision took shape in his mind. In the *Commentary on the Posterior Analytics*, his most mature account of the relation between intellect and objective reality, dating probably from the late 1220s, he speaks of truth as a simple thing in the world (*illud quod est*), with no mention of a comparison to God's ideal ([9.6] 99: 17–18). The source of this view goes back to *On Truth*, where for one uncharacteristic moment Grosseteste had recalled Augustine's definition of truth as 'what a thing is' (*id, quod est*), adding, in violation of traditional Boethian language, that this was the same as its being (*esse*) ([9.3] 141: 13–15). But what was merely an interesting aside in the early work now takes centre stage. Grosseteste in the Aristotle commentary is prepared to argue that the truth of a thing is exclusively its substantial presence in external reality. Another word for this is 'essence', taken as a thing's formal core shorn of all the accidents of material circumstance (*puritas essentiae suae non cum admixtione conditionum materialium* ([9.6] 406–7: 82–4). So patent a breach of Neoplatonizing principles appealed to William of Auvergne as well, for in his treatise *On the Universe* (*De universo*) from the early 1230s he similarly defines the objective truth of a thing as its 'substance, or essence, or being'. It is what is left to an object once all accidentals (*circumvestitio accidentium*) have been stripped away ([9.1] I: 836aE; also I: 794bF).

The new notion of truth opened the way for both thinkers to attack Neoplatonizing ontology and the conditions of knowledge it entailed. Referring to Plato and the *Timaeus*, William concedes in *On the Universe* that it is correct to posit an archetypal world of exemplary ideals (*exemplaria*) of which things in the perceived world are imitations (*exempla*), providing one locates the exemplary world in the mind of God. The problem with Plato is that he took the idea too far ([9.1] I: 823aC, 823bC, 835aA). As should be clear from the definition of an object's truth as its being or substance, the truth of something in the world and the truth of an idea in God's mind are not the same ([9.1] I: 837a(B–C)). Aristotle was right when he criticized Plato's notion of the reference of simple terms. Words such as 'earth', 'fire', 'water' and 'air' refer immediately to simple substances in the world and imply no comparison or reference to the Creator ([9.1] I: 835aB). A Neoplatonizing theory of truth – like that we have seen in Grosseteste's *On Truth* – is both semantically and ontologically misleading.

The Grosseteste of the *Commentary on the Posterior Analytics* agreed. A long, often misinterpreted passage outlines five sorts of object that might serve as immediate referent for terms of universal predication ([9.6] 139–41: 99–145). The first are the eternal reasons (*rationes*) in God, 'what Plato called ideas or the archetypal world'; the second are exemplary forms impressed by God on the minds of angels; the third are the causal reasons (*rationes causales*) of earthly things residing in the celestial spheres; the fourth, the inherent forms of real things themselves, taken as signifying the whole substance; and the fifth, accidents read as signs of the substantial reality to which they adhere. Grosseteste comments that it was according to the fourth way that Aristotle explained the predication of kinds and types (*genera et species*), and it is clear from what he says throughout the work that he accepts this as the norm for human knowledge in the world.[1] Echoing William, he claims that Plato's kinds and types – separate substances in an archetypal world held to be properly predicated of subjects in this, their exemplified imitator – are monsters produced by an erring intellect (*prodigia quae format error intellectus*) ([9.6] 224: 142–8).

For all their sympathy to Aristotle's theory of reference, however, William and Grosseteste shared an ontology of essence quite unlike anything Aristotle had in mind. William rejects the authentically Aristotelian position of Boethius whereby specific essences are individuated by the accidents of their particular – or material – instantiation ([9.1] I: 802a (E–F)). Instead he maintains that individuals are both fully particular and fully specific – that is to say, general – in their essence, which was, for him, their substance as well. Indeed, he insists that the numerical distinction of individuals of the same species can be reduced to what he calls an 'essential difference' (*differentia essentialis*): the fact that the essence of this thing is not precisely the essence of that ([9.1] I: 858b–59a(G–A)). Recognizing the awkwardness of his language, he hastens to add that the difference does not amount to a dissimilitude (*dissimilitudo*), which might sever the unity of the specific type, but should technically be referred to as a diversity (*diversitas*) among particulars ([9.1] I: 802aG). Grosseteste, too, held to the view that the essential nature of things was in and of itself individual ([9.6] 213: 221–4). Despite the philosophical ambiguity of such a position, it continued to be defended throughout the thirteenth century, nowhere more loyally than among Franciscans of the so-called Augustinian school, and provided the impetus for Scotus' famous theory of the formal distinction.

A notion of essence as of itself fully individualized naturally complicated the explanation of universal predication, which by the terms of William's and Grosseteste's semantics entailed direct reference to the very instantiated essences of which individuals were comprised. William never addressed the matter, but Grosseteste tried his hand at a solution that appears inspired by the terminist logic of his day. According to the *Commentary on the Posterior Analytics*, although universal predication cannot be reduced to an ontological configuration exactly the same as that of singularity, it must be founded on one that is not entirely different ([9.6] 245: 127–34). The notion of essence as simultaneously singular and general demanded as much. If, therefore, as Aristotle maintained, the universal is 'one thing from and in many' ([9.6] 161: 329–35) – a single predicate drawn from the knowledge of many singulars and referring to them all – this is because the universal taken in itself (*universale secundum se*) is neither one nor many (*nec unum nec multa*) but somehow capable of being construed as both. In Grosseteste's words, it 'falls to' (*accidit*) the universal, most probably through the agency of the intellect, to be one thing while representing many ([9.6] 244: 110–14). Certainly Grosseteste had in mind here the logician's understanding of the supposition of terms, by which linguistic markers that in themselves could signify either the singular or general aspect of an essence – words like 'horse' or 'man' – took on either universal or particular reference according to the demands of the propositions in which they were employed. Universals, in short, were terms: words denoting essence used for the purposes of universal predication (see [9.20] 185–7). The ambiguity of the term before supposition – of the 'universal in itself' – simply mirrored the fact that it signified an essence that was also in itself both singular and general.

By now we have reached an ontology and a semantics almost anticipating the nominalism of the fourteenth century. There was, however, at least for William still room for Neoplatonizing views. As he explains in *On the Universe*, while most words by which we describe created things refer directly to substances in the world, there are some that point more immediately to God and divine attributes. The reason is that the objective truth for which such words stand lies more precisely in God than in anything in the created world. When these words are used in discourse they consequently signify a divine object most properly – which is to say, univocally – and a created object only by equivocation, via an explicit or implied comparison (*comparatio*) to God ([9.1] I: 834a(F–G), 834b(G–H), 837b(A,B,D))). In short, for these cases the Anselmian view of reality and human knowledge of it seen earlier in Grosseteste's *On Truth* applies without qualification.

What is most interesting about these special cases is the kind of knowledge they entail. Although in *On the Universe* William speaks of words implicating the 'magnificence or excellence' of God (like 'being', 'good', 'true', 'power' and 'powerful') it is evident from what he says in his nearly contemporaneous treatise *On the Soul* (*De anima*) that he also has in mind a class of terms like 'whole', 'part', 'equal' and 'odd' out of which are constructed the fundamental propositions of rational argument. The latter are, William notes, what 'the philosophers' called 'axioms' (*dignitates*) or 'first impressions' (*primae impressiones*), what he refers to as the self-evident principles of science (*principia scientiarum nota per semetipsa*) ([9.1] II suppl.: 209b). They constituted Aristotle's common principles of demonstration, of which the most basic were the rules of non-contradiction and exclusive alternation. Relying on the Neoplatonizing interpretation of Avicenna, William adds that Aristotle posited a separate agent intellect – a higher intelligence hovering above human souls – to impress on the mind the intelligible forms (*signa vel formae intelligibiles*) by which such terms were known. He insists, instead, that it is God himself, the authentic archetypal world, who supplies the mind with these forms through his spiritual illumination ([9.1] II suppl.: 211a–b).

Substantial concession to Neoplatonizing concerns, this theory of principal cognition was, none the less, an anomaly, a flashback to a world-view fast disappearing in William's and Grosseteste's thought. In all other respects, they worked singlemindedly to tie their theories of knowledge ever more tightly to an ontology of absolutes in the perceived world. Indeed they thought they could lay out a taxonomy of cognition true to the principles of evidence and argumentation found in Aristotle, rivalling his ability to account for everything without recourse to a Neoplatonizing ideal in a world above. Nowhere is this more apparent than in their explanation of the greatest degree of certitude to which knowledge could lay claim. Here both scholastics fully accepted Aristotle's views. Grosseteste's *Commentary on the Posterior Analytics* was in fact a principal conduit by which Aristotelianizing epistemology was made available to the medieval university world.

The key was *scientia* or science, the Latinate equivalent of Aristotle's *epistēmē*, which constituted knowledge that could be regarded as absolutely certain. As Grosseteste makes plain in his *Commentary*, scientific knowledge is demonstrated knowledge: knowledge of the truth of a proposition that has been proved by means of syllogistic argument. What renders the syllogism scientific – that is, properly demonstrative – is that the middle term picks out the immutable, or necessary, cause making the subject – whether it be a simple nature or a complex state of affairs – what it is ([9.6] 99–100: 16–27, 406: 76–9, 407: 92–3). Of course all this has to be approached from the essentialist perspective of Aristotle, by which the reality of things was immutably determined according to fixed natures, but given this essentialism, one could easily believe that a clear understanding of the nature yielded the appropriate middle. From there it was simply a matter of logic to fashion a fully reasonable (*propter quid*) – and absolutely certain – defence of a statement of the truth ([9.6] 189: 23–30).

Naturally, any such demonstration of the truth of a statement – the demonstrated conclusion – depended on knowledge of the premisses from which the demonstrative syllogism was drawn, and if there were not to be an infinite regress in arguments for truth, there had to exist some premisses whose truth was evident without any syllogism at all. These were Aristotle's principles of science, whose truth was grasped immediately by *nous*, a non-discursive habit of mind Latinized as *intellectus* and translatable as something like propositional intuition. Following Aristotle to the letter, Grosseteste explains that it is by means of the two modes of cognition, *intellectus* and *scientia*, that all absolutely certain knowledge is attained, the former differing from the latter in involving no argument (no syllogism or middle term) and constituting the epistemic basis upon which the latter must reside ([9.6] 406–7: 76–89 and 98–9, 281: 89–91). It is, he says, the undemonstrated knowledge of first principles (*prima principia*), themselves the indemonstrable foundation for all demonstration ([9.6] 103: 92–3, 278: 3–7, 407: 91; and 281: 91–2, 407: 93–5). William, too, accepts Aristotle's epistemological scheme, referring to the classic exposition of it in the *Posterior Analytics* and directing his readers to its exemplary application in the *Physics* ([9.1] II suppl.: 210a).

In so far as the formal elaboration of this science-oriented epistemology entailed the application of the rules of propositional and syllogistic logic, it had little bearing on ontology, but there was at least one aspect of an Aristotelianized theory of science that raised questions about being and reality. Scientific truths were supposed to be immutable. For Grosseteste, that meant that they had somehow to be perpetual and incorruptible ([9.6] 139: 89–95).

One way to take this was simply to recognize that demonstrations consisted of propositions employing universal terms. The immutability of science was thereby reduced to the incorruptibility of universals, a quality easily accounted for with Grosseteste's essentially terminist theory of the universal in itself. As he says in the *Commentary*, universals are corrupted not in themselves (*ex non se ipsis*) but only in so far as the singular entities in which they are instantiated (*deferentia*) pass away ([9.6] 141: 145–9). The instantiating entities might be the words standing for universal terms in actual utterances or the existing referential base of such terms at any given time, but either way the universal itself as a term available for supposition – a logical entity – escapes the existential restraints of its real base. And just in case this answer is deemed insufficient, Grosseteste proposes another, focusing more on the real referents themselves. The perpetuity of universals can be saved even in a world of constant change because for all valid general terms, there is always somewhere at least one real individual to serve as referent and thus ontological anchor. After all, even though some things die away in winter, there is always summer somewhere on earth where objects of the same type can flourish ([9.6] 141: 149–54).[2]

Yet the immutability of science might also be taken to mean that the propositions themselves, and not just their conditions of truth, had to be perpetual. This demand was commonly made in the Neoplatonizing traditions from which both Grosseteste and William drew, and in *On Truth* Grosseteste presented a most Neoplatonizing way of satisfying it. Faithful to the tradition, he there takes perpetuity to mean eternity, as with the eternity of God. It is, he explains, possible to account for immutable truth in a world where no human utterances are incorruptible or unchanging so long as one concedes that it is legitimate to fall back on the eternal utterance propositions are given in God's mind ([9.3] 139–41). But such an account would have sat uneasily in the Aristotelianizing context of the *Commentary on the Posterior Analytics*, and in fact Grosseteste neither mentions it nor raises the question of the immutability of propositions in that work.

We must turn to William's writings for a theory to fill the gap. In *On the Universe* he states quite plainly that people commit a grievous error when they try to explain the eternal verity of statements which are always true by pointing to an eternal ontological base in the First Truth, God himself ([9.1] I: 793aA). Instead, it is possible to account for such truths without having recourse to any supratemporal conditions at all. One need merely take advantage of scholastic innovations in propositional logic. Drawing on a familiar definition of propositional truth (derived from Avicenna) as the accommodation of speech and reality (*adaequatio orationis et rerum*), William insists that the truth implicated in a true statement is nothing more than a relation. As such, it does not imply a reality beyond that of the related extremes: an utterance and its complex referent ([9.1] I: 795a(B–D)).

Here is where the new logic is relevant, for the precise words William uses for utterance and referent (*enunciatio* and *enunciabile*) reflect the increasing agreement among logicians that a true statement refers to a truth-bearing entity, what we would call the proposition, separate from any referential conditions in the real world.[3] Thus, as William makes clear, neither extreme of the relation of truth has more than a tenuous connection to real existence. Utterances are as fleeting as words or thoughts, and propositions (*enunciabilia*) are merely the logical representations of reality as it is or might be. This being so, truth, a relation that places no additional ontological burden on the extremes it relates, need have no greater existential presence than normal utterances or propositions, even if it is held to be immutable. Something can be said always to be true without there having to exist at every moment an utterance expressing the truth or an actual referential base ([9.1] I: 795b–96a(D–E)). Propositional truth is, William concludes, 'rational or logical' (*veritas rationalis sive logica*) and thereby formally independent of the question of actual existence ([9.1] I: 796aE). In short, the perpetuity of immutable truth was not so much an ontological as a logical condition, having little to do with the eternity of God.

There remained one kind of scientific truth particularly perplexing to Grosseteste just because his own attenuated account of the immutability of science seemed inadequate to explain it. He had predicated the perpetuity of universals partially upon his confidence that there was always somewhere at least one real instance of every general term, but this was not the case for some of the truths of what we would call natural science. There are not always lunar eclipses, although we feel justified in making universal statements about them. Or, to shift attention from the term to the proposition, we say it is universally true that heavy objects fall, even though any heavy object can be prevented from doing so. Such truths, Grosseteste notes in the *Commentary*, while not absolutely necessary, are regular enough – in scholastic parlance, their complex referents occur with sufficient frequency (*frequenter evenientia*) – to satisfy the demands of science ([9.6] 264: 119–22). Still, how can they be called immutable? Grosseteste offers two explanations, but the most relevant for us speculates that Aristotle intended to account for the perpetuity of such truths by insisting that their demonstrations specify the conditions under which they would be true ([9.6] 144–5: 200–19). Framed in conditional rather than categorical terms, such truths become just as immutable as those of the more necessary sciences, for whenever the conditions are met, they are indeed always true. Grosseteste appears here to be anticipating the notion of *ex suppositione* demonstration first fully elaborated later in the century by Albert the Great and by means of which even Galileo still defended the epistemic force of natural science.[4]

Aristotle, however, had also talked about experience; it was, as he said at the beginning of the *Metaphysics*, along with memory one of the fundamental sources of scientific knowledge. The same term had considerable resonance for Grosseteste and William, and not only in ways Aristotle might have intended. Grosseteste's ideas about experience have especially attracted the attention of historians of science ever since Crombie insisted that it was here we should look to find the medieval origins of the modern experimental method ([9.18] 1 and 10–11). Yet before accepting Crombie's judgement, we must remember that the words employed by thirteenth-century scholastics to talk about what can be loosely translated as 'experience' were varied, including most prominently *experientia* and *experimentum*, and it is not easy to ascertain the precise meaning of any of them. Historians must not assume too readily that their use has anything to do with our understanding of experimental method.

There is, in fact, only one occasion where Grosseteste talks about *experientia* in a way suggestive of what we most often mean by 'experiment'. The passage, in the *Commentary on the Posterior Analytics*, begins by stating the intention of sketching out a method for establishing what Grosseteste calls 'experimental universal principles' (*principia universalia experimentalia*) (see [9.6] 214–15: 252–71). In other words, he will propose an empirical way to certify some of the principles – that is, syllogistic premises – to be used for scientific demonstration. From the context it is clear that the principles in question will all belong to natural science, constituting truths that can be held neither with the absolute certitude of the principles of logic and mathematics nor with the still evident certitude of statements in natural science about the essential natures of things, for instance, the definitions of man or animal. Experimental principles are fundamental propositions for which there is no immediate or, in Aristotle's terms, purely analytical way to determine their truth.

According to Grosseteste, the first inkling of the shape of these truths comes to the mind after repeated sensory exposure to a sequence of events in the external world. For example, one might witness the eating of scammony followed by the passing of red bile often enough to suspect a relation of cause and effect. The intellect then goes on to form the proposition, 'Scammony purges red bile', but it is not yet able to claim with scientific certitude that the proposition is true. For this, it must turn to experiment (*convertere [se] ad experientiam*). In the example under consideration, one must feed scammony to a subject after having carefully removed all other agents that might purge red bile and then watch what happens. If one does this many times and the result is that the subject invariably passes red bile, then one is justified in holding the proposition about scammony and bile to be universally true.

It is impossible not to interpret all this as an account of experiment in the modern sense of the word, the controlled verification of a hypothesis or, in Grosseteste's terms, of a candidate for inclusion among the principles of science. Although there is no evidence that anyone in the thirteenth century considered the practical possibilities of a programme of experimentation set upon this theoretical foundation, or saw in any such programme the potential for a reformation of the sciences as was to be attempted in the seventeenth century, it is clear that at least Grosseteste appreciated the philosophical principle that classical experimenters would later employ to dramatic effect.

Yet this use of the idea of experiment constitutes an exception to the rule. For the most part, when thirteenth-century scholastics spoke of *experientia* or *experimentum* they had something quite different in mind. Often the reference was to what Hackett advises us to call personal experience, very like what Aristotle meant by his classic mention of *experimenta* in the *Metaphysics*. This is surely what William is thinking of with his numerous appeals to experience, combined with teaching (*doctrina et experientia*) as a source for scientific knowledge ([9.1] II suppl.: 212a, 214a; [9.2] 95: 54–64). He even directs the reader to the passage in the *Metaphysics* for clarification ([9.1] II suppl.: 216b). The cognitive process intended involved a complicated induction from sensation, bringing the intellect by means of Aristotle's logic of division to knowledge of one of the typical principles of natural science, such as those defining essential natures like 'dog' and 'man'. Grosseteste has the same noetic procedure of discovery in mind when in his *Commentary* he talks about the induction of universal principles (*universalia composita*) from sensible data ([9.6] 406: 67–72). Inductive experience of this sort was perfectly natural and commonplace, as is indicated by William's contrasting it to infused knowledge of the sort that Solomon received from God ([9.1] II suppl. 214a).

There was, however, yet another, dramatically non-Aristotelianizing notion one might have of the place of 'experience' in science, and this too appears in both Grosseteste's and William's thought. It was William who gave it the greatest attention. In the part of *On the Universe* investigating the powers and operations of demons, he refers with considerable fascination to the 'experimenters' (*experimentatores*), who in their writings describe the marvellous works they can do to the astonishment of the uninitiated ([9.1] I: 1059a–60a). He calls these writings 'books of experiments' (*libri experimentorum*), and it is clear that by this term he does not mean the controlled testing of hypotheses but rather the miraculous feats associated with magic (*opera magica*). Among the numerous examples he cites are fashioning a candle out of wax and serpent skin which, when lit, can make a room strewn with dried grass appear to be filled with writhing snakes, creating the illusion of water or a river where none really exists, and neutralizing the powers of enchanters or magicians by exposing them to certain snakes, or to quicksilver inserted just the right way into a reed tube. Such marvels and occult operations (*occultae operationes et mirabilia*) are, he adds, what physicians and natural philosophers are accustomed to call *empirica*, a term drawn from the lexicon of the medical arts ([9.1] I: 929bA).

According to William the ignorant gaze upon such works and attribute them erroneously to devilish powers, an error in which they are encouraged by the fact that some philosophers refer to the art by which the marvels are arranged as necromancy. The truth is, instead, that the 'experiments' of which he speaks, for all their miraculous appearance, can be traced back to the forces with which God has imbued his creation (*virtutes a Creatore inditae*). In this case the forces are deeply submerged, hidden to all but those trained to see them, but they are still fully natural, and their manipulation should be attributed to 'natural magic' (*magia naturalis*) ([9.1] I: 69bD).

Here William is mining an intellectual tradition of great antiquity and readily available to him and his scholarly contemporaries through translations from Hebrew, Arabic and Greek. In this tradition, the words 'experiment' and 'experience' evoke the illusory and the unexpected. According to William, the surprise and wonder are due to the fact that all the phenomena making up 'experience' in this sense arise from hidden forces (*virtutes occultae*) lying behind natural powers with which we are more familiar ([9.1] I: 1060a (E,H)). Grosseteste, too, was acquainted with the tradition and refers respectfully to the *experimentatores*, although he includes in this class those who simply have seen odd things and faraway places, like the north pole, and written down their experiences for us to share ([9.3] 68). He also counts among the experimenters scholars of optics who 'experiment' with lenses, the power of which to make far-away things seem near is itself wonderful (*admirandum, mirabile*) and thereby part of the marvellous world with which all experiment of this sort is tied ([9.3] 41, 73–4).

What must be kept in mind is that despite the suspicion and fear with which the writings of this tradition were often viewed, both William and Grosseteste believed that, if correctly received, they were not only benign but also a welcome addition to human knowledge.

214

William insists that natural magic, when not pursued with vain curiosity or used to do evil, is not harmful and does no offence to God ([9.1] I: 663bD). It constitutes, in fact, a legitimate part of natural science ([9.1] I: 69bD, 648aG). Those that know it, and perform the operations or experiments it reveals, are called *magi*, that is, doers of great things (*magna agentes*), and the association of them with evil, as well as the charge that *magus* means 'evil-doer' (*male agens*), is simply uninformed ([9.1] I: 1058bH). Grosseteste, too, understands that many associate the word *magus* with sorcerers (*malefici*), quoting Isidore to that effect, but he recognizes that others maintain that the true *magi* are wise men, like the learned divines of ancient Persia ([9.5] 23: 17–34). William even holds great expectations for the application of natural magic, asserting that it is not beyond magic's powers to produce things never before encountered on earth, including completely new animals ([9.1] I: 7aE). All that is wanting to see such things happen even in his own day is the right knowledge and an abundance of the proper tools and supplies ([9.1] I: 1058bH).

This was not to deny that there was evil magic, too, or that some experimenters and their experiments were malign and caught up with devils. William was familiar with what he thought were truly execrable magical books, like the *Sworn Book of Honorius (Liber sacratus)*, and he admits that even some potentially useful pieces of occult literature might mislead, just as the *On the God of Gods (De deo deorum)* attributed to Hermes (*Mercurius*) – whom he calls an Egyptian magician – had encouraged him in his youth to believe that with little effort he could raise himself to prophetic splendours ([9.1] I: 70aF, 1056a–b(H–E), 1060bF; cf. 78aF). Then, too, there was astrology, a science related to magic, which William said should be fought with sword and fire, at least in so far as it was taken to imply the necessity of all events ([9.1] 785aC, 785bB, 929bA). Grosseteste was likewise wary of astrology, although perhaps somewhat more ambivalent. In his early *On the Liberal Arts* he praises astronomy, clearly signifying judicial astrology, as most useful for the understanding and application of natural science ([9.3] 5–6). Yet in the *Hexaëmeron*, from the early 1230s, he sets the science of astral motion – astronomy – against the science of judging from the stars – astrology – condemning any attempt to use the latter to bind the will ([9.5] 41: 24–33). Later in the same work he warns Christians to have nothing to do with astrologers, or *mathematici*, and calls for their works to be burned ([9.5] 170: 4–7, 172: 3–5).

Even farther from Aristotle was an aspect of Grosseteste's science more deeply and authentically mathematical than astronomy or astrology. Again Crombie's picture of the thirteenth century must be recalled, for it was he who drew attention to Grosseteste as a medieval source for the modern orientation of science towards mathematics ([9.18] 60, 132–4). At a level not central to Crombie's view, Grosseteste's interest in mathematics takes us back to Aristotle. Grosseteste draws on the Aristotelian notion of the subordination of some sciences to others that explain more fully the subject of investigation and occasionally even supply demonstrative principles. He shows how it is common for scientific disciplines that investigate only the simple why and wherefore of a subject – in Aristotle's terms, pointing out only the fact (*quia*) – to stand in such subordination to other disciplines that can actually supply demonstrative reasons – again, in Aristotelian language, laying out the reasoned fact (*propter quid*) ([9.6] 194: 126–36). It is the various mathematical sciences that typically take this subordinating role, and Grosseteste mentions among other cases the science of radiant lines and figures (what we would call optics) subordinated to geometry, the science of harmony subordinated to arithmetic, and the science of navigation to astronomy.

Of greater interest to Crombie was a more ambitious theory inspired by Neoplatonic currents originating with Plotinus and taken to be the keystone of what is often called Grosseteste's 'metaphysics of light'.[5] Since most of what is attributed to this 'metaphysics' is not metaphysical at all, Lindberg wisely advises us to refer to it as a 'philosophy of light' ([9.19] 95). Of its four parts as Lindberg sketches them out, it is what he calls a 'cosmogony of light' (that concerns us here. In his treatise *On Light (De luce)* Grosseteste argues that light is the first corporeal form – corporeity, itself – by which matter, on its own absolutely simple and dimensionless, takes on extension or, as we would say, dimension. Light manages this through its quite special power of instantaneous self-diffusion in all directions from the point of origin, by which means as first form it literally carries all matter along with it ([9.3] 51: 10–52: 9). This is the way the universe was generated by God's command at the beginning of time, the reverberations of light from central point out to the limits of a spherical extreme, and then back and forth again and again, rarefying and condensing matter until it took the form of the nine celestial spheres and the elemental regions of the sublunar world ([9.3] 52: 17–21, 54: 11–56: 18). A cosmogony of this sort would seem to give light, and the mathematically-formulated optics by which it is understood, pride of place in our understanding of nature. That is, at least, what Crombie assumed.

Yet though Grosseteste must have been sensitive to the methodological implications of his cosmogony, it is instead a different element in his thought, the part of his 'philosophy of light' Lindberg calls the 'physics of light', upon which he based his principal argument for the relevance of mathematics to natural philosophy. Extrapolating not

216

only from Neoplatonism but also from the tradition of Arabic optics, Grosseteste fashioned a universal theory of natural causation referred to as the doctrine of the multiplication of species ([9.19] 97–8). The Neoplatonic element is laid out in *On Lines, Angles and Figures (De lineis angulis et figuris)*. According to this treatise, all natural agents work by multiplying or transmitting their power (*virtus*) in the form of species (*species*) or likenesses (*similitudines*) sent out into the surrounding medium, whether sensory or inert ([9.3] 60: 16–29). The significant thing about this multiplication is that it occurs in conformity to the rules of luminous radiation laid out in the science of optics. As both *On Lines* and *On the Nature of Place (De natura locorum)* make clear, any agent's species or likenesses are induced in all directions from the point of origin along straight lines which are bent, just like light rays, as they pass through media of contrasting density ([9.3] 60: 14–15, 66: 1–3). It is, therefore, possible to describe all natural causation by means of the geometrical principles of lines, angles and figures established in optics ([9.3] 65: 27–9).

Here Grosseteste turns again to the notion of subordination. The geometric explanation of all natural causation offered by optics – and Grosseteste uses the medieval name, *perspectiva* – is, because of its formal precision, also the most fundamental. It gives the 'reasoned' (*propter quid*) account of what the natural philosopher (*physicus*) otherwise knows only as fact ([9.3] 72: 12–13, also 60: 15–16). Indeed it is legitimate to say that one cannot truly know natural philosophy without recourse to the laws of optical science ([9.3] 59: 27–60: 1). Because of the way nature works, the science of natural philosophy is subordinate to optics, and therefore mathematics, to which optics itself is subordinated, must be the primary explanatory tool of the natural scientist.

Taken together, William and Grosseteste bequeathed a rich metaphysical and epistemological heritage to the rest of the thirteenth century. They were the first to weave the lines of Aristotelianism, Neoplatonism and Arabic and Jewish mathematics and magic into a texture alluring enough to engage the imagination of scholars in the new schools. From their fertile beginnings can be traced much of the scientific and philosophical achievement of the thirteenth century. But just as their own sources were varied, so the lines of inspiration trailing out from them into the rest of the century took several different paths. In so far as they sought to bring Neoplatonic traditions, especially in epistemology and noetics, into line with the logical and linguistic expectations of Aristotelianizing analysis, they laid the foundations for what is often called the Neo-Augustinianism of Bonaventure and his successors from the 1250s on. Equally important, however, was the debt owed to them by the more authentically Aristotelian current that emerged in the late 1240s with Albert the Great and continued with his even greater pupil, Thomas Aquinas.

Yet the figure who most literally reproduced the scientific ideal seen in William and Grosseteste – or perhaps who most dramatically amplified their idiosyncrasies – was Roger Bacon. Born in England around 1210, Bacon studied and taught arts at Oxford up to the late 1230s, moving on then to Paris where he lectured in the arts faculty until about 1247. Around 1257 he joined the Franciscan order, a decision which terminated his scholarly career for a decade until Pope Clement IV gave it new life with his request for Bacon's ideas on the reformation of learning. Perhaps in part because of this sign of papal favour, Bacon fell into an increasingly bitter conflict with his superiors, culminating in the condemnation of his work by the minister general of his order in 1278 and his probable incarceration. Apparently free again but still tormented by his fate, he died in 1292 or shortly thereafter.[6]

Like Grosseteste, whose lectures he may have attended while at Oxford, Bacon placed mathematics at the foundation of natural science – perhaps, indeed, of science altogether. He was even more insistent on this score than his illustrious forebear. In *The Character of the Natural Sciences (Communia naturalium)* he criticizes Aristotle for neglecting mathematics and excoriates renowned scholars of his day, among whom is certainly intended Albert the Great, for their ignorance of the subject ([9.10] 2: 5, 11), reserving his praise in the *Opus maius* and the *Opus tertium* for Grosseteste and the nearly idolized Peter Peregrinus of Maricourt, whom Bacon considered the mathematicizing prophets of his century ([9.8] I: 108; [9.7] 34–5). For Bacon – just as, he thought, for Grosseteste and the ancient sages and divines – only by means of mathematics, the 'door and key' to full knowledge, could the other sciences be grasped with absolute certitude ([9.8] I: 97, 98, 107).

His defence of this assertion is partly delivered in Grosseteste's Aristotelianizing language of the subordination of sciences, whereby mathematics supplies the reasoned explanation (*per causam*) of phenomena that the natural sciences can describe only as fact (*per effectum*) ([9.8] I: 169). Of greater weight for him, however, is the description of physical reality that Grosseteste had used to justify the subordination at the epistemic level, the doctrine of causation by the transmission of species or similitudes. Bacon enthusiastically embraces Grosseteste's view, embellishing it with a theoretical exactitude that made Bacon's version the model exposition of the matter for the next century and a half ([9.8] I: 111; [9.7] 37; [9.9] 2). He goes so far as to devote a whole treatise to the process, referring to it with the precise name by which it has since been known: *On the*

Multiplication of Species. Just as Grosseteste had argued in *On Lines* and *On the Nature of Place*, so Bacon reasons that, because the species by which all natural causality is achieved are generated in straight lines in exact replication of the phenomenon of luminous radiation, the science of optics offers the only universal means of accounting for all natural effects ([9.10] II: 24: 21–9; [9.8] I: 112, II: 31; [9.9] 90–4). This not only makes optics (*perspectiva*) the most special and very first of the natural sciences (*prima specialis scientia*) but also explains why natural phenomena cannot be truly understood without the power of mathematics ([9.10] II: 5: 25–31; [9.8] I: 110).

Yet it is what Bacon made of Grosseteste's and William's comments on experience or experiment for which he is best known, leading many to view him as the forerunner of his seventeenth-century namesake, Francis Bacon. To Roger's way of seeing things there is in fact a discrete experimental science, *scientia experimentalis*, which is the most certain of all and certifier for the others ([9.10] II: 9: 1–6). Despite its ostensible unity, this science is composed of three parts, each playing a different role – prerogatives or dignities as Bacon calls them – and for us to understand the whole we have to recognize that three constituents do not tend precisely to the same end ([9.10] II: 9: 9–12; [9.8] II: 172; [9.7] 43–4).

According to its first role, experimental science certifies by experience the demonstrated conclusions of the other sciences ([9.8] II: 172–3). Here Bacon has recourse to his conviction, surely evolved from weaker notions found in both William and Grosseteste, that while scientific demonstration in the Aristotelian sense can make known the truth, only experience removes all doubt ([9.8] I: 105–6, II: 167; [9.7] 297).[7] One might know by reasoned argument that fire burns, but only the experience of a scorched finger teaches one to avoid the flame. It is tempting to see in this a version of the theory of verification by experimentation, as many who praise Bacon have done. There is, after all, the precedent of Grosseteste with his example of testing the power of scammony to purge bile. But in fact Bacon, who is aware of the sort of verification Grosseteste described, takes it as having nothing to do with the 'experiment' he has in mind. Natural sciences often do, as Grosseteste realized, establish their principles by experiment or from experience; they then anchor their conclusions to the principles in Aristotelian fashion by demonstrative argument. Such methods, Bacon admits, have a legitimate place at the foundation of demonstrative science. Yet he wants his experimental science to go beyond Aristotle and bring the mind to adhere to conclusions, in contrast to principles, with the assent only experience, not argument, can induce ([9.8] II: 172–3; [9.7] 43). Experience in this case is not the controlled testing of a hypothesized principle but rather the empirical confirmation of an already proved conclusion. Bacon's first prerogative is thus a use of experience unlike anything Aristotle, or William and Grosseteste, had conceived, pointing to the growing prestige of singular perception in the noetics and epistemology of the late thirteenth and fourteenth centuries.

The second and third roles of experimental science are, if anything, even more un-Aristotelianizing, although not so novel. With them we return to the traditional notions of *experimenta* so well represented in William's thought. By its second prerogative, experimental science reveals truths about the subject-matter of the other sciences, which none of them can prove or dare to claim as true. The emphasis here is on practical accomplishments that are both marvellous and strange, as, for example, the construction of an astrolabe that would revolve daily on its own natural power, or a knowledge of how to use medicines dramatically to prolong human life ([9.8] II: 202–4). Experimental science's third prerogative is more awesome still, making known things not even dreamed of in the rest of scientific discourse. It penetrates all the way to the secrets of nature and surpasses judicial astrology, with which it seems to compete, by making firmer predictions about the future and doing far more miraculous works (*opera admiranda, mirabilia opera*) ([9.8] II: 215; [9.7] 44). It is primarily by this prerogative that experimental science commands all other sciences as their mistress (*domina*), and it is here that its practical value is realized in the extreme ([9.8] II: 221; [9.7] 46).

By now Bacon is clearly navigating in the waters of magical art, as is surely betrayed by his claim that the third prerogative explores the occult (*opera occulta*) ([9.10] II: 9: 11–12). Times have changed, however, and Bacon is far more squeamish than William was about being associated with anything labelled 'magic'. He not only refuses to call any aspect of experimental science 'magical' but also insists that one of his science's functions is to lay open the falsehood of the magical arts (*magicae artes*) ([9.10] II: 9: 21–6). Yet more than just fear of censure separates Bacon from William of Auvergne. He is, like William, willing to accept an art like astrology that is traditionally associated with magic, so long as it does not postulate the absolute necessity of all events or resort to the power of demons or fraud to impress its audience. He even gives acceptable astrologers the name of 'true mathematicians' (*veri mathematici*) in contrast to the 'false mathematician' (*falsi mathematici*) who dabble in magic ([9.8] I: 240–2). But Bacon's vision of experimental science, for all its debt to traditional magic, aspires to more than marvel. It presumes to draw the power of knowledge, especially scientific knowledge, into a campaign to transform the world. Indeed, the impetus behind most of Bacon's later work is his desire to lay the cognitive foundations for the reformation of human life. Such practical ideals are not foreign to the magic of William's mental landscape, but as distilled in Bacon's experimental science they savour for the first time of the ambition and energy of the seventeenth century.

 NOTES

1 For an analysis of the passage and an argument for what constituted Grosseteste's own view, see Marrone [9.20] 166–78.
2 How this sort of perpetuity might suffice for a Christian like Grosseteste, who held the world to have a temporal beginning and end, is argued in Marrone [9.20] 234–9.
3 See G. Nuchelmans, *Theories of the Proposition*, Amsterdam, North Holland, 1973, esp. ch. 10.
4 See W. A. Wallace, 'Aristotle and Galileo: The uses of hypothesis (*suppositio*) in scientific reasoning', in D. J. O'Meara (ed.) *Studies in Aristotle*, Washington, DC, Catholic University, 1981, pp. 47–77.
5 See Baur [9.29] and [9.30] 77–92; and the origin of the term (*Lichtmetaphysik*) in C. Baeumker, *Witelo, ein Philosoph und Naturforscher des XIII. Jahrhunderts*, Münster, Aschendorff, 1908, pp. 257–422.
6 For the dates of Bacon's life, see Hackett [9.40], especially pp. 46–7.
7 Marrone ([9.20] 36) points out William's assertion of the mildly obscurative effect of demonstration, echoed (p. 223) by Grosseteste's preference for principal cognition. A bias for particular experience appears in *On the Nature of Place* ([9.3] 66).

 BIBLIOGRAPHY

Original Language Editions

William of Auvergne

9.1 *Opera omnia*, 2 vols, Paris and Orleans, Hotot, 1674; repr. in 2 vols, Frankfurt on Main, Minerva, 1963.
9.2 Switalksi, B. (ed.) *De trinitate*, Toronto, Pontifical Institute of Mediaeval Studies, 1976.

Robert Grosseteste

9.3 Baur, L. (ed.) *Die philosophischen Werke des Robert Grosseteste, Bischofs von Lincoln*, Münster, Aschendorff, 1912.
9.4 Dales, R. C. (ed.) *Commentarius in VIII libros Physicorum Aristotelis*, Boulder, Colo., University of Colorado Press, 1963.
9.5 Dales, R. C. and Gieben, S. (eds) *Hexaëmeron*, London, British Academy, 1982.

9.6   Rossi, P. (ed.) *Commentarius in Posteriorum analyticorum libros*, Florence, Olschki, 1981.

Roger Bacon

9.7   Brewer, J. S. (ed.) *Fr. Rogeri Bacon Opera quaedam hactenus inedita*, London, Longman, 1859.
9.8   Bridges, J. H. (ed.) *The 'Opus Majus' of Roger Bacon*, 2 vols, Oxford, Clarendon Press, 1897; Suppl., London, Williams & Norgate, 1900.
9.9   Lindberg, D. C. (ed.) *Roger Bacon's Philosophy of Nature*, Oxford, Clarendon Press, 1983.
9.10 Steele, R. (ed.) *Opera hactenus inedita Rogeri Baconi*, Fasc. 2–4: *Communia naturalium*, Oxford, Clarendon Press, 1905?–1913.

English Translations

9.11 *The Opus Majus of Roger Bacon*, 2 vols, trans. R. B. Burke, Philadelphia, Pa., University of Pennsylvania Press, 1928.
9.12 *Robert Grosseteste On Light*, trans. C. R. Riedl, Milwaukee, Wis., Marquette, 1942.
9.13 *A Source Book in Medieval Science*, ed. E. Grant, Cambridge, Mass., Harvard University Press, 1974.

Bibliographies

9.14 Alessio, F. 'Un secolo di studi su Ruggero Bacone (1848–1957)', *Rivista critica di storia della filosofia* 14 (1959): 81–102.
9.15 Gieben, S. 'Bibliographia universa Roberti Grosseteste ab an. 1473 ad an. 1969', *Collectanea Franciscana* 39 (1969): 362–418.
9.16 Hackett, J. M. G. and Maloney, T. S. 'A Roger Bacon Bibliography (1957–1985)', *The New Scholasticism* 61 (1987): 184–207.
9.17 Huber, M. 'Bibliographie zu Roger Bacon', *Franziskanische Studien* 65 (1983): 98–102.

General Studies

9.18 Crombie, A. C. *Robert Grosseteste and the Origins of Experimental Science 1100–1700*, Oxford, Clarendon Press, 1953.
9.19 Lindberg, D. C. *Theories of Vision from Al-Kindi to Kepler*, Chicago, University of Chicago Press, 1976.
9.20 Marrone, S. P. *William of Auvergne and Robert Grosseteste: New Ideas of Truth in the Early Thirteenth Century*, Princeton, NJ, Princeton University Press, 1983.

9.21 Thorndike, L. *A History of Magic and Experimental Science*, vol. 2, New York, Macmillan, 1923.

Studies on William of Auvergne

9.22 Baumgartner, M. *Die Erkenntnislehre des Wilhelm von Auvergne*, Münster, Aschendorff, 1893.
9.23 Jüssen, G. 'Wilhelm von Auvergne und die Entwicklung der Philosophie im Übergang zur Hochscholastik', in W. Kluxen (ed.) *Thomas von Aquin im philosophischen Gespräch*, Freiburg and Munich, Alber, 1975, pp. 185–203.
9.24 —— 'Wilhelm von Auvergne und die Transformation der scholastischen Philosophie im 13. Jahrhundert', in J. P. Beckmann *et al.* (eds) *Philosophie im Mittelalter*, Hamburg, Meiner, 1987, pp. 141–64.
9.25 Masnovo, A. *Da Guglielmo d'Auvergne a s. Tommaso d'Aquino*, 3 vols, 2nd edn, Milan, Vita e Pensiero, 1945–6.
9.26 Moody, E. A. 'William of Auvergne and his *Treatise De anima*', in *Studies in Medieval Philosophy, Science, and Logic*, Berkeley, Calif., University of California Press, 1975, pp. 1–109.
9.27 Rohls, J. *Wilhelm von Auvergne und der mittelalterliche Aristotelismus*, Munich, Kaiser, 1980.
9.28 Teske, R. J. 'William of Auvergne on the individuation of human souls', *Traditio* 49 (1994): 77–93.

Studies on Robert Grosseteste

9.29 Baur, L. 'Das Licht in der Naturphilosophie des Robert Grosseteste', *Festgabe zum 70. Geburtstag Georg Freiherrn von Hertling*, Freiburg im Breisgau, Herder, 1913, pp. 41–55.
9.30 —— *Die Philosophie des Robert Grosseteste, Bischofs von Lincoln (gest. 1253)*, Münster, Aschendorff, 1917.
9.31 Callus, D. A. (ed.) *Robert Grosseteste, Scholar and Bishop*, Oxford, Clarendon Press, 1955.
9.32 Dales, R. C. 'Robert Grosseteste's scientific works', *Isis* 52 (1961): 381–402.
9.33 Eastwood, B. S. 'Medieval empiricism. The case of Grosseteste's optics', *Speculum* 43 (1968): 306–21.
9.34 —— 'Robert Grosseteste's theory of the rainbow: a chapter in the history of non-experimental science', *Archives Internationales d'Histoire des Sciences* 77 (1966): 313–32.
9.35 McEvoy, J. *The Philosophy of Robert Grosseteste*, Oxford, Clarendon Press, 1982.
9.36 Southern, R. W. *Robert Grosseteste: The Growth of an English Mind in Medieval Europe*, Oxford, Clarendon Press, 2nd ed., 1992.

Studies on Roger Bacon

9.37 Easton, S. C. *Roger Bacon and his Search for a Universal Science*, New York, Columbia University Press, 1952.

9.38 Fisher, N. W. and Unguru, S. 'Experimental science and mathematics in Roger Bacon's thought', *Traditio* 27 (1971): 353–78.

9.39 Hackett, J. M. G. 'The attitude of Roger Bacon to the *scientia* of Albertus Magnus', in J. A. Weisheipl (ed.) *Albertus Magnus and the Sciences: Commemorative Essays 1980*, Toronto, Pontifical Institute of Mediaeval Studies, 1980, pp. 53–72.

9.40 —— 'The meaning of experimental science (*scientia experimentalis*) in the philosophy of Roger Bacon', Ph.D. dissertation, University of Toronto, 1983.

9.41 Lindberg, D. C. *Studies in the History of Medieval Optics*, London, Variorum, 1983.

9.42 Molland, A. G. 'Roger Bacon as magician', *Traditio* 30 (1974): 445–60.

9.43 Williams, S. J. 'Roger Bacon and his edition of the pseudo-Aristotelian *Secretum secretorum*', *Speculum* 69 (1994): 57–73.

CHAPTER 10

Bonaventure, the German Dominicans and the new translations

John Marenbon

❦

As the previous chapter has illustrated, even in the first half of the thirteenth century the outlook of thinkers was much affected by the newly available translations of Aristotle and of Arabic commentaries and treatises.[1] By the mid-1250s, the arts course in Paris included almost the whole body of Aristotle's works and, within a couple of decades, nearly all the translations from the Greek and Arabic which would be used in the medieval universities were already available. The three leading theologians of this generation are the Dominicans, Thomas Aquinas and his teacher, Albert the Great, and the Franciscan, Bonaventure.[2] As philosophers, it may be argued, they form an unequal triumvirate. Aquinas is, by almost any account, among the greatest philosophers of his, or any, period; the next chapter will be devoted to him. Neither Bonaventure nor Albert came near to his ability at devising and interlinking, on a wide variety of philosophical questions, clear and powerful arguments which modern philosophers still find it worthwhile to scrutinize. Each, however, developed a range of distinctive positions. They include striking views on the nature of philosophy and its relation to their work as theologians; and, in Albert's case at least, these were adapted (and ultimately transformed) by a school of followers. It is these views on which the present, brief discussion will concentrate. But first some further details about the new translations are necessary, since they provide the background both to the thinking of Bonaventure and Albert, and to the work which all the following chapters will be examining.

∾ THE TRANSLATIONS ∾

Aristotle, the old textbooks used to say, reached the West through the Arabs. Literally, this statement is false. For the most part, Aristotle reached Western scholars in direct translations from the Greek: Boethius' translations of nearly all the logic (which became available gradually from the ninth to the twelfth centuries); James of Venice's versions (c. 1130–50) of the *Posterior Analytics, Physics, On the Soul*, some shorter scientific works; other twelfth-century translations of *On Generation and Corruption* and the *Physics*. As for the *Ethics* and the *Metaphysics*, there was a twelfth-century version of *Nicomachean Ethics* II and III (known as the 'Old Ethics'); the whole work was translated early in the thirteenth century, though only Book I (known as the 'New Ethics') circulated; and then (c. 1246–7) Robert Grosseteste and his assistants made a new translation of the whole work (they also translated part of *On the Heavens*). James of Venice translated *Metaphysics* I–III and part of IV; an early thirteenth-century revision of this translation, conflated with the unrevised text, formed the 'Old Metaphysics', whilst a twelfth-century translation of the whole work except Book XI was known as the 'Middle Metaphysics' (it seems not to have been used until the mid-thirteenth century). Finally, between 1260 and 1280 William of Moerbeke revised or retranslated almost all Aristotle's works, as well as making the *Politics* and *Poetics* available for the first time. William's translations became standard, except for the logic, for which Boethius' translations (and, for the *Posterior Analytics*, James of Venice's) were generally used.[3]

But there is, none the less, an important element of truth in the idea of 'Aristotle through the Arabs'. Some translations *were* made from the Arabic: for example those of Gerard of Cremona, who worked in Toledo, of the *Posterior Analytics, Physics* and some of the scientific works. A version of the *Metaphysics* (the 'New Metaphysics'; Book I, minus beginning, to X and most of XII) translated from the lemmata of Averroes' commentary was used in the early to mid-thirteenth century.[4] More important, Aristotle's non-logical works reached the West along with (or preceded by) a corpus of commentary by Arabic philosophers. In mid-twelfth-century Toledo, Dominic Gundissalinus, a canon of the cathedral there, helped by Arabic-speaking assistants, translated parts – including those corresponding to *On the Soul* and the *Metaphysics* – of Ibn Sina's (Avicenna's) paraphrase-commentary of Aristotle, the *Shifā'* (*Book of Healing*); further sections were translated late in the thirteenth century.[5] In the 1220s in Sicily, Michael Scotus translated a number of commentaries by Ibn Rushd (Averroes), including the 'great' commentaries (full-scale, detailed sentence by sentence discussions) on *On the Soul*, the *Physics*, *Metaphysics* and *On the Heavens*. Averroes' shorter 'middle' commentaries to a variety of Aristotle's works, including the logic, *On Generation and Corruption* and *Nicomachean Ethics*, were translated either by Scotus, or a little later by others. All these commentaries profoundly affected the ways Western thinkers read Aristotle. In addition, the Toledan translators of the twelfth century made Latin versions of various works by al-Kindī and al-Fārābī, more or less connected with Aristotle, as well as al-Ghazzālī's *Intentions of the Philosophers*.

Plato did not benefit directly from this busy period of translation. Although Henry Aristippus made Latin versions of the *Meno* and *Phaedo* in Sicily shortly before 1150, they hardly circulated, so the *Timaeus* in Calcidius' incomplete translation remained the one text by Plato himself well known in the Middle Ages.[6] A good deal of Neoplatonic material, however, became available, partly in the commentaries and other works related to Aristotle, because the Arab philosophical tradition before Averroes was heavily influenced by Neoplatonism in its approach to Aristotle, and also more directly: an Arabic adaptation of some of Proclus' *Elements of Theology* was translated into Latin by Gerard of Cremona as the *Book about Causes* (*Liber de causis*) and adopted into the Aristotelian curriculum (see below, pp. 230–1); later, William of Moerbeke translated the whole of the *Elements of Theology* directly from the Greek.

Jewish philosophy was also translated. The Toledan translators put into Latin Isaac Israeli's *Book on Definitions* and Solomon ibn Gabirol's ('Avicebron' or 'Avencebrol') *Fountain of Life*. Maimonides' great *Guide of the Perplexed* was put into Latin in the 1220s, from the Hebrew translation of Judah al-Harisi (see [10.32]).

❧ BONAVENTURE ❧

John of Fidanza, known as Bonaventure, was born *c.* 1217. He studied arts in Paris from 1234 or 1235 until 1243. He then joined the Franciscans and studied theology, also in Paris, where he was taught by Alexander of Hales, the first of the Franciscan masters of theology. Bonaventure himself held the Franciscan chair from 1253 to 1255. In 1257 he was elected Minister General of his Order, but he still maintained close contacts with the university and continued his theological writing up until nearly the time of his death in 1274. Among his most important works are his commentary on the *Sentences* (1250–5), a systematic textbook of theology called the *Breviloquium*, the brief *Journey of the Mind towards God* (1259) which expresses in a concise personal style many of his central ideas, and the sets of university sermons (*Collationes*) he gave in his last years, especially those on the Work of the Six Days (Hexaemeron), from 1273.

227

Bonaventure knew many of the newly translated texts and commentaries well. Theology, as he and his contemporaries recognized it, was a discipline which used arguments. Aristotelian logic had long been regarded as one of the theologian's essential argumentative tools, and by the 1250s the terminology and concepts of Aristotle's metaphysics and natural science were also indispensable. Bonaventure used this intellectual equipment, but his commitment to argument and conceptual analysis was far weaker than Aquinas', nor did he share much of Aquinas' belief that, on many questions, a full and accurate grasp of Aristotle's views was the best way to the right answer. Not surprisingly, then, he tended to adapt Aristotelian positions and combine them with others in the ways which best suited his overriding theological aims. For example, he accepted a roughly Aristotelian account of sense-cognition as the first stage of his theory of knowledge, but insisted that for knowledge of the truth direct divine illumination was required. Aristotle's theory of matter and form became, for Bonaventure (perhaps influenced by Solomon ibn Gabirol, see p. 75), a doctrine of universal hylomorphism. Everything, with the sole exception of God, is a composite of matter and form. Human body and human intellective soul are not, therefore, related – as in Aristotle, and Aquinas – as matter to form, but as matter-form composite to matter-form composite; a position which may be less satisfying than Aristotle's intellectually but fits well with Christian belief about individual immortality. The difference between Bonaventure and Aquinas is particularly pointed on the question of the eternity of the universe. This view, clearly contrary to Christian belief, was (rightly) recognized by many at the time to have been Aristotle's – though there were also doubts about the attribution. Aquinas insisted that, although 'the universe is not eternal' is a truth known by faith, it cannot be demonstrated; towards the end of his life, indeed, he argued that God could have created an eternal universe had he so chosen. By contrast, Bonaventure thought that he could demonstrate – using arguments based on Aristotle's own views about the infinite – that the universe is not and could not have been eternal.[7]

One of Aristotle's special failings, in Bonaventure's view, was his rejection of Platonic Ideas. In using the Ideas – considered, in the usual way since patristic times, as being in the mind of God – as a way of explaining the relationship between the creator and the universe, Bonaventure was merely doing the same as almost every other thirteenth-century theologian, Aquinas included. He was exceptional, however, in the weight he gave to explaining exemplarism which, along with the discussion of creation and divine illumination, he held constituted the whole of true metaphysics. This emphasis reveals the underlying direction of his thought. We reach the divine exemplars, and through them, God, by seeking in all things that which they exemplify. For Bonaventure, the main task of a Christian thinker is not so much to argue or analyse (though sometimes this is necessary) as to learn how to read creation, finding in it the hidden patterns and resemblances which lead back to God. We have been provided, he says, with a threefold aid for reaching 'the exemplary reasons' of things: sensibly-perceptible creation, where God has left his traces (*vestigia*); man's soul, which is made in the image of God; and Scripture, with its riches of inner meaning.

In *The Journey of the Mind*, Bonaventure develops this way of thinking in the most explicit way. The universe is 'a ladder for climbing to God': we must ascend through the traces of God, which we find in what is bodily, temporal and outside us, through the image of God, which we find within our immortal, spiritual selves, and finally raise ourselves to the eternal being. To these three stages correspond the threefold existence of things: in matter, in understanding and in God's mind, and Christ's threefold substance, bodily, spiritual and divine (I, 2–3). Each stage, however, is itself divided in two, for in each we can find God either *through* his mirror or *in* his mirror. The six steps yielded by this multiplication correspond to six powers of our soul: sense, imagination, reason, intellect (*intellectus*), intelligence (*intelligentia*) and the 'summit of the mind' or 'spark of synderesis'. Bonaventure also provides various scriptural parallels: the six days of creation, the six steps of Solomon's throne, the six wings of the Seraphim seen by Isaiah, the six days after which God called Moses from the midst of darkness and the six days after which Christ summoned his disciples on the mountain where he was transfigured (I, 5–6). This elaborate set of parallels and analogies is itself merely the framework for the analogies which make up each of the individual steps. So, for example, the fourth stage of ascent – contemplating God in his image – involves considering the Trinity in the image of man reformed by grace, his soul purified, illumined and perfected by the three theological virtues of faith, hope and charity. 'Hierarchized' in this way, the human spirit is compared to the hierarchy of angels (three groups of three), and a parallel is drawn between the three laws (of nature, of the Old Testament and of grace) and the three senses of Scripture, moral, allegorical and anagogical, which purify, illumine and perfect (IV, 1–6).

All the great Franciscan theologians of the thirteenth and fourteenth centuries looked back to Bonaventure with respect, and often his positions influenced their discussions of individual questions. But they did not share his fondness for reading signs and elaborating patterns as opposed to constructing and criticizing arguments; and it is on this point of difference, rather than on any of the intellectual debts they owed to the founder of their tradition, that depends their importance as philosophers.

❧ ALBERT THE GREAT ❧

Born in Swabia at the turn of the thirteenth century (1193, *c.* 1200, 1206–7 have been suggested), Albert died in extreme old age in 1280, outliving by six years his most famous pupil, Thomas Aquinas. After studying in Italy and Germany, and joining the Dominicans, he was a master of theology in Paris from 1245 to 1248 and then taught theology at Cologne until he became provincial of the German Dominicans (1254–7). Although he had no fixed teaching position after this, Albert continued his work on natural science, philosophy and theology with great energy until after 1270. His writings are among the most voluminous of any medieval thinker. They include, among many others, two comprehensive theological textbooks, a commentary on the *Sentences* completed in 1249, long paraphrase commentaries (in the manner of Avicenna) on many of Aristotle's works, including *On the Soul* (*c.* 1254–7), the *Ethics* (1252–3) and the *Metaphysics* (1263–7), a work *On the Causes and Procession of the Universe* based on the *Book about Causes* and on al-Ghazzālī (after 1263) and commentaries on pseudo-Dionysius (some, at least, written between 1248 and 1250).

As even this bare list indicates, Albert's attitude to the translations of Aristotle and of the related Arab material was, quite unlike Bonaventure's, one of unrestrained enthusiasm. Historians have indeed been agreed in giving him a central role in making Aristotle the supreme human authority for university theologians. Yet a glance at his Aristotelian commentaries shows that Albert's Aristotelianism is mixed with a host of characteristically Neoplatonic themes and views, and this – combined with the variety of his interests and works – has led to the impression that Albert was a muddled writer, overwhelmed by the mass of new material and unable to resolve the incompatible positions of his various sources or reach any coherent theories of his own. Thanks to Alain de Libera, however, it is now clear that, at least in one main aspect of his work, Albert is putting forward a bold and clear view, not so much about any individual problem in philosophy as about the nature and aim of the very practice of philosophizing.[8]

For Albert, Aristotelian metaphysics, the study of being, needed to be complemented and completed by an Aristotelian theology, the study of God. Albert found his Aristotelian theology in the *Book about Causes* which he took, along with his contemporaries, to be a work by Aristotle himself. When, late in Albert's life, Thomas Aquinas, using William of Moerbeke's translation of Proclus' *Elements of Theology*, showed that the *Book about Causes* was an adaptation of this Neoplatonic work, Albert took no notice. No wonder – for, had he done so, he would have had to give up the claim which runs through his life's work that he is expounding what he calls the 'peripatetic' position. Albert's peripateticism, then, builds on Aristotle, on the *Book about Causes* and on Avicenna's interpretation of Aristotle, which posits a hierarchy of Intelligences, each lower Intelligence emanating from the higher. Albert adapts these models, however, striving to maintain an absolute distinction between God, who is the being of all things only in so far as he is the *cause* of their being, and his creation, and to avoid any implication that the universe emanates eternally from God – a view which could not fit the Christian doctrine, which Albert accepted, of a created universe with a beginning.

Through our intellects, Albert believed, even in the present life we belong to the hierarchy of Intelligences. Here Albert both used and broke with his Arab mentors. Avicenna had identified the lowest of the Intelligences with the active intellect which Aristotle had mentioned briefly in *On the Soul* as being necessary if the potential intellect (*intellectus possibilis*), in itself purely receptive, is to be able to think. Averroes, in the view of Albert and all his Latin interpreters from the 1250s onwards, had gone even further and supposed that there was only one potential intellect for all men. Avicenna's position could easily be adapted to Christianity by taking the active intellect as God himself; Averroes', which precluded individual immortality, could not. Albert, however, holds that each human has its own individual active and potential intellect; like Bonaventure and Aquinas, he attacks the Averroist theory of a single intellect for all men; and yet he also proclaims his closeness to Averroes' theories about the intellect. These positions are not, as they might seem, in conflict with one another. Albert, like Averroes, held that human thought involves contact with an eternal, single intellect. But he considered that this came about through each human's individual agent intellect which was itself an emanation from the single, separate agent intellect. We engage in thought through the joining of our individual agent intellects to our individual potential intellects, which are predisposed to receive intelligible forms in the same way as our senses are predisposed to receive sensory ones. The conjunction is not a simple matter. Although the agent intellect is part of our soul, and in this sense is joined to it, the conjunction Albert has in mind is of its 'light, by which it activates the things understood' to the potential intellect.

By describing how this conjunction takes place, Albert sketches a view of the highest human happiness, which it is for philosophers to achieve ([10.49] III: 221–3). He bases himself on Aristotle's comments in *Nicomachean Ethics* X about theoretical contemplation as the best life for man. We can engage in intellectual speculation in two ways, he explains: through thinking the self-evident truths which we know simply by thinking of them, and through what we choose to learn by investigating and by listening to those who are learned. In both routes, we grasp intelligibles only because our agent intellect makes them intelligible, and 'in making them actually understood, the agent intellect is joined to us as an efficient cause'. What we are contemplating in this process, Albert believes, are not – as the description so far might suggest – eternal truths, but separate substances. The more our potential intellect is filled with these intelligibles, the more it comes to resemble the agent intellect, and when it has been filled with every intelligible thing, the light of the agent intellect has become the form to its matter, and the composite of agent and potential intellect is called the 'adopted' (*adeptus*) or divine intellect: 'and then the man has been perfected to carry out the work which is his work in so far as he is man – to contemplate perfectly through himself and grasp in thought the separate substances' ([10.49] III: 222: 6–9). 'This state of adopted intellect', Albert adds, 'is wonderful and best, for through it a man becomes in a certain way like God, because in this way he can activate divine things and bestow on himself and others divine understandings and in a certain way receive everything that is understood' ([10.49] III: 222: 80–4).

～ ALBERT'S SCHOOL: THE GERMAN ～ DOMINICANS

Albert's influence worked on three different groups in three different directions. Most explicitly associated with him, though most distant in time, are the fifteenth-century thinkers who set up Albert as their authority and described themselves as 'Albertists'; they are discussed below in Chapter 18. Albert was also an important figure for those in the arts faculties who looked to Averroes as the most faithful interpreter of Aristotle and who, while respecting Christian doctrine, considered their own role as arts masters was to reason without resort to revelation. Some of these thinkers from the thirteenth century are discussed below in Chapter 12; the movement they began lasted through to the end of the Middle Ages. John of Jandun (1285/9–1328) was one of the most outspoken advocates of Averroes (and learned from Albert), and Averroism was then taken up in Bologna and Padua, in Erfurt in the late fourteenth century and in Krakow in the mid-fifteenth.[9] But Albert's closest followers – those who carried on his tradition chronologically and developed what was most characteristic in his thought – were a group of thinkers who were all, like him,

German Dominicans.[10] They knew Albert's work well, both directly and through Hugh Ripelin of Strasbourg's *Compendium of Theological Truth* (*c.* 1260–8) which drew up some of the main themes of his work in textbook fashion. The first important member of the group was Ulrich of Strasbourg (born *c.* 1220–5), a student of Albert's at Paris and then Cologne. He returned to Paris in 1272 to complete his studies in theology, but died before he was finished. He had already written a large *summa*, *On the Highest Good*, which uses, and develops even more explicitly than Albert himself, the idea of the divinization of the intellect.

In the work of Dietrich of Freiberg, Albert's thinking is given a new and highly original twist. Dietrich (*c.* 1250–1318/20) belonged to a younger generation. He was active in Germany (from 1293 to 1296 he was provincial of the Dominican Province of Teutonia) but also in the University of Paris, where he studied between 1272 and 1274 and some time between 1281 and 1293, and where he was master of theology in 1296–7. He is an important figure in the history of natural science (see [10.73]), but his most remarkable philosophical ideas concern the human intellect. As mentioned above, medieval theologians generally accepted the view that God knows (and produces) his creation through ideas in his intellect. Dietrich accepted this common view with regard to the relation between God and all things *except* for intellects. The human intellect, he argues in *On the Intellect and the Intelligible*, is related to God in a different, closer way, which it has in common only with other intellects, such as (if they exist) the Intelligences posited by the philosophers. An intellect proceeds from God 'in so far as it is an image of God'. Like God's thinking, the object of the intellect's thinking is God himself. It is just this knowing God which constitutes the intellect; in the same act of knowing the intellect knows itself as that which knows God, and through knowing its essence it also knows all other things outside itself, since it is their exemplar: 'in one look (*intuitus*) knowing its origin and thus coming into being it knows the entirety of things.'[11] In this way, Dietrich argues that intellects exist in a special sort of way, which he describes as 'conceptional being': an intellect should not be considered as a something, which has a certain power – that of intellectually thinking. Rather, the thinking by which an intellect knows God is what the intellect is. Whereas Albert had explained how the human intellect could become God-like through what it could contemplate (the separate substances), Dietrich emphasizes the God-likeness of the intellect in its very manner of being. In another work (*On the Origin of the Things which belong to the Aristotelian Categories*), Dietrich argues that, in an important sense, the objects which we encounter in experience, and which can be described according to Aristotle's ten categories, are made by our intellects. Since the intellect knows these objects, it must bear a relation to them. The only three possible relations are that (1) it is identical to them, (2) they cause it, or (3) it causes them. Dietrich dismisses (1) and rejects (2) because a cause must have a 'greater power of forming' (*formalior virtus*) than that which it causes, whereas the intellect is 'incomparably more form-like and simpler than these things'.[12] Although Dietrich goes on to qualify his position, allowing that the intellect is not the only cause of these objects, he has given, to say the least, a surprisingly large role to the human intellect in constituting the world it grasps.[13]

The most celebrated of the German Dominicans is Eckhart (1260–1328). But Eckhart's fame has been linked more to his reputation as a mystic and as the instigator of a popular mystical movement, especially among women, than to his philosophical arguments. Unlike any other of the Western thinkers treated in this volume, Eckhart produced a body of work in the vernacular (Middle High German); and it is in these sermons that he develops some of his most striking ideas. Yet, until shortly before his death, when the process began which would lead to his posthumous condemnation in 1329, Eckhart had followed an outstanding career as a university theologian. He was a master of theology in Paris from 1302 to 1303 and, a rare honour, master again (*magister actu regens*) in 1311–13; from 1322 to 1325 he was in charge of the Dominican *studium* in Cologne. Recent scholars have emphasized the philosophical aspects of Eckhart's work (found both in the Latin *Parisian Questions* and *Three-part Work*, and in the German sermons and treatises) and have seen it as part of the tradition going back to Dietrich of Freiberg and Albert. Here there is room to touch on just three of these aspects of Eckhart's rich and many-faceted work.

In the second of his *Parisian Questions* (1302–3), Eckhart argues the position that in God, being (*esse*) and thinking (*intelligere*) are the same. In itself, there is nothing unusual about this position; Aquinas had held it too, and Eckhart quotes Aquinas' arguments for it. But Eckhart develops the idea in a particular direction, arguing – in a way which parallels what Dietrich of Freiberg says about the human intellect – that God is intellect, and his being follows from this: it is not 'because he is, that God thinks but because he thinks that he is; so that God is intellect and thinking and this thinking is the basis of his being'. The Gospel of John does not begin, Eckhart goes on to remark, with the words 'In the beginning was an existing thing (*ens*) and the existing thing was God', but 'In the beginning was the Word'; but the Word is 'in itself entirely relative to the intellect'. 'Neither being nor being existent (*ens*) is appropriate for God but something higher than what is existing.' Eckhart's line of argument threatens to undermine the whole tradition of theology based on God as supreme *being*;

although it too is rooted in theological tradition, the tradition of negative theology which goes back to pseudo-Dionysius.[14]

Eckhart's idea of the 'basis' (*grunt*) or the 'spark' (*vunke*) of the soul, developed especially in his German sermons, is even more daring, especially according to the interpretation recently advanced by Burkhard Mojsisch who, more than previous writers, has explored the philosophical, rather than the mystical, aspects of these writings.[15] Dietrich of Freiberg had already described the active intellect as the basis of the soul: the cause from which it springs. For Eckhart, however, the *grunt* or *vunke* does not belong to the soul, although it is in it. Eckhart must insist on this because he also claims that this 'something' is 'uncreated and uncreatable' (see [10.69] 133–4). When, in order to leave behind the false I and discover the true one, our possible intellect turns away from forms – wishing nothing, knowing nothing, letting nothing act upon it – it is to this 'something in the soul' which it must turn. Eckhart is willing to identify the uncreated *grunt* with God, but also, it seems, to go even further: the idea of God, he argues, implies a relation to something else, to creation; the *grunt*, or the 'I as I', by contrast, bears no relation to anything but itself. It is its own cause and even the cause of God (see [10.70] 27).

Eckhart thus transforms the theme he inherited from the tradition of Albert, according to which the highest part of man's soul, the intellect, is divinized through its ability to be filled with intelligible contents derived from God's thought itself. For Eckhart, the spark in the soul is itself divine or even more than divine, and only by turning away from anything outside myself and from any content whatsoever, do I discover myself as this 'I as I'. He also makes a parallel transformation of the moral outlook linked to Albert's theme. In place of the philosophical ideal of nobility, found in the contemplation enjoyed by the philosopher, Eckhart substitutes a nobility of renunciation which he expresses by the word 'detachment' (*abegescheidenheit*), and an ideal of poverty and humility: 'Were a man truly humble', he writes, 'God would have either to lose his own divinity and be entirely bereft of it, or else diffuse himself and flow entirely into this man. Yesterday evening I had this thought: God's greatness depends on my humility; the more humble I make myself, the more God will be raised up.'[16]

The tradition of Albert takes a different twist in the writings of Berthold of Moosburg (fl. *c.* 1335–*c.* 1361). His known work comprises just an incomplete, but none the less vast, commentary on Proclus' *Elements of Theology*. This choice of a life's work was no accident. Berthold believed that the 'Platonic philosophers', of whom he considered Proclus an outstanding example, had arrived at the true philosophy, by contrast with Aristotle and his followers. For Berthold, the main distinction to be considered is no longer between the teachings of the philosophers and those of Christian faith, but between the two main schools of ancient philosophy: the Aristotelians, whose metaphysics, the knowledge of being *qua* being, is seen in opposition to the theology developed by Christians and Neoplatonists alike (see [10.63] 317–442).

NOTES

1 Readers of this chapter are requested to look at what I say in my Introduction (above, p. 9, n. 8) about its aims and, especially, its limitations.

2 Aristotle was also studied intensively in Oxford: see above, Chapter 9, and Marenbon [10.34].

3 It is not certain that William was responsible for the revision of Grosseteste's translation that became standard.

4 For an authoritative summary of present knowledge about the translations of Aristotle, see Dod [10.30]. The preceding paragraph and a half is based especially on this study.

5 On Latin versions of Avicenna, see d'Alverny [10.27].

6 Part of the *Parmenides* was to be found in the lemmata of William of Moerbeke's translation of Proclus' commentary, but neither the commentary nor the text was generally known: see Steel [10.35] 306.

7 See Weber [10.47]. On the history of these arguments based on the idea of infinity, many of which appear to go back to the sixth-century Greek Christian thinker John Philoponus, see R. Sorabji, *Time, Creation and the Continuum*, London, 1983, esp. pp. 210–31.

8 See de Libera [10.64]. My comments on Albert draw especially from de Libera, but they offer only a crude reflection of de Libera's subtle views. See also de Libera [10.63] for a development of his views about Albert within a wider context.

9 See Schmugge [10.71] for John of Jandun and Kuksewicz [10.62] for later Averroism.

10 An excellent guide to this tradition, and argument for its unity, is provided in de Libera [10.63].

11 *De intellectu et intelligibili* II, 36; for the whole discussion, see II, 34–6, and III, 37; cf. Mojsisch [10.68].

12 *De origine rerum praedicamentalium* V2.

13 Flasch was the first scholar to bring out the nature and importance of Dietrich's position here: see [10.59].

14 For a thorough study of the background to the Parisian questions 1 and 2, see Zum Brunn and others [10.74] and Imbach [10.60].

15 See Mojsisch [10.69] and [10.70]. Not all Eckhart scholars accept Mojsisch's views: for a critique, see [10.72], esp. 307–12.

16 Sermon 14 [10.53, Deutsch. Werke, I 237: 1–5], quoted by de Libera [10.65] 325; on Eckhart's transformation of the ideal of nobility, see de Libera [10.65] 299–347.

❦❦❦ BIBLIOGRAPHY ❦❦❦

Editions of Latin Translations from Greek, Arabic and Hebrew

This is a list of some of the most important translations of philosophical works: for fuller lists, see Marenbon [Intr. 10] 194–7, with additions noted in Marenbon [10.33] 1009, n. 1.

10.1   Al-Ghazzālī (Algazel) *Intentions of the Philosophers*, sections on physics and metaphysics, in J. Muckle (ed.) *Algazel's Metaphysics*, Toronto, 1933.

10.2   Al-Ghazzālī (Algazel) *Intentions of the Philosophers* (complete text), Venice, 1506.

10.3–10.8 Aristotle: Logic (translations by Boethius, William of Moerbeke and others), ed. L. Minio-Paluello *et al.* (AL 1–6) Bruges and Paris, 1961–75).

10.9   —— *Metaphysics* (translations by James of Venice, *translatio vetus, translatio media*), ed. G. Vuillemin-Diem (AL 25), Bruges and Paris, 1970, 1976.

10.10   —— *Nicomachean Ethics* (various translations), ed. R. Gauthier (AL 26), Bruges and Paris, 1972–4.
        Aristotle's *On the Soul* (Michael Scotus's version) appears as lemmata in his translation of Averroes' Great commentary [10.14].

10.11   —— *On the Soul* (William of Moerbeke's version), as lemmata in Aquinas's commentary, ed. R. Gauthier (Leonine edition 45), Rome and Paris, 1984.

10.12   Ibn Rushd (Averroes) *Aristotelis opera cum Averrois commentariis*, Venice, 1560. (A large collection of his commentaries, uncritically edited.)

10.13   —— The 1562–74 edition of the above work, which contains fewer commentaries, has been reprinted in Frankfurt, 1962.

10.14   —— Great commentary on Aristotle, *On the Soul*, ed. F. Crawford, Cambridge, Mass., 1953.
        Averroes' Great commentary on Aristotle, *Metaphysics* is published as a whole in [10.13] vol. 8, and on individual books as follows:

10.15   —— on Book II, ed. G. Darms, Freiburg, Switzerland, 1966.

10.16   —— on Book V, ed. R. Ponzalli, Berne, 1971.

10.17   —— on Book XI, ed. B. Burke, Berne, 1969.

10.18   Ibn Sina (Avicenna): book on *On the Soul* from the *Shifā'*, in S. van Riet (ed.) *De anima*, 2 vols, Bruges and Paris, 1968, 1972.

10.19   —— book on the *Metaphysics* from the *Shifā'*, in S. van Riet (ed.) *Liber de philosophia prima sive scientia divina*, 3 vols, Bruges and Paris, 1977–83.

10.20   *Liber de causis* (*Book about Causes*), ed. A. Pattin, Louvain, undated.

10.21   Maimonides *Guide of the Perplexed*, Latin translation of the Hebrew translation by al-Harisi, *Dux seu director dubitantium vel perplexorum*, Paris, 1520; repr. Frankfurt, 1964.

10.22   Plato *Timaeus* (Calcidius' version, with his commentary), ed. J. Waszink, 2nd edn, London, 1975.

10.23   —— *Meno*, translated by Henry Aristippus, ed. V. Kordeuter and C. Labowsky, London, 1940.

10.24   —— *Phaedo*, translated by Henry Aristippus, ed. L. Minio-Paluello, London, 1950.

10.25   Porphyry *Isagoge*, translations by Boethius and others, ed. L. Minio-Paluello, (AL 1, fasc. 5–6), Bruges and Paris, 1966.

10.26   Proclus *Elements of Theology*, translated by William of Moerbeke, ed. H. Boese, Leuven, 1987.

Bibliographies and catalogues

Very full bibliographical information will be found in Daiber [10.29].

10.27   d'Alverny, M.-T. 'Avicenna Latinus', *Archives de l'histoire doctrinale et littéraire du moyen âge* (1961–72): 28, 281–316; 29, 217–33; 30, 221–72; 31, 271–86; 32, 259–302; 33, 305–27; 34, 315–43; 36, 243–80; 37, 327–61; 39, 321–41.

Studies

10.28   Brams, J. 'Guillaume de Moerbeke et Aristote', in Hamesse and Fattori [10.31] 315–36.

10.29   Daiber, H. 'Lateinische Übersetzungen arabischer Texte zur Philosophie und ihre Bedeutung für die Scholastik des Mittelalters', in Hamesse and Fattori [10.31] 203–50.

10.30   Dod, B. G. 'Aristoteles Latinus', in *CHLMP*, 45–79.

10.31   Hamesse, J. and Fattori, M. (eds) *Rencontres de cultures dans la philosophie médiévale*, Louvain and Cassino, 1990.

10.32   Kluxen, W. 'Literaturgeschichtliches zum lateinischen Moses Maimonides', *Recherches de théologie ancienne et médiévale* 21 (1954): 23–50.

10.33   Marenbon, J. 'Medieval Christian and Jewish Europe', in S. H. Nasr and O. Leaman (eds) *History of Islamic Philosophy*, vol. II, London, 1996.

10.34   —— (ed.) *Aristotle in Britain during the Middle Ages*, Turnhout, 1996.

10.35   Steel, C. 'Plato Latinus', in Hamesse and Fattori [10.31] 300–16.

Bonaventure

Original language editions

10.36   *Opera omnia*, ed. P. P. Collegii S. Bonaventurae, 10 vols, Quaracchi, 1882–1902.

10.37   *Collationes*, ed. F. Delorme (Bibliotheca Franciscana medii aevi 8), Quaracchi, 1934.

10.38   *Itinerarium mentis ad Deum* (text of *Opera omnia* with French parallel trans. and notes by H. Duméry), Paris, 1960.

Translations

10.39   *Breviloquium*, trans. J. de Vinck, Paterson, NJ, 1963.

10.40   *Itinerarium mentis ad Deum (The mind's journey to God)*, trans. P. Boehner, St Bonaventure, NY, 1956. (Other translations are also available.)

10.41   *De reductione artium ad theologiam*, trans. E. T. Healy, St Bonaventure, NY, 1955.

10.42   *Collationes* on the Hexaemeron, trans. (into French) M. Ozilon, as *Les six jours de la création*, Paris, *c.* 1991.

Studies

10.43   Bougerol, J. *Introduction à l'étude de Saint Bonaventure*, Tournai, 1961.

10.44   Gilson, E. *La Philosophie de Saint Bonaventure*, 3rd edn (Etudes de philosophie médiévale 4) Paris, 1953. (There is an English translation of the first, 1924, edn of this book: *The Philosophy of St Bonaventure*, trans I. Trethowan and F. J. Sheed, New York, 1938.)

10.45   Quinn, J. *The Historical Constitution of St Bonaventure's Philosophy*, Toronto, 1973.

10.46   Van Steenberghen, F. *La Philosophie au XIIIe siècle*, Louvain, 1966.

10.47   Weber, E. H. *Dialogue et dissensions entre Saint Bonaventure et Saint Thomas d'Aquin à Paris, 1252–73* (Bibliothèque thomiste 41), Paris, 1974.

Albert the Great and his Influence

Original language editions

10.48   Albert the Great *Opera omnia*, ed. A. and E. Borgnet, Paris, 1890–9.

10.49   —— *Opera omnia*, chief ed. B. Geyer, Münster, 1951–.

10.50   Berthold of Moosburg, Commentary on the *Elements of Theology*, partial ed. by L. Sturlese, Rome, 1974.

10.51   Dietrich of Freiberg *Opera omnia*, ed. K. Flasch *et al.*, Hamburg, 1977–83.

10.52   —— *De origine rerum praedicamentalium*, ed. F. Stegmüller, 'Meister Dietrich von Freiburg über den Ursprung der Kategorien', *Archives d'histoire doctrinale et littéraire du moyen âge* 24 (1957): 115–201. (This edition has been replaced by that in [10.51] but may be more readily available.)

10.53   Eckhart *Die deutschen und lateinischen Werke*, ed. J. Quint *et al.* (Stuttgart, 1930–).

Translations

10.54   Eckhart, Sermons and treatises, trans. M. O'C. Walshe, London and Dulverton, 1979.

10.55   *Meister Eckhart: the Essential Sermons, Commentaries, Treatises and Defence,* trans. E. Colledge and B. McGinn, London, 1981.
10.56   *Meister Eckhart: Teacher and Preacher,* trans. B. McGinn, NJ, 1986.
10.57   Eckhart *Parisian Questions and Prologues,* trans. A. Maurer, Toronto, 1974.

Bibliographies and catalogues

10.58   Larger, N. *Bibliographie zu Meister Eckhart* (Dokimion 9), Freiburg, Switzerland, 1989.
A wide bibliography to the whole area is given in de Libera [10.63].

Studies

10.59   Flasch, K. 'Kennt die mittelalterliche Philosophie die konstitutive Funktion des menschlichen Denkens? Eine Untersuchung zu Dietrich von Freiberg', *Kant-Studien* 63 (1972): 182–206.
10.60   Imbach, R. *Deus est intelligere,* Freiburg, Switzerland, 1976.
10.61   Krebs, E. *Meister Dietrich (Theodoricus Teutonicus de Vriberg): sein Leben, seine Werke, seine Wissenschaft* (BGPT MA 5, 5–6), Münster, 1906.
10.62   Kuksewicz, Z. 'L'influence d'Averroes sur les universités en Europe centrale: l'expansion de l'averroisme latin', in J. Jolivet (ed.) *Multiple Averroes,* Paris, 1978, pp. 275–86.
10.63   Libera, A. de *Introduction à la mystique rhénane d'Albert le Grand à Maître Eckhart,* Paris, 1984. Repr. as *La mystique rhénane,* Paris, 1994.
10.64   —— *Albert le Grand et la philosophie,* Paris, 1990.
10.65   —— *Penser au moyen âge,* Paris, 1991.
10.66   Lossky, V. *Théologie négative et connaissance de Dieu chez Eckhart,* Paris, 1960.
10.67   Meyer, G. and Zimmermann, A. *Albertus Magnus: Doctor Universalis 1280/1980* (Walberger Studien 6), Mainz, 1980.
10.68   Mojsisch, B. *Die Theorie des Intellekts bei Dietrich von Freiberg,* Hamburg, 1977.
10.69   —— *Meister Eckhart. Analogie, Univozität und Einheit,* Hamburg, 1983.
10.70   —— '"Le moi": la conception du moi de Maître Eckhart: une contribution aux "lumières" du Moyen-Age', *Revue des sciences religieuses* 70 (1996): 18–30.
10.71   Schmugge, L. *Johannes von Jandun (1285/9–1328),* Stuttgart, 1966.
10.72   Waldschütz, E. *Denken und Erfahren des Grundes. Zur philosophische Deutung Meister Eckharts,* Vienna, Freiburg and Basel, 1986.
10.73   Wallace, W. A. *The Scientific Methodology of Theoderic of Freiberg* (Studia Friburgensia, NS 25), Freiburg, Switzerland, 1959.
10.74   Zum Brunn, E., Kaluza, Z., Libera, A. de, Vignaux, P. and Wéber, E. *Maître Eckhart à Paris. Une critique médiévale de l'ontothéologie* (Bibliothèque de l'école des hautes études, sciences religieuses 86), Paris, 1984.

CHAPTER 11

Thomas Aquinas

Brian Davies OP

⚓

Thomas Aquinas, son of Landulf d'Aquino and his wife Theodora, was born sometime between 1224 and 1226 in what was then the Kingdom of Naples.[1] After a childhood education at the Benedictine monastery of Monte Cassino, he studied at the university of Naples. Here, possibly under Irish influence, he encountered the philosophy of Aristotle, which subsequently became a major source of philosophical inspiration to him.[2] The thinking of Aristotle and Aquinas differ in many ways. So it would be wrong to say, as some have, that Aquinas is just an 'Aristotelian', implying that he merely echoed Aristotle.[3] But he certainly used Aristotle to help him say much that he wanted to say for himself. And he did more than any other medieval philosopher to make subsequent generations aware of the importance of Aristotle.

In 1242 or 1243 Aquinas entered the Dominican Order of preaching friars founded by St Dominic (*c.* 1170–1221).[4] He subsequently studied under St Albert the Great (*c.* 1200–80) in Cologne and Paris, and by 1256 he was a professor at the University of Paris. The rest of his life was devoted to teaching, preaching, administration and writing – not only in Paris, but elsewhere as well. He taught, for example, at Orvieto and Rome. He was assigned to establish a house of studies in Rome in 1265. In 1272 he moved to Naples, where he became responsible for studies at the priory of San Domenico. But by 1274 his working life was over. In December 1273 he suffered some kind of breakdown. At around the same time he was asked to attend the second Council of Lyons. He set out for Lyons, but he became seriously ill on the way and he died in the Cistercian Abbey of Fossanova.

After his death Aquinas came near to being condemned at the University of Paris. And teachings thought to derive from him were condemned at Oxford in 1277. But his standing as a thinker grew steadily and, in spite of continued opposition to his teaching, he was canonized as a saint of the Catholic Church in 1323. Later medieval authors often quote him and discuss him, and, though his influence waned between the later medieval period and the age of the Counter-Reformation, his impact on post-Reformation figures was considerable, chiefly because St Ignatius Loyola arranged for his writings to be used in the training of Jesuits. After another period in which his thinking came to be lightly regarded, the study of Aquinas was encouraged by the papacy in the nineteenth century.

❧ PHILOSOPHER OR THEOLOGIAN? ❧

Does Aquinas deserve a place in a book on the history of philosophy? Anthony Kenny has described him as 'one of the dozen greatest philosophers of the western world' ([11.27] 1). But others have expressed a different view. Take, for example, Bertrand Russell. According to him:

> There is little of the true philosophic spirit in Aquinas. He does not, like the Platonic Socrates, set out to follow wherever the argument may lead. He is not engaged in an inquiry, the result of which it is impossible to know in advance. Before he begins to philosophize, he already knows the truth; it is declared in the Catholic faith.[5]

Russell had little time for Aquinas considered as a philosopher. And even Aquinas's supporters have sometimes characterized him as a theologian rather than a philosopher. According to Etienne Gilson, the philosophy in Aquinas is indistinguishable from the theology.[6] The same opinion is expressed by Armand Maurer. Commenting on Aquinas's *Summa theologiae*, he says that, in this work,

> everything is theological, even the philosophical reasoning that makes up such a large part of it. The water of philosophy and the other secular disciplines it contains has been changed into the wine of theology. That is why we cannot extract from the *Summa* its philosophical parts and treat them as pure philosophy.[7]

Russell's judgement will strike most modern philosophers as a dubious one. And, as Kenny nicely observes, it 'comes oddly from a philosopher who [in *Principia Mathematica*] took three hundred and sixty dense pages to offer a proof that $1 + 1 = 2$' ([11.27] 2). But there are good reasons for agreeing with Gilson and Maurer. Aquinas was a priest and a Dominican friar. And most of his writings can be properly classed as 'theology'. We have reason to believe that his greatest literary achievement, the *Summa theologiae*, was chiefly intended as a textbook for working friars.[8] And there is reason to suppose that his second best-known work, the *Summa contra Gentiles,* had an equally pastoral and Christian motive.[9]

Yet any modern philosopher who reads Aquinas will be struck by the fact that he was more than your average theologian. His writings show him to have been expert in matters of philosophical logic. And, like many medieval theology teachers, he presented his theology with an eye, not just on Scripture and the authority of Christian tradition, but also on what follows from what, what it is *per se* reasonable to believe, and what it makes sense to say in general. If Aquinas is first and foremost a theologian, he is also a philosopher's theologian who is worthy of attention from philosophers. He had an enviable knowledge of philosophical writings and he was deeply concerned to theologize on the basis of this knowledge. He was also a writer of considerable ability with theses of his own, which are not just restatements of positions received from the Christian tradition and the history of philosophy. Whether one calls him a 'theological' thinker or a 'philosophical' thinker does not really matter. The fact remains that his writings are full of philosophical interest.

❧ AQUINAS AND GOD ❧

Readers who want to get an overall sense of Aquinas's teaching are best advised to see it as defending what is usually called an *exitus-reditus* picture of reality ([11.12] ch. 11). God, says Aquinas, is 'the beginning and end of all things'.[10] Creatures derive from God (*exitus*), who is therefore their first efficient cause (that which accounts for them being there).[11] But God is also the final cause of creatures, that to which they aim, tend, or return (*reditus*), that which contains the perfection or goal of all created things.[12] According to Aquinas, everything comes from God and is geared to him. God accounts for there being anything apart from himself, and he is what is aimed at by anything moving towards its perfection. Aristotle says that everything aims for its good (*Ethics* I, i, 1094a3). Aquinas says that any created good derives from God who contains in himself all the perfections found in creatures. In so far as a creature moves to its perfection, Aquinas goes on to argue, the creature is tending to what is to be found in God himself.[13] As Father, Son, and Spirit, Aquinas adds, God is the special goal of rational individuals. For these can share in what God is by nature.[14]

Aquinas is sometimes reported as teaching that someone who claims rationally to believe in the existence of God must be able to prove that God exists. But this is not what Aquinas teaches. He says that people can have a rational belief in the existence of God without being able to prove God's existence.[15] And he holds that, apart from the question of God's existence, people may be rational in believing what they cannot prove. Following Aristotle, he maintains that people may rationally believe indemonstrable principles of logic.[16] He also maintains that one may rationally believe what a teacher imparts to one, even though one is in no position to demonstrate the truth of what the teacher has told one.[17] He does, however, contend that belief in God's existence is one for which good philosophical reasons can be given. This is clear from *Summa theologiae* Ia, 2, 2 and *Summa contra Gentiles* I, 9, where he says that 'we can demonstrate . . . that God exists' and that God can be made known as we 'proceed through demonstrative arguments'. 'Demonstrative arguments' here means what it does for Aristotle, i.e. arguments using premisses which entail a given conclusion on pain of contradiction.

Aquinas denies that proof of God's existence is given by arguing that 'God does not exist' is a contradiction. So he rejects the suggestion, commonly associated with St Anselm, that the existence of God can be demonstrated from the absurdity of denying that God exists.[18] He also rejects the view that human beings are naturally capable of perceiving or experiencing God as they perceive or experience the things with which they are normally acquainted. According to Aquinas, our perception and seeing of things is based on sensory experience.[19] Since God is not a physical object, Aquinas concludes that there can be no natural perception or seeing of God on the part of human beings.[20] He does not deny that people might have a knowledge of God without the medium of physical objects. In talking of life after death, he says that people can have a vision of God which is nothing like knowing a physical object.[21] But he denies that human beings in this world have a direct and unmediated knowledge of God. On his account, our knowledge of God starts from what we know of the world in which we live. According to him, we can know that God exists because the world in which we find ourselves cannot account for itself.

Aquinas considers whether we can prove that God exists in many places in his writings. But his best-known arguments for the existence of God come in Ia, 2, 3 (the 'Five Ways'). His thinking in this text is clearly indebted to earlier authors, especially Aristotle, Maimonides, Avicenna and Averroes.[22] And it would be foolish to suggest that the reasoning of the Five Ways can be quickly summarized in a way that does them justice. But their substance can be indicated in fairly uncomplicated terms.

In general, Aquinas's Five Ways employ a simple pattern of argument. Each begins by drawing attention to some general feature of things known to us on the basis of experience. It is then suggested that none of these features can be accounted for in ordinary mundane terms, and that we must move to a level of explanation which transcends any with which we are familiar.[23]

Another way of putting it is to say that, according to the Five Ways, questions we can raise with respect to what we encounter in day to day life raise further questions the answer to which can only be thought of as lying beyond what we encounter.

Take, for example, the First Way, in which the influence of Aristotle is particularly prevalent.[24] Here the argument starts from change or motion in the world.[25] It is clear, says Aquinas, that there is such a thing – he cites as an instance the change involved in wood becoming hot when subjected to fire.[26] How, then, may we account for it?

According to Aquinas, anything changed or moved is changed or moved by something else. *Omne quod movetur ab alio movetur.* This, he reasons, is because a thing which has changed has become what it was not to begin with, which can only happen if there is something from which the reality attained by the thing as changed somehow derives.[27] Therefore, he concludes, there must be a first cause of things being changed or moved. For there cannot be an endless series of things changed or moved by other things. If every change in a series of connected changes depends on a prior changer, the whole system of changing things is only derivatively an initiator of change and still requires something to initiate its change. There must be something which causes change or motion in things without itself being changed or moved by anything. There must an unchanged changer or an unmoved mover.

> Anything which is moved is moved by something else . . . To cause motion is to bring into being what was previously only able to be, and this can only be done by something that already is . . . Now the same thing cannot at the same time be both actually x and potentially x, though it can be actually x and potentially y: the actually hot cannot at the same time be potentially hot, though it can be potentially cold.
> Consequently, a thing which is moved cannot itself cause that same movement; it cannot move itself. Of necessity therefore anything moved is moved by something else . . . Now we must stop somewhere, otherwise there will be no first cause of the movement and as a result no subsequent causes . . . Hence one is bound to arrive at some first cause of things being moved which is not itself moved by anything, and this is what everybody understands by God.
>
> (*Summa theologiae* I q. 2, a. 3)

If we bear in mind that Aquinas believes that time can be said to exist because changes occur, the First Way is arguing that the reality of time is a reason for believing in God.[28] Aquinas is suggesting that the present becomes the past because something non-temporal enables the present to become past.

The pattern of the First Way is repeated in the rest of the Five Ways. According to the Second Way, there are causes in the world which bring it about that other things come to be. There are, as Aquinas puts it, causes which are related as members of a series. In that case, however, there must be a first cause, or something which is not itself caused to be by anything. For causes arranged in series must have a first member.

> In the observable world causes are found to be ordered in series; we never observe, nor ever could, something causing itself, for this would mean it preceded itself, and this is not possible. Such a series of causes must however stop somewhere; for in it an earlier member causes an intermediate and the intermediate a last ... Now if you eliminate a cause you also eliminate its effects, so that you cannot have a last cause, nor an intermediate one, unless you have a first.
>
> (ibid.)

According to the Third Way[29] there are things which are perishable (e.g. plants) and things which are imperishable (in Aquinas's language, imperishable things are 'necessary' beings or things which 'must be').[30] But why should this be so? The answer, says Aquinas, has to lie in something imperishable and dependent for its existence on nothing.[31]

> Now a thing that must be, may or may not owe this necessity to something else. But just as we must stop somewhere in a series of causes, so also in the series of things which must be and owe this to other things.
>
> (ibid.)

In the Fourth and Fifth Ways Aquinas turns to different questions. Why are there things with varying degrees of perfection?[32] And how does it come about that in nature there are things which, while not themselves intelligent, operate in a regular or goal-directed way?[33] Aquinas suggests that perfections in things imply a source of perfections. He thinks that where there are degrees of a perfection there must be something which maximally embodies that perfection and which causes it to occur in other things. And he thinks that the goal-directed activity of non-rational things suggests that they are governed by what is rational.

Some things are found to be more good, more true, more noble, and so on, and other things less. But such comparative terms describe varying degrees of approximation to a superlative; for example, things are hotter and hotter the nearer they approach to what is hottest. Something therefore is the truest and best and most noble of things. Now *when many things possess some property in common, the one most fully possessing it causes it in the others: fire,* to use Aristotle's example, *the hottest of all things, causes all other things to be hot.* There is therefore something which causes in all other things their being, their goodness, and whatever other perfections they have.

Some things which lack awareness, namely bodies, operate in accordance with an end . . . Nothing however that lacks awareness tends to a goal except under the direction of someone with awareness and with understanding . . . Everything in nature, therefore is directed to its goal by someone with understanding.

(ibid.)

❦ WHAT IS GOD LIKE? ❦

Aquinas is often described as someone who first tries to prove the existence of God and then tries to show that God has various attributes. But, though this description can be partly defended, it is also misleading. For Aquinas holds that the attributes we ascribe to God are not, in reality, anything distinct from God himself. According to Aquinas, God is good, perfect, knowledgeable, powerful and eternal. But he does not think that, for example, 'the goodness of God' signifies anything other than God himself. In the thinking of Aquinas, God does not *have* attributes or properties. God *is* his attributes or properties.[34] Aquinas also maintains that, though we speak of God and ascribe certain attributes to him, we do not know what God is. Aquinas is often thought of as someone with a precise or definite concept of God, someone who thinks he can explain just what God is. But in a passage immediately following the text of the Five Ways, he writes,

Having recognized that a certain thing exists, we have still to investigate the way in which it exists, that we may come to understand what it is that exists. Now we cannot know what God is, but only what he is not; we must therefore consider the ways in which God does not exist, rather than the ways in which he does.

(ibid.)

The same move is made in the *Summa Contra Gentiles*. Book I, Chapter 13 of the treatise is called 'Arguments in proof of the existence of God'. Chapter 14 begins with the assertion, 'The divine substance surpasses every form that our intellect reaches. Thus we are unable to apprehend it by knowing what it is.'

In saying that God and his attributes are identical, Aquinas is not saying that, for example, 'God is good' means the same as 'God exists'. And he is certainly not saying that God is a property.[35] He means that certain things that are true of creatures are not true of God. More precisely, he means that God is nothing material. On Aquinas's account, material things possessing a nature cannot be identified with the nature they possess. Thus, for example, Socrates is not identical with human nature. But what is it that allows us to distinguish between Socrates and other human beings? Aquinas says that Socrates is different from other human beings not because of his nature but because of his matter. Socrates is different from me because he was one parcel of matter and I am another. It is materiality which allows Socrates to be a human being rather than human nature. And, since Aquinas denies that God is something material, he therefore concludes that God and his nature are not distinguishable. He also reasons that angels and their natures are not distinguishable. The angel Gabriel is not a material object. And neither is the angel Michael. So, says Aquinas, Gabriel is his nature, and Michael is his nature. Or, as we may put it, God, Gabriel and Michael are not individual members of a species or genus.[36]

With respect to the question of knowing what God is, we need to be warned that Aquinas does not deny that we can know ourselves to speak truly when we make certain statements about God.[37] Aquinas spends a great deal of time arguing that many propositions concerning God can be proved to be true in philosophical terms. But he denies that we can understand the nature of God. On his account, our knowledge of what things are depends on our ability to experience them by means of our senses and to classify them accordingly. Since he holds that God is nothing material, he therefore denies that God is known by the senses and classifiable on the basis of sensory experience.

> The knowledge that is natural to us has its source in the senses and extends just so far as it can be led by sensible things; from these, however, our understanding cannot reach to the divine essence . . . In the present life our intellect has a natural relation to the natures of material things; thus it understands nothing except by turning to sense images . . . In this sense it is obvious that we cannot, primarily and essentially, in the mode of knowing that we experience, understand

immaterial substances since they are not subject to the senses and imagination ... What is understood first by us in the present life is the whatness of material things ... [hence] ... we arrive at a knowledge of God by way of creatures.

(*Summa theologiae*, Ia, 12, 12; 88, 1; 88, 3)

On Aquinas's account, our knowledge of God is derived from what we know of things in the world and from what we can sensibly deny or affirm of God given that he is not something in the world. So, says Aquinas, God is not a physical object which can be individuated as a member of a class of things which can be distinguished from each other with reference to genus and species. Among other things, Aquinas also argues that God is unchangeable and non-temporal (since he is the first cause of change, and since time is real since changes occur).[38]

In distinguishing God from creatures, however, Aquinas lays the greatest stress on the teaching that God is uncreated. One way in which he does so is to say that there is no 'potentiality' in God. To understand his teaching on God it will help if we try to understand what he means by saying this.

We can start by noting what Aquinas means by 'potentiality'. And we can do so by thinking of my cat Fergus. He is a lovely and loving creature, and I am deeply fond of him. But he is no Platonic form. Plato thought of the forms as unchangeable. But Fergus is changing all the time. He gets fat as I feed him. And he is constantly changing his position. So he is a serious threat to the local mice.

Aquinas would say that when Fergus weighs nine pounds he is also potentially eight and ten pounds in weight. Fergus might weigh nine pounds, but he could slim to eight pounds or grow to ten pounds. Aquinas would also say that when Fergus is in the kitchen, he is potentially in the living room. For Fergus has a habit of moving around.

What if Fergus ends up strolling on to a busy road? He stands a strong chance of becoming a defunct cat. Or, as Aquinas would say, Fergus is actually a cat and potentially a corpse. Fergus is vulnerable to the activity of things in the world. And some of them can bring it about that he ceases to be the thing that he is.

We can put this by saying that Fergus is potentially non-existent as a cat. And that is what Aquinas would say. But he would add that there is a sense in which Fergus is potentially non-existent quite apart from the threat of a busy road and the like. For there might be no Fergus at all, not just in the sense that there might never have been cats who acted so that Fergus was born, but in the sense that Fergus might not continue to exist. According to Aquinas, anything created is potential since its existence depends on God (since anything created is potentially non-existent). In his view, we are entitled to ask why anything we come across is there. And, so he thinks, in asking this question we need not be concerned with temporally prior causes or identifiable causes in the world which sustain things in the state in which they are. We can be asking about the fact that there is anything there to be produced or to be sustained. What accounts for the fact that such things exist at all? What accounts for there being a world in which we can ask what accounts for what within it?

Aquinas holds that, if we take these questions seriously, we must believe in the existence of something which is wholly lacking in potentiality, i.e. God. Fergus can change physically and he has potentiality accordingly. But God is no physical thing, and, since he accounts for there being a world, he cannot be potentially non-existent. He does not 'have' existence. His existence is not received or derived from another. He is his own existence (*ipsum esse subsistens*) and the reason why other things have it.

> Properties that belong to a thing over and above its own nature must derive from somewhere, either from that nature itself . . . or from an external cause . . . If therefore the existence of a thing is to be other than its nature, that existence must either derive from the nature or have an external cause. Now it cannot derive merely from the nature, for nothing with derived existence suffices to bring itself into being. It follows then that, if a thing's existence differs from its nature, that existence must be externally caused. But we cannot say this about God, whom we have seen to be the first cause. Neither then can we say that God's existence is other than his nature.
>
> (*Summa theologiae*, Ia, 3, 4)

In Aquinas's view, this would be true even if the created order contained things which are not material. For suppose there were immaterial beings other than God, as Aquinas took angels to be.[39] They would differ from material things since they would have no in-built tendency to perish or move around. In the language of Aquinas, they would be 'necessary' beings rather than 'contingent' ones. They would also be identical with their natures, for, as we have seen, Aquinas held that there are no two angels of the same kind or 'species'. But they would still be potentially non-existent since they would receive their existence from God. And, though they could not decay or perish at the hands of other creatures, it would be possible for God to de-create (annihilate) them. They would not therefore exist simply by being what they are. 'Without doubt', says Aquinas, 'the angels, and all that is other than God, were made by God. For only God is his existence; in all else essence and existence are distinct.'[40] Or, as he also explains,

Some things are of a nature that cannot exist except as instantiated in individual matter – all bodies are of this kind. This is one way of being. There are other things whose natures are instantiated by themselves and not by being in matter. These have existence simply by being the natures they are: yet existence is still something they *have*, it is not what they are – the incorporeal beings we call angels are of this kind. Finally there is the way of being that belongs to God alone, for his existence is what he is.

(*Summa theologiae*, Ia, 12, 4)

❧ GOD AND HIS CREATION ❧

How does Aquinas think of God as relating to his creation? In writing about the relation between God and creatures, one of the things he says is that God is not really related to creatures, though creatures are really related to God. In his own words:

Since God is altogether outside the order of creatures, since they are ordered to him but not he to them, it is clear that being related to God is a reality in creatures, but being related to creatures is not a reality in God.[41]

But what does he mean in saying this? And how does what he says connect with his belief that God is the creator and sustainer of everything other than himself?

One might suppose that the words of Aquinas just quoted constitute a flagrant violation of obvious truths. If A is related to B, then B must be related to A. What could be more obvious than that? But Aquinas's teaching on God and his relation to creatures is not a denial of the principle 'If aRb, then bRa'. If one reads him on the question of God's relation to creatures, one will find him endorsing all of the following propositions.

1   We can speak of God as related to his creatures in view of the purely formal point that if one thing can be said to be related to another, then the second thing can be said to be related to the first.
2   Since God can be compared to creatures, since he can be spoken of as being like them, he can be thought of as related to them.
3   Since God knows creatures, he can be said to be related to them.
4   Since God moves creatures, he can be said to be related to them.
5   Since God can be spoken of as 'first', 'highest' and so on, he can be said to be related to creatures since these terms are relational ones.[42]

In saying that 'being related to creatures is not a reality in God', Aquinas's primary concern is to deny that God is changed because he has created. Aquinas denies that God is something which has to create. In his view, God creates freely, and to understand what God is essentially would not be to see that he is Creator of the world. God, indeed, has created the world. But, says Aquinas, he does not produce the world as kidneys produce urine. For him, God is able to create, but he is not essentially a creator (as kidneys are essentially producers of urine).[43] So Aquinas reasons that the essence of God is in no way affected by the existence of created things and that being the Creator of creatures is not something in God. God does not become *different* by becoming the Creator of things. Nor does he change because his creatures change. For Aquinas, the fact that there are creatures makes no difference to God, just as the fact that my coming to know that Fred is bald makes no difference to Fred (my coming to know that Fred is bald does not change him, even though he might be deeply affected by learning that I have come to know of his baldness). In Aquinas's view, God is unchangeably himself. And he remains so even though it is true that there are things created and sustained by him.

This aspect of Aquinas's teaching allows him to take a view of God's activity which is quite at odds with that to be found in the work of many philosophers and theologians both ancient and modern. It has often been said that the action of God is a process undergone by God with effects in the world of created things. When I act, I do something in addition to what I have been previously doing. I go through a series of successive states. And my going through these states sometimes leads to changes in things apart from myself. By the same token, so it has often been argued, God acts by being a subject undergoing successive states some of which have effects in things other than him. But this is not Aquinas's position. On his account, the action of God is not a process undergone by him. It is a process undergone in things other than God. For Aquinas, God's action is the history of created things.

One of the things which Aquinas takes this to mean is that God cannot, strictly speaking, be thought of as intervening in the world. According to the usual sense of 'intervene', to say that X has intervened is to say that X has come to be present in some situation from which X was previously absent. Thus, for example, to say that I intervened in a brawl is to say that I moved into a fight of which I was not originally a part. But Aquinas holds that God can never be absent from anything. On his account, God is everywhere as making all places.[44] He also says that God is in all things as making them to be. Hence, for example, he refuses to think of miracles as cases of divine intervention. It is often said that to believe in miracles is to believe in a God who can intervene. The idea seems to be that a God capable of performing miracles must be one who observes a given scenario and then steps in to tinker with it. But God, for Aquinas, can never intervene in his creation in this sense. He therefore maintains that God is as present in what is not miraculous as he is in the miraculous. Miracles, for him, do not occur because of an extra added wonder ingredient (i.e. God). They occur because something is *not* present (i.e. a cause other than God, or a collection of such causes).[45]

This thought of Aquinas should be connected with another of his prevailing theses: that free human actions are caused by God. He frequently alludes to arguments suggesting that people cannot be free under God's providence. In *On Evil* VI, for instance, we find the three following arguments, from the twenty-four in all, against the thesis that human beings have a free choice of their actions:

> If change is initiated in the human will in a fixed way by God, it follows that human beings do not have free choice of their actions. Moreover, an action is forced when its originating principle is outside the subject, and the victim of force does not contribute anything to it. So if the originating principle of a choice which is made voluntarily is outside the subject – in God – then it seems that the will is changed by force and of necessity. So we do not have free choice of our actions. Moreover, it is impossible that a human will should not be in accordance with God's will: as Augustine says in the *Enchiridion*, either a human being does what God wills or God fulfils his will in that person. But God's will is changeless; so the human will is too. So all human choices spring from a fixed choice.

A similar kind of argument constitutes the third objection to Ia, 83, 1:

> What is *free is cause of itself*, as the Philosopher says (*Metaphysics* I.2). Therefore what is moved by another is not free. But God moves the will, for it is written (Prov. 21: 1): *The heart of the king is in the hand of the Lord; whithersoever He will He shall turn it*; and (Phil. 2: 13): *It is God Who worketh in you both to will and to accomplish*. Therefore people do not have free-will.

Yet Aquinas insists that the reality of providence (which means the reality of God working in all things as first cause and sustainer) is not incompatible with human freedom.

To begin with, he says, people certainly have freedom. For one thing, the Bible holds that they do (in Ia, 83, 1 Aquinas cites *Ecclesiasticus* 15: 14 to this effect). For another, people, as rational agents, have it in them to choose between alternative courses of action (unlike inanimate objects or animals acting by instinct).[46] They also have it in them to act or refrain from acting. In fact, says Aquinas, human freedom is a prerequisite of moral thinking.

> If there is nothing free in us, but the change which we desire comes about of necessity, then we lose deliberation, exhortation, command and punishment, and praise and blame, which are what moral philosophy is based on.
>
> (*On Power*, VI; *Summa theologiae*, Ia, 83, 1)

Secondly, so Aquinas continues, human actions falling under providence can be free precisely because of what providence involves. In his view we are not free *in spite of* God, but *because of* God.

> God does indeed change the will, however, in an unchanging manner, because of the manner of acting of God's change-initiating power, which cannot fail. But because of the nature of the will which is changed – which is such that it is related indifferently to different things – this does not lead to necessity, but leaves freedom untouched. In the same way divine providence works unfailingly in everything, but nevertheless effects come from contingent causes in a contingent manner, since God changes everything in a relative way, relative to the manner of existence of each thing . . . The will does contribute something when change is initiated in it by God: it is the will itself that acts, though the change is initiated by God. So though its change does come from outside as far as the first originating principle is concerned, it is nevertheless not a forced change.
>
> (*On Evil*, VI)

In other words, human freedom is compatible with providence because only by virtue of providence is there any human freedom. God, for Aquinas, really does act in everything. And since 'everything' includes human free actions, Aquinas concludes that God works in them as much as in anything else.

> People are in charge of their acts, including those of willing and of not willing, because of the deliberative activity of reason, which can be turned to one side or the other. But that someone should deliberate or not deliberate, supposing that one were in charge of this too, would have to come about by a preceding deliberation. And since this may not proceed to infinity, one would finally have to reach the point at which a person's free decision is moved by some external principle

superior to the human mind, namely by God, as Aristotle himself demonstrated. Thus the minds even of healthy people are not so much in charge of their acts as not to need to be moved by God.

(*Summa theologiae*, Ia2ae, 109, 3, ad. 1)

The same idea is expressed in Aquinas's commentary on Aristotle's *On Interpretation*:

If divine providence is, in its own right, the cause of everything that happens, or at least of everything good, it seems that everything happens of necessity ... God's will cannot be thwarted: so it seems that whatever he wants to happen happens of necessity ... [But] we have to notice a difference as regards the divine will. The divine will should be thought of as being outside the ordering of existent things. It is the cause which grounds every existent, and all the differences there are between them. One of the differences between existents is between those that are possible and those that are necessary. Hence necessity and contingency in things have their origin in the divine will, as does the distinction between them, which follows from a description of their proximate causes. God lays down necessary causes for the effects that he wants to be necessary, and he lays down causes that act contingently – i.e. that can fail of their effect – for the effects that he wants to be contingent. It is according to this characteristic of their causes that effects are said to be necessary or contingent, even though they all depend on the divine will, which transcends the ordering of necessity and contingency, as their first cause ... The will of God cannot fail: but in spite of that, not all its effects are necessary; some are contingent.

(*On 'On Interpretation'*, Bk I, lectio 14)

By 'necessary' here Aquinas means 'determined' or 'brought about by causes necessitating their effects'. By 'contingent' he means 'undetermined' or 'able to be or not to be'. His suggestion, therefore, is that God wills both what is determined and what is undetermined. Since he believes that each must derive from God's will, he locates them within the context of providence. But since he also believes that the determined and undetermined are genuinely different, he concludes that providence can effect what is undetermined as well as what is determined. And, on this basis, he holds that it can effect human free actions.

One may, of course, say that if my actions are ultimately caused by God then I do not act freely at all. But Aquinas would reply that my actions are free if nothing in the world is acting on me so as to make me perform them, not if God is not acting in me. According to him, what is incompatible with human free will is 'necessity of coercion' or the effect of violence, as when something acts on one and 'applies force to the point where one cannot act otherwise'.[47] As Herbert McCabe explains, Aquinas's position is that 'to be free means not to be under the influence of some other *creature*, it is to be independent of other *bits of the universe*; it is not and could not mean to be independent of God'.[48] For Aquinas, God does not interfere with created free agents to push them into action in a way that infringes their freedom. He does not act *on* them (as Aquinas thinks created things do when they cause others to act as determined by them). He makes them to be what they are, namely freely acting agents. In Aquinas's words,

> Free-will is the cause of its own movement, because by their free-will people move themselves to act. But it does not of necessity belong to liberty that what is free should be the first cause of itself, as neither for one thing to be the cause of another need it be the first cause. God, therefore, is the first cause, who moves causes both natural and voluntary. And just as by moving natural causes he does not prevent their acts being natural, so by moving voluntary causes he does not deprive their actions of being voluntary: but rather is he the cause of this very thing in them; for he operates in each thing according to its own nature.
>
> (*Summa theologiae*, Ia, 83, 1, ad. 3)

❧ HUMAN BEINGS ❧

On this account, people are totally dependent on God for all that they are. But the account is a very theological one. And one might wonder how Aquinas thinks of people without also thinking about God. What, for example, would he write if asked to contribute to a modern philosophical book on the nature of human beings?[49]

The first thing he would say is that human beings are animals. So they are, for example, capable of physical movement. And they have biological characteristics. They have the capacity to grow and reproduce. They have the need and capacity to eat. These characteristics are not, for Aquinas, optional extras which people can take up and discard while remaining people. They are essential elements in the make-up of any human being. And they are very much bound up with what is physical or material.

This line of thinking, of course, immediately sets Aquinas apart from writers who embrace a 'dualistic' understanding of human beings – writers like Descartes, for instance.[50] For Aquinas, my body is not distinct from me because it is a different substance or thing from me. On his account, if a human being is there, then so is a human body.

> For as it belongs to the very conception of 'this human being' that there should be this soul, flesh and bone, so it belongs to the very conception of 'human being' that there be soul, flesh and bone. For the substance of a species has to contain whatever belongs in general to every one of the individuals comprising that species.
>
> (*Summa theologiae*, Ia, 75, 4)

Aquinas often refers to the thesis that people are essentially substances different from bodies on which they act (a view which he ascribes to Plato). But he emphatically rejects this thesis.

> Plato and his followers asserted that the intellectual soul is not united to the body as form to matter, but only as mover to movable, for Plato said that the soul is in the body 'as a sailor in a ship'. Thus the union of soul and body would only be by contact of power . . . But this doctrine seems not to fit the facts.
>
> (*Summa contra Gentiles*, II, 57)

If our souls moved our bodies as sailors move ships, says Aquinas, my soul and my body would not be a unity. He adds that if we are souls using bodies, then we are essentially immaterial, which is not the case. We are 'sensible and natural realities' and cannot, therefore, be essentially immaterial.[51]

But this is not to say that Aquinas thinks of people as irreducibly material. He is not, in the modern sense, a philosophical 'physicalist'.[52] We have just seen that he is prepared to speak about people as having souls. And, on his account, a proper account of the human soul (*anima*) will deny that it is wholly material. By 'soul', Aquinas means something like 'principle of life'. 'Inquiry into the nature of the soul', he writes, 'presupposes an understanding of the soul as the root principle of life in living things within our experience'.[53] And, in Aquinas's thinking, the root principle of life in human beings (the human soul) is non-material. It is also something 'subsisting'.

In arguing for the non-corporeal nature of the human soul, Aquinas begins by reminding us what *anima* means, i.e. 'that which makes living things live'. And, with that understanding in mind, he contends that soul cannot be something bodily. There must, he says, be some principle of life which distinguishes living things from non-living things, and this cannot be a body. Why not? Because if it were a body it would follow that any material thing would be living, which is not the case. A body is alive not just because it is a body. It is alive because of a principle of life which is not a body.

> It is obvious that not every principle of vital activity is a soul. Otherwise the eye would be a soul, since it is a principle of sight; and so with the other organs of the soul. What we call the soul is the root principle of life. Now though something corporeal can be some sort of principle of life, as the heart is for animals, nevertheless a body cannot be the root principle of life. For it is obvious that to be the principle of life, or that which is alive, does not belong to any bodily thing from the mere fact of its being a body; otherwise every bodily thing would be alive or a life-source. Consequently any particular body that is alive, or even indeed a source of life, is so from being a body of such-and-such a kind. Now whatever is actually *such*, as distinct from *not-such*, has this from some principle which we call its actuating principle. Therefore a soul, as the primary principle of life, is not a body but that which actuates a body.
>
> (*Summa theologiae*, Ia, 75, 1)

In other words, if bodily things are alive just because they are bodies, all bodily things (e.g. my alarm clock) would be alive, which they are not. So what makes something a living thing cannot be a body.

But why say that the human soul is something subsisting? The main point made by Aquinas in anticipating this question is that the human animal has powers or functions which are not simply bodily, even though they depend on bodily ones. For example, people can know and understand, which is not the case with that which is wholly material. As Aquinas puts it, people enjoy an intellectual life and they are things of the kind they are (rational animals) because of this. Aquinas calls that by virtue of which people are things of the kind they are their 'souls'. So he can say that human beings are bodily, but also that they are or have both body and soul. The two cannot be torn apart in any way that would leave what remained a human being. But they can be distinguished from each other and the soul of a human being can therefore be thought of as something subsisting immaterially.

> The principle of the act of understanding, which is called the human soul, must of necessity be some kind of incorporeal and subsistent principle. For it is obvious that the under-standing of people enables them to know the natures of all bodily things. But what can in this way take in things must

have nothing of their nature in its own, for the form that was in it by nature would obstruct knowledge of anything else. For example, we observe how the tongue of someone sick with fever and bitter infection cannot perceive anything sweet, for everything tastes sour. Accordingly, if the intellectual principle had in it the physical nature of any bodily thing, it would be unable to know all bodies. Each of them has its own determinate nature. Impossible, therefore, that the principle of understanding be something bodily. And in the same way it is impossible for it to understand through and in a bodily organ, for the determinate nature of that bodily organ would prevent knowledge of all bodies. Thus if you had a colour filter over the eye, and had a glass vessel of the same colour, it would not matter what you poured into the glass, it would always appear the same colour. The principle of understanding, therefore, which is called mind or intellect, has its own activity in which body takes no intrinsic part. But nothing can act of itself unless it subsists in its own right. For only what actually exists acts, and its manner of acting follows its manner of being. So it is that we do not say that heat heats, but that something hot heats. Consequently the human soul, which is called an intellect or mind, is something incorporeal and subsisting.

(Summa theologiae, Ia, 75, 2)

Aquinas's notion that the human soul 'subsists' does not entail that it is a complete and self-contained entity, as, for example, Descartes thought the soul to be. For Aquinas, my human soul subsists because I have an intellectual life which cannot be reduced to what is simply bodily. It does not subsist as something with its own life apart from me, any more than my left hand does, or my right eye. Both of these can be spoken of as things, but they are really parts of me. We do not say, 'My left hand feels' or 'My right eye sees'; rather we say, 'I feel with my left hand' and 'I see with my right eye'. And Aquinas thinks that something similar should be said about my soul. I have a human soul because I have intellect and will. But it is not my soul which understands and wills. I do.

One might put this by saying that my soul is not I. And Aquinas says exactly this in his Commentary of St Paul's first letter to the Corinthians.[54] In that case, however, what happens to me when I die? Aquinas maintains that people are essentially corporeal. This means that I am essentially corporeal. For I am a human being. So am I to conclude from what Aquinas holds that I cease to exist at death? Can I look forward to nothing in the way of an afterlife?

Aquinas has a number of answers to these questions. Since he thinks of people as essentially corporeal, he agrees that there is a sense in which they cease to exist at death. But, since he believes that God can raise the dead to bodily life, he denies that the fact that I die entails that I cease to exist. On the other hand, he does not believe that most of those who have died have been raised to bodily life. He is certain that Christ has been raised to bodily life. But he would deny that the same can be truly asserted of, for example, Julius Caesar. He would therefore say that the soul of Caesar survives, though Caesar himself does not.

Given what we have now seen of Aquinas's teaching, it should be evident why he would deny that now, when he has not been raised to bodily life, Caesar survives his death. But why should Aquinas think that Caesar's soul would survive his death? Does he subscribe to the view that the human soul is immortal? Does he maintain that, though Caesar might die, his soul must survive the death of his body?

The answer to the last two questions is 'Yes'. Aquinas does believe that human souls are immortal. He also believes that they must survive the death of human beings. That by virtue of which I understand and think, he reasons, is not the sort of thing which can die as bodies can die.[55] He is well aware that people die and that their bodies perish. As we have seen, however, people, for Aquinas, are rational, understanding animals who are what they are by virtue of what is not material. He therefore concludes that there must be something about them capable of surviving the destruction of what is material. He does not think we can prove that the soul of Caesar must survive his death. In Aquinas's view, whether or not Caesar's soul survives the death of Caesar depends on whether God wills to keep it in being. And Aquinas does not think that we are in any position to prove that God must do that. For him, therefore, there is no 'proof of the immortality of the soul'. He holds that Caesar's soul could cease to exist at any time. But he also thinks that it is not the sort of thing of which it makes sense to say that it can perish as bodies can perish.

On the other hand, however, he does not think of it as the sort of thing which can survive as a human animal can survive. So the survival of Caesar's soul is not the survival of the human being we call 'Julius Caesar'. People, for Aquinas, are very much part of the physical world. Take that world away and what you are left with is not a human person. You are not, for example, left with something able to know by means of sense experience.[56] Nor are you left with something able to undergo the feelings or sensations that go with being bodily. On Aquinas's account, therefore, a human soul can only be said to survive its body as something purely intellectual, as the *locus* of thought and will.

Understanding through imagery is the proper operation of the
soul so far as it has the body united to it. Once separated
from the body it will have another mode of understanding,
like that of other disembodied natures . . . It is said, people are
constituted of two substantial elements, the soul with its
reasoning power, the flesh with its senses. Therefore when the
flesh dies the sense powers do not remain . . . Certain powers,
namely understanding and will, are related to the soul taken
on its own as their subject of inhesion, and powers of this
kind have to remain in the soul after the death of the body.
But some powers have the body-soul compound for subject;
this is the case with all the powers of sensation and nutrition.
Now when the subject goes the accident cannot stay. Hence
when the compound corrupts such powers do not remain in
actual existence. They survive in the soul in a virtual state
only, as in their source or root. And so it is wrong to say, as
some do, that these powers remain in the soul after the disso-
lution of the body. And it is much more wrong to say that
the acts of these powers continue in the disembodied soul,
because such powers have no activity except through a bodily
organ.

(*Summa theologiae*, Ia, 75, 6 ad. 3 and Ia, 77, 8)

Peter Geach observes that Aquinas's description of the life that would
be possible for disembodied souls is 'meagre and unattractive'.[57] And
many will agree. But the description now in question is all that Aquinas
feels able to offer as a philosopher. As a Christian theologian he feels
able to say that the dead will be raised to a newness of life of a highly
attractive kind. His final position is that, following the Incarnation of
God in Christ, people can be raised in their bodies to share in God's
life.[58] But the truth of this position, on Aquinas's own admission, is
in no way demonstrable by means of philosophical argument. It follows
from the teachings of Christ. On Aquinas's account, we are warranted
in believing what Christ taught. For Christ was divine. Yet, so Aquinas
adds, though we can give some rational grounds for believing in the
divinity of Christ, we cannot prove that Christ was God.[59] Belief in
the divinity of Christ is a matter of faith. It is not a matter of knowledge. Though it is not unreasonable, it is not demonstrably true. If
we subscribe to it, that can only be because God has given us the
theological virtue of faith.[60]

∽ FAITH AND PHILOSOPHY ∽

Aquinas's writings on faith provide good examples of texts which should lead us to challenge a view of medieval philosophy which has been referred to as 'separationism'.[61] Some students of Aquinas try rigidly to separate his theology from his philosophy. They then go on to write about him on the assumption that some of his texts are 'theological' while others are 'philosophical'. But Aquinas himself made no such sharp distinction between theology and philosophy. And even what he says of faith shows him to be weaving together what later authors separate under the headings 'theology' and 'philosophy'. The object of faith is God, he says.[62] Some will call this a statement of theology. The virtue of faith, he continues, involves holding fast to truths which philosophy cannot demonstrate.[63] That, too, might be called a theological conclusion. But in calling God the object of faith Aquinas draws on views about truth, falsity, belief and propositions which, in his opinion, ought to seem rationally acceptable to anyone. And in arguing that philosophy cannot demonstrate the truths of faith he defends himself with reference to what he thinks about human knowledge in general (apart from revelation) and what he thinks we must conclude given what our reason can tell us of God. So his teaching on faith can also be viewed as philosophical.

These facts bring us back again to the question touched on earlier. Is Aquinas really a philosopher? From what we have now seen of his thinking, it should be clear why the question cannot be answered if an answer must presume on our being able to draw a clear and obvious distinction between the philosophy of Aquinas and the theology of Aquinas. In his writings, philosophical arguments and theses are used to reach conclusions of theological import. And theses of theological import lead to judgements which can readily be called philosophical. And the result can be studied as something containing matters of interest to thinkers with any religious belief or none. In this chapter I have tried to give some indication of what these matters are. A complete account of Aquinas's thinking would have to report more than space here allows me. Those who read Aquinas for themselves, however, will quickly get a sense of what that might involve.

∽❖∽ NOTES ∽❖∽

1   For discussion of the date of Aquinas's birth see Tugwell [11.8], 291ff.
2   For the Irish influence on Aquinas see Michael Bertram Crowe, 'Peter of Ireland: Aquinas's teacher of the ARTES LIBERALES', in *Arts Liberaux et Philosophie au Moyen Age*, Paris, 1969.

3 As well as being influenced by Aristotle, Aquinas was also indebted to elements in the thought of Plato and to later writers of a 'Platonic' caste of mind. He commented on the *Book about Causes* (*Liber de causis*), an excerpted and adapted version of the *Elements of Theology* by the late Neoplatonist Proclus (*c.* 410–85). He also commented on Dionysu the Areopagite. And 'Platonic' theories and styles of argument abound in his writings.

4 Readers interested in understanding the origins and spirit of the Dominicans are best advised to consult Simon Tugwell OP (ed.) *Early Dominicans*, New York, Ramsey and Toronto, 1982.

5 Bertrand Russell, *A History of Western Philosophy*, London, 1946, pp. 484ff.

6 For an exposition of Gilson on this matter see John F. Wippel, 'Etienne Gilson and Christian philosophy', in [11.40].

7 *St Thomas Aquinas: Faith, Reason and Theology: Questions I–IV of his Commentary on the De Trinitate of Boethius*, translated with introduction and notes by Armand Maurer, Toronto, 1987, p. xv. Pegis elaborates his position in 'Sub ratione Dei: a reply to Professor Anderson', *The New Scholasticism* 39 (1965). Pegis is here responding to James Anderson's 'Was St Thomas a Philosopher?', *The New Scholasticism* 38 (1964). Anderson asked whether Aquinas was a philosopher and replied that he was.

8 Cf. Leonard E. Boyle, *The Setting of the Summa Theologiae of Saint Thomas* (Etienne Gilson Series 5), Toronto, 1982, pp. 17 and 30.

9 On the basis of a fourteenth-century life of St Raymund of Peñafort (*c.* 1178–1280), tradition holds that the *Summa contra Gentiles* was commissioned as an aid for Dominican missionaries preaching against Muslims, Jews and heretical Christians in Spain and North Africa. This theory has been subject to recent criticism, but it has also been recently defended. Cf. *Summa contra Gentiles*, I, text and French translation, with an Introduction by A. Gauthier, Paris, 1961, and A. Patfoort, *Thomas d'Aquin: les Clés d'une Théologie*, Paris, 1983.

10 Introduction to *Summa theologiae*, Ia, 2.

11 *Summa theologiae*, Ia, 44, 1.

12 *Summa theologiae*, Ia, 44, 4

13 *Summa theologiae*, Ia, 6, 1.

14 Cf. *Summa theologiae*, Ia, 12, 5; Ia2ae, 62, 1; Ia2ae, 110, 1; Ia2ae, 112, 1.

15 Cf. *Summa theologiae*, 2a2ae, 2, 4.

16 For Aristotle, see *Posterior Analytics*, I, 10. For Aquinas, see *Summa theologiae*, Ia, 2, 1; *On Truth*, I, 12; XV, 1. I am using 'believe' here in the loose sense of 'take to be true or accept'. Aquinas himself would not speak of believing first principles of demonstration. These, for him, are known or understood.

17 Cf. *Summa theologiae*, Ia, 1, 1; 2a2ae, 2, 3. See also Aquinas's inaugural lecture (*principium*) as Master in Theology at Paris (1256). This text can be found in the Marietti edition of Aquinas's *Opuscula theologica*, Turin, 1954, and is translated in Tugwell [11.8], 355ff.

18 For Anselm, see *Proslogion*, II and III. For Aquinas, see *Summa theologiae*, Ia, 2, 1; *Summa contra Gentiles*, I, 11. The argument discussed in the passages from Aquinas just cited was not so much Anselm's as a version of Anselm's argument current in the thirteenth century and offered by writers such as Alexander of Hales (*c.* 1186–1245). For a discussion of the matter, see Jean Chatillon,

'De Guillaume d'Auxerre à saint Thomas d'Aquin: l'argument de saint Anselme chez les premiers scholastiques du XIIIe siècle', in Jean Chatillon, *D'Isidore de Séville à saint Thomas d'Aquin*, London, 1985.

19 Cf. *On Truth*, X, 4–6; *Summa theologiae*, Ia, 84–8. For reasons of space I am not here going into details on Aquinas's teaching on the source of human knowledge. For an introductory account see Marenbon [Intr. 10], 116–31 and 134–5.

20 Cf. *Summa contra Gentiles*, I, 14; *Summa theologiae*, Ia, 12, 4 and 11.

21 Cf. *Summa theologiae*, Ia, 12, 1.

22 See William Lane Craig, *The Cosmological Argument from Plato to Leibniz*, London, 1980, ch. 5; Elders [11.16], ch. 3; van Steenberghen [11.36], 165ff.

23 One might reasonably deny that God is an 'explanation' of anything for Aquinas. One might say that an explanation of such and such is something we understand better than the thing with respect to which we invoke it as an explanation. Aquinas would agree with this observation. But if 'explanation' means 'cause', he would insist that God is an 'explanation' of what we find around us.

24 Aristotle presents an argument like that of Aquinas in *Physics* VII. Aquinas acknowledges his debt to Aristotle's argument in *Summa contra Gentiles*, I, 13 where he offers a longer version of what appears in the *Summa theologiae* as the First Way.

25 Aquinas here is concerned with what he calls *motus*. For him this includes change of quality, quantity or place (hence the legitimacy of translating *motus* as 'change' or 'movement').

26 Aquinas calls the First Way 'the most obvious' (*manifestior*) proof. That, I presume, is chiefly because what he calls *motus* is something which impinges on us all the time. Maimonides and Averroes are two other authors who thought that the truth of the reasoning which surfaces in the First Way is particularly evident. Cf. Maimonides (see [4.13], I, 70) and Averroes (see [3.17] IV).

27 Aquinas does not mean that the world does not contain things which can be thought of as changing themselves, e.g. people. He means that nothing in the world is wholly the source of its change. Cf. Christopher Martin [11.22] 61.

28 For Aquinas on time and change see *Summa theologiae*, Ia, 10, 1 and Lectures 15–20 of Aquinas's commentary on Aristotle's *Physics*. That the First Way is an argument from the reality of time is suggested by David Braine, *The Reality of Time and the Existence of God*, Oxford, 1988.

29 Some of the key concepts in the Third Way are found in Aristotle. Maimonides offers an argument very similar to that of the Third Way in *The Guide of the Perplexed* II, 1. One can also compare the Third Way with a proof of God's existence given by Avicenna (cf. Arthur J. Arberry, *Avicenna on Theology*, London, 1951, p. 25 for the text in English). But Aquinas's Third Way is a distinct argument and not just a straightforward repetition of earlier arguments with which it may be compared.

30 Cf. Patterson Brown, 'St Thomas' doctrine of necessary being', in Kenny [11.27].

31 There is a textual problem concerning the Third Way which my brief account of it bypasses. For a discussion of the issues and for a treatment of different interpretations of the Third Way see van Steenberghen [11.36] 188–201, and Craig, *Cosmological Argument*, pp. 182–94.

32 In the Fourth Way the background to the argument seems chiefly Platonic. Aquinas holds that perfection admits of degrees, a notion found in Plato,

St Augustine, St Anselm and many others. The Platonic theory which seems to lie behind the Fourth Way is expounded with reference to the Way in Kenny [11.28] ch. 5.

33 Here Aquinas invokes the notion of final causality or teleological explanation, which can be found in Book II of Aristotle's *Physics*. For Aristotle, a final cause or a teleological explanation was an answer to the question 'To what end or purpose is this happening?' For an exposition and discussion of Aristotle on purpose in nature, see Richard Sorabji, *Necessity, Cause and Blame: Perspectives on Aristotle's Theory*, London, 1980, chs 10 and 11. The argument of the Fifth Way is given in more detail by Aquinas in *On Truth*, V, 2.

34 For a more detailed account of this proposal see Brian Davies, 'Classical theism and the doctrine of divine simplicity', in Brian Davies (ed.) *Language, Meaning and God*, London, 1987.

35 In *Does God have a Nature?*, Milwaukee, 1980, Alvin Plantinga erroneously attributes to Aquinas the suggestion that God is a property.

36 *Summa theologiae*, Ia, 50, 4.

37 P. T. Geach properly draws attention to this point in *Three Philosophers*, Oxford, 1973, p. 117.

38 Cf. note 27 above.

39 Cf. *Summa theologiae*, Ia, 50, 2.

40 *Summa theologiae*, Ia, 61, 2.

41 *Summa theologiae*, Ia, 13, 7. Cf. also *Summa contra Gentiles*, II, 11 and *On Power*, VII, 8–11. For modern philosophical discussion of the suggestion, see Peter Geach, 'God's relation to the world', *Sophia* 8, 2 (1969): 1–9 and C. J. F. Williams, 'Is God really related to his creatures?', *Sophia* 8, 3 (1969): 1–10.

42 *On Power*, VII, 10.

43 Cf. *Summa theologiae*, Ia, 19, 1, 3, 10.

44 *Summa theologiae*, Ia, 8, 2.

45 Aquinas therefore holds that only God can produce miracles (*Summa theologiae*, Ia, 110, 4). Aquinas treats of miracles at some length in *Summa theologiae*, Ia, 105, *Summa contra Gentiles*, III, 98-102, and *De potentia*, VI.

46 *Summa theologiae*, Ia, 83, 1 and *On Evil*, VI.

47 *Summa theologiae*, Ia, 82, 1.

48 Herbert McCabe OP, *God Matters*, London, 1987, p. 14.

49 The honest answer to the question is, 'We do not know'. What follows is merely an opinion based on what Aquinas actually said.

50 Cf. René Descartes, *Meditations on First Philosophy*. For modern presentations of dualism see H. D. Lewis, *The Elusive Self*, London, 1982 and R. G. Swinburne, *The Evolution of the Soul*, Oxford, 1986.

51 *Summa contra Gentiles*, II, 57, 3–5.

52 I take physicalism to be the belief that people are nothing but bodies operating in certain ways. Cf. J. J. C. Smart, 'Sensations and brain processes', *Philosophical Review*, 68 (1950): 141–56.

53 *Summa theologiae*, Ia, 75, 1.

54 *Lecture on the first letter to the Corinthians*, XV; cf. *Summa theologiae*, Ia, 77, 8.

55 Cf. *Summa theologiae*, Ia, 75, 6.

56 Cf. *On Truth*, XIX.

57 Anscombe and Geach [11.11] 100.

58 *Summa contra Gentiles*, IV, 82–6.
59 Cf. *Summa theologiae*, 2a2ae, 1, 4, ad. 2.
60 For Aquinas on the virtue of faith see *Summa theologiae*, 2a2ae, 1–16.
61 Marenbon [Intr. 10], 83ff.
62 *Summa theologiae*, 2a2ae, 1, 1.
63 *Summa theologiae*, 2a2ae, 1, 4–5.

❦❦❦ BIBLIOGRAPHY ❦❦❦

Original Language Editions

The most authoritative study in English of Aquinas's works is I. T. Eschmann, 'A catalogue of St Thomas's works: Bibliographical notes', in Gilson [11.17]. It is supplemented by 'A brief catalogue of authentic works', in Weisheipl [11.9]. The definitive text of Aquinas's writings is being published by the Leonine Commission, established by Pope Leo XIII in 1880, which has already produced editions of Aquinas's most important works (e.g. *Summa contra Gentiles*, *Summa theologiae*). But the work of the Leonine Commission is still unfinished.

Publication of Aquinas's writings prior to the Leonine edition include *Opera omnia*, Parma, 1852–73 (the Parma edition), and *Opera omnia*, Paris, 1871–82 (the Vivès edition). Over many years most of Aquinas's writings have also been published in manual size by the Casa Marietti, Turin and Rome.

Translations

For a modern English translation of the *Summa theologiae*, with notes and commentary, readers are best advised to consult the Blackfriars edition of the *Summa theologiae*, London 1964–81. The translation is, unfortunately, sometimes unreliable. For a more literal rendering of the text, see *St Thomas Aquinas Summa Theologica*, translated by Fathers of the English Dominican Province, London, 1911 and Westminster, Maryland, 1981. For an English translation of the *Summa contra Gentiles* see *Saint Thomas Aquinas:* Summa contra Gentiles, translated by Anton C. Pegis, James F. Anderson, Vernon J. Bourke and Charles J. O'Neil, Notre Dame, Ind. and London, 1975. The best modern translation of *De ente et essentia* is *Aquinas on Being and Essence: a Translation and Interpretation* by Joseph Bobik, Notre Dame, Ind., 1965. For other English translations of Aquinas, see the Brief Catalogue in Weisheipl [11.9].

Bibliographical Works

11.1   Bourke, Vernon J. *Thomistic Bibliography: 1920–1940*, suppl. to *The Modern Schoolman*, St Louis, MO., 1921.

11.2   Ingardia, Richard (ed.) *Thomas Aquinas: International Bibliography 1977–1990*, Bowling Green, Oh., 1993.

11.3   Mandonnet, P. and Destrez, J. *Bibliographie Thomiste*, 2nd edn, revised by M.-D. Chenu, Paris, 1960.

11.4   Miethe, Terry L. and Bourke, Vernon J. *Thomistic Bibliography, 1940–1978*, Westport, Conn. and London, 1980.

Biographical Works

11.5   Ferrua, A. (ed.) *Thomae Aquinatis vitae fontes praecipuae*, Alba, 1968.

11.6   Foster, Kenelm (ed.) *The Life of Thomas Aquinas*, London and Baltimore, Md., 1959.

11.7   Torrell, Jean-Pierre, *Saint Thomas Aquinas*, vol. 1, *The Person and his Work*, Washington, DC, 1996.

11.8   Tugwell, Simon (ed.) *Albert and Thomas: Selected Writings*, New York, Mahwah and London, 1988.

11.9   Weisheipl, James A. *Friar Thomas D'Aquino*, Oxford, 1974: republished with corrigenda and addenda, Washington, DC, 1983.

General Studies and Introductions

11.10   Aertsen, Jan *Nature and Creature: Thomas Aquinas's Way of Thought*, Leiden, 1988.

11.11   Anscombe, G. E. M. and Geach, P. T. *Three Philosophers*, Oxford, 1961.

11.12   Chenu, M.-D. *Towards Understanding Saint Thomas*, trans. A. M. Landry and D. Hughes, Chicago, 1964.

11.13   Chesterton, G. K. *St Thomas Aquinas*, London, 1943.

11.14   Copleston, F. C. *Aquinas*, Harmondsworth, 1955.

11.15   Davies, Brian *The Thought of Thomas Aquinas*, Oxford, 1992.

11.16   Elders, Leo J. *The Philosophical Theology of St Thomas Aquinas*, Leiden, 1990.

11.17   Gilson, Etienne *The Christian Philosophy of St Thomas Aquinas*, London, 1957.

11.18   Kenny, Anthony *Aquinas*, Oxford, 1980.

11.19   Kretzmann, Norman and Stump, Eleonore (eds) *The Cambridge Companion to Aquinas*, Cambridge, 1993.

11.20   McInerny, Ralph *St Thomas Aquinas*, Notre Dame, Ind. and London 1982.

11.21   —— *A First Glance at St Thomas Aquinas: a Handbook for Peeping Thomists*, Notre Dame, Ind. and London, 1990.

11.22   Martin, Christopher (ed.) *The Philosophy of Thomas Aquinas*, London and New York, 1988.

Studies of Particular Topics

11.23   Boland, Vivian *Ideas in God according to Saint Thomas Aquinas*, Leiden, 1996.

11.24   Bonnette, D. *Aquinas' Proofs of God's Existence*, La Haye, 1972.

11.25 Hankey, W. J. *God in Himself: Aquinas's Doctrine of God as expounded in the Summa Theologiae*, Oxford, 1987.

11.26 Henle, R. J. *Saint Thomas and Platonism*, The Hague, 1956.

11.27 Kenny, Anthony (ed.) *Aquinas: a Collection of Critical Essays*, London and Melbourne, 1969.

11.28 —— *The Five Ways*, London, 1969.

11.29 —— *Aquinas on Mind*, London and New York, 1993.

11.30 Kretzmann, N. *The Metaphysics of Theism: Aquinas's Natural Theology in 'Summa contra Gentiles' I*, Oxford, 1996.

11.31 Lisska, Anthony *Aquinas's Theory of Natural Law*, Oxford, 1996.

11.32 Lonergan, Bernard *Verbum: Word and Idea in Aquinas*, ed. D. B. Burrell, Notre Dame, Ind., 1967.

11.33 McInerny, Ralph *Aquinas on Human Action*, Washington, DC, 1992.

11.34 Owens, Joseph *St Thomas Aquinas on the Existence of God: Collected Papers of Joseph Owens S.Ss.R.*, ed. J. R. Catan, Albany, NY, 1980.

11.35 Person, Per Erik *Sacra Doctrina: Reason and Revelation in Aquinas*, Oxford, 1970.

11.36 Steenberghen, Fernand van *Le Problème de l'existence de Dieu dans les écrits de S. Thomas d'Aquino*, Louvain, 1980.

11.37 —— *Thomas Aquinas and Radical Aristotelianism*, Washington, DC, 1980.

11.38 te Velde, Rudi A. *Participation and Substantiality in Thomas Aquinas*, Leiden, 1995.

11.39 Westberg, Daniel *Right Practical Reason: Aristotle, Action, and Prudence in Aquinas*, Oxford, 1994.

11.40 Wippel, John F. *Metaphysical Themes in Thomas Aquinas*, Washington, DC, 1984.

CHAPTER 12

The Paris arts faculty: Siger of Brabant, Boethius of Dacia, Radulphus Brito

Sten Ebbesen

Throughout the thirteenth century Paris overshadowed all other universities in the arts as in theology. This chapter will deal almost exclusively with Paris.

In pagan antiquity philosophy had not only been the pursuit of an ever better understanding in all sorts of fields, it had also been expected to provide the intellectuals with a sense of purpose in life, reconcile them with death and console them in difficult times. In a Christian society philosophy must leave the second task to religion. The division into arts and theology faculties at the universities institutionalized the division of tasks, leaving the artists with the obligation not to offer their own way to salvation, but also with a freedom to do penetrating research in a wide spectrum of disciplines, unfettered by demands that their insights be relevant to the achievement of existential satisfaction. On the whole, the division of tasks worked well, but problems arose when a considerable body of non-Christian literature on ethics, cosmology and natural theology became available to the artists and was taught in class. A crisis occurred in Paris in the 1270s.

An episcopal condemnation of thirteen theses in 1270 marks the beginning of the crisis. Then in 1272 the artists (that is, those teaching and studying in the arts faculty) think it necessary to codify their own obligation not to meddle in theological matters, 'overstepping, as it were, the limits set' for them. Finally, in 1277 the bishop, Stephen Tempier, issues a stern letter in which unnamed members of the arts faculty are accused of actually 'overstepping the limits of the faculty's competence', and of thinking that theories found in the writings of pagan philosophers could be true notwithstanding the fact that they conflict with the truth of Scripture. Tempier appends a list of 219 theses and threatens severe sanctions against anyone who may teach any such errors in the future or who has already done so.

Among the condemned theses some appear to deny creation, some to deny the immortality of individual souls, others are less obviously relevant to Christian dogma. The bishop had culled most of them from writings by arts masters. However, his attack on the artists was only the first move in a campaign designed, it seems, to culminate in a condemnation of a recently deceased theologian, Thomas Aquinas.

The artists had less powerful supporters than the theologians; attacking them first meant beginning with the weakest opponent, but it also meant striking at the root. It was the study of non-Christian writers that inspired the theories that Tempier would not tolerate, and that study had its permanent base in the arts faculty, whence it infiltrated the higher faculty of theology. Aristotelizing theologians could, in turn, influence the artists. In the 1260s and 1270s Thomas Aquinas made a strong impact; masters like Siger of Brabant borrowed freely from Thomas, though also occasionally polemicizing against him.

The contents of the arts had changed considerably since the twelfth century. Traditional Latin rhetoric had all but vanished. Grammar thrived, and conscious attempts were made to develop it into an axiomatized science of the type delineated by Aristotle in his *Posterior Analytics*. Logic underwent a deep transformation; the twelfth century had revelled in detailed propositional analysis; a technical vocabulary had been developed and theorems established that permitted much preciser determination of the possible interpretations of a sentence and of its truth-conditions than Aristotle's logic could provide. This was the 'native tradition' of Western logic, already highly developed before the entry of the 'New Aristotle' after 1130. At first the native tradition had been enriched by the encounter with the new books, in particular with the *On Sophistical Refutations* whose subject-matter, fallacious reasoning, lay within the existing sphere of interest. But in the thirteenth century the New Aristotle started to act as a cuckoo in the nest. His *Topics* killed the study of Boethius. His *Posterior Analytics*, *Metaphysics*, *Ethics*, *Physics*, etc. drew the attention away from the niceties of technical logic. The theorems (*regulae*, 'rules') formulated by the preceding generations were repeated in elementary handbooks but provoked little discussion and were not significantly added to. The foci of the masters' interest were elsewhere.

In logic, one focus of interest was metalogical problems; what sort of things are the objects (arguments, universals, topics, etc.) logicians deal with? Another was how to apply basic notions of metaphysics, such as substance, subject and accident, matter and form, movement and rest to the analysis of the meaning (*significatio*) of terms. Above all, there was a lively interest in the theory of *scientia*: knowledge, science. At the same time the old logic course expanded into a general course of philosophy, comprising metaphysics, ethics, natural philosophy and all.

It looks as if Oxford kept the native tradition more alive, and that this prepared for the spectacular breakthrough of English logic in the fourteenth century. But be that as it may, the thirteenth century was Paris's.

The present state of scholarship allows no clear picture of theoretical developments prior to *c.* 1265–70. We get fascinating glimpses only. Thus one anonymous logician from about the middle of the century considers the relations 'parenthood' (*paternitas*) and 'being a child' (*filiatio*); they are one species of relation, he says, in conformity with tradition, but then he proposes that a father plus his child will be one individual of that species, just as one unity plus another unity are an individual of the species 'set of two' (*binarius*). This seems to amount to treating dyadic relations as predicates or properties of (ordered) pairs of things. Is this theory peculiar to the one text in which I found it? Perhaps; but it is quite possible that an examination of unedited texts will show that it was widely known.

Though nobody can claim to be able to survey the extant writings from the early Parisian arts faculty, it is possible to name some of the most important masters. One was John Lepage, who was active in the 1230s. Another was Robert Kilwardby (d. 1279), archbishop of Canterbury from 1272, who, teaching in the years round 1240, was to influence his successors for several decades. When Albert the Great (*c.* 1200–80) compiled the logical part of his vast encyclopaedia, he relied on Kilwardby to an extent that nowadays would be called plagiarizing. Though full of inconsistencies, Albert's encyclopaedia became popular as a work of reference among the artists, much to the regret of Roger Bacon (d. 1292 or slightly later). Bacon seems to have taught at Paris in the 1240s, but the extent of his influence is difficult to gauge. John of Secheville was a prominent master in the 1240–50s who found a lot of inspiration in Averroes, who was now eclipsing Avicenna as the leading authority on what Aristotelian philosophy was about. Secheville is now best known for his *De principiis naturae* (*On the Principles of Nature*), a treatise on fundamental physics, probably written in the 1260s after the author's return to his native England. About 1250 there also was Nicholas of Paris, author of several logical works with some later success.

The generation who started their career as masters about 1265 are reasonably well known, though it must be admitted that modern research has been lopsided, the lion's share of attention going to texts and subjects relevant to the 1277 condemnation or Thomas Aquinas.

The fact that a Belgian and a Dane figured prominently among the masters targeted by the condemnation helped launch a Belgian and Danish project to edit each country's medieval philosophers, thus making the work of artists from those parts of Europe much better known than that done by their French or Italian colleagues. The Belgian was Siger of Brabant, the Dane Boethius of Dacia ('Bo from Denmark').

All evidence of Boethius' life before 1277 is contained in the epithet indicating his nationality and the number and nature of his extant or attested writings. He is likely to have commenced teaching about the mid-1260s. His best known works are the short treatises, *On the Highest Good* and *On the Eternity of the World*, but considerable parts of his *œuvre* in the fields of logic, natural philosophy and grammar have also survived. He wrote one of the very first Latin commentaries on Aristotle's *Rhetoric*, but unfortunately it has been lost, and little is known about the early reception of the *Rhetoric*. Extant sources suggest that the book was rarely taught and then with an emphasis on general problems of logic, ethics or psychology without much attention to the specific problems of rhetorical communication. Scholastics never quite got a firm grip of the art of persuasion.

It is the general, but unproven, assumption that Boethius was still teaching in 1277 and that the condemnation stopped his university career. He was almost certainly a secular during his regency in arts, yet his works occur in a medieval catalogue of books composed by blackfriars. It is permissible to speculate that the condemnation made him seek a new life among the friars, but actually his fate is unknown. While some of his works enjoyed wide diffusion, the author's person was soon forgotten. Only in the twentieth century has he re-emerged as an important figure in the history of philosophy.

Siger of Brabant always had more publicity, in life and in death. His very entry into history is spectacular: according to a document from 1265 he was suspected of complicity in the kidnapping of a member of the French nation of the university by scholars from the Picard nation. In 1271 the faculty of arts was split in two; the Normans and one Picard seceded from the rest. The Normans rewarded the Picard by electing him as rector. The Picard was Siger. When the nations were reunited in 1275 through the intervention of a papal legate, the blame was put on the Normans and this may have prompted Siger to leave Paris for Liège where he was a canon. In 1276 he was summoned to appear before an inquisitor to face charges of heresy; he was probably acquitted, but the next year propositions culled from his books were among those condemned in Paris. He himself may have been in Liège and thus out of harm's way. In 1281 or shortly afterwards he met his end in the papal residential town of Orvieto, stabbed by his own secretary who had gone insane, it is said.

Siger was *magister regens* (i.e. actually teaching) for some ten years (*c.* 1265–75) and several works from that period have survived, notably his questions on Aristotle's *Metaphysics*, on the *Liber de causis* (*Book about Causes*), some psychological works, and one about the eternity of the world.

Siger's name was never forgotten. Some decades after his death Dante portrayed him as a denizen of Paradise and let Thomas Aquinas point him out with the words:

This is the eternal light of Siger
who, when lecturing in rue de la Fouarre [site of the schools of
   arts],
concluded unwelcome truths.

(*Paradiso* 10.136–8)

In Italy some people continued to read Siger until the early sixteenth century.

The pope's legate who in 1275 reunited the university that Siger had helped split installed Peter of Auvergne (d. 1303) as rector – probably a wise choice. Peter's voluminous (and mostly unedited) writings reveal him as a mainstream thinker, a competent man, but a man of compromises rather than one of sharp or innovative positions. Peter later advanced to master of theology and in 1302 was awarded a bishopric. In the 1270s he and Boethius had some sort of collaboration as teachers, though they disagreed on many points, and discretely polemicized against each other. Peter was, after Thomas Aquinas, the first important Latin commentator on Aristotle's *Politics*, but his political philosophy is only just beginning to be seriously studied.

Simon of Faversham (d. 1306) is another mainstream author of some repute. He is likely to have been somewhat younger than Peter; his Parisian regency in arts probably fell around 1280. Later he taught theology in Oxford. Much of his *œuvre* is preserved but only some logical works have been edited and doctrinal studies have been sporadic.

About the early 1270s Martin of Denmark (Martinus de Dacia, d. 1304) composed a remarkably well-organized grammar, *Modi Significandi*, which became widely used. In the 1440s the humanist Lorenzo Valla paid tribute to its continuing actuality by specifically mentioning Martin and his 'sickening' *Modi Significandi* in a virulent attack on scholastic grammar. Martin became master of theology in the 1280s, served as chancellor to the Danish king about 1287–97, and then seems to have returned to Paris; at least he was buried in Notre Dame, of whose chapter he was a member.

Modus significandi, 'way' or 'mode of signifying', is a term with a long history before 1270, but now it had become a key concept of linguistics. Virtually all late thirteenth-century Parisian arts masters

273

were 'modists' in the sense that this concept with its complements, *modi intelligendi* (ways or modes of understanding) and *modi essendi* (ways or modes of being) played a major role in their thought.

The basic idea of modism is this: each constituent of reality (each *res*) has a number of ways or modes of being (*modi essendi*) which determine the number of ways in which it can be correctly conceptualized; the ways in which it can be conceptualized (*modi intelligendi*) in turn determine in which ways it can be signified.

Assume that pain is a constituent of reality. Pain is in a way like a substance: a stable thing in its own right that can have changing properties (be intense or weak, precisely located or diffuse, for example); in a way it is like a process occurring in some subject. The concept of pain will then be able to present itself to our mind in two ways and we will consequently be capable of signifying pain in two ways. Any word that signifies it as the stable carrier of properties (*per modum habitus et permanentiae*) is a noun; any word that signifies it as a process in a subject (*per modum fieri*) is a verb. The English words 'a pain' and 'to ache' signify the same thing or 'common nature' under two different modes. A third mode is expressed by the interjection 'ouch'.

'Whatever can be conceived of by the mind may be signified by any part of speech', says Boethius; his only restriction on this rule is that the mode of signifying of the part of speech must not be incompatible with the thing to be signified.

Fully elaborated theories of modes of signifying would, by similar means, account for all the traditional grammatical categories, not only parts of speech, but also cases, tenses, etc. Latin provided the examples used, but the modes were assumed to be completely independent of any particular language. What is around to be talked about is independent of the speaker's cultural background; 'what is there' (*ens*) is things (*res*) and their ways or modes of being; we can form concepts of no more things than there are and conceive of things only in as many ways as things are. Moreover, we can express whatever we can understand, but no more.

All peoples, then, have the same intellectual equipment (concepts plus ways of understanding) with which to grasp a common reality (things plus ways of being); the several ways of being of things determine the ways in which they may be known (*modi sciendi*), and those ways are what logic is about. So logic must be pan-human, says Boethius, and so must language in the sense that whichever thing can be signified in one tongue can be signified in another, and whichever mode of signifying is actualized in one tongue can be so (or even: is so) in any other. All languages have the same grammar and total translatability is guaranteed. True, some peoples may know things others don't and have a richer vocabulary, but this is accidental; new words can always be added to a language. Grammar is not disturbed by the fact that the same thing is called 'homo', 'anthropos', and 'man' in different languages; how to match sounds with concepts is a matter of convention (though it was generally assumed that some sort of mimetic system underlay the choice of sounds for the basic vocabulary of each language). Similarly, any device can be used to express masculinity (more precisely *modus significandi per modum agentis*) – suffixes, particles, whatever – but you cannot have a language incapable of expressing that fundamental category. Nor can you have a significative word with the lexical component [male human] and the grammatical category [female], as the result would be incomprehensible and hence non-significative. Such clashes between lexical component (*significatum*) and mode of signifying apart, there are no restraints on which combinations of significate and mode of signifying a particular language may choose to lexicalize by assigning them a certain sound value. Thus the same thing, *X*, may have a feminine name in language *A* and a masculine name in language *B*. The difference only means that the 'impositor', i.e. whoever introduced the word in *A*, paid attention to one mode of being of *X* ('as something acting'), whereas the *B*-impositor paid attention to another mode ('as something acted on').

Various strategies were used to block simple-minded inferences from surface grammar to reality; one would not like to be saddled with 'nothing' as a genuine thing in its own right just because 'nothing' is a noun, but at least in the 1270s and 1280s it must have seemed to most men as if such difficulties were surmountable. It was possible to describe a grammar that abstracted totally from phonetic realization, yet was easily correlatable to it, and which promised to yield a list of elementary modes of cognition all with a sure foundation in the reality subject to cognition.

Modistic theories promised easy shifts between the levels of being, understanding and signifying. Some went so far as to hold that the modes of signifying, understanding and being are fundamentally identical, just, said Martin, as the thing that is signified and the thing that is understood are basically identical with the thing out there. In other words, the mode of being is a mode of understanding when cognized by an intellect, and a mode of signifying when related to a linguistic sign.

Others, notably Boethius of Dacia, strongly opposed this identification, which threatened to leave the intellect as a mere mirror of extramental reality with the result that there could not be different sciences based on the same modes of being of things; thus logical relationships (*habitudines locales*) and grammatical modes of signifying would be strictly identical when derived from the same modes of being.

275

Moreover the way would be open to facile deductions from expressions and thoughts to extramental reality.

One weakness of all variants of modistic theory was that it was difficult to combine it with a theory of reference, for whatever the 'things' (res) of modistic theory were, they certainly were not singular extramental entities. On the other hand, no one wanted to be a full-fledged Platonist. There was a tendency to answer all questions about the relation between words and reality by referring to the set of significate and modes of signifying encoded in each lexical item when it was 'imposed'. Modistic semantics possessed few tools to deal with the contribution of linguistic context to the meaning of a term, and none at all to explain how extralinguistic context contributes to the way an expression is understood. Nor was it possible to offer a plausible modistic account of figurative expressions, metaphors, and the like. Desperate attempts were made to explain how 'man' can change its meaning from 'living rational body' into 'lifeless irrational body' on being joined by the adjective 'dead'. 'Man' was declared an 'analogical' term, and as such equipped on imposition not only with signification and modes of signifying but also with a rule to the effect that in isolation it signifies its primary significate (living human being), but its secondary significate (cadaver) when combined with the adjective 'dead'.

Radulphus Brito in the 1290s gave up many of the makeshift solutions proposed by the generation before him, but then he introduced instead a factor that simply does not belong in a modistic theory: the intelligent listener's ability to correct badly transmitted information and understand 'dead body' when the message strictly speaking says 'dead living body'.

Another, and ultimately related, difficulty was that it was not obvious why one should resist the temptation to describe all sorts of distinctions in terms of modes of signifying, thus endangering the position of grammar as a separate science. In works from the late thirteenth century there is an uneasy relationship between the properly grammatical modes of signifying (such as the substantive's modus per se stantis) and so-called modes of category (modi praedicamentorum, such as the modus substantiae of 'whatever').

Finally, the old trick of introducing non-things called modes to make distinctions without splitting one entity into several, always leaves the unpleasant question, 'What is the thing without the modes?' Perhaps the best answer is 'Nothing', for the 'common nature' hiding under the modes has no job in isolation. Its job is to glue together a number of items: thing-cum-mode-A, thing-cum-mode-B, etc.

Traditionally the common nature was identified with the essence of a thing which, according to Avicenna, is nothing except self-identical:

horsehood is horsehood, blackness is blackness (well, you may add a few trivial analytical statements, like 'blackness is a sort of colour', but that's all you can say about it). A common nature neither exists nor does not exist, it is neither universal nor particular. It can be thus modified, but in itself is beyond those oppositions.

There was in Avicenna and in the Latin tradition an ambiguity. On one hand the essence or common nature was thought to be prior to such determinations, on the other hand it was given positive determinations: it does not exist, but it has essential being; it is not concrete, but it is abstract.

The identification of the common nature with what was felt to be the least determinately modified alternative was a major source of theoretical inconsistency. Boethius may have sensed the problem, for he discusses whether it is possible to signify a thing under no mode. Since he believes we can think of it thus, he must – and does – hold that we can signify it thus, i.e. that it would be possible to institute a word for pain, for example, that would belong to no part of speech. However, he does not enter into a closer investigation of how such a word could be significative. The root of the trouble with the common nature seems not to have been localized till Radulphus Brito did so.

Brito may have been born about 1270. He was regent master of arts in the 1290s and possibly also in the first decade of the next century, while preparing for his degree in theology (obtained 1311/12). He may have died in the 1320s. The bulk of his extant *œuvre* is non-theological, consisting of questions on Aristotle, Manlius Boethius and Priscian plus some sophismata.

Brito's work may be seen as a clever attempt to mend and save a theoretical framework in crisis, though in his day the crisis of modism would not be obvious. Sometime around 1300 a new handbook was written by Thomas of Erfurt; called *Novi modi significandi* it was to dominate in German schools, while the old *Modi significandi* by Martin continued to be used in Italy. Philosophy began to drop the modes only about 1315, and in grammar they lived till much later.

Some of the problems besetting modistic theories had been realized as early as the 1270s. Thus it had been shown that explaining a lexical unity in terms of its modes of signifying had the awkward result that an equivocal noun, say *canis* = 'dog, dog-fish, dog-star', could not actually be one noun but would have to be as many nouns as it had meanings. An attempt was made to save the situation through a distinction: each of the things signified would possess its own passive mode of signifying (i.e. mode of being signified) as a noun, but to the three passive modes of signifying would correspond only one active mode on the vocal level. *Canis* would be one noun. This, on the other hand, threatened the basic modistic idea of isomorphy between the levels of being, understanding, and signifying. Radulphus therefore proposed that the distinction between active and passive modes is merely notional. It is, after all, a question of a relation of signification between word and thing. If you look at the relation from one end it is an accidental property of the word, if from the other, then of the thing. It is called active or passive according to which end it is viewed from. The lengths to which Brito had to go to save the fundamental ideas of modism are signs of a theory in trouble.

The greatest of the modists, Boethius, did not have to worry about any 'crisis for modism'. But he found other worries when Bishop Tempier in 1277 lashed out against him and Siger because he thought they had said objectionable things about the human soul, creation, and the ultimate aim of human life.

There always was a hot debate about the nature of the human soul, but it was unusually hot in the 1260–70s. It centred on four questions, namely:

(1) On the common presupposition that the intellect (= intellective soul) has two components, an active one (*intellectus agens*) which, *inter alia*, forms universal concepts on the basis of the particular pieces of information provided by the senses, and a passive one (*intellectus possibilis* or *potentialis* or *materialis*) which is the initially blank wax tablet on which the active one leaves its imprints in the form of concepts and knowledge acquired. On this presupposition, is the agent intellect a genuinely different thing from the 'possible' one, or are they fundamentally identical?

There was an old tradition for treating the two as genuinely different and considering the agent intellect to be an extra-human separate substance. Roger Bacon and many others had identified the agent intellect with God, others had held that this 'Giver of Forms' was a created intelligence, closer to God than men are but not identical with the First. On either view the agent intellect would be the same for all men; the common source of our intellectual insights would explain the possibility of communication. The individuality of our passive intellects would explain why we do not share all thoughts with one another.

However, the radical separation of the agent intellect from the possible one had become rather old-fashioned in the 1260s and 1270s; the main combatants of the time agreed that the two intellects are not as many substances.

(2) Is the intellect an extra-human separate substance? This was assumed to be Averroes' opinion (though earlier in the century he had been taken to represent the opposite view). Siger of Brabant seems to have gradually changed his mind on this question, but initially, at least, he thought Averroes was right.

This position allows the vegetative and sensitive souls to die without this affecting the intellect. Like the old assumption of a separate agent intellect it also accounts for men's ability to share knowledge, but it has a weakness that the old theory has not: however much such an 'Averroistic' intellect is supposed to exercise its activity in corporeal men it is hard to see how it can be individualized so that my intellect is different from yours. Siger accepted the consequence that there is just one shared intellect for all men, but tried to save some private thought for the individual by making the operation of the intellect in a particular human depend on representations (*intentiones imaginatae*) with an origin in sensation and formed without the help of the intellect. When explaining how the individual 'plugs into' (*continuatur*) the supra-individual intellect Siger relies heavily on Averroes, but is no less obscure than his master.

Contemporaries were alert to the 'Averroistic' theory's inability to explain how men can share an intellect without sharing all thoughts. However, the gravest objection against such 'monopsychism' (a modern term) was that it could leave no individual rational soul to carry responsibility for a deceased person's acts. Nor was it easy to see how an immaterial intellect could fail to be eternal; but it was Christian doctrine that God creates new souls every day and that they are in principle perishable (God could annihilate a soul, if he so wished).

(3) If each living man has his own intellect, this may be assumed to be the substantial form that makes him a member of the human species rather than of the asinine one. But is the intellect fundamentally identical with the sub-rational 'parts' of the soul? Or is a man constituted by a compound of hierarchically ordered substantial forms (corporeality, vegetative, sensitive and intellectual soul), corresponding to the definition 'man is a rational animal' = 'man is a rational, sensitive, vegetative body'? Such was the traditional view about 1270. It could be used to explain how human semen develops into an irrational embryo and thence into a genuine human by successive acquisition of higher forms, and it might seem to allow the highest form to survive bodily death.

However, it may be doubted if the notion of a plurality of substantial forms is at all consistent; a substantial form is supposed to make its thing into the kind of thing it is; several such forms would seem to dissolve it into several things, as was often pointed out by medieval critics. Thomas Aquinas was the leading proponent of the thesis that one substance can have one substantial form only: a nobler form enables its owner to do anything a lower form would, and so no independent 'vegetative soul' is needed to explain the fact that intelligent beings metabolize. A main problem with this theory is that the embryo cannot acquire rationality without shedding its previous substantial form and thus becoming a new thing; nor can the dead Christ's body have been identical with that which existed before he expired on the cross or that which existed after the resurrection.

The form-question was intensively debated both among theologians and among artists. Boethius of Denmark was for the unity of form. John of Denmark – a contemporary about whose life nothing is known – believed in a plurality; in the short run, at least, he was on the winning side, for Stephen Tempier had the same belief and so had Robert Kilwardby, who in 1277 made the University of Oxford condemn the unity thesis.

(4) How can the corporeal man's form survive bodily death? Aristotle had indicated that the intellect should not be treated as an ordinary material form; for a material form to be there, is for some matter to be organized in some particular way. The intellect, he felt, was of a different type; matter is no essential ingredient of thought.

If Aristotle could sit on the fence, so can we, many medievals thought. Thus Aquinas came to argue that the intellect is a self-subsistent form, substance-like in its capability of being on its own, but like a material form in that it is an incomplete entity if deprived of its matter. A disembodied Thoman intellect has the capacity for metabolizing, it just does not have the requisite tools for so doing. Siger of Brabant scoffed at this notion and Boethius did not like it either. He agreed that a man has just one substantial form, namely his soul, which, of course, is rational. It is a material form and can only in a very weak sense be called a substance. It must perish if it ceases to inform its body. If the intellect survives somehow – and Boethius does leave this possibility open – it does not do so as a disembodied Thoman form craving for a body; a separate intellect is neither a soul nor a form at all, it is a substance. One would like to ask Boethius which sort of identity such a substance has with the living man's form, and whether separate intellects can have individuality. It is a fair guess that he would answer 'No' to the second question, but I have no idea how he would tackle the first one.

The discussions about the soul ended in an impasse. The soul was required to do too many jobs. It was required to be a form that vivifies a body, yet to be a substance capable of surviving the body; to be individualized, yet to be totally immaterial *qua* intellect; to bestow identity over time, yet be able to acquire or lose essential properties; to have an intellective ingredient which is immaterial and not naturally generable, yet with a beginning in time and capacity for being annihilated as well as a capacity for lasting forever.

There are clear signs that many artists felt that all these requirements could not be simultaneously satisfied. Stephen Tempier forbade them to obtain consistency by dropping one or more of the requirements. Although his ruling was legally binding only in Paris, it effectively provided the framework within which philosophers could move for the next two and a half centuries, and it became a standard procedure to describe first the philosophically tenable theories, namely (1) the whole soul is a material form and perishes with bodily life (ascribed to Alexander of Aphrodisias); (2) the intellect is as a whole an eternal and supra-individual substance (ascribed to Averroes). Then, after indicating which alternative he favours, the author will add, 'But according to truth and the catholic faith neither of these theories is acceptable, but . . .', without seriously trying to provide reasons for the 'true' theory. Incidentally, such tactics had already been used by Siger and others before 1277 and were denounced by Tempier, but to no avail.

The late ancient philosophical way to salvation was an ascent from the miserable world of matter towards ultimate being or even to the transcendent One. This ascent was effected via the theoretical study of ever more exalted objects: from the earthly you pass to the heavenly, etc. This way of thinking with its strict hierarchy of beings gained new impetus in the thirteenth century. Avicenna's theory of emanation from The First played a major role and the anonymous *Book about Causes* (based on Proclus' *Elements of Theology*) helped cement the notion of a hierarchically structured universe in which each species of thing was ultimately conditioned by its relative proximity to The First (Cause), no two species being equidistant from The First. Averroes' and Greek authors' panegyrics of the blessings of the theoretical life lent support to the belief that an intellectual ascent up the ladder of being was possible, and when Aristotle's *Nicomachean Ethics* became commonly known after 1250 everybody could see in Book X that ultimate happiness for man consists in theoretical insight.

Such intellectualism appealed to an age which had reasons for epistemological optimism in view of the rapid growth of knowledge, as all the disciplines treated by Aristotle plus some more were coming to the artists' attention. It was, of course, agreed on that no man can know all particular things, but both Siger of Brabant and others held that a human intellect may in principle achieve exhaustive knowledge of all genuine objects of knowledge. This would be impossible if the proper objects of knowledge were infinitely many, or if there were infinitely many avenues to knowledge, or if knowledge of some object could be more or less clear on a scale going on to infinity. But none of these cases obtain, they held. There is a limited number of proper objects, the natural species; there is a limited number of avenues to knowledge: demonstration and definition; demonstration does not go on *ad infinitum* and definition provides an insight which is not just optimal in the sense that we cannot manage better, but in the sense that it exhausts what there is to be known about the object.

The climate was there for claiming that immaterial beings ('separate substances'), and even The First, are not outside the reach of the human intellect. Proud assertions to this effect almost became a commonplace in introductions to Aristotelian commentaries; mastering the theoretical sciences is what makes a man a man in the fullest sense, says one artist, echoing Averroes. Simon of Faversham invokes the support of Proclus for the claim that all things strive to assimilate themselves to the things that are one step higher up the ontological ladder, and that it is therefore natural for man to desire knowledge, which is the means through which we may assimilate ourselves to the separate substances. Radulphus Brito also repeatedly says that philosophizing can make us godlike, and gives the thought a special twist by also stressing Seneca's Stoic description of the effects of philosophy: it makes a man free. Such exaltations of the intellectual's life hardly ever contain any reference to the standard doctrine of two types of highest good, one obtainable in this life, another obtainable only afterwards. Few appear to have been shocked.

There is no sign either that any authority was shocked by Boethius' disparaging remark that 'laymen ... are only quasi-human (*deminuti homines*) since they do not have the human perfection bestowed by theoretical sciences'. But Stephen Tempier did not like Boethius for saying that 'when a man is occupied with this [the best and most perfect of the operations of the intellective power] he is in the best state possible for a man. And the people [who get into that state] are the philosophers, for they spend their life in the study of wisdom.' The formulation is provocative because it seems to allude to the theological notion of a 'state of perfection' attaching to the taking of religious vows. Moreover, Boethius' views on perfection enter into a fairly coherent set of views about human knowledge, and he also declares that

> there can be no question which is debatable with reasons and which nevertheless the philosopher ought not debate and determine how it is with truth in the matter as far as it [i.e. the truth] can be grasped by human reason. This is so because all reasons by means of which the debate is carried out are derived from reality, or else they would be a figment of the mind. Now, the philosopher teaches the natures of all things, for as philosophy teaches being, so the parts of philosophy teach the parts of being ... Therefore it is the philosopher's job to determine every question that is debatable with reasons,

> for every question which is debatable with reasons falls in some part of being, and the philosopher investigates every being, the natural, the mathematical and the divine alike.

Boethius' philosopher is the perfect man, he studies and gains an understanding of all sections of reality and in particular the most noble of all, the First Cause; his is human happiness in this life. On one occasion Boethius says that such earthly perfection also brings its possessor closer to happiness in the next life. Only the repeated phrase 'debatable with reasons' suggests there may be questions about which it is no use to reason.

Up to the early 1270s there had been some intense debates about the compatibility of certain Aristotelian doctrines and Christianity, and whether un-Christian doctrines could be refuted without using arguments from faith. By the early 1270s it must have been clear to nearly everybody in the arts faculty that Aristotle did not think the world as a whole or any of its biological species has once begun to be. It was further clear that his sempiternalism is logically coherent, *and* it was clear that creationism is so too. This had not always been obvious; Siger of Brabant seems to have realized only gradually that the main argument against creationism relies on an unwarranted subsumption of the un-Aristotelian concept of creation under the Aristotelian notion of change (*mutatio*); considered as a species of change, creation is an inconsistent concept, since change presupposes the existence before the change of that which was changed.

But does not Aristotelian science require the sempiternity of the world? If scientific axioms are necessary, and necessity means being always true, a biological axiom like 'every man is an animal' would seem to require sempiternal existence of men to act as verifiers. A standard question in our period was 'Is the proposition "every man is by necessity an animal" true if no man exists?' Some answered 'Yes' and held it was enough if some intelligent being still had a concept of man and animal; some used the Avicennian idea that existence is an accident of essences to hold that even with no men around the essence of man could be, though could not exist, and could act as verifier. Siger thought the question involved a pragmatic inconsistency, for the condition that there exists no man can never be fulfilled, he held. In an Aristotelian universe any species is always represented by existing members, and so there are always individuals to verify the proposition.

Boethius answered 'No'. He accepted the permissibility of the hypothesis that there might at some time be no men, and firmly held that with no existents around there would be no essences, and that analyticity is no guarantee of truth; with no men in existence even 'man is man' would be false. He held a simple correspondence theory of truth; an affirmative proposition is true if and only if such things as its subject and predicate signify are actually combined in the way the proposition indicates; a negative proposition is true if and only if such things are not combined. This means that all negative propositions about non-existents are true and all affirmative propositions about non-existents are false.

As 'every man is an animal' would be false in the case posited, so 'every man is by necessity an animal' would *a fortiori* be so. But even when men exist the modal proposition is false, for there can be no necessary, i.e. unchangeable, truths about changeable and corruptible beings.

Apparently, then, God and the separate substances (intelligences, angels) are the only objects about which there can be scientific knowledge. But Boethius holds that natural science is possible, for science only requires a weaker form of necessity, namely that the causal relationships stated in its propositions obtain without fail *presupposing that such things as the propositions are about exist*. Whenever there is a man there is in him a cause why 'animal' should inhere in him. Boethius does not go so far as to call categorical scientific propositions covert conditionals ('man is an animal' = 'if there is a man, he is an animal') – that was left for the next century – but he comes close to so doing.

Natural science takes the existence of the physical world with its population of natural species for granted. And it has to do so, Boethius thought, for every science must presuppose the existence of its subject and the truth of its axioms. Aristotelian natural science is a science about the material world and thus cannot incorporate a theory of how things may come to be otherwise than through matter acquiring a form.

Boethius stresses that each science is an autonomous system of primitive terms, axioms and derived theorems. There is, he admits, more to be said about the structure of reality than natural science can say, and in fact there are causes stronger than those proper to the sublunary sphere and thus capable of eliminating the work of natural causes. Hence in a particular case, the expected effect may fail to follow its natural causes, or an effect may be due to other causes than natural ones. Reality is organized in a hierarchy of entities of increasing causal power the closer one gets to the First Cause. When doing natural science we deal with cause–effect relationships that hold invariably *provided no superior, non-natural cause intervenes*. Similarly within natural science there may be sub-sciences, it seems, the causal laws of one of which may occasionally annihilate the effects of those of another.

The important thing for Boethius' scientist is always to remember which science he is doing at the moment; whatever he may know as a metaphysician, for example, he is not permitted to use it in any other science unless it is incorporated in the principles of that science. And men have access to information which simply cannot be incorporated into the principles of natural science, because it would turn it into an inconsistent set of propositions. This is the case with some information which only faith provides, such as that the world started its existence a definite time ago and there was a first couple of humans. Such revealed information the Christian has to accept; but when he is doing biology he has to stick to the principle that every human being has two parents, and, Boethius expressly says, he has to deny the allegation that someone was the first man.

Boethius' terminology suggests that to him a scientist at work was like someone participating in one of the formalized 'games' of disputation practised at the university. Doing science, then, is partaking in an activity governed by rules about what you have to concede or deny, these being the 'principles' of the science in case. In a dialectical disputation it is a rule that only generally accepted propositions be taken as premisses, and Boethius explicitly says that a disputant commits a mistake and 'lies' if he uses a premiss which is not generally acceptable, although it may as a matter of fact be true.

In other words, saying that a universal theorem p is true in science A does not amount to a claim that p is true in the fundamental sense of corresponding with particularized reality. It only means that it follows from the rules (axioms) of that science and will apply to particular cases if no causality the description of which belongs in another science intervenes. Scientific truth is truth relative to some assumptions, not truth *simpliciter*.

The superior cause could impede the applicability of p by failing to provide entities of the sort p describes or by making some of them have other causal relationships than described by p. It could not, of course, make all instantiations of p false, for then p would be a theorem of a pseudo-science whose axioms could not be based or tested on observation.

But wouldn't it be possible to create a super-science that would take all causes into account? Couldn't metaphysics provide an adequate description of all matter-less causes, including the First Cause? No, Boethius holds, metaphysical reasoning can lead to some knowledge of The First, but given the assumption of a Free Divine Will, there is no way to give a full account of causation. It can be rationally inferred that the world is created, but not that it is not co-eternal with its creator. The First Cause endowed its creation with a causal structure that we can partly understand; but part of a correct understanding is the realization that at the head of the causal chain stands an inscrutable cause.

Thomas Aquinas would allow no genuine conflicts between scientific propositions and articles of faith; apparent conflicts arise from flaws in the scientific argumentation; in principle a unified system of knowledge must be possible. Scripture is an answer book which can tell us if a rational theory needs revision. Thomist man may have a hard job to spot the flaw in the theory, but he is not troubled by the spectre of an inconsistent world.

Siger of Brabant rather took the attitude that there are irresolvable inconsistencies between the data of revelation and correctly derived scientific theorems. To Sigerian man the clash between science and revelation is catastrophic, because he has to sacrifice one of the two; if he does not want to become a heretic, he must decide that the results of rational enquiry are wrong though he cannot see how they could be so.

To Boethian man it comes as no surprise that historical facts do not always exemplify the causal mechanisms described in scientific propositions. It is exactly what scientific metaphysics should make us expect: it leads to the assumption of a first cause, but cannot possibly tell exactly how this cause wields its power. Boethian man bows to Scripture without abandoning any scientific theorems.

Boethius toiled to find a philosophically tenable way out of the apparent contradiction between Christian dogma and philosophy. His deference to faith was probably sincere. Siger's is more suspect; his true belief may have been that philosophy was right but that Christianity could be shown to conform with philosophy if properly demythologized. In his *Questions on the Metaphysics* he follows Averroes in holding that man-made religions (*leges*) contain mythological elements, falsehoods designed to scare the plebs and make them behave. As an example the Pythagorean doctrine is mentioned that a good man's soul will migrate to that of a good body after death, while a bad man's will enter a beast's body. It is easy to see a parallel to Christian doctrines about purgatory, heaven and hell, and, in fact, Siger once tried to show that fire could not affect a disembodied soul. Stephen Tempier did not forget to condemn that view, just as he remembered one that Siger did not openly profess, but very nearly did so, namely that there are mythological falsehoods in *all* religions, including the Christian one.

Sometimes the reader feels that Siger is mocking would-be censors or other philosophical opponents. Investigating whether there must be just one first principle and cause, he refutes all serious arguments for the necessity of this and then presents various bad arguments for it as if they were conclusive. When discussing whether any natural desire could be in vain, he introduces the class of those desires which are directed to aims that cannot possibly be achieved, like immortality.

Isn't that mocking the idea espoused by, among others, Thomas, that there must be an eternal life since men have a desire for it and no natural desire can be in vain?

The debate about philosophy versus faith did not stop in 1277, but for a long time it was rather low-key. Philosophers avoided any Boethian attitudes that were provocative, while generally following the trail he had blazed, considering creation and other unpredictable manifestations of divine power as irrelevant to the construction of scientific theories.

Important as the collision between philosophy and religion was, it should be stressed that there is no sign that the driving force behind the philosophers was a wish to do away with traditional Christian doctrine. Their primary occupation was with a rational enquiry into all aspects of reality, including the divine. They just happened to arrive at conclusions that did not harmonize well with standard beliefs.

The 'invention' for which Radulphus Brito was best known to posterity is a good example of theologically neutral everyday work from the arts faculty. Radulphus invented a fourfold division of 'intentions' to account for the genesis and ontological status of universals.

There was a well-entrenched distinction between primary intentions such as 'horse' and secondary ones such as 'species', which presuppose the primary ones. Some would say that 'species' etc. are concepts of concepts, but Brito wished to tie them more securely to extramental reality. He then divided both primary and secondary intentions into abstract and concrete ones.

The abstract primary intention is a formal concept like 'humanity'. It is based on the modes of being or manifestations (*apparentia*) of some essence (or 'nature'); reasoning, for example, is a manifestation of human nature. An abstract primary intention is a mental entity, a thought (*cognitio*) whose object is man, but it does not include its object.

The concrete primary intention is the object of the abstract one, but it is not a purely extramental thing. It is the thing (man, for instance) *qua* thought of by means of the formal concept (humanity).

The concrete primary intention has one foot in the mental and one in the extramental world. Brito also describes it as an aggregate of the thing out there and the thought by which we grasp it. This ontological duplicity was often criticized in later times, but Brito's theory was at least a brave attempt to secure the lifeline between concepts and their objects without moving the objects into the mind. True, he would need a mechanism by which an essence can function as quiddity, i.e. basis of understanding, via its manifest modes of being, but such a mechanism was provided by fairly standard theory of sensation and abstraction.

Apart from the primary intentions Brito operates with a set of two secondary ones; once again the modes of being form the basis of concept-formation, but this time we are not dealing with modes proper to some nature but common ones, as follows.

The abstract secondary intention, universality for instance, is a concept derived from the common feature (mode of being) of being capable of occurring in several individuals or types; this feature is shared by man and donkey, for example, both of which can occur in several individuals, and also by animal which can occur in several species. Our intellect can grasp this, and it can do so without comparison: it can construct a Porphyrian tree on the basis of sensory acquaintance with a single individual, recognizing, for instance, that sensing (which characterizes animals) is a trait apt to be shared by more beings than is reasoning (which is reserved for humans).

The corresponding concrete secondary intention (in our example: 'universal') is the thing (man, for example) *qua* conceived of by means of the formal concept of universality.

Concrete secondary intentions like universals and syllogisms are the sort of things logic is about – that was commonly agreed. Some forty or fifty years before Brito, Robert Kilwardby had said that secondary intentions are thus called because they arise from inspection and comparison of things already grasped by the mind. Brito wants to generate secondary intentions through direct inspection of the entities that gave rise to the first intentions. Why will he not allow the mind to operate on the products of its primary inspection, and why will he allow no comparison? Because this might leave the mind too much power over which secondary intentions there are to be and make them much too mental – thoughts of thoughts.

If secondary intentions were mere mental constructs, the whole of logic would be so. And it could quickly be shown that grammar, physics, in fact any science would be in the same situation, for all theoretical entities – modes of signifying, causes, effects, whatever – must have a genesis similar to that of the secondary intentions of logic.

If one endeavour pervaded the work done by Parisian artists in the second half of the thirteenth century it was the endeavour to secure an extramental anchoring of scientific knowledge by deriving its categories from features of reality. That was what the modistic triad of ways of being, understanding, and signifying was all about, and that was Brito's central preoccupation. He tried relentlessly to mend the cracks that had appeared in the edifice of theories built with and around the modistic triad. There was no easy way to fix the cracks, the complexity of Brito's own theories showed that; the time was ripe for a radically new approach such as the one that John Buridan was to introduce in Paris about the 1330s.

━◆❖◆━ BIBLIOGRAPHY ━◆❖◆━

Original Language Editions

12.1 Ebbesen, S., Izbicki, T., Longeway, J., del Punta, F. and Stump, E. (eds) *Simon of Faversham, Quaestiones super Libro Elenchorum* (Studies and Texts 60), Toronto, PIMS, 1984.

12.2 Fauser, W. F. *Der Kommentar des Radulphus Brito zu Buch III De anima* (BGPTM n.f. 12), Münster, Aschendorff, 1974.

12.3 *CIMAGL* (journal with a large number of relevant text editions).

12.4 Enders, H. W. and Pinborg, J. (eds) *Radulphus Brito, Quaestiones super Priscianum minorem* (Grammatica Speculativa 3.1–2), Stuttgart, Bad Cannstatt, Frommann-Holzboog, 1980.

12.5 Roos, H., Otto, A., Pinborg, J. and Ebbesen, S. (eds) *Corpus Philosophorum Danicorum Medii Aevi*, Copenhagen, Gad/DSL, 1955–. (Contains several relevant works, including those of Boethius, John and Martin of Denmark.)

12.6 Pinborg, J. 'Radulphus Brito's sophism on second intentions', *Vivarium* 13 (1975): 119–52.

12.7 Van Steenbergen, F. (ed.) *Philosophes Médiévaux*, Louvain, Institut Supérieur de Philosophie de l'Université de Louvain, 1948–. (Contains several relevant works; the works of Siger of Brabant are in vols 12–14 and 24–5.)

English Translations

12.8 McDermott, A. C. S. *Godfrey of Fontaine's Abridgement of Boethius of Dacia's Modi Significandi sive Quaestiones super Priscianum maiorem* (Amsterdam Studies in the Theory and History of Linguistic Science 22), Amsterdam, John Benjamins, 1980.

12.9 Wippel, J. F. *Boethius of Dacia, On the supreme good, On the eternity of the world, On dreams* (Mediaeval Sources in Translation 30), Toronto, Pontifical Institute of Mediaeval Studies, 1987.

Studies

12.10 Ebbesen, S. 'Concrete accidental terms: late thirteenth-century debates about problems relating to such terms as "album"', in N. Kretzmann (ed.) *Meaning and Inference in Medieval Philosophy*, Dordrecht, Kluwer, 1988.

12.11 Gauthier, R. A. 'Notes sur Siger de Brabant, I–II', *Revue des Sciences Philosophiques et Théologiques* 67 (1983): 201–32 and 68 (1984): 3–49.

12.12 Hisette, R. *Enquête sur les 219 articles condamnés à Paris le 7 mars 1277* (Philosophes Médiévaux 22), Paris and Louvain, Publications Universitaires and Vander-Oyez, 1977.

12.13 Marmo, C. *Semiotica e Linguaggio nella Scolastica: Parigi, Bologna, Erfurt 1270–1330. La semiotica dei Modisti* (Nuovi studi storici 26), Rome, Istituto storico italiano per il medio evo, 1994.

12.14 Pinborg, J. *Die Entwicklung der Sprachtheorie im Mittelalter* (BGPTMA 42.2), Münster and Copenhagen, Aschendorff and Frost-Hansen, 1967.

12.15 —— *Logik und Semantik im Mittelalter*, Stuttgart and Bad Cannstatt, Frommann-Holzboog, 1972.

12.16 —— *Medieval Semantics: Selected Studies on Medieval Logic and Grammar*, London, Variorum, 1984.

12.17 Rosier, I. *La Grammaire spéculative des Modistes*, Lille, Presses Universitaires de Lille, 1983.

12.18 Van Steenbergen, F. *Maître Siger de Brabant* (Philosophes Médiévaux 21), Paris and Louvain, Publications Universitaires and Vander-Oyez, 1977.

comprised in large measure the more extreme Aristotelian and Arabic philosophical positions taught in the arts faculty. Henry certainly represented a critical attitude to Aristotelianism on the commission, and indeed several articles on Tempier's syllabus appear traceable to him. Henry was also present at the immediately ensuing meetings of the theology faculty that resulted in the censure of the younger theologian, Giles of Rome, and in the masters' own condemnation (*damnatio per sententiam magistrorum*) of Aquinas's doctrine of unicity of substantial form. Henry's Augustinian orientation, so evident in Tempier's actions, continued throughout his career, encountering new Aristotelian foes within the faculty after 1285, when Giles of Rome was rehabilitated at the order of Honorius IV and Godfrey of Fontaines became master. A secular, Henry was also known as a strident critic of the mendicant privileges granted by Martin IV in 1281. His opposition was such that he was reprimanded and suspended in 1290 by the future Boniface VIII. Henry's death is usually given as 29 June 1293.

Henry's two major works are the direct products of his long teaching career at Paris. The first is his *Summa of Ordinary Questions* and the second his fifteen series of *Quodlibetal Questions*. Cross-references establish that both works were disputed and written concurrently over the length of his career. His regular or 'ordinary' questions derived from his disputations held as master during the normal course of term. Revised for publication as a massive *Summa*, these ordinary questions represent Henry's systematic investigation of the nature of theology (articles 1–20), the divine nature and attributes (articles 21–52), and the Trinity (articles 53–75). Henry intended his *Summa* to include a part on creatures, but he never completed it. As such, Henry's *Summa* corresponds roughly in plan to the first forty-three questions of the first part of Aquinas's own *Summa theologiae*, yet approaches Aquinas's entire work in length. Unlike ordinary questions, which were disputed by the master at regular class hours throughout the academic year, quodlibetal questions were special university disputations only held before Christmas and Easter. Here the questions were not posed by the master himself on controlled topics, but by the audience, on any issue of interest. Hence they were designated *quodlibetales* or 'on anything whatever'. Accordingly, while ordinary questions allowed for systematic investigation, quodlibetal questions forced the master to address the current controversies in the university community that at times involved the master himself. Henry's fifteen quodlibetal disputes represent one for nearly every academic year from 1276 to 1292. Each dispute itself contains up to forty separate questions, which were considerably expanded and revised by Henry for publication, including lengthy insertions, cancellations and digressions. Henry brought the quodlibetal question to its apex as a literary form of scholastic theology and was the first to make the quodlibet a principal vehicle for his thought.

Duns Scotus

It is perhaps no exaggeration to claim that less is known with certainty about the life, career and works of Duns Scotus than about any scholastic thinker of his rank. Aside from his own writings, only six slight documents provide what scattered facts are known of his life. Of Scottish origin, Scotus is thought to have been born about 1266, on the basis of the established date of his ordination to the priesthood on 17 March 1291. The once widely accepted details of Scotus's place of birth, family, early education and entry into the Franciscan order are now considered unreliable owing their source to the discredited chronicle *Monasticon Scoticanum* of Marian Brockie. From about 1288, Scotus studied theology at Oxford, although it is disputed whether this was interrupted after his ordination in 1291 by several years of study at Paris. In either case, Scotus was certainly studying theology at the Oxford convent by 1300. On 6 July 1300, he was one of twenty-two Franciscans from the Oxford diocese presented to John Dalderby, bishop of Lincoln, for permission to hear confessions. About this same time, he was beginning to revise his lectures on the *Sentences*, given as a bachelor at Oxford. This revised commentary on the *Sentences*, known as the *Ordinatio* (see below), was under way in 1300, because in the prologue Scotus himself says that he is writing in that year. Further evidence of his activities as bachelor at Oxford during this same period is given by his participation in a disputation of the Franciscan master Philip Bridlington, who was also in the same group presented to Dalderby. Scotus, however, never incepted as master at Oxford. He was instead sent in the autumn of 1302 to study theology at Paris, where he began a new set of lectures on the *Sentences*. These were interrupted in June 1303 when, together with some eighty other Franciscans, he was expelled from France for declaring allegiance to Pope Boniface VIII against Philip the Fair in their escalating dispute over taxation of church property. Where Scotus went during his exile from Paris is unknown, but it is commonly assumed that he either returned to Oxford or went to Cambridge, where he is believed to have lectured at some point in his career. Scotus was back in Paris at the latest by the autumn of 1304 to finish lecturing on the *Sentences*. It is inferred that Scotus must have incepted as master at Paris by early 1305, because in a letter dated 18 November 1304, Gonsalvus of Spain, the newly elected Minister General of the Franciscans and the Franciscan regent master when Scotus first arrived at Paris, recommended Scotus as next in line for promotion to master. In his letter, Gonsalvus testifies to Scotus's reputation, which he says had 'already spread everywhere'. During his regency at Paris, Scotus held one quodlibetal disputation and debated with the Dominican William Peter Godinus on the principle of individuation. For reasons unknown, Scotus was replaced as the Franciscan regent at Paris by Alexander of Alexandria in the autumn of 1307 and abruptly transferred to the Franciscan convent in Cologne, where he is listed as a lector in early 1308. Nothing is known of his activities during his Cologne period. Before his career could reach full maturity and with his major work the *Ordinatio* still in a state of revision, Scotus died in Cologne later that year, where he remains buried today. The date of his death is traditionally given as 8 November 1308.

As with the details of his life and career, uncertainty about Scotus's writings is unparalleled for a medieval thinker of his stature. While much progress has been made in establishing Scotus's genuine corpus, important questions of chronology and canon still remain. Scotus's genuine works can be divided into philosophical and theological writings, and roughly speaking the former are regarded as earlier. Scotus's logical works are generally considered to be his earliest. These include sets of questions on Porphyry and the *Categories*, two works on *De interpretatione*, and questions on the *Sophistical Refutations*. The important *Questions on the Metaphysics* have traditionally been considered an earlier work as well, though somewhat later than the logical treatises, but this has been disputed by commentators since the sixteenth century. Current evidence suggests that the latter books, VII–IX (only the first nine books are authentic), show revision from later in Scotus's career, perhaps even very late. Finally, there are two philosophical works that fall outside this main group owing to uncertainty over their dating and degree of authenticity: questions on *On the Soul* and the *Theoremata*. While *On the Soul* is surely Scotistic, manuscripts attest that it has been edited by a follower of Scotus (*scotellus*), perhaps Antonius Andreas (d. *c.* 1320). Both manuscripts and contemporaries assign the *Theoremata* to Scotus, but their authenticity has been debated owing to a section entitled *Treatise on Articles of Faith* (*Tractatus de creditis*), which denies the philosophical demonstrability of the existence of God.

The bulk of Scotus's reputation rests, however, on his more mature and longer theological writings. These are essentially four: various versions of his commentaries on the *Sentences*, two sets of disputes known as *Collationes*, a set of twenty *Quodlibetal Questions*, and the *Treatise on God as First Principle* (*De primo principio*). The textual situation of Scotus's commentaries on the *Sentences* is one of the most complicated in medieval scholarship. First of all, Scotus lectured on the text at Oxford, again at Paris and, at an undetermined time, at Cambridge. Second, his secretaries and students conflated these different versions in an effort to fill in places apparently left incomplete at his death. Finally, Scotus revised by means of numerous additions and annotations to the primitive text, so that these had to be distinguished from the intrusions inserted by his students and secretaries. The better part of modern textual criticism on Scotus has been devoted to teasing apart these various versions and layers of his *Sentences*. This research has established that there are two versions of his Oxford *Sentences*, an earlier *Lectura*, which was then considerably expanded to form the *Ordinatio*, previously termed the *Opus oxoniense*. As indicated, Scotus read the *Sentences* again when he went to Paris in the autumn of 1302, which commentary survives as neither a *lectura* nor an *ordinatio* but as what students' reports called *reportationes*. A major point of dispute is the chronological relation of these *Parisian Reports* (*Reportationes parisienses*) to the Oxford *Ordinatio*. The long-held view was that Scotus constructed the *Ordinatio* from both the early Oxford *Lectura* and the Parisian *Sentences*, rendering the *Ordinatio* later than the Parisian commentary and according it a status as the most definitive of Scotus's works. Recent studies have tended to revise this view, placing at least the first book of the *Ordinatio* before rather than after the corresponding part of the Parisian *Sentences*. This revised chronology seems required not only by Scotus's own statement dating the prologue of the *Ordinatio* to 1300, two years prior to his theological studies in Paris, but also by the Parisian commentary's noticeable independence in organization, topic and treatment relative to both of its Oxford counterparts. Scotus's two series of *Collationes*, one held at Oxford and the other at Paris, are known from the eye-witness testimony of his secretary, William of Alnwick, to represent the proceedings of oral disputation. It has been suggested that these *Collationes* were exercises carried out by Scotus within the Franciscan houses while still a bachelor, but this is not certain. His *Quodlibetal Questions* are assigned to his regency at Paris, perhaps in the academic year 1306/7. As the product of a formal university disputation by a regent master in theology, they must certainly be regarded as Scotus's mature thought. Finally, the *De primo principio* is a systematic treatise on the transcendentals, containing Scotus's proof for the existence and infinity of God. While the authenticity of the *De primo* is uncontested, it none the less betrays the influence of an editor. More than half of the *De primo* has been supplied verbatim from the *Ordinatio*, indicating that it is to some extent a compilation of material. Despite this, it has received more contemporary attention by way of translation and commentary than any other single work in Scotus's corpus.

295

∾ RELATION OF HENRY OF GHENT ∾
TO DUNS SCOTUS

Henry's significance, both historically and philosophically, stems from his position in the thirteenth century of having an important and immediate relationship to both Aquinas and Scotus. On the one side, Henry mounted the most sustained and sophisticated Augustinian response in the later thirteenth century to the Aristotelianism of Aquinas. Adopting a critical attitude towards Aristotle on fundamental points, Henry returned to more Augustinian principles, which he infused with certain elements of Avicenna. In comparison with Aquinas, Henry can fairly be said to exhibit a doctrinal tendency called 'Avicennizing Augustinianism', a label coined by Etienne Gilson to describe the exploitation by certain scholastic thinkers of similarities between Augustine and Avicenna, such as their mutual denial of knowledge by abstraction. Thus, where Aquinas argues 'according to Aristotle and the truth' (*secundum Aristotelem et veritatem rei*), Henry will instead argue 'according to Augustine, Avicenna, and the truth' (*secundum Avicennam et veritatem rei; secundum Augustinum et Avicennam*).[1] In particular, Henry reverted to certain positions considered Augustinian by thirteenth-century standards, such as the compatibility of faith and demonstration, a need for a special divine illumination in natural knowledge, a heavy emphasis on the reality of the divine ideas and their role in both knowledge and creation, and above all a strong voluntarism against the intellectualism of Aristotle. Henry specifically criticized Aquinas on numerous points, including the concept of theology as a subalternated science, the exclusivity of faith and demonstrative reasoning, the definition of self-evidence and related criticism of Anselm's ontological argument, the pre-eminence given to Aristotle's argument for the unmoved mover, the denial of any positive knowledge of God's essence (*quid est*) in the present life, the limitation of each Aristotelian separate form or angel to a species in itself, the real distinction of essence and existence (at least as defended by Giles of Rome), the indemonstrability of the temporal beginning of the world, and a variety of theses connected to the relationship of the intellect to the will. In the words of one of Henry's editors, 'No theologian immediately after the death of Aquinas so sharply criticized the philosophical basis of his theology as Henry of Ghent.'[2]

On the other side, Henry's own revised Augustinian outlook was itself subjected to an extensive, critical evaluation by Duns Scotus. What led Scotus to focus on Henry is not known. Perhaps in view of the restrictions placed by the Franciscans in 1282 on reading Aquinas's *Summa*, the Order turned to Henry's *Summa* to supply the systematic training in current theology during Scotus's formation. A high regard for Henry is evident in Oxford Franciscans just prior to Scotus, such as Roger

Marston, who in 1283 described Henry as 'a recent, solemn doctor, renowned and studious in philosophy from infancy'.[3] Whatever the explanation, Henry constitutes not just a source, but the source, for Scotus's thought. This is in fact so true that Scotus appears to be the first major scholastic thinker to base his principal work explicitly on the systematic examination of a contemporary. On many important questions, Scotus develops his own position as a critical reaction to that of Henry, often after extensive reporting, analysis and refutation of Henry's reasoning. This is the case, for example, on such fundamental issues as the relation of faith and reason, natural knowledge of God, the nature of transcendental concepts, the primary object of the intellect, necessity and contingency, the divine ideas, creation, illumination, causality of the will, connection of the virtues and on numerous points of Trinitarian theology. All the same, however, it would be a distortion to see Scotus as simply rejecting Henry's positions. Even when clearly repudiating a view of Henry, Scotus will none the less presuppose much of Henry's underlying philosophical framework and formulate his own position in terms of Henry's basic concepts, distinctions and technical vocabulary. This is not to say that Scotus was unoriginal and derivative but only that his originality cannot be fully understood apart from his relationship to Henry. Nowhere is the relationship between Scotus and Henry better illustrated than in their dispute over the nature of the transcendental concepts.

❧ UNIVOCITY AND ANALOGY ❧

One of the most striking results of the metaphysics of Duns Scotus was that the concepts of being and the other transcendentals applied univocally to God and creatures, substance and accidents. Scotus broke with the unanimous and traditional view that being, conceived in its utmost generality, could only be predicated analogously and not univocally of substance and accident, much less of God and creatures. Scotus made his innovative move to univocity in specific and explicit response to the peculiar version of analogy advanced by Henry of Ghent. Indeed, it would be more accurate to say that Scotus's path to univocity was paved by Henry's prior and equally innovative interpretation of the traditional view of analogy itself. Here, perhaps more than in any other area of disagreement between them, it would be a distortion to portray Scotus as simply rejecting, rather than building upon, an antecedent position of Henry. None the less, in advancing beyond Henry's own version of analogy to univocity, Scotus had to solve fundamental difficulties connected with univocity that had always been compelling motivations for the traditional view of analogy, difficulties which Henry evidently saw but could not resolve.

Scotus advances his theory of univocity as part of a critical and exhaustive revision of Henry's account of our natural knowledge of God. At issue was an abiding concern of the period: how to reconcile the possibility of attaining some knowledge of the divine nature from creatures with God's total transcendence of creatures. The difficulty involved was long recognized, having a formulation as far back as Gaunilo's reply to Anselm that the argument of the *Proslogion* appeared to put God in a genus or species. In order for God to be totally transcendent, the divine nature can have no reality in common with creatures. But if God and creatures agree in nothing real, then a creature can never yield a positive notion of the divine nature that conveys any of its reality. One standard solution was to stress the negative character of natural knowledge of God. For instance, Aquinas attempted to reconcile divine transcendence with our natural knowledge of God by way of the Aristotelian distinction between knowing that something is (*quia est; si est*) versus knowing its essence or nature (*quid est*). According to Aquinas, our intellect in its present, natural state can only know through sensible creatures that God is or exists (*si est*). As for the divine essence, we cannot know what it is (*quid est*) but only what it is not.[4] This solution was attacked in the condemnations issued by Stephen Tempier on 7 March 1277. Article 215 on Tempier's syllabus repudiated such attempts to protect the transcendence of God at the expense of restricting natural knowledge of the divine nature to the bare fact of its existence. As censured the article read, 'That it can only be known that God is, or that God exists.' (*Quod de Deo non potest cognosci nisi quia ipse est, sive ipsum esse.*) Both Henry and Scotus agreed that some positive knowledge of the divine nature and attributes was naturally attainable from creatures, thereby fully reinstating the tension between the transcendence and knowledge of God. Henry, for his part, attempted to account for this positive knowledge while maintaining the traditional view that being and the other transcendentals were only analogously common to God and creatures. Henry none the less saw that he had to revise the traditional doctrine of analogy, and in so doing extended that traditional view as far as it could go without actually becoming a doctrine of univocity. Scotus rejected Henry's revised theory as unworkable and argued that only univocity could ensure a naturally attainable concept of the divine essence.

Henry of Ghent on Analogy

Henry of Ghent followed the common opinion in holding that being is predicated of God and creatures neither univocally, nor purely equivocally, but analogously.[5] The traditional understanding of the terms was based on Aristotle. The definitions of univocity and equivocity derived from the opening chapter of the *Categories*, while the notion of analogy was taken chiefly from the treatment of being as an equivocal by reference (πρὸς ἕν; *ad unum*) in the *Metaphysics*.[6] Thus, a term is univocal if it has a single meaning or concept (*ratio, intentio, intellectus, conceptus*) when applied, such as 'animal' when predicated of a horse and a human being. It is a pure or chance equivocal (*aequivocum in casu*) if it is applied according to completely discrete and unrelated meanings, such as the 'bark' of a dog and a tree. Analogy, however, is intermediate between these two extremes of univocity and equivocity. An analogous term has different but connected meanings, so that one is primary and the other is related to it, usually either as a cause or an effect. Aristotle's own example of 'healthy' served as the standard illustration. The primary meaning of 'healthy' is the state of a well-functioning, living organism, yet clearly things are said to be healthy which do not possess health in this sense. Both medicine and urine, for example, are called 'healthy' not because they possess health in the primary sense, for they are not living at all, but because they bear some relationship to it. Medicine is a cause of health and urine a sign or effect of it. The scholastics adapted Aristotle's conception of analogy as a middle way between the extreme positions of univocity and equivocity, to account for some knowledge of God based on creatures while ensuring divine transcendence. Being was not univocal to God and creatures, but rather analogous, so that it applied to God primarily and to creatures in a secondary but related sense, although appropriate distinctions had to be made to avoid equating the relation of divine and created being with that of substance and accident. In this regard, Henry was in conformity with the common view.

> Being therefore does not belong to God univocally . . . nor purely equivocally . . . but in a middle way, namely, by analogy, because it signifies one thing primarily and principally and the other as in some way ordered, related, or proportional to what is primary . . . And in this way, being in the most common sense primarily signifies God, secondarily creature, just as created being primarily signifies substance and secondarily accidents, although the relation in each case is different.
>
> (*Summa* a.21 q.2 (ed. 1520, I, f.124r))

Aristotle, however, was not the only authority on the transcendentals. Even more important for the scholastics was Avicenna, who had not only made being, in explicit contradistinction to God, the subject of metaphysics, but also one of the primary conceptions of the mind. These claims of Avicenna for the primacy of being had to be addressed, for together they implied that there was a concept of being antecedent to either God or creatures. Henry's formulation of the Avicennian objection is important, not only because it states sharply the impediment to univocity, but also because in Henry's reply Scotus clearly saw that the denial of univocity involved highly unacceptable consequences.

> What is predicated of several things, but has an essential concept different from the concepts of those things [of which it is predicated], is something really common to them, for every concept is based upon some thing. Being is this sort, because according to Avicenna, 'Being is imprinted on the mind by a first impression,' even before the concept of God or creature are impressed on it. [Therefore, being is something really common to God and creatures.]
> (*Summa* a.21 q.2 (ed. 1520, I, f.123v))

The argument is that being must have a concept different from those of God or creature, because it is known prior to either one. Since being is predicated of both God and creature, that concept must also be common. Thus, the noetic primacy of being entails that it have a concept distinct from and common to those proper to God and creatures. Because any such common concept must be based on some common reality, being must be something really common to God and creature.

It is the major premiss which constitutes the underlying impediment to making any concept univocally common to God and creatures: every concept must be based on some reality (*omnis conceptus fundatur in re aliqua*). Accordingly, a common concept must be of some common reality. But, obviously, no reality can be admitted as common to God and creatures. This will prove to be the most formidable difficulty for Scotus's doctrine of univocity: how to sustain a real concept univocally common to God and creatures without positing any reality common to them. The minor premiss, based on Avicenna's famous text on the primary intelligibles, is meant to establish that being has a concept outside of those of God and creatures owing to its position as a primary notion. The burden of Henry's reply will be to deny that there is any concept of being apart from those of God and creatures. It is in this reply that Scotus will find his argument that, on the contrary, being must be a distinct concept, and hence univocal.

In reply to Avicenna's text, Henry is emphatic that there can be no concept of being absolutely taken apart from the concepts of God and creature, as if there were some single, simple concept of being common to them (*aliquis unicus intellectus simplex communis*), for there can be no such concept. Rather, any real concept of being is either of the being proper to God or of the being proper to creatures, but not of anything common to them. Henry's position is governed by the requirement in the major premiss that a real community must underwrite a real, common concept. Since there can be no such real community between God and creatures, there can be no real common concept. Demanding therefore a strict correspondence in unity between a real concept and its foundation in reality, Henry concludes that at the transcendental level being forms two proper and distinct concepts corresponding to the two separate and diverse realities of divine and created being. These concepts, while proper and diverse, none the less have a community of analogy, the real foundation for which is the causal dependence of the creature on God. This agreement in being by virtue of the connection cause and effect, while real, is not sufficient to support a single, common notion of being but only two proper concepts related as primary and secondary.

Had Henry gone no further than this in his reply to Avicenna, his account would have conformed to what Peter Aureoli later identified as the common opinion. Being conceived at its most general level does not form a single, simple *ratio* common to God and creatures, but two proper *rationes* related in attribution as primary and secondary. Henry, however, did go further in his reply, motivated by a need not only to explain Avicenna's text on the primary intelligibles, upon which he would depend heavily in his proof for the existence of God, but also to account for how the mind could move from a concept proper to creatures to one proper to God.

Henry explains that if there appears to be some common concept of being, this is only because the divine being or created beings have been conceived in an indistinct or indeterminate way. But to conceive of either the being proper to God or proper to creatures in an indistinct way is not to have some third, distinct concept of being as absolutely undetermined and common to both. That is, there is no separate concept of being as absolutely undetermined that can be abstracted from the proper concepts of God and creature, as if each proper concept comprised a common notion of being as undetermined and a determining concept, such as finite and infinite or created and uncreated. Rather, the proper concepts of God and creatures are in each case already concepts of being as undetermined. Any concept of being as absolutely undetermined, which appears to be single, simple, and prior to the proper concepts of God and creature, is merely the result of confusing the two different ways in which the being proper to God and creatures is in each instance undetermined.

Divine being is undetermined in the sense that it cannot be determined by any advening perfection or entity. This is what it means to say that the divine being is infinite, for it cannot be determined or limited. Created being, however, when taken in its utmost generality as common to all creatures, is undetermined in the sense that it has been abstracted from all determinations with which it is found in reality, such as 'existing in itself' and 'existing in another', which determine or limit created being to substance and accident. Henry's technical terminology for this distinction is that divine being is undetermined negatively, for it is to be denied all determination, and created being privatively, for it can be conceived without the determinations with which it is found. As Henry explains in slightly different terms elsewhere, to conceive of being absolutely, that is, without any determination or qualification, can mean two different things. It can mean either being in its singular, most perfect instance (*in quadam singularitate*) or in its widest generality (*in quadam universalitate*). Being taken absolutely in the first way is God, in the second way is the notion of being common to the categories. There is no sense in which being can be conceived as undetermined apart from these two.[7]

Having made this distinction, Henry replies to the objection that what appears to be an absolutely undetermined concept of being univocally common to God and creatures is in fact a confusion of the two different ways in which being is undetermined. The divine being is undetermined by negation, because it lacks all determination in both act and potency; created being is undetermined by privation, because it is conceived as lacking determination in act but not in potency. The confusion between the two arises because both are concepts of being without determination, and to this extent they are similar. The mistake is to think that from this similarity one can extract a single notion of being as absolutely undetermined common to both God and creatures. Rather, what appears to be a simple, common notion of undetermined being is in fact a conflation of two proper notions of being, which resemble each other in their removal of determination.

Against the challenge presented by Avicenna's text that there is a concept of being common to God and creatures because, as a primary notion of the mind, the concept of being is prior to both, Henry upholds the traditional position of analogy. Being, conceived in its utmost generality, cannot be reduced to a single notion but only to two distinct concepts, one proper to God and the other to creatures, which are none the less related through attribution or analogy. Yet, in his answer to Avicenna Henry went considerably beyond this traditional view by explaining that being could be conceived with sufficient indeterminacy so as to *appear* univocal. While insisting that there was in truth no univocal notion of being, Henry none the less allowed that the being of either God or creatures could be conceived so indistinctly that the concept proper to the one actually was known in a confused way along with the concept of the other, because both were concepts of being without determination. This was a critical move past the traditional view of analogy and was clearly but a step away from Scotus's univocity, where a simple common concept would replace a confusion of two proper but similar concepts. After Henry went so far as to admit an apparently univocal concept of being, Scotus would conclude that such a concept must in fact be univocal.

Thus Henry revised the common opinion on analogy, according to which the concepts of being proper to God and creatures were united through attribution, by adding that they were also united by confusion in an indistinct notion that appeared univocal. Henry's underlying motivation for this extension of the traditional view was to provide some cognitive bridge between the two proper notions of being which allowed the human mind to pass from its knowledge of creatures to one of the divine nature. This bridge could not be provided by any concept common to both, so Henry supplied it by allowing the two concepts to be conceived together as though they were one. That is, Henry permitted the being of a creature to be conceived in such an indeterminate fashion that it in fact comprised, in an indistinct and confused fashion, the concept of being proper to God. In this way, Henry was attempting to explain, where the traditional view of analogy had not, how one could arrive at a proper concept of the divine nature from creatures. This is clear from Henry's account of the mind's ascent from creatures to God.

In the context of Tempier's condemnation of the position that we can only know that God exists (*si est*), but not what God's nature is (*quid est*), Henry undertook an extensive examination in nine questions of the categories of *si est* and *quid est* as they applied to our knowledge of God, paying particular attention to the extent to which knowledge of the divine nature had to be negative (*quid est non*). In express opposition to the assertion of Aquinas, Henry denied that in the present life we cannot know what God is but only what God is not. If our knowledge of the divine nature were limited only to negations about creatures, then we would know no more about the nature of God from creatures than we would about Socrates by saying that he is not a rock. That is, to have purely negative knowledge of the divine essence is to have no knowledge of it at all. The reason is that negation is always negation of something, so that all meaningful knowledge of what something is not presupposes, to some degree, knowledge of what it is. Furthermore, a purely negative knowledge of the divine nature could not account for our love and desire of God in the present life, for, as Augustine says, we can love what is unseen but not what is unknown. Accordingly, against the assertion of Aquinas, Henry concludes that there must be some positive knowledge of the divine *quid est* naturally available in the present life from creatures.

In effect, Henry sees a complete reduction of our knowledge of the divine nature to negations about creatures as inconsistent with analogy, because it is tantamount to making all predication about God purely equivocal. On the other hand, the positive knowledge of the divine nature provided by analogy does not compromise the transcendence of God to the human mind, because it is not of God's essence in its own particularity and individuality. Analogy can only yield a knowledge of God's *quid est* which is general, indistinct and, as it were, incidental to the substance of the divine nature itself. Yet, even this imperfect knowledge of the divine nature provided by analogy requires a sophisticated manoeuvre by Henry, utilizing his special understanding of the doctrine of analogy itself.[8]

Henry's account of the mind's ascent to the divine *quid est* from creatures involves three main stages, designed to conform broadly to the traditional understanding of the pseudo-Dionysian ways of causality, eminence and negation. At each stage the divine essence is known in a progressively less general fashion, so that ascent is made by degrees to an increasingly distinct knowledge of God, which none the less always remains in some way general and universal. In these three stages Henry says that God is known most generally (*generalissime*), less generally (*generalius*), and least generally (*generaliter*), which involve, respectively, abstraction, eminence and negation. The first or *generalissime* stage is both the most elaborate and important, for it is here that the initial move is made from creatures to God. This first stage itself comprises three degrees of knowledge based on two types of 'abstraction' (*abstractio*).

According to Henry, a formal perfection can be abstracted from its instances in two ways: either as a universal or as something separate. In the first type of abstraction, for example, goodness can be abstracted from this or that particular good as a common and universal form in which they share (*commune quoddam et universale*). Here, while the form is abstracted from its instances, it is none the less still seen in relation to them as that in which they all participate, for the universal is 'one in many'. In the second type, the form is considered in absolute separation from any material instance, for it is seen not as something common divided among many particulars but as transcendent and subsistent in itself (*in se subsistens*). Quite clearly, these two types of 'abstraction' are for Henry the noetic procedures that result in the concepts of being, goodness or any other perfection as indeterminate by privation and negation. These two kinds of abstraction produce the three steps of the *generalissime* way of knowing the divine nature.

In the first step of most general knowledge of God, any perfection in a creature already reveals, at least in a very confused and indistinct fashion, something of the divine nature. For instance, in knowing this or that particular, created good, Henry says that we know two things: the 'this' and 'that', which are proper to creatures, and 'good' which is something common to God and creatures. Thus, even in 'this created good' we know something of the divine good, even if it is not known as distinct from the creature. If, however, by the first type of abstraction we remove the 'this' proper to the creature, we attain a notion of the good that is less determined to the creature than before, and this is the second step of the *generalissime* stage. Here the good is not seen as proper to creatures or God but as something analogously common to both (*commune analogum ad Deum et creaturam*). Although in fact the good of God and of the creature form two diverse and distinct concepts (*diversos intellectus distinctos faciunt*), just as is the case with being, nevertheless these notions are so similar that our intellect at this point conceives both together in a confused way as one (*quia tamen proximi sunt, intellectus noster concipit modo confuso utrumque ut unum*).[9] By performing a second abstraction, we can distinguish within this confused, analogous notion those two proper concepts, so that we differentiate between what is abstract in the sense of universal and in the sense of separate. This is the third and final step of most general knowledge of the divine nature, where some perfection, such as goodness or being, is viewed as subsistent in itself. Such a concept is proper to God alone.

Once Henry has reached this point, he can easily apply the Dionysian techniques of eminence (*prae-eminentia*) and negation (*remotio*) to this proper concept to ascend to respectively the *generalius* and *generaliter* levels of knowing the divine essence. In eminence, the note of excellence is added to that of subsistence to result in the notion of God as a most perfect nature. In negation, all composition and diversity are removed from this most perfect nature, so that its goodness, wisdom and so forth are taken to be identical with its being. In this way, Henry concludes, we can know what God is, not just what God is not, from creatures in the present life, although 'by comparison to the beatific vision of God's nature, this knowledge is almost nothing'.

Henry's claim for a natural knowledge of the divine *quid est* from creatures would appear to face an insuperable obstacle in his denial of any conceptual community between God and creatures. By restricting our knowledge of God and creatures solely to two wholly proper, simple, and diverse notions, Henry seems to have completely undermined any epistemological basis for claiming that we can derive any concept of the one from the other. Henry clearly saw this obstacle and used considerable ingenuity to overcome it. He conceded that God and creature could be brought together in a common concept, yet found a way to deny that such a notion was univocal.

Henry's strategy, naturally enough, is to explain the derivation of knowledge of God from creatures by means of abstraction. Thus, as outlined above, we begin with some perfection of a creature, such as being or goodness, and detach the particularizing and determining elements with which that perfection is found in its material existence to reach a universal and general notion of it. In Henry's above scheme this abstraction marks the transition from the first level of most general knowledge, in which being and goodness are conceived as most proper to creatures, to the second. Henry is clear that in this step he has in mind the familiar and broadly Aristotelian kind of abstraction that yields common and universal concepts. When taken to its end, however, this process of abstraction does not result merely in a universal concept of being or goodness applicable to creatures alone, which is to say one proper to them, but in one that is *common* to both creator and creature (*quod dicitur 'bonum', hoc est commune creatori et creaturae.*)[10] To be sure, this notion is not univocally common, for it is not a distinct concept *included in both* those of God and creature. It is rather 'analogously common', for it *includes both* the concepts of God and creature in a confused way as one. Thus, for Henry, a perfection can be abstracted from a creature and conceived with such indeterminacy that it is not just the universal knowledge of a creature but a confused knowledge of *both* God and creature. This exceedingly abstract notion, which Henry calls 'analogously common', provides the necessary epistemological bridge from creature to God by constituting a concept of both at once.

Henry attempts to span the cognitive gulf between God and creatures, the knowledge of which he has otherwise limited to proper, simple and diverse notions, by means of his 'analogously common' concept. He has constructed it to perform the required epistemological functions of a truly common concept, for it is universal and applicable to both of its instances, but in such a way that it cannot be called univocal. None the less, Henry's solution is remarkable for how close it comes to an admission of univocity. Indeed, his analogous common concept so nearly functions as a univocal one that even Henry himself at times slips into seeing it as such. In describing how we abstract the general notions of being and the other transcendentals from creatures, so that we do not distinguish in such a notion what is proper to God from what is proper to creatures, Henry adds, 'just as also in univocal things we abstract a common nature' (*sicut etiam in univocis abstrahitur natura communis*). Elsewhere, Henry describes the universal concept of being abstracted from creatures as 'indifferently common to what belongs to God and creature' (*conceptus generalis ut entis . . . qui indifferenter communis est ad id quod est creatoris et ad id quod est creaturae*).[11] It is little wonder that Scotus will argue that

Henry cannot consistently deny univocity, if for no other reason than he appears to have all but admitted it.

As will be clear, the distance between Henry's revised analogous concept and Scotus's univocal one is accordingly not as great as the opposition in their positions might suggest. They both agree that being and the other transcendental perfections can be thought of without determination to either God or creature and that this is the result of abstraction from creatures. They diverge sharply, however, on the exact nature of this indeterminate conception. Henry denies that it is in fact a separate and distinct concept but holds rather that it is a confusion of two proper notions of being which are themselves simple, ultimate and irreducible. Scotus argues against Henry that to admit such an indeterminate apprehension of being and then to deny that it forms a bona fide, distinct, simple and univocal concept is a contradiction. However, in seeking to avoid the inconsistencies that he sees lurking within Henry's analogously common concept, Scotus must show that a truly univocal notion does not violate the real transcendence of God, which Henry's revised doctrine of analogy, whatever its faults, tried to preserve.

Duns Scotus on Univocity

In his commentaries on the *Sentences*, Scotus addresses the issue of the univocal concept of being in three separate but related contexts: the natural knowledge of God, the primary object of the human intellect and divine simplicity. All three discussions are closely connected, as Scotus's own numerous cross-references indicate. The first, on natural knowledge of God, is a lengthy, critical examination of Henry's position and contains Scotus's most sustained arguments for univocity.[12] After a detailed and systematic summary of Henry's account of our knowledge of God, Scotus replies that, while agreeing with Henry that such knowledge is possible, he departs from his position on five points. In the second of these five points, Scotus maintains against Henry that God is known not only in a concept analogous with, but also in one univocal to, creatures. It is an important but at times overlooked point that Scotus is not here rejecting the traditional view, upheld by Henry, that we have proper notions of God and creatures united by analogy or attribution. Rather, he is rejecting Henry's view that there can be *only* such proper concepts united only in that way. Scotus's point against Henry is that when perfections such as being and goodness are conceived in their utmost generality, they must be univocal not analogous notions. The precise target of Scotus's attack, then, is not Henry's commitment to a traditional doctrine of analogy, a version of which they both concede, but his conclusion that such excludes any univocal conception of being.

In an annotation to his criticism of Henry, Scotus at one point itemizes as many as ten arguments in favour of univocity, but gives five main proofs in the body of his discussion. Three of these are generally singled out as most important. The first of the five, the so-called arguments from 'certain and doubtful concepts', Scotus's own contemporaries labelled the 'Achilles' of his position. It runs as follows:

Major: An intellect certain about one concept, but doubtful about others, has a concept about which it is certain that is different from the concepts about which it is doubtful.

Minor: We can be certain that God is a being, but doubt whether God is infinite or finite being.

∴   The concept of being is different from the concept of infinite or finite being, and hence univocal, since asserted of both.

Scotus takes the major premiss to be evident, for one cannot be both certain and doubtful of the same concept. That is, one and the same concept predicated of the same subject cannot result in a proposition whose truth is both certain and doubtful. The minor premiss is *de facto* true, because past thinkers, such as the pre-Socratics, never doubted that the first principle was a being, but disagreed as to whether it was even material or immaterial, much less finite or infinite. Since the concept of being is different from those of infinite and finite being, but obviously predicated of both, it must be univocal.

Scotus's point, which he establishes more explicitly in the ensuing arguments, is that some univocal notion of being is presupposed in any natural knowledge of God. Ultimately, however much one doubts whether the concepts of infinite being or uncaused cause apply truly to God, such concepts are doubtful with respect to something that is certain. To be doubtful in all respects of some notion of God is simply to concede that one has no meaningful concept at all.

While Scotus has formulated his argument in sufficiently general terms to give it a universal force and appeal, he has none the less engineered it to expose what he sees as a fundamental absurdity lurking in Henry's analogously common concept of being. In effect, Scotus has crafted the minor premiss around Henry's analogous concept, substituting his own terminology of infinite and finite being for Henry's corresponding notions of negatively and privatively undetermined being. According to Henry, this analogously common notion of being is so abstract that we are in doubt as to whether it is a concept of negatively or privatively undetermined being. At the same time, Henry denies that there is any concept of being apart from these two proper concepts about which we are in doubt. Scotus's argument points out the inconsistency of these two claims: Henry must either concede that we have no certain knowledge of being at all in this analogous concept, for he allows only the two proper concepts of which we are admittedly doubtful, or that we are both certain and doubtful of the same concept. Thus, Henry's abstract, indeterminate notion of being is either vacuous or else it must be distinct from, and hence common to, either of the concepts proper to God and creature.

Recall that Henry's explanation was that there is no concept of being distinct from these two proper ones, but only a confused notion of both which *appears* univocal owing to their similarity. Accordingly, Henry would reply to Scotus that we are not certain of some distinct, common concept, as Scotus concludes, but only of a confused notion that seemed common. Scotus perceives Henry's manoeuvre as introducing scepticism at the most fundamental level of human knowledge. According to Scotus, it would destroy all univocity, for any allegedly univocal concept could always be denied on the grounds it was not one but two very similar notions which merely seemed to be one. Scotus's evident point is that if univocity cannot be ascertained with certainty at the level of our most abstract concepts, which are therefore primary, simple and irreducible, then it can never be determined. Furthermore, according to Henry, these two proper concepts of being must be ultimate and hence wholly simple – otherwise they would be resolvable into more primitive notions – and are therefore known in their totality and distinctly or not at all. Therefore, either they will always be seen as one or never will be, for, being wholly simple, no distinguishing element can be discovered in them which was not evident in the first place. Finally, either they were initially seen as wholly different concepts of being proper to God and creatures, and then it seems impossible in view of their disparity that they could have ever been confused as one, or they were seen in a relation of similarity owing to analogy. In the latter case they could not be initially known as one, for any two things seen as united in some relation must first be known as distinct. Therefore, these two notions would never appear to be one, simple concept, but only as distinct under a relation of similarity.

Scotus's first argument, then, attempts to draw out the apparent inconsistency in Henry's open admission, on the one side, that the intellect can conceive of being without determining it to God or creature, and his emphatic denial, on the other, that there is any concept of being distinct from those proper to God and creature. Scotus argues that Henry cannot claim that this indeterminate conception contains any certain knowledge of being at all unless he admits that it is a concept distinct from the concepts of being proper to God and creature. The reason is that, by Henry's own admission, the intellect is not certain at this point that it has either proper concept, for it has not yet distinguished between the two. It thus is either certain of no concept of being or is certain and doubtful of the same concept. Henry's device of making this analogous concept an *apparently* common and univocal concept, which is then later discerned to be two proper notions, collapses under scrutiny. Even if the simplicity of these two proper concepts of being did not make it impossible for them to be confused at one time and distinguished at another, they can only be seen as similar, and hence one, after first having been known as distinct and proper. As an epistemological explanation for the natural origin of our proper concept of God, Henry's analogously common notion simply begs the question. It presupposes the very proper concept of God that it is supposed to explain.

In his second argument, Scotus is explicit that denial of a univocal concept renders natural knowledge of God impossible. Specifically, Scotus attacks Henry's position on the grounds that no creature can be the immediate cause of a concept which is both simple and wholly proper to God. Yet this is Henry's only available account for the natural origins of our knowledge of God, given that he admits only two proper and simple concepts of being and excludes any which is common. Scotus maintains that it is patently absurd to hold that a creature can directly cause a simple and wholly proper concept of God, simply because such cannot be the concept of anything contained within the creature. Scotus argues that an object can only cause a concept of that which it contains either as an essential part (e.g. its *differentia* or genus) or virtually (e.g. an essential property). Obviously, the creature contains nothing proper to God as an essential part. Similarly, a creature cannot virtually contain anything proper to God, for one thing virtually contains another as the naturally prior contains the posterior or the cause its effect. For instance, premises virtually contain their conclusions in the sense that their greater truth and certitude has the 'power' (*virtus*) to produce or cause certitude of the conclusion. The creature, however, is naturally posterior and inferior to divine nature as its effect and therefore cannot virtually contain anything proper to God. Rather, just the reverse is true; God virtually contains the creature. Thus, if a creature can produce any concept of God at all, it must be one that is common to both, which Henry denies.

Scotus pursues a similar line of reasoning in his fourth proof, which examines the commonly admitted basis for natural knowledge of God, the so-called 'pure perfections' (*perfectiones simpliciter*), such as intellect, will or wisdom. Scotus argues that either these perfections have some meaning common to God and creature or not. If not, this is either because they are wholly proper to creatures, which no one admits, or they are wholly proper to God. If they are wholly proper to God, then they are not attributed to God because they are pure perfections, but are rather pure perfections because they are attributed to God. This, however, would violate the traditional and universally accepted procedure given by Anselm for determining what can be assigned to the divine nature. According to Anselm, we attribute to God those perfections which are pure in the sense that they contain of themselves no imperfection. As defined by Anselm, such a perfection is 'what absolutely taken is better to be than not'.[13] (For instance, colours are not pure perfections, since it is not absolutely better to be coloured than not.) But on Anselm's definition, one can determine what is a pure perfection without any reference to God. That is, on the received and accepted account of natural knowledge of God, something is first determined to constitute a pure perfection and then on that basis attributed to God, not the reverse. Consequently, something is not a pure perfection precisely because it is attributed to God but is such prior to that attribution. Pure perfections must therefore have some meaning that is common apart from the meaning it has as attributed and proper to God alone.

Once again Scotus argues that some common and hence univocal notion is presupposed by our analogous, proper concepts of God. In this case, the traditional doctrine of 'pure perfections' is seen to entail just such a common notion. If there were no common but only proper concepts of these perfections, then they could not be known apart from their attribution to God. Yet, exactly the opposite is prescribed by the traditional concept of pure perfections, for they are known independently of and prior to any relation to God.

Scotus makes the same point in a confirmation of this argument, this time using the equally traditional Dionysian procedures of removal and eminence. According to Scotus, all metaphysical enquiry about God proceeds by taking some formal notion (*ratio formalis*) and removing from it all imperfections with which it is found in a creature. For example, we take the formal notion of the will – a power for opposites – and remove any limitations connected with its existence in a creature, such as variability in its act of willing over time. We then attribute will to God by conceiving of it not just as lacking imperfection, but as possessing the greatest degree of perfection, such that it is infinitely powerful. This process presumes that the formal notion of the will which has been stripped of creaturely limitations is the same notion of will as is assigned the highest degree of perfection. If this is not the case, so that nothing of the notion of will abstracted from creatures remains when we attribute will to God, then perfections found in creatures tell us nothing about the perfection of God. As Scotus puts it, we could then no more say that the divine nature was an intellect, a will or wise than it was a rock. That is, the distinction traditionally made within creatures between pure perfections, which can be applied to God, and their other formal features, which cannot, would be meaningless on denial of any common notion of such perfections. If to be a 'perfection' has absolutely no common meaning as applied to God and creature, then perfection in creatures becomes tantamount to imperfection. Thus, 'wisdom' would be no more applicable to God than 'rock'.

The point of Scotus's fourth proof and its confirmation is that the traditional concepts and methods that are the accepted basis for natural knowledge of God presuppose a common notion of being and other such perfections. Elsewhere Scotus is more pointed: 'All masters and theologians seem to use a concept common to God and creature, although they deny this verbally when they apply it'.[14] There can be little doubt, however, that Scotus has Henry specifically in view. This is particularly evident in Scotus's corroborative argument based on the Dionysian procedure, from which, as shown, Henry constructed his own three-stage ascent to God. Scotus has pared this procedure to the two minimal steps of removal and eminence, which correspond respectively to what Henry calls knowing God *generalissime* and *generalius*. (In his third point of disagreement with Henry, Scotus discards Henry's final stage of conceiving God as wholly simple through negation and limits our highest simple concept of God to that of a pre-eminent or infinite being.) Scotus's point is that the Dionysian procedure requires that the notion or meaning (*ratio*) yielded by removal be the same notion to which eminence is applied, otherwise the first step would simply have no relevance to the second. Removal and eminence would not, as all theologians assume, form two stages of a continuous process of reasoning leading from a knowledge of creatures to God. As Scotus says, 'There would be no such process, but inquiry of this kind would have to be avoided' (*nullus esset talis processus, sed vitanda esset talis inquisitio*).[15] But this is exactly the situation in Henry's interpretation of the Dionysian process, for he holds that the *ratio* of a perfection arrived at by the abstraction and removal of created limitations is wholly other than that to which eminence is applied (*illud est alterius et alterius rationis*). Distinguishing between the epistemological functions of the ways of causality and eminence, Scotus denies that these two diverse *rationes* can be sufficiently connected by means of causal dependence, as Henry maintains. Something is not formally or essentially predicated of God, in the manner of a pure perfection, simply because it is an effect. A rock is an effect of God as exemplary cause in so far as it has an idea in the divine mind, yet the formal notion of 'rock' cannot be predicated of God in the same way as that of goodness, justice, truth or any other such perfection. Rather, perfections found in creatures must have some univocally common concept if they are to be predicated essentially of God as divine attributes, whereas things predicated of God as their cause need not have such a common notion. Henry cannot therefore use the way of causality to underwrite the way of eminence, for the epistemological requirements for the latter are greater than for the former. Thus, he must admit that his first stage issues in some notion common to God and creature.

The force of all this argumentation is that Henry cannot consistently uphold natural knowledge of the divine nature and then deny that being has some concept common to creatures and God. If being and the other perfections have only two simple and wholly diverse *rationes* or notions, one proper to creatures and the other to God, then creatures simply cannot yield any concepts relevant to the divine nature. The causal dependence of the creature on God is irrelevant here, because being, goodness and such are seen as divine *attributes* revelatory of God's nature, not because they are effects, but because they are perfections of a certain sort. Henry himself seems to have appreciated the limitations of the way of causality and attempted to supply the required conceptual unity by means of an 'analogously common notion', in which the two proper and diverse *rationes* were conceived in a confused way so as to appear univocal. Scotus saw this as an unworkable contrivance vulnerable to the most obvious of absurdities, such as that the intellect could lack certitude about its most fundamental concepts. In the face of Henry's strained and artificial attempts to sustain natural knowledge of God while denying any bona fide common concept, Scotus replaced Henry's 'analogous', confused notion of two proper *rationes* that appeared univocal with a distinct concept of a single, simple *ratio* that in fact was univocal. Accordingly, where for Henry being conceived in its utmost generality and community was a complex and confused concept, and the concepts proper to God and creatures were simple and distinct, for Scotus just the reverse became the case. The most general and indeterminate concept of being was irreducibly simple and common, and thus known in a distinct rather than a confused way, while the concepts of being proper to God and creature were complex, or at least not irreducibly simple. By admitting a simple and univocal concept of being, Scotus provided a true conceptual community between God and creature and placed the project of natural knowledge of the divine nature on a firm epistemological footing.

Scotus's univocal concept of being clearly had great epistemological advantages over Henry's revised version of analogy. It eliminated Henry's unsatisfactory attempt to make an unstable conflation of equivocal notions do the epistemological work of a genuinely univocal concept merely because such a conflation appeared univocal. Univocity not only provided a true conceptual community between God and creature, but made being suitable as a primary object of the mind by rendering its conception certain, simple and prior. In granting univocity, Scotus replaced Henry's two concepts of being with a single one, his doubtful concepts with a certain one, his relational concepts with an absolute one, and his confused concepts with a distinct one. Yet these epistemological advantages of univocity came at a very high metaphysical cost, which is precisely why Henry went to such extreme lengths to deny that there was in truth any such concept. The cost of Scotus's univocal concept of being, as one objector put it, was nothing less than 'to destroy the whole of philosophy'.[16]

While Scotus portrayed univocity as contained with the tradition of natural theology, so that it could be found in 'arguments frequently made or implied by doctors and the saints', he had to reconcile it with a daunting array of philosophical authorities to the contrary. Scotus himself did not fail to raise and confront the various conflicts that a univocal concept of being appeared to present to the philosophical tradition, particularly that of Aristotle. Thus, for instance, univocity would remove a pillar of Aristotle's metaphysics, namely, that 'being is said in many ways', which meant that being was not univocal but a type of equivocal. It would destroy the categories as ultimate classifications or genera, for they would become species under the higher class of being. Similarly, it would render the five predicables of Porphyry inadequate, for being would form a sixth universal. Worst of all, God would enter a community of being with creatures. The divine nature would not be a wholly simple and pure act, but a composite of being and difference.

All of these impossible conclusions really expressed one and the same difficulty in different ways. Scotus's univocal concept of being appeared to his contemporaries to destroy all of philosophy – Aristotle's conception of metaphysics, the categories, the predicables, and even the distinction between God and creatures – because it appeared to destroy being itself as a transcendental. On the common view, a 'univocal transcendental' was a contradiction in terms, precisely because the categories or supreme genera were regarded as the highest classes of univocal predicates. Since a transcendental was by definition beyond the categories, it could not be univocal. This conviction was clearly stated by Peter Olivi, a theologian writing in the generation before Scotus: 'The nature of being, one, and true is so common to all things that it transcends the nature of a genus and everything univocal.'[17] In other words, on the common view, univocity destroyed being as a transcendental because it reduced being to a genus. Indicative of this common view was the use of Aristotle's claim that being and one could not fall under a genus as a standard authority against univocity.

This conventional identification of univocal and generic concepts resulted from the requirement, explicitly invoked by Henry in this connection, that there must be a strict correspondence between real and conceptual community. Any real, univocal concept, as opposed to a purely logical or mind-dependent notion, had to be based on some type of corresponding real community or agreement. Since the categories by definition constituted the highest classes of reality, they formed the outer boundaries of real agreement. Accordingly, there could be no univocal concept of anything more universal than these categories or genera, for to such a notion would correspond no real community. If this was true of the categories, so much more of God and creatures, whose real diversity was immeasurably greater than that between any two genera. The challenge facing Scotus was thus clear if his doctrine of univocity was not to destroy all of philosophy by reducing being to a genus. He had to explain how there could be a truly univocal notion of being to which there corresponded no real agreement. Scotus himself was completely aware that this was the universally perceived impasse to making being and the other transcendentals univocal. The central difficulty to be overcome was that 'God and creatures are wholly diverse in reality, agreeing in no reality . . . and nevertheless agree in one concept' (*Deus et creatura realiter sunt primo diversa, in nulla realitate convenientia . . . et tamen conveniunt in uno conceptu*).[18]

This is the problem Henry saw but could not solve. He could not see how to unite God and creatures under some common concept of being without also uniting them in some common reality, that is, without bringing them under being as a genus. For Henry the one required the other, as exemplified by Plato, who held being was univocal because it was a genus (*Plato ponens ens esse genus, tanquam sit nominis entis unum aliquid commune conceptum*).[19] Because Henry could not resolve this difficulty, he tried to construct a type of conceptual community by conflating proper concepts rather than admit a single, common one. Scotus was the first to find a way around this impasse, and his solution involved some of the most innovative aspects of his metaphysics.

Scotus's solution is found in his question on divine simplicity, which he specifically formulated to draw out just his difficulty: 'Is it compatible with divine simplicity that God, or anything formally predicated of God, be in a genus?'[20] As the lead objection to the question makes clear, the issue is whether Scotus's position of univocity, previously established in distinction 3, entails that God is in a genus.

It seems that [God is in a genus], because God is formally a being. Being, however, signifies a concept predicated of God

315

quidditatively (*in quid*). This concept of being is not proper to God, but common to God and creature, as was said in distinction 3. Therefore, in order for this common concept to become proper [to God] it must be determined by some determining concept. That determining concept is related to the concept of being just as a qualitative concept (*quale*) to a quidditative concept (*quid*), and consequently as the concept of a *differentia* to a genus.

(*Ord.* 1 d.8 n.39 (Vat. 4.169))

The above line of argument is precisely why Henry so adamantly refused to admit both a common and proper concept of divine being and allowed only a proper one. It is impossible to admit both concepts of God without conceding that the proper one itself is a composite of common and distinguishing notions which must be related in effect as potency and act, or as the objection puts it, as determined and determining. This is simply to admit that the common notion is a genus and the distinguishing one a *differentia*. This conclusion follows especially from Scotus's position, because he admits that the common concept of being applies to God quidditatively, which means that it is the concept of a 'what' (*quid*). The distinguishing concept will accordingly specify or qualify being as a kind (*quale*), so that the two will conform exactly to the classical relation of genus to *differentia* as *quid* to *quale*.

In his lengthy reply to the objection, Scotus concedes that there is a common concept of being and that it is 'contracted' or determined by the notions of infinite and finite to result in concepts proper to God and creatures. He even concedes that the common and contracting or determining concepts are related as *quid* and *quale*. He denies, however, that they are respectively concepts of a genus and its *differentiae*. As for the first point, Scotus argues that the univocal concept of being cannot be that of a genus. The reason is that being so conceived is common to both the finite (creatures) and the infinite (God), and this community exceeds that of any genus. No generic concept can be so common, for by definition the concept of a genus is that of a reality potential to some further, perfecting reality added by the *differentia*. What is infinite in being, however, cannot be potential to any further reality. Accordingly, since a genus by definition involves potentiality, the concept of being common to God and creatures cannot be that of a genus, for the infinite being of God can never be conceived, however commonly or indeterminately, as some reality potential to further perfection. The second part of Scotus's response is that the determining concepts of infinite and finite do not correspond to those of specific *differentiae*. Here the reason is that infinity and finitude do not indicate the addition of some reality outside that given in the common concept of being, but only degrees or grades of perfection intrinsic to the reality of being. The concept of a *differentia*, however, is always of some reality outside of and added to that of the genus.

Scotus's response relies on his technical conception of a formal, extramental distinction of two realities, on the one hand, and his so-called 'modal' distinction between a reality and its intrinsic grades or modes of perfection, on the other. As for the first, Scotus recognizes within one and the same thing (*res*) a distinction of realities, formalities or entities (*realitates, formalitates, entitates*), as he variously calls them, corresponding to our different concepts of that thing. Such realities are said to be 'formally distinct', but really identical or united within one and the same thing.[21] Such a 'formal distinction' is for Scotus not merely conceptual but real in the sense that it obtains prior to any consideration of the intellect. Scotus holds that at minimum this formal distinction between two realities is required to provide a real basis for the concepts of genus and *differentia*. According to Scotus, this degree of distinction is minimally needed to sustain any real relationship of potency to act required for genus and difference. The concept of a genus is taken from the one reality, which is perfected by and potential to, the formally distinct reality from which the difference is taken. Scotus argues that unless genus and *differentia* are at least formally distinct realities, the concept of the genus would coincide with the entire reality of the species, rendering the addition of specific *differentia* in a definition redundant.

In addition to this formal distinction of realities in one and the same thing, Scotus recognizes a lesser distinction between a reality and its degree of perfection, or in Scotus's terminology, its intrinsic mode. This is the distinction, for instance, between an accidental form, such as white, and the degrees of intensity with which it is actually found. For example, white can be differentiated into degrees or shades, yet these degrees do not form different species of colour. Or again, a species of precious stone, such as diamond, can be distinguished according to the various degrees of perfection that make up the gemmologist's scale, from imperfect to flawless, yet these gradations do not each one constitute a different species of gem. Such grades or modes are said to be 'intrinsic' because they do not add, as a specific *differentia* does to a genus, a new reality extrinsic to the form of which they are the grades. They rather indicate different quantitative degrees, as it were, of one and the same reality or form. Scotus's model here is the medieval theory of intension and remission of accidental forms. According to this theory, accidental forms, such as colours, heat, and cognitive and moral habits, are said to have a certain extension or 'latitude' (*latitudo*) within which they can be increased (*intensio*) or decreased (*remissio*) without a change in the essence or species of the form itself.[22]

In light of these technical refinements, Scotus's answer to the above objection is that the relationship of the common concept of being to its contracting or determining notions of infinity and finitude does not correspond to that of genus and *differentia*, for this requires two formally distinct realities related as potency and act. The common concept of being cannot involve the element of potentiality found in a genus, for this would render it inapplicable in any way to the divine being, and hence not common to God and creatures. Rather, being and its qualifying concepts of infinity and finitude correspond to the relation of a reality and its intrinsic modes of perfection. The categorical analogue for the common concept of transcendental being is not therefore a genus and its specific differences, but rather a specific form and its grades of intension and remission. Clearly, Scotus thinks he has found in this categorical analogue of intension and remission a model for common and differentiating concepts which escapes the real relation of potency and act required in genus and *differentia*. The various degrees of intensity are *real* but not *specific differentiae* of a form. As it actually exists, white is found in different degrees of brilliance or intensity, and these are *real differentiae* of that form. Yet this diversity within the form of whiteness is not one produced by specific *differentiae*, otherwise every shade of white would constitute a different species of colour. Rather, the intensive grades of a form result from *differentiae* less than specific, albeit real, because they are intrinsic to the nature of the form itself. Specific *differentiae* by contrast always add a new reality in kind. By appealing to a recognized distinction within the categories between a form and its degrees, which is less than that of genus and *differentia*, Scotus thinks he can explain how the common concept of being can be 'contracted' by the finite and infinite without reducing being to a genus.

Yet Scotus realizes that this reply does not fully resolve the difficulty of the real basis for this common concept of being, so that univocity still poses a threat to divine simplicity. The problem is that Scotus holds that the concept of being univocally common to God and creatures is both *real* and distinct from the concept of infinite being proper to God. Since this common concept is *real*, it must be taken from some corresponding reality in God that is common. The original objection now reappears, because Scotus still has to admit that there will be two realities in God, one which is common to account for the real, common concept of being and another to account for the proper concept of God. These realities will be related as potency to act and hence as genus and *differentia*. The problem thus seems inescapable. If the common concept of being is real, it must be of something real in God. But to admit a common reality in God is nothing less than to place God under a genus. Scotus himself sharply focuses the difficulty: 'Here is doubted how a real concept common to God and creature is possible unless it is taken from some reality of the same genus.'[23]

Scotus replies that both the common concept of being univocal to God and creatures and the concept proper to God are taken from one and the same reality of infinite being. The implicit assumption of the objection denied by Scotus is that in order for a common concept to be real, it must always be an adequate or perfect concept of the reality conceived. Rather, the common and proper concepts of God are related as imperfect and perfect conceptions of one and the same reality, not as perfect or adequate concepts of two distinct realities. Scotus's response exploits his distinction between a reality and its intrinsic mode or grade of perfection to account for how one and the same reality can cause both a perfect concept, which is proper, and an imperfect concept, which is common. For example, some particular instance of white existing at the tenth grade of intensity can be conceived perfectly, and then it is known according to the degree of perfection with which it is actually found. That same instance of white can be conceived imperfectly, and then only the nature of 'whiteness' as such, apart from the real condition of its grade of intensity, is known. The former is a proper concept of whiteness in some determinate grade, the latter a concept common to the various instances of white differing in degrees. No concept common as a genus, however, can ever result simply from conceiving a reality in an imperfect way. Rather, as just seen, to the concepts of genus and *differentia* there must correspond two different realities, and, in each case, there can be a perfect and adequate concept of the corresponding reality.

As applied to the renewed form of the initial objection, Scotus's distinction means that our univocally common concept of being does not entail a corresponding common reality in God, because that common concept is not a perfect or adequate concept of any reality. Rather, it is an imperfect concept of the reality of infinite being proper to God or of finite being proper to creatures. To put it another way, that concept of being is common to God and creatures because in it the two wholly diverse realities of infinite and finite being are conceived in an imperfect way. In an annotation to this reply, Scotus expresses in technical language his answer to the difficulty of the real basis for the univocal concept of being:

> Note [in this answer] how there can be a primary intention [i.e. a real as opposed to a secondary or merely logical

concept] of 'a' and 'b' that is common and nothing of a single
nature corresponds in reality, but two wholly diverse formal
objects [i.e. God and creature] are understood in one first
intention, although *either imperfectly.*

(*Ordinatio* 1 d.8 n.136 (Vat. 4.221))

This constitutes Scotus's ultimate resolution of the metaphysical
impasse to a univocal concept of being. It consists of recognizing a
distinction that is real but less than that of two different realities. Only
given such a lesser distinction is it possible to provide an ontological
foundation for common and proper concepts that not are related as
genus and *differentia.* Scotus himself is clear that the solution to the
objective basis for a univocal concept of being requires such a lesser
distinction, namely, that of a reality and its intrinsic mode: 'Therefore,
a distinction is required between that from which the common concept
[of being] is taken and that from which the proper concept is taken,
not a distinction of reality and reality, but of reality and the proper
and intrinsic mode of the same reality' (*Ord.* 1 d.8 n.139 [13.29] 4,
222). In Scotus's view, Henry and his contemporaries were led to deny
univocity because they demanded that every distinction in real concepts
be based upon a corresponding distinction of realities. They failed to
see that the boundaries between our concepts can be more refined, so
that they do not always answer to a distinction of realities but can be
based on one between a reality and its degree of perfection. Such is
sufficient for perfect and imperfect conceptions of the same reality,
which are related as proper and common concepts of it. A concept of
being which is common by virtue of its imperfection is all that is
required for it to be univocal to God and creature.

Having solved this problem, however, Scotus faced a final hurdle
to univocity in the authority of Aristotle, who repeatedly states that
being is a type of equivocal. From this it is concluded that being
cannot be univocal. Scotus replies that this reasoning assumes that
analogy and univocity are incompatible, which he denies. First,
according to Aristotle himself, there is a first in every genus, which is
the measure of all in that class (*Metaphysics* 10.1 (1052b18)), such as
is the case with human being in the genus of animal. Despite this
relationship of attribution, in which human being constitutes the
primary instance of animal to which all others are referred, Scotus
argues that all still admit a single notion of animal univocal to all in
the genus. Similarly, the order and attribution existing between the
proper and analogous concepts of being is consistent with some
univocal notion common to both. Second, the real or natural philosopher (i.e. the physicist, who deals with material beings) takes as
equivocal the diverse genera which the logician sees as univocal, for

320

in reality only the form of the ultimate species is truly univocal. So, Scotus concludes, all of the citations of Aristotle where being is claimed to be analogous should be read as referring to a real diversity of beings among which there is attribution, which is none the less consistent with some univocally common concept abstracted from them.[24] Scotus's second response will form the basis for ensuing attempts by Scotists to reconcile his doctrine of univocity with Aquinas's position on analogy. In reconciling the two views, Aquinas is portrayed as maintaining real analogy among beings, while Scotus is seen as holding a purely conceptual unity.

CONCLUSION

There can be no question that in maintaining a concept of being univocally common to God and creatures, Scotus moved beyond the common view of the transcendentals in a dramatic and important way. The doctrine of univocity counts as one of the genuinely original results of Latin medieval philosophy, and its impact was felt well into the modern period. At the same time, Scotus's achievement depended in an intimate way on prior developments by Henry of Ghent. As has been repeatedly stressed, this is in fact so true that Scotus's doctrine of univocity should properly be seen not as a complete rejection but as a revision of Henry's own unique understanding of analogy. Specifically, Scotus's simple, univocal concept was a modification of Henry's revised 'analogously common' notion of being. Henry's extended sense of an 'analogous concept' had many features in common with Scotus's univocal one: it was a conception of being as completely undetermined, the result of abstraction from creatures, and the epistemological foundation for natural knowledge of the divine nature. Scotus accepted these aspects of Henry's indeterminate conception of being, and then argued that Henry could not consistently deny that such a conception formed a truly unified, distinct, and common notion unto itself. Scotus accordingly abandoned Henry's analogous notion of being, but did so by making it into the very univocal concept Henry claimed it appeared to be, but in truth was not. In other words, the univocal concept of being for which Scotus argues is, in many important respects, the very one that Henry described but rejected as merely apparent: a single, simple concept common to God and creature and different from concepts of both (*aliquis unicus intellectus simplex communis ad Deum et creaturam, alius praeter intellectum Dei aut creaturae*).[25] These words of Henry answer quite closely to the concept demonstrated by Scotus, particularly in his first argument for univocity. To be sure, in upholding the univocal notion which Henry had rejected Scotus had to move beyond

Henry's understanding of univocity in an important and creative way, most notably by detaching univocal community from the ontological limitations of a genus. On the other hand, it is not true that Scotus advanced a univocal concept of being which Henry had simply failed to see altogether; Henry saw a good part of it, but could not see how to sustain it.

The close connection between Scotus and Henry examined here in their disagreement over the nature of transcendental concepts is found to various degrees in many other areas of their thought. For example, Scotus rejects more and appropriates less in his attacks on Henry's version of Augustinian illumination and his theory of exemplar causality, according to which creatures have a necessary and eternal 'essential being' (*esse essentiae*) as divine ideas. In other areas, Scotus appropriates more and rejects less, such as in his proofs for the existence of God. In nearly all cases, however, a proper understanding of Scotus will depend on appreciating his relationship to Henry.

 NOTES

1 Henry, *Summa* a.22 q.5 ([13.2] I f. 134v).

2 L. Hödl, 'Introduction à l'edition de la *Summa* d'Henry de Gand', in Macken's edition of Henry's *Summa* articles 31–4 [13.3] xiii–xiv.

3 Roger Marston, *Quaestiones disputatae De emanatione divine, De statu naturae lapsae, De anima*, Grottaferrata, 1932, p. 412.

4 Aquinas's own position is more nuanced, but this is the aspect of it stressed by Henry. See J. Wippel [13.27] 215–42.

5 Henry's express treatment of analogy is given in *Summa* a.21 q.2 ([13.2] I f. 123v–125v).

6 See Aristotle, *Categories* 1 (1a1–15) and especially *Metaphysics* 4.1 (1003a32–b5). For Aristotle's notion of equivocity, which the scholastics called analogy, see J. Owens, *The Doctrine of Being in the Aristotelian Metaphysics*, 3rd edn, Toronto, 1978, pp. 107–36.

7 Cf. Henry, *Quodlibeta* 13 q.10 ([13.3] (1985) 65–7).

8 Henry's account of natural knowledge of the divine *quid est* occupies *Summa* a.24, especially qq. 4, 7 and 9. See the second article by Pegis in [13.23].

9 *Summa* a.24 q.6 ([13.2] I f. 142v).

10 *Summa* a.24 q.6 ([13.2] I f. 142v).

11 For these two quotations, see Henry *Summa* a.24 q.7 ([13.2] I f. 144v).

12 This part of Scotus's discussion, which is the basis of what follows, is found translated according to the Vivès edition in Wolter [13.35] 13–33.

13 Scotus cites Anselm, *Monologion c.*15 (ed. Schmitt [6.11] I: 28–9) in this connection, but the association of this doctrine with Anselm was a commonplace.

14 Duns Scotus 1 *Lectura* d.3 n.29 ([13.29] 16.235).

15 1 *Lectura* d.8 n.79 ([13.29] 17.27).

16 1 *Lectura* d.3 n.105 ([13.29] 16.264).

17 S. Brown, 'Petrus Joannis Olivi, *Quaestiones logicales*: critical text', *Traditio* 52 (1986): 36–7.
18 1 *Lectura* d.8 n.129 ([13.29] 17.46).
19 *Summa* a.21 q.2 ([13.2] I f. 124v).
20 Scotus, 1 *Ordinatio* d.8 p. 1 q.3 ([13.29] 4.169–230).
21 See the entries under 'Formal Distinction' in the bibliography. Scotus varied both his terminology and definition of the formal distinction between Oxford and Paris, but this does not affect the present point.
22 On this theory, see for example J. Wippel, 'Godfrey of Fontaines on intension and remission of accidental forms', *Franciscan Studies* 39 (1979): 343–55.
23 1 *Ordinatio* d.8 n.137 ([13.29] 4.221).
24 1 *Ordinatio* d.8 n.48, 83 ([13.29] 4.172, 191–2).
25 *Summa* a.21 q.2 ([13.2] I f. 124v).

❧❧❧ BIBLIOGRAPHY ❧❧❧

Henry of Ghent

Original language editions

13.1 *Quodlibeta Magistri Henrici Goethals a Gandavo Doctoris Solemnis*, Paris, I. Badius, 1518; repr. in 2 vols, Louvain, Bibliothèque, SJ, 1961. (Referred to as the Badius edition, after its printer.)

13.2 *Summae quaestionum ordinariarum*, Paris, 1520; repr. in 2 vols, St. Bonaventure, NY, Franciscan Institute, 1953 (*Summa*).

13.3 *Henrici de Gandavo opera omnia*, general editor R. Macken, Leuven, University Press, 1979– . (The planned critical edition is expected to run to some 40 volumes including several on the manuscripts of Henry's works and his life. To date eight *Quodlibeta* have appeared: I (ed. R. Macken, 1979), II (ed. R. Wielockx, 1983), VI (ed. G. Wilson, 1987), VII (ed. G. Wilson, 1991), IX (ed. R. Macken, 1983), X (ed. R. Macken, 1981), XII qq. 1–30 (ed. J. Decorte, 1987), XII q. 31 = *Tractatus super facto praelatorum et fratrum* (ed. L. Hödl, 1989) and XIII (ed. J. Decorte, 1985). The edition of the *Summa* is also under way, and two volumes have appeared: articles 31–4 (ed. R. Macken, 1991) and articles 35–40 (ed. G. Wilson, 1994).)

English translations

13.4 Wippel, J. F. and Wolter, A. B. (eds) *Medieval Philosophy*, New York, Free Press, 1969, pp. 378–89. (Translation of Henry of Ghent's proof for the existence of God in *Summa* a.22 q.4).

13.5 *Quodlibetal Questions on Free Will*, trans. R. J. Teske, Milwaukee, Wis., Marquette University Press, 1993.

Bibliographies

13.6   Laarmann, M. 'Bibliographia auxiliaris de vita, operibus et doctrina Henrici de Gandavo', *Franzikanische Studien* 73 (1991): 324–66.

13.7   Macken, R. *Bibliographie d'Henri de Gand*, Leuven, 1994. (More a bibliography of late thirteenth-century philosophy. Inaccurate in places.)

Studies

13.8   Brown, J. V. 'Duns Scotus on Henry of Ghent's arguments for divine illumination: the statement of the case', *Vivarium* 14 (1976): 94–113.

13.9   —— 'Duns Scotus on the possibility of knowing genuine truth: the reply to Henry of Ghent in the *Lectura prima* and in the *Ordinatio*', *Recherches de théologie ancienne et médiévale* 51 (1984): 136–82.

13.10 Brown, S. 'Avicenna and the unity of the concept of being: the interpretations of Henry of Ghent, Duns Scotus, Gerard of Bologna and Peter Aureoli', *Franciscan Studies* 25 (1965): 117–50.

13.11 —— 'Henry of Ghent', in *Individuation in Scholasticism: the Later Middle Ages and the Counter-Reformation, 1150–1650*, ed. J. J. E. Gracia, Albany, NY, State University of New York Press, 1994, pp. 195–220.

13.12 Dumont, S. D. 'The *quaestio si est* and the metaphysical proof for the existence of God according to Henry of Ghent and J. Duns Scotus', *Franziskanische Studien* 66 (1984): 335–67.

13.13 —— 'Time, contradiction and free will in the late thirteenth century', *Documenti e studi sulla Tradizione Filosofica Medievale* 3.2 (1992): 199–235.

13.14 Macken, R. 'La temporalité radicale de la créature selon Henri de Gand', *Recherches de théologie ancienne et médiévale* 38 (1971): 211–72.

13.15 —— 'La théorie de l'illumination divine dans la philosophie d'Henri de Gand', *Recherches de théologie ancienne et médiévale* 39 (1972): 82–112.

13.16 —— 'La volonté humaine, faculté plus élevée que l'intelligence selon Henri de Gand', *Recherches de théologie ancienne et médiévale* 42 (1975): 5–51.

13.17 —— 'The metaphysical proof for the existence of God in the philosophy of Henry of Ghent', *Franziskanische Studien* 68 (1986): 247–60.

13.18 Marrone, S. P. *Truth and Scientific Knowledge in the Thought of Henry of Ghent*, Harvard University Press, Cambridge, Mass., 1985.

13.19 —— 'Matthew of Aquasparta, Henry of Ghent and Augustinian epistemology after Bonaventure', *Franziskanische Studien* 65 (1983): 252–90.

13.20 —— 'Henry of Ghent and Duns Scotus on the knowledge of being', *Speculum* 63 (1988): 22–57.

13.21 *Mediaevalia: Textos e Estudos* (Porto), ed. M. Pachecho, 3 (1993). (Special issue devoted to Henry of Ghent.)

13.22 Paulus, J. *Henri de Gand: Essai sur les tendances de sa métaphysique*, Paris, Vrin, 1938.

13.23 Pegis, A. 'Toward a new way to God: Henry of Ghent', *Mediaeval Studies* 30 (1968): 226–47; 31 (1969): 93–116; 33 (1971): 158–79.

13.24 Porro, P. *Enrico di Gand: La via delle proposizioni universali*, Bari, 1993. (Contains complete bibliography on Henry, arranged chronologically.)

13.25 Wielockx, R. (ed.) *Aegidii Romani Opera Omnia III.1: Apologia*, Florence, Olschki, 1985. (Contains much material on Henry of Ghent, especially concerning his role in the condemnations of 1277 and the censure of Giles of Rome.)

13.26 Wippel, J. F. 'The relationship between essence and existence in late thirteenth-century thought: Giles of Rome, Henry of Ghent, Godfrey of Fontaines, James of Viterbo', in *Philosophies of Existence: Ancient and Medieval*, ed. P. Morewedge, New York, Fordham University Press, 1982, pp. 131–64.

13.27 —— 'Divine knowledge, divine power and human freedom in Thomas Aquinas and Henry of Ghent', in *Metaphysical Themes in Thomas Aquinas*, Washington, DC, Catholic University of America Press, 1984, pp. 243–70.

Duns Scotus

Original language editions

13.28 *Opera omnia. Editio nova iuxta editionem Waddingi XII tomos continentem a patribus Franciscanis de observantia accurante recognita*, 26 vols, Paris, Vivès, 1891–5. (Vivès edition. Modernized reprint of the Wadding edition (Lyons, 1639). Contains many spurious works. For the certainly authentic works, see C. Balić, *John Duns Scotus: Some Reflections on the Occasion of the Seventh Centenary of his Birth*, Rome, 1966, pp. 29–44. Since the critical, Vatican edition is far from complete, this is still the only text for many of Scotus's writings. Even for those texts which have been critically edited, the edition remains valuable for the scholia, parallel citations and commentaries by later Scotists.)

13.29 *Opera omnia studio et cura Commissionis Scotisticae ad fidem codicum edita*, Vatican City, Typis Polyglottis Vaticanis, 1950– . (Vatican edition. Planned critical edition of Scotus's writings. To date: vols 1–7 = *Ordinatio* (to 2 d. 3); vols 16–19 = *Lectura*.)

13.30 *John Duns Scotus: a Treatise on God as First Principle*, ed. A. B. Wolter, Chicago, Franciscan Herald Press, 1966; 2nd rev. edn, 1983. (The revised edition adds an extensive commentary.)

13.31 *Obras del Doctor Sutil, Juan Duns Escoto: Cuestiones Cuodlibetales*, ed. F. Alluntis, Madrid, Biblioteca De Autores Cristianos, 1968. (Revision of Vivès text of the *Quodlibetal Questions*.)

English translations

13.32 *A Scholastic Miscellany: Anselm to Ockham*, ed. E. Fairweather, Philadelphia, Pa., Westminster Press, 1956, pp. 428–39. (Translation of *Ordinatio* question on whether God's existence is self-evident.)

13.33 *Contingency and Freedom: John Duns Scotus, Lectura I 39*, trans. A. Vos, Dordrecht, Kluwer, 1994. (Translation of *Lectura* questions on divine foreknowledge.)

13.34 *Duns Scotus on the Will and Morality*, ed. and trans. A. B. Wolter, Washington, DC, Catholic University of America Press, 1987.

13.35 *Duns Scotus, Philosophical Writings*, trans. A. B. Wolter, Indianapolis, Ind. and Cambridge, Hackett, 1987. (Translation of selections from the *Ordinatio* with facing Latin text of the Vivès edition.)

13.36 *Five Texts on the Medieval Problem of Universals*, trans. P. V. Spade, Indianapolis, Ind. and Cambridge, Hackett, 1994, 57–113. (Translation of *Ordinatio* questions on the principle of individuation.)

13.37 *God and Creatures: the Quodlibetal Questions*, trans. F. Alluntis and A. B. Wolter, Princeton, NJ, Princeton University Press, 1975; repr. Washington, DC, Catholic University of America Press, 1987. (Includes helpful glossary of Scotistic vocabulary.)

13.38 Wippel, J. F. and Wolter, A. (eds) [13.4] 402–19. (*Lectura* or early version of Scotus's proof for the existence of God.)

13.39 Wolter, A. 'Duns Scotus on the necessity of revealed knowledge', *Franciscan Studies* 11 (1951): 231–71. (Translation of the prologue to the *Ordinatio*.)

13.40 Wolter, A. and Adams, M. 'Duns Scotus' Parisian proof for the existence of God', *Franciscan Studies* 42 (1982): 248–321.

13.41 Wolter, A. B. and Frank, W. A. *Duns Scotus, metaphysician*, West Lafayette, Ind., Purdue University Press, 1995. (Selected texts with facing Latin and commentary.)

Bibliographies

13.42 Schaefer, O. *Bibliographia de vita operibus et doctrina Ioannis Duns Scoti, Saec. XIX–XX*, Rome, Orbis Catholicus-Herder, 1955.

13.43 —— 'Resenha abreviada da bibliographia escotista mais recente (1954–1966)', *Revistas Portuguesa de Filosofia* 23 (1967): 338–63.

13.44 Cress, D. 'Toward a bibliography on Duns Scotus on the existence of God', *Franciscan Studies* 35 (1975): 45–65.

Collections of articles

(The first five items below are proceedings of the International Scotistic Congress (*Congressus Scotisticus Internationalis*) and contain many articles on all aspects of Scotus's thought.)

13.45 *De doctrina Ioannis Duns Scoti*, 4 vols, Rome, Cura Commissionis Scotisticae, 1968.

13.46 *Deus et homo ad mentem I. Duns Scoti*, Rome, Societas Internationalis Scotisticae, 1972.

13.47 *Regnum hominis et regnum Dei*, 2 vols, ed. C. Bérubé, Rome, Societas Internationalis Scotistica, 1978.

13.48 *Homo et Mundus*, ed. C. Bérubé, Rome, Societas Internationalis Scotistica, 1981.

13.49 *Via Scoti. Methodologica ad mentem Joannis Duns Scoti*, 2 vols, ed. L. Sileo, Rome, Edizioni Antonianum, 1995.

13.50 *Duns Scotus*, ed. A. B. Wolter, *American Catholic Philosophical Quarterly*, 67 (1993).

13.51 John Duns Scotus, 1265–1965, in J. K. Ryan and B. Bonansea (eds) *Studies in Philosophy and the History of Philosophy* 3, Washington, DC, Catholic University of America, 1965.

13.52 *Metaphysik und Ethik bei Johannes Duns Scotus: Neue Forschungsperspektiven*, ed. M. Dreyer and R. Wood, Leiden, E. J. Brill, 1996.

13.53 *Philosophy of John Duns Scotus in Commemoration of the 700th Anniversary of his Birth*, Monist 49 (1965).

13.54 Wolter, A. B. *The Philosophical Theology of John Duns Scotus*, ed. M. Adams, Ithaca, NY, Cornell University Press, 1990. (Collection of many of Wolter's articles on Scotus.)

General studies

13.55 Gilson, E. *Jean Duns Scot: Introduction à ses positions fondamentales*, Paris, Vrin, 1952. (A comprehensive book on Scotus's philosophy, but of limited value owing to its failure to take account of Henry of Ghent.)

13.56 Honnefelder, L. *Ens inquantum ens. Der Begriff des Seienden als solchen als Gegenstand der Metaphysik nach der Lehre des Johannes Duns Scotus* (BGPTMA, n.f. 16), Münster, Aschendorff, 1979. (Extensive work on Scotus's conception of the science of metaphysics.)

13.57 Wolter, A. B. *The Transcendentals and their Function in the Philosophy of Duns Scotus*, St Bonaventure, NY, Franciscan Institute, 1946. (A study still regarded as the best introduction to Scotus's metaphysics.)

Univocity

13.58 Boulnois, O. *Jean Duns Scot: Sur la connaissance de Dieu et l'univocié de l'étant*, Paris, Presses Universitaires de France, 1988.

13.59 Dumont, S. D. 'The univocity of being in the fourteenth century', *Mediaeval Studies* 49 (1987): 1–75; 50 (1988): 186–256; (with S. Brown) 51 (1989): 1–129.

13.60 —— 'Transcendental being: Scotus and Scotists', *Topoi* 11 (1992): 135–48.

13.61 Marrone, S. P. 'The notion of univocity in Duns Scotus's early works', *Franciscan Studies* 43 (1983): 347–95.

Individuation

13.62 Dumont, S. D. 'The question on individuation in Scotus's *Quaestiones in Metaphysicam*', in [13.49] I, 193–227.

13.63 King, P. 'Duns Scotus on the common nature and the individual difference', *Philosophical Topics* 20, 2 (1992): 51–76.

13.64 Rudavsky, T. 'The doctrine of individuation in Duns Scotus', *Franziskanische Studien* 59 (1977): 320–77 and 62 (1980): 62–83.

13.65 Wolter, A. B. 'Scotus's individuation theory', in [13.54] 98–124.

Formal distinction

13.66 Adams, M. M. 'Universals in the fourteenth century', in *CHLMP* pp. 411–39.
13.67 Wolter, A. B. 'The formal distinction', in [13.54] 45–60.

Epistemology

13.68 Dumont, S. D. 'The scientific character of theology and the origin of Duns Scotus's distinction between intuitive and abstractive cognition', *Speculum* 64 (1989): 579–99.
13.69 Marenbon, J. *Later Medieval Philosophy (1150–1350)*, London, Routledge, 1987, pp. 154–68.
13.70 Wolter, A. B. 'Duns Scotus on intuition, memory and our knowledge of individuals', in [13.54] 98–124.

Virtues, will and freedom

13.71 Boler, J. 'Transcending the natural: Duns Scotus on the two affections of the will', *American Catholic Philosophical Quarterly* 67 (1993): 109–22.
13.72 Dumont, S. D. 'The necessary connection of prudence to the moral virtues according to John Duns Scotus – revisited', *Recherches de théologie ancienne et médiévale* 55 (1988): 184–206.
13.73 —— 'The origin of Scotus's theory of synchronic contingency', *The Modern Schoolman* (1995): 149–68.
13.74 Frank, W. A. 'Duns Scotus on autonomous freedom and divine co-causality', *Medieval Philosophy and Theology* 2 (1992): 142–64.
13.75 Ingham, M. E. *Ethics and Freedom: an Historical-Critical Investigation of Scotist Ethical Thought*, Washington, DC, University Press of America, 1989.
13.76 Prentice, R. 'The voluntarism of Duns Scotus as seen in his comparison of the intellect and the will', *Franciscan Studies* 28 (1968): 63–103.
13.77 Wolter, A. B. 'Native freedom of the will as the key to the ethics of Scotus', in [13.54] 148–62.
13.78 —— 'Duns Scotus on the will as rational potency', in [13.54] 163–80.

CHAPTER 14

Ockham's world and future

Arthur Gibson

━ PHILOSOPHICAL BIOGRAPHY ━

Ockham was born in about 1285, certainly before 1290, probably in the village of Ockham, Surrey, near London. If his epitaph is accurate, he died on 10 April 1347. Yet Conrad of Megenberg, when writing to experts in the know, appears to assign to Ockham a piece written after November 1347, so perhaps the epitaph was doctored. It has been affirmed that he died in Munich, possibly of the Black Death, though perhaps the Plague had not yet reached Germany or Bohemia by that date (see [14.55] 27–8). Whatever the correct view, the beginning and end of his biography are subject to some uncertainty.

Ockham's intellectual life is replete with confident redefinition of contemporary philosophical concepts, often drawing on, or sharing in, the work of other theologians doing philosophy. This redefinition was not a source of pleasure to the powers that be. Medieval Christian philosophy was the manifestation of complex axioms, the restatement of which was a constant attraction as well as a risky endeavour. Arriving at Oxford in 1309, the Franciscan Ockham was eventually perceived by the Chancellor of the university and secular theologian, John Lutterel, to have fallen from grace. This was partly because Ockham did not accept this Chancellor's own Thomistic doctrines. Lutterel was fighting a rather lonely rearguard defence of Aquinas, since Ockham's philosophy was preoccupying most of the English scholars in his subject.[1] Ockham had studied under the previous Oxford Chancellor, Henry Harclay (who died in 1317),[2] and he had embraced the latter's criticism of Duns Scotus on universals. In about 1315 we find Peter Aureoli developing similar criticism. Ockham was not, then, the sole dissenting original thinker in a burgeoning trend of new reflection, which was stimulated in part by the unexpected revival, and modification, of concepts of supposition (denotation) theory. Scotus's work

329

acted as both a major focus for and influence upon scholars at Oxford. He had reformulated aspects of recently past scholarship in ways that attracted Ockham's debt, often through disagreement.

Moving to London, after a less than peaceful time at Oxford, Ockham continued undeterred to compose his philosophy until 1324, even though in the previous year John Lutterel had already attempted to procure from the Pope in Avignon a judgement of heresy on fifty-six of Ockham's theses. The papal legal process was commenced in spring 1327, and, even in June 1328, after a year's work of the inquisition on Ockham, it had not yet managed to furnish a case against him using Lutterel's evidence.[3] Francis of Meyronnes counselled that Franciscan scholars in the interim should eschew public and unqualified *determinationes* of their traditional position (see [14.55] 57–9). Ockham's conscience, leading him to open dispute, aggravated the situation. When at Oxford Ockham was carefully listened to by a number of scholars, including Walter Chatton and Adam Wodeham. Chatton was the most likely source of Lutterel's indirect knowledge of Ockham's views, though he did not purposely act as an inside-dealer against Ockham. Rather, Chatton was attentive to him because of his own interest in Ockham's epistemology, which departed from the perspectivist theories with which he was familiar. The political conflict between Ockham's Franciscan order and Pope John XXII (concerning the criterion of application for poverty) occupied a central place in his attention at Avignon, not least since he was asked to read the disputed papal bulls on this issue (see [14.11] xvii). By the time Ockham left Avignon he was a defendant in a heresy accusation concerning his earlier writings. But the principal reason Ockham departed was that he accused the Pope of heresy regarding his teaching on rights and poverty. Ockham departed from Avignon for the protection of the Holy Roman Emperor, Louis of Bavaria. Excommunicated, he thenceforth composed political philosophy for the rest of his life.

⚓ A PRELIMINARY PICTURE OF OCKHAM'S ⚓ WRITINGS AND PHILOSOPHY

Ockham had finished writing his non-political philosophy by 1324. He had lectured on the *Sentences* at Oxford between 1317 and 1319. The next compositions were his *Expositio aurea* ('Golden Exposition', of Aristotle's logic) and the *Exposition of Aristotle's 'Physics'* (Books I–IV); all these were written during 1321–3. In addition to these, by 1324 he had produced his *Summa logicae* (*Textbook of logic*), the *Quodlibets*, the remainder of the *Exposition of Aristotle's 'Physics'* (Books V–VII), and his two treatises on quantity. As well as a *reportatio* of his Oxford *Sentences*

330

commentary, Books II–IV, there is a revised version of his lectures on Book I, an *Ordinatio*, probably dating from 1319–24. With the implicit reference to and condemnation of Ockham as a heretic by Pope John XXII (6 June 1328) in his bull *Quia quorundam*, Ockham's work was disrupted. By 1332–4 Ockham commenced writing his, eventually very extensive, political philosophy, the first volume of which is *Opus nonaginta dierum* (*Work of Ninety Days*). Its extraordinary length and impartiality are amazing in view of his personal circumstances. Yet by late 1334 he had also composed and sent his *Epistola ad Fratres Minores* (*Letter to the Franciscans*), as well as having written *I Dialogus*, a very long neutral treatise on the concept of heresy and its application to papal authority, both now in English thanks to the fine editions of Stephen McGrade and John Kilcullen (see [14.11] and [14.7]).

As with other medieval scholars, we should reckon on our possessing less than Ockham's complete works. Non-extant writings and their detail, deemed to be obscure or of marginal significance, may not have been so regarded by Ockham or some of his contemporaries. It is possible that his lost writings, if rediscovered, would change topics in his philosophy. For example, Rega Wood draws attention to citations attributed to Ockham which do not occur anywhere in his extant writings ([14.102] 30–1; cf. her n. 25). These appear in the sole extant copy of John of Reading's *Sentences*. This Reading, a Franciscan, typifies the lesser, yet ecclesiastically significant, type of figure who contributed to the battleground of dispute with Ockham. By 1323 Reading, interestingly a former student of Lutterel's, was to be found as a consultant to the Pope at Avignon prior to Ockham's arrival. Reading disputed Ockham's view of intuitive cognition. He maintained that intuitive cognition of non-existents is possible ([14.2]). Although he was influenced by Duns Scotus, Reading here disagrees with him (see [14.93] 166–74), and he bases his case on God's absolute power.

God was central to Ockham's philosophy. He was a theologian who did philosophy, with a penchant for logic. Although his researches in logic are detailed and widespread, they are not a formal system in our modern sense. Ockham was more explicitly interested in formal questions of logic than Aquinas, yet his instinct and understanding fall short of Aquinas's.

His fundamental principle for God and logic is simplicity. This is not a project about presentation – it is easy to think him ironic about simplicity when we view the often torturous complexities of his logic, though his writings betray no sense of whimsicality. His simplicity has its ideal in God: the unity, the necessity. 'Ockham's razor' is a label for the philosophical counterpart of God: a principle to reduce, or keep, entities to a minimum. Just as a theologian views polytheism as a corruption threatening monotheism, so Ockham's philosophy treated the multiplication of species as a corrosive infecting our perception of world-structure that mirrored God. Ockham's programme relies on the reduction of ontological categories to just two, substance and quality – though he has no systematic logic worked out for implementing such a scheme.

Ockham produced an extensive formal philosophy. Yet, rather like Bertrand Russell, he did not integrate his formal interests with his dialectical (for example, ethical) writings. This perspective is only slightly misleading, since Ockham's dialectically presented political philosophy only obliquely embodies some of his other philosophical concerns. But Ockham sometimes makes an explicit, albeit unexpected, connection between the dialectic of *obligationes* and the logic in his *Summa Logica*. For example, Ockham's philosophical logic there deals with the concept of 'consequence' and impossibility in its varying paradoxical forms under this general heading. In twentieth century terms, Ockham might be described as carrying out a thought experiment. Eleonore Stump illuminates the way Ockham connects the topics of 'obligations' and 'insolubles' (see [14.92] ch. 12). 'Insolubles' were forms of conundrums or paradoxes, and this linking of the two topics together was usual in Ockham's lifetime. He attempted to show how impossible propositions might not, in disputations, obviously entail a contradiction. As Spade shows,[4] Ockham permits self-reference in his logic. Ockham's technique modifying Walter Burley's, is to submerge the collisions in premisses concerning relevance to yield a possible world which both satisfies typical conditions of possibility, yet produces a state of affairs that unexpectedly reconfigures subjunctive conditional boundaries. This is not unlike Lewis's [14.59] wider pluralising of worlds, increasing entities, not reducing them. Gensler has recently shown how one might discover such interconnections, more secure than Ockham's ([14.39]). Although Ockham did not develop his work on obligations theory within his political philosophy, it seems clear that he was implicitly injecting the results of research into his political and ethical theory, in the way he combines canon law, logic and case-precedent technique, for example in his *III Dialogus* ([14.7]).

Research on logic readily inclines a philosopher to give attention to the mental bedrock that facilitates the use of logic, and the perceptual spheres which are its media of operation. Although Ockham was committed to Aristotle's maxim that 'man is a rational animal', he believed that this truth is often submerged by other psychological and dispositional tendencies, and certainly his political philosophy (see below) indicates that this is true of humanity. But unfortunately, Ockham's own stress on the roles of the mind and universals provoked him too readily to internalize the grounds of knowing. A contemporary of Ockham's, Durandus of Saint-Pourçain, stressed the person who observes – the agent, rather than the object known – as the ground for knowledge. Ockham was so impressed with this approach, that with the aid of divine intervention he supposed that one might have an intuitive cognition of a non-existent thing. But in usual circumstances, 'intuitive cognition' for Ockham marks the knowledge of a present singular individual with properties. This situation is partially causal and conjoins with one's simultaneous abstractive cognition of the individual with properties. Abstractive cognition of this state of affairs lays the perceptual and propositional mental grounds for repeating, and thus extending, the process and cognitions to like individuals. Memory is partly composed from such cognitions, and when there is a temporal lapse after intuitive cognition, there remains an imperfect intuitive cognition permitting the observer to infer the truth of the relevant past tense proposition representing a given experience (see [14.64] 186). These distinctions were the subject of extreme technical debate, bound into the science of the times. Adam Wodeham (see [14.93] ch. 10) was inclined to follow John Duns Scotus and dispute Aureoli's view that intuitive cognition is understanding by means of which the individual is either present *or* appears to be. Wodeham nevertheless learnt from Aureoli that it would be possible for a perception to satisfy the same truth conditions if an absent entity were simulated, and so, on Ockham's hypothesis, delude the observer by causing intuitive cognition. This is quite a different problem, Ockham thought, from having intuitive cognition by means of miracle. It is interesting to consider how the science and technology of a period affect philosophical theorizing: would televised individuals have been a convenient 'presence' for Wodeham with which to challenge Ockham?

❧ OUR DIFFICULTY IN DEFINING OCKHAM ❧

Controversy and misrepresentation attended Ockham's philosophy in his own time and later. Philosophers of today display some qualified parallels with Ockham's relation to his, not always intended, deconstruction of elements in medieval philosophical traditions. His philosophy contributed to the medieval 'new modernism'; this is a designation Stephen Nicholls employed to characterize French medieval cultural contexts (see [14.71]). One might extend the depiction of this 'new modernism' to Ockham, and to others, by describing it as a claim to return to the past whilst reinventing it as a new future for, and to dispute with, the present. Typical of this is Ockham's break with the medieval world in his treatment of logical and metaphysical relations. As with post-Enlightenment French romantic modernists, however, Ockham wished to look back to past archetypes (such as Aristotle) whom he moulded in his own image for the future.

Central to the assessment of Ockham is the problem of measuring our own sounding-boards. In the late nineteenth, and twentieth century, what can be termed modernist logic[5] and its philosophy of language are often presupposed by philosophers, in differing ways and sometimes indirectly by contrast, as the correct or true frequencies for observing the quite different universe of Ockham. These modernist logic developments stem principally from the work of Gottlob Frege([14.34]–[14.36]), though there have been many developments since his last publication in 1923.[6] Conversely sometimes there is a romantic disposition to give the privileged status to Ockham's logic as if it should remain unchallenged by our analytical philosophy's research and logic. This priority has not entirely escaped the epoch-making study by Marilyn McCord Adams,[7] to which the reader is referred as the principal research resource on Ockham. For example, Adams judges 'Peter Geach [to be one] who writes from a Fregean bias' ([14.12] 393 and n. 34). Geach criticized Ockham's two-name theory of predication.[8] Adams does not attempt to prove her curt partisan dismissal of Geach and Frege. The problem here is not a matter of local in-house debate. It is a dispute about the identity of logic; to what extent should a logician's work be judged by timeless, absolute standards? To what extent must it be seen in the context of its times?

Some fresh general considerations expressed here require more research, not least since the generality and boldness of Ockham's theories lay claim to answers outside his, and sometimes our, logical ken. But as we now attempt to look back at him, a straight contrast between, say, twentieth-century philosophical logic and Ockham's medieval world obscures, fails to account for, explore, or sufficiently query, complex interconnections and differences between Ockham's own philosophical prehistory and our contemporary philosophy (cf. [14.80]). Assuming that there is such a thing as logical truth, however, or if we presuppose that humans have made some progress in understanding logic, it would be surprising to conclude that Ockham's position did not need revision or development after over 600 years.

For Ockham, the expression of language which is the soul-home of concepts and utterance is in the mind – the mental language (peculiarly like, but not quite identical to Latin) – as Paul Spade points out (see [14.89]). In Ockham the strongest version of meaning is an internal utterance within the mind. This mental model is accordingly psychologistic, and it is reductionist. Is the concept of a mental language that is not itself the intention with which one speaks credible? Could Ockham's philosophy benefit from modern work which argues

that all natural languages can be treated as manifestations of underlying neurophysiological genetic syntaxes or semantics? Even were there
to be an affirmative answer to this question, do we yet possess the, or
most of the, formal elements which would constitute understanding
of the logical ingredients of such a map? Does the Latin of Ockham
display relativity which is in tension against this purported universality? Is it proper to employ our modern formal logic 'languages' to
symbolize (and thus to interpret) Ockham's philosophical language
and logic? Our contemporary logics are highly formalized and explicit,
with their symbolically refined artificial functions and operators. These
logic languages are partially alien to Ockham's philosophical language.
For example, as Spade remarked,[9] Ockham's *significatio* (signification)
cannot be translated by Frege's *Sinn* (sense) without distortion. This
is not because of untranslatability, however; it is owing to their
competing theses: Frege's is semantic logic, whereas Ockham's is based
on mental understanding. The medieval Latin he used, a hybrid of
oral and written forms evolved into a sort of formal – often obscure
– technical 'dialect', falls far short of the explicit and technical
symbolism of our own logics. So an upshot of these questions is another
one: when a medievalist paraphrases philosophical Latin employing
our logics, can synonymy be preserved between the medieval ambiguity, and our contemporary often complex razor-sharp logic?

Geach has demonstrated how well Buridan initiated the resolution
of problems in 'quantification into opaque contexts' which are still
partly intractable in our current philosophical research (see [14.38]
161–3, then 129–38, 148). One of these topics is intentional identity,
i.e. only seeming to refer to a referent by use of a quasi-name with
intentional verbs, as in, 'I believe that I am referring to a square-circle
drawn on the ground.' Could this sort of intentional approach unexpectedly be utilized to map Ockham's own thesis that there is a 'mental'
language to which he only intentionally refers? Is the mental language
a non-existent intentional identity falsely invoked by a quasi-name and
quasi-language? Is it a conceptual fiction? Ockham's supposition theory
is itself so subject to equivocation that confusion over intentional verbs
cannot be clarified. Ockham posits (in his actual Latin analytical
language) his alleged mental language as a vehicle by which to over-
ride and secure his logic and reference. If his (linguistic) analytical
language in Latin is itself an intentional medium of expression, then
he cannot actually succeed in referring to his ideal mental language
since it would be an intentional fictive object. On this account,
Ockham's mental language, and its two class domains, inhere solely
as a myth: a complex abstract object of his imagination.

Perhaps we should look synchronically at differences within our
own contemporary philosophical traditions and controversies to gain a

clearer sense of the diachronic problem for us of identifying Ockham's philosophy. Difficulties of paraphrasing Ockham into modern philosophy are *not* like problems in (in the required sense and to the relevant degree) unexpectedly new developments of our analytical philosophy. For example Russell's basic logic has been developed in directions of which, one would judge, he did not or would not approve. A case in point is David Lewis (see [14.59]); he is rather like an Ockham in reverse. Where Ockham wanted to reduce ontological plurality, Lewis goes forth and multiplies it. His theory is that we can 'invent' ontologies by making counterpart universes for other space-times. The universes he reproduces are modelled from our own indexicals of location (here/there), person (you/me), time (now/then), etc., that mirror our own world. I believe that Russell would have thought that this sort of subjunctive conditional philosophizing to be like confusing 'fairy tales' with real-life ontology.[10] But we can derive Lewis's logic from Russell's (and thus choose to ignore the latter's lifelong neglect of modal logic), even though some ingenuity is required. Yet we cannot derive Whitehead and Russell ([14.98]) from Ockham's logic. This sort of enterprise, generalized, indicates that Ockham cannot consistently, in this arena, be paraphrased into modern analytical philosophy without inventing a logic and philosophy.[11] In any case, what it is to be a criterion of logical possibility, as a basis for refining or transforming a concept, is obviously not the criterion to assess what Ockham thought. Beyond this issue is another one: if one classifies logic as a subset of scientific knowledge, then one is committed to admitting some type of invariance to allow for the increasing explanatory power of theory. But this presupposes a questionable form of individuation in the philosophy of history, and of originality. Can we properly offer an intellectual biography of Ockham that in some way does not consider non-scientific creative originality in Ockham's philosophy?[12] We may wish to direct such queries to the ethical and political domains of Ockham, but the interplay of logic as a discovery procedure for inference, and creative intuition, requires more attention in research, though it would take us too far to investigate this axis for tracing Ockham's consciousness in his compositions.[13]

Impinging on attempts to access Ockham for us in our worldviews is the issue of the status of extending a concept beyond its framed origin. Using a 'function' to formulate a predicate and quantifier logic (as Russell did, following Frege [14.34]) has revolutionized the identity of inferences involving generalization. We should not underestimate the scope of this revolution, though problems remain (see [14.84]). The logical power of the predicate calculus also enables sentence-forming operators ('and', 'or', 'if', etc.) and quantifiers ('some', 'all', 'the', 'few', 'scarcely') to be defined using logical predicates. This calculus has many other transforming roles, which contrast with Ockham's doctrine of terms.

These issues compound the simple problem of what it is for a modern logical concept to be 'contained in Ockham's general premisses'.[14] Can there be a relation of inference between Ockham's philosophy of logic and the achievements in logic research over 600 years later? When we consider our contemporary philosophical defence and criticism of Ockham, do they embody merely the sort of narrow-mindedness Russell might have displayed toward Lewis, and did show Ockham?[15] Consideration of such questions will contribute to our assessing Ockham's modernity, limitations and potential more clearly, while guarding against charges of anachronism or overestimation.

❧ OCKHAM AND REFERENCE ❧

Names are fundamental for Ockham. Adams mentions that Ockham adopts the traditional distinction (see [14.12] 71), inspired by Aristotle's *On Interpretation*, that there are three kinds of names: spoken, written and mental.[16] Ockham uses the word for 'name' that he employs to classify a subject *and* a predicate. Yet they are functionally different. For Ockham, the proposition 'The Titanic is wrecked' is composed of two names: one for the subject 'The Titanic'; and the same 'name' for the quite differently functioning predicate 'wrecked'. Logic should preserve differences of use in language; Ockham's naming strategy destroys it: the subject and the predicate in the above proposition are actually asymmetric in use. 'The Titanic' refers to an object. The predicate 'is wrecked' is a state of affairs which is true *of* its subject (if or when true). Once wrecked, the Titanic has the contingently necessary property of 'is wrecked'. This predicate is a self-inhering term, though before striking the iceberg it was not even a property of the Titanic. The notion of identity is bound into 'the Titanic' in a way in which it is not in 'is wrecked'. And that is not preserved by using 'name' for both parts of the proposition 'The Titanic is wrecked.'

If, before the Titanic sank, someone called out and named: 'The Titanic!', it could logically yield the question: 'Where?' and the answer: 'There!' But if someone called out: 'is wrecked', at most this peculiar response would attract the question: 'What is?' This latter question advertises the problem: with a predicate one does not know the identity of the thing of which the predicate is true (or false, as the case may be). Contrariwise, with the subject 'Titanic', the identity of the subject referred to *is* the self-contained sense which is the use of the term.[17]

This difference is fundamental in oral, written and the mental language accessible for us to test.

Therefore it is basic to a knowledge of Ockham's use of names to appreciate that his theory about 'name' is contradicted by the foregoing argument. His explanation does not work for linguistic use, and if a language were constructed according to his rules, we could not communicate when using a large portion of it (witness, 'I name this ship "is wrecked"').

Although he regarded Aristotle as his general inspiration, Ockham's application of names to propositions is quite contrary to Aristotle's concept of the asymmetry of subject and predicate in *On Interpretation*, as Geach observes ([14.38] 290–1).[18] In claiming to retrieve Aristotle's teaching, Ockham followed medieval contemporary tradition which reinterpreted some aspects of Aristotle's later doctrine of terms. Ockham uses 'name' to represent two allegedly identical mental universals which constitute a proposition: the subject and the predicate. These are often translated nowadays into the letter-names: 'N' and 'P'. For Ockham, there is here no naming difference between a subject and predicate. But in the above work by Aristotle, the subject and predicate are asymmetrical in functions, even though in the *Prior Analytics* Aristotle later dropped the scheme in favour of a doctrine of terms. (Although Plato's *Sophist* was not available to Ockham, it is worth noting that elements of Aristotle's asymmetry conception parallel distinctions in the *Sophist*, though for Plato the verb is classified in relation to its extension, whereas for Aristotle it is as a function in a statement. It is true that the distinction between name and predicate (or verb) in Aristotle is not as explicitly and exclusively defined as it is in our contemporary logic; but the central ingredients are there.) Now one would therefore think that Ockham was, in principle, in a position to choose to adopt the distinction of the functional asymmetry identities of logical subject and predicate, especially with his devotion to Aristotle. Yet he did not. Did it dawn on him that this asymmetry was in Aristotle, citing as he did from the same work in which this doctrine appears? It might be replied that since the doctrine of terms appears later in Aristotle, it is not surprising that Ockham, in any case, chose this instead of the concept of asymmetry between logical subject and predicate. Even so, for those who wish to 'modernize' Ockham's logic, or paraphrase it into our logics, Ockham's not choosing Aristotle's asymmetry distinction, fundamental to most modern logics, implies a judgement against Ockham's instinct for the deeper foundations of logic as they have been developed long after Aristotle's, and then subsequent to his, lifetime.

For Frege, for Russell, and most analytical philosophers, the predicate has no reference of its own because it is incomplete. It is like a function. On this interpretation, a predicate has to be linked to a logical name, which refers. By the mediation of the logical subject the predicate is attached to the name that refers, and is thereby true (or false) of the name's referent; it has an ascriptive function to create its link with the referent. There are issues to be addressed in these areas, such as the need to concentrate on the role of quantified general terms, rather than Russell's own views of 'definite descriptions', and the effect it has had on interpretation of the predicate calculus. But, after all this is assessed, the difference between the enormous capabilities of the predicate calculus, as against the two-name theory with its supposition doctrine, is like contrasting alchemy with nuclear physics with regard to the transformation of metals.

Ockham had absorbed the common doctrine of terms (in which a proposition is made up of names). The enormous grip that this doctrine, together with supposition theory, had on Ockham, and much of the medieval world, is hardly to be explained by this, less than ideal, at points implausible, interpretation of Aristotle and its amalgam of supposition. Why did Ockham adopt this position? One answer, apart from it being a trend at the time, is that a doctrine of terms, or names, enables one to play more freely with imaginative possibility. A reason for this is that the doctrine of terms helps one evade the features of the actual relations required by language to represent the external world, while pretending a logical guarantee of true meaning. In other words, it is a covert theory of equivocation which subverts the relations between semantics, ontology and mental understanding.

Ockham's two-name theory is undermined by two other considerations which reflect thinking by Dummett ([14.30] 223–4, 294). The target of the two concepts is the relation of a predicate to the mental realm, as they go proxy for parts of the external world. Dummett's research has explored some hitherto ill-defined areas of reference. First, if predicates were to have the sort of name-reference Ockham ascribes to them and their mental and ontological counterparts, then to what does this commit Ockham? We would have to admit quantification over the *referents* of these predicates.[19] Ockham opposed Aquinas's view that 'matter, already understood under corporeity and dimensions, can be understood as distinct in different parts'.[20] For Ockham, the referents would need to be the indivisible 'essence' or 'substance' which is prior to quantification. But second, even if quantification over predicate-referents were compatible with Ockham's philosophy, then this would commit him to an impossible position. That is to say, if we presuppose with Ockham that predicates refer – as his subjects do – they cannot refer to a complete entity. For if a predicate refers, its *referent* would have to be *incomplete* (i.e. 'is wrecked' is a semantic mirror of its ontology: there is no subject *in it* by which to refer to pick out this ontological subject). This is exactly the opposite of what Ockham needs. He requires a nominal universal in the mental realm to be referred to, which would have to be complete. Ockham could hardly allow an incomplete entity referred to by supposition. Ockham's theory of naming is rather like one's pointing to a ship-wreck in thick fog, or down through deep water; the 'name' does not locate its own object, and it locates a wrong position because it has no knowledge of the effect of refraction on perception.

The conflation of subjects with predicates, we have seen above, is triggered by Ockham's use of a 'name' category for subject and for predicate. Ockham absorbed the common doctrine of terms. He and Walter Burley, with some differences, embraced the theory of suppo-sition, which had been strangely restored from near-oblivion. Yet Aquinas, before Ockham, employed applicatives (quantifiers) such as 'some', 'every', 'only' to explain that a predicate does not itself refer but indicates a nature.[21]

Ockham attempted to avoid the problem, created through his failure to recognize the asymmetry of subject and predicate, by looking to his idea of mental language. Ockham viewed mental language as a phenomenon that mediated us directly to the world it represents. Shortcomings when trying to implement his two-name theory in oral and written language provoke him to download the elusive mental language.[22]

How did Ockham suppose that the theory of supposition, linked to naming, connects with the mind? He supplied the connection through a theory of signification. An important study by Spade exposes aspects of the relation. Spade cites Buridan and Augustine to indicate concepts of signification which were influential in Ockham's time ([14.87] 215). According to them, signification establishes the under-standing of a thing, and that signs are causal lexemes which produce mental effects beyond the impression the thing makes on the senses. As Spade notes ([14.87] 218), the stress on mentality reflects, minus the sense-impression element, Aristotle's *On Interpretation* (I, 16a3f): 'Spoken words are the symbols of mental experience.' Stated very roughly, the later medieval trend is to treat supposition theory as a semantic hypothesis (proposing connections between a term's referring and its referent). In contrast, signification is an epistemological theory, concerned with understanding. The conjunction of these two approaches targets the conditions for knowing and learning in the medium of language. Ockham claimed to have direct knowledge of individuals. A term deployed in simple supposition in this perspective goes proxy for the concept to which it is subject. As Spade explains ([14.87] 222), by contrast, Burley's view is that terms stand in simple supposition for what they signify. This involves a social view of language as a tool to communicate with others. Ockham proposed, in other contexts,[23] that there is a triangular relation in some acts of assent between mental language, spoken language and the referent. In these contexts he argued that the consequence of such a relation is that a person may know something which is the product of it (for example, that one entity is not another), yet (to express it in a way Ockham does not) the person may not possess the recognitional capacity for having a concept of that concept (see [14.61]). Ockham's main emphasis is on the grounds of a person's own knowledge, not social interaction, and on the causal efficacy of signification for mental states, together with the denial of natures.

From various twentieth-century philosophical standpoints, Ockham's causal theory of understanding is not well grounded in its own or our terms. Two contemporary views on the philosophy of mind are first, that of the theory-theorists (see [14.58]) (i.e. those who maintain that to speak of the mind at all we have (at least implicitly) to have a theory of it); second, that of the simulationists ([14.48]) (i.e. those disposed to argue that we have no adequate theory of the mental, and in any case we simulate the mental states of others in our mental activity without presupposing a theory). Both could be partially integrated by utilizing the function of 'implicit' in the theory-theory view. This could mark an innate mental capacity tantamount to a theory, along the lines of Fodor (see [14.33]), which is partially activated by a simulationist model. Each of these approaches is concerned with the role of collective social learning in the way Ockham was not, and as such they complement Burley's attitude.[24] As the simulationist Heal points out ([14.48]), justification or epistemic status is a holistic notion, and the notion of relevance is extraordinarily complex and undetermined. These points count against Ockham's signification. His signification is a semantics which naïvely causes mental language effects. Or, more precisely, mental states (thoughts, etc.) cause linguistic (spoken, written) signification. Ockham had no grasp of the instantiation of relevance theory, complexity theory, or simulation of others' states.

In relation to these issues, we now have fairly firm grounds for accepting the instability of linguistic signs, and their frequent indeterminacy relating to mental and oral uses, originally from research by Saussure into written Latin (and its interpretation by Starobinski, see [14.91]) and work by Jakobson (see [14.54]) as well as Anscombe's rather different work on intention and mental causality in the contexts of their expression (see [14.16], [14.17]). We also have the latter author's study on the difficulties of classifying the first pronoun (in agreement with Kant). To this one can add, for example, Chomsky's more recent theories on indeterminacy in mind and orality in relation to the abstract identities of concrete entities. As Chomsky remarks, 'the abstract character of London is crucial to its individuation' ([14.24]

341

21). These have generally been taken to have fractured and dismantled the almost mechanistic symmetry that the Ockham scenario presupposes between spoken, written and mental terms. Even if there are criteria of identity appropriate to each, it does not follow that for each there is a fixed content to the criterion of identity (Moses' identity may be fixed in varying ways (see [14.99] §§20–110)). One cannot sustain the view that there is a mapping criterion for which there is an equivalence of the relevant sort between Ockham's supposition in respect of spoken, written and mental terms. Ockham had a naïve realist view about the way terms fix to referents.

Adams speaks of Ockham's view that the division between personal, material and simple supposition applies equally to spoken, written and mental terms.[25] This has been criticized by Spade (see [14.89] XIII). He judged that it follows from Ockham's way of relating concept, thought, personal supposition and signification, that, with mental terms which may have personal or material supposition, we do not always know what we are asserting. Spade's view has been countered by Adams supposing

> that the issue is not really whether or not one of our thoughts could be about something (in the sense of a term's standing for some particular) without our knowing it. Ockham allows that when I think 'Every man is an animal', the term 'man' supposits for lots of things without my knowing that it does, since I have no awareness of those particular men. Rather the question is whether on the above proposal anything would make it the case that the term was suppositing for these rather than those.
>
> (see [14.12] 351 n. 104)

It is wrong to argue here that, 'the term "man" supposits for lots of things without my knowing that it does, since I have no awareness of those particular men'. If a person knows the meaning of the term 'men', that person will know from experience and cognition that it is true or false that there are men. So at the very least, for those terms for which that person holds concepts which supposit in the singular and have (even conjecturally) more than one referent, it is not possible that 'the term "man" supposits for lots of things without [that person] knowing it does'. This advertises the problem that, in Ockham, equivocation and ignorance are functions of his failure, not only to possess a viable theory of reference in his signification, but also of his system's inability to explain the complex presence and scope of relevance. His system does not explain introspection of pertinent contents in one's own consciousness. The presence of equivocation in Ockham's supposition and signification is a mask for his failure to explain mental choice and the invasive role of complex relevance conditions in holding, knowing as well as using concepts. A suppressed general premiss behind Ockham's positions here is his misconception that if one conjoins the functioning mind to the world, then it will 'read off' the true interpretation of both regarding terms. Consequently, his need for equivocating between supposition and signification is hardly surprising in view of his principle of parsimony.

In practice, however, Ockham's procedure is sometimes the negation of simplicity, since he approaches a simple situation by multiplying entities. He invents mental classes to which the signifiers supposedly refer, though people using language seem strangely unaware that these classes exist. For Ockham, 'Socrates is a man' is an instance of a categorical proposition. But Ockham has no general account of what it is to be a proposition. Following Ockham, Marilyn Adams paraphrases this sort of proposition as: 'N is P if and only if N has P-ness or P-ness inheres in N.'[26] This contravenes Ockham's razor, since it multiplies entities for 'N is P' (and the technique requires increasingly complex *ad hoc* devices). The paraphrase mediates on behalf of 'N is P', intervening allegedly to make explicit the mental-language contract with the simple statement. This is at the centre of the two-class theory. In Ockham's two-name theory 'man' is a mental sign, a nominal or conceptualist-nominalist supposition that inheres not only in Socrates but other male humans. So, in the term 'man' employed of Socrates, it also denotes all humans. Aquinas would have had none of this,[27] since he did not allow that a general term, such as 'nature', had direct reference, for it is true *of* individuals – ascribed, not referring to an identity. The appeal to 'P-ness' invents a class that is not derivable from P, without the addition of a new entity: abstractions of the mind. Since 'Socrates' is symmetric in logical form to 'man' (in 'N is Socrates'), we should be able to redistribute its 'Socrates'-ness over other men. Obviously Ockham wanted to construe 'Socrates' as a uniquely suppositing term, with 'is a man' differently represented as a class name term. Yet he classifies them as names, which Adams formalizes identically. So here their representation in logic is uniform. But their interpretation as to function is distinct; that is inconsistent. We should here insist on that to which Ockham commits himself. Symmetry of syntactic formalization (the predicate has a unitary symbol, 'P', as has the subject) is the identity of its entities. No doubt we will be told Ockham did not intend this by his depicting the predicate-name as a complete entity. Quite so; but that is the problem: intentionality. Intentions do not rule words.

Can the two-name theory of Ockham be salvaged? It appears not. But imagine Ockham reading the foregoing with the foresight of (and disagreements in) our contemporary analytical philosophy. Ockham might respond:

'I see the explanatory power of a logical singular term which presupposes a criterion of identity. It strikes a fundamental distinction with the logical predicate which I did not understand, and I admit that it is more accurate to represent the predicate as a function, asymmetric in role to the logical subject, along the lines of *Fn*. Despite these concessions, it seems that their scopes have been overstated. Your predicate calculus is correct, and my formalism crude, and I consider that supposition might be replaced with the following strategy, which I think achieves the same results. I restore something parallel with my two-name theory as follows, using your philosophical logic.

'I want to disturb your confidence by exposing some weaknesses in twentieth-century analytical philosophy and logic, to make space for my own use of your distinctions. First, Frege used the analogy of a logical name to craft part of his concept of a logical predicate. And I understand that this analogy collapsed in a messy way ([14.29]). I can reconstruct my two names by taking the analogy, though I am unclear whether or not I was incorrect in degree or type to use "name" of the predicate. Second, twentieth-century philosophers when pushed have some difficulty making *definitively* explicit what they mean by "referring". There is the "pointing" origin of the word for "reference" (German *Bedeutung*) in Frege.[28] Many twentieth-century philosophers sympathetic to Frege do not seem able precisely to inform me what "referring" semantically is, except to say that it is what a singular term does: it picks out a single referent, by acting to implement one of the subject's criteria of identity. Well, I wish to come back to this concession of ignorance. Why can this singular ability be achieved *only* by your logical *name*? I agree that my use of "name" was itself foggy, but I was aiming at a label for a particular, not the narrower sense later ascribed to me. I am willing to drop, for my predicates, what you term "referring", and Geach's analyses have convinced me that supposition theory is best eliminated completely, including from logically proper names. But I would like to conclude, with Recanati ([14.77] 401), that the differences between indexicals and proper names is largely pragmatic.

'Now here is my original move. You have developed a logic of indexicals: "here", "there", "me", "you", "past", "present" (David Lewis builds a whole universe from them). But I understand that you have a problem with the first person pronoun "I". Logicians often deem that the first person "I" can be replaced by the person's proper name. But of course that will not do, it fails some truth-conditions, including the third person proper name contexts when you substitute it with a proper name. And if Kant and Anscombe ([14.16]) are right to affirm that "I" does not refer, we have an indexical particular. It is more like a unique (categorial) predicate. It picks out a person in particular

344

context. Now why may I not generalize this over large sets of indexicals? I can paraphrase my predicate-name scheme into an indexical programme. If I may borrow an expression from Heal, this procedure can be called 'indexical predication'.[29] I appreciate that this leads to complex semantic analysis, and a proposal to analyse propositions according to a deep structure which I cannot describe within my own terms. But for any abstract form such as "the property of whiteness" there is a paraphrase back to the surface form, e.g. "The donkey is white".[30] So a two-name theory can be replaced with something that is almost parallel, yet it satisfies the notion of asymmetry between the subject and predicate. Although we had no refined quantifier logic in the medieval world that treated quantifiers as predicates in the Frege manner, I see no reason why indexical predication cannot be extended to general terms and variables. As for the mental language, I shall have to exchange it for the Fregean metalanguage according to which object-languages are its manifestation. All this does not augur well for my principle of parsimony, but I may have to resort to the larger questions of cosmology to re-state it.'

❧ OCKHAM'S RAZORS ❧

When Ockham was a young man, his fellow Franciscan Roger Bacon (1220–92) had only recently died. Ockham's razor (as his principle of parsimony was later to be termed) is to some degree a reaction against Bacon's theory of the multiplication of species. Bacon broke with other perspectivists (though their influence was less pervasive than Aristotle's theory of knowledge)[31] to argue that, for example, light multiplies in time, though this thesis was not, in his view, a matter of observation ([14.93] 16–26). Bacon's notion of multiplication of entities has some concurrence in a modern logician such as Arthur Prior, with Prior's counter-maxim: *Entia non sunt subtrahenda praeter necessitatem* ([14.75] 31) (Entities should not be subtracted unless it is necessary). Later in Bacon's career (*On Signs*, 1267, and his final work, the *Compendium of Theology*, 1292), he began to restore and re-state aspects of the confused doctrines of *supposition*, while intending to remove some of its confusions, rejecting the notion of univocal supposition. It was left to the young Ockham to mull over the relation of his aversion to Bacon's multiplication sum, and his attraction to Bacon's late change of heart on supposition.

Ockham was averse to Platonism, and conceived Aristotle as a champion of this dislike. Everything in the world was singular, and there was no principle of individuation. Real universals do not exist. Ockham believed that the grammar of propositions might bewitch us

345

into thinking that their complexity mirrored structures in the world, but below this semantic surface the universe's ontology has a proclivity for singularity, and so does our mental structure. He was convinced that we must therefore reduce the number of entities appropriate to these circumstances. Semantic expressions can be universal, as can mental concepts. Ockham's synthesis of these hypotheses comprised an original, not to say problematic, equation of semantics and ontology, not least when Ockham conferred his unexpected gaze on a similar tradition or the fragmentarily parallel views of his peers. In practice 'the' parsimonious razor, which is the emblem of the perceived influence of Ockham, is often applied piecemeal, and episodically, by his successors, which in effect falsifies it as a universal principle. There was also contemporary opposition from writers such as Walter Chatton, who asserted a rule contravening Ockham's: 'If three things are not sufficient to verify an affirmative proposition about things, a fourth must be added, and so on.'[32]

'Ockham's razor' simplifies the quite various attempts by Ockham to formulate a principle of parsimony. This state of affairs could be evidence that Ockham did not succeed in specifying the vaunted singular razor. The popularizing aphorism, 'do not multiply entities beyond necessity', does not occur in Ockham. It arises from a number of sources, mediated, for example, by the editor John Ponce of Cork, in a 1639 note added to Duns Scotus.[33] This aphorism is usually taken to echo the spirit of Ockham's ontology, however. In the form just given, one might be excused for giving it short shrift, by remarking that the only entity which exists by necessity is God, so according to this maxim nothing else exists. Therefore is it not false? But the razor is resonant with Aristotle's maxim, according to which a single means, rather than plurality, is favoured by nature and transcendent power.[34] In this form Aristotle has no use for 'necessity', though his 'plurality' is akin to one of Ockham's versions: 'Plurality is not to be assumed without necessity.'[35] Quite what 'necessity' has supposedly to entail according to Ockham is not, by him, definitively or consistently specified, though he does seem aware of some of the variety of different modal necessities.

Perhaps intuitively sensitive to some counter-intuitive modal complexities, Ockham in some contexts excises 'necessity' and, for example, introduces us instead to: 'No plurality is to be assumed except it be proved by reason, experience or infallible authority.'[36] Ockham's razor use of 'proved by experience' conflates practical reason with logical theory (as a logical axiom). In the required sense, logically necessity is not derivable from experience. That, in this type of rule, 'experience' should be taken as a criterion for logical uses of 'plurality' (elsewhere in Ockham guaranteed by 'necessity') is a category-error.

346

Possibly such blemishes kept Ockham on the move to attempt other formulae to meet his taste for restricting plurality, or they reflect his confusion, despite his central logical motivation, i.e. his wish to follow a law of non-contradiction. Ockham does not prove his principle of parsimony. This inclination is compatible with an anti-realist position, and with the admission of truth-conditions for a minimal set of statements, which serve as the core for a theory of meaning (see [14.28]). But there is a problem with this approach and the various forms of Ockham's principle of parsimony. As Wright argues in the context of late twentieth-century anti-realist versus realist debates (see [14.103] 120–4 etc.), there is no way anyone could possibly arrive at a conception of what it is for a verification-transcendent state of affairs to be true as a result of training in the use of language. Ockham did not leave us with one principle. The plural occurrence of his parsimony itself reduces to a contradiction of the principle. And even if we allow this to pass by, it follows that we have no consistent criterion by which to identify the form or test the purported existence of the razor, and so on.

Marilyn Adams claims that the principles Ockham states as versions of the razor are, 'in the first instance, methodological principles, and it is not obvious how they are related to truth or probability' ([14.12] 157). It is not formally evident what a 'methodological principle' is here, and anyway many cases of Ockham's use of philosophical or logical terms in his formulations of the principle might be drawn upon to illustrate that Ockham is not in the first instance expressing what would normally be considered methodological principles. Let us consider the foregoing employment of 'assumed' (*ponenda*) in the form (also quoted by Adams): 'plurality is not to be assumed without necessity'. This version seems to presuppose the negation of Adams's view, since its terms are those employed in Ockham's discussion of logic to express logic, in the first instance, not those of method or the logic of method. There are problems in mapping razor terminology on to our modern logics. For example, 'assumed' (*ponenda*) is rooted in the term for 'possibility', in its use here. Generally in medieval uses it has something to do with modally positing (what we would term) a propositional function, whilst it does not fully comply with this latter type of modern usage.[37] If one were to attempt an equation of it with terms in our predicate calculuses, it tends towards a premiss, whilst also partially contributing a function independently of that, of sharing a property of a presupposition, together with a weakened sense of the 'assertion' sign.[38] In other words, there is a breakdown in an attempt to fit it uniformly and broadly, or narrowly, into the concepts attending our standard logical terminology. Nevertheless, this version of Ockham's razor is no mere 'methodological principle', since it displaces space in logic otherwise occupied by different axioms and makes claims on the domain of logic and its putative ontology. If we draw on the traditions of *ponenda* on which Ockham rests, and attempt a partial alignment with our logics, we meet a complex hybrid of assumption, premiss, assertion and presupposition, bound into the conditional negation of 'necessity', generalization ('plurality'), and axiom, applied with some confusion extensionally to ontology. It is thus apparent that Ockham is talking logic, not methodological principles. He is proposing a logic for ontology, not devising methodological principles, and is asserting reductionist logic rules of quantification, not methodological principles.

One of the difficulties in aligning Ockham's use of 'assumption' and other logical terms, including those in his razor versions, is that in typical cases he accepts generalized logical laws, whilst he deems that they have exceptions in theology (for example, in his view of the Trinity). His belief was that arguments of given general logical forms of syllogism are universally valid when applied to all matters in the world; but the same logical forms are invalid if applied to the Trinity, or need to be so interpreted through a nominalist or conceptualist supposition theory that they cannot 'properly' be so applied. As Geach makes clear,[39] Ockham was confused about the relation of inference to ontology, and muddled about logical relations between first and second intention terms in logic. I leave aside here, as far as is practicable, other issues of 'nominalism' and doctrine, so as to isolate difficulties in his philosophy of logic. These exceptions are also ones often anticipated and rejected by, for example, Aquinas. So it is not self-evident that Ockham theologically needed to contravene the scope of logical laws, while it is clear that he held such collisions of his interpretations between logic and theology as a matter of sincere conviction. Consequently a reader of Ockham has to face a problem in Ockham's examination of the Trinity. Where one might hope for a resolution of tension in the use of assumption and razor, there at the centre of the theological conception most important to him, Ockham admits that he has exceptions to logic.

Unfortunately this is not a deployment of methodological principle. Clearly it is a contradictory exception involving accepting true premisses that imply false conclusions which, therefore, disprove his inferences, the razor rule, or his theological interpretation. This follows from Ockham's own rule of non-contradiction. It was an embarrassment to Ockham that Chatton employed the law of non-contradiction to demonstrate the (alleged) truth of the anti-razor by considering the multiple components that constitute causal relations in an action (for example, wood burning) (see [14.66] 469f.). Ockham attempts to head off a possible accusation of heresy by limiting the scope of his logic and introducing a nominal or conceptualist inter-pretation of abstract nouns into incarnation theology. So at this juncture he opts for semantic speculation to warrant rigging his logic, which is itself a violation of his 'necessity' and adoption of a law of non-contradiction.

Ockham's attempted justification of his failure to apply the razor in some doctrinal contexts appears in his extended version of the razor: 'No plurality is to be assumed unless it can be proved ... by some infallible authority', in which, in addition to his appeal to Scripture, he adds 'certain sayings of the saints and the determinations of the Church'.[40] As Adams acknowledges: 'Ockham always allows the claims of reason and experience to be defeated by contrary pronouncements of the Church, which should lead "every thought captive".'[41] But Ockham does not feel obliged to take the further step of embracing the fully general theory of which such ecclesiastical determinations are instances. Although he prizes generality as a desirable feature in theo-ries, he is more committed to the maxim: a theory-maker should not multiply miracles, i.e. theses contrary to reason and experience, beyond necessity.[42] There are deep fractures in these viewpoints. First, there is no logical or philosophical necessity at all to accept pronouncements of an institution, especially if they are contrary to reason.

Second, there is a suppressed contrariety in his employment of the foregoing quotation, 'every captive thought'. Ockham himself distinguishes between the authority of Scripture, which is infallible, and of the authority of the Church, which can on occasions – according to him – be wrong. But the quotation about 'every captive thought' comes from the New Testament, not from the Church's pronounce-ments (which are clearly distinct from the New Testament in this context, on his own interpretation). It is wrong, then, on Ockham's own terms, to use this quotation form as infallible authority, to under-write the authority of an external institution which, he agrees, can be wrong in its judgements. Ockham deployed that guarantee to prevent himself allowing his razor its full generality. It is tragic, in the perspec-tive of the medieval contemporary opposition to Ockham, to observe this internal inconsistency in Ockham's philosophy: a sincere believer painfully doing his best, as he sees it, to pacify antagonistic inconsis-tent Church authorities by attempting artificially to manufacture agreement with them, when neither logic nor his razor demands it. Clearly we should position all this with problems any thinker has when living in a quasi-totalitarian regime in which the threat against life is not uncommon, as a device for achieving conformity in belief. In contrast, Ockham's campaign, in the last twenty years of his life, to convict the Pope of heresy manifests a certain resilience and indepen-dence of mind.

We stand outside the limitations of Ockham's own life situation (but, as he would have done, have difficulty in standing outside our own) and are aware of the influence of our own times on our picture of Ockham. Nevertheless, could we attempt some damage-limitation or reconstruction of the fragments of Ockham's philosophy criticized above? First, he could have dropped his nominalist analysis and reinterpretation of the Trinity. Second, one might argue, irrespective of his *presentation* of the razor's exceptions, that Ockham should accept (what we would now term) deviant logics as having equal status to the bivalent one, and allow him subjunctive conditional certainty in a plural world. This of course would not leave him happy, since it would entail that his options are only possibly true. Third, someone could designate the Trinitarian doctrine itself as incorrect, and so the false conclusions thereby implied by the true antecedents simply identify a route on which Ockham did not continue (or of which he was not aware). This issue might be expressed as follows: in the foregoing discussion we have seen that Ockham used the Bible to develop some of his positions (as he did more extensively in his political philosophy, as the section below shows). Almost none of the defining terms of the Trinity occur in the Bible (nor do synonyms of them). So Ockham could have redefined the incarnation so as to avoid the troublesome terms which he judged require a restriction in the scope of his logic. Unfortunately, incarnation terminology in the Bible is not nominalist-conceptualist, and the propositions there do not fit the two-name theory.

Fourth, one might utilize Alféri's research (see [14.14]), and propose that a post-structuralist estimation of Ockham's razor removes the need for the type of logical consistency which Ockham sought in formal theory. Fifth, one could transform hints in Ockham, and argue that his unconscious is ahead of his formal consciousness. One would thus propose that the solution to his formal logic problems is to dump his formal programme, and accept that, underneath his apparently 'logical inferences', at the crossroads where the collision occurs between inference using the razor and the incarnation, the answer to some of Ockham's problems could be to metaphorize, as a 'game', areas of his whole logic. Although of course Wittgenstein did not suggest this type of enterprise,[43] it might be envisaged as a possible upshot of his analyses of what it is 'to follow a rule' in his *Philosophical Investigations*.[44] Of course, this is revolutionary even by our contemporary standards. Sixth, an Ockhamist could attempt to circumvent the foregoing and other criticisms by adopting the sort of paraconsistent logic that Priest devises,[45] fragments of which occupied some medieval logicians. In a paraconsistent scenario, there are limits to cognition (in Ockham's case the Trinity), and there are semantic closures smaller than the set of all propositions, yet which facilitate access to transcendence in part using set-theoretic reductionism. A paraconsistent approach has the drawback that it requires a given proposition to be (or that it could be) true and false. This would help support Ockham's treatment of the Trinity, whilst eliminating his law of non-contradiction. A reason for mentioning some of these ideas is to indicate that, taken together, Ockham's philosophy of logic and his philosophy amount to a partial hybrid of competing logics.

But brute forms of Ockham's razor have been accepted and popular since his time, increasingly with the emergence of experimental science, though with exceptions. J. S. Mill is rightly regarded as a mediator of Ockham's logic from the medieval world to modern philosophy ([14.69]). Nevertheless, in respect of parsimony, Mill was appalled by Ockham's razor. In 1865 Mill attacked Sir William Hamilton for his use of a version of the razor ([14.70] 418–19). Hamilton's own positions on logic were sometimes incompatible with Ockham's. He was moving towards a quantification theory which, if it had any relation to Ockham, was one of contrast,[46] in which there is a closer relation to Frege's quantificational logic than the sort of Ockhamist logic that Mill (apart from the razor) had espoused. Later, Russell's practice of eliminating, where possible, existential quantification, and Hans Reichenbach's concern with simplicity evinced in his idea of logical empiricism, as Sober ([14.86]) notices have similarities with some uses of Ockham's razor, though neither philosopher is generally compatible with Ockham. Dummett applies a restrained use of Ockham's razor in mathematical theory, while he notes that denying a thought by the process of negation is intrinsically complex ([14.29] 38, 317).

❦ ANTI-REALISM'S TRUE RAZOR? ❦

The foregoing challenged Adams's claim that the various versions of Ockham's razor are 'in the first instance, methodological principles, and it is not obvious how they are related to truth or probability'. Surely it is, in relevant respects, clear how Ockham relates at least some of them to truth. Adams's view does not account for at least one version of Ockham's razor, which she quotes: 'When a proposition comes out true for things, if two things suffice for its truth, it is superfluous to assume a third.'[47] The expression 'comes out true' (*verificatur*) and the word 'truth' are related to truth explicitly, by being the purported measure for true propositions in a thesis canvassing for a reductionist use of numerical principles as the basis for an austere ontology regulating generalization in logic. For Ockham, number relations are real. Such relational propositions have truth-conditions and substitution instances.

351

They accord with a rough correspondence theory (not as well developed as those of Paul of Venice, and adopted without Duns Scotus's full realism, while yet they are not mind-dependent). Of truth, Ockham states that, 'truth, i.e. the concept *truth*, in addition to the proposition it signifies, connotes that things are such in reality as they are conveyed to be by means of the proposition'.[48] Although Ockham's theses are distinct from the semantics of Tarski–Davidson (in which to give the truth-conditions is a way of giving the meaning of a sentence),[49] yet the various features of Ockham's 'correspondence' presuppositions partially parallel these modern authors, principally because of the way he is attracted to anti-realism.[50] Ockham's 'correspondence' position was pressed by his anti-realism, a view which had some similarity with Peter Aureoli's and Henry Harclay's disposition to dismantle direct realism.

Marenbon's view appears to offer the most explanatory promise: Ockham's rejection of essential essence realism, together with his acceptance of truth-conditions for the semantics of the external world, eventually imply that his adoption of a conceptual system for understanding the world in terms of species and genera is merely one possible system – whereas for his contemporary opponents it is a system which has to be used if one is to achieve a full understanding of reality. Any of these interpretations involve a use of truth which restores to it the role not accorded it by Adams's opinion that the above forms of the razor are methodological and that it is not obvious how they are related to truth.[51] Indeed, the razor's purported theory-generating informativeness seems to be its merit. But on occasions the razor is contradicted by the presence of informative complexity in a new more productive theory (as with fundamental physics and superstrings[52]), which is more informative than a previous simpler theory. Although scientists appeal to Ockham's razor, their use of it often explicitly conflicts with Ockham's own express claim that it should only be employed outside the scope of observation statements,[53] which complies well with his desire to press demonstrative science into admission of uncertainty.

Ockham was aiming at a reduction of individuation in ontology, and he denied that some relational states between propositions have to be distinct.[54] Ockham's use of a complex procedure using negation to achieve reduction of entities, is itself also a negation of parsimony, since its strategy is to acknowledge complex propositions while positing them as such, then negating them to achieve their elimination.[55]

Ockham's desire to bring parsimony to ontology internalizes a tension between realism and epistemology. If one conceives that necessity in reason is a criterion of identity for restricting ontological plurality, then ontological contingencies may be unwarrantably censored (and this can cut against empirical productivity, as much as it can against semantics). Ockham's way of meeting this tension is to internalize a version of anti-realism into his epistemological programme. But this 'anti-realism' is precariously positioned in relation to the traditions which he controverts, in particular if contrasted with twentieth-century opponents of realism. Ockham, after what appears to be an early position in which he agrees with Scotus, attacks Duns Scotus's strong realism,[56] though concurring with Duns Scotus that real relations are mind-independent.[57] His aim is commendable, in his parsimonious wish to place limits on excessively strong claims about empiricism, and at a time when scientific mythology and ignorance falsely generalized local experience.

We can concur with Goddu that this tendency is in keeping with our contemporary physics ([14.44] 208–31). Goddu furnishes us with the Quantum Mechanical Bell theorem's scope, as an example to flesh out Ockham in current physics. This theorem is to the effect that, in universalizing realist claims in science, we must relinquish claims on locality or determinism respecting universal claims for empiricism. Clearly Ockham is a far cry from Bell. Ockham was concerned to argue that positing additional entities is not in principle a strategy for resolving realist problems in favour of a strong realism, just as the proposal that there are hidden variables in quantum mechanics does not resolve the issue of action at a distance without a medium. It seems clear that his view was being opposed by William of Crathorn, who lectured at Oxford in 1331 ([14.93] 255–74, etc.). Crathorn held that viewing was through a medium. He devised an original theory of knowledge that disagreed with Ockham (and Holcot, [14.93] 93). In particular, Crathorn, concerned with the purported uncertainty involved in intuitive cognition, affirms that incomplete objects in a propositional context are complex, disputing Ockham's reductionism and epistemological certainty. Although Crathorn's theories are often uneven and cavalier in their attention to views of opponents, they illustrate that Ockham was part of a general trend of exploration in Oxford. Crathorn's comprehension of propositional complexity in the context of incomplete objects is an unexpected partial parallel with our modern concepts of the incompleteness of a logical predicate (to be attached to a subject term), which pulls against Ockham's two-name theory. But while disagreeing with Crathorn and others, Ockham was impelled by the razors to admit incompleteness as a conceptual condition, so as to meet the restrictions of ignorance and yet adequacy according to empirical reductionism.[58]

∾ FUTURE CONTINGENTS ∾

Looking from the present at the universe, Ockham was to some degree aware that we are observing its past. If psychoanalysis has any lesson to teach here ([14.22] 38–46), it is that analysis of the future is intentional, and the future is a sort of metonymy for present concerns, as well as a series of codes for covert absorption and transference of our pasts. No doubt such matters can be overstated. But with Ockham and his contemporaries, the most obvious constituent in their talk of future contingents, only slightly off stage, is their personal interest in that future. The study of God's knowledge of the future is an understanding of how he deals with his people. The conditionality of present life requires guidance by instruction in the principles according to which God knows the future in relation to people in the present.

In practice, however, the scholarly debates about such topics were often highly abstract technical affairs, and even used to feed earthly vendettas, networking through generations. Boethius refined the conception (cf. Chapter 1), which is followed by Peter the Lombard in his *Sentences*, that God is timeless and has present capacity to know from all eternity everything he knows in the present. Thomas Buckingham took up this thesis in his *On the Contingency of the Future, and Free Will*. His thesis was an attack on Thomas Bradwardine's *De causa Dei contra Pelagium* (*In God's defence, against Pelagius*). Bradwardine's view was that humanity exercised freedom to choose, or not, to obey God's will without the interference of preordination. As de la Torre has demonstrated (14.94] ch. 5), Buckingham carefully refrains from explaining that Bradwardine accepted that the First Cause regiments people, yet they are able to act freely in secondary cause contexts. For Bradwardine, God, from all eternity, chose freely from the array of future contingents. Such contingency (*contingentia ad utrumlibet*) applies also to humans in the secondary cause contexts.

A generation earlier Ockham had attempted to apply his sense of simplicity to reduce confusion. For him, duration was the foundation feature of time. God has knowledge of the future. Ockham was troubled by Aristotle's *On Interpretation*. In accordance with the standard medieval view, Ockham took Aristotle to have argued that singular propositions about future affairs are not, prior to the time of which they speak, true or false. Since for Ockham this violates the doctrine that all propositions are true or false (to cut a long story short), there must never have been future contingents, or they are illogical.[59]

Ockham, then, interprets Aristotle as maintaining that God is, in a special sense, possibly ignorant of a future contingent. A reason for this is that – expressed that way – it is not an epistemological existent.

That is to say, the future does not exist, thus future contingents do not instantiate, self-inhere, or obtain now, for the future, since it is not there nor here to refer to. But God's absolute power, for Ockham, alters this bald state of affairs. Although in a narrow sense an individual, for Ockham and for Scotus, only intuition can deform this boundary for God ([14.64] 184–5), if and can only exercise intuitive cognition of an existing thing, the conjunction of God's absolute power and if the law of non-contradiction is not violated. We should appreciate in this context that for Ockham logic is possibility for ontology as well as for propositions; this is partly why he was agreeable to 'limiting' God's knowledge of future contingents: in a strict sense, they do not exist, do not supposit. Despite this, God's omnipotence infinitely empowers his intuition, and God is also able, as well as willing, to make and implement promises about the future,[60] which both inform his use of epistemological possibility and construct intuitive cognition.

～ OCKHAM'S ETHICS AND POLITICAL ～ PHILOSOPHY

Ockham has waited over 600 years for the first publication in any modern language of his political philosophy.[61]

The castigation of Ockham by the 'humble' Christian Lutterel, with his complaint to the Pope at Avignon in 1323, embodied and generated an attitude to Ockham which outlawed him for some of his contemporary, and later, would-be readers. Lutterel was generally disliked and opposed at Oxford university. His appointment seems one of those conundrums that can attend an institution: the contrary of its identity is appointed to lead it. Possibly, since Ockham bore the brunt of Lutterel's vehemence, as part of a tactic for the latter to ingratiate himself with the Pope's power-base, this was a cause of the alienation Ockham increasingly experienced, though we ought to contend with his own sense of embodying the Oxford tradition which Lutterel dared to change.

No doubt, alienation was nevertheless a growing component in Ockham's identity, while yet it is only one thread in a complex fabric. Alienation is a property of 'romantic modernism', for example in French modernism, emerging in the early eighteenth century. Holland has identified schizoid behaviour in Baudelaire, induced by his alien-ation. In this case, narcissism encouraged by an elitist perspective was projected on to the society, which was challenged to conform to the writer's perspective.[62] Offler judged that Ockham was prisoner of his own elitism and had no interest in following the democratizing move to popularize scholasticism in the vernacular ([14.72] 341–2) such as

Conrad of Megenberg displayed. Indeed, Offler mentions that the latter was fighting against the vogue of Ockhamist 'modernism'.

Fundamental to a modernism is individualism, and this held true for Ockham's ethics and political action. As McGrade explains (see [14.62] 17ff.), there is a puzzling tension between Ockham's individualism in practice (Ockham emphasizes not just individuality, but this property for sets of individuals) in contrast with the explicit abstractness, or impersonal style (even when writing of personal matters) of much of his writing on the topic. One could interpret this as a splitting of psychological identity along modernist lines. We do not know enough about his time at Avignon, nor of Lutterel's, to understand what party politics made up the pressure on Ockham to provoke, or Lutterel act as foil for, his fracture with the Church. It was quite usual for a theologian of Ockham's ilk to write political philosophy and ethics, not least if he were following Aristotle as the ideal. Offler observed that it looks as if Ockham seriously attended to Aristotle's *Politics* and *Ethics* in 1339–40 ([14.72] 340), after he had written a considerable amount of the political philosophy. (See Ockham's reference in III *Dialogus*, I, to Aristotle's *Politics* V, 8.)

It was some time later, in the 1340s, subsequent to more general compositions on political philosophy, that Ockham responded to the Pope's assertion of supreme political authority and its relation to poverty, with his *A Short Discourse on the Tyrannical Goverrnment: Over Things Divine and Human, but Especially the Empire and Those Subject to the Empire Usurped by Some Who Are Called Highest Pontiffs* (see [14.11]). Hardly a basis for ecumenical *rapprochement*. In the convention of the time this title measures Ockham's antagonism, individualism and pragmatism. It is a surprise if one is familiar only with the intellectual range circumscribed by his theoretical philosophy and logic. Consider for example Ockham's intensive use of the Bible, for example in *The Work of Ninety Days* (in [14.7]). In his confrontation of the Pope's extravagant riches, he sounds like a member of a theological underground of, say, Peter Waldo of Lyon in the twelfth century. He reminds the Pope that Jesus and the Apostles had no riches, concluding with the allegation that in such matters the Pope follows Constantine, not Peter ([14.7] 105). This policy-aim to contextualize the Bible does not expand to its internal limits, however, though one should not minimize its radical strategy. For example, it does not occur to Ockham to use the function of implication or dialectic within the New Testament narrative presuppositions to discover their own internal limiting parameters. (He uses the citations, instead, as checks for excesses in papal misuse of its rightful original position.) Ockham might, for example, have questioned, within the foregoing debate, how it is that the authority of Peter in Matthew 16 extends beyond the lifetime of Peter to others. Nevertheless his philosophical questioning about the relation of divine narratology to political institutions is bold and his new recognition of a repressed connection, in an atmosphere of intolerance, should not be underestimated.[63]

Ockham can be usefully placed by seeing him in relation to John of Paris,[64] a Dominican who had supported Aquinas against Ockham's order, the Franciscans. These two theologians, the former a disciple of the latter, spoke of law, discipline, and education as ruling functions of the state over the individual, though Aquinas stressed the natural law, in accordance with his view of Aristotle in his *Nicomachean Ethics*. Like Aristotle, John is interested in what it is to be human, rather than secular power-bases, whilst the state is the decision-maker and custodian of the common good. John's synthesis, which was influential in the law of states, lays a foundation for fourteenth-century individualism and the state authority which denies it. So Ockham came at a time when there was a growing awareness of individualism and yet a lack of a counterpart discrimination in its corollary: the state should not obtrude on rights and liberty. Ockham argues that these come from God, instantiated in nature.[65] Consequently papal authority should not usurp God's power and provision by countermanding individualism. It is in the identity of a human experiencing this nature that general laws are derived from nature, and from revelation, on personal liberty and its collective form. There is some similarity on facets of individualism and freedom between Ockham and more recent philosophies of freedom.[66] Holopainen has proposed that Ockham advanced a single theory of divine command ethics ([14.51] 133–49, etc.), which allows two moralities. Divine morality, transcendent with respect to cultural variables, supervenes on, and yet is manifest in, nature.[67] But the relation between Ockham's individualism and the logic of his various analyses is complex. The reader may with particular profit read Adams's work on the extent of Ockham's use or manifestation of individualisms (see [14.13]). She writes of the polyvalency of individualism, plausibly arguing that Ockham's variety of individualisms are logically independent of each other, and warning against the seductive lure to integrate this variety into a singularity which can then easily be fitted into a grand historical sweep. These are important points, and ones which can be used to probe the extent and veracity of his parsimony.

There are other considerations to complement such explorations. Logically, independence does not of course imply that separate individualisms cannot be consistent with each other, just as tokens are values of a single type. When we are attempting to assess a complex original figure such as Ockham, who also derives many of his patterns of thought from his contemporaries, it is problematic to develop connections, as Adams is aware. Given his sometimes original use of contemporary influences, Ockham can be elusive and difficult; he is a nuanced mirror of his era, which dislocates his period's self-perception of continuity.

 NOTES

Ockham is a central figure in fourteenth-century philosophy and his thought is discussed in a number of chapters. Readers may find the presentation of some of his main ideas in Chapters 15 and 17 below a useful introduction to the wider-ranging and more speculative discussion in the present chapter. [EDITOR]

1 At least, those of whom manuscripts are extant. See Courtenay [14.26].

2 See Ockham [14.5] *Ordinatio*, I, d. 2, q. 7.

3 See Knysh [14.55] 25-6, who suggests that the *liber suus* of 1327 was a technical stumbling-block for the authorities.

4 Spade [14.89] IV shows how Thomas Bradwardine's research on insolubilia assisted him to craft a theory of signification that has correspondence-theory properties.

5 I propose that 'modernist logic' be used to mark philosophical trends that run contemporarily with the familiar use of the term 'modernism' for a general cultural context. There is a need for research on cross-currents between these contexts and philosophy in nineteenth-century European modernisms.

6 See Frege, 'Compound logical thoughts', in [14.36]; cf. Dummett [14.30].

7 Adams [14.12]. Adams has only one brief reference to Frege (p. 388), and four to Russell (pp. 136–7, 150, 536, 797).

8 Adams [14.12] refers to the 1st edn (Ithaca, NY, 1962) of Geach's book. There have in fact been two edns of the book since 1962. The 2nd in 1964, 3rd in 1980. Adams was published in 1987. In his 3rd edn, Geach ([14.37] 13), explains that he rewrote parts of the book, noting, 'The sections most affected by these changes are sections 32, 34, and 35 … The only major change in Chapter Three is in section 36.' These include the main sections to which Adams refers. Adams ([14.12] 388), having only one brief reference to Frege, offers no presentation or proof of what the 'Frege bias' is supposed to be.

9 See Spade [14.87] 216, and the section below, 'Ockham on reference'.

10 Russell was unable to judge that work. Smiley [14.84] assesses Russell on descriptions.

11 Adams ([14.12] 897–9) briefly refers to David Lewis in a taxonomical remark on Ockham, noting his indexical theory of actuality. She observes that Ockham's 'uniform assumption that temporal indicators cannot be eliminated in favour of an eternal-present show that he was not an Indexicalist'.

12 The relation between metaphoric language in scientific theory and logical space in philosophy is a facet of 'logic as a work of art'. A starting point for this new area of research is the use in Wittgenstein [14.100] of a proposition as a projection in space, together with the role of space and geometry in Mallarmé [14.63]. For studies on this latter aspect, see Bowie [14.21], Gibson [14.42], Reynolds [14.79], Scott [14.83].

13 Bowie [14.22] 37–42, 103–4, etc., relates logic to creativity.

14 Russell [14.98] regularly confuses premises with assumptions.

15 Someone might wish to adapt Ockham's theory of a 'mental language' by using the sort of innate syntaxes devised by Chomsky. Chomsky [14.24] proposed a thesis that incorporates indeterminacy into his theories of mind, however. According to Chomsky, our ordinary uses, not some ideal language, are nested innately. This would be the opposite of what Ockham needs. Chomsky's generalization of indeterminacy is also alien to Ockham, and it destabilizes his nominal and causal relations. Russell's misinterpretation of Ockham has been noted by Offler [14.72] 338 and n. 1.

16 Ockham [14.5] *Summa logicae* I, c. 1.

17 Dummett ([14.29] 59–62, etc.) offers valuable analysis of proper names and other subject/predicate differences.

18 See Aristotle *On Interpretation* 1–3, 10, 11.

19 This argument follows Quine's work as presented by Dummett [(14.30] 223–4, 294).

20 Aquinas *Summa theologiae* I, q. 76, a. 6, ad 2. Cf. [14.12] 13–16, 679–997.

21 As Geach [14.37] 201–2.

22 On links between these ideas of Ockham's and Wodeham and Rodington, see Tachau [14.93] 203–5. Walter Chatton attacked this aspect of Ockham's thought.

23 As White [14.97] 173, referring to Ockham [14.5] *Quodlibet* III q. 8.

24 Kripke's [14.56] approach amplifies in a different mould social and causal roles, for which, if adjusted, one could develop aspects of Burley's approach.

25 As Adams ([14.12] 329) states it. On the different types of supposition see below, Chapter 17, pp. 412–14.

26 Adams [14.12] 387–8 mentions that Frege's use of 'is' could be brought into the semantic analysis; but Frege's approach to predication and the role of 'is' in such uses is the contrary of Ockham's.

27 Aquinas, *Summa*, Ia, q. 13, art. 12.

28 Frege uses this one German term with the three senses of 'referring', 'referent' and the relation of 'reference'. Dummett [14.29] maintains that Frege does not confuse these separate uses. So do we here have one term, also containing two polysemes, or a metaphor?

29 Suggested by Jane Heal. I should stress that this whole 'Ockham' reconstruction has nothing to do with Heal's theory and is not suggested by her, though I am indebted to her reaction to my above idea.

30 A suggestion about paraphrasing (e.g. 'she's a right one') indexicality, not in a referential role, not in an Ockham context, and without my generalizing thesis over whole general predicates, comes from Heal's working paper delivered at the Cambridge Moral Sciences Club, 21 January 1997. I acknowledge her permission to mention it.

31 Marenbon [14.65], [14.64] 57 for Bacon's Paris study and teaching of Aristotle.

32 See Walter Chatton [14.4] I, d. 30, q. 1, a. 4.

33 Duns Scotus, *Opera omnia*, ed. L. Wadding, J. Ponce *et al.*, Duran, Lyons, 1639, vol. VII, p. 723.

34 Aristotle *On the Heavens* II, xii, 292a–b25.

35 Ockham [14.5], *Ordinatio* I, d. 30, q. 2.

36 Ockham [14.5], *Treatise on Quantity* II i, q. 1.
37 Aspects of this use of *ponenda* are not unlike a notion that Dummett ([14.29] 309) pointed out in Gentzen's use of 'suppose'. Gentzen formalized inference to allow for a use similar to natural language reasoning, 'Suppose that . . .'. If contradictory inferences follow from that use, one can withdraw the premisses which led to it. This complies well with Ockham's desire for non-contradiction.
38 See Haack's [14.46] treatment of Frege's 'presupposition'. For scrutiny of 'assertion-sign' see Dummett [14.29] 328–9.
39 Geach [14.38] 288–301. Adams [14.12] 989–90 quotes him ([14.38] 296–7), concerning Ockham's use of *humanitas* and regarding Nestorianism. Although demurring from Geach's view, Adams never attempts to fault Geach's use of logic.
40 Ockham [14.5], *Treatise on Quantity* I, q. 1.
41 Adams [14.12] 1008–10. She is citing Ockham [14.5], *Ordinatio* I, d. 2. q. 1.
42 Adams [14.12] 1008–10 numbers this maxim 7.
43 White [14.97] serves as a framework for this suggestion.
44 This point could be applied with profit to any of Ockham's logic. There is a profound treatment of the research in Boghassian [14.19].
45 Priest [14.74]; cf. Smiley's [14.85] criticisms.
46 Geach ([14.37] 27) points out that the expression 'quantify' and 'quantification' appear to derive from Hamilton.
47 Adams [14.12] 156: 'Quando propositio verificatur pro rebus, si duae res sufficiunt ad eius veritatem, superfluum est ponere tertiam.' Adams refers to its use in Ockham [14.5], *Quodlibet* IV, q. 24.
48 Ockham [14.5], *Quodlibet* VI, q. 29.
49 D. Davidson, 'Truth and meaning', in *Inquiries into Truth and Interpretation*, Oxford, 1984, pp. 24ff.
50 Boler ([14.20] 470; see Spade [14.87]) suggests that Ockham might be committed to adopting a sophisticated coherence theory of truth. Coherence theory (inadvertently) allows internal contradictions: they only have internally to cohere.
51 A response to defend this use of 'methodological principle' might be envisaged: does not Dummett [14.31] 164 employ the expression to describe an approach advocated by Wittgenstein [14.99], and is not criticism of Adams's 'methodological principles' unwarranted? No, because Dummett is contrasting Frege's (and others') truth-conditional theory of meaning with Wittgenstein's methodological principle concerning *use*, whereas Ockham's 'razors' use logical terms to govern logic and its ontology, in which Ockham proposed truth-conditional logic.
52 See Gross [14.45], and resumption of this theme below in the section *Antirealism's true razor?*
53 Ockham [14.5], *Reportatio* II, q. 150.
54 Ockham [14.5], *Ordinatio* I, d. 30, q. 1.
55 Cf. Horst [14.52] 365–70 (from a perspective outside Ockham studies).
56 See Ockham [14.5], *Ordinatio* I, d. 30, q. 1, and *Quodlibet* VI, qq. 8–19, etc.
57 See Ockham [14.5], *Ordinatio* I, d. 30, q. 1.
58 An interesting extension of the principle of parsimony is provided by the astrophysical cosmology of the early universe, where some scientists seek a single equation functioning as *the* universal for the whole universe: see Rees [14.78], but cf. Hunt [14.53]. On the problems posed by such science (can its formulations be taken literally?), see Dallaporta [14.27] and Bell [14.18]. Perhaps

Ockham, like these cosmologists, arrives at counter-intuitive consequences in his search for simplicity. On this whole question see Popper [14.73], Lewy [14.61] and Gibson [14.40].

59 See Aristotle *On Interpretation*, IX, 1–16, 18–25. Few modern interpreters would accept this view. Cf. Anscombe [14.15] 53. See also Milbank [14.67] on Ockham's confusion in this case.

60 Ockham [14.5], *On Predestination* q. 1.

61 McGrade [14.11] ix. As he points out (n. 1) E. Lewis [14.60] translated 23 chapters, and F. Oakley 4 chapters, in Lerner [14.57].

62 This term is used in the sense of Holland [14.50]. In Gibson [14.42] Pt I, there is a comparative conception of 'modernism' complementary to the present study.

63 On the problems about connecting theoretical with political philosophy, and on criteria for difference and identity, see Milbank [14.68] chs. 7 and 8; Ward [14.96] 24–8, and also, more broadly, Dummett [14.29] 73–80.

64 John of Paris, *On Royal and Papal Power*.

65 *On the Power of Emperors and Popes*, in Ockham's Opera Politics IV, ed. H. S. Offler, Oxford, British Academy, 1997, 278–355. Volumes I–III are edited by J. Sikes *et al.*, Manchester, 1940–63.

66 Rawls [14.76], and with regard to Aristotle *Ethics* V; Dworkin [14.32] on inalienability of individual rights.

67 See Coleman ([14.25] 27) and generally for a concise valuable study on Ockham's nature and rights.

❧❧ BIBLIOGRAPHY ❧❧

Original Language Editions and Manuscripts

14.1 Adam Wodeham *Sentences* 1, I, I, ed. G. Gál, in 'Adam of Wodeham's question on the "complexe significabile" . . .', in *Franciscan Studies* 37 (1973): 66–102.

14.2 John of Reading *Sentences* I, Florence, Biblioteca Nazionale Centrale, MS conventi soppressi D.IV.95.

14.3 Thomas Buckingham *De contingentia futurorum et arbitrii libertate*, in B. R. de la Torre, *Thomas Buckingham* [14.94].

14.4 Walter Chatton *Reportatio*, Paris, Bibliothèque Nationale, lat. 15887.

14.5 William of Ockham *Opera philosophica et theologica*, 17 vols, St Bonaventure, NY, Franciscan Institute, 1967–88.

Translations

14.6 William of Ockham 'Five Questions on Universals' (from the *Ordinatio*), in P. V. Spade (ed. and trans.) *Five Texts on the Medieval Problem of Universals*, Indianapolis, Ind., Hackett, 1994.

14.7 ―― *A Letter to the Friars Minor and Other Writings*, ed. A. S. McGrade and J. Kilcullen, trans. J. Kilcullen, Cambridge, 1995. (Note: this is the volume announced before publication, in the Preface, p. ix, to *A Short Discourse* [14.11], as *Selections from the Major Political Works*.)

14.8 —— *Philosophical Writings*, trans., intro. and notes by P. Boehner, Latin text and trans. revised by S. F. Brown with new Foreword, Indianapolis, Ind., Hackett, 1990.

14.9 —— *Predestination, God's Foreknowledge and Future Contingents*, 2nd edn, trans., intro., notes and appendices by M. M. Adams and N. Kretzmann, Indianapolis, Ind., Hackett, 1983.

14.10 —— *Quodlibetal Questions*, vols 1 and 2, trans. A. J. Freddoso and F. E. Kelley, New Haven, Conn., Yale University Press, 1991.

14.11 —— *A Short Discourse on the Tyrannical Government*, ed. A. S. McGrade, trans. J. Kilcullen, Cambridge, Cambridge University Press, 1992.

Editor's Bibliographical Note

Since the 'Studies' section of Arthur Gibson's bibliography is mainly occupied by details of the wide range of comparative material cited in his chapter, it may be useful to give a quick guide to the basic secondary bibliography on Ockham and his followers. Where the works are listed by Gibson below, just the author's name and reference number are given.

Biography

L. Baudry, *Guillaume d'Occam: sa vie, ses oeuvres, ses idées sociales et politiques*, Paris, Vrin, 1949.

Bibliography

V. Heynck, 'Ockham – Literatur: 1919–1949', *Franziskanische Studien* 32 (1950): 164–83; J. Reilley, 'Ockham bibliography, 1950–67', *Franciscan Studies* 28 (1968): 19–214.

General philosophical studies

Adams [14.12] is fundamental. Other general studies include Alféri [14.14], L. Baudry, *Lexique philosophique de Guillaume d'Occam: étude des notions fondamentales*, Paris, Léthielleux, 1975; G. Leff, *William of Ockham: the Metamorphosis of Scholastic Discourse*, Manchester and Totowa, NJ, Manchester University Press/Rowman & Littlefield, 1975; and C. Panaccio, *Les Mots, les concepts et les choses: la sémentique de Guillaume d'Occam et le nominalisme d'aujourd'hui* (Analytiques 3), Montreal and Paris, Bellarmin/Vrin, 1991 (this compares Ockham's semantics with modern Anglo-American discussions; a useful foil for the rather different comparison made in this chapter). P. Boehner's important articles are collected as *Collected Articles on Ockham*, ed. E. Buytaert, St Bonaventure, NY, Louvain and Paderborn, Franciscan Institute,

Nauwelaerts and Schöningh, 1958. Vossenkuhl [14.95] contains excellent articles by specialists on different aspects of Ockham's work.

Particular areas

Logic   E. Moody, *The Logic of William of Ockham*, London, Sheed & Ward, 1935, was groundbreaking but is now rather dated. Adams [14.12] covers this area thoroughly in volume I of her study; see also Chapter 17 below and bibliography there.
Epistemology   Tachau [14.93] places Ockham's views in context and assesses their influence.
Ethics   Holopainen [14.51].
Future contingents   A. Plantinga, 'On Ockham's way out', *Faith and Philosophy* 3 (1986): 171–200, repr. in T. V. Morris (ed.) *The Concept of God*, Oxford, Oxford University Press, 1987; D. Perler, *Prädestination, Zeit und Kontingenz: philosophisch-historische Untersuchungen zu Wilhelm von Ockhams 'Tractatus de praedestinatione et de praescientia Dei respectu futurorum contingentium'* (Bochumer Studien zur Philosophie 12), Amsterdam, Grüner, 1988.
Political theory   McGrade [14.62] and J. Miethke, *Ockhams Weg zur Sozialphilosophie*, Berlin, De Gruyter, 1969.

Contemporaries, followers and the next generation of Oxford philosophers

Tachau [14.93] revises previous views about Ockham's relation to his contemporaries and his influence; see also Chapters 15 and 16 below. Important general studies and collections include: J. Biard, *Logique et théorie du signe au XIVe siècle*; A. Hudson and M. Wilks (eds) *From Ockham to Wyclif*, Oxford, Blackwell Publishers, 1987; Z. Kaluza and P. Vignaux (eds) *Preuve et raisons à l'Université de Paris: Logique, ontologie et théologie au XIVe siècle*, Paris, Vrin, 1984.
Particular thinkers: Adam Wodeham   W. J. Courtenay, *Adam Wodeham: an Introduction to his Life and Writings*, Leiden, E. J. Brill, 1978;
Henry of Harclay   C. Balić, 'Henricus de Harclay et Ioannes Duns Scotus', *Mélanges offerts à Etienne Gilson*, Toronto, Pontifical Institute of Mediaeval Studies, 1959.
Oxford *calculatores* (in general)   E. D. Sylla, 'The Oxford Calculators', ch. 27 in *CHLMP*, provides a good introduction; see also M. Clagett, *The Science of Mechanics on the Middle Ages*, Madison, Wis., University of Wisconsin Press, 1959; E. D. Sylla, 'Medieval concepts of the latitude of forms: the Oxford Calculators', *Archives de l'histoire doctrinale et littéraire du moyen âge* 40 (1973): 223–83.
Richard Swineshead   J. A. Weisheipl, 'Roger Swyneshed, OSB, logician, natural philosopher and theologian', in *Oxford Studies Presented to Daniel Callus*, Oxford, Oxford University Press, 1964.
Robert Holcot   F. Hoffmann, *Die theologische Methode des Oxford Dominikanlehrers Robert Holcot* (BGPTMA) (Münster, Aschendorff, 1972) (wider in scope than its title suggests).
Thomas Bradwardine   G. Leff, *Bradwardine and the Pelagians*, Cambridge, Cambridge University Press, 1957; H. A. Oberman, *Archbishop Thomas Bradwardine: a Fourteenth-century Augustinian*, Utrecht, Zemink and Zoon, 1957; E. W.

Dolniowski, *Thomas Bradwardine: a View of Time and a Vision of Eternity in Fourteenth-century Thought*, Leiden, E. J. Brill, 1995.
Thomas Buckingham J.-F. Genest, *Prédétermination et liberté crée à Oxford au XIVe siècle: Buckingham contre Bradwardine* (Etudes de philosophie médiévale 70), Paris, Vrin, 1992.
William Heytesbury W. Curtis, *William Heytesbury: Medieval Logic and the Rise of Mathematical Physics* (University of Wisconsin Publications in Medieval Science 3), Madison, Wis., University of Wisconsin Press, 1956.

Studies

14.12 Adams, M. M. *William Ockham*, 2 vols, Notre Dame, Ind., University of Notre Dame Press, 1987.
14.13 —— 'Ockham's individualisms', in [14.95].
14.14 Alféri, P. *Guillaume D'Ockham le singulier*, Paris, Minuit, 1989.
14.15 Anscombe, G. E. M. 'Aristotle and the sea battle', in *The Collected Philosophical Papers of G. E. M. Anscombe*, vol. 1, Oxford, Blackwell Publishers, 1981.
14.16 —— 'The first person', in *The Collected Papers of G. E. M. Anscombe*, Oxford, Blackwell Publishers, 1981.
14.17 —— *Intention*, Oxford, Blackwell Publishers, 1957.
14.18 Bell, J. S. *Speakable and Unspeakable in Quantum Physics*, Cambridge, Cambridge University Press, 1987.
14.19 Boghassian, P. 'The rule-following consideration', in *Mind* 98 (1989): 507–49.
14.20 Boler, J. F. 'Intuitive and abstractive intuition', in *CHLMP*.
14.21 Bowie, M. *Mallarmé and the Art of Being Difficult*, Cambridge, Cambridge University Press, 1978.
14.22 —— *Psychoanalysis and the Future of Theory*, Oxford, Blackwell Publishers, 1993.
14.23 Butler, C. *Early Modernism*, Oxford, Oxford University Press, 1994.
14.24 Chomsky, N. 'Language and nature', in *Mind* 104 (1995): 1–62.
14.25 Coleman, J. 'The individual and the medieval state', in J. Coleman (ed.) *The Individual in Political Theory and Practice*, Oxford, Oxford University Press, 1996.
14.26 Courtenay, W. J. 'Theology and theologians from Ockham to Wyclif', in J. I. Catto and R. Evans (eds) *The History of the University of Oxford*, vol. II, *Late Medieval Oxford*, Oxford, Clarendon Press, 1992.
14.27 Dallaporta, N. 'The different levels of connection between science and objective reality', in G. Ellis, M. Lanza and J. Miller (eds) *The Renaissance of Generality, Relativity and Cosmology*, Cambridge, Cambridge University Press, 1993.
14.28 Dummett, M. *The Elements of Intuitionism*, Oxford, Oxford University Press, 1977.
14.29 —— *Frege: Philosophy of Language*, 2nd edn, Duckworth, London, 1980.
14.30 —— *Frege and Other Philosophers*, Oxford, Oxford University Press, 1991.
14.31 —— *Origins of Analytical Philosophy*, Duckworth, London, 1993.

14.32 Dworkin, R. *Taking Human Rights Seriously*, London, Duckworth, 1977.

14.33 Fodor, J. 'A theory of the child's theory of mind', in *Cognition* 44 (1992): 283–96.

14.34 Frege, G. *The Foundations of Arithmetic*, 2nd edn, trans. J. L. Austin, Oxford, Blackwell Publishers, 1953 (German and English texts).

14.35 —— *Nachgelassene Schriften*, vol. 1, ed. H. Hermes, F. Kambartel and F. Kaulbach, Hamburg, Meiner, 1969.

14.36 —— *Logical Investigations*, trans. P. T. Geach and M. Black, Oxford, Blackwell Publishers, 1977.

14.37 Geach, P. T. *Reference and Generality*, 3rd edn, Ithaca, NY, Cornell University Press, 1980.

14.38 —— *Logic Matters*, corrected reprint, Oxford, Blackwell Publishers, 1981.

14.39 Gensler, H. *Formal Ethics*, London, Routledge, 1996.

14.40 Gibson, A. *Counter-Intuition* (forthcoming).

14.41 —— *Divining Cosmology* (forthcoming).

14.42 —— *What is Literature?* (forthcoming).

14.43 —— 'Transcending the "limits" of logic?' (forthcoming).

14.44 Goddu, A. 'William of Ockham's "empiricism" and constructive empiricism', in [14.95].

14.45 Gross, D. J. 'Strings at superplanckian energies', in M. Atiyah *et al.* (eds) *Physics and Mathematics of Strings*, Proceedings of a Royal Society discussion, London, 1989.

14.46 Haack, S. *Deviant Logic*, Cambridge, Cambridge University Press, 1974.

14.47 Heal, J. 'Wittgenstein and dialogue', in T. Smiley (ed.) *Philosophical Dialogues*, Proceedings of the British Academy, Oxford, Oxford University Press, 1995.

14.48 —— 'Simulation, theory, and content', in P. Carruthers and P. K. Smith (eds) *Theories of Theories of the Mind*, Cambridge, Cambridge University Press, 1996.

14.49 Henninger, M. G. *Relations: Medieval Theories 1250–1325*, Oxford, Clarendon Press, 1989.

14.50 Holland, E. *Baudelaire and Schizoanalysis*, Cambridge, Cambridge University Press, 1993.

14.51 Holopainen, T. M. *William Ockham's Theory of the Foundations of Ethics*, Publications of the Luther Agricola Society B20, Helsinki, 1991.

14.52 Horst, S. W. *Symbols, Computation and Intentionality*, Berkeley, Calif., University of California Press, 1996.

14.53 Hunt, G. M. K. 'Is philosophy a "theory of everything"?', in A. P. Griffiths (ed.) *The Impulse to Philosophise*, Royal Institute of Philosophy Supplement 33, Cambridge, 1992.

14.54 Jakobson, R. *Questions de poétique*, Paris, Seuil, 1873.

14.55 Knysh, G. *Ockham Perspectives*, Ukrainian Academy of Arts and Sciences in Canada (UVAN), Winnipeg, 1994.

14.56 Kripke, S. A. *Wittgenstein on Rules and Private Language*, Oxford, Blackwell Publishers, 1982.

14.57 Lerner, R. and Mahdu, M. (eds) *Medieval Political Philosophy*, Glencoe, Ill., Free Press and Toronto, Collier Macmillan, 1966.

14.58 Lewis, D. 'An argument for the identity theory', in *Journal of Philosophy* 63 (1966): 17–25.

14.59 —— *On the Plurality of Worlds*, Oxford, Oxford University Press, 1986.

14.60 Lewis, E. *Medieval Political Ideas*, London, 1954.

14.61 Lewy, C. *Meaning and Modality*, Cambridge, Cambridge University Press, 1976.

14.62 McGrade, A. S. *The Political Thought of William of Ockham*, Cambridge, Cambridge University Press, 1974.

14.63 Mallarmé, S. *Un Coup de Dés*, Paris, Bonniot, 1914.

14.64 Marenbon, J. *Later Medieval Philosophy (1150–1350)*, London, Routledge, 1987.

14.65 —— Review of Tachau *Vision and Certitude*, in *Journal of Ecclesiastical History* 41 (1990) 105–6.

14.66 Maurer, A. 'Ockham's razor and Chatton's anti-razor', in *Mediaeval Studies* 46 (1984): 463–75.

14.67 Milbank, J. *Theology and Social Theory: Beyond Secular Reason*, Oxford, Blackwell Publishers, 1990.

14.68 —— *The Word Made Strange*, Oxford, Blackwell Publishers, 1997.

14.69 Mill, J. S. 'A system of logic, ratiocinative and inductive', in *Collected Works*, 2nd edn, ed. J. M. Robson, Introduction by R. F. McRae, London, Routledge, 1996.

14.70 —— 'An examination of Sir William Hamilton's philosophy', in *Collected Works*, ed. J. M. Robson and A. Ryan, London, University of Toronto and Routledge, 1996.

14.71 Nicholls, S. G., Brownlee, M. S. and Brownlee, K. (eds) *The New Medievalism*, Baltimore, Md. and London, Johns Hopkins University Press, 1991.

14.72 Offler, H. S. 'The "influence" of Ockham's political thinking', in [14.95].

14.73 Popper, K. R. *Objective Knowledge*, Oxford, Oxford University Press, 1972.

14.74 Priest, G. *Beyond the Limits of Thought*, Cambridge, Cambridge University Press, 1995.

14.75 Prior, A. 'Entities', in P. T. Geach and A. Kenny (eds) *Papers in Logic and Ethics*, Duckworth, London, 1976.

14.76 Rawls, J. *A Theory of Justice*, Cambridge, Mass., Harvard University Press, 1972.

14.77 Recanati, F. *Direct Reference: from Language to Thought*, Oxford, Blackwell Publishers, 1993.

14.78 Rees, M. *Perspectives in Astrophysical Cosmology*, Cambridge, Cambridge University Press, 1995.

14.79 Reynolds, D. *Symbolist Aesthetics and Early Abstract Art*, Cambridge, Cambridge University Press, 1995.

14.80 Rorty, R. 'The historiography of philosophy', in R. Rorty, J. B. Schneewind and Q. D. Skinner (eds) *Philosophy in History*, Cambridge, Cambridge University Press, 1984.

14.81 Ryan, J. J. *The Nature, Structure, and Function of the Church in William of Ockham* (AAR Studies in Religion 16), Missoula, Mont., Scholars Press, 1979.

14.82 Sainsbury, R. M. *Paradoxes*, 2nd edn, Cambridge, Cambridge University Press, 1995.

14.83 Scott, D. *Pictorialist Poetics*, Cambridge, Cambridge University Press, 1988.

14.84 Smiley, T. J. 'The theory of descriptions', *Proceedings of the British Academy*, Oxford (1982): 321–37.

14.85 —— 'Can contradictions be true?', *Proceedings of the Aristotelian Society*, suppl. vol. 67 (1993): 17–33.

14.86 Sober, E. *Simplicity*, Oxford, Clarendon Press, 1975.

14.87 Spade, P. V. 'Some epistemological implications of the Burley–Ockham dispute', *Franciscan Studies* 35 (13) (1975): 212–23.

14.88 —— 'Medieval philosophy', in A. Kenny (ed.) *The Oxford Illustrated History of Western Philosophy*, Oxford, 1994.

14.89 —— *Lies, Language and Logic in the Middle Ages*, London, Variorum Reprints, 1988.

14.90 —— 'Quasi-Aristotelianism', in N. Kretzmann (ed.) *Infinity and Continuity in Ancient and Medieval Thought*, Ithaca, NY and London, Cornell University Press, 1982.

14.91 Starobinski, J. *Les Mots sous les mots: les anagrammes de Ferdinand de Saussure*, Paris, Gallimard, 1971.

14.92 Stump, E. *Dialectic and its Place in the Development of Medieval Logic*, Ithaca, NY, Cornell University Press, 1989.

14.93 Tachau, K. H. *Vision and Certitude in the Age of Ockham*, Leiden, E. J. Brill, 1988.

14.94 Torre, B. R. de la *Thomas Buckingham and the Contingency of Futures*, a study and edition of Thomas Buckingham's *De contingentia futurorum et arbitrii libertate*, Notre Dame, Ind., University of Notre Dame Press, 1987.

14.95 Vossenkuhl, W. von and Schonberger, R. (eds) *Die Gegenwart Ockhams*, Weinheim, VCH Acta humaniora, 1990.

14.96 Ward, G. *Theology and Contemporary Critical Theory*, London, Macmillan, 1996.

14.97 White, G. 'Ockham and Wittgenstein', in [14.95].

14.98 Whitehead, A. N. and Russell, B. *Principia Mathematica*, Cambridge, Cambridge University Press, 1910.

14.99 Wittgenstein, L. *Philosophical Investigations*, ed. G. E. M. Anscombe, R. Rhees and G. H. von Wright, trans. G. E. M. Anscombe, Oxford, Blackwell Publishers, 1953.

14.100 —— *The Tractatus Logico-Philosophicus*, trans. D. F. Pears and B. McGuinness, London, Routledge, 1963.

14.101 —— *On Certainty*, ed. G. E. M. Anscombe and G. H. von Wright, trans. D. Paul and G. E. M. Anscombe, corrected reprint, Oxford, Blackwell Publishers, 1974.

14.102 Wood, R. 'Ockham on essentially-ordered causes: logic misapplied', in [14.95].

14.103 Wright, C. *Realism, Meaning and Truth*, Oxford, Blackwell Publishers, 1987.

CHAPTER 15

Walter Burley, Peter Aureoli and Gregory of Rimini

Stephen Brown

❦

Immediately after the glorious age of Bonaventure and Thomas Aquinas, the University of Paris, as we have seen, had a number of outstanding teachers. Henry of Ghent, following in the path of Bonaventure, was the reigning figure until about 1285 ([15.14] 121–78; 221–3).[1] Godfrey of Fontaines, the pupil of Aquinas and his defender against the 1277 condemnation of propositions associated with the great Dominican thinker, developed his own voice and gradually replaced Henry as the principal master at the university ([15.32] xv–xxi, 382–5; [15.14] 3–41 and *passim*; [15.21] 193–207). Giles of Rome, a student of Aquinas from 1269 to 1272, whose teaching was delayed by a censure against him in 1277, was restored to good standing by Pope Honorius IV in 1285 ([15.14] 223–5). He established an early form of Augustinian teaching that held sway with the Augustinian Hermits until a more English-influenced approach was established in 1342–4 by Gregory of Rimini ([15.29] 182–207). As the fourteenth century began, the most out-standing figure was a visitor from Oxford, John Duns Scotus. His lec-tures at Paris survive in the form of student reports, bearing the appropriate name, *Reportata Parisiensia*. With the death of the Subtle Doctor in 1308, an era of famous Parisian teachers came to an end.

The influence of these great thinkers, however, remained at Paris in the period (1308–50) that now concerns us. Henry, as we shall see, is the opponent of Peter Aureoli on the unity of the concept of being and on God's knowledge of future contingents. Although many Parisian authors continued to criticize his theory of illumination, Henry

368

still found a staunch ally in Hugolinus of Orvieto (see [15.16] 151–4). Godfrey was a strong influence on the Carmelite John Baconthorpe, who taught in Paris as well as England and on John of Pouilly, who quoted him favourably in his *Quodlibeta* ([15.32] 386). Giles influenced members of his order at Paris in different ways: Gerard of Siena and Thomas of Strasbourg stayed close to Giles in their teaching, whereas Michael of Massa in his later writings sacrificed the metaphysical interests of Giles to the study of natural philosophy in order to refute William of Ockham's teachings on physics ([15.36] 196–214). Scotus had so many followers at Paris in the decade after his death that one might even speak of them (William of Alnwich, Antonius Andreas, Hugh of Newcastle, Francis of Marchia, Francis Meyronnes, and others) as forming the first Scotist school ([15.14] 9–24).

❧ WALTER BURLEY ❧

If, however, we want to move beyond the echoes of Henry, Godfrey, Giles and John Duns to the new philosophical voices of the era after Scotus's death, we might well begin with Walter Burley. Burley, as is known, did his early and his late work in England. However, he arrived in Paris before 1310 to study theology and he stayed there until 1327. In effect, then, the central years of the life and activity of Walter, who was born around the year 1275, were spent in Paris. The *Tractatus primus* (*First Treatise*), which is Walter's defence of certain theses of his *Commentary on the 'Sentences'* that were attacked by Thomas Wilton, was written in Paris. So was his *Treatise on Forms*, perhaps his first reaction to William of Ockham's physics. If the first version of his *De puritate artis logicae* (*On the Purity of the Art of Logic*), with its attack on Ockham's theory of supposition, did not have its origin in Paris, it at least existed there in a number of copies – one, an abbreviation – before 1350. His detailed attack on Ockham's physics began with his *Exposition of Aristotle's 'Physics'*, whose books I–VI were completed at Paris ([15.31] 180–6). Around 1340 Walter's continued influence at Paris is confirmed by the Danish commentator on the *Prior Analytics*, Nicholas Drukken, who defended Ockham's position on supposition against Burley, whom he explicitly names and cites ([15.27] 51–3). Certainly he must be considered one of the great voices of Parisian realism. Burley served as an envoy of Edward III at the papal court in Avignon from 1327 to 1330. Although he finished his career in England, often under the patronage of Richard of Bury, the Bishop of Durham, he made frequent trips to the Continent ([15.30] 30–8). During his later years in England, he commented on the *Ethics*, wrote his *Super artem veterem* (*On the 'logica vetus'*), and produced an

Exposition of Aristotle's 'Politics', books VII and VIII of which were heavily indebted, even in phraseology, to the Parisian commentary of Peter of Alvernia ([15.31] 186–8; [15.27] II: 13–22).

The early works of Walter Burley place him at Oxford in 1301 and 1302, though he seems to have lectured there even earlier. We have, for example, at least four different commentaries by him on Aristotle's *On Interpretation* that have survived. It is the *Questions on 'On Interpretation'* that dates from 1301. This work, however, in a *quaestio* format, is somewhat advanced. There is a more basic commentary, a précis of Aristotle's work, found along with parallel abbreviations of Porphyry's *Isagoge* and Aristotle's *Categories* in Cambridge, MS St. John's College 100, ff. 47ra–54vb. Such cursory *lectiones*, which simply list the general content of Aristotle's works for beginners, most likely antedated the more developed *quaestiones* arising from the Aristotle's text and aimed at an advanced group of scholars. Such summary works do not reveal much about Burley. Anyone could have done such summaries. Also among the works associated with the years 1301 and 1302 is a *Treatise on Supposition* ([15.1] 16, [15.3] 200–1).

What is characteristic of these early works, as we should well expect, is the total absence of any reference to William of Ockham or his philosophy. In other words, during his early days at Oxford we find no conflict between Burley's form of realism and the nominalistic realism of Ockham. The *Treatise on Supposition* is very instructive, since it was both a positive and negative source for Ockham's *Summa logicae*. Ockham, in his presentation of the supposition of relative terms, copied extensively from Burley's work, and in treating improper supposition, summarized his statements. Ockham, however, disagrees with Burley over simple and personal supposition. One must, however, tread softly in establishing the interplay of the two authors. The Venerable Inceptor's own words inform us that Burley is not his only opponent: 'From this argument the falsity of the common opinion which declares that simple supposition takes place when a term supposits for its significate is clear' ([14.5] II, 141). Burley himself, when he attacks Ockham's *Summa logicae* in the later *De puritate artis logicae*, implies his own agreement with the traditional way by informing us that William is out of accord with the ancients ([15.11] 7).

❦ BURLEY'S REALISM AND OCKHAM'S ❦ NOMINALISM

Walter Burley did not see his form of realism as something new. Yet, despite its claim to roots in the ancients, it does have its own peculiarities. In his 1301 *Questions on 'On Interpretation'* he asks: Does a spoken word signify a thing (*res*) or a concept (*passio animae*)? Realizing that Aristotle had answered this question by saying that a spoken word does not signify a thing but the *passio animae* or concept, Burley explains: a spoken word does not signify the thing (*res*) with its individuating differences; it signifies the *passio animae*. But what is this *passio animae* or concept, for him? Claiming to follow Ammonius, Burley contends that the *passio animae* is the thing itself in so far as it is proportionate to the intellect. A name is imposed on something only to the degree that it is known by the mind. Now nothing is known by the mind except in so far as it is capable of moving the intellect. So a name cannot be imposed on anything unless it is proportionate to the mind. There is, according to Burley, a parallel between the act of signifying and the act of knowing. In regard to the act of knowing, Burley explains, there are three things to be considered: the thing known, the intellect knowing, and the species by means of which a thing is known. The species is not what is first known; the *res* or thing is the first object known even though it is known by means of the species. Likewise, the act of signifying has three elements: the word which is signifying, the thing signified, and the species by means of which the thing is signified. And just as the species is not that which is first known, so it is not that which is first signified. The thing itself is that which is first signified, though by means of the species ([15.3] 211).

In a later commentary on *On Interpretation*, which bears the title *Middle Commentary* because it fits between the *Questions* and the late Commentary of 1337 both in size and time, he holds the same position as in the *Questions*. He adds, however, a second point: not only are there universal concepts and singular concepts, but because the concept is the thing itself, there are in propositions universal things as well as singular things ([15.2] 84–5). In the last redaction of his *On Interpretation* commentary, he underscores this point even more forcefully: 'Supposing, nonetheless, that universals are things outside the mind – which is the more true position – we have to state that the name of a first intention is the name of a thing as it falls under the first concept of the intellect.' In a direct attack on William of Ockham in the same work he establishes a third point, declaring, 'It can be noted that outside the mind there are some universal things and some singular things . . . Propositions are composed of things outside the mind which are universal and things that are singular. These are both outside the mind. And still such noteworthy considerations are not pleasing to the moderns who do not posit universals outside the mind and who do not admit that propositions are made up of things outside the mind' ([15.9] ff. 67va, 75vb).

When one sees these three theses of Burley's commentaries on *On Interpretation*, it is hard to resist the conclusion that William of

Ockham had him (and perhaps also Walter Chatton) in mind in the prologue to his *Commentary on 'On Interpretation'*, when he attacks an opinion that claims:

> That the concept is the thing outside the mind as conceived or understood (*res extra concepta sive intellecta*) in the way that some grant that besides singular things there are universal things, and that singular things conceived are subjects in singular propositions and universal things conceived are subjects of universal propositions. Now this opinion, in regard to this: that it places some things outside the mind besides the singulars and existing in them, I think altogether absurd and destructive of the whole philosophy of Aristotle and all science and all truth and reason, and that it is the worst error in philosophy and rejected by Aristotle in Book VII of the *Metaphysics*, and that those holding such a view are incapable of science.

([14.5] Op. Phil. II: 362–3)

For Ockham himself there are no such *res universales* in singular things which correspond to our common names. As he declares near the end of the Book II of his *Commentary on 'On Interpretation'*, 'Names of this type, "man", "animal", "lion", and universally all first intention names primarily and principally signify the things themselves outside the mind. The word *man* primarily signifies all men, and the word *animal* primarily signifies all animals. And the same holds for other words of this type' ([14.5] Op. Phil. II, 502). For Ockham, 'man' and 'animal' signify that men and animals are really alike, and they are really alike prior to any activity of the mind that recognizes that they are alike; yet they are similar because they are men or animals, not because of some common similarity that exists in each of them ([14.5] Op. Th. IV: 287–310). These competing theories concerning common nouns and the objects they signify took on the already existing labels 'realism' and 'nominalism', even though in the works of Burley and Ockham these positions might have some particular characteristics of their own.

The debate over the significates of common nouns led realists – and Burley claims his position is the traditional one – to hold that supposition is simple when a common noun stands for its significate ([15.11] 7). The nominalists – and Ockham claims that he is opposing the common position – hold that supposition is personal when a common noun stands for its significate. For the nominalists, supposition is simple when a term stands for the intention or concept in the mind, which properly is not the significate of the term, for such a first intention term signifies true things and not concepts (see [14.5] Op. Phil. I: 196). In brief, Ockham, whose theory of supposition

372

parallels his theory of universals, rejects any common reality existing among and in individuals and interprets earlier theories of simple supposition, like that of Burley, as holding a common reality corresponding to our common concepts. Ockham redefines simple supposition by declaring that the supposition of a term is simple when the term supposits for what is common: the concept. For Ockham and the nominalists, when the suppositing term in a proposition stands for its significate (a real thing) then you have personal supposition, since the only true things are individuals. It is, in Ockham's judgement, this error – the error of those realists, like Burley, who believed that there is something in things besides the singular thing itself, and that humanity, for example, is some thing distinct from singular men and found in them, and that this distinct thing is their essence – that led them astray both in their theories of signification and supposition ([14.5] Op. Phil. I: 204). Both camps held that common nouns signified things. The realists and nominalists differed because the first focused on common things, while the second denied the existence of common realities. Burley entitled his work *De puritate artis logicae*, to return to the pure logic of the ancients in contrast to the contaminated logic of Ockham's *Summa logicae*. In this work, Burley claims to follow Aristotle, Boethius, Priscian and Averroes when he argues that when someone employs the word 'man' in a meaningful or significative way, he is not directing his attention to Peter or John or any other particular person that is now present. He is rather focusing on that which is common to Peter, John or anyone else. In other words, 'man' does not signify particular men but rather the common reality by which each individual is a man ([15.11] 7–8).

Perhaps the example that Burley believes best illustrates the differences in signification and supposition theory between the realist and nominalist positions is the proposition 'Man is the most noble of all creatures.' What possibly could you mean when you make such a statement? Surely you do not want to say, when you make this declaration, that some particular man is the most noble of all creatures. In this statement, 'man' has simple supposition since it stands for its significate, i.e. for something common, the species 'man', which is the most noble of all creatures ([15.1] 24, [15.11] 7).

Burley also disagreed with Ockham in regard to the nature of the ten categories. In cases where they are dealing with singular substances, both men would treat such substances as things, and there would be no controversy. However, as we have seen, Ockham denies that there are universal substances. Since science is of the universal, then, for Ockham, science cannot, strictly speaking, be about things, since all things are particular. For Walter Burley, scientific propositions stand for universal things outside the mind. This understanding was, in his judgement, the only way to guard real sciences. Since, in Ockham's theory, universals are only concepts, all sciences are about concepts. According to him, this does not obliterate the distinction between real and rational sciences. Such a division, he argues, depends not on whether the science is about things or concepts, but whether the concepts which are the components of all scientific propositions stand for things or for other concepts. In the former case we have a real science; in the latter we have a rational science ([14.5] Op. Th. II: 136–8; [15.18] 112–15).

When they deal with inhering qualities, such as whiteness, sweetness or heat, both William and Walter consider them to be things. In Ockham's analysis of reality, however, not all qualities are inhering qualities and thus not all qualities express things distinct from their substances. The same holds for all the remaining categories: they signify something real but not a distinct thing existing subjectively in singular substances like individual inhering qualities.

Ockham's favourite example should help us understand what he means. 'Similarity' signifies something real. It does not, however, signify a thing over and above the really inhering quality (e.g. whiteness) in two or more subjects. 'Similarity' does not itself signify a further really existing quality (i.e. similarity) in the white subjects. If this were the case, argues Ockham, the distinction of the categories would be obliterated, since the category of relation would be reduced to the category of quality ([14.5] Op. Phil. I: 167–8). If Socrates is white and Plato is white, then Socrates is, without the addition of any other thing, similar to Plato. The white Socrates does not gain a new reality in Plato's becoming white. He gains a new predicate, a new denomination, and it is a real predicate he gains, but it is not a new predicate signifying a new *res* or thing. By the very fact that both Socrates and Plato are white, they are similar. Given this condition that both are white, even God cannot take away their similarity. Furthermore, they are similar independently of our mind, so they are really similar. Yet neither Socrates nor Plato has similarity as a quality subjectively inhering in them. If Plato ceases to be white, he would lose an inhering quality of whiteness, but he would not lose an inhering quality of likeness to Socrates according to whiteness. He would lose such a predicate or denomination, but not a *res* (see [15.18] 120).

As it is in the case of 'similitude', which expresses one type of relation, so is it with the remaining categories. They do not signify things, but are *nomina* (concepts or words) which signify something real but not things distinct from substances and inhering qualities. Even some terms in the category of quality do not signify inhering qualities. Some terms indicating the figure of something, e.g. that something is curved or straight, do not signify a new *res* added to that thing. As Ockham states in the *Summa logicae*, 'Such predicables "curved" and "straight" are able to be affirmed successively just because of local motion. When something is straight, if its parts afterwards, simply by local motion and without the arrival of any new thing, are closer together so that they are less distant than before, it is said to be curved' ([14.5] Op. Phil. I: 180).

A discrete quantity also is a concept or word which does not signify a distinct reality over and above the things which are numbered. When we speak about two men, one in Cambridge and one in Paris, we do not signify by the term 'two' a duality that exists subjectively in them. If 'two' signified a thing over and above the men, would it exist subjectively in each? In this case each man would be two, since this thing 'duality' would exist in each. If one part of the accident 'duality' existed in one man and another part in the other, then two parts of an accidental quality distinct in subject and place, even by hundreds of kilometres, would make one accidental quality or *res* – which seems unimaginable. 'Two' thus does not signify a distinct thing over and above the two things, which makes the two things two; it stands for the two things themselves and connotes that the two things do not make a *per se unum* ([15.18] 121).[2] Ockham in the *Summa logicae* goes through each of the categories attempting to show that they do not signify distinct things from substances and inhering qualities and arguing that terms in each of the distinct categories do not necessarily signify distinct things.

Burley, in his late *Commentary on Aristotle's 'Categories'*, attacks the nominalistic view of the categories presented by Ockham. The categories cannot simply signify names or concepts; they must signify things. If we look at Ockham's favourite example, that of similarity, we see that there are many reasons that militate against similarity being reduced to a name or concept. A likeness, for instance, admits of degrees: things can be more or less like one another. When we look at two things we can see that they are more alike than two other things. Yet names or concepts do not admit of degrees. Furthermore, it is impossible to know one of the things that are relative without knowing the other. But you can know one noun or concept without knowing another noun. Moreover, according to Aristotle, relative things exist at the same time, so that if one of them is destroyed, then the other is affected. If a father is killed, then his son ceases to be actually a son anymore. But if you destroy a word, such as 'father', the word 'son' is not affected ([15.7] ff. e4vb–e5ra).

Neither is the nominalist account of discrete quantity acceptable to Burley. What a nominalist like Ockham assumes is that every accident that is numerically one has to have a subject that is numerically one. Yet this is not the way that Averroes explains discrete quantities in his *Commentary on Book III of Aristotle's 'Physics'*. There he explains that it is characteristic of a discrete quantity that it is present in many subjects by reason of its parts. When we are talking about two things, then, this does not mean that 'duality' taken as a whole is in each subject. What it means is that the parts of a duality each exist in a subject, so that one of its parts is in one subject and another of its parts is in another subject. It is in this way that an accident that is numerically one can be in diverse subjects even separated by great distances. There is no reason why an accident that is *per se* one in the sense of being one discrete quantity has to have a subject that is *per se* one ([15.7] f. e2rb).

In a way parallel to Ockham's treatment in the *Summa logicae* and his *Commentary on Aristotle's 'Categories'*, Burley thus unfolds his realistic interpretation of all the categories in his *On the 'logica vetus'*. Nor is the story different if we compare Ockham and Burley's views concerning natural philosophy. Basically the same principles are at work. For Ockham, many of the terms of natural philosophy, i.e. 'change', 'motion', 'time', 'instant', etc., are interpreted as absolute terms that point to things that exactly correspond to them. According to Ockham, many such terms of physics are not absolute terms; they are connotative terms. What does this distinction mean? If you take a word like *albedo* ('whiteness'), it is an absolute term that signifies a colour. However, if you take a word like *albus*, it signifies more than one thing. To avoid complications, let us say *albus* signifies 'a man who is white' or 'whiteness in a man'. In short, it just doesn't signify one thing; it signifies one thing and co-signifies or connotes another. Ockham explains that a word like 'motion', because it is a noun, can lead us into thinking that there is an absolute thing that corresponds to it. In fact, he argues, 'motion' is not an absolute term, but is a short hand way of saying 'something is moving'. Another way of saying this is that 'motion' is a connotative term that signifies more than one thing. It is a term that we should really translate into connotative language ('something is moving') in order to avoid thinking it is an absolute term that has a distinct or separate reality corresponding to it. In his *Exposition of Aristotle's 'Physics'* he expresses well the problem he sees: 'Wherefore, this proposition "Something is moving" is more explicit and more clear than the proposition "A motion exists". The latter statement is ambiguous, because some understand by it that there is something distinct from a movable object and other permanent things that exists, the way some moderns do. Others, however, do not understand by the statement "A motion exists" anything more than "Something is moving", where you convert the noun form into a verbal form. It is for this reason alone that Aristotle says that "motion" is not something that you can point to; and he says the same about other terms of this kind' ([14.5] Op. Phil. V: 243).

Walter Burley certainly belonged to the first, realist group of interpreters. 'Motion', 'change', 'time', 'instant' – all such words point to exactly corresponding realities. In Book I of his *Exposition on the Books of Aristotle's 'Physics'* he announces boldly, 'Fourthly, I prove that an instant is something in reality, something that is completely indivisible' ([15.10] col. 38A).

Burley is not the only champion of realism at Paris in the first half of the fourteenth century, but his is a strong voice and one that found followers and opponents during this period. Ockham, likewise, is not the only champion of nominalism. In fact, he was not then an actual presence, except through some of his writings and followers, as well as through the voice of some of his opponents like Burley (see [15.23] 53–96). Burley's voice is a real one. It was in Paris that he began his attacks on Ockham's logic and physics.

PETER AUREOLI

If one could debate whether Burley was an English thinker or a Parisian one, there is no doubt about the Parisian association of Peter Aureoli. He was in Paris during the first decade of the century and perhaps was a student of Scotus. Even if he was not an actual student of Scotus, he later became central in the life of Parisian Scotism. After teaching at Bologna (1312) and Toulouse (1314), this French Franciscan returned to Paris where he lectured from 1316 to 1320. His most famous work, the *Scriptum in primum Sententiarum* (*Writing on the First Book of the 'Sentences'*), was produced before he taught at Paris. His Paris production is a complex issue that will not be settled until the First Book of his *Reportatio* (student reports) there is edited. Two important issues from the First Book show the independent character of his thought.

The Unity of the Concept of Being

The first issue concerns the unity of the concept of being. Aureoli treated the matter both in his earlier *Scriptum* and in his Paris *Reportatio*. The treatments are substantially the same, even though Aureoli has reworked his *Reportatio* presentation in such a way that the two works have no text in common. The account in both is the same, although the *Scriptum* rendition provides names. Aureoli has a number of authors as opponents. Henry of Ghent, for example, sets the framework for Aureoli's discussion. For Henry, our concept of 'being' is a confused concept. This has to be understood in a very precise sense: 'Confused' has the sense of 'con-fused'. In other words, we do not have one concept of being unless we take one concept in the sense of a psychological unity. When we analyse what we at first think is one concept we find that we have two concepts. One of these concepts is the concept of 'privatively undetermined being'. In short, this concept of being is arrived at by examining creatures and then leaving aside or depriving them of their many differences. The other concept is the concept of 'negatively undetermined being'. This concept of being is proper to God alone, since God cannot be determined or limited at all; he is totally undetermined or unlimited. Since the concept of being predicable of creatures is a concept that is a common concept of created being without the differences included and the concept of being predicable of God is a concept of a being that admits no limits or differences, our mind mistakes them and views the two kinds of indetermination as one. When we analyse the nature of the indetermination and divide it into privatively and negatively undetermined being, we realize that we are dealing with two different concepts of being: one predicable of God, the other predicable of creatures.

Furthermore, for Henry, because of his theory of illumination, the first concept we have is the concept of negatively undetermined being, or of God. We only know other things because of the light of divine being. We are not aware of the divine being when we perceive created beings, but when we examine how we can know created beings, we realize that God provides the light that makes their being and truth shine forth – somewhat in the way that the light behind a stained glass window allows us to see the colours and shapes of the windows. We focus on the colours and shapes, so that is what we think we know first. Yet, when we analyse the situation of seeing the colours and shapes we realize that the light is in a sense the first thing we know, even though it is not the first thing we focus on.

John Duns Scotus rejected Henry's theory of illumination and had to find another explanation for our knowledge of being. For Scotus, our concept of being is not a confused concept in the way that Henry meant 'con-fused'. 'Being' is the most distinct concept we have. 'Being' leaves aside all determinations or differences. Of course, the realities have their differences: created beings are finite and the uncreated being is infinite. But we can, according to Scotus, leave these differences outside our concept of being. Modes of being, such as 'infinite' or 'finite', if left outside our concept of being, provide us with a distinct concept of being in contrast to the con-fused concept that Henry affirms. Whatever could confuse it is left outside. We thus end up, according to Scotus, with a concept of being that is univocal. It is predicable of God and creatures in the same sense, since whatever could compromise this single sense is left outside the concept.[3]

Aureoli's third set of opponents are the Dominican Hervaeus Natalis (Hervé Nedellec or Hervé Nöel) and the Carmelite Gerard of Bologna. Each of these Parisian thinkers treads a middle way between the equivocal concept of being that is affirmed by Henry of Ghent and the univocal concept of being defended by John Duns Scotus. In effect, they lean more toward Henry by declaring, like Aristotle, that 'being is said in many ways'. They follow the model of Aristotle in Book IV of the *Metaphysics*: 'Being' is like 'health'. We say that many different kinds of things are healthy. Not only is a man healthy, but also the diet that preserves his energy, the complexion that indicates that he is robust, the urine sample that a doctor takes to test the state of his condition, all are called 'healthy'. They have this name because they all are connected with the health of a man. So with 'being': whatever is related to a substance, the primary meaning of 'being', is also called 'being'. The colour of a substance, the size of a substance, the location of a substance also are 'being' in some sense, since they are all related to the substance in the same way that diets, complexions, and urine samples are related to the health of a human being or other animal. 'Being', then is said 'in many ways', but because of the relation of all the different types of being to the substances to which they are linked, they are united in some way. There are thus many concepts of being, but because of the connection among the realities they signify, they are in a certain way unified. They are, in short, analogous.

Peter Aureoli's own position will contest each of these three opposing theories concerning the unity of the concept of being, yet it will in a way include elements from each of them. In contrast to Henry, Gerard and Hervaeus, he will side with Scotus and stress the true simple unity of the concept of being. Yet the concept of being is not univocal in the sense that it leaves outside its ambit the differences. It is thus not a distinct concept, since it includes all the differences of being within it. Like Henry, at least in his vocabulary, Aureoli's view of the concept of being is that it is a confused concept. However, he does not understand it as a con-fused concept that needs to be corrected. It is confused in the sense that the simple concept of being includes all differences within it. The realities that can have 'being' predicated of them have, of course, their real differences; but still we can, Aureoli argues, have a most indistinct concept that can be predicated of all of them. The transcendental concept of 'being' is a certain total implicit *ratio* and the categorical concepts of substance and accidents are explicit partial *rationes*. There is not in a stone one *ratio* which makes it a being and a diverse *ratio* which makes it a stone. The *ratio* making it a stone and everything in a stone is formally being. In this way, Aureoli separates himself from the 'health' employed by Aristotle that is so strongly stressed by Gerard of Bologna and Hervaeus

379

Natalis. 'Healthy' points to the formal presence of health in a man or other animal; diets, complexions, etc. are not formally healthy. With 'being' the case is different. Each kind of being is formally being. The analogy of extrinsic attribution, exemplified by 'healthy', does not tell the whole story, according to Aureoli. All realities and all aspects of reality are formally being. There must be a concept predicable of all of them. It is an implicit concept containing all *rationes* of being. A proper concept of a particular thing is attained not by adding some *ratio* that is not being or some *ratio* that is being in another sense of the term 'being'; it is an explicit concept of 'a particular kind of being' in contrast to the implicit concept of being that is predicable of all that is not nothing (see [15.17] 117–50; [15.19] 118–120).

Aureoli's position on the unity of the concept of being was attacked by a number of the followers of John Duns Scotus. Walter Chatton defended Scotus against Aureoli's challenge both in his London *Reportatio* of 1321–3 and his Oxford *Lectura* of 1328–30 (see [15.4] 127–77). Peter Thomae attacked Aureoli's teaching in his *Questions on Being*, disputed at the Franciscan house of studies in Barcelona around 1325 (see [15.25] 216). Gerard Odon, at Paris, distinguished between Aureoli's logical concept of being and the meta-physical concept of being that was defended by Duns Scotus (Geraldus, MS Paris BN 6441, ff. 7va–9rb).

God's Knowledge of Future Contingent Events

The second issue that garnered immediate attention for Aureoli was his theory concerning God's knowledge of future contingent events. Although his treatment of this issue arises immediately from the discussion of it in John Duns Scotus, the problem, as he treats it, has its more precise origin in William de la Mare's representation of Thomas Aquinas's position on God's knowledge of future contingent events, an interpretation that Henry of Ghent judged to be true and to be the position of Aquinas. According to this view temporal things, not just causally but actually, have a reality in the eternal 'now' of God. Most likely, Henry introduced this understanding to establish the point that changes in this world do not entail any change in God's knowledge of them. To escape the implication that the eternal presence of things to God's knowledge entails their actual eternal existence, Aureoli refuses to speak of the presence of creatures in the eternal 'now'. It is improper to speak of future things as present to eternity, since what is not present in itself is not able to be present to something else. He forges a new word to describe how God knows temporal things. Temporal things are non-distant (*indistantes*) to God's eternity. Aureoli's new term 'non-distant' expresses a negative relation: it means 'present, but not in a temporal way'. Future contingent events, then, are not future to God; but neither are they present in a present-tense manner that points to a present temporal moment (see [15.13] 114–24).

Since God's knowledge of events that for us are future is not future, and thus does not precede the event, Aureoli contends that singular propositions about future contingent events are neither determinately true nor determinately false in themselves. For him, they are completely neutral or indeterminate. If, he argues, they were determinately true or false because God knew them before they happened, then all future events would take place immutably. This position was strongly attacked by John Baconthorpe, Francis Meyronnes, Francis of Marchia, Landulph Caracciolo and a number of other masters who taught at Paris before 1350 (see [15.13] 126–31, 78). Aureoli had to wait for Peter of Candia, who commented on *Book I of the Sentences* at Paris in 1378, before he found an ally for the possibility of his position. Aureoli's effect on this issue, however, was long-lasting: his position was revived by Peter of Rivo at Louvain in the 1460s in a battle with Henry of Zomeren. This debate led to the censure of Peter of Rivo in 1473 for 'opinions ill-sounding, scandalous and offensive to Christian ears'. Some of the censured statements also might be attributed to Peter Aureoli (see [15.26] 12–15).

If Aureoli is significant for the independent power of his thought, he is also important for the thorough knowledge of his contemporaries whom he blended into his own synthesis. Francis Meyronnes praises him highly for his portrait of the positions of others when he simply declares, 'If you want to see the opinions of others presented distinctly, look everywhere in Aureoli' ([15.24] 24). Almost a hundred years later, Capreolus uses Aureoli as a main source book. This is immediately evident in the question on the unity of the concept of being, where it is easy to see that Capreolus does not know Henry of Ghent, Duns Scotus, Gerard of Bologna or Hervaeus Natalis directly. All of them people his text, yet all their citations are taken verbatim from the text of the *Scriptum* of Peter Aureoli. In short, Capreolus' knowledge of these and many other authors is through the reports of Peter Aureoli (see [15.12] xxii).

❧ GREGORY OF RIMINI ❧

Our final focus will be on Gregory of Rimini, an Augustinian Hermit, who brought to Paris a more detailed knowledge of William of Ockham, along with a developed knowledge of Ockham's English critic, Walter Chatton, as well as Ockham's somewhat independent follower, Adam Wodeham. It was also Gregory who introduced the thought of Richard Fitzralph, and to a lesser degree that of Thomas Bradwardine, Richard Kilvington, William of Heytesbury, Thomas Buckingham, and Robert of Halifax to Paris. In effect, these influences led Gregory in his own works to supplant the Augustinian Hermit tradition of Giles of Rome with his own more English-initiated philosophy and theology (see [15.22] 311–13).[4]

Gregory had been a student in Paris from 1323 to 1329, before teaching at the Augustinian houses of Bologna, Padua, and Perugia. He returned to Paris in 1341 or 1342 to prepare for his lectures on the *Sentences* of Peter Lombard. His *Lectures on Books I and II of the Sentences* (1342–3 or 1343–4) show that during this preparatory year he deepened his acquaintance with Ockham, Chatton and Wodeham. When we spoke above of Ockham's and Burley's views of science, we stressed that science is of the universal and necessary. Since there are universal and necessary realities for Burley, science has as its object the universal and necessary realities that exist in individual things and make them to be the kind of things they are. Since there are no universal realities for Ockham, the objects of science for him are then the propositions or conclusions that alone are universal and necessary. Ockham's position was not only attacked by Burley; it was also attacked by Walter Chatton. Ockham's student Adam Wodeham disagreed with both his teacher and Chatton and forged a new alternative, which was endorsed by Gregory. The alternative was based on the argument against Chatton that there are no necessary beings besides God. Creatures then cannot be the objects of science since they are neither necessary nor universal. Yet Adam Wodeham and Gregory disagreed with Ockham as well. The objects of science are not identified with propositions, but are somehow real. They are not the real contingent things, but rather a real state of affairs. The universal and necessary knowledge of science is located by them in the total overall significate of the conclusion of a syllogism. The total significate of the proposition 'Man is rational' is thus neither the proposition 'Man is rational', nor individual contingent men, but rather the state of affairs that might be expressed as 'man-being-rational'. It is thus the *dictum* or state of affairs that is expressed by the proposition that is the object of scientific knowledge (see [15.5] 66–70; [15.35] 40–3).[5]

If Gregory disagrees with Ockham on the object of knowledge, there are other places where he follows him quite closely. He argues that 'a universal is not some thing outside the mind but is rather a concept created (*fictus*) or formed by the soul that is common to many things' ([15.6] I: 396). This *fictum* theory concerning the nature of the concept seems to have originated with Henry of Harclay. It was frequently defended as one alternative explanation by Ockham. Ockham does not make it his explanation of choice in his *Quodlibet*, where he has to pick one explanation over any other, but (as Gregory shows) Walter Chatton's critique of the *fictum* theory was not definitive.

In his natural philosophy, Gregory follows the more economical theories of Ockham, denying that motion, time, and sudden change are distinct entities in themselves. 'Sudden change' does not, for Gregory, signify some thing beyond the permanent things involved in the change. There is the subject that is changed, the form gained by the subject that was not there before, and the form lost by the subject that previously had it. There is no need to posit any extra entities.

The Augustinian background of Gregory is very developed. He chides Peter Aureoli for inexact citations of Augustine. He quotes long passages from the *On Free Will* to establish our intellectual knowledge of singulars. His claims of loyalty to Augustine appear most staunch, however, when he criticizes Ockham and Wodeham about man's powers. He accuses them of being modern Pelagians and underscores the weakness of fallen human nature. According to Gregory, we are wounded both in our ability to know what we should choose or avoid and also in our ability to carry out properly our tasks even if we were to have the correct knowledge (see [15.22] 194).

Philosophy at Paris in the first half of the fourteenth century is still in need of a great deal of exploration. As we indicated, one of the principal conflicts that developed gradually was the debate between the realists and the nominalists. But the labels of realism and nominalism swelled from an affirmation or denial of real entities corresponding to our universal concepts to include numerous other points. The investigation of the exploding aspects of these two orientations will complete the introductory treatment and manifestation of some of the riches to be found that we have presented.

 NOTES

1 See also above, Chapter 13.
2 See also below, Chapter 17, pp. 418–20, for Ockham's idea of connotation.
3 For a detailed discussion of Henry of Ghent's and Duns Scotus' contrasting views on whether 'being' is an equivocal or univocal term, see above, Chapter 13, pp. 297–321.
4 Further discussion of Gregory of Rimini's relation to Oxford thought will be found in Chapter 16, pp. 391–3.
5 See also below, Chapter 17, pp. 410–11 for discussion of the *complexe significabile*.

➻❈❖❈➺ BIBLIOGRAPHY ➻❈❖❈➺

Original Language Editions

15.1   Brown, S. F. 'Walter Burley's *Tractatus de suppositione* and its relation to William of Ockham's *Summa logicae*', *Franciscan Studies* 32 (1972): 15–64.

15.2   —— 'Walter Burley's Middle Commentary on Aristotle's *Perihermenias*', *Franciscan Studies* 33 (1973): 42–139.

15.3   —— 'Walter Burley's *Quaestiones in librum Perihermenias*', *Franciscan Studies* 34 (1974): 200–95.

15.4   Fitzpatrick, N. 'Walter Chatton on the univocity of being: a reaction to Peter Aureoli and William of Ockham', *Franciscan Studies* 31 (1971): 88–177.

15.5   Gál, G. 'Adam Wodeham's question on the complexe significabile as the immediate object of scientific knowledge', *Franciscan Studies* 37 (1977): 66–102.

15.6   Gregory of Rimini *Lectura super primum et secundum Sententianum*, 7 vols, ed. D. Trapp, V. Marcolino, Berlin, De Gruyter, 1979–87.

15.7   Walter Burley *In Categorias etc.*, Venice, 1478.

15.8   —— *Super artem veterem*, Venice, 1497.

15.9   —— *In artem ueterem*, Venice, 1541.

15.10 —— *In Physicam Aristotelis*, Venice, 1589.

15.11 —— *De puritate artis logicae tractatus longior*, ed. P. Boehner (Franciscan Institute text series 9), St Bonaventure, NY, Franciscan Institute, 1955.

15.12 Paban, C. and Pèques, T. *Joannes Capreolus, defensiones theologiae Thomae Aquinatis*, Turin, Albred Cattier, 1900.

15.13 Schabel, C. 'Peter Aureoli on divine foreknowledge and future contingents: *Scriptum in primum librum Sententiarum*, dd. 38–39', *CIMAGL* 65 (1995): 63–212.

15.14 Wielockx, R. *Aegidii Romani, Apologia* (Opera omnia III.1), Florence, Olschki, 1985.

Studies

15.15 Berubé, C. 'La première école scotiste', in Z. Kaluza and P. Vignaux (eds) *Preuve et raisons à l'Université de Paris: logique, ontologie et théologie au XIVe siècle*, Paris, Vrin, 1984.

15.16 Beumer, J. 'Erleuchteter Glaube: die Theorie Henrichs von Gent und ihr Fortleben in der Spätscholastik', *Franziskanische Studien* 37 (1955): 129–60.

15.17 Brown, S. F. 'Avicenna and the unity of the concept of being', *Franciscan Studies* 25 (1965): 117–50.

15.18 —— 'A modern prologue to Ockham's natural philosophy', *Miscellanea Mediaevalia* 13, 1 (Sprache und Erkenntnis in Mittelalter) (1981): 107–29.

15.19 —— 'Nicholas of Lyra's Critique of Scotus' Univocity' in B. Mojsisch and O. Pluta (eds) *Historia Philosophiae Medii Aevi. Studien zur Geschichte der Philosophie des Mittelalters. Festschrift für Kurt Flasch zu seinem 60. Geburtstag.* Amsterdam, Philadelphia, B. R. Grüner, 1991: 115–127.

15.20 —— 'Guido Terrena, O. Carm., and the analogy of being', *Documenti e studi sulla tradizione filosofica medievale* II–1 (1994): 237–69.

15.21 —— 'Godfrey of Fontaines and Henry of Ghent: individuation and the condemnations of 1277', *Société et église* (Rencontres de philosophie médiévale, 4) (1995): 193–207.

15.22 Courtenay, W. J. *Schools and Scholars in Fourteenth-century England*, Princeton, NJ, Princeton University Press, 1987.

15.23 Courtenay, W. J. and Tachau, K. 'Ockham, Ockhamists, and the English-German nation at Paris, 1339–1441', *History of Universities* 2 (1982): 53–96.

15.24 Dreiling, R. *Der Konzeptualismus in der Universalienlehre des Franziskanererbischofs Petrus Aureoli* (BGPTMA, XI, 6). Münster, Aschendorff, 1913.

15.25 Dumont, S. 'The Univocity of the Concept of Being in the Fourteenth Century: II: The De ente of Peter Thomae' *Mediaeval Studies* 50 (1988): 186–256.

15.26 Etzkorn, G. J. and Brown, S. F. 'A Symposium on God's Knowledge of Future Contingents', *Miscellanea Francescana* 96 (1996): 561–620.

15.27 Flüeler, C. *Rezeption und Interpretation der Aristotelischen 'Politica' im späten Mittelalter* (Bochumer Studien zur Philosophie 19), Amsterdam and Philadelphia, Pa., B. R. Grüner, 1992.

15.28 Green-Pedersen, N. J. 'Nicholaus Drukken de Dacia's commentary on the *Prior Analytics*, with special regard to the theory of consequences', *CIMAGL* 37 (1981): 42–69.

15.29 Trapp, D. 'Augustinian theology of the 14th century', *Augustiniana* 6 (1956): 146–274.

15.30 Uña Juárez, A. *La filosofia del siglo XIV: contexto cultural de Walter Burley*, Real Monasterio de el Escorial, 1978.

15.31 Weisheipl, J. 'Ockham and some Mertonians', *Mediaeval Studies* 30 (1968): 163–213.

15.32 Wippel, J. *The Metaphysical Thought of Godfrey of Fontaines: a Study in Late Thirteenth Century Philosophy*, Washington, DC, Catholic University of America Press, 1981.

15.33 Würsdorfer, J. *Erkennen und Wissen nach Gregor von Rimini* (BGPTMA 20), Münster, Aschendorff, 1917.

15.34 Zumkeller, A. 'Die Augustinerschule des Mittelalters: Vertreter und philosophisch-theologische Lehre', *Analecta Augustiniana* 27 (1964): 167–262.

CHAPTER 16

Paris and Oxford between Aureoli and Rimini

Chris Schabel

Oxford ideas in logic and natural philosophy were readily received, analysed, and partially incorporated into corresponding writings of a logical or natural philosophical nature at the University of Paris throughout the 1320s, 1330s, and 1340s. Precise dating, however, is usually not possible. There was a strong Parisian reaction to Ockham's physics before 1327, particularly on the part of Walter Burley, and Ockham's *Summa logicae* was available to the influential Parisian arts master John Buridan.[1] Statutes of the Parisian arts faculty show that Ockham's logic was playing a significant role there by 1339 ([16.10], [16.26]). The logical writings of the Oxford Calculators from the late 1320s and 1330s were important in Parisian works of natural philosophy from the 1340s and afterwards ([16.19]). Buridan and Nicole Oresme used the more abstract Oxford geometrical and mathematical concepts, but made their application to physical theory a fundamental aim, and this contributed to their interesting treatments of such topics as the motion of projectiles and the Earth's rotation.

With philosophical theology the story is different. A common view of theology at the University of Paris in the quarter century between Peter Aureoli and Gregory of Rimini is that Paris ignored Oxford just when Oxford was experiencing its golden age. After Aureoli lectured on the *Sentences* in 1316–18, Parisian scholars busied themselves in stagnant isolation refuting his opinions for a few years until about 1326, when Parisian thought went into what has been labelled as a 'dormition', only to be reawakened in 1343–4 by Rimini, who brought much of the new Oxford thought into Paris. Thus in this period Paris not only lost its customary dominance to Oxford, it actually went into sharp decline in absolute terms because it failed to maintain intellectual contacts with the main English *studium generale* (see [16.9] 153).

The aim of this chapter is to review and revise this scenario. Although Parisian theology *was* isolated from Oxford, for the most part, between 1318 and 1343, Oxford was equally ignorant of Paris. Moreover, where scholars have looked, Paris was alive, awake, and productive at least until 1330, and remained the intellectual focal point of *continental* education. The Parisian 'products', of course, differed from those of Oxford, as one would expect from such mutual isolation, but when *both* rigorous currents came together at Paris in the 1340s, they created a dynamic synthesis.

❧ THE BEGINNINGS OF ISOLATION ❧

In the thirteenth and early fourteenth centuries, Paris was the top school in philosophy and theology for the secular clergy, and the international and hierarchical educational systems of the mendicant orders helped ensure that the leading students in Barcelona, Bologna, Cologne and Oxford eventually made their way to Paris. When scholars left this international market of ideas, they carried those ideas with them. For reasons that are unclear, however, English scholars began to stay at home in the 1310s, and most of the English had left Paris by 1320. Some remained, but few new English students arrived at Paris in the 1320s and 1330s. This fact alone accounts for Oxford's rise in these decades: the best of Britain's students stayed at home.

In Paris it was business as usual, with two exceptions: first, it lost its English scholars; second, the end of the 1320s and the early 1330s were troubled times for the Church. Scholarly energies were sometimes turned to issues like the quarrel between John XXII and the mendicants, and John XXII's other doctrinal 'interests', such as the beatific vision, matters which produced some important writings in political philosophy, for example, although not always directly connected with Paris. Otherwise, things went on without the English. Between 1315 and 1340 we find at Paris many significant Spanish, Italian and of course French scholars, although a few Germans also left a mark, such as Thomas of Strasbourg. Only in the early 1320s were there any 'leftover' English, such as John Baconthorpe, Thomas Wilton and Walter Burley. Moreover, this composition of Spanish, Italian and French scholars continued even after Rimini's 'recovery', so that in the 1340s we find that our remaining *Sentences* commentaries come from Alphonsus Vargas of Toledo of Spain; Rimini, Hugolinus of Orvieto, Paul of Perugia, and John of Ripa from Italy;

and John of Mirecourt and Pierre Ceffons from France. The English never really did return in force to Paris, whereas the German presence increased there markedly, until the creation of the new German universities in the wake of the Great Schism.

To a degree English thought had always played a role in Paris, but it was primarily English scholars who had also studied theology in Paris, such as Scotus, William of Alnwick, Wilton, Baconthorpe and Burley, who were known to their fellow Parisians. This was consistently the case even in the thirteenth century, and continued until around 1340. One can take Henry of Harclay as an example: he was cited by name in, for example, distinction 39 of Peter Aureoli's *Scriptum* version of his commentary on book I of the *Sentences* ([16.4] 185–6). Through Aureoli, almost all Parisian theologians came to learn of Harclay's position. Furthermore, Aufredo Gonteri Brito OFM literally absorbed the whole of Harclay's Parisian *Sentences* commentary into his own, when lecturing at Paris in the 1320s. English influence at Paris in the 1320s did *not* depend on their physical presence there.

What about the influence of contemporary Oxford scholars in this period, in Paris? Before 1326 we have practically no evidence of the new English theology in Paris, and yet this was a highly productive period. There are several possible reasons for the lack of English influence at Paris after 1326, however: Pope John XXII's movements after 1326 against the suspect opinions and actions of Ockham, Peter Olivi, Meister Eckhart, Michael of Cesena and Thomas of Wales, which may have stifled philosophical flamboyance; the straining of cross-Channel relations at the approach of the Hundred Years War; and the extreme decrease in the numbers of English scholars at Paris after 1325 (see, e.g. [16.7] 45–6). The most plausible explanation for the Parisian attitude toward Oxford in both periods is that Parisian thinkers were too busy dealing with Aureoli.

Peter Aureoli's stature in medieval thought has not been fully appreciated, partly because until recently few have bothered to look at Parisian thought in the decade after him, when we would expect his impact to be felt most intensely. Aureoli comprehensively dismantled the systems of Aquinas and Scotus, and created a new, internally coherent system of thought that could not be ignored. It was so large, however, that it left little room for anyone else. Thus Landulph Caracciolo, for example, sometimes seems content to attack Aureoli as if there were no one else. Looked at from this perspective, it is no wonder Ockham and the English failed to make an impact.

❧ SOURCES FOR STUDYING PARISIAN ❧ THEOLOGY, 1315–40

Between 1315 and 1340 many significant scholars studied at the University of Paris. When we look at Parisian thought in this era we are struck with the large number of extant *Sentences* commentaries from the period 1315–30. In this period, these commentaries are the main source for current issues not only in theology *per se*, but also science and philosophy more generally (see [16.17] 274–80). There are about twenty named authors with major extant theological works, several anonymous commentaries (mostly Franciscan) that can be assigned to this period, and we find many of Wilton's ideas via Baconthorpe and Pierre Roger's from Francis Meyronnes (see [16.23]). We have only two commentaries that we can assign with certainty to the 1330s, those of Strasbourg and Peter of Aquila, both conservative thinkers. Although we do have the fascinating letters between Nicholas of Autrecourt and Bernard of Arezzo, their *Sentences* commentaries do not survive. Autrecourt's was in fact burned. Thus we have about thirty theologians participating in a twenty-five-year discussion, but most of the discussion had apparently ended by the early 1330s.

There is some evidence for the lasting influence of the theologians in these decades. Although Early Modern motives in publishing were complex, it is still interesting that at least ten Parisians of this period, for the most part not well known to us, had major theological works printed in the late fifteenth through to the early seventeenth centuries, but this could be said for only five Oxford scholars from the same era.[2] Yet very few historians have tried to trace the course of any debate in the Paris of that time. Even the editors of Rimini had little success in finding the Parisian sources with whom he agreed, though this was partly because he did not cite them himself. In truth, later theologians, especially Franciscans, looked back upon these decades as a golden age in *Parisian* thought, at least Franciscan thought. The fifteenth-century English Scotist John Foxoles placed the ultimate origin of three schools of roughly Scotist thought in the 1320s and 1330s: Meyronnists, Bonetists and pure Scotists (see [16.5] 270–1). In some areas of philosophy there arose a 'Marchist' school as well, arising from Francis of Marchia, and further articulated by Michael of Massa and William of Rubione. By Rimini's time some of their ideas were common enough to be used without reference.

It is too early to tell the story of Paris between Aureoli and Rimini with any degree of accuracy. Indeed, we are unsure of important basic dates for many works, e.g. the versions of Aureoli's *Sentences* commentary; Peter Thomae's and Peter of Navarre's lectures; and Rubione's commentary (see [16.1] 199–207; [16.4] 78–82). Recently changes have been made to the chronology of several figures in the 1330s: Peter of Aquila, Thomas of Strasbourg, Nicholas of Autrecourt and Bernard of Arezzo (see [16.13]). Book I of Marchia's *Sentences* commentary, from lectures given just after Aureoli's, survives in two main versions in at least fifteen manuscripts and five fragments, but remains unedited. In light of the inchoate nature of the research, a general view of the period is simply impossible. Therefore, let us examine the theory of Oxford superiority and Parisian isolation, stagnation, dormition and reception of Oxford thought by comparing more closely the discussion of Parisian and Oxford scholars in two of the four areas in philosophical theology that Courtenay deems 'worthy of special mention' in *Oxford* theology in the very same period: epistemology and future contingents ([16.11] 22–9).

✦✦ FUTURE CONTINGENTS ✦✦

No fewer than ten theologians active from 1315 to 1340 have had all or much of their Oxford treatments of future contingents published in modern critical editions.[3] For Paris, by contrast, this is true for two figures only: Aureoli and Navarre. Lest this philosophical issue be considered an area of particular strength for Oxford and weakness for Paris, it must be added that Gregory of Rimini, the Parisian theologian who is considered most responsible for the integration of the 'New English Theology' into the Parisian milieu in the early 1340s, devoted most of his energy to refuting Aureoli, building on *Parisian* tradition. Moreover, during the celebrated quarrel over future contingents at Louvain in the later fifteenth century, a controversy that grew to include issues of divine power and will, Aureoli, Meyronnes, Marchia and Nicholas Bonet played explicit roles, but none of the Oxford theologians did (see [16.21] 407–8). So we must be prepared from the outset to admit that the supposed superiority of Oxford thought in this era is perhaps more a reflection of modern scholarly interests than of medieval considerations.

Aside from the verbatim copying (reading *secundum alium*) of Durandus by Bernard the Lombard and Dionysus de Burgo Sancti Sepulchri, and of Harclay by Gonteri as mentioned, scholars active between 1318 and 1330 focused on Aureoli's opinions. The main elements of Aureoli's position have been outlined above. Temporal things are indistant or non-distant to God's eternity, and future-tensed propositions are neither true nor false determinately; nor does God's knowledge make them so, since it does not temporally precede the future. In addition, Aureoli's emphasis on absolute divine necessity left little room for any divine action, so Aureoli developed an awkward division between the intrinsic divine will of 'complacency' which was immutable and absolutely necessary, and the extrinsic will of 'operation', by which God actually acts, as in creation.[4]

The reaction to Aureoli's theory in England was slight. Ockham showed no awareness. Chatton knew some of Aureoli, and quoted the basics of his ideas on propositions and prophecy, so he must have known Aureoli's distinction 38, article three. In refuting this fragment of Aureoli's treatment, Chatton even said, 'this would be a nice explanation, if it were true'. Adam Wodeham demonstrated about the same cognizance of Aureoli as had Chatton, and perhaps knew a bit more about the Parisian debate generally. Otherwise, there was little response. Some of Bradwardine's remarks in his *De causa Dei* which appeared to some scholars to refer to Aureoli personally, really did not, and Bradwardine was a bit confused if he meant that the *position* that he heard defended in Avignon and Oxford was Aureoli's own. Aureoli never played a big role in the Oxford debate, which instead went in other, interesting directions, examining in depth issues surrounding prophecy, the ontological status of divine foreknowledge (and the *complexe significabile*), and finally the different types of necessity with respect to both the past and future.[5]

These last 'Oxford' issues only came to prominence in Paris with Rimini. In the intervening years, almost every Parisian theologian whose pertinent works can be securely dated to between 1318 and 1330 focused much of his discussion on Aureoli. Every one of Aureoli's main points was attacked, since he appeared to have denied foreknowledge and prophecy altogether. In the 1320s, Baconthorpe, Caracciolo, and his follower the anonymous author of Vienna ÖNB 1439 criticized Aureoli's vulnerable concept of the twofold divine will; Caracciolo wondered whether creation came from God at all under Aureoli's scheme, if the act of creation were somehow 'extrinsic' to God. Meyronnes, Caracciolo, Gerard of Siena, Bonet, and in an odd way Gerard Odon rejected Aureoli's notion of indistance, maintaining that such a negative relation made little positive sense. Meyronnes, Marchia, and Michael of Massa opposed the neutrality of future contingent propositions, making use of both logical arguments and Scripture in their defence of bivalence.

Several scholars defended Scotus's account and appealed to the traditional distinctions between the composite and divided senses of such propositions as 'what God foreknows will necessarily come about', and between the necessities of the consequent and of the consequence (and parallel distinctions) in such consequences as 'God foreknows X; X will be'. All of these Aureoli had refuted at length, so this constitutes the major 'conservative' point shared by many of these thinkers. Nevertheless, interesting positive theories came out of the debate. For

Wilton, whose ideas in this context we know via Baconthorpe, what was needed was to show that there are different levels of determination in human activities anyway, and that we need not fear all such 'predetermination'. Thus God can know 'contingent' futures. Francis of Marchia developed a similar solution, although in much greater depth. In short, he distinguished between different types of determinations and indeterminations *de inesse* and *de possibili*. Humans in fact determine themselves beforehand with respect to what they are actually going to do; this is determination *de inesse*, about what is in reality, without which no one would or could actually do anything. This does not mean that they are determined *de possibili*, however, in a way that the *possibility* to do otherwise is removed. Determination *de inesse* was the basis of divine foreknowledge and was required for human action, while *in*determination *de possibili* preserved human freedom and left God's foreknowledge intact. Aureoli would have found several problems with this theory, but it was expressed eloquently and systematically. Massa and Rubione accepted Marchia's solution as their own, and by Rimini's time it seems to have been a commonplace. Through Rimini it was passed to later theologians, and used in the late fifteenth century by the well-read Fernand of Cordoba against Peter of Rivo's defence of Aureoli's doctrine.

Rimini does not cite Marchia by name in his *Sentences* commentary in this context, nor do the editors trace Marchia's influence. Like most scholastics, Rimini was not in the habit of citing by name those with whom he agreed. When he devoted an entire question to refuting Aristotle and Aureoli's opinion on future contingent propositions, he did not cite his Parisian predecessors who did the same thing. His Augustinian confrère Massa, in particular, focused much energy on this very point, and may have been Rimini's immediate source for Marchia's *de inesse*/*de possibili* distinction. Nevertheless, he was not cited by name either and historians have doomed him to oblivion even in his own order. Moreover, the Parisian Nicholas Bonet was probably Rimini's reason for treating propositions yet again after so many others had. During the Louvain controversy in the 1470s, Cardinal Bessarion and Francesco della Rovere (Pope Sixtus IV) would remember and applaud their fellow Franciscan Bonet's refutation of Aureoli's indistance notion in the former's *Natural Theology* of around 1330, but they looked less favourably on Bonet's apparent agreement with Aureoli that future contingent propositions could not be true or false without entailing fatalism. Indeed, Bonet seems to have limited the certainty of divine foreknowledge, in a way Aureoli himself would not have approved (see [16.20] 127–279, 714–69).

Rimini's main goal in his impressive and exhaustive treatment is to defeat Aureoli once and for all on the issue of propositions. In doing so, Rimini defended foreknowledge *per se*, and only then did he go on to other sub-issues, some of which came from Oxford. Rimini shows his familiarity in this context with Wodeham, Chatton, Ockham and the Monachus Niger. This is well known, but it does not seem possible with future contingents to show when exactly these Oxford ideas were in circulation in Paris. Probably it was not before 1330, but certainly by 1343. Unfortunately the paucity and conservative nature of pertinent sources from the 1330s do not allow any more specificity.

❧ EPISTEMOLOGY ❧

Katherine Tachau has looked at the Oxford discussion of epistemology in these decades, and at Aureoli and some of his Parisian successors. With the help of other works, we are able to piece the Parisian picture together fairly comprehensively. In epistemology as in future contingents Aureoli played a pivotal role. Although he was emphasizing vision, Aureoli's successors interpreted his theories as a radical departure from previous epistemologies, primarily Scotus's. Scotus had differentiated between intuitive and abstractive cognition basically by saying that intuitive cognition was of objects immediately present, and abstractive cognition was the knowledge one had when the object was absent. Aureoli put forth a redefinition of intuition and abstraction, taking various erroneous visual 'experiences' (he gives eight examples) as his starting point to define intuition. In doing so, Aureoli maintained that intuition occurred when one *thought* the object was immediately present, and in that case the 'apparent being' (*esse apparens*) was in fact present to the mind, even with veridical intuition. For example, when one is on a moving ship, one experiences the motion of objects on the shore. Since one intuits the apparent being of such motion without its real presence, or even existence, outside the mind, and since even in 'veridical' intuition one in fact intuits only apparent being, then one cannot infer the real presence or existence of the objects of 'normal' experiences, Aureoli argued. Moreover, if produced by God, an erroneous intuition would be indistinguishable from a veridical one. For some of Aureoli's successors, this jeopardized all certainty, although Aureoli apparently did not intend this (see [16.24] 85–112).

By his own admission, Ockham had limited access to Aureoli's *Scriptum*, but Ockham learned enough about Aureoli to treat the latter's position in a confused way in his *Ordinatio*, written while at the London convent in 1320–4. The most idiosyncratic aspects of Ockham's treatment are his claims that one can have a true intuition that something does *not* exist, and that God could give us a false intuition of something not present, but we would still discern its falsity. These awkward opinions were easy targets for those who followed in the English discussion. In debates with his confrère Walter Chatton, Ockham modified some of his views ([16.24] 113–53). Chatton himself, composing his *Sentences* commentary in 1321–3, knew Aureoli's *Scriptum* better, but Chatton's readers were not able to distinguish clearly between Ockham and Aureoli in Chatton's work, and this led to further confusion ([16.24] 180, 185–6, 207–8). Adam Wodeham was Chatton's *rapporteur* at the Franciscan London *studium*, and when he in turn lectured on the *Sentences* at Norwich, London and Oxford, beginning perhaps in 1328 or even earlier, Wodeham came to explore Aureoli's views directly, so that he knew him better than anyone else in England.[6]

From the discussions of future contingents and epistemology we can perhaps infer that the Franciscans' London convent housed the only manuscript of Aureoli's *Scriptum* in England, since Ockham, Chatton and Wodeham, who show the most extensive knowledge of Aureoli, seem to have examined his work there. Unfortunately we know less about epistemology at Oxford after Wodeham, but the London convent and Adam Wodeham may be the key to the passage of English theology to Paris beginning in the 1330s.

As in the case of future contingents, Aureoli's thought played a significant role in Parisian epistemological discussions in the 1320s and 1330s. Of the theologians Tachau inspected from this period, she found that only Strasbourg appeared unfamiliar with Aureoli's epistemology, and even Strasbourg has been added to those who treated Aureoli in that context (see [16.13] 455). The same can be said of some of the theologians Tachau has not studied, such as Baconthorpe (see [16.14] 57). In many cases, these theologians had difficulty understanding Aureoli's position because they approached his text wearing Scotist glasses, reading into Aureoli Scotus's definition of intuition and abstraction. Still, the epistemological debate that followed Aureoli in Paris had a continuing impact even after the full reception of English thought. Caracciolo's treatment, for example, was well known to Pierre Ceffons, lecturing in 1345 (see [16.24] 321).

In epistemology, however, English thought is already present by 1332. Parallel passages in Chatton and William of Rubione reveal a close connection in the context of epistemology, and other evidence reinforces such an early cross-Channel link (see [16.15] 39–40; [16.13] 447–8). Rubione's commentary could have been written any time between 1323 and 1332, however, so Chatton's commentary may have even been available in Paris immediately following his own *Sentences* lectures. There is another difficulty: we cannot be certain about

Rubione's testimony until we examine Marchia's works exhaustively. In other contexts, Marchia influenced both Chatton and Rubione, and although an inspection of the two main versions of Marchia's *Sentences* commentary did not reveal the relevant discussion of abstractive and intuitive cognition, perhaps there was another source. It would be odd for such an original thinker as Marchia to have been perhaps unique in ignoring Aureoli on this issue.

Chatton's impact is certainly present, however, in the most famous epistemological debate of the time, perhaps of the entire Middle Ages, the exchanges of letters between Nicholas of Autrecourt and Bernard of Arezzo in 1336–7. Taking the lead from Aureoli and the Parisian discussion following his lectures, Autrecourt took the next step and denied the possibility of certainty based on sensory perception. No apparent perception of an extramental object could provide certainty of the existence of that object. Moreover, even assuming the existence of those objects, one could never be certain of cause and effect relations, the bases of natural philosophy. If it is possible for us to be mistaken about the external world and efficient causation because of God's action, Autrecourt maintained that it is possible without qualification to be so mistaken. There have been many treatments, even monograph-length accounts, of the radically sceptical aspects of Autrecourt's thought. Until recently this debate was seen as evidence of the influence of that ubiquitous 'Ockhamism', but Tachau shows convincingly that this historiographical interpretation is based on a long series of errors and false suppositions. In fact, there is no evidence for Ockham's influence on Autrecourt in the debate (see [16.24] 335–52; [16.13] 453–9; [16.25] 248–50).

Still, there are strong indications that Autrecourt knew Chatton's work, if not Ockham's. In 1340 the arts faculty restricted a proposition that Autrecourt, while being reviewed in 1346, admitted he had held, presumably in the 1330s: 'God and a creature are nothing.' Although in 1346 Autrecourt used the term *complexe significabile* to describe what he had held, and Tachau therefore links the proposition to Wodeham, it could just as easily be the case that Autrecourt came to hold the proposition via Chatton's influence, and only later learned Wodeham's terminology. Indeed, Tachau says that Autrecourt conflated the views of the two English Franciscans ([16.24] 353–6).

The first strong evidence for Wodeham's presence, and for Ockham's, comes again with Rimini. As in the case of future contingents, Rimini combined a concern with Aureoli and Parisian currents with a close knowledge of the English debate, although he was less negative toward Aureoli in this context. Rimini opposed Ockham's position, as had most Oxford scholars, but Wodeham played a positive part in the development of the Italian Augustinian's opinion. Here as well we see the introduction of the *complexe significabile* to yet another philosophical problem, and in the decade following Rimini the English and Parisian trends merged ([16.24] 357–83).

THE IMPACT OF ENGLISH THOUGHT IN PARIS AFTER 1340

The impact of English thought in Parisian philosophical theology in the 1330s appears to be mostly limited to Oxford writers active in London before 1323, e.g. Ockham in his non-theological works, Chatton in his *Sentences* commentary, and perhaps Wodeham. By 1343, however, Rimini was using a very wide range of English philosophical and theological works. There is reason to believe that there was an important Italian connection here. William of Alnwick was named lector at the Franciscan *studium* in Bologna in 1323, and Thomas Waleys was lector at the Dominican convent there in 1326–7. Walter Burley, who by 1327 knew so much of the intellectual currents of both Oxford and Paris, was in Bologna in 1341. Ockham himself was in Italy for a while after 1328, although it is doubtful that he had much of an impact there just then. These English scholars brought their minds and their books, and by about 1340 parts of Burley's, Ockham's, Rodington's and Chatton's *Sentences* commentaries and no doubt many other English works were available in Bologna. Finally, before returning to Paris in 1342, Gregory of Rimini lectured in Bologna, Padua and Perugia (see [16.6] 13–32; [16.13] 449–50). This may help explain how Rimini brought so much with him, and why the full introduction of English thought into Paris seems so abrupt.

After 1343 there was definitely an English influence in Paris, but how much of an impact? In theology, Courtenay points to four English trends. First, *Sentences* commentaries shrank in size. Second, *Sentences* commentaries were restructured, so that they departed from Lombard's organization and focused on sophismata. Third, schools of thought disappeared, and more emphasis was placed on individual thinking than on system building. Finally, new logical, physical and mathematical ideas were applied to theological issues ([16.8] 111–14).

The size of *Sentences* commentaries at Paris does not seem to have shrunk appreciably after 1343, although we must remember that the size of commentaries depended on whether they were revised by the author into longer forms (*ordinationes*). The structuring of commentaries is a different matter. Here we find that after 1343 theologians such as Mirecourt, Henry Totting of Oyta, Peter d'Ailly and Peter of Candia do depart from Lombard's distinction organization, the last three, writing in the 1370s, asking a mere handful of very large questions. Still, many stuck close to Lombard's system, such as John of Ripa and John Hiltalingen of Basel. And even Mirecourt and Candia followed Lombard's basic order, usually finishing off their commentaries on the first book with questions on divine knowledge, foreknowledge, power and will. Moreover, some of this was already present in, for example, Francis of Marchia. Although Marchia superficially keeps to Lombard's distinctions, the contents of the questions do not correspond to Lombard's. Thus in one version Marchia devoted all of distinctions 35, 36, 38 and 39 to future contingents.

It is a difficult question as to whether school traditions existed in an important way in Paris before 1343, or whether there was a big change afterwards. Both before and after 1343, mendicants for the most part kept their discussion within their own orders, at least. The traditional view, however, has been that Paris was pretty much a Scotist university in these early decades, or that Parisians were less individualistic than their Oxford counterparts. We have seen that there are a few examples of reading *secundum alium*, hardly an original activity. It is also true that Marchia and Caracciolo, for example, had their own groups of close followers on certain issues, and that many theologians were content to modify a Scotist account in reply to Aureoli. The trend of paraphrasing and even copying others continued, however, long after the Oxford currents had been absorbed into the Paris environment. But how do we assess this situation? Their aim continued to be system building: Aureoli had a new system; Marchia tried to develop a new system, leaving much of Scotus behind; his followers tried to hammer it out; Rimini himself wanted a system. The Parisian scholars may have looked at the big picture more than did those at Oxford, who focused on individual problems. This does not mean that Parisians did not criticize. They had no choice but to be fundamentally negative in their works in response to Peter Aureoli's complete revision of most aspects of philosophical theology. It is simply that after their attacks on Aureoli, they tended to either develop new systems or seek refuge in old ones. It did no good if one's ideas did not hold together, after all. Especially telling in this regard was a tendency, already in Wilton and later in Bonet (at least in future contingents), to throw up one's hands where no systematic solution could be found. This is exactly what Hiltalingen and Candia did later on (see [16.20] 713, 804).

Finally, there is the new logic, mathematics and physics in theology. This was a trend already evident in Paris in the late 1310s and 1320s in the writings of Aureoli, Marchia, Massa and Odon. Scholars of the 1340s make increasing use of Oxford geometrical, mathematical and logical 'measure' language to discuss such topics in philosophical theology as the infinite, already one of Rimini's favourite subjects. Even if the new *language* of Oxford was not developed in Paris, certainly the problems associated with and presupposed in that language were explored before 1343, however. In this way, Oxford thought reinforced a Parisian trend already in motion, and the writings of Rimini, Mirecourt and Ceffons abound with the fruits of the new merger, both in terms of new tools and in terms of new topics. Ceffons even develops the tools and techniques further (see [16.16], [16.18]).

Ultimately, the safest basis for claiming that English scholarship played a big new role in Paris after 1343 is citations. One need look no further than the master of citations himself, the Augustinian John Hiltalingen of Basel, who lectured on the *Sentences* at Paris in 1365–6. He cited some twenty Oxford scholars from the previous fifty years, and in his discussion of foreknowledge and predestination alone, Hiltalingen cited Bradwardine, Heytesbury, Richard of Kilvington, Wodeham, Fitzralph and Nicholas Aston (see [16.27] 242–50; [16.20] 789–807). English thought had permanently penetrated the 'mainstream' of European philosophy by 1365. One finds impressive numbers of English citations in the 1340s with Rimini and Hugolino of Orvieto. In many places John of Mirecourt's commentary appears to be a simple matter of cutting and pasting from Wodeham, Halifax, Bradwardine, Kilvington, Langeley and Buckingham, which suggests that Parisians may have used Oxford material, without attribution, to show off and gain a reputation as innovators (see [16.12]).

This may even be the case with Rimini himself. It is telling that in the period after Scotus, Rimini's editors found that he cited Aureoli and Ockham about 200 times each. Only three other scholars between 1320 and 1343 have more than ten references in Rimini: Wodeham (66), Fitzralph (34) and Burley (58), although the editors have found a few references to several other theologians from the period on both sides of the Channel. It is hard to believe that Rimini would treat Aureoli so often while ignoring the intervening Parisian debates which undoubtedly provided ammunition. As we have seen, Rimini was less likely to cite Parisians explicitly (although he used their material), but it is also the case that English citations and ideas would have been more interesting to an audience who had heard all of the anti-Aureoli arguments before.

❧ CONCLUSION ❧

There is no doubt that Oxford thought between 1315 and 1340 was truly exciting. The main reason for this was that more English scholars simply stayed at home. There is also little doubt that Rimini to a large extent was responsible for first explicitly introducing many of the stimulating English developments into the Parisian discussion, and that English thought outside of natural philosophy and logic was largely ignored in Paris in the meantime, at least until around 1330, when Walter Chatton's *Sentences* commentary was probably available in Paris. But Rimini's Aureoli citations and much present research show that there is also considerable evidence that Parisian theology, at least until the 1330s, continued to be illuminated by brilliant minds as it had before 1318 and as it would after 1343. What happened after 1343 was that newer English techniques and even English theological problems further enriched what was already a lively affair at the continental university. After 1343, in future contingents for example, there are more issues to discuss. But from the period 1318 to 1343, Oxford, although to a lesser extent than Paris, was not conversant with trends in the other city, and in many cases awareness of, say, the Parisian debate on future contingents, would have stimulated the English treatment of the same issue.

Whether Oxford thought was 'better' than Parisian thought in this period, or vice versa, is in the final analysis a matter of taste. Modern taste thus far has leaned heavily toward Oxford. Late medieval and Early Modern tastes, perhaps more conservatively, went in the direction of Paris. It really does not matter. Surely, however, the continued flourishing of Paris and the unique developments at Oxford between 1315 and 1350 can only mean a high point in *European* philosophy generally, both universities contributing and deserving further study.

NOTES

1. On Burley's reaction to Ockham, see above, Chapter 15, pp. 369–77; on Buridan and the *Summa logicae*, see John Buridan [16.2] xxx–xxxv.
2. For Paris there are all or part of the *Sentences* commentaries of Durandus, Aureoli, Meyronnes, Baconthorpe, Landulph Caracciolo, Gerard of Siena, William of Rubione, Strasbourg and Aquila, and Nicholas Bonet's *Natural Theology*; for Oxford, those of Ockham, Holcot, Wodeham and Buckingham, and Bradwardine's *De causa Dei*.
3. For some Oxford theologians, see above, Chapter 14, pp. 354–5; for Paris, Aureoli's contribution to the dispute is edited by Schabel [16.4] and Peter of Navarre's in Petrus de Navarra [16.3].
4. See above, Chapter 15, pp. 380–1 and cf. Schabel [16.4] 75–8, 175–80.
5. Some of these issues are discussed in Chapter 17, below: see especially pp. 410–11 (complexly significables).
6. [16.24] 276, 290; and see above, Chapter 14, pp. 330, 333, 346 and 348–9 on Chatton and Wodeham.

❦ BIBLIOGRAPHY ❦

Original Language Editions

16.1 Brown, S. F. 'Peter Aureol: *De unitate conceptus entis (Reportatio Parisiensis in I Sententiarum* dist. 2, p. 1, qq. 1–3 et p. 2, qq. 1–2)', *Traditio* 50 (1995): 199–248.

16.2 John Buridan *Questiones Elencorum*, ed. R. van der Lecq and H. Braakhuis, Nijmegen, 1994.

16.3 Peter of Navarre *In Primum Sententiarum Scriptum* I, ed. P. Azcona, Madrid, 1974.

16.4 Schabel, C. 'Peter Aureol on divine foreknowledge and future contingents: *Scriptum in Primum Librum Sententiarum*, distinctions 38–39', *CIMAGL* 65 (1995): 63–212.

Studies

16.5 Catto, J. I. 'Theology after Wycliffism', in Catto and R. Evans (eds) *The History of the University of Oxford*, vol. II, *Late Medieval Oxford*, Oxford, 1992, pp. 263–80.

16.6 Courtenay, W. J. 'The early stages in the introduction of Oxford logic into Italy', in A. Maierù (ed.) *English Logic in Italy in the 14th and 15th Centuries*, Naples, 1982, pp. 13–22.

16.7 —— 'The reception of Ockham's thought at the University of Paris', in Z. Kaluza and P. Vignaux (eds) *Logique, ontologie, théologie au XIVe siècle: preuve et raisons à l'Université de Paris*, Paris, 1984, pp. 43–64.

16.8 —— 'The role of English thought in the transformation of university education in the late Middle Ages', in J. Kittelson and P. Transue (eds) *Rebirth, Reform, and Resilience: Universities in Transition 1300–1700*, Columbus, Ohio, 1984, pp. 103–62.

16.9 —— *Schools and Scholars in Fourteenth-century England*, Princeton, NJ, 1987.

16.10 —— 'The registers of the University of Paris and the statutes against the *Scientia Occamica*', *Vivarium* 29 (1991): 13–49.

16.11 —— 'Theology and theologians from Ockham to Wyclif', in *The History of the University of Oxford*, vol. II, 1992, pp. 1–34.

16.12 Genest, J-F. and Vignaux, P. 'La bibliothèque anglaise de Jean de Mirecourt: *subtilitas* ou plagiat?', in O. Pluta (ed.) *Die Philosophie im 14. und 15. Jahrhundert. In memoriam Konstanty Michalski (1879–1947)*, Amsterdam, 1988, pp. 275–301.

16.13 Kaluza, Z. '*Serbi un sasso il nome*: une inscription de San Gimignano et la rencontre entre Bernard d'Arezzo et Nicolas d'Autrecourt', *Historia Philosophiae Medii Aevi* 1 (1991): 437–66.

16.14 Michalski, K. *Le Criticisme et le scepticisme dans la philosophie du XIVe siècle*, Cracow, 1926; repr. in Michalski, *La Philosophie au XIVe siècle*, ed. K. Flasch, Frankfurt, 1969, pp. 67–149.

16.15 —— *Les Courants critiques et sceptiques dans la philosophie du XIVe siècle*, Cracow, 1927; repr. in Michalski, *La Philosophie au XIVe siècle*, 1969, pp. 151–203.

16.16 Murdoch, J. '*Mathesis in philosophiam scholasticam introducta*'. The rise and development of the application of mathematics in fourteenth-century philosophy and theology', in *Arts Libéraux et Philosophie au Moyen Âge*, Montreal, 1969, pp. 215–49.

16.17 —— 'From social into intellectual factors: an aspect of the unitary character of late medieval learning', in Murdoch and E. Sylla (eds) *The Cultural Context of Medieval Learning*, Dordrecht, 1975, pp. 271–348.

16.18 —— '*Subtilitates Anglicanae* in fourteenth-century Paris: John of Mirecourt and Peter Ceffons', in M. Cosman and B. Chandler (eds) *Machaut's World: Science and Art in the Fourteenth Century*, New York, 1978, pp. 51–86.

16.19 Sarnowsky, J. 'Natural philosophy at Oxford and Paris in the mid-fourteenth century', in A. Hudson and M. Wilks (eds) *From Ockham to Wyclif*, Oxford, 1987, pp. 125–34.

16.20 Schabel, C. 'The quarrel with Aureol: Peter Aureol's role in the late-medieval debate over divine foreknowledge and future contingents, 1315–1475', Ph.D. dissertation, University of Iowa, 1994.

16.21 —— 'Peter de Rivo and the quarrel over future contingents at Louvain: new evidence and new perspectives (Part I)', in *Documenti e studi sulla tradizione filosofica medievale* 6 (1995): 363–473.

16.22 —— 'Peter de Rivo and the quarrel over future contingents at Louvain: new evidence and new perspectives (Part II)', *Documenti e studi sulla tradizione filosofica medievale* 7 (1996): 369–435.

16.23 Schabel, C. and Friedman, R. L. 'The vitality of Franciscan theology at Paris in the 1320s: MS Wien Österreichische Nationalbibliothek, Palatinus 1439', *Archives d'histoire doctrinale et littéraire du moyen âge* 63 (1996): 357–72.

16.24 Tachau, K. *Vision and Certitude in the Age of Ockham: Optics, Epistemology, and the Foundations of Semantics 1250–1345*, Leiden, 1988.

16.25 Thijssen, J. M. M. H. 'John Buridan and Nicholas of Autrecourt on causality and induction', *Traditio* 43 (1987): 237–55.

16.26 —— 'Once again the Ockhamist statutes of 1339 and 1340: some new perspectives', *Vivarium* 28 (1990): 136–67.

16.27 Trapp, D. 'Augustinian theology in the 14th century', *Augustiniana* 6 (1956): 146–274.

CHAPTER 17

Late medieval logic

Paul Vincent Spade

∿ I ∿

Medieval logic encompassed more than what we call logic today. It included semantics, philosophy of language, parts of physics, of philosophy of mind and of epistemology.

Late medieval logic began around 1300 and lasted through at least the fifteenth century. With some noteworthy exceptions, its most original contributions were made by 1350, particularly at Oxford. Hence the focus of this chapter will be on the period 1300–1500, with special emphasis on Oxford before 1350.

But first some background concerning the earlier period. The logical writings of Aristotle were all available in Latin by the mid-twelfth century.[1] In addition, except for the theory of 'proofs of propositions'[2] (see section VIII below), the characteristic new ingredients of medieval logic were already in place or at least in progress by the end of the twelfth century or the beginning of the thirteenth.

The theory of inference or 'consequence', for example, was studied as early as Peter Abelard (1079–1142). Again, after about 1120 the circulation of Aristotle's *Sophistical Refutations* in Latin stimulated a study of fallacies and the many features of language that produce them. Out of this investigation there arose twelfth- and thirteenth-century writings on semantic 'properties of terms', like 'supposition' and 'ampliation' (see section VI below).[3] At the same time, treatises on *sophismata* or puzzle-sentences in logic, theology or philosophy of nature began to be produced. (A good analogy for this literature may be found in modern discussions of Frege's 'The morning star is the evening star'.) Likewise, studies were written about the logical effects of words like 'only', 'except', 'begins' and 'ceases' that offer many opportunities for fallacies and involve complications going far beyond syllogistic or the theory of topical inferences.[4] Treatises on 'insolubles' or semantic

402

paradoxes began to appear late in the twelfth century ([17.42], [17.49]). Simultaneously, a literature developed on a new kind of disputation called 'obligations'.[5] Collectively, these new logical genres are known as 'terminist' logic because of the important role played in them by the 'properties of terms'.

These developments continued into the thirteenth century. By mid-century, authors such as Peter of Spain, Lambert of Auxerre and William of Sherwood were writing summary treatises (*summulae*) covering the whole of logic, including the material in Aristotle's writings as well as new terminist developments.[6]

Then, after about 1270, something odd happened, both in England and on the Continent. In France, terminism was eclipsed by an entirely different theory called 'speculative grammar', which appealed to the notion of 'modes of signifying' and is therefore sometimes called 'modism'. This theory prevailed in France until the 1320s, when John Buridan (b. *c*. 1295/1300, d. after 1358) suddenly restored the theory of supposition and associated terminist doctrines. After Buridan, supposition theory was the leading vehicle for semantic (as distinct from grammatical) analysis until the end of the Middle Ages.

Modism never dominated England as it did elsewhere; terminism survived there during its period of neglect on the Continent. Still, few innovations in supposition theory or its satellite doctrines were made in England during the last quarter of the thirteenth century. But then, in the very early fourteenth century, Walter Burley (or Burleigh, b. *c*. 1275, d. 1344/5) began to do new work in the terminist tradition.

This temporary decline of terminism on both sides of the Channel at the end of the thirteenth century, and its sudden revival shortly after 1300, are mysterious events. But, whatever the underlying causes, when supposition theory and related doctrines re-emerged in the early fourteenth century, they were importantly different from how they had been earlier.[7]

--- II ---

This section will survey the main stages of late medieval logic, and introduce important names. Later sections will focus on particular theoretical topics.[8]

In England,[9] logic after 1300 may be divided into three stages: first, 1300–50, when the best work was done. Burley and William of Ockham (*c*. 1285–1347) were the paramount figures during this period. Both made important contributions to supposition theory, and Ockham in particular developed sophisticated theories of 'mental language' and 'connotation'.

In the next generation, several men associated with Merton College, Oxford, were influential in specific areas. Richard Kilvington (early fourteenth century, d. 1361) and William Heytesbury (b. before 1313, d. 1372/3), among others, applied the techniques of *sophismata* to questions in natural philosophy, epistemic logic and other fields. Thomas Bradwardine (*c.* 1295–1349) wrote an *Insolubles* that was perhaps the most influential treatise on semantic paradoxes throughout the Middle Ages. Around 1330–2, Adam Wodeham devised an important theory of 'complexly significables' (*complexe significabilia*), the closest medieval equivalent to the modern notion of 'proposition'. Richard Billingham (fl. 1340s or 1350s) seems to have originated the important theory of 'proofs of propositions'. His treatise *Speculum puerorum* or *Youths' Mirror* will be discussed in section VIII below.

The second stage of English logic after 1300 lasted from 1350 to 1400. This was a time of consolidation, of sophisticated but no longer especially original work. The period has not yet been well researched, but at least three trends can be distinguished. First, there was a remarkable number of school-manuals written in logic, compilations of standard doctrine with little innovation. Works of Richard Lavenham (d. 1399 or after) provide a good example. Gradually, certain of these school-texts congealed into two collections called the *Libelli sophistarum* (*Little Books for Arguers*), one for Oxford and one for Cambridge. These were printed in several editions around 1500.

Second, English logic from 1350 to 1400 had a special interest in the doctrine of 'proofs of propositions' associated with Billingham. As time passed, the labour devoted to this topic grew enormously. John Wyclif dedicated a large part of his *Logic* (before 1368) and especially of his *Continuation of the Logic* (1371–4) to this theory. So did Ralph Strode, a contemporary of Wyclif's, in his own *Logic*. John Huntman wrote a *Logic* sometime near the end of the century, showing the continued expansion of the Billingham tradition.

A third concern of English logic in this period was the signification of propositions. The most influential work here was probably *On the Truth and Falsehood of Propositions* by Henry Hopton (fl. 1357). There Hopton discussed and rejected several previous views before setting out his own theory.[10] (See section V below.)

Several other English authors during this period should be mentioned, although their works are not yet fully understood. They include Richard Feribrigge (fl. probably 1360s), author of an important *Consequences* and a *Logic or Treatise on the Truth of Propositions*. Of lesser importance are: Robert Fland (fl. 1335–60); Richard Brinkley, the author of a *Summa* of logic probably between 1360 and 1373; Thomas Manlevelt (or Mauvelt), who wrote several treatises around mid-century that were influential on the Continent; and near the end of the century, Robert Alington, William Ware, Robert Stonham, and others.

One of the most significant events in English logic late in the century was the arrival at Oxford in 1390 of the Italian Paul of Venice (*c*. 1369–1429). Paul studied there for some three years. On his return to Italy, he taught at Padua and elsewhere, and was an important conduit through which English logic became known in Italy in the fifteenth century. His writings include a widely circulated *Little Logic* (*Logica parva*) and the enormous *Big Logic* (*Logica magna*).

The third stage of late medieval English logic includes the whole fifteenth century. This was a period of shocking decline. Except for a few insignificant figures around 1400, not even second-rate authors are known. The manuscripts from this period – and by 1500, early printed books – offer little hope that further research will change this assessment. The Oxford and Cambridge *Little Books for Arguers*, already mentioned, testify to the deterioration of logic during this period. Medieval logic was effectively dead in England after 1400.

Logic on the Continent during these same two centuries cannot be so neatly divided into stages. Still, there as in England, the most important work was done before about 1350. The pre-eminent figure was doubtless Buridan. His writings include a *Consequences*, a *Sophismata* and a *Summulae of Dialectic*. Buridan's students included many influential logicians of the next generation, among them: Albert of Saxony (d. 1390), the author of a *Sophismata* and *A Very Useful Logic*, and the first rector of the University of Vienna; and Marsilius of Inghen (*c*. 1330–96), the first rector of the University of Heidelberg and the author of an *Insolubles* and of treatises on 'properties of terms'.

On many points, Buridan's logical views were like Burley's or especially Ockham's in England. There are differences, but the similarities are more striking, especially when contrasted with logic on either side of the Channel before 1300. The extent of Ockham's own influence on Buridan is doubtful, but Ockham's confrère Adam Wodeham was instrumental in transmitting much English learning to Paris. In particular, Wodeham's theory of 'complexly significables' was adopted by Gregory of Rimini (*c*. 1300–58).

The Parisian Peter of Ailly (1350–1420/1) wrote several interesting logical works, including: *Concepts and Insolubles*, a pair of treatises on 'mental language' and the Liar Paradox; *Destructions of the Modes of Signifying*, against 'modism'; *Treatise on Exponibles* (see section VIII below); and *Treatise on the Art of 'Obligating'* (perhaps by Marsilius of Inghen instead).

Before 1400, the Italian Peter of Mantua (fl. 1387–1400) wrote a *Logic* that already shows knowledge of earlier English work, particularly that stemming from Billingham. Around 1400 Angelo of

Fossombrone, who taught at Bologna (1395–1400) and Padua (1400–2), wrote an *Insolubles* maintaining an elaborated version of Heytesbury's theory. About the same time, the newly returned Paul of Venice spread the gospel of Oxford logic further in Italy. Among his students, Paul of Pergula (d. 1451/5) wrote a *Logic* and a treatise *On the Composite and the Divided Sense* (on the scope of certain logical operators) based on Heytesbury's own work of that name, and Gaetano of Thiene (1387–1465) wrote detailed commentaries on works by Heytesbury and Strode. Other authors in Italy and elsewhere continued to write on logic to the end of the Middle Ages and beyond.[11]

Even these few names will suffice to show that the logical landscape after about 1400 was by no means so desolate on the Continent as in England. Still, on either side of the Channel logical work after 1350 was largely derivative and, while sometimes very sophisticated, not very innovative. There was certainly no one, for example, with the stature of Burley, Ockham or Buridan.

∾ III ∾

This and the following sections will concentrate on five important topics in late medieval logic: (a) the theory of 'mental language', (b) the signification of propositions, (c) developments in supposition-theory, (d) semantic paradoxes, and (e) connotation-theory and the 'proofs of propositions'.

In *On Interpretation*, 16a3–4, Aristotle stated that 'spoken sounds are symbols of affections in the soul, and written marks symbols of spoken sounds'. These words were translated by Boethius and interpreted as implying three levels of language: spoken, written and mental. Through Boethius this three-level hierarchy of language became a commonplace in medieval logical literature.

Of the three, mental language was regarded as the most basic. Its semantic properties are natural ones;[12] they do not originate from any convention or custom, and cannot be changed at will. Unlike spoken and written languages, mental language is the same for everyone.

Careful authors sometimes distinguished 'proper' from 'improper' mental language. The latter occurs when we think 'in English' or 'in French'. Thus a public speaker might rehearse a speech by running through silently the words he will later utter aloud. What goes on there is a kind of 'let's pretend' speaking that takes place in imagination and is in that sense 'mental'. But it is not what most authors meant by 'mental language'. Since silent recitation varies with the spoken language one is rehearsing, it is not the same for everyone. Proper mental language is different. It includes, for example, what happens when one suddenly 'sees' the force of a mathematical proof; in that case there is a 'flash of insight', an understanding or judgement that need not yet be put into words, even silently. This kind of mental language, the theory goes, *is* the same for everyone.[13]

Spoken language, by contrast, has its semantic function parasitically, through a conventional correlation between its expressions and mental ones. The arbitrariness of this convention is what allows the multitude of spoken languages. Written language plays an even more derivative role, through a conventional correlation between its inscriptions and the sounds of spoken language. The arbitrariness of this convention too allows for different scripts among written languages. Only through the mediation of spoken language, the theory went, are inscriptions correlated with thoughts in mental language. This view implies that one cannot read a language one does not know how to speak. Most medieval authors accepted this consequence.

Following Boethius, the correlations between written and spoken language and between spoken and mental language were often regarded as relations of 'signification'. This claim had theoretical consequences, since signification was a well-defined notion in the Middle Ages. A term 'signifies' what it makes one think of ('establishes an understanding of' = *constituit intellectum* + genitive).[14] While there was dispute about what occupies the object-pole of this relation, there was agreement over the criterion. Signification is thus a special case of causality, and so transitive. (Certain authors added to signification in general the particular notions of immediate and ultimate signification. The general relation of signification thus became what modern logicians call the 'ancestral' of the relation of immediate signification;[15] a term t then ultimately signifies x if and only if t signifies x and x does not signify anything else.) Terms in mental language signify (make one think of) external objects only in the degenerate sense that they *are* the thoughts of those external objects.

According to this view, to say that expressions of spoken language immediately signify expressions of mental language is to say that the function of speech is to convey thoughts. Certain authors, e.g. Duns Scotus (*c.* 1265–1308), Burley and Ockham, regarded this as too restrictive. For them, spoken (and written) terms may be made to signify anything, not only the speaker's thoughts. In fact spoken words do *not* always make us think of thoughts; sometimes we are made to think directly of external objects. For these authors, the relations between written and spoken language and between either of these and mental language are not relations of signification. Ockham described them neutrally as relations of 'subordination'.[16]

~~ IV ~~

Although authors since Boethius had recognized mental language, it was not until the fourteenth century that it began to be investigated in detail. Ockham was the first to develop a full theory of mental language and put it to philosophical use. Shortly thereafter, Buridan began to work out his own view. His theory agrees with Ockham's on the whole, although Ockham's is the more detailed. In the early 1340s, Gregory of Rimini refined certain parts of the theory, and applied it to a solution to the Liar Paradox. In 1372, Peter of Ailly's *Concepts and Insolubles* incorporated the work of both Ockham and Gregory.[17] Other authors made contributions to the theory, but these were the major ones. The presentation below will follow Ockham's account except as indicated.

Terms in mental language are concepts; its propositions are judgements. The fact that mental language is the same for everyone explains how it is possible to translate one spoken (or written) language into another. A sentence in Spanish is a correct translation of a sentence in English if and only if the two are subordinated to the same mental sentence. More generally, any two spoken or written expressions – from the same or different languages – are synonymous if and only if they are subordinated to the same mental expression. Again, any spoken or written expression is equivocal if and only if it is subordinated to more than one mental expression.

If mental language accounts for synonymy and equivocation in spoken and written languages, can there be synonymy or equivocation in mental language itself? The textual evidence is mixed. There are passages in Ockham (*Summa logicae* I, 3 = [17.7] *OP* 1: 11; *Summa logicae* I, 13 = [17.7] *OP* 1: 44) supporting a negative answer in both cases. Nevertheless other texts (*Ordinatio*, I, d. 3, q. 2 = [17.7] *OT* 2: 405; *Ordinatio* I, d. 3, q. 3 = [17.7] *OT* 2: 425; *Quodlibet* 5, q. 9 = [17.7] *OT* 9: 513–18), where Ockham is discussing the semantics of certain connotative terms (see section VIII below), perhaps imply the existence of mental synonymy. As for equivocation, Ockham's theory of tense and modality, as well as his theory of supposition (see section VI below), commits him outright to certain kinds of equivocation in mental language.[18] But apart from textual considerations, there are philosophical reasons for saying that, given other features of Ockham's theory, mental synonymy or equivocation makes no sense.[19]

What is included in mental language? In two passages (*Summa logicae*, I, 3 = [17.7] *OP* 1: 11.1–26; *Quodlibet* 5, q. 8 = [17.7] *OT* 9: 508–13), Ockham remarks that, just as for spoken and written language, the vocabulary of mental language is divided into 'parts of speech'. Thus there are mental nouns, verbs, prepositions, conjunctions, etc. But not all features of spoken and written language are found in mental language. Ockham acknowledges doubts about mental participles (their job could be performed by verbs) and pronouns (presumably 'pronouns of laziness', as for example in 'Socrates is a man and *he* is an animal'). Moreover, not all characteristics of spoken and written syntax are found in mental language. While mental nouns and adjectives have case and number, and mental adjectives admit of positive, comparative and superlative degrees, they do not have gender and are not divided into grammatical declensions (like Latin's five declensions). Mental verbs have person, number, tense, voice and mood, but are not divided into grammatical conjugations.

Ockham's mental language looks remarkably like Latin. This fact led some modern writers to reject the theory as a foolish attempt to 'explain' features of Latin by merely duplicating them in mental language, which is then regarded as somehow more 'basic' ([17.39] § 23). But more is involved than that. Ockham's strategy is to admit into mental language exactly those features of spoken or written language that affect the truth-values of propositions. All other features of spoken and written language, Ockham says, are only for the sake of decorative style, or in the interest of brevity. They are not present in mental language.[20]

Mental language is thus a logically perspicuous language for describing the world. It has whatever is needed to distinguish truth from falsehood, nothing more. In this respect, mental language is reminiscent of the 'ideal languages' proposed by early twentieth-century philosophers ([17.51]).

How are mental words combined in mental propositions? What is the difference, for example, between the true mental proposition 'Every man is an animal' and the false 'Every animal is a man'? In written language, the difference is the spatial configuration of the words. But the mind does not take up space, so that there can be no such difference there. In speech the difference lies in the temporal sequence of the words. But since proper mental language at least sometimes involves a 'flash of insight' that happens all at once, neither can temporal word order account for the difference between the two mental propositions.

Because of such difficulties, authors such as Gregory of Rimini and Peter of Ailly held that mental propositions (although not all of them for Peter) are simple mental acts not really composed of distinct mental words at all.[21] Ockham too had considered such a theory (*In Sententias* II, qq. 12–13 = [17.7] *OT* 5: 279; *Exposition of 'On Interpretation'*, proem = [17.7] *OP* 2: 356). It is hard to reconcile this view with the claim that mental vocabulary is divided into 'parts of speech'; distinct mental words would appear to have no job to do if they do not enter into the structure of mental propositions.

❧ V ❧

Besides the disagreement over the immediate signification of spoken and written terms (see section III above), there was a dispute over ultimate signification. Metaphysical realists, such as Burley, maintained the traditional view that general terms ultimately signify universal entities, while nominalists (e.g. Ockham and Buridan) held that they ultimately signify only individuals.

Some authors extended the notion of signification to ask not only about the signification of terms but also about the signification of whole propositions. Do they signify anything besides what their component terms signify separately? Do they signify, for example, states of affairs or facts?

Ockham did not explicitly address this question. But Buridan did, and his answer was no. For him ([17.16] II, conclusion 5), a proposition – and in general any complex expression – signifies whatever its categorematic terms signify, nothing more. ('Categorematic' terms are those that can serve as subject or predicate in a proposition; they were regarded as having their own signification. Other words were called 'syncategorematic' and were regarded as not having any signification of their own; they are 'logical particles' used for combining categorematic terms into propositions and other complex expressions.) Thus in the spoken proposition 'The cat is on the mat', when I hear the word 'cat' I am, on Buridan's account, made to think of all cats and when I hear 'mat' I am made to think of all mats. That is all the proposition makes me think of, and so all it signifies.

Elsewhere Buridan maintained a different and incompatible theory ([17.16] II, sophism 5 and conclusions 3–7). The proposition 'Socrates is sitting', for example, signifies *Socrates to be sitting*. And what is that? Buridan held that if Socrates really is sitting, then *Socrates to be sitting* is just Socrates himself. But if he is not sitting, then *Socrates to be sitting* is nothing at all.[22] This view bears some similarity to a theory held earlier at Oxford by Walter Chatton (1285–1344) and discussed as the first previous view in Henry Hopton's *On the Truth and Falsehood of Propositions*. Similar views were defended by Richard Feribrigge and John Huntman. The details of their texts have not been thoroughly investigated, and there is much that is still obscure; it is not certain that all these authors maintained variants of the same doctrine. Still, the motivation is the same in each case: to find something to serve as the significate of a proposition in an ontology that does not allow anything like facts, states of affairs or 'propositions' in the modern sense.

But there were other opinions. As early as Abelard, some authors held that what propositions signify falls outside the Aristotelian categories, and is something like the modern notion of 'proposition'.

Sometimes this new entity was called a 'mode', sometimes a *dictum*.[23] In the fourteenth century, such theories continued to find their defenders. Perhaps a version of it may be seen in the early 1330s in William of Crathorn. Perhaps too Henry Hopton intended such a theory as the second previous view he considered, according to which a proposition signifies a 'mode' of a thing, where a 'mode' is not a *something* but a *being-somehow* (*esse aliqualiter*). But an unequivocal statement can be found in the theory of 'complexly significables' ([17.38]; see also [17.35] chs 14–15). According to this theory, complexly significables are the bearers of truth-value. They are not propositions in the medieval sense, not even mental propositions, but are what is expressed by propositions. They are the significates of propositions, and the objects of knowledge, belief and propositional attitudes generally. Complexly significables do not exist in the way substances and accidents do. Before creation, for example, only God existed. But even then God knew *that the world was going to exist*. This complexly significable cannot be identified with God himself, since God is a necessary being but it was contingent that the world was going to exist. Yet as distinct from God, it cannot have existed before creation. Such extralogical considerations were an important motivation for the theory of complexly significables. Authors such as Buridan and Peter of Ailly rejected the theory; Peter, for example, claimed that the argument about God's knowledge before creation is based on an illegitimate substitution of identicals in an opaque context involving necessity ([17.27] 62).

All these theories offered a real entity (even if an odd one, like a 'complexly significable') as the correlate of a true proposition, and so as the ontological basis for a 'correspondence' theory of truth. Other authors took a different approach. They too maintained a correspondence theory, often expressed as: a proposition is true if and only if it 'precisely signifies as is the case', or if and only if 'howsoever [the proposition] signifies, so it is the case'. For them, the proper question is not *what* but *how* a proposition signifies. This 'adverbial' notion of signification allowed a correspondence theory without being obliged to find any ontological correlate for a true proposition to correspond to. After rejecting earlier views, Henry Hopton's own theory was like this. Heytesbury had earlier held a similar view, as did Peter of Ailly later ([17.22] 61–5; [17.27] 10, 48–54 and nn.).

~~ VI ~~

The theory of 'supposition' is a mystery. Although it is central to the theories of 'properties of terms' that developed from the twelfth century on, it is not clear what the theory was intended to accomplish, or indeed what the theory as a whole was about.[24]

Throughout its history, there were two main parts to supposition theory. One was a theory of the reference of terms in propositions, and how that reference is affected by syntactic and semantic features of propositions. The question this part of the theory was intended to answer is, 'What does a term refer to (supposit for, stand for) in a proposition?' That much is clear. But from the beginning, there was another part of supposition theory, an account of how one might validly 'descend to singulars' under a given occurrence of a term in a proposition, sometimes combined with a correlative account of 'ascent from singulars'. The mystery surrounds this second part.

Before the decline of terminism after 1270, there is some evidence that the second part of supposition theory, like the first, was intended to answer the question of what a term refers to in a proposition. The first part of the theory says what kind of thing a given term-occurrence refers to, while the second specifies how many such things it refers to (in much the way one finds even today accounts purporting to say whether the terms of a syllogism are about 'all' or 'some' of a class). The evidence for this is mixed, but even if this was the original intent of the second part of supposition theory, some authors quite early realized its theoretical difficulties.

When supposition theory re-emerged with Burley in England and later with Buridan in France, the two parts of the theory had been separated once and for all. By that time the theory of descent and ascent clearly was not about what a term refers to in a proposition. What it was about instead is uncertain.

The account below will mainly follow Ockham, although other authors will be mentioned. Their theories differed from his in detail, sometimes in important detail, but Ockham's is fairly typical.

The first part of supposition theory divided supposition or reference first into proper (literal) and improper (metaphorical). The latter is illustrated by 'England fights', where 'England' refers by metonymy to England's inhabitants. Medieval logic, like modern logic, did not have an adequate theory of metaphor. Ockham, Burley and a few others list some haphazard subdivisions of improper supposition, but really mention it only to set it aside. Their emphasis is on proper supposition.

Proper supposition was divided into three kinds: personal, simple and material. The origin of these names is unclear, although the term 'personal' suggests a connection with the theology of the Trinity and the Incarnation. But it should not be thought that personal supposition has anything especially to do with persons.

Personal supposition occurs when a term refers to everything of which it is truly predicable. Thus in 'Every man is running', 'man' refers to all men and so is in personal supposition. But so too 'running' refers there to all things now running, and hence is likewise in personal supposition. It does not refer there only to some running things, for example, only to the running men. Again, in 'Some man is running', 'man' refers to all men, not just to running ones.

A term has material supposition when it refers to a spoken or written word or expression and is not in personal supposition. Thus, 'man' in 'Man has three letters' has material supposition. Although there are obvious similarities, material supposition is not merely a medieval version of modern quotation marks. For in 'It is possible for Socrates to run', the phrase 'for Socrates to run' has material supposition. But it refers to the proposition 'Socrates is running', of which the phrase 'for Socrates to run' is not a quotation. (For Ockham, there are no states of affairs or complexly significables that can be said to be possible. Only propositions are possible in this sense.)

The definition of simple supposition was a matter of dispute, depending in part on an author's metaphysical views and in part on his theory about the role of language in general ([17.46]). As a paradigm, 'man' in 'Man is a species' has simple supposition. In general, terms in simple supposition refer to universals. But for nominalists like Ockham, there are no metaphysical universals; the only universals are universal terms in language, most properly universal concepts in mental language. Thus for Ockham terms in simple supposition refer to concepts. It is they that are properly said to be species or genera. To prevent the term 'concept' in 'Every concept is a being' from having simple supposition (it has personal supposition, since it refers to everything it signifies – to all concepts), Ockham added that a term in simple supposition must not be 'taken significatively', i.e. that it not be in personal supposition.

But for a realist like Burley, terms in simple supposition refer to real universals outside the mind. It is they that are species and genera. Furthermore, for Burley and certain others, general terms in language signify those extramental universals. Thus the term 'man' signifies universal human nature, not any one individual man or group of men, and not all men collectively. For Burley, therefore, it is in simple supposition that a term refers to what it signifies. For Ockham, general terms do not signify universals, not even universal concepts; they signify individuals. Even a term like 'universal' signifies individuals, since it signifies concepts, which are metaphysically individuals and are 'universal' only in the sense of being predicable of many things. Hence for Ockham, it is in personal supposition, not simple, that a term refers to what it signifies.

Personal supposition is the default case. Any term in any proposition can be taken in personal supposition. It may alternatively be taken in simple or material supposition only if the other terms in the proposition provide a suitable context. In such cases, the proposition is strictly ambiguous and may be read in either sense.[25]

From this first part of supposition theory alone, certain authors, e.g. Ockham and Buridan, although not Burley, developed a theory of truth-conditions for categorical propositions on the square of opposition. Thus, a universal affirmative 'Every *A* is *B*' is true if and only if everything the subject term refers to the predicate term also refers to (although it may refer to other things as well). Truth-conditions for other propositions on the square of opposition can be derived from this.

Subordinated to this first part of supposition theory was a theory of 'ampliation', accounting for the effects of modality and tense on personal supposition. A term in personal supposition may always be taken to refer to the things of which it is presently predicable. But in the context of past or future tenses, the term may also be taken to refer to the things of which it was or will be predicable. Likewise, in a modal context (possibility, necessity), the term may also be taken to refer to the things of which it *can* be truly predicable. This expansion of the range of referents was called 'ampliation'.

Ockham and Burley regarded the new referents provided by ampliation as alternatives to the normal ones. Thus in the proposition 'Every man was running', 'man' may be taken as referring either to all presently existing men or to all men existing in the past. The proposition is thus equivocal. But on the Continent, Buridan and others regarded the new referents as additions to the normal ones. For them, in the proposition 'Every man was running' 'man' refers to all presently existing men and all past men as well.[26]

The second main part of supposition theory, the theory of descent and ascent, was a theory subdividing personal supposition only, into several kinds. First, there is discrete supposition, possessed by proper names, demonstrative pronouns or demonstrative phrases (e.g. 'this man'). All other personal supposition is *common*, and was typically subdivided into: determinate (e.g. 'man' in 'Some man is running'), confused and distributive (e.g. 'man' in 'Every man is an animal'), and merely confused (e.g. 'animal' in 'Every man is an animal'). The details varied with the author.

Sometimes these subdivisions were described via the positions of terms in categorical propositions. Subjects and predicates of particular affirmatives, and subjects of particular negatives, have determinate supposition. Subjects of universal affirmatives and negatives, and predicates of universal and particular negatives, have confused and distributive supposition. Only predicates of universal affirmatives have merely confused supposition.

414

More helpful is the description in terms of descent and ascent. For Ockham (Burley's and Buridan's theories are equivalent), a term has determinate supposition in a proposition if and only if it is possible to 'descend' under that term to a disjunction of singulars, and to 'ascend' to the original proposition from any singular. The exact specification of the notions of 'descent', 'ascent' and 'singular' is subtle, but an example should suffice. In 'Some man is running' one can 'descend' under 'man' to a disjunction: 'Some man is running; therefore, this man is running or that man is running', etc., for all men. Likewise one can 'ascend' to the original proposition from any singular: 'This man is running; therefore, some man is running.' Hence 'man' in the original proposition has determinate supposition.

A term has confused and distributive supposition in a proposition if and only if it is possible to 'descend' under that term to a conjunction of singulars but *not* possible to 'ascend' to the original proposition from any singular. Thus in 'Every man is running' it is possible to descend under 'man': 'Every man is running; therefore, this man is running and that man is running', etc., for all men. But the ascent from any singular 'This man is running; therefore, every man is running' is invalid. Hence the term 'man' in the original proposition has confused and distributive supposition.

A term has merely confused supposition in a proposition if and only if (a) it is not possible to descend under that term either to a disjunction or to a conjunction, but it is possible to descend to a *disjoint term*, and (b) it is possible to ascend to the original proposition from any singular. Thus in 'Every man is an animal' it is not possible to descend under 'animal' to either a disjunction or a conjunction, since if every man is an animal, it does not follow that every man is this animal or every man is that animal, etc. Much less does it follow that every man is this animal *and* every man is that animal, etc. But it does follow that every man is *this animal or that animal or*, etc. Again, if it happens that every man is this animal (i.e. there is only one man and he is an animal), then every man is an animal. Hence the term 'animal' in that proposition has merely confused supposition.

It is hard to see what this doctrine was intended to accomplish, particularly with its appeal to odd 'disjoint terms' in merely confused supposition. At first, modern scholars thought it was an attempt to provide truth-conditions for quantified propositions in terms of (infinite) disjunctions or conjunctions. But if that was its purpose, the doctrine is a failure. The predicate of the particular negative 'Some man is not a Greek' has confused and distributive supposition according to the above definitions, but the conjunction to which one can descend under 'Greek' does not give the truth-conditions for the original proposition. Suppose Socrates and Plato are the only men.

415

Then the conjunction 'Some man is not this Greek [Socrates] and some man is not that Greek [Plato]' is true, but the original proposition is false.

The problem is that rules for ascent always concern ascent from any one singular, never from a conjunction. Certain later authors, e.g. Ralph Strode, Richard Brinkley and Paul of Venice, do explicitly discuss ascent from conjunctions.[27] But earlier writers such as Burley, Ockham and Buridan conspicuously did not.

Another attempt to explain this second part of supposition theory suggests that the rules for ascent and descent were used in detecting and diagnosing fallacies. This is doubtless correct as far as it goes, but does not account for the details in the theory as we actually find it. In the end, the exact function of this part of the theory in the early fourteenth century remains a mystery.

～ VII ～

Medieval discussions of 'insolubles' (semantic paradoxes like the Liar Paradox, 'The sentence I am now saying is false') began in the late twelfth century. By around 1200, theories on how to solve them can be distinguished. Thereafter, three periods in the medieval insolubles literature can be distinguished: (1) *c.* 1200–*c.* 1320, (2) *c.* 1320–*c.* 1350 and (3) everything after that.

The earliest known medieval theory of insolubles (*cassatio* or cancelling) maintained that one who utters an insoluble is simply 'not saying anything', in the sense that his words do not succeed in making a claim. This view, although it has its supporters today, quickly disappeared in the Middle Ages. Other early theories rejected some or all self-reference; these too have their modern counterparts. Still other early theories sound less familiar to modern ears. A few authors argued that, despite the surface grammar, the reference in insolubles is always to some *previous* proposition. For example, 'What I am saying is false' really amounts to 'What I said a moment ago is false'. The insoluble is true or false depending on whether I did in fact say something false a moment ago. Others, e.g. Duns Scotus, appealed to a distinction between signified acts and exercised acts. This is the distinction between what the speaker of an insoluble proposition says he is doing (the signified act) and what he is really doing (the exercised act). Although the distinction is suggestive, it is far from clear how it solves the paradoxes.

Many of these early views are cast in the framework of Aristotle's fallacy of what is said 'absolutely' and what is said 'in a certain respect'. Discussing that fallacy in his *Sophistical Refutations*, Aristotle made some enigmatic remarks (180a38–b3) that suggested the Liar Paradox [17.42]. Consequently, many medieval authors tried to treat insolubles as instances of that fallacy, although there was little agreement on the details. Some held that insoluble propositions are true 'absolutely' but false 'in a certain respect'. Some had it the other way around. Others said they were both true and false, each 'in a certain respect'. Still others applied the Aristotelian distinction not to truth but to supposition, so that they distinguished between supposition absolutely and supposition in a certain respect. Long after the early period in the medieval literature, the fallacy *absolutely/in a certain respect* was retained as an authoritative framework for many authors' discussions, even when the real point of their theories was elsewhere.

These early theories predominated until about 1320; some of them survived much longer. Burley and Ockham offered nothing new here. Both maintained a theory that merely rejected problematic cases of self-reference without being able to identify which those problematic cases were.

The first to break new ground was Thomas Bradwardine, in the early 1320s. Bradwardine's theory was based on a view linking signification with consequence. He appears to have been the first to hold that a proposition signifies exactly what follows from it.[28] Since he was also committed to saying that *every* proposition implies its own truth (e.g. Socrates is running, therefore 'Socrates is running' is true), this means that the insoluble 'This proposition is false' signifies that it itself is true. Since it also signifies that it is false, it signifies a contradiction, and so is simply false. The paradox is broken.[29]

Bradwardine's view was enormously influential. Buridan later maintained a broadly similar theory, and others held variants of it to the end of the Middle Ages; it was one of the predominant theories.

Shortly after Bradwardine, Roger Swyneshed (fl. before 1335, d. *c.* 1365), an Englishman associated with Merton College, proposed a theory in which truth is distinguished from correspondence with reality. For a proposition to be true, it must not only correspond with reality ('signify principally as is the case'), it must also not 'falsify itself', i.e. not be 'relevant to inferring that it is false'. (This notion of 'relevance' is not well understood.) Swyneshed drew three famous conclusions from his theory: (1) There are false propositions (namely, insolubles) that nevertheless correspond with reality. (2) Valid inference sometimes lead from truth to falsehood. Validity does not necessarily preserve truth, although it does preserve correspondence with reality. (3) Sometimes, two contradictory propositions are both false. The insoluble 'This proposition is false' is false because it 'falsifies' itself. But its contradictory 'That proposition is true' (referring to the previous proposition) is also false, since it fails to correspond with reality – the previous proposition is *not* true. These conclusions generated much discussion in the later literature. Swyneshed's theory did not have many followers, but it had at least one important one: Paul of Venice maintained a version of Swyneshed's theory in his *Big Logic*.

In 1335, William Heytesbury proposed a theory that rivalled and may have surpassed Bradwardine's in influence. He maintained that in circumstances that would make a proposition insoluble if it signified just as it normally does ('precisely as its terms pretend'), it *cannot* signify that way only, but must signify some other way too. Thus 'Socrates is uttering a falsehood', if Socrates himself utters it and nothing else, cannot on pain of contradiction signify only that Socrates is uttering a falsehood, but must signify that and more. Depending on what else it signifies, and how it is related to the ordinary signification of the proposition, different verdicts about the insoluble are appropriate. Heytesbury himself refused to say what else an insoluble might signify besides its ordinary signification; that could not be predicted. But some late authors went on to fill in Heytesbury's silence. They stipulated that insolubles in addition signify that *they are true*, thus linking Heytesbury's theory with Bradwardine's.

Heytesbury's view has an important consequence. Since signification in mental language is fixed by nature, not by voluntary convention, mental propositions can never signify otherwise than they ordinarily do. Given Heytesbury's account of insolubility, this means that *there can be no insolubles in mental language*. Heytesbury himself did not draw this conclusion, but it is there none the less.

All important developments concerning insolubles between 1320 and 1350 originated with Englishmen and are associated in one way or another with Merton College. Later writers, in the third and last stage of the medieval insolubles literature, sometimes developed this English material in interesting new ways. Thus Gregory of Rimini and Peter of Ailly took the above consequence of Heytesbury's theory to heart. They maintained that there are no insolubles in mental language, and that insolubles arise in spoken and written language only because they correspond (are subordinated) to *two* propositions in the mind, one true and the other false. Apart from these developments of earlier views, there seem to be no radically original theories of insolubles in the Middle Ages after about 1350.

• VIII •

Ockham's theory of connotation has antecedents in Aristotle's remarks on paronymy (*Categories*, 1a12–15). It is the most highly developed such theory in the Middle Ages.

For Ockham, some categorematic terms are absolute; others are connotative. 'Bravery' is absolute since it signifies only bravery, a quality in the soul. But 'brave' is connotative since it signifies certain persons (brave ones), but only by making an oblique reference to ('connoting') their bravery. Connotative terms have nominal definitions; absolute terms do not. The notion of a nominal definition is difficult to state exactly ([17.44]), but all nominal definitions of a connotative term are 'equivalent' for Ockham in a sense that is perhaps as strong as synonymy. Furthermore, it appears that the connotative term itself is synonymous with each of its nominal definitions, and may be viewed in fact as a kind of shorthand abbreviation for them. Thus the adjective 'white' is a connotative term having the nominal definition 'something having a whiteness' or 'something informed by a whiteness'. All three expressions are synonymous for Ockham.

Since Ockham's 'better doctrine' is that there is no mental synonymy, the elementary vocabulary of mental language (simple concepts) includes no connotative terms. Mental language contains the absolute term 'whiteness' and syntactical devices to form nominal definitions like those above. But it does not, on pain of synonymy, contain a distinct mental adjective 'white'. (But see section IV, above.)

All primitive categorematic mental terms are thus absolute. This has important consequences for Ockham's philosophy. For (barring miracles) the mind has simple concepts only for things of which it has had direct experience ('intuitive cognition'). The supply of absolute concepts is therefore a guide to ontology.

There is a related theory in Ockham, the theory of 'exposition' or analysis (see [17.34] 412–27). The outlines of this theory were established by the mid-thirteenth century. In brief, an exponible proposition is one containing a word (the 'exponible term') that obscures the sense of the whole proposition. It is to be analysed or 'expounded' into a plurality of simpler propositions, called 'exponents', that together capture the sense of the original. Thus 'Socrates is beginning to run' might be expounded by 'Socrates is not running' and 'Immediately hereafter Socrates will be running'.

Ockham's own theory of exposition is not especially innovative, except that he explicitly links it with the theory of connotation. This is an attractive move, since whereas the theory of connotation provides explicit nominal definitions for connotative terms, it is plausible to view exposition theory as providing contextual definitions of exponible terms treated as incomplete symbols. Hence, just as the absence of synonymy in mental language means that it contains no simple connotative terms, so too it would mean that mental language contains no exponible propositions, but only their exponents. Since contextual definitions provide the more general approach, it is not surprising that connotation theory quickly declined after Ockham, and is treated only perfunctorily in Strode and Wyclif. Its place is taken there by much more elaborate treatments of exponibles. Buridan does retain a fairly full theory of connotation, but it is not so detailed as Ockham's.[30]

Although the theory of exposition continued to have a life of its own, by mid-century it had also been incorporated into the theory of 'proofs of propositions'.[31] Billingham's *Youth's Mirror* was a seminal work here.

The notion of 'proof' involved in this literature was broader than the Aristotelian demonstration of the *Posterior Analytics*. It meant any argument showing that a certain proposition is true. Not all propositions can be 'proved'. Some of them serve as ultimate premisses of all proofs; they must be learned another way. Such elementary propositions Billingham calls 'immediate' propositions, containing only 'immediate' terms that cannot be 'resolved' into more elementary terms. Immediate terms include indexicals such as 'I', 'he', 'this', 'here' and 'now', and very general verbs such as 'is' and 'can' and their tenses. Hence a proposition like 'This is now here' is immediate.

Other propositions can ultimately be 'proved' from immediate propositions. Billingham recognized three methods for such proofs: exposition, 'resolution' and proof using an 'auxiliary' *(officialis)* term.

Exposition has already been explained. Resolution amounts to proof by expository syllogism. Thus 'A man runs' is 'proved' by the inference 'This runs and this is a man; therefore, a man runs'. But there is a problem. The premisses of this inference are not immediate, since their predicates are not immediate terms. And there appears to be no way to reduce them to yet more basic propositions by any of the three ways Billingham recognizes.

'Auxiliary' terms govern indirect discourse. They include epistemic verbs such as 'knows', 'believes', etc., and modal terms such as 'it is contingent'. To 'prove' a proposition containing an auxiliary term is to provide an argument spelling out the role of the auxiliary term. One of the premisses of this argument states how the proposition referred to in indirect discourse 'precisely signifies'. Thus 'It is contingent for him to run' is proved by: ' "He runs" is contingent; and "He runs" precisely signifies for him to run; therefore, it is contingent for him to run.'

There are still many obscurities in the theory of 'proofs of propositions'. But it was very widespread.

◆◆ IX ◆◆

Our knowledge of late medieval logic has advanced enormously since the 1960s. The availability of previously unpublished texts has shed great light on this fertile period. Yet, as this chapter shows, there is still much that is unknown. The general reader should regard the claims in this chapter as tentative. Readers with specialized training or interest should regard them as an invitation to further research.

 NOTES

1 *CHLMP*, pp. 46, 74–5. See also Chapter 7 above, p. 176.
2 In medieval terminology, a 'proposition' is a declarative sentence, often a sentence-*token*. The term was not typically used in its modern sense, to mean what is expressed by a sentence(-token). I shall use 'proposition' in its medieval sense throughout this chapter except where indicated.
3 De Rijk [17.29], especially vol. 1. On *consequentiae* in the twelfth century, see Chapter 7 above, pp. 157–8, 175–6.
4 *CHLMP*, ch. 11.
5 *CHLMP*, ch. 16. Despite the name, these disputations had nothing to do with ethics or morality. They were not about deontic logic. Their exact purpose is still uncertain.
6 There were also anonymous works of this kind, dating back to the twelfth century. See De Rijk [17.29].
7 With these last three paragraphs, see Spade [17.50], especially pp. 187–8, and references there. See also *CHLMP*, chs 12 and 16B.
8 For information on authors mentioned in this section, see *CHLMP*, pp. 855–92 ('Biographies').
9 On English logic as discussed in this section, see Ashworth and Spade [17.28] and references there.
10 In the 1494 edition of Heytesbury, Hopton's treatise is wrongly attributed to Heytesbury himself.
11 On Angelo, see Spade [17.45] 49–52. For other authors mentioned in this paragraph, see Maierù [17.34], 34–6.
12 There is potential for confusion here. In twentieth-century philosophy, a 'natural' language is one like English, in contrast to 'artificial' languages like Esperanto or the 'language' of *Principia Mathematica*. In medieval usage, the latter would likewise count as 'artificial' languages, but so would English; the only truly natural language is mental language.
13 See Peter of Ailly [17.27] 9, 19–21, 36–7, and references there.
14 See Aristotle, *De interpretatione*, 16b19–21.
15 Something a bears the ancestral of relation R to z if and only if a bears R to something b that bears R to something c that … that bears R to z.
16 With this section, see *CHLMP*, ch. 9.
17 For Gregory and Peter, see Peter of Ailly [17.27].
18 Buridan's theory does not imply this, and Peter of Ailly flatly denies it for supposition.
19 With these last two paragraphs, see Spade [17.47].
20 See the reply to Geach in Trentman [17.51]. For a critique of Ockham's strategy, see Spade [17.47].

21 See Peter of Ailly [17.27] 9 and 37–44, and references there.
22 A similar approach is used in Buridan's discussion of opaque epistemic and doxastic contexts. See *Sophismata* [17.16], IV, sophisms 9–14. With the remainder of this section, see Ashworth and Spade [17.28].
23 Kretzmann [17.40]. See also Chapter 7 above, pp. 157–8.
24 With this section, see Spade [17.50], and *CHLMP*, ch. 9.
25 Spade [17.43]. In so far as such contexts can arise in mental language, this view requires equivocation there. See Spade [17.47].
26 [17.47]. See also n. 18, above.
27 Spade [17.50] n. 78 and the Appendix. For Brinkley I am grateful to M. J. Fitzgerald.
28 In the 'adverbial' sense of propositional signification, described in section V above.
29 For qualifications and complications, see Spade [17.48].
30 Buridan's name for connotation is *appellatio* or 'appellation' (*Sophismata*, IV).
31 With this last part of section VIII, see Ashworth and Spade [17.28] and references there.

BIBLIOGRAPHY

Original Language Editions

17.1   Albert of Saxony, *Perutilis logica*, Venice, 1522; repr. Olms, Hildesheim, 1974.
17.2   —— *Sophismata*, Paris, 1502; repr. Olms, Hildesheim, 1975.
17.3   Alessio, F. (ed.) *Lamberto d'Auxerre: Logica (Summa Lamberti)*, Florence, La nuova Italia editrice, 1971.
17.4   Boehner, B. (ed.) *Walter Burley: De puritate artis logicae tractatus longior, with a Revised Edition of the Tractatus Brevior*, St Bonaventure, NY, Franciscan Institute, 1955.
17.5   Brown, M. A. (ed.) *Paul of Pergula: Logica and Tractatus de sensu composito et diviso*, St Bonaventure, NY, Franciscan Institute, 1961.
17.6   De Rijk, L. M. (ed.) *Peter of Spain: Tractatus, Called Afterwards Summule Logicales*, Assen, Van Gorcum, 1972. (translated in [17.21])
17.7   Gál, G. *et al.* (eds) *Guillelmi de Ockham: Opera philosophica et theologica*, 17 vols, St Bonaventure, NY, Franciscan Institute, 1967–88. (*OT = Opera theologica*; *OP = Opera philosophica.*)
17.8   Geach, P. and Kneale, W. (general editors) *Pauli Veneti logica magna*, Oxford, Oxford University Press, 1978– . (Latin edition and English translation, in several fascicles. Editors and translators vary.)
17.9   Grabmann, M. (ed.) *Die Introductiones in logicam des Wilhelm von Shyreswood*, Munich, Verlag der Bayerischen Adademie der Wissenschaften, 1937. (translated in [17.26])
17.10 Gregory of Rimini, *Super primum et secundum Sententiarum*, Venice, 1522; repr. Franciscan Institute, St Bonaventure, NY, 1955.
17.11 Heytesbury, W. *Tractatus guilelmi Hentisberi de sensu composito et diviso, Regulae ejusdem cum sophismatibus . . .* , Venice, 1494.

17.12 Hubien, H. (ed.) *Johannis Buridani Tractatus de consequentiis*, Louvain, Publications Universitaires, 1976. (translated in [17.17])

17.13 Maierù, A. (ed.) 'Lo *Speculum puerorum sive Terminus est in quem* di Riccardo Billingham', *Studi Medievali* (3rd series) 10.3 (1969): 297–397.

17.14 Paul of Venice, *Logica* (= *Logica parva*), Venice, 1484; repr. Olms, Hildesheim, 1970. (translated in [17.20])

17.15 Peter of Ailly, *Conceptus et insolubilia*, Paris, *c.* 1495. (translated in [17.27])

17.16 Scott, T. K. (ed.) *Johannes Buridanus: Sophismata*, Stuttgart, Fromman–Holzboog, 1977. (translated in [17.18])

See also [17.19], [17.29] II, pt 2.

English Translations

17.17 *John Buridan's Logic: The Treatise on Supposition, the Treatise on Consequences*, trans. P. King, Dordrecht, Reidel, 1985.

17.18 *John Buridan: Sophisms on Meaning and Truth*, trans. T. K. Scott, New York, Appleton-Century-Crofts, 1966. (translation of [17.16])

17.19 *John Buridan on Self-Reference: Chapter Eight of Buridan's 'Sophismata', with a Translation, an Introduction, and a Philosophical Commentary*, trans. G. E. Hughes, Cambridge, Cambridge University Press, 1982. (The paperback edition omits the Latin text, and has different pagination and subtitle.)

17.20 *Paul of Venice: Logica parva*, trans. A. R. Perreiah, Washington, DC, Catholic University of America Press, and Munich, Philosophia Verlag, 1984. (translation of [17.14])

17.21 *Peter of Spain: Language in Dispute*, trans. F. P. Dinneen, Amsterdam, J. Benjamins, 1990. (translation of [17.6])

17.22 *William Heytesbury, On 'Insoluble' Sentences: Chapter One of His Rules for Solving Sophisms*, trans. P. V. Spade, Toronto, Pontifical Institute of Mediaeval Studies, 1979. (translated from [17.11])

17.23 *William of Ockham: Ockham's Theory of Propositions: Part II of the Summa logicae*, trans. A. J. Freddoso and H. Schuurman, Notre Dame, Ind., University of Notre Dame Press, 1980.

17.24 *William of Ockham: Ockham's Theory of Terms: Part 1 of the Summa logicae*, trans. M. J. Loux, Notre Dame, Ind., University of Notre Dame Press, 1974.

17.25 *William of Ockham: Predestination, God's Foreknowledge, and Future Contingents*, trans. M. M. Adams and N. Kretzmann, New York, Appleton-Century-Crofts, 1969; 2nd edn, Indianapolis, Ind., Hackett, 1983.

17.26 *William of Sherwood's Introduction to Logic*, trans. N. Kretzmann, Minneapolis, Minn., University of Minnesota Press, 1966. (translation of [17.9])

17.27 *Peter of Ailly: Concepts and Insolubles, an Annotated Translation*, trans. P. V. Spade, Dordrecht, Reidel, 1980. (translation of [17.15])

See also [17.8].

Collections of Articles, General Studies and Surveys

17.28   Ashworth, E. J. and Spade, P. V. 'Logic in Late Medieval Oxford', in *The History of the University of Oxford*, vol. II, Oxford, Clarendon Press, 1992.

17.29   De Rijk, L. M. *Logica Modernorum*, vol. I, *On the Twelfth Century Theories of Fallacy*, Assen, Van Gorcum, 1962; vol. II, *The Origin and Early Development of the Theory of Supposition*, Assen, Van Gorcum, 1967. (Vol. II is bound in 2 parts: 1, De Rijk's own discussion; 2, Latin texts and indices.)

17.30   *CHLMP*.

17.31   Kretzmann, N. (ed.) *Meaning and Inference in Medieval Philosophy: Studies in Memory of Jan Pinborg*, Dordrecht, Kluwer, 1988.

17.32   Lewry, P. O. (ed.) *The Rise of British Logic: Acts of the Sixth European Symposium on Medieval Logic and Semantics, Balliol College, Oxford, 19–24 June 1983*, Toronto, Pontifical Institute of Mediaeval Studies, 1983.

17.33   Maierù, A. (ed.) *English Logic in Italy in the 14th and 15th Centuries: Acts of the Fifth European Symposium on Medieval Logic and Semantics, Rome, 10–14 November 1980*, Naples, Bibliopolis, 1982.

17.34   —— *Terminologia logica della tarda scolastica*, Rome, Edizioni dell'Ateneo, 1972.

17.35   Nuchelmans, G. *Theories of the Proposition: Ancient and Medieval Conceptions of the Bearers of Truth and Falsity*, Amsterdam, North Holland, 1973.

17.36   Pinborg, J. *Die Entwicklung der Sprachtheorie im Mittelalter*, Münster: Aschendorff, 1967.

17.37   —— (ed.) *The Logic of John Buridan: Acts of the Third European Symposium on Medieval Logic and Semantics, Copenhagen, 16–21 November 1975*, Copenhagen, Museum Tusculanum, 1976.

Studies of Particular Topics

17.38   Gál, G. 'Adam of Wodeham's question on the 'complexe significabile' as the immediate object of scientific knowledge', *Franciscan Studies* 37 (1977): 66–102.

17.39   Geach, P. *Mental Acts: Their Content and Their Objects*, London, Routledge & Kegan Paul, 1957. (Section 23 is on mental language.)

17.40   Kretzmann, N. 'Medieval logicians on the meaning of the *Propositio*', *Journal of Philosophy* 67 (1970): 767–87.

17.41   Pinborg, J. 'The English contribution to logic before Ockham', *Synthese* 40 (1979): 19–42.

17.42   Spade, P. V. 'The origin of the mediaeval *insolubilia* literature', *Franciscan Studies* 33 (1973): 292–309.

17.43   —— 'Ockham's rule of supposition: two conflicts in his theory', *Vivarium* 12 (1974): 63–73.

17.44   —— 'Ockham's distinction between absolute and connotative terms', *Vivarium* 13 (1975): 55–75.

17.45   —— *The Mediaeval Liar: A Catalogue of the Insolubilia Literature*, Toronto, Pontifical Institute of Mediaeval Studies, 1975.

17.46 —— 'Some epistemological implications of the Burley–Ockham dispute', *Franciscan Studies* 35 (1975): 212–22.

17.47 —— 'Synonymy and equivocation in Ockham's mental language', *Journal of the History of Philosophy* 18 (1980): 9–22.

17.48 —— '*Insolubilia* and Bradwardine's theory of signification', *Medioevo: Rivista di storia della filosofia medievale* 7 (1981): 115–34.

17.49 —— 'Five early theories in the mediaeval *insolubilia* literature', *Vivarium* 25 (1987): 24–46.

17.50 —— 'The logic of the categorical: the medieval theory of descent and ascent', in [17.31] 187–224.

17.51 Trentman, J. 'Ockham on mental', *Mind* 79 (1970): 586–90.

CHAPTER 18

Late medieval philosophy, 1350–1500

Zénon Kaluza

❧

❦ INTRODUCTION ❦

No fact in philosophical or other history underlies the commonly-made division of fourteenth-century philosophy around the year 1350, except perhaps the Black Death of 1348–9, which overcame the Oxford masters and destroyed an original style of thinking and doing philosophy. Things happened differently on the Continent, at least in 1348–9, so that this division does not apply there. The great philosophers of the Middle Ages who have a place in history were not all dead before 1350; and some, indeed, continued to think and write after this time. The chapter-division in this volume is, then, more than anything a reflection of the state of knowledge of historians, who have been more interested in the first half of the fourteenth century than in the second, so that our knowledge of the years 1300–50 is surer than that of the years 1350–1400. And since, as a general rule – to which this chapter is an exception – historians prefer to speak of what they know, they also adopt the breaks which indicate the limits of their knowledge of the past: breaks which are 'historical' only by convention. This applies also to the other limit of the period, the year 1500, the rough textbook boundary between the Middle Ages and modern times. Such text-book divisions exist to show that there is a moment when every beginning comes to its end and makes way for a new beginning.

The period 1350–1500 is, then, little studied. This is true not only of the philosophers and theologians, but also of the universities where they taught. For speculation – what is called 'medieval speculation' – did not take place outside universities except to a very limited degree. It was always the work of clerics teaching in *studia*. The only important exception is Italy, where the development of humanism began by introducing philosophical thought into chancelleries and then later made itself a place of its own – the academies. But that is another story which, traditionally, does not belong to 'medieval philosophy'.

The century and a half from 1350 is precisely the period of development of the universities. It saw the foundations of several dozen universities everywhere in Europe, especially in Central Europe, but also in Italy, the south of France, Scandinavia and Scotland. Although they are not entirely indistinguishable, the history of medieval philosophy is also, at least in its origins, the history of the university as an institution. That is why, before discussing doctrines, we must consider the intellectual and institutional context of late medieval philosophy.

❧ THE INSTITUTIONAL CONTEXT ❧

After the tragic years of 1349–50, the University of Oxford became an important centre for realist philosophy, where logicians (who were already well known) worked alongside philosophers and theologians, such as the two secular clerics, Nicholas Aston and Richard Billingham, the Franciscan Richard Brinkley, the Carmelite Osbert Pockingham and the Augustinian Hermit Godfrey Hardeby. The years 1360–80 are notable for the intellectual activity of John Wyclif (c. 1328–84), the author of various works in English and Latin, of logic, philosophy and theology, politics, of sermons and of polemic. Pope Gregory XI condemned a set of his political positions in 1377, but it was not until 1380 that the criticisms of his theological doctrines began in England. In the following years, his positions and his writings would be condemned several times at Oxford and London, at Prague and at the Council of Constance. Among his critics we find several outstanding and prolific philosophers and theologians, such as the two Carmelites, Richard Lavenham (d. 1381/3) and Thomas Netter (in his *Doctrinale antiquitatum*). To the same group belongs the Dominican Thomas Claxton (d. 1430), a Thomist and member of the commission which condemned the writings of Wyclif in 1411. With Netter and Claxton we are already in the fifteenth century.[1]

John Wyclif has a decisive position in the intellectual history of Europe for two reasons. First of all, he added weight to the attack on nominalism, and his realism and reformism would profoundly influence the new University of Prague. They underlie the Czech reform and all its political and religious repercussions.[2] Second, after the fairly universal rejection of nominalism at the beginning of the fifteenth century, the criticisms of Wyclif and his condemnation stimulated and perhaps accelerated the return to the great scholastic thinkers of the thirteenth century. This return (which seems to us today to be the first version of neoscholasticism) took place in England at the very time of the anti-Wyclifite polemics. It was thus earlier than the parallel movement on the Continent.

In Paris, the second half of the fourteenth century continued on the path already set until the beginning of the Great Schism (1378–1414), a period of political and doctrinal crisis for the university. After 1378 the influence of Oxford on Paris was diminished and relations between the two universities, which had already been weakened by the Hundred Years War, became openly hostile. Two schools engaged in explicit polemic: the nominalists (the followers of John Buridan) and the Scotists. A third, Thomism, was attacked brutally and publicly by Peter d'Ailly. In the faculty of theology a number of doctrines were current, and this led in the general direction of eclecticism. But the faculty of arts was dominated by the nominalist school, which seemed to have imposed its textbooks and methods. This position would change in about 1395, the time when Pierre d'Ailly gave up the position of Chancellor. From this date onwards, the realists – especially the Thomists, but also the followers of Albert the Great – made up lost ground and ended the nominalists' monopoly. The 1339 prohibition on teaching Ockham's doctrines, which was considered in the fifteenth century to be a ban on all forms of nominalism, would remain in force until 1481, when Louis XI lifted the prohibition of books and doctrines held to be nominalist.

Italian universities, sometimes older than those north of the Alps, developed in a different way from other *studia*. This came about for three main reasons. First, the great universities of Padua and Bologna opened their theology faculties (the faculties in which doctrinal speculation tended to be most developed) relatively late: Padua in 1363, Bologna in 1364. Other theology faculties would be opened even later. Without the natural support which theology gave it in the northern universities, philosophy as practised in Italy did not succeed, in our period, in producing doctrinal schools. But, for this very reason, the most gifted philosophers, Francis of Marchia, Gregory of Rimini, John of Ripa and many others, went to Paris and became famous there. Second, in Italy the faculties of liberal arts prepared young people for practical careers as physicians or lawyers and placed little emphasis on philosophical speculation. In Italy philosophy consisted most of all in the task of commenting on the writings of Aristotle and the set-books of grammar, astronomy and optics. Indeed, the important Italian philosophers of this period were often also medical doctors. All the same, towards the end of the fourteenth century, a tradition was born, and some people set themselves to studying English logicians and

428

philosophers, then to studying Averroes, Aquinas and Duns Scotus, whilst others were drawn to the novelty which is called 'humanism'.

Humanism is the third important factor in the development of philosophy in late medieval Italy. Everything which is most original and productive in the intellectual life of the late Middle Ages belongs to the broad movement of humanism, which Petrarch and an extraordinary series of chancellors of Florence, beginning with Coluccio Salutati (1375–1406) and Leonardo Bruni (1410–11, 1427–44), created and continued ([18.47]). These chancellors, assisted later by many 'humanists' (grammar teachers), brought into being the movement which would finally change the course of philosophy. They were attracted to a different sort of philosophy from that of the universities. For, whereas the university philosophers devoted themselves especially to logic, natural philosophy and metaphysics, the humanists were particularly interested in moral and political philosophy, ancient philosophy, literature and philology. The fifteenth century witnessed at once scholastic resistance to humanism and a mingling of the two currents of thought.[3] Their exponents did not always have friendly relations. Sometimes the humanists attacked university philosophy, which was heavily influenced by the English, complaining of *Suissenicae quisquiliae, subtilitates Anglicanae* and *barbari Britanni*.[4] Perhaps they were right, since not only the fourteenth century, which finished with Peter of Mantua (d. 1400), but also the fifteenth, which began with the teaching of Biagio Pelacani (d. 1416) and Paul of Venice (Paolo Nicoletti, d. 1429), and continued with Gaetano da Thiene, was very influenced by English logic and philosophy, that of the *calculatores* and Merton College in particular. In the second half of the fifteenth century, however, and later, humanist philology also conquered the universities and did great service for philosophy, encouraging work on texts, new translations and paraphrases and new commentaries. To it Aristotelianism owed its vigorous revival.[5]

The situation with regard to philosophy was different in the Empire and the countries bordering on it. The University of Prague, which was established in 1347, developed normally until about 1400. Its theologians were allowed great freedom and were influenced by the Church Fathers and twelfth-century writers such as St Bernard, the Victorines and Alan of Lille. Among the philosophers, who enjoyed a similar liberty, John Buridan's doctrines, equated with nominalism, were popular; but, from 1390 to the early 1400s, Wyclif often replaced Buridan as the model. Fairly soon, to Wyclifite philosophy there was linked Wyclifite theology and various attempts at ecclesiastical reform. The Wyclifites became a part of the reform movement and were linked with nationalism. The statute of Kutná-Hora (1409), abolishing the system of voting by nation, shook the university. Those who objected to it – the Germans especially – left to teach and study in German universities, especially Leipzig (founded in 1409). After the condemnation of Jan Hus and Jerome of Prague at the Council of Constance and their burning at the stake (in 1415 and 1416), the Hussite revolution broke out, destroying the economic base of the university, the system of colleges and benefices. By cutting off the university from the rest of Europe, it caused philosophy to disappear from Prague for many years.

The University of Kracow, though established in 1364, only began functioning properly in 1400, with masters trained at Prague. Students of the following generations sometimes went to study at Cologne, Erfurt or Leipzig. The University of Vienna, founded in 1365, and refounded in 1384, was able to continue despite its difficult beginnings, thanks to the untiring work of Albert of Saxony and of the reorganizers of the university, Henry of Langenstein and Henry of Oyta. All three had previously studied at Paris. At Kracow, Vienna and in the new German universities of the fourteenth century – Cologne, Heidelberg and Erfurt – John Buridan had become the unchallenged authority in the faculty of philosophy. This nominalist *schola communis* persisted for varying lengths of time from place to place: in Paris until about 1395, at Cologne up until 1420/1, in Heidelberg until the 1450s, in Vienna right up until almost the end of the fifteenth century. Each of these schools made its own decision on whether it should continue with this or that philosophy.[6]

❧ ENGLISH PHILOSOPHY ❧

The mainstream of English philosophy after 1350 was realist. Realist philosophers looked to two points of reference in the recent past, which they used in order to define their own identity: the philosophy of William of Ockham and Thomas Bradwardine's *De causa Dei* (*In God's Defence*). As a general rule, the writers rejected Ockham's teaching. Such, for instance, was the attitude of the Franciscan Richard Brinkley. His *summa* of logic continues, in this respect, the pseudo-Campsall's tradition of anti-Ockhamist logic.[7] For Wyclif, Ockham and his followers would always be *doctores signorum*, masters whose teaching is about words which signify things, but tells us nothing about the things themselves. By contrast, Bradwardine's masterpiece was criticized only on points of detail, whilst it is very often a rich source of inspiration, particularly in the cases of Thomas of Buckingham and Nicholas Aston.

Nicholas Aston, a theologian and philosopher, is interesting in a number of ways. He read the *Sentences* between 1352 and 1354, and then in 1358 he became a doctor of theology. He was Chancellor of the university from 1358 or 1359 to 1361, and finally Dean of Chichester in 1362. Aston seems to have wanted to make theology and philosophy subordinate to his logical concerns. His treatise on *insolubilia*, which remains lost, is quoted in his commentary on the *Sentences* (still unpublished). This commentary raises a good many logical problems, such as the signification of affirmative and negative propositions, the nature of contradictory, contingent and false propositions, and the rules of inference. It is as a logician that he raised the great question of God's existence, since he believed that logic is the only discipline accepted by everybody without reservation and that the proof which it could provide would not depend on any philosophical presuppositions. This is to say that he rejected the proofs of God which had been devised previously. In particular, he criticized Bradwardine's proof, which is based on the concept of possibility (*De causa Dei*, I, 1). Yet Aston is also Bradwardine's follower, especially in his critique of Duns Scotus's notion of impossibility and in his discussion of the view that the propositional content *Deum non esse* (that God is not) necessarily contains a contradiction (*De causa Dei* I, 13 and 14).[8]

Aston's own demonstration of God's existence is based on three definitions, three suppositions and two principles, one of which is important for us: 'every false proposition is either contingent or includes a contradiction' (*omnis propositio falsa est contingens vel contradictionem includens*). The main proof (called 'Achilles') takes the following form:

1   If God exists, and if there is a proposition *p* which asserts that God does not exist, then *p* contains a self-contradiction.
2   *p* contains a self-contradiction if it is the case that God does not exist just as it does if it is the case that God does exist.
3   Therefore, in both cases, *p* is self-contradictory.

(2) is based on the principle that no change in things can prevent a self-contradictory proposition from being self-contradictory. Aston proves (1) in this way. Granted that God exists, suppose that the *p*, which denies his existence, is not self-contradictory. It must then be false. Now, according to the principle mentioned above, every false proposition is either contingent or self-contradictory. But *p* is not contingent because, by virtue of the definition of contingents, the statement 'God exists' would equally be contingent and so God, what is designated by the subject term, would be a contingent being. And so the statement 'God does not exist' is and will always be self-contradictory and so 'impossible'.[9]

This proof – one which, to our eyes, shows as much, or more faith in logic than in God – gave rise to lengthy discussion in England,

France, Bohemia and even in Italy. These discussions are interesting not for what they prove, but because of the subjects they touch on, the main one of which is the definition of impossible and self-contradictory propositions. This is, for example, the problem faced by the Augustinian, Godfrey Hardeby, and the Franciscan, Brinkley. Brinkley did not think that a 'simple negative' consisting of a subject and a verb, could be self-contradictory, but merely true or false.[10] In the final years of the fourteenth century, Biagio Pelacani, an Italian physician and philosopher, went on with the discussion of the same problem, and now linked it to causality. He knew very well the English debates about the statement 'God does not exist' ([18.40]). As far as we can discern today, the discussions which took place at Paris seem to have taken another direction. The scholars there tried to show the contradictory character of 'God does not exist' in a more commonplace way, by reference to the Neoplatonic definition of God as pure being (*esse purum*), or by recourse to Anselm's concept of the most perfect being. In each case this being cannot not exist.

Brinkley's discussion of the 'logical proof' of God's existence was just one of the reasons for the popularity in Paris of his commentary, dating from 1350 to 1360. In fact the Parisian masters were also interested just as much in problems about the first contingent being (*prima contingentia*) and how contingent beings can be produced by a necessary cause, and those about the status of theology as a science and about the causes and nature of assent to the articles of faith. The two first problems are linked. They concern the reply to the question of whether the notion of creation is conceivable and, if so, whether the contingency of the effect presupposes a certain contingency in its cause. Bradwardine had followed others in putting this question. He had replied that the first and highest freedom and contingency, which causes all other freedom and contingency, is in the divine will (II, 5; 624B). This position was taken up by the Franciscan, John of Ripa and his disciple, Louis of Padua, but it was condemned in 1362 by the theology faculty of Paris. But Brinkley had already rejected it. He held that contingency derives from created things, not God: only being which changes is contingent. To answer the question, however, Brinkley presents God's productive action in an original way – by noun and by adverb: *modo necessario* and *necessario* ('in a necessary way', 'necessarily') *modo contingenti* and *contingenter* ('in a contingent way' and 'contingently'). The noun *modus* implies and determines the nature of the cause which acts. It cannot, therefore, be the case that God can act *modo contingenti* because, being a necessary being, he always acts *modo necessario*. By contrast, the adverb describes God's action in terms of its result, which is sometimes necessary (as in the persons of the Trinity), sometimes contingent (as in created things).

The two assertions, that God acts *modo necessario* and that he acts *contingenter* are not concerned with the same thing and do not rule each other out. Rather, they are complementary.

With regard to proving God's existence, Richard Brinkley rejects every sort of proof, whether a priori or a posteriori. Most frequently he makes clear his differences from the tradition of Duns Scotus and Ockham, in particular on whether *passio* can be demonstrated, rejecting any formulation of the univocity of being and arguing against the trinitarian theology of Scotus.[11]

Brinkley bases his semantics on two concepts: imposition and subordination. To summarize it very briefly: Brinkley maintains that a conventional sign (such as a word) signifies exactly the same thing as the corresponding natural sign (a concept) does – that is to say, an object outside the mind, not a concept. The only conventional signs that signify concepts are those especially imposed to do this. Otherwise, signification is immediate (sign natural/conventional > thing), so we can move from language directly to the world of things. Since conventional signs come after natural signs, their function as signifiers is based on a temporal relationship (*prius/posterius*). Brinkley adds that no conventional sign depends on any other conventional sign; and he rules out any hierarchy of languages, since every language depends in the same way on natural signs. The relations between mental, spoken and written propositions are explained in the same way, and so is the concept of truth. Brinkley's view of imposition also affects his theory of obligations.[12]

John Wyclif became a member of Merton College in 1356, a master at Balliol in 1360 and a doctor of theology in 1372. A number of the writings of this energetic polemicist are gathered in two collections, the *Summa de ente* (*Textbook on Entities*) and the *Summa theologiae* (*Textbook of Theology*). Wyclif considered himself close to the tradition of Richard Fitzralph and Thomas Bradwardine, and he often described himself as a 'realist philosopher', in this way marking his opposition to the 'doctors of signs'.

Wyclif's metaphysics is founded on two principles, the one positive, the other negative. The negative principle, 'Nothing is and is not at the same time' (*nihil simul esse et non esse*) is one of the many variants of the principle of non-contradiction. Wyclif considers it as a first and pure negation. The positive principle, that being exists (*ens esse*), is the first indubitable and indemonstrable truth. Being, the existence of which is asserted by this principle, is taken in general (*in communi*). Being is transcendent, and everything which exists participates in it. It exists, then, in singular things: it is impossible to know transcendent being without knowing a singular, and vice versa. Being is identical to entity, one, the true and the good and it is the first object of knowledge (*primum cognitum*) of our intellect. As the first object known, it is also the first *signabile*, that is to say, the first that is able to be designated by a word, to be signified by an expression. Being is eternal, not because the singulars which contain it are eternal, but by virtue of the first, uncreated being and also by virtue of the universals which are ideal reasons (*rationes ydeales que vocantur universalia*) and other eternal truths, such as the future and past states of things, negations, distinctions and numbers. This transcendent being is unique and the attributes which apply to created things cannot be predicated of it except analogously. It is not made of parts, but the human intellect is capable of distinguishing six transcendental attributes: being, thing, something (*aliquid*), one, true and good: the last three are 'qualities of being' (*passiones entis*).

It should, all the same, be emphasized that for Wyclif the notion of analogous being has a special sense, derived from Augustine's theology of creation. He holds analogous being to have been created by a sudden and simultaneous act of creation, and he defines it – looking to the *Book about Causes* (*Liber de causis*) IV, 37 as the 'first created being' (*esse primum creatum*) or 'first of created things' (*prima rerum creatarum*). When he created it, God placed in this being the models and measures of the genera and species. Afterwards, all particular things were made according to these models. This second act of creation is called by Wyclif 'administration' (*administratio*). Wyclif's two-stage scheme of creation echoes Augustine's distinction between 'first creation' (*prima conditio*) and 'administration'. For this reason it is legitimate to think of the models contained in analogous being as Wyclif's version of the causal reasons (*rationes seminales*) discussed by Augustine.[13]

The ideal reasons mentioned in the paragraph before last are just one group among universals. In fact, universals are divided in two different ways into three groups. Following Avicenna (*Logica* 3) and Eustratius, Wyclif distinguishes between universals *ante rem*, the divine ideas; universals *in re*, the common natures in singulars; and universals *post rem*, concepts. In fourteenth-century fashion, he also distinguishes universals by causality, by communication, and by representation. The first way of dividing follows the universals' way of being, whereas the second mixes their way of being and their function. For instance, the divine ideas are universals by causation, because they cause genera, species and singular things, but they are also *ante rem*, for the very reason that they precede everything of which they are the cause.[14] Universals by communication are the common natures in which singulars participate, although they are formally distinct from them. Universals by representation are terms predicated in propositions.

Wyclif goes against tradition by identifying real universals with the genera and species listed in Genesis – that is, roughly speaking, with natural kinds. In this way he combines the word of Scripture, philosophical analysis and our everyday perception of biological differences. Yet the point of his consideration of universals is simply to gain fuller knowledge of the Bible and the mystery of the Trinity: 'The knowledge of universals is particularly useful because it enables the literal sense of the scriptural passages which talk of universals to be understood and it reveals the paralogisms which arise in talking about the Trinity.'[15] In fact the mystery of the Trinity is explained by using the idea of formal distinction (that between the persons and the divine essence) and of communication (the divine essence which communicates itself to the persons). But Wyclif denies that there are any real distinctions in God (so as not to make his essence plural) and that what is common, the divine essence, is in any way prior to what is individual (the persons) – although this priority *is* found in the theory of universals. The formal nature of the distinction between God's essence and the divine persons is based on the epistemological idea of the 'first known' or that which is 'known principally' (*principaliter intellectum*) in God: at one moment this is essence (communicability), at another a person (incommunicability); but the two remain unmixed ([18.6] XIV: 143, 149).

Wyclif's doctrine of universals by causality was inspired by the passages in St Augustine on divine ideas. These universals – also called exemplars, ideas and archetypes – are in God. They are the very essence of God, and so 'essentially' God, whilst formally they are the reason by which God knows created things. The only distinctions between themselves, and between themselves and God, are formal. Wyclif and his followers used this opinion of St Augustine's to show that, thanks to the (universal) ideas, the action and the result of creation are intelligible: without them God would have created something without having knowledge of it. There is another way, too, in which universals make the world intelligible. Granted the priority of what is common and of the universal over the particular, we know a singular in so far as we contemplate its intelligibility, its 'passive intellection', which is the universal in God, placed in the Word, but present in the whole Trinity.[16] As for the number of the ideas, Wyclif merely distinguishes between ideas of singulars, those of universals and that of analogous being (the ontological status of which is not easy to grasp). Every created thing is singular in its existence, belongs to a natural kind, participates in being and reflects in itself the ideal world of causal reasons. And, since the causal chain is finite and infinite regress is impossible, there is no room for talk of ideas of ideas ([18.5] I, c. X: 72).

Wyclif's theory of universals must be clearly distinguished from the ontology of forms devised by the Franciscan Francis of Meyronnes. Whereas Wyclif identified the ideas in the mind of God, taken from

435

Augustine, with universals, Francis left ideas in the mind of God to the theologians, whilst as a philosopher keeping Platonic ideas. His theory is, indeed, a new interpretation of Platonism – and a more philosophical one than Wyclif's.[17] Spurred by Duns Scotus and Avicenna, Meyronnes imagines a world of formal quiddities, which gives the lie to Aristotle's caricature of Platonic ideas: 'If they exist, they are monsters.' Francis argues that, in Plato's view, essential predication, definition, demonstration and division are all based on ideas, since all these intellectual operations imply a specific nature which is unchangeable and unmoveable and set apart from any material conditions. These operations cannot even take place without there being formal quiddities: if they are to be true and necessary, the links between the terms must be made in the first instance outside the mind and not depend in any way on its workings. These quiddities must be pure and separated from everything which would determine them in a concrete being. For this reason, they must be attributed the same sort of being as Avicenna's essences. And so, if it is necessary to posit ideas, they must be formally separated from everything which has put them into an individual being: place, duration, *haecceitas* (this-ness). To put it in another way: their being is abstract by their nature, not as a result of an intellectual operation. To the final question, 'How can the *esse in pluribus* (being in many) which defines universals fit with quiddities?', Meyronnes has a simple reply: *accidit*. It so happens that a universal is in particulars or in our concept. But, from the point of view of its nature, it is there by accident; whereas from the point of view of the particulars, it is there by necessity.[18]

To return to Wyclif himself. Older views of the 'extreme realism' of his philosophy are not justified, if such extremism is taken to embrace the existence of genera and species outside singulars, and the existence of divine ideas outside the divine essence or really distinct from it. Wyclif rejects such a philosophy. On the question of universals, he places himself between Thomas Aquinas and Walter Burley, and with regard to ideas he accuses Aristotle of having been foolish to claim that Plato thought that ideas were separate essences. Wyclif's realism is not, then, extreme. Its unwonted nature reflects its unusual source of inspiration: it is a theological realism, because it derives from a literal reading of the word of Scripture.

Several Oxford masters adopted Wyclif's doctrine of universals, along with the metaphysics and logic which underpinned it. They carried on teaching a sort of Wyclifism until the 1420s, but they are hardly known to us.[19] At the same time, in the last decade of the fourteenth century, the University of Prague provided excellent ground for the development of Wyclifism, first in the person of Stanislas of Znaim (later the enemy of Wyclif and Hus; d. 1414) and his followers,

John Hus (d. 1415) and Stefan Palec (later the enemy of Wyclif and Hus; d. 1423), and later still in Jerome of Prague (d. 1416), Jacobellus of Misa (d. after 1430) and others.[20] All of these men shared Wyclif's teaching, especially his doctrine of universals as being at once divine ideas, common forms and terms or concepts. For the Wyclifites of Prague, however, universals were of especial interest in their first function, as ideas. Znaim, Palec and Jerome presented, as the basis of their teaching, a flourishing world of ideas, which merited love and adoration because of their real identity with God's essence – a view once rejected by Duns Scotus. None the less, only Znaim – so far as we know – set out to demonstrate at length the existence of universals on the basis of Genesis (cf. [18.26] n. 795).

❦ PHILOSOPHY IN PARIS ❦

If, at Oxford, the second half of the fourteenth century and the fifteenth century were dominated by realism, the situation was very different in Paris, despite the ban on teaching Ockham's doctrines. To consider just the second half of the fourteenth century: the faculty of arts was dominated by 'Parisian nominalism', or the school of Buridan, and this went on to win over the other universities on the Continent. The most famous masters of this school were Albert of Saxony (who went on to become the first rector of the University of Vienna), Themo the Jew, Dominic of Clavasio, Marsilius of Inghen (who became the first rector of Heidelberg), Henry of Langenstein, Peter d'Ailly, Henry Totting of Oyta and John Dorp, all of them famous in the history of science, or the history of logic, or as theologians.[21]

Given the relative silence of the other schools, it was the disputes between the 'Ockhamists' (*hereditas filiorum Ocham*) and the different intellectual inheritors of Duns Scotus which were witnessed by the faculty of theology. These 'Scotists' showed unceasing originality and independence of mind in relation to their doctrinal master. The case of a Spanish Dominican, Juan of Monzon, shows the sad state of Thomism in Paris at the time. It also gave Peter d'Ailly, the future chancellor, a better chance than he could have hoped to attack Aquinas's teaching publicly, at the university and at the court in Avignon. In the aftermath, the Dominicans withdrew from the University of Paris (1388–1403).

The nominalist school in theology is not well known: we cannot even be sure that it existed between the time of Gregory of Rimini and Peter d'Ailly. True, a statute of Louis XI, dated 1474, forbidding nominalism names as nominalist theologians Ockham, Wodeham, John of Mirecourt, Gregory of Rimini and Peter d'Ailly. Yet, of the three Parisians, Gregory and Peter are considered followers of Ockham, whilst John was rather a realist, who followed English writings closely and plagiarized them energetically. All the same, since Peter d'Ailly also seems to have been as much of a plagiarist, it is hard to speak of his original ideas with confidence until there is a critical edition of his writings and their sources have been established. None the less, for our present purposes it is tempting to reconstruct the main decisions taken by the university and the main disagreements between the schools, since the first as much as the second affected the doctrinal teaching and the institutional life of the University of Paris. We have arranged them around three events which made apparent the situation of the various doctrinal schools: the statutes of 1339 and 1340; Peter d'Ailly's fight against Thomism; and Gerson's fight against the Scotists.

On 25 September 1339, the faculty of arts of Paris instituted a ban on commenting in public or private on the writings of Ockham, and on citing his opinions in disputations. This statute should not be taken, as some scholars have exaggeratedly read it, as a decision made against nominalism, but as a measure directed personally against Ockham, his writings and his teachings. And, since the faculty did not take the statute to go beyond these limits, nominalism was able to develop in Paris better than elsewhere. It was during the doctrinal struggles of the beginning of the fifteenth century, when Ockham was identified as the father of nominalism, that the broader interpretation of the statute was probably first entertained. Louis XI's law of 1 March 1474, which forbade all nominalist teaching and books, refers to the decision of 1339 as a prohibition of nominalism. Between 1339 and 1474 the meanings of terms had slipped and coalesced, and Ockham, Ockhamism and nominalism were considered one and the same. We should note, all the same, finally that the same Louis XI, in 1481, gave permission for nominalist doctrines to be taught, and, at the same time, removed all the earlier prohibitions.

The statute of 29 December 1340 was not a condemnation of Ockham and his own doctrine, nor a decision taken by the realists against the interest of the nominalists. Rather, it was a faculty measure taken against certain Parisian masters who said they were Ockhamists. No other reading is possible, since the text of the statute follows the letter and spirit of Ockham's and Buridan's doctrine.

The central problem in the statute, which occurs in four out of six articles, is that of the distinction between two senses of a proposition: the proper or literal sense (*virtus sermonis, sensus proprius*) and the improper sense, which however is considered as proper when it fits the imposition and use of the words, and when it is determined by a *materia subiecta*, that is to say, according to Aristotle and his commentators, a subject belonging to and treated in a determinate discipline.²² We can call them 'proper sense' and 'improper sense' (which is 'proper' in a given language). With these two possibilities in mind, the authors of the statute set out to consider every proposition in the light of two rules:

1   If a proposition *p* is false in the proper sense but true in the improper sense, it is accepted.
2   If a proposition *p* is true in the proper sense, but false in the improper sense, it is rejected.

These rules were known to Buridan, but they were used especially in theology by Peter d'Ailly and Gerson. They determine whether propositions are accepted or rejected, since, by the statute, only those propositions which accord with the first rule can be admitted, and all those which fall under the second rule must be rejected and left to 'sophists'.

The statute of 1340 can be judged as favouring nominalism. It derives from fresh thought about the idea of 'the force of speech' (*virtus sermonis*) and about the division of knowledge into disciplines, each of which has its own language with its special characteristics. Altogether, logic apart, the *virtus sermonis* exists only within a language determined either by the subject being treated, or by the discipline to which the language and the subject belong. By stressing, like Aristotle, the importance of subject matter, the statute introduces another meaning of the term 'certainty' besides the certainty of our act of knowing (already the subject of epistemological discussion): the certainty of a demonstration within a given discipline. In this way, the statute takes the problem of certainty from the domain of epistemology and places it within the context of questions about how we build up a scheme of knowledge and about probability and evidence.

With these remarks in mind, we can see the position of the Parisian Ockhamists. The statute criticizes them for having too rigid a view of the proper meaning of terms, a meaning which can be verified always and everywhere, especially using personal supposition, to which they gave absolute priority. They limited themselves to this universal, logical analysis probably because their interests did not go beyond signs, for the simple reason that they thought that terms and propositions are the only object of human knowledge. The School of Buridan answered this 'Ockhamist' position by showing the flexibility of language and adopting rules of analysis for the technical languages of the different branches of knowledge.

What has come to be known as 'the Monzon affair' (1387-9) was a dramatic series of events with important institutional repercussions. The events are well known, but more often than not the institutional repercussions are presented solely as the abandonment of the University by the Dominicans. The subject of the dispute was the Immaculate Conception, in which Peter d'Ailly, his brilliant pupil Gerson and the faculty of theology believed, but which Monzon and the Dominicans rejected. The dispute acted as a pretext for a battle between the theology faculty and the powerful Dominican Order, and between nominalists and realists. Quickly, the Monzon affair came to centre on Thomas Aquinas and his doctrine, and it was exactly this development which made the Dominicans leave the university. The decisive episode in the struggle took place at Avignon, before the Pope, his court, some Dominican doctors and a delegation of Paris theologians ([18.49] 197–8).

Peter d'Ailly's long and skilful sermon raised a number of fundamental problems for the Church and the Paris theology faculty: in particular the question of the order of the jurisdiction of the various different ecclesiastical authorities which are empowered to define doctrine, and the hierarchical order of those who are allowed to teach the Word. Here d'Ailly holds that Aquinas is at the bottom of the hierarchy, placed after Peter the Lombard, among his commentators. In the course of giving his answers to these questions, d'Ailly also examines the value of the teaching of Aquinas itself. And it is here that we can see the young theologian attacking the authority of the 'holy doctor'. He gives his views in two sets of three conclusions. The first series gives a general estimation of the doctrine, and the second consists of a wide-ranging demonstration of Aquinas's errors. Conclusions 1–3 state the following: although Aquinas's doctrine might be accepted as being useful and probable, we must not believe that it is true in every part, nor that it is entirely without error or heresy. And Conclusions 4–6: in the *Summa contra Gentiles* (II, 29–30), Aquinas's doctrine on the absolute necessity of created things is literally false (*de virtute sermonis*), blemished with errors and in part suspect. Even if, when understood correctly in accord with its author's intention, it is to a certain extent correct (*aliqualiter vera*), it should not be taught without its correct meaning first being established.[23] The final conclusion has the air of a gratuitous concession, although it fits perfectly with the first of the 1340 rules, which d'Ailly quotes and uses in this very sermon. D'Ailly admits that he has been using the style of the polemic, where one must show up an enemy's weaknesses (*de virtute sermonis*) and disguise his strong points: in the end, Aquinas's thesis can be taught when the distinction of the two senses of *virtus sermonis* is made.

Peter d'Ailly was able to show at Avignon the errors and contradictions of Thomism, and to make himself noticed. In the aftermath of this victory, the faculty of theology succeeded in making the Dominicans leave the university and the office of almoner, whilst d'Ailly was given two appointments: first, to be the royal almoner, and second (on his nomination from Avignon) the chancellorship of the university (1389). The Monzon affair took place, then, when the university was dominated by the nominalists, and this would continue until d'Ailly left the chancellorship in 1395. We know very little about this period and we cannot talk about it with confidence. It seems very likely, however, that the ban on commenting Aristotle following a realist author, which is mentioned by John of Nova Domus (Maison-neuve) at the beginning of the fifteenth century, could well have come between 1388 and 1395.

We know of several conflicts between theological schools, thanks to the work of Ehrle on Peter of Candia. They are of interest to historians of philosophy in so far as they concerned speculative matters, and also because they afford a precious opportunity to trace the divisions of schools as they were perceived and described by the very participants in these disputes. One of the rivalries, in the 1370s and perhaps later, was between the nominalists and the *formalizantes* mentioned above. Although there was some slowing down in the production of Scotist books towards the end of the fourteenth century and at the beginning of the next century, Gerson sustained this conflict up to his death in 1429. He accused the Scotists and *formalizantes* (formalists) of three errors. First, they introduced into theology a principle of causality – 'from the same in so far as it is the same nothing but the same can come' (*ab eodem in quantum idem non provenit nisi idem*) – which turns free creation into a necessary act. Second, in order to safeguard the reality of our knowledge, they asserted that a thing in the extramental world corresponds to each of our concepts. Third, by distinguishing between the divine essence and its attributes, they introduced a formal distinction within God.[24] To Gerson, the thinker principally responsible for these errors was John of Ripa.

At this time, the Scotist school was not particularly important at Paris. During the first half of the fourteenth century the school had developed quickly (we need merely mention Francis of Meyronnes, Nicholas Bonet and Peter Thomae); and at the end of the fifteenth it would flourish again (in the treatises *de formalitatibus* by Stephen Brulefer and Antonius Sirect, on which several commentaries were written at Padua). But, during Gerson's working life, Scotism was going through a period of torpor. None the less, there were good reasons for Gerson to criticize the Scotists. Their ontology of forms – especially the priority of *formalitates* to the act of knowing them – contradicted the bases of Gerson's own thought, which owed much to the tradition of Buridan and d'Ailly. Moreover, when eighteen articles of Louis of Padua were condemned in 1362, this was also a condemnation of John of Ripa. When they introduced formal distinction into the absolutely simple being of God, Louis and John had asserted, among other things, that 'something in God is his real being which is not his formal being' and that 'something intrinsic in God is contingent'.[25] Finally, there was the question of theological language, linked to Buridan's idea that the proper meaning of words is limited to a determinate discipline. Throughout his work, Gerson held that the theological vocabulary of Scotus and the Scotists (and that too of Raymond Lull) was improper and had departed from the tradition of an Aristotelian way of speaking ([18.55] 39–40, 51).

CONCLUSION: FIFTEENTH-CENTURY STAGNATION

In a letter which he wrote in 1400 to the young theologians of the College of Navarre, Gerson advised his readers to study the great scholastics of the thirteenth century. As for more recent theologians, Gerson said that they were excellent in many ways, but beneath the covering of theological language they had busied themselves with problems of physics, metaphysics and logic ([18.1] II, n. 5). This call for a return to classical scholasticism was in harmony both with Gerson's own underlying ideas and with the new intellectual tendencies of his time. Faithful to the school of Buridan, to the 1340 statute and to the programme which Pope Clement VI had given the university in a letter of 1346, Gerson always fought against the mixing of disciplines and their languages.

The revival of realism in Paris began in 1395–1400 (see [18.54] and [18.76] 279–394). Here, as at Cologne, it took the form of a minor intellectual rebellion against the obligation to study only nominalist treatises, in particular those about the properties of terms. Among the rebels there were also a good number of Thomists and Albertists. As the conflict developed, three different ideas of university freedom came into play. There was that of the conservative establishment, who upheld the exclusive position of nominalism although they allowed the chance for realist philosophers to be mentioned (Cologne, 1414). There was that of the Albertist John of Nova Domus, who proposed confining himself to the Christian – that is to say, Aristotelian – tradition, from which he excluded the nominalists (Paris, before 1418). Finally, there was that of the Cologne realists who allowed all the university traditions.

By contrast with the tradition of the school of Buridan, which separated the disciplines and their principles, the realists put forward the old model in which knowledge is unified: its basis is metaphysics, from which all the particular disciplines derive. They also insisted on the unity of the principles governing all philosophical and theological speculation. Clearest about this was the University of Cologne which, in 1425, declared that the links binding philosophy and theology were indissoluble, and took St Thomas for its model, because 'in his two *Summae* he uses the same principles as he does in expounding the works of Aristotle' (*in omnibus Summis suis utitur eisdem principiis, quibus usus est libros Philosophi exponendo*).

The nominalists responded to this exaltation of the great thirteenth-century scholastics by looking to the founders of their own school, John Buridan and Marsilius of Inghen. Indeed, strange to say, round about the year 1400 philosophers decided that they would no longer do philosophy on their own account and no longer take any personal responsibility for their philosophical positions. Rather, they spent the whole of the fifteenth century fighting among themselves, with prescriptions and prohibitions as their weapons, not in order to impose on everybody their own thought, but that of their distant models: Thomas Aquinas, Albert the Great, Duns Scotus, Giles of Rome and Buridan. Universities passed statutes to remove undesirables and to close themselves to new ideas. None of these decisions rose above the level of factional in-fighting.

This upholding of traditions and the related and unceasing conflicts (especially in the German universities) were institutional rather than doctrinal in their basis. Historians describe them by the German word *Wegestreit*. Sometimes by their violence and length these conflicts turned universities into a battleground where scholars fought to re-establish one of the old schools, whether realist or nominalist. The courses in these universities were limited to the revival of the thought of one or another great master of the past. Likewise, the practice of teaching centred on the great names of the past. In England, Wyclif was attacked in the name of St Thomas. In Paris, a predominantly Thomist realism became the established doctrine by the last quarter of the century. In Germany, the choice of doctrine was regulated by the statutes of the different universities. Since this return to old scholasticism was the first of a series of such deliberate returns, it is certainly right to call it *the first neoscholasticism*. In Italy alone this type of institutional conflict had no place: there philosophers at once followed the English tradition of 1300–50 and the Parisian traditions of Averroism and Buridanism, as well as the traditions of Thomas Aquinas and Duns Scotus.

(translated by John Marenbon)

•••❧•••❧••• NOTES •••❧•••❧•••

1 For a general picture, see Catto and Evans [18.37], Hoenan *et al.* [18.52], Robson [18.72] and Courtenay [18.39] 327–80; 384–413, with bibliography.

443

Richard Billingham's theological writing has not yet been recovered; that of Nicolas Aston is unpublished; that of Richard Brinkley is known only in abbreviated form; that of Godfrey Hardeby, preserved in two manuscripts, has recently been identified by A. Tabarroni [18.75] 341, 348–53. Thomas Netter's *Doctrinale antiquitatum fidei ecclesiae catholicae* (completed in 1437) has been printed several times: see Stegmüller [18.27], n. 9055. Thomas Claxton was critical of Wyclif as well as of Ockham and Duns Scotus. He wrote a commentary on the *Sentences* and a *Quodlibet* consisting of seven questions (which is why it is – wrongly – called *Quodlibeta*); qq. V and VI were edited by M. Grabmann in 1943: see Riva [18.71].

2　H. Kaminsky, *A History of the Hussite Revolution*, Berkeley and Los Angeles, Calif., 1967; F. Smahel, *La révolution hussite, une anomalie historique*, Paris, 1985.

3　See, on the whole of the period 1350–1500, B. Nardi, *Saggi sull'aristotelismo*; A Poppi, *Introduzione*, Padua, 1970; and the studies by Kristeller listed in the bibliography. C. B. Schmitt has given especial attention to problems of methodology in [18.73] and [18.74] ch. 1.

4　See Garin [18.45] 141–77; Vasoli [18.77] 9–27; Murdoch [18.69]. We should remember, as Kristeller has pointed out, that these mocking comments were not always taken in earnest.

5　For details, see notes 3 and 4; Maierù [18.67]; Garin [18.44]; Schmitt [18.73] ch. 3; Federici Vescovini [18.41].

6　Gabriel [18.42] 457–83. It seems that it was only in the faculties of arts that a *via* ('method', later: 'school') had to be followed.

7　Fitzgerald [18.10] 18 n. 44, suggests 'the possible identification of Richard Brinkley with the author of the *Logica contra Ockham*'. But I have shown in my study of Brinkley ([18.11] 266 n. 38, 269 n. 60) that this identification must be rejected.

8　Thomas Bradwardine, *De causa Dei* I, 13, 207C: 'aliter et forte melius potest dici, quod Deum non esse necessarissime contradictionem includit'; and I, 14, 209E–210A. The ground for this idea is prepared through a long discussion of *esse* (being) and *necesse esse* (necessary being). But the doctrine as a whole and its consequences rely on a type of metaphysics called by Etienne Gilson a 'metaphysics of Exodus' (in reference to Exodus 3: 14), where the primacy of *esse* is emphasized. In accord with this metaphysics, Bradwardine defines the first necessary, affirmative principle (ibid., I, 11–12). Thus it is the necessary divine being which makes its negation a contradiction. Aston's thought would leave metaphysics and examine the question from the logical point of view. But the Parisian thinkers would return to Bradwardine's more congenial way of thinking.

9　Ms. Worcester, Cathedral Library, F 65, f. 46va; Oxford, Oriel College, 15, f. 221rb: 'Aliter arguo quod Deum non esse contradictionem includit, et hoc argumentum est mihi Achilles. Et arguo sic. Si Deus est, et aliqua propositio est significans praecise Deum non esse, propositio sic praecise significans contradictionem includit; igitur, sive Deus sit sive non sit, si aliqua propositio est significans praecise Deum non esse, ipsa propositio praecise sic significans contradictionem includit. Primo probo consequentiam. Propositio aliqualiter significans et contradictionem includens, quacumque mutatione facta ex parte rei, dummodo ipsa sit semper eodem modo significans praecise, ipsa semper erit contradictionem includens. Verbi gratia, ista propositio "Rex sedet et nullus rex sedet" contradictionem includit rege existente; consimiliter . . . rege non existente . . . Item probo antecendens . . . et arguo sic. Antecedens est una consequentia, quae si non valeat, pono oppositum consequentis stare cum antecedente, utpote quod Deus est et quod propositio aliqua est significans praecise Deum non esse, et tamen propositio sic praecise significans contradictionem non includit . . .' See Bender [18.32]; Courtenay [18.39] 343–6; Kaluza [18.54].

10 Godfrey Hardeby has been known for some time as the *Augustinensis subtilis* of Oxford. A copy of his commentary of the *Sentences* is found in Paris, Bibl., nat., lat 16535, f. 75–110. Q. III: *Utrum Deum non esse contradictionem inferat manifestam*, has been edited by L. A. Kennedy, 'A fourteenth-century Oxford Augustinian on the existence of God', *Augustiniana*, 36 (1986): 28–47. A. Tabarroni has found a new manuscript of the commentary which has allowed him to make the identification between Godfrey and *Augustinensis subtilis* (see n. 1). On Richard Brinkley, cf. Kaluza [18.11] 230–2, 262–5, nn. 29–33.

11 For a general account, see Kaluza [18.11].

12 Gál and Wood [18.43]; Fitzgerald [18.10] 18–28; Ashworth [18.30] 15ff. We summarize briefly here the *Summa logicae*, Treatise I and part of Treatise V, which is still unpublished.

13 Wyclif [18.4] I, tr. I, c. 1–3. These three chapters are dependent on the *On the Nature of Genus* c. 1, attributed to Thomas Aquinas; cf. S. Thomae Aquinatis *Opuscula philosophica*, I, ed. J. Perrier, Paris, 1949, pp. 495–9. See also Catto [18.37]. On double creation, see Augustine, *Literal Commentary on Genesis*, IV, iii–xii and V, xx–xxiii; Wyclif [18.5] II, ch. 3 and [18.14] ch. 12, and Kaluza [18.56], which also discusses univocity and analogy of being.

14 See especially [18.4], I, tr. 1, c. 4–5, and *Tractatus de universalibus*, *passim*. For an account of the doctrine, cf. P. V. Spade, in the Introduction to the translation of Wyclif's *On Universals* [18.14] and A. D. Conti, in the doctrinal study following his edition [18.2] 298–309. The second distinction is found here and there in the fourteenth century. Most frequently, it is used to explain the word *universale* (taken either as a noun or an adjective). For example, John Buridan recognizes a causal universal, which he distinguished from the universal as a term: 'Uno modo aliquid dicitur universale secundum causalitatem, quia causa est multorum. Et sic universalissimum in causando esset Deus, et consequenter intelligentiae, et corpora caelestia . . . Alio modo docitur universale secundum praedicationem vel significationem' (*In Metaphysics*, I, q. 15, Paris 1518, f. 50va). Making the distinction between *universale* and *particulare*, Ockham (*Summa logicae*, I, 14; *Opera philosophica*, I, p. 49, 47–52) asserts: 'Indeed, we call the sun a universal cause, because it is the cause of several things.' The origin of the distinction is unknown. The shift in its meaning is also found in Wyclif: 'From all this it is clear – I think – that all envy or actual sin is caused by the lack of an ordered love of universals, . . . because every such sin consists in a will preferring a lesser good to a greater good, whereas in general the more universal goods are better'; [18.14] 3, p. 22, 145–50.

15 [18.4] I, tr. I, c. 5, p. 57, 17–20; cf. Conti [18.2] 298. For the whole discussion, see the texts and studies cited in n. 14. A sign is called 'universal' by metaphor: 'magis remote dicitur universale quam urina dicitur sana'; [18.4], p. 55, 3–6. Wyclif recognizes three distinctions: essential, real and formal. Formal distinction

is not 'by reason' or 'notional' but by 'formal reason'. Conti [18.2] 301–3, indicates various difficulties raised by the relations between the three types of distinction. Wyclif's English followers would abandon this part of his teaching.

16 Wyclif [18.5] I, c. VIII–IX, p. 66, defines 'idea' thus: 'ydea est essentialiter natura divina, et formaliter ratio, secundum quam Deus intelligit creaturas'. The treatise *De ideis* (part of the *Summa philosophica*) is still unpublished. It is probably with the 'ontological place' of the ideas in the Word that Wyclif's partisans put into his mouth the adage, *Qui negat ideas, negat Filium Dei*. The adage is almost always attributed to Augustine and it was certainly coined before the time of Wyclif: it was known by John of Paris, *In I Sent.*, q. 119; by Master Eckhart, *Expos. Gen.*, I, 5; Thomas Aquinas, *De ver.*, q. 3, a. 1, sed contra; Albert the Great, *In II Sent.*, d. 35, a. 7, n. 4; and William of Auxere, *S. aur.*, II, tr. I, c. 1. The formalist ontology of Francis Meyronnes presents an analogous case. Here the being of essence (the quiddity, the idea) has a separate formal being, which can become concrete 'by chance'. Francis asserts that whoever denies the existence of quiddities must deny the existence of everything (*qui negat quidditates habet omnia negare*), *Quodl.*, q. 8.

17 Nicholas of Autrecourt provides a third example, but sadly only a sketch of it, preserved on the last page of his unfinished *Exigit ordo*, is known.

18 For a general account, see Vignaux [18.78] 265–78, cited here.

19 Cf. Conti [18.2] 226–7, 309–17. The main figures are John Sharp (Rector in 1403), Robert Alyngton (d. 1398), William Milverley, John Tarteys, Roger Whelpdale (d. 1423), several of whose works have been edited by Conti, and William Penbygull (d. 1420). See also Hudson and Wilks, *From Ockham to Wyclif*.

20 See Spunar [18.26], s.v., and Bartos and Spunar [18.16]. On Znaim, see also Nuchelmans [18.70].

21 On the history of the school of Buridan, see Michael [18.68] 321–89.

22 *Chartularium Universitatis Parisiensis*, II, n. 1042. Art. 1: 'nulli magistri, baccalari vel scolares . . . audeant aliquam propositionem famosam illius actoris cuius librum legunt dicere simpliciter esse falsam, vel falsam de virtute sermonis . . . ; sed vel concedant eam, vel sensum verum dividant a sensu falso . . . ; *cum sermones sint recipiendi secundum materiam subiectam*'; art. 3: 'nullus dicat quod nulla propositio sit distinguenda'; art. 4: 'nullus dicat propositionem nullam esse concedendam, si non sit vera in eius sensu proprio'; 'Magis igitur oportet in affirmando vel negando sermones ad materiam subiectam attendere, quam ad proprietatem sermonis'; art. 6: 'nullus asserat absque distinctione vel expositione, quod Socrates et Plato, vel Deus et creatura nihil sunt'. The distinction between suppositions had been known and followed for a long time. What was new in the 1340 statute was the distinction in the sense of propositions according to their 'matter'. Article 1 refers to the *Nicomachean Ethics*, II, 2, 1104a 3, but the problem is in fact considered in Book I, c. 3. For the detailed interpretation of this text, see Kaluza [18.57] 223–55.

23 Full edition in C. Du Plessis D'Argentré, *Collectio judiciorum*, I–2, Paris, 1728, p. 116a, concl. 1; 116b, concl. 2; 117a, concl. 3; 124a, concl. 4; 125a, concl. 5; 128b, concl. 6.

24 A. Combes, *Gerson commentateur dionysien*, pp. 305–11; 568–687; Kaluza [18.55] 50–60; de Libera [18.65]. Gerson's criticisms of John of Ripa some-

times follow those of Peter d'Ailly. The formal distinction is also called a distinction *ex natura rei sed non realis*, so as to differentiate it from a distinction *ex natura rei*, which is not formal. Scotists made either three distinctions (*rationis, formalis, realis*), or five (adding a *distinctio modalis* and a *distinctio essentialis*), or eight (adding distinctions: *ex natura rei, se totis subiectiva* and *se totis obiectiva*). A formal distinction pertains between two formalities, that is to say two quiddities or formal reasons, one of which does not belong to the essence of the other and each of which is known by a distinct act of the thought – for instance, all the quiddities, definable or indefinable, which are most specific (humanity), subalternate (animality), most general (quantity) and transcendent (entity). These formalities exist before they are known by the human intellect: *ante omnem operationem intellectus*. It is for precisely this realism that Gerson criticizes the Scotists.

25   A. Combes, p. 644ff.

 BIBLIOGRAPHY

Original Language Editions

18.1   Jean Gerson, *Oeuvres complètes*, 10 vols, ed. P. Glorieux, Paris, Tournai, Rome, New York, Desclée & Cie, 1960–73.

18.2   Johannes Sharpe, *Quaestio super universalia*, ed. A. D. Conti, Florence, Olschki, 1990.

18.3   John Wyclif, *Tractatus de universalibus*, ed. I. J. Mueller, Oxford, Oxford University Press, 1985.

18.4   John Wyclif, *Summa de ente, Libri primi tractatus primus et secundus*, ed. S. H. Thompson, Oxford, 1930.

18.5   John Wyclif, *Trialogus*, ed. G. Lechler, Oxford, 1869.

18.6   John Wyclif, *Tractatus de Trinitate*, ed. A. duPont Breck, Boulder, Colo., University of Colorado Press, 1962.

18.7   Paul of Venice *Summa philosophiae naturalis*, Venice, 1503; repr. Hildesheim and New York, G. Olms, 1974.

18.8   —— *Super primum Sententiarum Johannis de Ripa Lecturae abbreviatio. Prologus*, ed. F. Ruello, Florence, Olschki, 1980.

18.9   Peter d'Ailly *Tractatus contra Johannem de Monzon (Apologia universitatis)*, in C. Du Plessis D'Argentré, *Collectio iudiciorum*, Paris, 1728, I, pars 2, pp. 71–135.

18.10 Richard Brinkley's *Theory of Sentential Reference: 'De significato propositionis' from Part V of his Summa nova de logica*, ed. M. J. Fitzgerald, Leiden, E. J. Brill, 1987.

18.11 (Richard Brinkley), Kaluza, Z. 'L'Oeuvre théologique de Richard Brinkley, O.F.M.', *Archives d'histoire doctrinale et littéraire du Moyen Age*, 56 (1990): 169–273.

18.12 Thomas Buckingham, *De contingentia futurorum*, in B. de la Torre *Thomas Buckingham and the Contingency of Futures*, Notre Dame, Ind., University of Notre Dame, 1987.

18.13 Thomas Buckingham, *De contingentia futurorum*, in J.-F. Genest, *Prédéstination et liberté créée à Oxford au XIVe siècle: Buckingham contra Bradwardine*, Paris, Vrin, 1992.

English Translations

18.14 John Wyclif, *On Universals (Tractatus de universalibus)*, Text translated by A. Kenny, with Introduction by P. V. Spade, Oxford, Oxford University Press, 1985.

18.15 (John Wyclif), *Selections from English Wycliffite Writings*, ed. A. Hudson, Cambridge, 1978.
       Richard Brinkley *De significato propositionis* [18.10] contains an English translation.

Bibliographies and Manuscript Catalogues

18.16 Bartoš, F. and Spunar, P. *Soupis pramenů k literárni činnosti M. Jana Husa a M. Jeronýma Pražskeho*, Prague, 1965. (A new edition is planned at Wrocław, Ossolineum, in Studia Copernicana.)

18.17 Gabriel, A. L. *Summary Bibliography of the History of the Universities of Great Britain and Ireland up to 1800 covering publications between 1900 and 1968*, Notre Dame, Ind., 1974.

18.18 Guenée, S., *Bibliographie de l'histoire des universités françaises des origines à la Révolution*, I: Paris, 1981; II: Paris, 1978.

18.19 Hoenen, M. J. F. M. 'Einige Notizen über die Handschriften und Drucke des Sentenzenkommentars von Marsilius von Inghen', *Recherches de théologie ancienne et médiévale* 56 (1989): 117–63.

18.20 —— 'Marsilius von Inghen, bibliographie', *Bulletin de philosophie médiévale* 31 (1989): 150–67.

18.21 Lohr, C. H. *Commentateurs d'Aristote au Moyen-Âge latin. Bibliographie de la littérature secondaire récente*, Fribourg, Switzerland, Editions Universitaires; (Vestigia 2) Paris, Editions du Cerf, 1988.

18.22 —— Medieval Latin Aristotle commentaries', *Traditio* 23 (1967): 313–413; 24 (1968): 149–245; 26 (1970): 135–216; 27 (1971): 251–351; 28 (1972): 281–396; 29 (1973): 93–197; 30 (1974): 119–44; *Bulletin de philosophie médiévale* 14 (1972): 116–26; 15 (1973): 131–6.

18.23 Markowski, M. 'Katatog dziel Marsyliusza z Inghen z ewidencją rękopisów', *Studia Mediewistyczne* 25, 2 (1988): 39–132.

18.24 Rothschild, J.-P. *Bibliographie annuelle du Moyen Âge tardif, auteurs et textes latins, vers 1250–1500*, rassemblée à la section latine de l'IRHT (CNRS), I–VI, Turnhout, Brepols, 1991–1996.

18.25 Schmitt, C. B. *A Critical Survey and Bibliography of Studies on Renaissance Aristotelianism, 1958–1969*, Padua, 1971.

18.26 Spunar, P. *Repertorium auctorum Bohemorum provectum idearum post Universitatem Pragensem conditam illustrans*, I (Studia Copernicana 25), Wrocław-Varsovie-Cracow, Ossolineum, 1985.

18.27   Stegmüller, F. *Repertorium commentariorum in Sententias Petri Lombardi*, Würzburg, 1947.

18.28   Thomson, W. R. *The Latin Writings of John Wyclif* (Subsidia mediaevalia 14), Toronto, Pontifical Institute of Mediaeval Studies, 1983.

Studies

18.29   *Aristotelismo padovano e filosofia aristotelica*, in *Atti del XII Congresso Internazionale di Filosofia*, vol. 9, Florence, 1960.

18.30   Ashworth, E. J. *La sémantique du XIVe siècle vue à travers cinq traités oxoniens sur les Obligationes* (Cahiers d'épistémologie, no. 8915), Montreal, University of Montreal, 1989.

18.31   *L'Averroismo in Italia*, in *Atti dei Convegni Lincei* 40, Rome, 1979

18.32   Bender, J. 'Nicholas Aston: a study in Oxford thought after the Black Death', Ph. D. dissertation, University of Wisconsin, Madison, 1979.

18.33   Bernstein, A. E. *Pierre d'Ailly and the Blanchard Affair*, Leiden, 1978.

18.34   Bianchi, L. (ed.) *Filosofia e teologia nel Trecento*, Studi in ricordo di Eugenio Randi, Louvain, Brepols, 1994.

18.35   Biard, J. (ed.) *Itinéraires d'Albert de Saxe: Paris-Vienne au XIVe siècle*, Paris, Vrin, 1991.

18.36   Catto, J. I. and Evans, R. (eds) *The History of the University of Oxford*, vol. II, *Late Mediaeval Oxford*, Oxford, Oxford University Press, 1992.

18.37   Catto, J. I. 'Wyclif and Wyclifism at Oxford 1356–1430', in [18.37] 175–261.

18.38   Conti, A. D. *Esistenza e verità. Forme e strutture del reale in Paolo Veneto e nel pensiero filosofico del tardo Medioevo*, Rome, 1996.

18.39   Courtenay, W. J. *Schools and Scholars in Fourteenth-century England*, Princeton, NJ, Princeton University Press, 1987.

18.40   Federici Vescovini, G. 'Discorso logico e discorso teologico secondo Biagio Pelacani da Parma', *Archives d'histoire doctrinale et littéraire du Moyen Âge* 45 (1978): 33–44.

18.41   —— *Astrologia e scienza: La crisi dell'aristotelismo sul cadere del Trecento e Biagio Pelacani da Parma*, Florence, Nuova edizioni E. Vallecchi, 1979.

18.42   Gabriel, A. L. ' "Via antiqua" and "via moderna" and the migration of Paris students and masters to the German universities in the fifteenth century', *Miscellanea Mediaevalia* 9 (1974): 439–83.

18.43   Gál, G. and Wood, R. 'Richard Brinkley and his *Summa logicae*', *Franciscan Studies* 40 (1980): 59–101.

18.44   Garin, E. 'Le traduzioni umanistiche di Aristotele nel secolo XV', *Atti e memorie dell'Accademia Fiorentina di scienze morali 'La Colombaria'* 2 (1947–50): 55–104.

18.45   —— *L'età nuova: Ricerche di storia della cultura dal XII al XVI secolo*, Naples, 1961.

18.46   —— *Italian Humanism: Philosophy and Civic Life in the Renaissance*, trans. P. Muntz, Oxford, Blackwell Publishers, 1965.

18.47   —— *Science and Civic Life in the Italian Renaissance*, Doubleday, 1969.

18.48 —— *Aristotelismo veneto e scienza moderna*, Padua, 1981.

18.49 Guenée, B. *Entre l'Eglise et l'Etat: Quatre vies de prélats français à la fin du Moyen Age*, Paris, Gallimard, 1987.

18.50 Hoenen, M. J. F. M. *Marsilius of Inghen: Divine Knowledge in Late Medieval Thought*, Leiden, New York and Cologne, 1993.

18.51 Hoenen, M. J. F. M. and Libera, A. de (eds) *Albertus Magnus und der Albertismus. Deutsche philosophische Kultur des Mittelalters*, Leiden, New York and Cologne, 1995.

18.52 Hoenen, M. J. F. M., Schneider, J. H. J. and Wieland, G. (eds) *Philosophy and Learning in the Middle Ages*, Leiden, New York and Cologne, E. J. Brill, 1995.

18.53 Hudson, A. and Wilks, M. (eds) *From Ockham to Wyclif* (Studies in Church History, Subsidia 5), Oxford, Blackwell Publishers, 1987.

18.54 Kaluza, Z. 'L'Oeuvre théologique de Nicolas Aston', *Archives d'histoire doctrinale et littéraire du Moyen Age* 45 (1978): 45–82.

18.55 —— *Les querelles doctrinales à Paris: Nominalistes et réalistes aux confins du XIVe et du XVe siècles* (Quodlibet 2), Bergamo, Lubrina, 1988.

18.56 —— 'Jérôme de Prague et le *Timée* de Platon', *Archives d'histoire doctrinale et littéraire du Moyen Âge* 61 (1994): 57–104.

18.57 —— 'Les sciences et leurs langages. Note sur le statut du 29 décembre 1340 et le prétendu statut perdu contre Ockham', in Bianchi [18.34] 197–258.

18.58 —— 'Les débuts de l'albertisme tardif (Paris et Cologne)', in Hoenen and de Libera, [18.51] 207–95.

18.59 Kenny, A. *Wyclif*, Oxford, Oxford University Press, 1988.

18.60 Kristeller, P. O. *Studies in Renaissance Thought and Letters*, Rome, 1956.

18.61 —— *Renaissance Thought: the Classic, Scholastic, and Humanist Strains*, New York, 1961.

18.62 —— *Le thomisme et la pensée italienne de la Renaissance*, Institut d'Etudes médiévales, Montreal and Paris, Vrin, 1967.

18.63 —— *Medieval Aspects of Renaissance Learning*, Durham, NC, 1974.

18.64 —— *Renaissance Thought and its Sources*, New York, 1979.

18.65 Libera, A. de '*Ex uno non fit nisi unum*: La *Lettre sur le Principe de l'univers* et les condamnations parisiennes de 1277', dans *Historia philosophiae medii aevi* (Festschrift für K. Flasch, hrsg. von B. Mojsisch and O. Pluta), Amsterdam, B. R. Grüner, 1991, I, pp. 543–60.

18.66 —— *La Querelle des universaux: de Platon à la fin du Moyen Âge*, Paris, 1996.

18.67 Maierù, A. (ed.) *English Logic in Italy in the 14th and 15th Centuries* (History of Logic I), Naples, Bibliopolis, 1982.

18.68 Michael, B. *Johannes Buridan: Studien zu seinem Leben, seinen Werken und zur Rezeption seiner Theorien im Europa des späten Mittelalters*, Inaugural-Dissertation, 2 vols, Berlin, Freie Universität, 1985.

18.69 Murdoch, J. 'Subtilitates Anglicanae in fourteenth-century Paris: John of Mirecourt and Peter of Ceffons', *Annals of the New York Academy of Science* 314 (1978): 51–86.

18.70 Nuchelmans, G. 'Stanislaus of Znaim (d. 1414) on truth and falsity', in *Mediaeval Semantics and Metaphysics*, Studies dedicated to L. M. de Rijk, edited by R. P. Bos (Artistarium, Supplementa II), Nijmegen, Ingenium Publishers, 1985, pp. 313–38.

18.71   Riva, F. *Tommaso Claxton e l'analogia di proporzionalità*, Milan, 1989.
18.72   Robson, J. A. *Wyclif and the Oxford Schools: the Relation of the 'Summa de ente' to Scholastic Debates at Oxford in the Later Fourteenth Century*, Cambridge, Cambridge University Press, 1961.
18.73   Schmitt, C. B. *Aristotle and the Renaissance*, Cambridge, Mass. and London, Harvard University Press, 1983.
18.74   —— *La tradizione aristotelica: fra Italia e Inghilterra*, Naples, Bibliopolis, 1985.
18.75   Tabarroni, A. 'Nuovi testi di logica e di teologia in un codice palermitano', in Bianchi [18.34] 337–66.
18.76   Tewes, G.-R. *Die Bursen der Kölner Artisten-Fakultät bis zur Mitte des 16. Jahrhunderts*, Cologne, Weimar and Vienna, 1993.
18.77   Vasoli, C. *La dialettica e la retorica dell'Umanesimo. 'Invenzione' e 'Metodo' nella cultura del XV e XVI secolo*, Milan, Feltrinelli, 1968.
18.78   Vignaux, P. *De Saint Anselm à Luther*, Paris, Vrin, 1976.
18.79   Wlodek, S. 'Der Begriff des Seins bei Thomas Netter von Walden', *Salzburger Jahrbuch für Philosophie* 26–7 (1981–2): 103–16.

CHAPTER 19

Suárez (and later scholasticism)

Jorge Gracia

❧❦❧

❧ THE SILVER AGE OF SCHOLASTICISM ❧

The golden age of scholasticism covered a period of roughly one hundred years, from around 1250 to 1350. There were important scholastic developments before 1250 and after 1350, but it is generally thought that they cannot compare with the achievements of the years in between. The sheer number of productive authors during this period and the extraordinary originality and intellectual rigour of their thought makes this one of the periods of highest achievement in the history of ideas. The silver age of scholasticism came roughly one hundred and seventy-five years later and also lasted for a period of about one hundred years, from about 1525 to 1625. Again, there was an extra-ordinary level of intellectual productivity in terms of both quantity and quality, but as a whole the silver age cannot rival the golden age either philosophically or historically. First, philosophically, because it depended to a great extent on the achievements of the earlier period; thus the silver age cannot be regarded as original as the golden age. Second, historically, because the philosophy that followed it largely moved in a different direction; while many of the thinkers who came after the golden age looked back on it for inspiration, most thinkers who followed the silver age looked away from it, rejecting much that characterized it.[1]

There are, however, remarkable similarities between the golden and silver ages. Both ages were guided by the scholastic aim of under-standing the Christian faith. They exerted considerable effort in the defence of that faith and of orthodox doctrine against actual or perceived threats. Scholastics of both ages were heavily Aristotelian, giving 'the Philosopher' a prominent place in matters philosophical, but relying on authoritative patristic and scriptural sources for their theological doctrines. Both ages followed or were concurrent with periods of translation during which newly discovered works written in other languages were rendered into Latin. The centre of activity in both cases was the university, and the literary forms of expression used were largely a result of curricular activity. Finally, most scholastics were members of religious orders and, thus, had a strong commitment to the goals of those orders.

In spite of these points of similarity, there are profound differences between the two periods. Although both periods had the same aim of understanding the Christian faith, the overall theological emphasis that inspired most activities of the earlier scholastics had decreased in the sixteenth century. In theory and in some aspects of practice, philosophy remained the servant of theology, but a progressive independence of reason, as demonstrated by its increasing use apart from faith, developed in the later period. The traditional scholastic format of argument, in which both theologically authoritative sources and arguments based on reason were given in support of the positions to be defended, ceased to be the norm in non-theological works, and a greater emphasis was put upon reason. Moreover, the political structure and ideological situation of Europe during the silver age – and, in particular, the discovery of the New World – raised new important philosophical and legal issues of a secular nature that encouraged speculation independent of theology. For example, matters that had to do with the rights of conquered peoples produced a body of literature largely purged of theological considerations. There were, of course, many issues discussed by masters of arts and others in the earlier period that had nothing or little to do with theology, and in the discussion of which theological authorities were largely ignored. But the number of these secular issues increased substantially in the later period.

With respect to the apologetic spirit of both periods, again there are substantial differences. In the golden age the defence of Christian doctrine was primarily directed against infidels, as illustrated by Thomas's *Summa contra Gentiles*, or against those who were thought to have accepted too much of the thought of pagan philosophers, as is evident from the list of doctrines officially condemned in Paris in 1277. Yet there was no overall sense of urgency in the Church, nor was there a unified and institutional effort to deal with the challenges to orthodoxy. During the silver age, however, the situation was different. The challenges to the Church came from two different sources within the Christian community and one of them had considerable political power. The first source was humanism. The discovery of new literary, philosophical and artistic works from the ancient world had given rise not only to a renewed interest in pagan ideas, but to a change of attitude in the intellectual community that seemed to many to pose a threat to the integrity of the Christian faith. The second source was the Reformation, a movement of rebellion against institutionalized Christianity that gained considerable political support. As a result, a sense of urgency among members of the hierarchy and an organized Church-wide effort to meet these challenges developed, culminating in the Council of Trent (1545–63). There was, therefore, much apologetic literature written during this time, and its tone appears more urgent and compelling than that produced in the golden age. Medieval scholastics were fighting ideas, but scholastics from the silver age were fighting not only ideas, but also worldly power.

There is, as noted, remarkable agreement in the sources of both periods, with the later period depending heavily on the first as well. By the sixteenth century, scholasticism had become parcelled out into three traditions according to the author followed by each of them: Thomism, Scotism and Ockhamism. Moreover, these traditions had become identified with certain religious orders that looked upon the founders of these traditions with proprietary interests. For example, Dominicans were generally Thomistic, while Franciscans tended to follow Scotus or Ockham. This sort of ideological alignment had already begun in the thirteenth century, but it was not as rigid as it eventually became during the silver age. Moreover, the influence of Thomas Aquinas became increasingly pervasive in the silver age, particularly in the Iberian peninsula, a fact which has led some scholars to speak of a school of Spanish Thomism.

The heavy use of Aristotelian and medieval scholastic sources by scholastics of the silver age points to another interesting difference between the silver age and the golden age. While both ages coincided with or followed periods of intense translation activity, in the golden age the resulting translations helped shape the thought of the period and were the immediate source of much of that thought.[2] By contrast, scholastics of the silver age largely ignored the new translations. There may be many reasons for this relative neglect, but surely one of them was the heavily Aristotelian character of scholasticism, which must have found distasteful the overwhelmingly Platonic material being translated.

The activity in both periods was concentrated in the university, but again there is an important difference. In the golden age, Paris was the unchallenged centre of both scholasticism and the intellectual life of Europe; it was the 'new Athens'. There were other important universities such as Oxford, Cambridge, Bologna and Naples, but none rivalled Paris. Moreover, an intellectual axis developed along a line which went from Rome to Oxford, passing through Paris. By contrast, the scholasticism of the silver age was most concentrated in the universities of the Iberian peninsula: Coimbra, Alcalá, and, above all, Salamanca. There were significant places of learning in Italy too, but they were much less influential than the Iberian universities. Intellectual communication now extended from Coimbra, through Salamanca, and ultimately to Rome. These are two other important points to note. First, as in the earlier period, these strongholds of silver-age scholasticism were not alone in promoting great intellectual ferment. Paris, Oxford and Cambridge, for example, were also important, and there was considerable work done in the Netherlands and Germany. Second, these centres of silver-age scholasticism did not hold a monopoly on the intellectual life of Europe. By the sixteenth century scholasticism had become a regional, albeit powerful intellectual force – perhaps the most powerful at the time – but it had ceased to be the only intellectual force in Europe, as it had been during the golden age.

The scholastic literary genres favoured in the golden age, namely, the *summa*, the *quaestio*, and the commentary, were also used in the silver age, but with an important new development in this later period. Iberian scholastics, particularly Fonseca and Suárez, helped develop a new genre that became the standard form of expression among scholastics after the sixteenth century: the systematic and comprehensive treatise. There are plenty of examples of systematic and comprehensive treatises produced in the Middle Ages. Indeed, medieval *summae* are both systematic and comprehensive. But there are some important differences between medieval *summae* and the treatises produced during the silver age and thereafter. First, medieval *summae* tended to follow the established arrangement of the discourse in whatever subject-matter they explored. These patterns were derived from textual traditions going back to original paradigmatic works or particular doctrines. Thus, for example, the pattern of theological *summae* generally reflected an order of progression from God to creatures and back to God, the Neoplatonic *exitus–reditus* theme.

Second, the new type of literature differed from the medieval *summae* in that it abandoned the *quaestio* format, which had been used very frequently by earlier scholastics, in favour of an unbroken exposition of topics. Finally, these treatises were put together and organized into complete courses (*cursus*) of study that extended beyond particular disciplines, and included logic, natural philosophy and other philosophical disciplines. Sometimes these 'courses' were the result of co-operative efforts, as was the case with the well-known *Cursus Conimbricensis*, the main author of which was Fonseca. At other times, they were the result of a single author's effort (or that of his editors), as was the case with John of St Thomas's *Cursus philosophicus*.

The didactic advantages of the new genre should be obvious, for it organized materials in a continuous, comprehensive and logical way which facilitated teaching and made these works ideal textbooks. On the other hand, it introduced an element of dogmatism that was lacking in most of the earlier literature, for it veered toward the expository and away from the polemical, losing the sense of the controversial character of the topics discussed. This was not the case with all the philosophical treatises of the period; some still presented the *status questionis* of the issues they discussed in a polemical or quasi-polemical manner, but it certainly applied to a considerable portion of the philosophical literature produced at the time. Moreover, the adoption of the systematic and comprehensive format contributed to the neglect of the commentary and, therefore, the further estrangement of scholasticism from humanism. Primary sources were read in conjunction with these secondary sources, resulting in the neglect of the original authors and the frequent misunderstanding of their views (cf. [19.40] 835–7).

Finally, although the most prominent members of both periods belonged to religious orders, the leading order during the silver age was the Society of Jesus, which had been founded by Ignacio de Loyola in 1540 in response, first, to the challenges that the Reformation posed to the Catholic Church and, second, to the need to convert the heathen. The mission of the Jesuit order, then, was from the start an apologetic one; and the order was organized like an army – a clear indication of its aim. By contrast, the Franciscan and Dominican orders, which had dominated the golden age, had less defined and militant missions. The aim of the Franciscans was one of service, and the aim of the Dominicans was instruction through preaching. The latter was in part a response to the need to defend the faith against infidels and heretics – Domingo de Guzmán was a Spaniard and was quite aware of the needs of a frontier church – but the Dominican order was never intended to be an army for the Church.

Understanding the similarities and differences between the golden and silver ages of scholasticism should help us understand Suárez, for he eminently displayed most of the characteristics of the scholasticism of the silver age we have discussed. He pursued the medieval aim of understanding faith, but granted philosophy a sphere of operation separate from and largely independent of theology. As a theologian, he was at the forefront of the defence of Catholic doctrine and the Catholic Church against the attacks of the Reformation. He was aware of the rigid conceptual traditions associated with the medieval religious orders and moved easily within their frameworks, although he frequently tried to break down the barriers among them. His thought was strongly Aristotelian, ignoring to a great extent the recently produced translations of non-Aristotelian works, but he showed extensive and firsthand acquaintance with traditional Christian sources. Suárez spent his professional life almost entirely within the confines of the leading Iberian universities of the period. He never taught at Paris, and most of his exchanges took place with either Iberian or Italian authors. He was the first to apply a systematic approach to metaphysics, and finally, as a member of the Jesuit order, Suárez displayed some of the combative traits associated with that order in several of his more polemical works. In short, it would be hard to find among scholastics of his time one that displayed more clearly the traits that characterized the silver age.

❧ SUÁREZ'S LIFE, WORKS, AND INFLUENCE ❧

Suárez was born in Granada, Spain, on 5 January 1548, at the height of Spanish imperial power. Under Isabella of Castile and Ferdinand of Aragon, known as *los Reyes Católicos* (the Catholic Kings), a large part of the Iberian peninsula had become unified (1479) and power consolidated after the final defeat of the Moors at Granada (1492). Also in 1492 America was discovered, opening up unheard-of resources to the newly united kingdom. In a matter of fifty years, Spain became the pre-eminent political and economic power in Europe. As a result, artists and intellectuals flocked to Madrid, stimulating the development of arts and letters. Indeed, the period that goes roughly from 1500 to 1650 is generally known as the *Siglo de Oro* of Spanish letters because of the abundance and extraordinary quality of the literature produced. Spain became an intellectual leader in Europe and the undisputed leader of the Counter-Reformation. The Spanish mystics of the time, Teresa of Avila, Juan de la Cruz and Fray Luis de León, were among the most renowned anywhere. Antonio de Nebrija composed the first grammar of any romance language in 1492. The music of Victoria, Cabezón and other Spanish composers was played all over Europe. The theatre flourished under the pens of Lope de Vega and Calderón de la Barca. The novel reached new heights in the work of Cervantes. And Spanish painting achieved international acclaim with Ribera, Zurbarán and Velázquez.

Philosophy, of course, could not be left behind, and so we find a score of Iberian figures of high rank. Among the most celebrated are Juan Luis Vives (1492–1540), Francisco de Vitoria (1492/3–1546), Domingo de Soto (1494–1560), Alonso de Castro (1495–1558), Melchior Cano (1509–60), Pedro Fonseca (1528–99), Domingo Bañez (1528–1604), Francisco Toletus (1532–96), Luis de Molina (1535–1600), Juan de Mariana (1536–1624), Gabriel Vázquez (1549–1604) and Juan de Santo Tomás (1589–1644). The greatest of the philosophers, however, is Francisco Suárez (1548–1617). Indeed, his work surpasses in depth, originality and comprehensiveness that of any other of these, and his influence, both in modern philosophy and in subsequent scholastic thought, has been substantial.

Suárez decided early in life that he would pursue an ecclesiastical career. Accordingly, he went to Salamanca to study canon law. While engaged in his studies there, he requested admission into the Society of Jesus. At first he was refused admission for reasons of health and what was perceived as a lack of proper intellectual capacity. Insistence paid off, however, and he was allowed to join the order in 1564. After completing his studies, he began a teaching career that would last for over fifty years, taking him to some of the most renowned institutions of his time: Segovia, Valladolid, Rome, Alcalá, Salamanca and Coimbra. Suárez died in Lisbon, at the age of 70, on 25 September 1617.

Suárez did not publish early in his life. His first work, *De incarnatione verbi*, appeared in 1590 when he was 42. After this initial publication, however, a steady stream of works followed. Suárez's contributions are important in three areas in particular: philosophy, law and theology. From a philosophical standpoint his most important works are *De anima* (*On the Soul*, 1621), which contains his psychology, epistemology and philosophy of mind; *De gratia* (*On Grace*, 1619–51), which deals with issues of philosophical theology involving free will and determinism; and the monumental *Disputationes metaphysicae* (*Metaphysical Disputations*, 1597). The last is undoubtedly one of the great works of Western philosophy: the first systematic and comprehensive treatise on metaphysics composed in the West that is not a commentary on Aristotle's *Metaphysics*. Furthermore, it summarizes and evaluates medieval metaphysical thought and remains the most complete exposition of Aristotelian metaphysics ever produced.

De legibus (1612) is Suárez's most important work dealing with legal and political theory. In it he explores in detail the nature of law and of civil society. His views on *ius gentium* make him, together with Vitoria and other Spanish authors of the time, a founder of international law.

Suárez's contributions to theology are contained in his numerous books on the subject. He touched upon almost every aspect of sacred doctrine, from the Trinity to questions pertaining to the spiritual life. This has made his theological writings a standard source of Catholic theology. Moreover, his role in helping to shape the response of the Catholic Counter-Reformation to the rise of Protestantism guarantees him a place in history.

Suárez's position in the history of philosophy is frequently disputed. Some historians locate him firmly in the medieval tradition, claiming that he should be seen as perhaps the last world-class figure of that tradition, before modern philosophy changed the philosophical direction of the West. Others, however, see Suárez as providing the foundation for some of the views that came to form the core of subsequent developments, and thus as a precursor of modern philosophy.

There are bases for defending both of these interpretations. Indeed, if one looks at Suárez carefully, it becomes evident that he is both the last major medieval theologian and the first major modern philosopher. This can be best illustrated, perhaps, with reference to the stated intention and method of the *Disputationes metaphysicae*.

With respect to the intention of the work, we need to look no further than the Preface to see that Suárez follows the theological emphasis of the Middle Ages. His purpose is the same as that expressed by the Anselmian saying: *Fides quaerens intellectum* (Faith seeking understanding). Suárez tells us, first, that he deals with metaphysics precisely because his aim is theological, for the good theologian will set down the foundations of metaphysics before he goes on to theology. Accordingly, he postponed his theological commentaries on Aquinas until after he had finished the *Disputationes* in order to provide a proper foundation for theology. Moreover, like Aquinas and other medieval theologians before him, Suárez points out that he never loses sight of Christian doctrine while he philosophizes and, indeed, that he intends his philosophy to be both Christian and an instrument of theology. This end is what guides not only the way he deals with the issues he discusses, but also the very opinions and views he presents, leading him to favour those that appear to him more useful for piety and revealed doctrine. Finally, in strict medieval fashion, he closes the Preface by hoping that the work will lead to God's greater glory and be of use to the Catholic Church.

From this, it appears quite conclusively that Suárez's aim in the *Disputationes metaphysicae* is theological rather than philosophical, and that he fits squarely within the main medieval scholastic view in which philosophy is seen as a handmaiden of theology. However, in the very Preface to which reference has been made there are indications of a different attitude at play as well. First, Suárez speaks of giving back to metaphysics the place and position that rightly belongs to it, and that place and position are interpreted as being separate from and anterior to theology. Second, he states that his role as author of the *Disputationes* is not that of the theologian, but of the philosopher. And, third, he apologizes for the occasional digressions into theological matters found in the work, even though he does not discuss theological issues in depth, since that would certainly be beyond the bounds of the subject-matter of the book. Indeed, even a superficial perusal of the *Disputationes* reveals that, when theological topics come up, Suárez generally suggests to the reader that they do not pertain to the subject-matter and should be discussed, or are, in fact, discussed, elsewhere.

All this indicates Suárez's rigorous view of the distinction between metaphysics and theology and of his role as philosopher and theologian. The fact that he calls himself a philosopher, that in philosophy he avoids arguments based on faith, and that he apologizes for dealing, even incidentally, with theological matters in a work of philosophy should be sufficient to make the point. Although many of the masters who taught liberal arts in the Middle Ages were not theologians and taught subjects independently of theology, the most famous scholastics of the age considered themselves theologians and their philosophical views were generally presented within theological works. Moreover, even though many scholastics distinguished between theology and philosophy, none of them would have apologized for the introduction of theological matter in a philosophical context, and most of them used both faith and reason to argue for both philosophical and theological views. But such a procedure is abandoned in Suárez's *Disputationes*.[3] Occasionally, he does bring up a theological point, but in such cases the aim is to show the reader how to apply metaphysical principles to theology rather than to use theology to prove philosophy. This secular emphasis in metaphysics both sets Suárez apart from his medieval predecessors and situates him at the beginning of the modern tradition.

Another point that sets him apart from medieval scholasticism is the very structure and procedure he follows in the *Disputationes*. The work does not adopt the standard medieval scholastic literary genres used in works of metaphysics. Medieval authors generally presented their metaphysical views in commentaries on Aristotle, which were sometimes internally organized in *quaestiones*; or they presented them in the course of theological works, such as theological *summae* or commentaries on the *Sentences* of Peter Lombard. Occasionally, short didactic or polemical tracts (*opuscula*) such as Thomas's *De ente et essentia* or *De unitate intellectus contra Averroistas* were also composed. But no systematic and comprehensive metaphysical treatises were produced. Suárez, however, adopted precisely this format. Nor did he follow the popular custom of structuring works as *quaestiones* reflecting current controversies and polemics. Rather, he adopted a logical procedure in which metaphysical issues are discussed according to their relation to overall topics. Suárez is the first to apply this procedure to metaphysics. His originality in this is what distinguishes him from his predecessors and points to modern philosophy.

In short, Suárez cannot be considered exclusively a medieval scholastic or a modern philosopher. He has to be seen in context, as restating the past and anticipating the future. His overall aims and views go back to the Middle Ages, but some of his procedures point toward the modern period. He should be seen as both a medieval scholastic and a modern philosopher.

Before concluding this section I should say something about Suárez's influence on the Catholic tradition, modern thought and Latin American scholasticism. Along with Augustine, Aquinas and other figures of similar stature, Suárez is one of the most influential figures in Catholicism. He played a major role in the response to the growing challenge of Protestantism and the secularizing impact of humanism. Many of his theological ideas were considered highly original at the time and have become part of the common stock of Catholic theology. His analogical understanding of the doctrine of the Trinity, his position concerning the motivation for the Incarnation, and his views on morality have all played important roles in Catholic teaching. But perhaps it is his doctrine of the relation between divine grace, merit and human freedom that has most firmly established his influence and most evidently contrasts him with the Protestant ideas of the time.

Suárez's influence, however, is not confined to the Catholic tradition. Most early modern philosophers learned metaphysics from his *Disputationes*, and many of their ideas can be traced to that work. Among those most clearly influenced by Suárez are Jungius, Descartes, Leibniz, Spinoza, Wolff, Berkeley, Schopenhauer and Vico, but echoes of his language and views can be seen in many others, including Locke.[4] Indeed, Suárez is often blamed for contributing to the development of the mentalistic metaphysics characteristic of modern philosophy. Whether this attribution is correct is a matter of debate, but what is clear is that his terminology seeped into early modern philosophy and became a part of the common philosophical way of speaking. In addition to his metaphysics, moreover, his legal and political views had considerable impact on modern legal theorists such as Holdsworth and Grotius. Indeed, some consider Suárez's thought in these areas to be as influential and valuable as, if not more so than, his metaphysical views.

Finally, there is Suárez's impact on Latin American thought. The New World was discovered in 1492, and by the middle of the next century, schools and universities teaching scholastic thought were already functioning in Mexico and elsewhere. Thus, by the time Suárez's *Disputationes metaphysicae* was published in 1597, there was a ready audience available for them. The result was to be expected: his metaphysical and theological views established themselves as alternatives to the already popular views of Aquinas, Scotus and Ockham.

◆◆ SUÁREZ'S METAPHYSICS ◆◆

The core of Suárez's philosophical, theological and legal thought is his metaphysics. The rest of this essay will therefore be devoted to the

461

exploration of two key elements of Suárez's metaphysical thought, which illustrate both the transitional role it played between medieval scholasticism and modern philosophy and the innovation within traditional parameters that is so characteristic of it. These elements are his conception of metaphysics and the doctrine of the transcendentals.

Suárez's Conception of Metaphysics

Most conceptions of metaphysics fall into one of two categories: views that regard metaphysics as concerned with the real as opposed to the mental, and views that conceive it as concerned with the mental rather than the real. Aristotle (*Metaphysics* 1, 1–3) and his medieval commentators are usually identified as proponents of the first view. Metaphysics in this context is conceived as a science not very different from other sciences, except for some peculiarities of the object it studies and the method it employs. Like other sciences its aim is to describe the world, noting its characteristics and the causal relationships that hold among the entities that are part of it. There is, then, nothing mental about the object that metaphysics studies; its object of study is extramental reality, not concepts or other mental entities.

In contrast, the mentalistic conception of metaphysics is a favourite in contemporary philosophical circles.[5] According to it, metaphysics is not concerned with the description of the extramental world or the way it functions; it is concerned with our concepts about the world, rather than the world itself. In that sense, metaphysics is not realistic but mentalistic.

The mentalistic conception of metaphysics did not come about as a result of a single drastic change in the history of philosophy. Descartes, Hume, Kant and many others figure prominently in the slow process that produced a change from realism to mentalism. Among the figures that are often cited as having contributed to that process is Suárez.[6]

Suárez conceives metaphysics as a perfect and a priori science. Something is perfect if it is complete, that is, if it lacks nothing for it to be the sort of thing it is (*Disputationes metaphysicae* 10, 1, 15; [19.1] 25: 333). Thus a perfect science is a science that lacks none of the conditions required of sciences. Such conditions stipulate that sciences provide certain and evident knowledge of the objects they study through knowledge of the properties, principles, and causes of those objects (1, 3, 2, and 1, 1, 27; 25, 22 and 11). Moreover, since metaphysics is an a priori science, such knowledge is not based on experience.

A property, in the Aristotelian context within which Suárez works, is a feature of a thing which necessarily characterizes the members of the species to which the thing belongs but is not part of the essence of the thing in question and thus does not appear in its definition (3, 1, 1; 25, 103). The capacity to laugh, for example, is a property of human beings because it necessarily characterizes human beings, although it is not part of the definition of human being. A property, in contrast with an accident, always accompanies each member of a species. The task of science, and therefore of metaphysics, is twofold: first, to identify the properties of the object it studies and, second, to demonstrate the necessary connection of those properties to the object in question through an analysis of the principles and causes of that object.

The object of metaphysics was a matter of intense discussion in the Middle Ages. The origin of the debate can be traced back to Aristotle's *Metaphysics*, where he presents four different understandings of its object: being *qua* being, substance, divine entities, and primary causes and principles (*Metaphysics* 4, 1; 7, 1; 6, 1; 3, 2). Settling the issue was important, for most medievals believed that the unity of a science is derived from the unity of its object. Yet, the four objects that Aristotle identified as objects of metaphysics were not easily collapsed into one.

By the time Suárez was addressing this issue, the possible objects of metaphysics had grown in number and certain precisions had been introduced. Suárez considers and rejects six different opinions on the object of metaphysics: (1) being taken most abstractly and generally so that it includes not only all real beings, whether substantial or accidental, but also mental beings; (2) only real being, leaving out mental beings, so that its object includes both substantial and accidental beings; (3) the supreme, real being, namely God; (4) immaterial being or substance; (5) categorical being, namely, being as divided into the ten Aristotelian categories; and (6) substance *qua* substance, that is substance considered apart from whether it is material or immaterial, finite or infinite (1, 1, 2–18; 25, 2–8).

Suárez's view is that the object of metaphysics is 'being insofar as it is real being' (*ens in quantum ens reale*). As such, metaphysics includes the study of God, immaterial substances, and the real accidents of immaterial substances. It excludes, however, the study of purely mental beings (*entia rationis*) and the study of beings which are completely accidental, and abstracts from all matter (1, 1, 26; 25, 11).

If Suárez had said nothing else about the nature of metaphysics and its object than what I have presented in summary so far, he could have been interpreted only as having a realistic conception of metaphysics, albeit a somewhat different one from those of his predecessors. Moreover, it would have been very difficult to accuse him of having moved in the direction of mentalistic metaphysics. After all, he clearly states that metaphysics deals with real being and only real being, and argues against it having to do with mental being. However, Suárez did not stop there. He went on to discuss the nature of the object metaphysics studies. It is what he says on this matter in particular, coupled with how his views were used by later philosophers, that has given rise to speculation about his role in the history of metaphysics and its development toward mentalism.

The view that Suárez contributed substantially to the mentalization of metaphysics is based, first, on his conception of real being and, second, on his statement that the object of metaphysics is the objective concept of being. Real being for Suárez is not the same as actual being. Actual being is the kind of being existing things have. Real being need not be actual; it can be possible. Thus, real being encompasses both actual being (e.g. my existing cat Minina and the colour of her fur) and possible being (e.g. my non-existing cat Misifus and the colour of his fur). The difference between non-real beings and possible beings is that possible beings have an aptitude for existence, even though they do not exist, whereas non-real beings do not. A possible being like Misifus, has an aptitude such that it could exist even if it does not; but a non-real being like a goatstag, lacks such an aptitude and neither exists nor can exist (31, 2, 10; 26, 232).

Real being, then, includes possible, unactualized essences in addition to actualized ones. This means that the object of science, and thus of metaphysics, is not restricted to actually existing being, but extends to and includes possible being (31, 2, 10; 26, 232). This conception of metaphysics, as the study of not only actual essences but also possible essences, has been identified as one of the sources of the mentalism of modern philosophy; for possible being, so the argument goes, can be nothing but mental, and thus the door is open to a conception of metaphysics as a science of the mental.

This interpretation is disputable, however, for Suárez does not identify possible being with mental being. He understands mental being as 'what has objective being only in the intellect or as what is thought by the mind as a being, although it has no being in itself', that is, what has no being outside the mind (54, 1, 5; 26, 1016). Blindness is a good example of a mental being, for blindness is a lack of something rather than having something and, as such, has no reality outside the mind.[7]

From this it follows that possible beings for Suárez are not the same as mental beings. For possible beings, even though they do not exist, have an aptitude for existence. But it is impossible for mental beings ever to exist, so they cannot have an aptitude for existence. Consequently, that metaphysics includes the study of possible beings does not mean that it is concerned with mental entities.

The second source of the charge that Suárez's conception of meta-physics contributed substantially to the mentalization of the discipline is his claim that the object studied by metaphysics is the objective concept of being (2, 1, 1; 25, 65). This claim may be interpreted as implying mentalism because objective concepts, *qua* concepts, presumably cannot be anything but mental; therefore, it turns out that metaphysics studies something mental rather than something real.

The notion of objective concept is one of two members of a distinction widely used by later scholastics. The other member of the distinction is the formal concept. The formal concept, according to Suárez, is an act of our minds whereby we conceive something. As an act of the mind, it is a quality and thus an accident of the mind. The formal concept is called 'formal' because it informs the mind in the way any form informs its subject, and it is the end of the process of conception. Moreover, it is by means of the formal concept that the mind knows an object, for the formal concept represents the thing known to the mind (2, 1, 1; 25, 65).

The objective concept, on the other hand, is what is represented in the act, or quality, which is the formal concept. The objective concept is not a concept in the way a formal concept is, namely as a form that modifies the mind, determining its conception. Indeed, it is called a concept only derivatively because of the relation it has to the formal concept. It is objective in so far as it is the object with which the formal concept is concerned; it is not objective in the sense of being an image or representation of something else ([19.42] 41). On the contrary, the objective concept is what is represented by the formal concept and, as Suárez states elsewhere, 'the thing signified' by it (29, 3, 34; 26, 59).

In short, we might say that the distinction between the objective concept and the formal concept is the distinction between what I think about (objective) and that through which I think it (formal). So, whereas 'the formal concept cat', for example, is the mental act whereby someone thinks of 'cat', 'the objective concept cat' is whatever one thinks about when one thinks of 'cat', namely cat.

Put this way, it does not look as if objective concepts are mental in any way. As Suárez states, they are not concepts strictly speaking; they are not representations or images; and they are not mental acts or qualities. Instead, they are the objects of the (formal) concepts the mind forms. This would seem to indicate that they are not mental at all.

This inference is corroborated by the fact that the being and unity of objective concepts turn out to be the same being and unity of their objects and, thus, that objective concepts can be mental or real depending on those objects. Suárez makes quite clear that whereas the formal concept is real, always 'a true and positive thing', the objective concept need not always be something real; it can be mental or real, depending on the objective concept in question. If, for example, the objective concept in question is 'blindness', what we have is a mental being because blindness is not a real entity. If, on the other hand, the objective concept in question is 'humanity', what we have is a real being, namely an actual or possible substance (i.e. a human being). Indeed, Suárez says that this is the case with the objective concept of being (2, 3, 7; 25; 83).

From these considerations we must conclude that not all objective concepts have only a mental status; some objective concepts exist in reality. This entails, then, that to be an objective concept does not necessarily imply mental existence alone. Whether that is the case depends not on the nature of objective concepts as such, but on the particular objective concept involved. In the case of 'blindness', it does imply mental existence alone because blindness does not and cannot exist outside the mind; but in the case of 'humanity', it does not because human beings can and do exist outside the mind. This same point is corroborated when we look at the unity of objective concepts.

Do objective concepts, *qua* objective concepts, have universal or individual unity? Suárez's answer is unequivocal. The formal concept is always present in some mind that produces it and is, therefore, individual. With respect to the objective concept, however, the case is different, for an objective concept is universal or individual depending on the particular objective concept involved (2,1,1; 25, 65). If the objective concept in question is 'man' or 'substance', the objective concept is universal. If, on the other hand, the objective concept in question is something determinate, like 'Socrates', then the objective concept is individual. From this it also follows that only those objective concepts that are individual can exist extramentally and therefore be real, since for Suárez universals have no such existence (5, 1, 4; 25, 146).

The situation with respect to the unity of objective concepts, then, is quite similar to the one with respect to their being. Objective concepts can be individual or universal; therefore, they cannot, *qua* objective concepts, be one of these to the exclusion of the other. In cases where there is an exclusion, as it happens with 'blindness', the exclusion arises from the nature of the objective concept in question, not from the fact that it is an objective concept.

The implication of what Suárez says concerning the being and unity of objective concepts is that objective concepts have the ontological status, that is, the being and unity, of their objects. We know, for example, that the objective concept 'blindness' has the same ontological status as blindness, and that the same applies to the objective concepts 'humanity' and 'Minina'. The being and unity of the objective concept of Minina is the being (real) and unity (individual) of Minina; the being and unity of the objective concept of tree is the being (real) and unity (universal) of tree; and the being and unity of the objective concept of blindness is the being (mental) and unity (universal) of blindness. This seems quite clear. Now, since the objective concept that metaphysics studies is 'real being', the object of metaphysics cannot be anything but real, and Suárez's conception of metaphysics cannot be anything but realistic.

The Transcendentals

Suárez's conception of metaphysics prompts an interesting objection. The function of science, as already noted, is to identify the properties of its object, demonstrating their necessary connection with it through an analysis of principles and causes. It follows, then, that metaphysics, as a science of being *qua* being, must be concerned with identifying the properties of being and demonstrating how those properties are necessarily tied to being through an examination of the principles and causes of being. The difficulty posed by this view is that being *qua* being does not have any properties, for considered this abstractly, being is common to every being and its properties. Thus it does not appear that being *qua* being can have any properties which are peculiarly its own.

Suárez is aware of this difficulty and gives an explicit answer to it (1, 1, 28; 25, 11). The answer is important both philosophically and historically. It is philosophically important because it makes clear that, even though Suárez never explicitly says so, metaphysics for him turns out to be the science of the transcendentals; it is historically important because this conception of metaphysics may have served to prepare the way for the growth of transcendentalism in later European Continental philosophy.[8]

Suárez's solution to the difficulty is to propose that, although being *qua* being has no properties that are really distinct from it, it does have properties that are conceptually distinct from it (1, 1, 28; 25, 11). These properties are unity, truth and goodness. They are coextensional with being because whatever is a being is also one, good and true, and whatever is one, good or true is also a being.

It is the coextension of these properties with being that makes them transcendental, for they are common to the ten categories into which being is divided. These properties are not cointensional with being, however, because their conceptual analyses do not coincide with that of being or with those of each other. In short, although whatever is a being is also one, good and true, to be and to be one, to be good, and to be true are not the same.

Metaphysics can be conceived as the study of being *qua* real being so long as it is understood that it deals with properties of being that are only intensionally distinct from it. Moreover, since what is coextensional but not cointensional with being are precisely its transcendental attributes (unity, truth, goodness), it turns out that what metaphysics studies as principles and what it studies as properties of being are the same. Under these circumstances, metaphysics turns out to be the science of the transcendentals.

Suárez's answer to the difficulty posed by the fact that being does not appear to have any properties is to argue that indeed being has properties even though they are not the same sort of property other things have. According to Suárez, properties must fulfil several conditions: they must be real, and really distinct from their subjects, and they must be coextensional with their subjects but not included in their essences (3, 1, 1; 25, 103). The capacity to laugh, for example, fulfils all these conditions with respect to human beings and thus is a property of them. But it is obvious that none of the transcendental properties of being Suárez accepts, namely, one, true, and good, fulfil all these conditions.

Suárez grants this conclusion (3, 1, 8; 25, 105), but he argues that being can still have properties because it has some 'attributes which are not mere products of the mind, but are truly and really predicated of it' (3, 1, 10; 25, 106). But how, then, are these attributes related to being? What kind of properties are they if they cannot be properties in the usual way? Suárez's answer is that these attributes add to being negations, privations, or real extrinsic denominations taken from real relations; unity adds a negation or privation, and truth and goodness add real extrinsic denominations (3, 1, 11; 25, 106).

For Suárez, both negations and privations are lacks, but there is an important difference between the two. Privations are lacks of what things ought to have by virtue of their natures. Thus, a privation is a lack or absence in a thing of what naturally belongs to it, such as blindness in a human being. A negation, by contrast, is an absence of what is not natural to a subject, such as the absence of wings in a human being. The issue of what is or is not natural to a thing is determined by a definition which specifies those features that make the thing what it is (54, 5, 7; 26, 1036).

Strictly speaking, therefore, negations and privations are not real if by real one means, as Suárez often does, actual or possible being, for negations and privations are not beings at all, but lacks of being (31, 2, 10; 26, 232). Their only ontological status is as mental beings (*entia rationis*).

Still, this does not entail that negations and privations are fictitious constructs of the mind. The mind may arrive at truth or falsity regarding reality through negations and privations, for 'negations and privations can be truly and absolutely predicated of a thing without involving any kind of intellectual fictions' (54, 5, 5; 26, 1032). A person X who concludes that another person Y is blind has understood something true about Y if Y is in fact blind and something false about Y if Y is not blind, even though blindness is not something in the world. In either case, the truth or falsity arrived at by X is not dependent on X's understanding, but on Y, that is, on reality, even if the truth is that Y lacks sight.

From this we may gather that 'one', which is predicated of being as a negation of privation, is not real in the sense of being either an actual or possible entity. Its reality lies only in that it is not a fictitious product of the mind and thus can be truly predicated of being. Suárez is using two senses of 'real', then, which allow him to say that unity is both real (i.e. non-fictitious) and not real (i.e. neither actual nor possible) without contradiction.

The other properties of being, namely truth and goodness, are not conceived as negations and privations. Rather, they express real extrinsic denominations based on real relations. For Suárez, real extrinsic denominations have four terms: denomination, thing denominated, denominating form, and relation founding the denomination (54, 2, 14; 26, 1021). In the case of a wall, for example, which is extrinsically denominated as 'seen', the terms of the denomination break down as follows:

denomination:	seen
thing denominated:	a wall
denominating form:	the act of seeing
founding relation:	relation of seeing the wall

Relations for Suárez also have four elements: relation, subject, term and foundation. Consider the case of the relation of similarity of S, a white "3×5" card, to T, another white "3×5" card. In this example, S is what Suárez calls the *subject*; T is the *term* of the relation, the white colour of S is the *foundation* of the relation; and the similarity of S to T is the *relation* (47, 6, 1; 26, 809).

In a real relation, the subject, the term, and the foundation of the relation must be, according to Suárez, real, and the term must also be actual and really – or at least modally – distinct from the foundation (47, 6–9; 26, 809–19). (It must be remembered that for Suárez real being includes not only actual, but also possible being.) Thus, for the relation of similarity of S to T to be real, S and the white colour of S must be real, and T must actually exist. That does not entail, however, that the relation is something really distinct from its foundation; the relation and its foundation are only conceptually distinct (47, 8, 14; 26, 818). In the example given above, the white colour of S, a form in S

which is the foundation of the relation, is not really distinct from the similarity of S to T.

If any of these conditions is not met, that is, if some of the elements of a relation are not real, or if the term is not actual, or if the distinction between the term and the foundation is not at least modal, then the relation is mental (54, 6, 2 and 47, 6–8; 26, 1039 and 808–18). The reason is that in none of these cases would the relation describe accurately the way things are, and thus would have to be considered, at least in part, a mental construct.

A key difference between a real extrinsic denomination founded on a relation and a real relation is that the real extrinsic denomination applies to the term of the real relation on which the denomination is founded and not to the subject of that relation. It could not be otherwise, for if it were, a real extrinsic denomination would posit in the thing it denominates, namely, in the subject of the relation, a form really distinct from it, which is impossible according to Suárez (54, 2, 9; 26, 1020). That the real extrinsic denomination applies to the term and not the subject of the real relation becomes clear if we use the real relation of similarity of S to T as the basis for a real extrinsic denomination. In this case, the thing denominated is not S, the subject of the relation, but T, its term. Thus:

denomination	similar
thing denominated:	T (the term of the relation)
denominating form:	the whiteness of S
founding relation:	similarity of S to T
subject of founding relation:	S
term of relation:	T

Now let us apply what has been established concerning real extrinsic denomination to being and its transcendental attributes true and good:

denomination:	true	good
thing denominated:	being	being
denominating form:	act of intellect	act of will
founding relation:	understanding of being by intellect	desiring of being by will
subject of founding relation:	intellect	will
term of relation:	being	being

Thus, we see what Suárez means when he says that being, true and good are convertible in reality but not conceptually, for whatever is a being is capable also of being the term of a real relation between an intellect or a will and being itself. Such a relation does not affect being, nor do the transcendental attributes true and good refer to a form in being really distinct from it. True and good express extrinsic denominations of being founded on real relations between an intellect or a will and being. The subjects of the relations are intellects and wills, and the forms on which the relations are founded are the acts which modify those intellects and wills. As such, therefore, true and good are neither real properties of being, strictly speaking, nor real or mental relations of being to something else. If they were real properties or real relations, it would imply a kind of distinction between being and them, or their foundation (in the case of real relations), which would be impossible. If they were mental relations, it would imply that true and good are the result of mental activity and, therefore, fictitious.

∾ CONCLUSION ∾

Suárez is, without a doubt, one of the key figures in the transition from medieval thought to modern philosophy. He played a substantial role in this transition in so far as he worked within a scholastic tradition that went back to the thirteenth century and beyond but introduced modifications in it that anticipated and prepared the way for modern thought. Nowhere else is this more evident perhaps than in his metaphysics. Indeed, his conception of both metaphysics and the transcendentals illustrate well how he was able to introduce innovations within the strict parameters of the tradition within which he worked, thus serving to move Western thought out of the Middle Ages and into the modern period.

This is evident in his conception of metaphysics in so far as he still substantially adheres to the realistic conception of the discipline defended by such medieval scholastics as Aquinas. But the extension of the object of study of metaphysics to possible being and some of the mentalistic language he uses to refer to such an object anticipates and prepares the way for the mentalism so characteristic of modern philosophy.

In the doctrine of the transcendentals, Suárez again works within the parameters he inherits, but he introduces modifications in the doctrine by understanding two of the transcendental properties of being – true and good – as expressions of real extrinsic denominations of being rather than as mental relations, the popular view among scholastics. This understanding of the transcendentals opens the way to interpretations that, again, pave the way for future developments. In short, Suárez is a figure in whom both the scholastic past and the modern future of philosophy meet and interact in interesting and peculiar ways. From studying his works, one can learn much about both the Middle Ages and modern philosophy.

 NOTES

1 There is wide disagreement as to how to refer to the scholasticism of the sixteenth and seventeenth centuries. Carlo Giacon has proposed the term 'second scholastic' [19.26]. But this expression seems to suggest a break between the scholasticism of the thirteenth and fourteenth centuries and that of the sixteenth and seventeenth centuries, while, in fact, there is no such break. For a challenge to the general view about the decline of scholasticism after 1350, see Chapter 18 above.

2 Cf. Bernard G. Dod, 'Aristoteles latinus' and C. H. Lohr, 'The medieval interpretations of Aristotle', in *CHLMP*, pp. 45–98.

3 J. Marenbon, 'The theoretical and practical autonomy of philosophy as a discipline in the Middle Ages', in Monika Asztalos *et al.* (eds) *Knowledge and the Sciences in Medieval Philosophy*, Helsinki, Yliopistopaino, 1990, pp. 262–74, and Jorge J. E. Gracia, 'Philosophy in the Middle Ages', *Diálogos* 9 (1977): 233–43.

4 See Cronin [19.18], Ferrater Mora [19.25], Iriarte [19.33], and others in the bibliography.

5 Cf. P. F. Strawson, *Individuals*, London, Methuen, 1959, p. 9.

6 Cf. R. P. D. Dubarle, 'Intervention', *Archives de Philosophie* 42 (1979): 274; Courtine [19.16]; and Cronin [19.18], ch. 3.

7 For the details of Suárez's doctrine of mental beings, see Doyle [19.23] (1).

8 This transcendentalism was given an epistemic turn in later thinkers that was not intended by or present in Suárez. See Doyle [19.24].

 BIBLIOGRAPHY

Original Language Editions of Suárez

19.1   Berton, C. (ed.) *Opera omnia*, 28 vols, Paris, Vivès, 1856–61. (*Disputationes metaphysicae*, reprint of vols 25 and 26, Hildesheim, G. Olms, 1965.)

19.2   Castellote, Salvador (ed.) *De anima*, Madrid, Sociedad de Estudios y Publicaciones, 1978– .

19.3   Pereña, L. *et al.* (eds) *De legibus*, 8 vols, Madrid, Consejo Superior de Investigaciones Científicas, 1971–81.

19.4   Vicente, L. P. (ed.) *De bello* (*De triplice virtute theologica*, treatise 3, disputation 13), Madrid, Instituto Francisco de Vitoria, 1954.

19.5   Elorduy, E. and Pereña, L. (eds) *Defensio fidei III*, Madrid, Consejo de Investigaciones Científicas, 1965.

English Translations with Commentaries

19.6   *Metaphysical Disputations X and XI and Selected Passages from Disputation XXIII and Other Works*, trans. Jorge J. E. Gracia and Douglas Davis, in *The Metaphysics of Good and Evil According to Suárez*, Munich and Vienna, Philosophia Verlag, 1989.

19.7   *On the Essence of Finite Being as Such*, trans. Norman Wells, Milwaukee, Wis., Marquette University Press, 1983.

19.8   *Metaphysical Disputation V: Individual Unity and its Principle*, trans. Jorge J. E. Gracia, in *Suárez on Individuation*, Milwaukee, Wis., Marquette University Press, 1982.

19.9   *On Formal and Universal Unity*, trans. James F. Ross, Milwaukee, Wis., Marquette University Press, 1964.

19.10   *On the Various Kinds of Distinctions*, trans. Cyril Vollert, Milwaukee, Wis., Marquette University Press, 1947.

19.11   *On Efficient Causality: Metaphysical Disputations 17–19*, trans. Alfred J Freddoso, New Haven, Conn., Yale University Press, 1994.

19.12   *Selections from Three Works (De legibus, Defensio fidei catholicae, De triplici virtute theologica)*, 2 vols, trans. G. W. Williams and James Brown Scott, Oxford, Clarendon Press, 1944.

Studies

19.13   Adams, Robert M. 'Middle knowledge and the problem of evil', *American Philosophical Quarterly* 14 (1977): 109–17.

19.14   Alejandro, J. M. *La gnoseología del Doctor Eximio y la acusación nominalista*, Comillas, Universidad Pontificia, 1948.

19.15   Ashworth, E. J. 'Traditional logic', in *CHRP*, pp. 143–72.

19.16   Courtine, Jean-François 'Le project suarécien de la métaphysique', *Archives de Philosophie* 42 (1979): 235–74.

19.17   —— *Suárez et le système de la métaphysique*, Paris, Presses Universitaires de France, 1990.

19.18   Cronin, Timothy *Objective Being in Descartes and Suárez*, Rome, Gregorian University Press, 1966; repr. New York and London, Garland Publishing, 1987.

19.19   Daniel, William *The Purely Penal Law Theory in the Spanish Theologians from Vittoria to Suárez*, Rome, Gregorian University Press, 1968.

19.20   Doyle, John P. 'Suárez and the reality of the possibles', *The Modern Schoolman* 45 (1967): 29–48.

19.21   —— 'Suárez on the analogy of being', (1) and (2), *The Modern Schoolman* 46 (1969): 219–49 and 323–41.

19.22   —— 'Prolegomena to a study of extrinsic denomination in the work of Francis Suárez, SJ', *Vivarium* 22 (1984): 121–60.

19.23   —— 'Suárez on beings of reason and truth', (1) and (2), *Vivarium* 25 (1987): 47–75 and 26 (1988): 51–72.

19.24   —— ' "Extrinsic cognoscibility": a seventeenth-century supertranscendental notion', *The Modern Schoolman* 68 (1990): 57–80.

19.25   Ferrater Mora, José 'Suárez and modern philosophy', *Journal of the History of Ideas* 14 (1953): 528–47.

19.26   Giacon, Carol *La seconda scolastica*, 2 vols, Milan, Fratelli Bocca, 1946.

19.27   Gnemi, Angelo *Il fondamento metafisico: Analisi di struttura sulle 'Disputationes metaphysicae' di F. Suárez*, Milan, Società Editrice Vita e Pensiero, 1969.

19.28 Gracia, Jorge J. E. 'Evil and the transcendentality of goodness: Suárez's solu-
tion to the problem of positive evils', in Scott MacDonald (ed.) *Being and
Goodness: the Concept of the Good in Metaphysics and Philosophical Theology*,
Ithaca, NY, Cornell University Press, 1991, pp. 151–78.

19.29 —— (ed.) *Francisco Suárez*, issue of *American Catholic Philosophical Quarterly*
64, 1 (1991). (Articles by Douglas P. Davis, John P. Doyle, Jorge J. E.
Gracia, John Kronen, Carlos Noreña, Thomas Sullivan and Jeremiah
Reedy, and John L. Treloar.)

19.30 —— 'Suárez on the transcendentals', in Jorge, J. E. Gracia (ed.) *The
Transcendentals in the Middle Ages*, issue of *Topoi* 10 (1992): 121–33.

19.31 Hamilton, Bernice *Political Thought in Sixteenth-century Spain*, Oxford,
Oxford University Press, 1963.

19.32 Hellin, J. *La analogía del ser y el conocimiento de Dios en Suárez*, Madrid,
Editora Nacional, 1947.

19.33 Iriarte, J. 'La proyección sobre Europa de una gran metafísica', *Razón y Fe*
(1948): 229–65.

19.34 Iturrioz, J. *Estudios sobre la metafísica de Francisco Suárez, SJ*, Madrid, Fax,
1949.

19.35 Kronen, John D. 'Essentialism old and new: Suárez and Brody', *The Modern
Schoolman* (1991): 123–51.

19.36 Lohr, Charles H. 'Metaphysics', in *CHRP*, pp. 537–638.

19.37 Owens, Joseph 'The number of terms in the Suárezian discussion on essence
and being', *The Modern Schoolman* 34 (1957): 147–91.

19.38 Scorraille, R. de *François Suárez de la Compagnie de Jésus*, 2 vols, Paris,
Lethiellieux, 1912–13.

19.39 Scott, J. B. *The Catholic Conception of International Law*, Washington, DC,
Georgetown University Press, 1934.

19.40 Trentman, John A. 'Scholasticism in the seventeenth century', in *CHLMP*,
pp. 818–37.

19.41 Wells, Norman 'Suárez on the Eternal Truths', (1) and (2), *The Modern
Schoolman* 58 (1981): 73–104 and 159–74.

19.42 —— 'Objective reality of ideas in Descartes, Caterus, and Suárez', *Journal
of the History of Philosophy* 28 (1990): 33–61.

19.43 Wilenius, Reijo *The Social and Political Theory of Francisco Suárez*, Helsinki,
Akateeminen Kirjakauppa, 1963.

Glossary

The Glossary should be used in conjunction with the index, where pages containing good introductory discussion of a term are printed in bold. An 'I' after an entry here indicates where reference to such discussions will be particularly useful.

absolute/connotative terms: according to Ockham, a term (such as 'man' or 'whiteness') that signifies something directly (a man, the quality whiteness) is absolute, whereas a term that signifies something obliquely, by means of indicating one of its attributes ('white (thing)', which signifies the thing that is white by indicating its attribute of whiteness) is connotative. The distinction corresponds closely to that used earlier in the Middle Ages between words for substances, *differentiae* and accidents on the one hand (= absolute terms) and denominative words on the other hand (= connotative terms). **I**

accident: a property which a substance could conceivably lose or have added to it without ceasing to be the substance it is: wearing a hat is an accident of Socrates; so too is having a snub nose (although his nose is always this shape); see also **categories**.

actuality, in act (*in actu*) / potentiality, in potency (*in potentia*): Aristotle was fond of contrasting what or how things actually are with what or how they will or might be by using the pair 'act/potency'. An acorn is an oak tree in potency; when it grows up into a tree, then it is a tree in act. A movable but still body is moving in potency, and a cold body is hot in potency.

ampliation (*ampliatio*): the extension of the supposition (reference) of a word brought about by the use of the past or future tense or by words such as 'possibly'.

analogy: when a word is used in connection with different sorts of things in such a way that its different **significations** in each case, though not the same, are related to each other, it is said to signify analogously. Often, this similarity between analogous significations

475

consists in their each bearing a different relation to the same thing. For instance, 'healthy' is used analogously of a person (i.e. he is in a healthy state), of a medicine (i.e. it makes people healthy) and of a blood-sample (i.e. it is a sign of health). I

apodictically: using a **demonstration**.

beatific vision: according to most Christian theologians, after death the souls of the blessed will be separated from their bodies and enjoy a vision of God which will make them completely happy.

'Bertrand Russell': Bertrand Russell was an English philosopher who lived from 1872 to 1970. His name is used metonomously by some historians to stand for any modern analytical philosopher who values qualities they believe inappropriate to consider in relation to medieval thinkers (for instance, clarity, precision and cogency in argument).

categorematic / syncategorematic terms (*categoremata / syncategoremata*): as used by medieval authors, this distinction builds on the analysis of categorical statements as: Subject–(copula)–Predicate. Strictly speaking, categorematic terms can stand alone as the subject or the predicate (for instance, '*homo*' ('(the) man'), ('*currit*' ('runs'); a syncategorematic term cannot be used meaningfully in a statement without (at least) a subject and a predicate (for instance, '*si*' ('if'), '*non*' ('not'). Logicians often extended the class of syncategorematic terms to include ones such as 'begins' ('*incipit*') which could be used categorematically, but were usually used to modify the **signification** of categorematic terms. One of the branches of the *logica modernorum* was the study of those syncategorematic terms, in this wider sense, which logicians found especially interesting.

categories (*categoriae, praedicamenta*): in medieval discussions, these are almost always the ten categories, or most general *genera* distinguished by Aristotle in his *Categories*: **substance** / essence (*ousia* (Greek), *substantia, essentia*) and the nine categories of **accident**: quantity, quality, relation, place, time, posture, state, action, being-acted-on. Whether Aristotle's classification concerned things, words, perceptions or some combination of these three was a matter of controversy in late antiquity and the Middle Ages.

causes, material / formal / efficient / final: following Aristotle, medieval writers regularly distinguished between four types of 'cause': the material cause of something is what it is made from, the formal cause that which makes it the sort of thing it is, the efficient cause that which makes it, and the final cause that for the sake of which it is made. In the case of this table, then, the material cause is the wood it is made from, the formal cause the form of being a table (which would have guided a carpenter when he made the wood into a table, not a chair or a bench), the efficient cause is the carpenter and the final cause my wish to have something to write on.

complexly significable (*complexe significabile*): the term used by some fourteenth-century writers, such as Adam Wodeham and Gregory of Rimini, for what statements signify: the exact ontological status of these significates was debated. I

composite / divided sense: a distinction used to define the scope of certain logical operators. For example, 'It is possible that the sitting man is standing' would be read in the composite sense to mean: the following is possible, that the man is sitting and standing (M(p & -p)). In the divided sense it would be read: the man is sitting, and it is possible that he stands (p & M-p). A reading in the composite was also called a '*de dicto*' modality, and that in the divided sense a '*de re*' modality.

connotation / denotation: in modern usage, a word's denotation is its extension (the objects to which it refers) and its connotation is its intension or abstract meaning, which provides the principle by which its denotation is determined. Some writers, however, use the distinction more loosely.

connotative terms: see **absolute / connotative terms**

consequences (*consequentiae*): either (1) 'if . . . then . . .' statements, or (2) arguments consisting of a single (perhaps composite) premiss and a conclusion (for example, (1) 'if he's a man, he's rational' or (2) 'he's a man; so he's rational'). Medieval writers rarely distinguished clearly between (1) and (2).

copula: 'is' (and its other forms) when used to link the subject and predicate of a statement (e.g. 'Socrates is white'). Most medieval philosophers gave a three-part analysis of predication, distinguishing between the subject ('Socrates'), the predicate ('white') and the copula. But some (for instance, Abelard) also suggested a two-part analysis, closer to that used by logicians today, in which the copula is part of the predicate: the logical form of 'Socrates is white' is then 'Socrates whites' (in modern terms, 'Fa', where 'F' stands for being white, and 'a' is a designator for Socrates).

demonstration: in medieval usage, a demonstration is a logically valid argument from premisses which are 'necessary' in the sense that they state a truth about what is unchanging.

denomination: a word 'd' is 'denominated' from a word 'w' when (1) the signification of 'd' is related to that of 'w' and (2) verbally 'd' is similar to, but not the same as, 'w'. For example, 'white' is denominated from 'whiteness' and 'virtuous' from 'virtue'. As these examples indicate, adjectives which can be predicated of concrete objects often are denominated from nouns for the abstract qualities which they attribute.

dialectic (*dialectica*): in medieval use (and that of modern historians of medieval philosophy), 'dialectic' is usually just a synonym for 'logic'.

emanation: if *A* emanates from *B*, *A* is produced by *B* without *B*'s being in any way changed (as, for instance, light is produced by a source of light). Neoplatonists described intelligible reality as a series of emanations.

epistemology: the theory of knowledge.

equivocation (*aequivocatio*): a word is equivocal if it has two or more different significations (e.g. 'bank' signifying a river bank and a place where money is kept).

essence (*essentia*; from Greek *ousia*): minimally, something's essence is the formula which states the sort of thing it is. If 'E' is the essence-formula for Socrates, then (1) Socrates is necessarily E and (2) 'E' tells one what is centrally important in understanding what Socrates is.

exponibles: a term *t* is exponible when a statement in which it occurs can be clarified for logical purposes by analysing it into a conjunction of statements ('exponents') which do not contain *t*. For example, 'it is beginning to' is an exponible term in 'Socrates is beginning to run', which is clarified by analysis into 'Socrates was not running a moment ago' and 'Socrates is now running'. I

form (*forma*): (1) in the period up to *c.* 1200, '*forma*' often meant an accident or a *differentia*; I (2) for writers influenced by Aristotle's metaphysics (directly after 1200, or indirectly before then) a '*forma*' was an Aristotelian form which, with matter, makes a concrete whole (Aristotle also considered whether some forms could exist without matter; these were called 'separate forms'); (3) platonic **Ideas** were sometimes called *formae*.

formal distinction: according to Duns Scotus, two things, which are not really distinct may be 'formally distinct'. A formal distinction is not merely a conceptual distinction ('distinction of reason') since it obtains apart from its being considered by any intellect. For instance, a thing's singularity (or 'haecceity' – a term which has been resurrected in modern metaphysics), its existence and its essence are formally distinct from each other. These formally distinct aspects of a thing are usually called *formalitates* ('formalities') by Scotus and his successors. I

genus and species: according to Aristotle, substances can be hierarchically ordered according to a series of increasingly more general essential definitions which give their species and genera. For instance, Socrates is a man, an animal, a living thing and a bodily thing. Man, Animal, Living Thing and Bodily Thing are species or genera: more precisely, Animal is the species of Living Thing, but the genus of Man (and so on – 'genus' and 'species' are used relatively). See also **universals**. I

gloss: medieval manuscripts often contained many glosses as well as the main text. Glosses of one or a few words, written between the lines, explain the meanings of difficult words or phrases. Longer glosses, written in the margins of the manuscript and often keyed to the text by reference letters or signs, paraphrase or discuss the text or bring extra information.

homonymy: means the same as 'equivocation'.

hylomorphism: the doctrine that things consist of matter and form.

hypothetical statements / propositions, hypothetical syllogisms: a hypothetical statement is a molecular statement: a statement comprising two or more individual statements, linked by a connective such as 'and', 'when' or 'if ... then'; a hypothetical syllogism is a syllogism in which at least one of the premises is a molecular statement.

Ideas / Forms, Platonic (theory of): the view that universals are independently really existing entities, graspable by the intellect.

illumination: some medieval philosophers (in the West usually under the influence of Augustine) held that humans could not know any proposition with certainty without receiving in each case an 'illumination' from God.

indexicals: words such as 'now', 'then', 'I', 'there', the reference of which is determined by the context of its utterance.

insolubles (*insolubilia*): semantic paradoxes, such as the Liar Paradox (e.g. 'The sentence I am now saying is false.'). I

Intellect, potential and active: according to Aristotle in *On the Soul*, the human intellect is a receptive capacity, which is put into activity by receiving the universal forms of things. In an obscure passage, he suggests that there is also an active intellect, responsible for putting this potency into activity. Some commentators in antiquity and the Middle Ages held that there is just one agent intellect, others that each human being has an active as well as a potential intellect. Christian thinkers sometimes identified the single active intellect with God; Islamic thinkers often considered that the active intellect was the Agent Intelligence, the last of the series of Intelligences to be emanated.

Intelligences: according to the Neoplatonists, from the Intellect (*nous*) – the Platonic World of Ideas – there comes, by a process of successive **emanations**, a series of Intelligences, which are incorporeal, thinking beings. The last of these is the Agent Intelligence (see **Intellect, potential and active**). The scheme of Intelligences was taken up by many Islamic thinkers in their interpretation of Aristotle, and through them it influenced Latin thinkers. I

intension/remission: an accidental **form** can have different grades of intension or remission whilst remaining the same form. For instance, when I put the kettle on the fire, the form of heat in the water it contains becomes more intense; when I take it off the flame, the form is remitted – the water cools. I

intentions, primary and second(ary) (*intentiones primae/secundae*): primary intentions are the concepts we can apply directly to reality: for instance, the concept of man, which is a concept we apply directly to a certain sort of real thing – men. Second(ary) intentions are concepts we use in thinking about primary intentions: for instance, the concept of species, which we use in order to distinguish one sort of primary intention (man, horse, donkey) from others. I

intuitive cognition: discussed widely from Duns Scotus onwards, intuitive cognition (which may be sensible or intellectual) is a type of immediate cognition like sight (*intueor* = 'to see, contemplate') of a particular as existent and present. The exact definition of 'intuitive cognition' was, however, debated.

kalām: Islamic scholastic theology.

liberal arts: the seven subjects made up by the **trivium** and the **quadrivium**.

logos: Greek for 'word', 'reason'. Christian theologians often called the second person of the Trinity, the Son, the *logos* or (as a Latin equivalent) the *verbum* ('word') of God.

macrocosm, microcosm: the macrocosm is the greater (*makros*) world (*kosmos*) (usually, the whole universe), the microcosm – literally the small (*mikros*) world – the human being. Many ancient and medieval authors drew parallels between the structure of the macrocosm and the microcosm.

metaphysics: in medieval writing, metaphysics is the study of those questions considered by Aristotle in his *Metaphysics*. These were usually considered to centre around the study of being as (*qua*) being, and especially around the attempt to arrive at some general characterization of existing things which applies to members of all the ten Aristotelian categories or most general genera.

modism, modes: (1) see **speculative grammar**; (2) medieval writers also use *modus* ('mode') in a different way, when they talk about the intrinsic 'modes of being', by which they mean finite being or infinite being. I

Muʿtazilites: one of the schools of *kalām*.

Neoplatonism: the most influential philosophical school of late antiquity. It was founded by Plotinus (205–*c*. 270 AD) who claimed he was reviving Plato's true thought. In fact, he and, especially, successors such as his pupil, Porphyry, and the fifth-century philosopher, Proclus, developed an elaborate system strikingly different from anything Plato himself attempted.

Nestorians: the Christians who follow what Catholics consider to be the heresy, first propounded by Nestorius, that Christ consisted of two separate persons, one human, one divine.

noetic: of or appertaining to the intellect.

obligations: an argument-game, originating in the twelfth century, but most important in the fourteenth and fifteenth centuries. One contestant, the 'respondent' obligated himself to something – in *positio*, the most straightforward form of the game, to maintaining the truth of a statement, the *positum* put forward by the 'opponent'. He also accepted, for the purpose of the game, a certain statement of how things are in reality (the *casus*). The opponent would then put forward a series of sentences which the respondent would have to declare true or false according to a set of strict rules. His object would be to force the respondent into self-contradiction.

ontology: ontology is the discussion of what sorts of thing, according to their broadest types, exist. For instance, are there **universal** things as well as particulars? Are facts a sort of entity or not? To ask what is a philosopher's ontology is usually to enquire what sorts of things that philosopher claims exist.

opaque contexts: are created by 'necessarily', 'possibly' and verbs such as 'know', 'believe', 'wish'. Normally if a and b are two words which refer to the same thing, one may be substituted for the other in a statement without altering its truth value (e.g. 'Cicero wrote this work' is true; so 'Tully wrote this work' is also true). This is not the case in certain opaque contexts (e.g. 'he believes that Cicero wrote this work' is true, but 'he believes that Tully wrote this work' is false, since he has never heard 'Tully' used as a name for Cicero; 'necessarily, 9 is greater than 7' is true, but not 'necessarily, the number of the planets is greater than 7'.

Organon, **Aristotle's:** Aristotle's logical works. *Organon* is the Greek for 'tool', and it became the name for these works because some late ancient thinkers held that logic was not a part of philosophy, but rather a tool used by it.

paronymy: means the same as '**denomination**'.

participation: particulars are said to 'participate' in universals when universals are considered to exist independently, apart from particulars: on this view, if a is F, it is F in virtue of participating in the form of F-ness.

potentiality: see **actuality** (etc.).

predicables: the five terms discussed in Porphyry's *Isagoge* were known as the five predicables: '*genus*', '*species*', '*differentia*', '*proprium*', accident, (*accidens*). For some writers, these terms are words which signify other words, not things; for others, they signify things as well as words.

predication: the attribution of a property to something. In 'Socrates is white', whiteness is predicated of Socrates. According to most medieval analyses, the word 'white' would be regarded as the 'predicate', linked to 'Socrates' by the copula 'is'; see also **copula**.

proposition (*propositio*): in medieval usage, a declarative sentence: truth or falsehood is almost always attributed by medieval authors to *propositiones* (although some would say that they are not the primary bearers of truth and falsehood). A *propositio* is usually understood as a token sentence rather than a type sentence: 'I am sitting' said by me now is a different *propositio* from 'I am sitting' said by me in a minute's time, or said by you. The meaning of *propositio* is therefore different from that of 'proposition' used in its modern sense, to designate that which is expressed by a sentence. The nearest medieval equivalents to 'proposition' in the modern sense are Abelard's '*dictum*' and the fourteenth-century '**complexly significable**'.

quadrivium: the four mathematical arts: arithmetic, geometry, music and astronomy.

quaestio: literally 'question'. Texts based on university teaching were usually written up in '*quaestio*-form'. A problem would be phrased in the form of a yes-or-no question: '*p* or not-*p*'. Suppose the author wished to argue that not-*p*. First a set of arguments would be given for the view which the writer did *not* wish to advance (for *p*), preceded by the qualification *videtur* ('it seems that'). Then arguments would be advanced for the opposite view (for not-*p*), preceded by the comment *sed contra* ('but against this'). These might just consist of a single authoritative quotation. There followed the 'body' of the *quaestio*, the author's discussion of his view (that not-*p*) along with his reasons for holding it, preceded by the comment *respondeo dicendum* ('I reply that it ought to be said that . . .'). Finally, each of the arguments for *p* would be answered in turn.

quiddity (*quidditas*): was used in the thirteenth century and later to mean **essence**; sometimes the phrase *quod quid est* was used with the same meaning. A 'quidditative definition' is an essential definition.

regent (master): in the medieval university system, a student became a master of arts or of theology at the end of the arts or theology course. He then taught as a master for a short period, usually one or two years, during which he was a *magister regens* ('regent master') before vacating his post for someone else. Most exceptionally (as in the cases of Aquinas and Eckhart) a master was allowed a second period of regency some years after his first one.

scholastics, scholasticism: the philosophers and theologians of the universities of Latin Europe from the thirteenth to the fifteenth or sixteenth centuries are often called 'scholastics' and their work described as 'scholasticism'. Sometimes eleventh- and twelfth-century thinking is described as 'early' or 'pre-scholasticism', and the age of 'high scholasticism' (roughly 1250–1300) is distinguished from 'late(r) scholasticism'. The value of these labels is doubtful.

science (Aristotelian): a branch of knowledge (for instance, geometry or physics) with its own self-evident first principles. See also **subalternation**.

semantics: the theory of meaning; see **signification, supposition**.

semiotic: that which pertains to the study of semiotics, which is the study of symbolic systems in general. Language is one of these symbolic systems.

Sentences: used in connection with medieval philosophy without further qualification, 'the *Sentences*' almost always refers to the *Liber sententiarum* of Peter the Lombard (written *c.* 1155). From the early thirteenth century until the end of the Middle Ages, Peter the Lombard's *Sentences* and the Bible were the two textbooks of university theology faculties. Commenting on all or part of the *Sentences* was part of the requirements for becoming a master of theology. These commentaries – among which are included the most important works of Duns Scotus, Ockham and many others – offered plenty of opportunity to develop philosophical discussions only tenuously related to the Lombard's text.

separate form: see **form**.

separated soul: the human soul in separation from the body after death.

signification (*significatio*): the broadest of terms used in medieval discussions of semantics. Although 'signifies' could be given a special meaning by qualification (e.g. 'signify by nomination'), usually a word's signification is x if and only if x is that of which it makes its hearers think.

singular / universal statements or propositions: a singular statement is one about a particular thing ('Socrates is white'); a universal statement is one about all things of a sort ('All men are rational').

sophisms (*sophismata*): puzzle sentences (in logic, theology or natural philosophy), often ambiguous ones which are true under one interpretation and false under another. Mediaeval interest in sophisms seems to have been stimulated by study (from *c.* 1130 onwards) of Aristotle's treatise on fallacies, *On Sophistical Refutations*.

speculative grammar: the attempt by certain writers, especially in the mid- and late-thirteenth century, to treat grammar as an Aristotelian science. It involved analysing words in sentences according to their various 'modes of signifying' (*modi significandi*) and discussing the relation between modes of signifying, modes of being and modes of understanding. Its practitioners were therefore sometimes known as 'modists' (*modisti*). I

square of opposition: a diagrammatic way of representing the relationship between statements of the forms (A) 'All S are P', (E) 'No S is P', (I) 'Some S is P', (O) 'Some S is not P'.

subalternation: every Aristotelian **science** (or branch of knowledge) is based on first principles, which cannot themselves be demonstrated within that science. Some sciences derive their first principles from another science, to which they are then said to be 'subalternate': for example, optics was considered to be subalternate to geometry, whilst it was much disputed whether theology, as practised by scholars here on earth, was subalternate to the theology practised by the souls of the blessed, enjoying the **beatific vision.**

substance (*substantia*): according to the Aristotelian view, generally accepted in the Middle Ages, a substance is (1) a particular member of a natural kind (particular substance) or (2) the **species** or **genus** of some (1) (universal substance). Some medieval thinkers denied, however, that there are in reality any substances of type (2).

supposition (*suppositio*): the reference of a word within a sentence. Supposition was classified into various types from the late twelfth century onwards. This classification is sometimes called the 'theory of the properties of terms'. I

syllogism: a syllogism has two premisses, each with two terms, one of which is common to them both (the 'middle (term)'): for instance, 'All men are mortal', 'All philosophers are men'. From the premisses there follows a conclusion in which the middle term does not appear ('All philosophers are mortal').

syncategoremata: see **categorematic** . . . **terms.**

synonymy: means the same as '**univocation**'.

terminist logic: the work of those logicians who laid emphasis on the theory of the properties of terms – the classification of the different sorts of **supposition.** The most popular of terminist textbooks was Peter of Spain's *Tractatus* (known as his *Summule logicales*) (probably 1230–9).

Thomist: this term is usually applied to those nineteenth- and twentieth-century philosophers and historians who have taken (an often simplified view of) the ideas of Aquinas as an accurate guide to the truth in philosophical and theological matters.

transcendentals: attributes which, it was believed, all things have. They included being an existing thing (*ens*), truth, goodness, unity and, according to some thinkers, beauty. I

trivium: the three linguistic arts: grammar, logic (dialectic) and rhetoric.

truth, correspondence theory of: a theory of truth which, at minimum, requires that for a statement to be true it signify exactly what is the case; it may or may not also treat what is the case as some sort of real entity (e.g. a **complexly significable**).

universals: a word is universal if it is of a type suited to be predicated of many things. 'Man', 'white', 'animal', 'run(s)' are all universals, but not 'Socrates' or 'Trinity College'. It was a matter of great dispute throughout the Middle Ages whether there were not just universal words and concepts, but also universals things: Man the species as well as particular men, whiteness in general as well as this or that white thing.

world soul: that which, according to Plato's *Timaeus*, is responsible for the movements and regularity of the universe.

Index

The two indexes cover the text of all the chapters and the glossary, and the notes in so far as they add material not discussed in the text. The bibliographies are not indexed. The *index nominum* includes the names of all writers and their works (but not e.g. kings or popes) and towns, monasteries, convents and universities (but not countries). The *index rerum* is a selective guide to the themes and ideas discussed in the book. Details of individual manuscripts cited in the text and notes are given in the *index rerum* under 'manuscripts, individual'. In cross-references between the two indexes, *IN* abbreviates *index nominum*, *IR* abbreviates *index rerum*. *SC* abbreviates *Sentence Commentary*, i.e. a commentary on all or part of the *Sentences* of Peter the Lombard. Page numbers in bold indicate a detailed discussion dedicated to the author, work or theme in question. Page numbers preceded by an asterisk are those of the glossary-entry for the term indexed. The principles of nomenclature and alphabetization followed are that (a) ancient authors are referred to by their usual names (e.g. Boethius, Cicero); (b) post-classical Latin or Western vernacular writers working before c. 1500 are referred to by Christian name first, almost always in English form (e.g. Walter Burley, under 'W' – not Gualterus Burlaeus, under 'G' or 'B'), and connective particles, such as 'of', are ignored in the ordering; those working after c.1500 are referred to by surname first (e.g. Descartes, Renée, under 'D') (c) Arabic and Jewish writers are referred to by their last name first – often beginning with 'al' or 'ibn'; the commonly accepted Latin and English forms of the name are used for Averroes, Avicenna and Maimonides but not otherwise; (d) names of works are generally given as in the text, but often shortened; (e) a few exceptions to these rules have been made where following them would go against normal usage (e.g. Bonaventure is listed under this name, not under John of Fidanza), but there are cross-references here and elsewhere to avoid confusion.

Index Nominum

Index Rerum